Introduction to Belgian Law

General Editors of the Series: Prof. Tuğrul Ansay & Prof. Don Wallace, Jr.

List of the Introduction books already published are as follows:

Introduction to the Law of Israel (1995)
Introduction to Hungarian Law (1998)
Introduction to Belgian Law (2001)
Introduction to Italian Law (2002)
Introduction to the Law of the United States (second edition 2002)
Introduction to the Law of South Africa (2004)
Introduction to Swiss Law (third edition 2004)
Introduction to German Law (second edition 2005)
Introduction to Polish Law (2005)
Introduction to French Law (2008)
Introduction to Greek Law (third edition 2008)
Introduction to Turkish Law (sixth edition 2011)
Introduction to the Law of Kazakhstan (2012)
Introduction to the Law of Croatia (2014)
Introduction to the Law of Austria (2015)
Introduction to Brazilian Law (second edition 2017)

Introduction to Belgian Law

Second Edition

Edited by

Marc Kruithof
Walter De Bondt

Wolters Kluwer

Published by:
Kluwer Law International B.V.
PO Box 316
2400 AH Alphen aan den Rijn
The Netherlands
Website: www.wklawbusiness.com

Sold and distributed in North, Central and South America by:
Wolters Kluwer Legal & Regulatory U.S.
7201 McKinney Circle
Frederick, MD 21704
United States of America
Email: customer.service@wolterskluwer.com

Sold and distributed in all other countries by:
Turpin Distribution Services Ltd
Stratton Business Park
Pegasus Drive, Biggleswade
Bedfordshire SG18 8TQ
United Kingdom
Email: kluwerlaw@turpin-distribution.com

ISBN 978-90-411-6704-0

e-Book: ISBN 978-90-411-8728-4
web-PDF: ISBN 978-90-411-8729-1

Editors

Marc Kruithof is Professor at Ghent University, where he teaches civil liability (torts) and comparative law. He holds a Ph.D. in Law (Ghent University, 2009), LL.M. (Yale Law School, 1986), Licentiate in Economics (Ghent University, 1985), and Licentiate in Law (Ghent University, 1983). His current research focuses on torts and on general concepts of the law of obligations. Previously, his work focused on financial services law and client protection in investment services.

Walter De Bondt is Emeritus Professor at Ghent University and at Vrije Universiteit Brussel (VUB). He holds a Ph.D. in Law (Ghent University, 1982), LL.M. (UC Berkeley, 1978), and Licentiate in Law (Ghent University, 1973). He taught courses on contracts and on comparative law. His research mainly focused on the formation of contracts, the precontractual process, the consent of the parties and the free will of a patient asking for euthanasia.

Contributors

Robert Andersen, Professor Emeritus at Université Catholique de Louvain (UCL), First President Emeritus at the Council of State of Belgium (*Conseil d'Etat – Raad van State*), Ph.D. in Law (UCL, 1977), Licentiate in Applied Economic Sciences (UCL, 1966), and Doctor in Law (UCL, 1965).

Diederik Bruloot, Professor at Ghent University, Ph.D. in Law (Ghent University, 2012), and Licentiate in Law (Ghent University, 2005).

Ignace Claeys, Professor at Ghent University, Attorney: Partner at Eubelius in Brussels, Ph.D. in Law (KU Leuven, 2002), LL.M. (University of Chicago, 1996), and Licentiate in Law (KU Leuven, 1994).

Miguel De Jonckheere, Professor at Vrije Universiteit Brussel (VUB), Ph.D. in Law (VUB, 1995), Special Licentiate in Tax Law (VUB, 1988), and Licentiate in Law (VUB, 1986).

Francis Delpérée, Member of the Belgian House of Representatives elected in 2014, Former Member of the Belgian Senate 2004–2014, Professor Emeritus at Université Catholique de Louvain (UCL), Former Assessor at the Council of State (*Conseil d'Etat – Raad van State*), Doctor Honoris Causa of universities d'Aix-Marseille III (1987), Geneve (1993), Ottawa (1993), Szeged (2002), Athens (2003) and Sud Toulon-Var (2008), Doctor in Law (Paris, 1968), and Doctor in Law (UCL, 1964).

Christian De Wulf, Professor Emeritus at Ghent University, Honorary Notary at Dendermonde, D.Phil. (Oxford University, 1963), MCL (Columbia University, 1960), Doctor in Law (Ghent University, 1959), and Licentiate in Notarial Law (1958).

Hans De Wulf, Professor at Ghent University, Ph.D. in Law (Ghent University, 2001), LL.M. (Karl-Eberhards Universität Tübingen, 1994), and Licentiate in Law (Ghent University, 1993).

Johan Erauw, Professor Emeritus at Ghent University, Attorney: Member of the Ghent Bar, Arbitrator, Honorary Dr (East China University of Politics and Law, 2005), Ph.D. in Law (Ghent University, 1979), and Licentiate in Law (Ghent University, 1972).

Dirk Heirbaut, Professor at Ghent University, Member of the Royal Flemish Academy of Belgium for Science and the Arts, Ph.D. in Law (Ghent University, 1997), Licentiate in Law (Ghent University, 1993), and Licentiate in History (Ghent University, 1988).

David Renders, Professor at Université Catholique de Louvain (UCL), Attorney: Member of the Brussels Bar, Ph.D. in Law (UCL, 2002), Bachelor in Philosophy (UCL, 1994), and Licentiate in Law (UCL, 1994).

Joëlle Rozie, Professor at University of Antwerp, Ph.D. in Law (Vrije Universiteit Brussel (VUB), 2004), and Licentiate in Law (VUB, 1997).

Vincent Sagaert, Professor at KU Leuven and at University of Antwerp, Attorney: Off Counsel at Eubelius in Brussels, Ph.D. in Law (KU Leuven, 2002), and Licentiate in Law (KU Leuven, 1999).

Patrick Senaeve, Professor at KU Leuven, Ph.D. in Law (KU Leuven, 1981), Licentiate in Political and Social Sciences (KU Leuven, 1977), and Licentiate in Law (KU Leuven, 1974).

Piet Taelman, Professor at Ghent University, Former Dean of the Ghent University Law School (2008–2014), Ph.D. in Law (Ghent University, 1994), and Licentiate in Law (Ghent University, 1982).

Sebastiaan Vandenbogaerde, Post-Doctoral Researcher at Ghent University, Ph.D. in Law (Ghent University, 2014), Master of Law (Ghent University, 2010), and Licentiate in History (Ghent University, 2006).

Willy van Eeckhoutte, Professor at Ghent University, Attorney at the Court of Cassation: Partner at Van Eeckhoutte, Taquet & Clesse in Ghent, Ph.D. in Law (Ghent University, 1985), and Licentiate in Law (Ghent University, 1975).

Mark Van Hoecke, Professor at Queen Mary University of London, Professor Emeritus at Ghent University, Ph.D. in Law (Ghent University, 1979), and Licentiate in Law (Ghent University, 1972).

Claudia Van Severen, Research Assistant at Ghent University, and Master of Laws (Ghent University, 2010).

Eddy Wymeersch, Professor Emeritus at Ghent University, Former Chairman of the Committee of European Securities Regulators (CESR), Former Chairman of the Supervisory Board of the Belgian Banking, Finance and Insurance Commission, LL.M. (Harvard Law School, 1968), and Doctor in Law (Ghent University, 1966).

Summary of Contents

Table of Contents

CHAPTER 1

The Belgian Legal Tradition: Does It Exist?

Dirk Heirbaut[*]

Belgium came into existence as an independent state in 1830, when the southern part of the then United Kingdom of the Netherlands seceded. Though not of as recent origin as some other European states, Belgium is still relatively young. It is therefore justified not only to ask what legal tradition Belgium has, but also, most of all, whether the country has any such tradition at all. The answer should vary according to the period concerned: before or after 1830.

§1.01 A BELGIAN LEGAL TRADITION BEFORE BELGIAN INDEPENDENCE IN 1830?

[A] Belgian Political History Before 1830

It is hard to find any antecedents of Belgium before the end of the sixteenth century. The divisions of the Carolingian empire in the treaties of Verdun (843) and Meersen (870) split up the territories that now form Belgium and the Netherlands between France and Germany, the river Scheldt serving as frontier. The French part became an autonomous principality at the end of the ninth century under the counts of Flanders. The German kings managed to keep their Duchy of Lotharingia under better control until the eleventh century. Thereafter it also fell under the sway of local rulers. Thus in the twelfth century the Low Countries were a patchwork of autonomous principalities, like Flanders, Hainault, Brabant, Luxembourg, Liège, Holland, Utrecht and Guelders.

* I wish to thank Prof. em. dr. R. Van Caenegem, Prof. em. dr. D. Lambrecht, Patricia Carson, Gerard Sinnaeve, Luk Burgelman, S. Huygebaert and M. Van Der Haegen who have read drafts of this text. I greatly benefited from their comments and suggestions. Any remaining errors are entirely my own.

Although these principalities were united by economic and, sometimes, dynastic ties, they did not coalesce into a larger unit in the twelfth and thirteenth centuries.

However, from 1386, the dukes of Burgundy gradually brought most of these principalities under their control. To distinguish them from the Burgundian homelands, these new possessions received the name *pays de par deça* (Burgundy and the Franche-Comté being the *pays de par delà*). The Habsburgs, who succeeded the dukes of Burgundy as rulers, finished the process of unification in the sixteenth century. At that time, the *pays de par deça* were in learned circles known as Belgium. This Belgium of sixteenth century humanists, however, was not today's Belgium. It roughly covered the territory of the modern states of Belgium, the Netherlands and Luxembourg and even a part of northern France. Thus, the term Belgium in the sixteenth century has to be translated as the Low Countries. The same is true for its popular equivalent: Netherlands, which does, again, not mean today's Netherlands, but Low Countries (which is in fact the literal meaning of the term Netherlands).

The political unity of the Low Countries did not survive the sixteenth century. Due to religious and other reasons, the Low Countries revolted against their Habsburg overlord, Philip II, king of Spain. The North, the so-called Northern Netherlands, became independent and came to be known as the United Provinces. The Habsburgs managed to keep the South, the so-called Southern Netherlands. Thereafter, the old name of Belgium was still used for both the North and the South. In the eighteenth century, however, it was almost exclusively used for the South, which, by then, had been passed from the Spanish to the Austrian Habsburgs. Yet, even the Southern Netherlands were not completely equivalent to today's Belgium. The principalities of Liège and Stavelot-Malmédy stayed autonomous under their own rulers (a bishop and an abbot). On the other hand, the whole of Luxembourg and the northernmost part of France belonged to the Southern Netherlands (the latter until it was conquered by Louis XIV). The French revolution led to an annexation of the Southern and later also of the Northern Netherlands by France.

In the aftermath of the Napoleonic wars, North and South were reunited in 1815 in the United Kingdom of the Netherlands. As in the sixteenth century, the terms Netherlands and Belgium were, again, used indiscriminately for the whole Low Countries. By now, the French forms of the word Belgium, like *Belgique*, had ousted the original Latin word. Thus, the inhabitants of the new state could both be called *Nederlanders* (in Dutch) and *Belges* in French.[1] North and South had grown estranged in the time spent apart between the end of the sixteenth century and 1815, so that their reunion did not last long. For various reasons, the South broke away in 1830.[2] As its ruling elite was French-speaking, the new state called itself in French *Belgique* (Belgium). The Dutch-speaking North continued to call itself in Dutch *Nederland* (Netherlands).

1. J. Stengers, *Le vocabulaire national dans le royaume des Pays-Bas*, *in* ACTA: COLLOQUIUM OVER DE GESCHIEDENIS VAN DE BELGISCH-NEDERLANDSE BETREKKINGEN TUSSEN 1815 EN 1945. COLLOQUE HISTORIQUE SUR LES RÉLATIONS BELGO-NÉERLANDAISES ENTRE 1815 ET 1945, 9–28 (Ghent: Erasmus 1982).
2. On the United Kingdom of the Netherlands, *see* G. DENECKERE & R. AERTS, HET (ON)VERENIGD KONINKRIJK DER NEDERLANDEN. EEN POLITIEK EXPERIMENT IN DE LAGE LANDEN (Rekkem: Ons Erfdeel 2015).

[B] The Legal History of the Southern Netherlands Before 1830

One can distinguish the following periods:

(1) The Middle Ages (till the end of the fifteenth century);
(2) The Early Modern period (end of the fifteenth century to 1795);
(3) The French period (1795–1815); and
(4) The Dutch period (1815–1830).

[1] The Middle Ages (Until the End of the Fifteenth Century)

It is hard to see how a 'Belgian' legal tradition could have existed in the autonomous principalities. There was no political unity between them and, thus, also no unified law. Even within each of these principalities, there was no common legal system. Medieval law in the Southern Netherlands was largely customary and each place had its own customs and, thus, its own laws. One exception to this was the Prince-Bishopric of Liège, where legal unification was largely achieved in the thirteenth century.[3] Apart from local differences, customs could vary because of the status of persons or goods. The result was therefore not one legal system, but a variety of legal systems.[4]

Yet, the chaos was not total. Some legal rules were of more than local importance, but even then, most of them were not common to the whole Southern Netherlands. That some legal rules were more widespread, was not due to the influence of legislation. Legislation did exist, but it was mostly an urban phenomenon.[5] From the twelfth century onwards, city aldermen could legislate and they used this right extensively. This municipal legislation was not without importance as cities were widespread. The county of Flanders, for example, was as urbanised as was northern Italy. In contrast to their cities, the various counts and dukes mostly abstained from law making. This changed under the dukes of Burgundy. Their legislation even began to rival the city ordinances. Yet, its effect was still limited. The Burgundians did not promulgate general laws. They made individual laws for each of their principalities.[6]

Jurisprudence did not remedy the lack of a general legislation. From the thirteenth century, the learned law – i.e., Roman and canon law that were studied at

3. On Liège, *see* S. Dubois, B. Demoulin & J.-L. Kupper, Les institutions publiques de la principauté de Liège (980–1794) (Brussels: State Archives 2012).
4. D. Van Den Auweele, *De evolutie van het recht in het Zuiden. 12de-14de eeuw*, *in* 3 Algemene Geschiedenis der Nederlanden 145, 149–150 (Haarlem: Fibula – Van Dishoeck 1982).
5. P. Godding, *Les ordonnances des autorités urbaines au moyen âge. Leur apport à la technique législative*, in Peasants and Townsmen in Medieval Europe. Studia in Honorem Adriaan Verhulst 185–201 (J. Duvosquel & E. Thoen eds., Ghent: Snoeck-Ducaju 1995).
6. For Hainault, *see* J. Cauchies, La législation princière pour le comté de Hainaut. Ducs de Bourgogne et premier Habsbourg. (1427–1506). Contribution à l'étude des rapports entre gouvernants et gouvernés dans les Pays-Bas à l'aube des temps modernes (Brussels: Publications des facultés universitaires Saint-Louis, XXIV, 1982).

the universities – began to penetrate.[7] Because of the central position of the church in medieval society, canon law influenced the matters for which the ecclesiastic courts were competent, like marriage. Roman law had less impact. Even princes only began to use it from the fourteenth century onwards. Scientific study of customary law was almost non-existent. Even when customary law was written down, this was by practitioners, who mostly limited themselves to local customs. It is telling that the most influential work on customary law was the *Somme Rural* of Jehan Boutillier, a Frenchman.[8]

In the absence of professors and legislators, other factors contributed to some legal unity in the Southern Netherlands during the Middle Ages. The most important was the mechanism of the *recours au chef de sens*, the practice of asking the advice of another court, the chief court.[9] This allowed the spread of legal rules from the head-court to other courts. From the fourteenth century, central princely courts also began to influence the decisions of lower courts through appeals and other procedures.[10]

Because of these and other mechanisms, groups of customs can be distinguished. A well-studied division distinguishes Flemish and Picard-Walloon customs. Both groups of customs tend to protect the interests of the family, while still caring for the surviving spouse. In a conflict between the family and the surviving spouse, Flemish customs are more inclined to choose the side of the family; Picard-Walloon customs rather prefer the widow or widower.[11] However, it should be stressed that this distinction is only valid for inheritance law and matrimonial property law, and even then it is only valid for broad tendencies rather than for individual legal rules. In short, during the Middle Ages no Belgian law existed.

[2] The Early Modern Period

Political unification being achieved in the sixteenth century, legal unification could follow. Yet, it was late to come and achieved only limited results. The Habsburg princes did not legislate as king or emperor, but as Duke of Brabant, Duke of Luxembourg,

7. On the reception of Roman law in Belgium, *see* D. Heirbaut & J.-F. Gerkens, *In the Shadow of France. Legal Acculturation and Legal Transplants in the Southern Netherlands/Belgium, in* The Belgian Reports at the Congress of Washington of the International Academy of Comparative Law 3–34 (E. Dirix & Y.H. Leleu eds., Brussels: Bruylant 2011).
8. D. Van Den Auweele, *De evolutie van het recht in het Zuiden 12e-14e eeuw, in* 3 Algemene Geschiedenis der Nederlanden 145, 152 (Haarlem: Fibula – Van Dishoeck 1982).
9. R. Van Caenegem, Geschiedenis van het strafprocesrecht in Vlaanderen van de XIe tot de XIVe eeuw 300–314 (Brussels: Koninklijke Vlaamse academie voor wetenschappen, letteren en schone kunsten van België 1956).
10. P. Godding & J. De Smidt, *Evolutie van het recht in samenhang met de instellingen, in* 4 Algemene Geschiedenis der Nederlanden 172, 172–173 (Haarlem: Fibula – Van Dishoeck 1980).
11. P. Godding, Le droit privé dans les Pays-Bas méridionaux du 12e au 18e siècle 318–321 (Brussels: Académie royale de Belgique 1987); R. Jacob, Les époux, le seigneur et la cité. Coutume et pratiques matrimoniales des bourgeois et paysans de France du Nord au moyen âge (Brussels: Publications des facultés universitaires Saint-Louis, 1990); E. Meijers, Het Ligurische erfrecht in de Nederlanden II-III (Haarlem: Tjeenk Willink 1932–1936); J. Yver, *Les deux groupes de coutumes du Nord,* 35 Revue du Nord 197–220 (1953), 36 Revue du Nord 5–36 (1954).

Count of Flanders, etc. Consequently, each of the former principalities still had its own set of laws. General legislation was exceptional in the sixteenth century, though by the eighteenth it had become common. Even then, the number of princely ordinances was small. On average fifty new ordinances were issued each year.[12] The best known is the *Edictum Perpetuum* of 1611, promulgated by the Archdukes Albert and Isabella. This short text was the first, and last, major attempt by the legislator at unifying some rules of private law in the Southern Netherlands.[13] Also well-known are the Criminal Ordinances of 1570. Their intention was to unify criminal procedure, but in practice they were largely disregarded.[14]

Jurisprudence did not contribute much to legal unification. The first great author was Philip Wielant around 1500.[15] He made a synthesis of the law of the county of Flanders as it existed in his time. His major works were devoted to criminal law and criminal procedure (*Practijcke criminele*) and to civil procedure (*Practijcke civile*). Wielant's work has one drawback: it was only concerned with Flemish law, not with the law of other principalities. Moreover, it was written in Dutch, as it was aimed at the practitioners of law, who could not always understand Latin very well. Therefore, Latin translations could be published by Joos de Damhouder, who forbore from mentioning Wielant's name. In its Latin form and under Damhouder's name, Wielant's work became widely known in the Southern Netherlands and abroad.[16]

After the split between the Northern and Southern Netherlands and stimulated by the *Edictum Perpetuum* and French examples, some authors began to study law in the Southern Netherlands as a whole. Their work was mostly descriptive. Authors like Gudelinus, Zypaeus or Anselmo were looking for common elements, but they did not themselves create a unified legal system. After the middle of the seventeenth century, most legal works are mediocre.[17]

A third unifying factor, beside jurisprudence and legislation, were the provincial and supra-provincial courts. The supra-provincial court was the Great Council of Malines. Its jurisdiction was disputed, as the provincial councils claimed to be sovereign, i.e., that no appeal against their decisions was possible. Some of them managed to obtain recognition of this sovereignty, so that at the end of the eighteenth

12. J. Gilissen, *Essai statistique de la législation en Belgique de 1506 à 1794*, 40 REVUE DU NORD 9–13 (1958).
13. G. MARTYN, HET EEUWIG EDICT VAN 12 JULI 1611, ZIJN GENESE EN ZIJN ROL IN DE VERSCHRIFTELIJKING VAN HET PRIVAATRECHT (Studia 81, Algemeen Rijksarchief en Rijksarchief in de provinciën 2000).
14. J. Monballyu, *Strafprocesrecht in Vlaanderen voor en na de criminele ordonnantien van 1570*, 36 HANDELINGEN VAN DE KONINKLIJKE COMMISSIE VOOR DE UITGAVE VAN OUDE WETTEN EN VERORDENINGEN VAN BELGIË 117–133 (1996).
15. J. MONBALLYU, FILIPS WIELANT. VERZAMELD WERK. I. CORTE INSTRUCTIE IN MATERIE CRIMINELE 7–18 (Brussels: Koninklijke academie voor wetenschappen, letteren en schone kunsten van België 1995).
16. J. Dauwe & J. Monballyu, *Joos de Damhouder (1507–1581) en zijn Practycke ende handbouck in criminele zaken*, epilogue to the anastatic reprint of J. DE DAMHOUDER, PRACTYCKE ENDE HANDBOUCK IN CRIMINELE ZAEKEN 1555 (Roeselare: Den Wijngaert 1981); J. Monballyu & J. Dauwe, *Joos de Damhouder en zijn 'Practycke in civile saecken'*, epilogue to the anastatic reprint of J. DE DAMHOUDER, PRACTYCKE IN CIVILE SAECKEN, 1626 (Ghent: s.n. 1999).
17. J. GILISSEN & M. MAGITS, DE BRONNEN VAN HET RECHT IN DE BELGISCHE GEWESTEN SEDERT DE DERTIENDE EEUW 115–116 (Antwerp: Kluwer rechtswetenschappen 1989).

century the Great Council of Malines was only competent for Flanders, Namur and Malines.[18] In these circumstances, it should come as no surprise that it could not contribute much to the creation of a unified law for the Southern Netherlands. The provincial councils had marginally more success, but were confined to their own individual provinces.[19]

Even if central legislation, jurisprudence and supra-provincial courts had been more prominent, their chances of realising legal unity would have been small. In 1531, Emperor Charles V ordered the homologation of local customs. They were to be written down, and, after revision by the central authorities, promulgated by the prince. One of this homologation's aims was to bring about legal unification. At first sight, it was fairly successful. About 600 customs were abrogated and fewer than 100 were homologated. In Namur and Luxembourg, for example, the local customs were replaced by one regional custom. However, in the most important provinces, Flanders and Brabant, local customs still prevailed. Moreover, though homologation had abolished many local customs, it had strengthened the position of those that were left by putting them in writing and giving them official recognition. Thus, the homologation's effect was maintaining the diversity of customary law rather than abolishing it. Homologation had one other negative effect. As long as a custom is not written down, it can and will easily change, as there is no fixed point of reference. Homologation changed that. One could now refer to the text of the homologated custom. This meant that the development of customary law largely stopped after homologation. Consequently, most evolution of customary law took place in the Middle Ages rather than in the sixteenth to eighteenth centuries.[20] On the positive side, homologation put up a bulwark against the growing influence of Roman law.[21] A special case was the homologation of Antwerp law during the sixteenth and early seventeenth centuries. Antwerp was unique in that its customs were written down four times. Moreover, this Antwerp law influenced the law of commerce in Amsterdam and London, which displaced it as Europe's main port in the seventeenth and eighteenth centuries.[22] Antwerp was also

18. A. Wijffels, *Grote Raad voor de Nederlanden te Mechelen*, *in* De centrale overheidsinstellingen van de Habsburgse Nederlanden 1482–1795, 454–455 (E. Aerts et al. eds., Brussels: Algemeen rijksarchief 1994); C.H. Van Rhee, *The Low Countries Until 1800*, *in* European Supreme Courts. A Portrait Throughout History 204–217 (A. Wijffels & C.H. Van Rhee eds., London: Third Millennium 2013).
19. Cf. J. Monballyu, *De gerechtelijke bevoegdheid van de Raad van Vlaanderen in vergelijking met de andere 'Wetten' (1515–1621)*, in Hoven en banken in Noord en Zuid 1–26 (B. Jacobs & P. Nève eds., Assen: Van Gorcum 1994).
20. P. Godding, 'Nouveaux itinéraires en droit' dans l'espace belge du 12e au 18e siècle, in: Nouveaux itinéraires en droit. Hommage à François Rigaux 242–244 (Brussels: Bruylant 1993); R. Van Caenegem, An Historical Introduction to Private Law 36–38 (Cambridge: Cambridge University Press 1992).
21. Cf. G. Macours, *De visie van de Belgische 19de-eeuwse rechtspraak op de subsidiaire rol van het oude Romeinse recht. Een verkennend onderzoek*, *in* 'Houd voet bij stuk'. Xenia iuris historiae G. Van Dievoet oblata 256–286 (F. Stevens & D. Van Den Auweele eds., Louvain: KULeuven, Law Faculty, Section of Roman law and legal history 1990).
22. On Antwerp law, *see* B. Van Hofstraeten, Juridisch humanisme en costumiere acculturatie. Inhouds- en vormbepalende factoren van de Antwerpse Consuetudines compilatae (1608) en het Gelderse Land- en Stadsrecht (1620) (Maastricht: Universitaire pers 2008); D. De Ruysscher,

essential for the work of Leonardus Lessius, who, around 1600, used his acquaintance with Antwerp business practices to write on finance and commerce.[23]

During the Early Modern Period political unity did not lead to legal unity. In the second half of the eighteenth century the influence of the enlightenment and natural-law theories made itself felt. This was mostly due to an external development. Most lawyers in the Southern Netherlands distrusted the writings of the natural lawyers.[24] Notable exceptions were some proponents of reforms in the administration or in criminal law, for instance Goswin de Fierlant and Vilain XIV.[25] In these circumstances, changes had to be initiated from above. However, the Austrian Habsburgs[26] hesitated for a long time to overhaul the existing structures of the Southern Netherlands. In 1780, Joseph II came to power, and he started an ambitious programme of reform. Before him, the princes of the Southern Netherlands promulgated on average fifty new ordinances a year. Now that number more than doubled. Crucial were Joseph's plans for sweeping reforms of the administrative and judicial organisation and two codes for civil and criminal procedure respectively. The population of the Southern Netherlands did not like these abrupt changes, and in October 1789 a revolt put an end to Joseph's power and his reforms. Austrian authority was later restored, but any plans of reform had to be given up.[27]

[3] The French Period[28]

The restoration of Austrian power did not last long. In 1795 revolutionary France annexed the Southern Netherlands. Henceforward, all French revolutionary legislation was also in force in the annexed departments. Even some older legislation, i.e., French

NAER HET ROMEINS RECHT ALSMEDE DEN STIEL MERCANTIEL. HANDEL EN RECHT IN DE ANTWERPSE RECHTBANK (16DE-17DE EEUW) (Heule: UGA 2009).

23. T. VAN HOUDT & W. DECOCK, LEONARDUS LESSIUS: TRADITIE EN VERNIEUWING (Antwerp: Belpaire 2005).
24. G. Van Dievoet, *De ontwikkeling van de rechtswetenschappen*, *in* 7 ALGEMENE GESCHIEDENIS DER NEDERLANDEN 311, 318 (Haarlem: Fibula - Van Dishoeck 1980).
25. J. Monballyu, *De Raad van Vlaanderen en de hervormingen van het strafrecht (1756–1787)*, 64 TIJDSCHRIFT VOOR RECHTSGESCHIEDENIS 47–75 (1996); F. Stevens, *Jean Vilain XIIII (1712–1777)*, *in* GESTALTEN UIT HET VERLEDEN. 32 VOORGANGERS IN DE STRAFRECHTSWETENSCHAP, DE STRAFRECHTSPLEGING EN DE CRIMINOLOGIE 1-9 (C. Fijnaut ed., Brussels: Kluwer Rechtswetenschappen 1993); D. Van Den Auweele & P. Nefors, *Goswin de Fierlant (1735–1804)*, *in* GESTALTEN UIT HET VERLEDEN: 32 VOORGANGERS IN DE STRAFRECHTSWETENSCHAP, DE STRAFRECHTSPLEGING EN DE CRIMINOLOGIE 11–22 (C. Fijnaut ed., Brussels: Kluwer Rechtswetenschappen 1993). *See also* more in general, J. MONBALLYU, HISTORY OF CRIMINAL LAW IN THE SOUTHERN NETHERLANDS AND BELGIUM (1400–2000) (Leyden, Brill 2014).
26. For a monumental work on the Austrian Habsburgs in the Southern Netherlands, *see* L. DHONDT, VERLICHTE MONARCHIE, ANCIEN RÉGIME EN REVOLUTIE: EEN INSTITUTIONELE EN HISTORISCHE PROCESANALYSE VAN POLITIEK, INSTELLINGEN EN IDEOLOGIE IN DE HABSBURGSE, DE NEDERLANDSE EN DE VLAAMSE POLITIEKE RUIMTE (1700/1755–1790), 5 Vol. (Brussels: State Archives 2002).
27. L. Dhondt, *Politiek en institutioneel onvermogen 1780–1814 in de Zuidelijke Nederlanden*, *in* 9 ALGEMENE GESCHIEDENIS DER NEDERLANDEN 139–159 (Haarlem: Fibula - Van Dishoeck 1980).
28. The French era is the subject of: E. Berger, D. Heirbaut, H. Leuwers & X. Rousseaux, *La justice avant la Belgique: tentatives autrichiennes, influences françaises et expériences néerlandaises (1780–1830)*, *in* DEUX SIÈCLES DE JUSTICE. ENCYCLOPÉDIE HISTORIQUE DE LA JUSTICE BELGE 26–50 (M. De Koster, D. Heirbaut & X. Rousseaux eds., Bruges: die Keure 2015).

royal ordinances from the sixteenth to eighteenth centuries, like the *Ordonnance civile pour la réformation de la justice*, were introduced in the Southern Netherlands.[29]

As the former Southern Netherlands were a part of France under Napoleon, all his codifications and other reforms also came into force there, among them:

- the *Code civil* (1804);
- the judicial organisation (1800);
- the *Code de procédure civile* (1806);
- the *Code de commerce* (1807);
- the *Code d'Instruction criminelle* (1808); and
- the *Code pénal* (1810).[30]

Revolutionary and Napoleonic legislation finally ended legal diversity in the Southern Netherlands. However, this did not mean that a 'Belgian' legal tradition was born. The new legal system was French. To the extent that the old law disappeared, this was a break with the past, but to the extent that it was French, it was less of a break. As far as the sources of the law are concerned, France at that time could be divided into the regions of customary law (*pays de droit coutumier*), where customary law of Germanic origin dominated, and the regions of written law (*pays de droit écrit*), where Roman law had been supreme. The Southern Netherlands belonged to the *pays de droit coutumier.*[31] More specifically, they were part of the so-called *pays de nantissement* (literally: regions of pledging), regions where the publicity of transfers of rights to real property was assured by the intervention of the competent court.[32] Besides, French laws, French authors and French practices had already been influencing the Southern Netherlands for a long time.[33] During the second half of the eighteenth century that influence had grown even stronger.[34] The complete 'reception' of French law at the beginning of the nineteenth century was a continuation, though a very drastic one, of an already existing trend. To all this should be added that the first generation of lawyers

29. J. GILISSEN & M. MAGITS, DE BRONNEN VAN HET RECHT IN DE BELGISCHE GEWESTEN SEDERT DE DERTIENDE EEUW 153–154 (Antwerp: Kluwer rechtswetenschappen 1989).
30. Of the many commemorative volumes of the bicentennials of Napoleon's codes, only a few can be mentioned here: LE CODE NAPOLÉON. UN ANCÊTRE VÉNÉRÉ? MÉLANGES OFFERTS À JACQUES VANDERLINDEN (R. Beauthier & I. Rorive eds., Brussels: Bruylant 2004); UN HÉRITAGE NAPOLÉONIEN. BICENTENAIRE DU CODE CIVIL EN BELGIQUE (D. Heirbaut & G. Martyn eds., Mechelen: Kluwer 2005); THE FRENCH CODE OF CIVIL PROCEDURE (1806) AFTER 200 YEARS. THE CIVIL PROCEDURE TRADITION IN FRANCE AND ABROAD 159–192 (D. Heirbaut, C.H. Van Rhee & M. Storme eds., Mechelen: Kluwer 2008); BICENTENAIRE DU CODE DE COMMERCE EN BELGIQUE (G. Martyn & D. Heirbaut eds., Brussels: KVAB 2009).
31. Cf. R. VAN CAENEGEM, AN HISTORICAL INTRODUCTION TO PRIVATE LAW 27 (Cambridge University Press 1992).
32. P. GODDING, LE DROIT PRIVÉ DANS LES PAYS-BAS MÉRIDIONAUX DU 12E AU 18E SIÈCLE 233 (Brussels: Académie royale de Belgique 1987).
33. For example the homologation of customary law. *See* R. VAN CAENEGEM, AN HISTORICAL INTRODUCTION TO PRIVATE LAW 36 (Cambridge University Press 1992).
34. J. Bosch, *Remarques sur quelques influences exercées en matière de droit, par les provinces méridionales sur les provinces septentrionales des Pays-Bas jusqu'en 1795*, 19 TIJDSCHRIFT VOOR RECHTSGESCHIEDENIS 154 (1951).

after the French and Napoleonic legislation still continued to work in the framework of the old laws.[35]

[4] The Dutch Period

The end of the French occupation in 1814 did not lead to independence, nor did it lead to a restoration of Austrian rule. Instead, the United Kingdom of the Netherlands was created, which reunited the Southern and the Northern Netherlands and Liège under William I of the House of Orange. The new state wanted to have its own codifications. Some differences had to be overcome to create a new national law. In the South, French influence was very great, whereas the North was more inclined to use German ideas and theories. The Southerners wanted law to be practical; on the other hand, the Northerners loved theory. In spite of all that, by 1829 a new law on judicial organisation and four new codes, dealing with civil law, commercial law, civil procedure and criminal procedure were ready. By royal decree, they would come into force on 1 February 1831. However, in 1830 the South seceded. Consequently, the new codes were never introduced there. Exceptions were titles VI and VII of the second book of the new civil code. The French civil code had not dealt with long leases and building leases. Therefore, that part of the new civil code had already been introduced in 1825.[36] Apart from that, the United Kingdom of the Netherlands has not left many traces of its existence in Belgian law.

§1.02 A BELGIAN LEGAL TRADITION AFTER BELGIAN INDEPENDENCE IN 1830?

[A] The Belgian Revolution

The Belgian revolution of 1830 had many causes. The United Kingdom of the Netherlands had been discriminating against the South from its start. The state debt of the new kingdom had to be paid equally by North and South, although the debts were mainly Northern. In the parliament the North had as many delegates as the South,

35. *See* the articles by Beauthier, Stevens and Heirbaut in LE CODE NAPOLÉON. UN ANCÊTRE VÉNÉRÉ? MÉLANGES OFFERTS À JACQUES VANDERLINDEN (R. Beauthier & I. Rorive eds., Brussels: Bruylant 2004).

36. J. Gilissen, *Codification et projets de codification en Belgique au XIXe siècle (1804–1915)*, 14 BELGISCH TIJDSCHRIFT VOOR NIEUWSTE GESCHIEDENIS 219–229 (1983); *Ibid.*, *De Belgische commissie van 1816 tot herziening van het ontwerp burgerlijk wetboek voor het Koninkrijk der Nederlanden*, 35 TIJDSCHRIFT VOOR RECHTSGESCHIEDENIS 383–443 (1967); H. KOOIKER, 1 LEX SCRIPTA ABROGATA. DE DERDE RENAISSANCE VAN HET ROMEINSE RECHT. EEN ONDERZOEK NAAR DE DOORWERKING VAN HET OUDE RECHT NA DE INVOERING VAN DE CIVIELRECHTELIJKE CODIFICATIES IN HET BEGIN VAN DE NEGENTIENDE EEUW 346–356 (Nimeguen: Ars Aequi 1996); S. Van Brakel, *De geschiedenis van de totstandkoming van het Burgerlijk Wetboek van 1820 tot 1838, in* GEDENKBOEK BURGERLIJK WETBOEK 1838–1938, 277–326 (P. Scholten & E. Meijers eds., Zwolle: Tjeenk Willink 1938); J. Van Den Broeck, *Het Burgerlijk Wetboek en de invloed van de Duitse rechtshistorische school in België tijdens de 19de eeuw, in* WETBOEK EN GRONDWET IN HISTORISCH PERSPECTIEF. LIBER AMICORUM JOHN GILISSEN 417–425 (Antwerp: Kluwer Rechtswetenschappen 1983); E. VAN DIEVOET, HET BURGERLIJK RECHT IN BELGIË EN NEDERLAND VAN 1800 TOT 1940. DE RECHTSBRONNEN 15–53 (Antwerp, De Sikkel, 1943).

although the population of the South was nearly twice that of the North. The constitution of the United Kingdom of the Netherlands had only been approved in the South in 1815 by some very creative counting (the abstentions and no-votes for religious reasons were counted as yes-votes). Events after 1815 mostly strengthened Southern dislike of the United Kingdom of the Netherlands. The Catholics were enraged because the king interfered too much with education and was not willing to give Catholicism a privileged position in the south. The French-speaking bourgeoisie did not like the linguistic policy of the king, who wanted to promote the Dutch language. They also wanted to have a liberal state, in which there would be no place for the autocracy of the king.

[B] The Constitution

The 1830 revolution led to one major legal document: the Constitution. It came into force on 25 February 1831. This Belgian Constitution has been considered to have been very innovative. Its success can be seen as a testimony of that. It was very influential in the nineteenth century and was imitated in Spain, Greece, Romania and Luxembourg. It also inspired the framers of the Italian, Prussian, Bulgarian and Dutch constitutions. In the twentieth century, it was still a source of inspiration in Poland, Hungary and Czechoslovakia. Yet, the Belgian Constitution was not original at all. Forty per cent of it was borrowed from the constitution of the United Kingdom of the Netherlands, 35% of the French *Charte constitutionnelle* of 1830, 10% of the French constitution of 1791 and 5% was derived from English constitutional practice. This leaves only 10% that has not been borrowed from elsewhere. If one weeds out some articles without much importance, only about ten articles were really new in 1831.[37]

[C] French Influence in the Nineteenth Century

Although the Constitution itself was not so original, Article 139 called for a quick revision of the existing French codifications.[38] If this had happened as soon as the framers had wanted, a Belgian legal tradition might have come into existence. In reality, however, the opposite happened.[39] Paradoxically enough, independence was one of the worst things that ever happened to legal science in Belgium. The French had first abolished the study of law in the Belgian territories and later created some kind of vocational school for law studies. Consequently, after the French occupation there

37. J. Gilissen, *Die belgische Verfassung von 1831. Ihr Ursprung und ihr Einfluss*, *in* Beiträge zur deutschen und belgischen Verfassungsgeschichte im 19. Jahrhundert 38–69 (Stuttgart: Klett 1967); *Ibid.*, *La constitution belge de 1831: ses sources, son influence*, 10 Res publica 107–141 (1968).

38. J. Gilissen, *Codification et projets de codification en Belgique au XIXe siècle (1804–1915)*, 14 Belgisch tijdschrift voor nieuwste geschiedenis 229 (1983).

39. *See* for a general survey, D. Heirbaut, Hadden/hebben de Belgische ministers van justitie een civielrechtelijk beleid (Mechelen: Kluwer 2005) and also F. Stevens, *Der Code civil in Belgien seit 1804. Ein fester Halt*, *in* 200 Jahre Code civil. Die napoleontische Kodifikation in Deutschland und Europa 207–224 (Cologne: Böhlau 2005).

were few natives who were learned enough to teach law at a university. The government of the United Kingdom of the Netherlands had to bring in foreigners, mostly Germans. However, the efforts to create an academic study of law came to a halt after the revolution. The Constitution promoted the liberty of education. Anyone, who wanted to, could teach law. To assure at least some level of ability, in 1835 a central commission was instituted in Brussels. Only this commission could, after an examination, award a legal diploma. Original thinking was to be avoided, as that only lessened one's chances of passing the central exam.[40] In these circumstances, it is hard to see how an original Belgian legal tradition could have developed.

However, there was hardly a need for it. For a long time, Belgium could still count on some of the foreigners who had become professors in the 1815–1830 era. Jacques-Joseph Haus, for example, had become professor in Ghent in 1817 and only stopped teaching there in 1880. Most of all, after 1830, the Belgian elite was French-speaking. Although more than half the population was Dutch-speaking, the legal language was French. For lawyers it was easier to keep working with the French codes. That way, they could have a free ride by copying French laws, citing decisions of French courts and using French literature, sometimes in pirated editions of French works printed in Brussels.[41]

The result of this was that during most of the nineteenth century independence of the legal system was further away than ever. The judicial organisation still ran along Napoleonic lines.[42] There were few changes to the French codes.[43] Most attempts at revising them failed. Projects of the two procedural codes only led to new preliminary titles in the existing codes. The Civil Code was even worse off. A first commission to revise it was installed in 1841. The commission's efforts only led to a revision of the title on real securities. However, in 1879 François Laurent was charged with writing a new civil code.[44] Laurent was, beyond any doubt, the greatest legal mind ever working in Belgium. His new code was finished in 1883. It was a well-crafted document that also

40. B. Coppein, *Rechtsonderwijs en rechtsleer*, *in* DEUX SIÈCLES DE JUSTICE. ENCYCLOPÉDIE HISTORIQUE DE LA JUSTICE BELGE 111–112 (M. De Koster, D. Heirbaut & X. Rousseaux eds., Bruges: die Keure 2015).
41. E. VAN DIEVOET, HET BURGERLIJK RECHT IN BELGIË EN NEDERLAND VAN 1800 TOT 1940. DE RECHTSBRONNEN 89–90 (Antwerp, De Sikkel, 1943); F. VERBEKE, BELGIAN LAW: AN ANNOTATED BIBLIOGRAPHIC GUIDE TO REFERENCE MATERIALS, 1803–1993, 115–135 (Brussels: Belgische commissie voor bibliografie en bibliologie 1994).
42. J. GILISSEN, L'ORDRE JUDICIAIRE EN BELGIQUE AU DÉBUT DE L'INDÉPENDANCE (1830–1832), CII JOURNAL DES TRIBUNAUX 565–596 (1983); J. NANDRIN, 1 HOMMES, NORMES ET POLITIQUE: LE POUVOIR JUDICIAIRE EN BELGIQUE AUX PREMIERS TEMPS DE L'INDÉPENDENCE (Ph.D. dissertation Université Catholique de Louvain-La-Neuve 1995).
43. About these, *see* E. Holthöfer, *Belgien*, in HANDBUCH DER QUELLEN UND LITERATUR DER NEUEREN EUROPÄISCHEN PRIVATRECHTSGESCHICHTE III/1, 1070, 1089–1098 (H. Coing eds., Munich: Beck 1982) and III/3, 3277, 3287–3345 (H. Coing eds., Munich: Beck 1986); J. Gilissen, *Codification et projets de codification en Belgique au XIXe siècle (1804–1915)*, 14 BELGISCH TIJDSCHRIFT VOOR NIEUWSTE GESCHIEDENIS 229–269 (1983); E. SPANOGHE & R. FEENSTRA, HONDERDVIJFTIG JAAR RECHTSLEVEN IN BELGIË EN NEDERLAND, 1830–1980. PREADVIEZEN UITGEBRACHT VOOR EEN COLLOQUIUM GEORGANISEERD DOOR DE JURIDISCHE FACULTEITEN VAN DE UNIVERSITEITEN VAN GENT EN LEIDEN (Leyden: University Press 1981).
44. On Laurent and his project for a new civil code, *see* D. Heirbaut, *Een hopeloze zaak François Laurents ontwerp van burgerlijk wetboek voor België*, 2013 PRO MEMORIE 261–283.

showed some of the author's social preoccupations. Its quality was marred by his virulent hate of the Catholic church, which permeated his work. Even in Laurent's own 'liberal' party his zealotry was frowned upon. The Catholics, who came to power in 1884, immediately installed a commission that would make something more to their liking.[45] That commission could not achieve much before it stopped its activities in 1929. The Penal Code saw more change. A new Penal Code, mainly written by Jacques-Joseph Haus, came into force in 1867. It did not really deviate from the French pattern. The French had already made modifications to their penal code by 1867, and the new Belgian code only revised the Napoleonic code to a limited extent.[46]

One Napoleonic code, the Commercial Code, was greatly changed in the nineteenth century. Its structure stayed intact, but one chapter after another was replaced by new laws between 1851 and 1891.[47] This did not happen by chance. Industrialisation came earlier to Belgium than to France. Moreover, the country had in relative terms more industry, railroads, etc. than France.[48] Therefore, it was confronted with the legal problems the new technologies posed much earlier and to a greater extent than France.[49] Consequently, in these cases the Belgians could not imitate French solutions, but had, out of necessity, to look to other countries, like England, or develop their own laws.[50] This explains also why the title on real securities in the civil code was revised. The power structure of nineteenth century Belgium explains why legislative change remained limited to rules impacting on commerce and industry. As only the rich had the right to vote, they dominated Parliament. Catholic and liberal members of Parliament were deeply divided on the issue of church-state relationships, but they were just as strongly united in their willingness to give Belgian industrialisation the best legal instruments possible.[51] In sharp contrast, they were unwilling to

45. F. Stevens, *'Où est donc passée la commission de révision?' La révision du Code civil en Belgique à la fin du XIXe et début du XXe siècle*, *in* LES DÉMARCHES DE CODIFICATION DU MOYEN-ÂGE À NOS JOURS 213–221 (G. Macours & R. Martinage eds., Brussels: KVAB 2006).

46. F. Stevens, *La codification en Belgique. Héritage français et débats néerlandais*, in *LE PENAL DANS TOUS SES ETATS* 287–302 (Brussels: Facultés universitaires Saint-Louis 1997). The hotly debated issue of the death penalty in this code is the subject of J. DE BROUWER, LA PEINE DE MORT EN BELGIQUE: LES CONDITIONS D'ÉMERGENCE DU SYSTÈME ABOLITIONNISTE DE FAIT (1830–1914) (PhD dissertation Université Catholique de Louvain-La-Neuve 2009).

47. D. HEIRBAUT, EEN BEKNOPTE GESCHIEDENIS VAN HET SOCIAAL, HET ECONOMISCH EN HET FISCAAL RECHT IN BELGIË 87–89 (Ghent: Academia Press 2013).

48. Cf. H. COING, 2 EUROPÄISCHES PRIVATRECHT, 19. JAHRHUNDERT. ÜBERBLICK ÜBER DIE ENTWICKLUNG DES PRIVATRECHTS IN DEN EHEMALS GEMEINRECHTLICHEN LÄNDERN 81 (Munich: Beck 1989).

49. Cf. E. Holthöfer, *Belgien*, in HANDBUCH DER QUELLEN UND LITERATUR DER NEUEREN EUROPÄISCHEN PRIVATRECHTSGESCHICHTE III/1, 1138 (H. Coing eds., Munich: Beck 1982); E. VAN DIEVOET, HET BURGERLIJK RECHT IN BELGIË EN NEDERLAND VAN 1800 TOT 1940. DE RECHTSBRONNEN 388 (Antwerp, De Sikkel, 1943).

50. *See* for the example of bankrupcy law, D. DE RUYSSCHER, GEDISCIPLINEERDE VRIJHEID: EEN GESCHIEDENIS VAN HET HANDELS- EN ECONOMISCH RECHT 107–108 (Antwerp: Maklu 2014). For non-French foreign influences in Belgian case law, *see* G. Martyn, *In Search of Foreign Influences Other Than French in Nineteenth Century Belgian Court Decisions*, *in* 2 RATIO DECIDENDI. GUIDING PRINCIPLES OF JUDICIAL DECISIONS. FOREIGN LAW 155–167 (G. Martyn, S. Dauchy, W. Hamilton Bryson & M. Mirow eds., Berlin: Duncker & Humblot 2010).

51. D. HEIRBAUT, HADDEN/HEBBEN DE BELGISCHE MINISTERS VAN JUSTITIE EEN CIVIELRECHTELIJK BELEID 38–40 (Mechelen: Kluwer 2005).

improve the legal conditions of the working classes. For example, although working place accidents had become more common because of the rapid expansion of Belgium's industry, legislation on it had to wait until the early twentieth century.[52]

Fortunately, not all changes had to be initiated by the legislature. The first to encounter the challenges of industrialisation were the judges. Although they were willing to help the victims of industrialisation, their attitude towards it was rather benevolent. Judges were willing to award damages, but they did not forbid dangerous activities. At first, they sometimes based their decisions on the pre-1804 laws. In the second half of the nineteenth century the judiciary became more self-conscious and only referred to its own precedents.[53] The role the judges played in developing new legal rules has long been underestimated. For example, Article 1384, paragraph 1, of the Civil Code was creatively interpreted by the Brussels Court of Appeal, so that a new strict liability for damage caused by defective objects could be based on it. Laurent later made this theory popular and thus, it was believed to be his.[54]

'The country most faithful to Napoleon's codes',[55] or, 'a French province',[56] these expressions neatly sum up Belgium during the nineteenth century. Only a few changes to the French codes were made. Even these changes should not be overestimated and be seen as the embryonic developments of a legal tradition of its own. They were made only when necessary. Besides, some of them were not very Belgian. Laurent was a native of Luxembourg, and many other more or less original legal thinkers, like Haus, were of German origin.[57] It is hard to see how a Belgian legal tradition could have come into existence with only French codes and foreign scholars to nurture it.[58] Paradoxically, throughout the nineteenth century Belgium's highest magistrates paid lip service

52. B. Debaenst, Een proces van bloed, zweet en tranen! Juridisering van arbeidsongevallen in de negentiende eeuw in België (Brussels: KVAB 2011).
53. D. Heirbaut, *Les juges belges face au Code civil*, *in* Richterliche Anwendung des Code civil in seinen europäischen Geltungsbereichen außerhalb Frankreichs 253–272 (B. Dölemeyer, H. Mohnhaupt & A. Somma eds., Frankfurt: Klostermann 2006). *See also* G. Martyn, *The Judge and the Formal Sources of Law in the Low Countries (19th–20th Centuries): From 'Slave' to 'Master'?*, *in* 1 Ratio Decidendi: Guiding Principles of Judicial Decision. Case Law 201–222 (W. Hamilton Bryson & S. Dauchy eds., Berlin: Duncker & Humblot 2006).
54. Cf. L. Cornelis, De buitencontractuele aansprakelijkheid veroorzaakt door zaken. Rechtsvergelijkend onderzoek: België, Frankrijk, Nederland, Bondsrepubliek Duitsland en Engeland 23–24 (Antwerp: Kluwer Rechtswetenschappen 1982).
55. Cf. R. Piret, *Le Code Napoléon en Belgique*, 6 Revue internationale de droit comparé 754 (1954).
56. E. Holthöfer, Beiträge zur Justizgeschichte der Niederlande, Belgiens und Luxemburgs im 19. und 20. Jahrhundert 147 (Frankfurt: Klostermann 1993).
57. C. Hennau & J. Verhaegen, *Jacques-Joseph Haus (1796–1881)*, *in* Gestalten uit het verleden: 32 voorgangers in de strafrechtswetenschap, de strafrechtspleging en de criminologie 73–81 (C. Fijnaut eds., Brussels: Kluwer Rechtswetenschappen 1993).
58. Some recent doctoral theses (F. Muller, La cour de cassation belge à l'aune des rapports entre pouvoirs. De sa naissance dans le modèle classique de la séparation des pouvoirs à l'aube d'une extension de la fonction juridictionnelle 1832–1914/1936 (Bruges: die Keure 2011); S. Vandenbogaerde, Vectoren van het recht. Geschiedenis van de Belgische juridische tijdschriften (PhD dissertation Ghent University 2014)), however, may open the debate on Belgian autonomy towards France during the nineteenth century, as they show that some law reviews and the Court of Cassation took a more autonomous stand than has hitherto been assumed. *See also* De Belle Époque van het Belgisch recht (1870–1914) (B. Debaenst ed., Bruges: die Keure, 2016).

to the country's old legal traditions and its great jurists of the past, as if to compensate for a reality which went completely against their discourse.[59]

[D] The Waning of French Influence

Belgian law still has ties with French law,[60] but there is no denying that from the end of the nineteenth century[61] the dependence on France has lessened. The process has been very gradual, and its effects differ. It has many causes, but only the most important of them can be mentioned here.

[1] Changes in Legal Education and Legal Science

In 1876, the organisation of legal education in Belgium was drastically changed. The universities themselves could confer degrees in law. This meant that a law student was no longer examined by a central commission in Brussels, but by the professors who had taught him. This gave more freedom to law professors. Consequently, legal science in Belgium took off in a new direction.[62] Before 1876 the exegetical method dominated in the law faculties. Its adherents stated that statutes were the only source of law and that they had to be interpreted literally. Now, other ways of studying law became possible. As in France, the exegetic method came under fire from the proponents of the scientific method. They wanted legal research to be free from the constraints of the codes. Other sources of law than statutes and even social influences had to be studied.[63] A typical representative of this new method around 1900 was Adolphe Prins, who developed the theory of social defence (maintaining order is the sole goal of justice) and stimulated the reform of criminal law.[64] Another leading author of the 'socialisation of law' around 1900 was Edmond Picard, a prolific legal writer, patron of the arts and politician.[65]

---

59. Cf. F. Stevens, *Histoire du droit et nationalisme en Belgique aux XIXe siècle, in* HISTOIRE DE L'HISTOIRE DU DROIT 203–215 (J. Poumarède ed., Toulouse: Presse de l'université 2006); A. HENDRICK, 'DES MOTS DE CIRCONSTANCE'. LES DISCOURS DE RENTRÉE DE LA HAUTE MAGISTRATURE BELGE AU XIXE SIÈCLE (PhD dissertation Université Saint Louis Brussels 2012).
60. Cf. C. MALLIET, ELEMENTAIRE BIBLIOGRAFIE BELGISCH RECHT 65 (Ghent: Mys & Breesch 1999).
61. On this pivotal era for Belgian law, *see* DE BELLE ÉPOQUE VAN HET BELGISCH RECHT (1870–1914) (B. Debaenst ed., Bruges: die Keure, 2016).
62. F. Stevens, *Het rechtsonderwijs in de Zuidelijke Nederlanden in het begin van de 19de eeuw*, 9 CAHIERS DU CENTRE DE RECHERCHES EN HISTOIRE DU DROIT ET DES INSTITUTIONS (CHRIDI) 67–70 (1998).
63. Cf. J. GILISSEN & M. MAGITS, DE BRONNEN VAN HET RECHT IN DE BELGISCHE GEWESTEN SEDERT DE DERTIENDE EEUW 254–256 (Antwerp: Kluwer rechtswetenschappen, 1989); J. Van Biervliet, *L'interprétation belge du code civil, in* 2 LE CODE CIVIL. 1804–1904. LIVRE DU CENTENAIRE 652 (Paris: Rousseau 1904).
64. S. Christiaensen, *Adolphe Prins (1845–1919), in* GESTALTEN UIT HET VERLEDEN: 32 VOORGANGERS IN DE STRAFRECHTSWETENSCHAP, DE STRAFRECHTSPLEGING EN DE CRIMINOLOGIE 109–123 (C. Fijnaut ed., Brussels: Kluwer Rechtswetenschappen 1993); B. De Ruyver, *De transformatie van het Belgisch strafrecht in de achtergrond van de politieke en sociaal-economische ontwikkelingen in het laatste kwart van de negentiende eeuw, in* HANDELINGEN VAN HET XVE BELGISCH-NEDERLANDS RECHTSHISTORISCH CONGRES 207–210 (Antwerp: Kluwer Rechtswetenschappen 1998).
65. Picard will be an inexhaustible subject of study for many years to come. On him, *see* B. COPPEIN, DROMEN VAN EEN NIEUWE SAMENLEVING: INTELLECTUELE BIOGRAFIE VAN EDMOND PICARD (Ghent: Larcier 2011); F. RINGHELHEIM, UN JURISCONSULTE DE RACE, EDMOND PICARD (1836–1924) (Brussels: Larcier

The great figures of the scientific school after the Second World War[66] were Henri De Page and René Dekkers, who wrote authoritative studies of Belgian civil law, which are still used today.[67] In spite of the popularity of their works, their scientific method has had little impact. The formalism of the exegetic method still dominates Belgian legal thinking, the main difference with the nineteenth century being that case law has become more important, with the decisions of the Court of Cassation (*Cour de cassation – Hof van Cassatie*) in practice having nearly the same status as acts of Parliament.[68] Apart from Chaïm Perelman, who worked about argumentation theories, the scientific method has not led to much original scientific work. To be fair, the situation seems to have changed in the last decades. Since the seventies, more work is being made of a scientific study of law, but this has, to date, little influenced the mainstream of Belgian lawyers.[69] However small the results of the scientific method may be in this respect, it has achieved one of its goals, an unfettered research of the law, and thus lessened French influence.

[2] Social and Economic Changes

Already in the middle of the nineteenth century, Belgium sometimes had to make its own laws because France's economic development lagged behind. This took on even more importance from the end of that century, as the rate of technological change accelerated and the legal system began to reflect not only the interests of the bourgeoisie, but also of other social groups. In 1887, for example, the first social laws were voted by Parliament, and a huge body of labour law and social security law has been created in the years after.[70] Ever since, Belgians have prided themselves on their

2012); P. Aron & C. Vanderpelen-Diagre, Edmond Picard (1836–1924); un bourgeois socialiste belge à la fin du dix-neuvième siècle. Essai d'histoire culturelle (Brussels: Musées royaux des beaux-arts 2013); Genius, grandeur & gêne: Het fin de siècle rond het justitiepaleis te Brussel en de controversiële figuur van Edmond Picard (W. Van Eeckhoutte & B. Maes eds., Brussels: Knops 2014).

66. This text cannot deal with the special situation during the World Wars and their aftermath. For that, *see* M. Bost & S. Horvat, *Une première crise majeure. L'impact de la Grande Guerre sur la justice belge, in* Deux siecles de justice. Encyclopedie historique de la justice belge 517–537 (M. De Koster, D. Heirbaut & X. Rousseaux eds., Bruges: die Keure 2015); K. Peters, R. Roden & L. Vanhaecke, *La Seconde Guerre mondiale et la répression d'après-guerre, in* Deux siecles de justice. Encyclopedie historique de la justice belge 538–561 (M. De Koster, D. Heirbaut & X. Rousseaux eds., Bruges: die Keure 2015); K. Aerts, *De repressie en juridische reïntegratie van collaborateurs na de Tweede Wereldoorlog, in* Deux siecles de justice. Encyclopedie historique de la justice belge 562–577 (M. De Koster, D. Heirbaut & X. Rousseaux eds., Bruges: die Keure 2015).
67. R. Dekkers, Handboek burgerlijk recht, 3 Vols. (Brussels: Bruylant 1971); H. De Page, Traité élémentaire de droit civil belge, 10 Vols. (Brussels: Bruylant 1952–1975).
68. Cf. R. Kruithof, Naar een 'gouvernement des juges' in het Belgische verbintenissenrecht en andere opstellen 39–45 (Antwerp: Maklu 1992).
69. Cf. F. Ost & M. Van Hoecke, *La jurisprudence en Belgique*, 33 Revue interdisciplinaire d'études juridiques 107–137 (1994).
70. *Honderd jaar sociaal recht in België*, 88 & 89 Arbeidsblad (1987–1988); B. Chlepner, Cent ans d'histoire sociale en Belgique (Brussels: Editions de l'université de Bruxelles 1972); J. Nandrin, *La genèse du droit du travail en Belgique. Plaidoyer pour la chronologie, in* Auctoritates. Xenia R.C. Van Caenegem oblata 256–288 (S. Dauchy, J. Monballyu & A. Wijffels ed., Brussels:

social system, even though, taking into account its early industrialisation, Belgium was a latecomer.

The most interesting evolution in this story happened in family law (in its broadest sense). The Napoleonic Civil Code had given the man as husband and father an authority over his wife and children that mirrored the absolute power Napoleon himself exercised over France. This patriarchal vision of the family was strengthened by the discrimination against the surviving spouse (which was mostly disadvantageous to women) and children born out of wedlock. From the end of the nineteenth century, all this was challenged and the family structure was gradually reorganised along more 'democratic' lines.[71] This process was stimulated by research into legal history.[72] Many customs in the Southern Netherlands had generally promoted a more democratic family structure before the coming of the French[73] and new legislation returned, if not to the details, then at least to the spirit of pre-French era family law. It is strange to realise that the evolution of Belgian family law from the nineteenth century has largely been a return to the past. This is exceptional. Most other legal developments cannot be linked to the old law of the Southern Netherlands. In 2001 the transformation of Napoleonic family law was completed, when Parliament abolished the family council, a typically French institution, which had never taken root in Belgium.[74] In the twenty-first century Belgian law has finally broken away from both the Napoleonic and older concepts of the family, introducing civil solidarity pacts, same sex marriage and legal voluntary euthanasia. A common element of the changes in both the twentieth and the twenty-first century seems to be a more democratic family life with a greater freedom for individuals to make their own choices.[75] Further changes, for example a modification of the rules on forced heirship, are on the horizon.

Koninklijke academie voor wetenschappen, letteren en schone kunsten van België, Wetenschappelijk comité voor rechtsgeschiedenis 1997); G. Vanthemsche, De beginjaren van de sociale zekerheid in België, 1944–1963 (Brussels: VUBPress 1994; D. Heirbaut, Een beknopte geschiedenis van het sociaal, het economisch en het fiscaal recht in België 15–80 (Ghent: Academia Press 2013); D. Heirbaut & B. Debaenst, *Het sociaal en het economisch recht: twee grote werven voor de justitiegeschiedenis, in* Deux siècles de justice. Encyclopedie historique de la justice belge 502–509 (M. De Koster, D. Heirbaut & X. Rousseaux eds., Bruges: die Keure 2015).

71. Cf. B. Bouckaert, *De herziening van het Burgerlijk Wetboek: een tweede adem voor de rechtsstaat?, in* Liber memorialis François Laurent 231 (J. Erauw, B. Bouckaert, H. Bocken, H. Gaus & M. Storme eds., Brussels: Story Scientia 1989); W. Delva, *Honderd jaar burgerlijk recht. Het civiel recht – inzonderheid het familierecht – gisteren, vandaag en morgen, in* Gedenkboek. De Vlaamse conferentie der balie van Gent 1873–1973, 341–355 (G. Baert ed., Ghent: Vlaamse conferentie der balie van Gent 1974).
72. Cf. G. Van Dievoet, *Geschiedenis van de Commissie*, 37 Handelingen van de Koninklijke Commissie voor de uitgave van oude wetten en verordeningen van België 15–57 (1996).
73. For the old persons and family law, *see* P. Godding, Le Droit Privé dans les Pays-Bas Méridionaux du 12e au 18e Siècle 47–138, 295–413 (Brussels: Académie royale de Belgique 1987); J. Monballyu, Geschiedenis van het familierecht van de late middeleeuwen tot heden (Leuven, Acco, 2006).
74. On the changes in postwar Belgian family law, *see* J. Gerlo, *Het familierecht in het zicht van het jaar 2000, in* Liber amicorum prof. dr. G. Baeteman 119–140 (Deurne: Story-Scientia 1997); M. Meulders-Klein, *La famille, le législateur et le juge à la croisée des chemins*, 63 Revue régionale de droit 31–56 (1992).
75. D. Heirbaut, *Vijftig jaar privaatrecht in het TPR: er is in die tijd veel veranderd*, 51 Tijdschrift voor Privaatrecht 44–49 (2014).

[3] *The Rise of Dutch as a Language for Law*

Today's Belgium has three official languages: Dutch, spoken in Flanders in the north and by a small part of the population of Brussels; French, spoken in Wallonia in the south and by the largest part of the population of Brussels; and German, spoken in the so-called eastern districts. The German-speakers form only a small part of the population. About 60% of Belgium speaks Dutch and about 40% French. Although the Flemings form the majority of the population, the language of law after Belgian independence was French. French was the language of the elite, even in Flanders, and thus of the lawyers. For example, if one does not count vulgarising publications, between 1830 and 1890 only a few more than twenty books on law were published in Dutch. Legislation was only published in French, and only in a small minority of the courts was Dutch used.[76]

From 1856 the dominant position of the French language came under attack from the so-called Flemish movement. At first, the Flemings did not demand much: equality of Dutch and French in Flanders. In 1873 a first language law[77] was passed in Parliament. It made the use of the Dutch language compulsory in Flanders in criminal proceedings in which the accused could not understand French. Laws of 1878 and 1883 introduced comparable rules for administrative matters and education. From 1898 all statutes, royal decrees and government regulations had to be published both in French and in Dutch.

After the First World War, language legislation entered a new stage. A 1921 act of Parliament introduced the territoriality principle: in principle, the language of the authorities should be the language of the region in which they act. In 1932 this led to the recognition that Flanders and Wallonia are unilingual (Dutch, respectively French) and that Brussels is bilingual. A 1935 law applied this principle also to judicial proceedings. Thus, a linguistic boundary was created in Belgium. However, a regular language census was held regularly and the linguistic boundary could be changed according to its results. However, in 1962–1963 this boundary was fixed by statute and in 1970 even by the Constitution.[78] In the 1960s the most important statutory instruments which date from before 1898 were also officially translated into Dutch (e.g., the Civil Code in 1961, the Constitution in 1967).[79] The 1930s and 1960s are also crucial for legal education. Ghent University, where Dutch had been used next to

76. H. Van Goethem, *De Nederlandse rechtstaal in België in de negentiende eeuw*, *in* 'Houd voet bij stuk'. Xenia iuris historiae G. Van Dievoet oblata 587–599 (F. Stevens & D. Van Den Auweele eds., Louvain: KULeuven, Law Faculty, Section of Roman law and legal history 1990); H. Van Goethem, De taaltoestanden in het Vlaams-Belgisch gerecht 1795–1935 (Brussels: Koninklijke academie voor wetenschappen, letteren en schone kunsten van België 1990).
77. On Belgium's language legislation, *see* B. Coppein & M. Muller, *La législation linguistique en Belgique*, *in* Deux siecles de justice. Encyclopedie historique de la justice belge 477–499 (M. De Koster, D. Heirbaut & X. Rousseaux eds., Bruges: die Keure 2015).
78. L. Wils, *Bestuur*, *in* Nieuwe encyclopedie van de Vlaamse beweging, I, 480–486 (Tielt: Lannoo 1998); H. Van Goethem, De taaltoestanden in het Vlaams-Belgisch gerecht, 1795–1935 (Brussels: Koninklijke academie voor wetenschappen, letteren en schone kunsten van België 1990).
79. J. Gilissen & M. Magits, De bronnen van het recht in de Belgische gewesten sedert de dertiende eeuw 201 (Antwerp: Kluwer rechtswetenschappen, 1989).

French from 1923, began to use only Dutch from 1930. In Louvain, however, French was still used until 1969.[80]

The rise of Dutch as an official language and a language for education inevitably led to the development of a legal literature in Dutch. The great stages run close to the legal developments: a first real start at the end of the nineteenth century, a breakthrough in the 1930s, and well established after 1960. Today law articles in Dutch are in all respects equal to those in French.[81] Needless to say, the appearance of Dutch-speaking lawyers has greatly contributed to the weakening of French influence.

[E] A French-Speaking and a Flemish Belgian Legal Culture?

The decline of French influence has not led to the creation of a distinct Belgian legal culture. In fact, an evolution is visible towards the development of two new legal cultures: one Flemish, i.e., Dutch-speaking, the other French-speaking. Some examples can illustrate the growing rift between Belgian lawyers on both side of the linguistic border:

- The leading reviews are different: for Flemings the *Rechtskundig Weekblad* and *Tijdschrift voor Privaatrecht*; for the French-speakers the *Journal des tribunaux* and *Revue critique de jurisprudence belge*. It has to be stressed that the divide is far from absolute here. For example, some law reviews have become bilingual.[82]
- The decisions of courts may vary according to the linguistic background of the judges. This has been most visible for the Council of State (*Conseil d'Etat – Raad van State*), the highest administrative court. Some of its decisions have come under attack by members of one linguistic group because they had been taken by justices of the other linguistic group.[83]
- Flemish lawyers are more influenced by Dutch, German and Anglo-American legal thinking, whereas in the French-speaking part of the country the presence of French jurisprudence is still strong.[84]

---

80. R. Verstegen, *L'enseignement du droit en Belgique. Evolution de la législation aux XIXe et XXe siècle, in* 'Houd voet bij stuk'. Xenia iuris historiae G. Van Dievoet oblata 154, 191 (F. Stevens & D. Van Den Auweele eds., Louvain: KULeuven, Law Faculty, Section of Roman law and legal history 1990).
81. Cf. G. Van Overwalle, *Het Nederlandstalig juridisch tijdschrift in België*, 1988/4 Vlaams jurist vandaag 16–20. *See also* H. Sabbe & L. Huyse, De juristen in België. Een beroepsgroep in beweging 5 (Leuven: Instituut recht en samenleving 1994); S. Vandenbogaerde, *Vijftig jaar grensoverschrijdende rechtswetenschap: Het Tijdschrift voor Privaatrecht (1964–2014)*, 51 Tijdschrift voor Privaatrecht 60–103 (2014).
82. G. Van Overwalle, *Het Nederlandstalig juridisch tijdschrift in België*, 1988/4 Vlaams jurist vandaag 19–21.
83. G. Baeteman, *De Raad van State op de drempel van de 21ste eeuw, in* 50 jaar Raad van State 8 (Bruges: die Keure 1998); F. Remion, Le conseil d'état 225 (Brussels: Bruylant 1990); J. Sohier, *'Forumshopping' bij de Raad van State: realiteit of waanidee?*, 1998/5 Vlaams jurist vandaag 19.
84. Cf. J. Herbots, *Belgium, in* 1 International Encyclopedia of Laws, Contract Law 30 (The Hague: Kluwer Law International 1998); F. Ost & M. Van Hoecke, *La jurisprudence en Belgique*, 33 Revue interdisciplinaire d'etudes juridiques 107, 115 (1994).

That Dutch-speaking, i.e., Flemish, and French-speaking lawyers are different becomes clear, when one consults surveys of legal science in Belgium. Both parts of the country are dealt with separately.[85]

Differences will only grow stronger in the future. Belgium was originally conceived as a unitary state, though with a lot of freedom for local authorities. Nowadays, it no longer is a unitary state. Since 1993, the first article of the Constitution states that Belgium is a federal state. Subsequent revisions of the Constitution and constitutional bylaws in 1970, 1980, 1988–1989, 1992–1993, 2001 and 2012–2013 (the reader will notice a ten-year pattern) have created one of the most original types of federalism in the world. Three 'communities' (Dutch-speaking, French-speaking and German-speaking) are competent for educational and cultural matters, and three 'regions' (Flanders, Wallonia and Brussels) are competent for economic matters.[86] Communities and regions have their own legislative and executive branches of government. For the areas of their competences, these new entities are making their own legislation, thus assuring that Dutch-speaking and French-speaking lawyers in these areas no longer share the same laws. Not to be neglected is the fact that education is no longer organised by the federal State, as it falls under the jurisdiction of the communities. Dutch-speaking and French-speaking universities are already now organised along different lines.[87] It is to be expected that, in time, this will contribute to the growing break-up of Belgian law. On the other hand, constitutional amendments have also introduced a new player in the world of Belgian law. In 1980 the Constitution established the Court of Arbitration, which was in spite of its name a constitutional court, albeit with limited powers. Thereafter its jurisdiction expanded, so that from 2007 its name is 'Constitutional Court' (*Cour constitutionnelle – Grondwettelijk Hof*). Its prestige has grown rapidly, and it has even displaced the Court of Cassation as Belgium's leading court.[88]

The people of Belgium have been mostly apathetic toward law, unless it interfered with the more important linguistic, social or religious problems.[89] In 1996 a scandal broke out over the paedophile Marc Dutroux, who was responsible for the disappearance of several young children. Although Dutroux was caught, the bungling way in which judicial and police authorities handled this case, has led to a situation in which disrespect for the courts has nearly become common sense.[90] Most striking was

85. For example F. Ost & M. Van Hoecke, *La jurisprudence en Belgique*, 33 Revue interdisciplinaire d'études juridiques 107, 113–137 (1994).
86. On Belgian federalism, *see infra* Chapter 3, §3.09 [D].
87. In Flanders university education and organisation were reformed in 1991, but in French-speaking Belgium there have been no comparable reforms.
88. Cf. e.g., K.-J. Vandormael, Het Grondwettelijk Hof: Rechter of regelgever? Analyse van de draagwijdte van de rechtspraak van het Grondwettelijk Hof (Ghent, Larcier, 2015).
89. Cf. L. Huyse, De lange weg naar Neufchâteau 192 (Leuven: Van Halewijck 1996); L. Huyse & A. Verdoodt, *Dertig jaar justitiebeleid. Kroniek van een aangekondigde crisis*, 20 Panopticon 3–12 (1999); M. Storme, *Slotrede*, *in* Vertrouwen in het gerecht 124 (Diegem: Kluwer Rechtswetenschappen 1995).
90. Cf. S. Gutwirth, K. Raes & D. Roef, *België, een rechtstaat met vormgebreken*, 23 Recht en kritiek 4 (1997).

the so-called spaghetti-decision of the Court of Cassation, in which the popular instruction judge Connerotte who had arrested Dutroux was taken of the case because he as a special invited guest had attended a fundraising dinner for the legal defence costs of some of the victims in that case.[91] A march, the so-called White March, with about 300,000 participants (on a population of 10 million) against this decision was held in Brussels: 'une grande première qui mérite attention par son caractère atypique'.[92] Consequently, justice, law and order have suddenly come to the forefront of political life.[93] Reforms in criminal law, in the organisation of the police and the judiciary have since been realised,[94] but much work is still to be done. Moreover, the new reforms have made even clearer that Flemings and French-speaking Belgians have different ideas about law. Instead of bringing both parts of the country together, the events after the Dutroux-scandal have driven them even more apart.[95] Before 1996, it was beyond discussion that justice, law and order had to be federal matters.[96] Now doubts are beginning to surface. It remains to be seen what will come of them, but it is significant that the country no longer has a national bar association.[97]

It is not clear what the future may bring. On the one hand Belgium is becoming more divided, on the other there are countervailing tendencies, such as the Constitutional Court which has already been mentioned. Other elements are both the growing Europeanisation and globalisation[98] and the rise of a multicultural society.[99] Belgian law used to reign supreme. Now it is just part of a multi-layered legal order with regional, European and international elements. In comparison with other countries, Belgium is rather open to influences from foreign legal systems. Proximity and language ensure that the law of neighbouring countries, together with American law, is the main influence. Belgium is also very accommodating towards European and

91. *See* about this decision C. Van Den Wijngaert, *De naweeën van het spaghetti-arrest van 14 oktober 1996*, 18 Panopticon 72–74 (1997); P. Traest, *Zijn gevoel en recht niet met elkaar te verzoenen?*, 18 Panopticon 75–77 (1997).
92. R. Perrot, *Exposé général, in Crise de société-crise de justice*, 7 Actualités de droit 114 (1997).
93. Cf. L. Huyse, De lange weg naar Neufchâteau 192 (Leuven: Van Halewijck 1996); L. Huyse & A. Verdoodt, *Dertig jaar justitiebeleid. Kroniek van een aangekondigde crisis*, 20 Panopticon 18–19 (1999). *See also* D. Deli, *Het onderwijs in de basisbeginselen van ons rechtssysteem: geen overbodige luxe voor het secundair onderwijs*, 1996–1997/5 Tijdschrift voor onderwijsrecht en onderwijsbeleid 312–315.
94. F. Muller & X. Rousseaux, *Politiques et pratiques pénales à l'aune des transformations de l'État belge (1830–2012), in* Deux siecles de justice. Encyclopedie historique de la justice belge 204–212 (M. De Koster, D. Heirbaut & X. Rousseaux eds., Bruges: die Keure 2015); J. Campion, M. De Koster, L. Keunings, B. Majerus, X. Rousseaux & F. Welter, *L'appareil policier en Belgique (1830–2010)*, in: Deux siecles de justice. Encyclopedie historique de la justice belge 410–416 (M. De Koster, D. Heirbaut & X. Rousseaux eds., Bruges: die Keure 2015).
95. Cf. B. De Smet, *De justitie in de steigers. Beschouwingen over het ontwerp Franchimont als steunpijler van een moderne gerechtelijke samenleving*, 18 Panopticon 219–220 (1997).
96. Cf. C. Coudron, P. Daeninck & I. Vos, *Proeve van een grondwet voor Vlaanderen. Een grondwet voor de Vlamingen?*, 33 Jura Falconis 350 (1996–1997).
97. B. Quintelier, *Opkomst en ondergang van de nationale orde van advocaten van België*, 2009 Pro Memorie 341–360.
98. Cf. however C. Brunner, *Nationale codificaties en de eenwording van het privaatrecht*, 33 Tijdschrift voor Privaatrecht 357–359 (1996).
99. E. Dirix, Privaatrecht en multiculturaliteit (Antwerp, Intersentia, 2007).

international law.[100] In this context, it has become harder to make significant new legislation on the federal level, as that requires both a conciliation of conflicting viewpoints on both sides of the linguistic border and a respect for European and international norms. For a long time it seemed that the 1967 Judicial Code would be Belgium's last great legislative monument.[101] Since 1996, however, there is a revival of the codification idea. Several new codes have appeared: the Companies Code (1999), the Code of Private International Law (2004), and the Code of Economic Law (2014). A draft Code of Maritime Law awaits approval by Parliament, and major revisions of other codes (including the Civil Code) are in preparation. Following the example of neighbouring countries Belgium has also redrawn its judicial map in 2014.[102] In short, in spite of growing obstacles there have also been considerable achievements proving that Belgians can still find common ground. A drawback of the latter is that new legislation may be more remarkable for its compromises than for its innovations.

§1.03 THE PRAGMATIC ATTITUDE OF BELGIAN LAW

A quest for a Belgian legal identity will leave the seeker with empty hands. Before the coming of the French there was no Belgian legal tradition, because there were only local and regional customs. Thereafter, French law dominated. Now that French influence has become less, certainly not a Belgian, but maybe a Flemish, i.e., Dutch-speaking, and a French-speaking Belgian legal culture are emerging. As there is no Belgian legal tradition, it is very hard to find anything in the field of law for which Belgium is remarkable. It may have had throughout its history some lawgivers and authors who have been of note, but very few of them have made a significant contribution to the development of legal thought in Europe.[103]

The picture is less bleak, when one looks at it from another angle. True, Belgium has not produced laws and professors of European importance. But, that can be linked to the character of 'Belgian' law throughout the centuries. Law in Belgium is and has always been a law of the practitioner. The leading personalities of the law are not the legislators and professors, but the judges, advocates, notaries and the like.[104] Their attitude towards law has always been pragmatic. There may not be a Belgian legal

---

100. D. Heirbaut & M.E. Storme, *The Belgian Legal Tradition: From a Long Quest for Legal Independence to a Longing for Independence*, 14 EUROPEAN REVIEW OF PRIVATE LAW 663–671 (2006).
101. On the code and its history, *see* D. Heirbaut, *Efficiency: The Holy Grail of Belgian Justice? Civil Procedure in Belgium (1806–2008)*, *in* ACCESS TO JUSTICE AND THE JUDICIARY. TOWARDS NEW EUROPEAN STANDARDS OF AFFORDABILITY, QUALITY AND EFFICIENCY OF CIVIL ADJUDICATION 89–117 (A. Uzelac & C.H. Van Rhee eds., Antwerp-Oxford: Intersentia 2009).
102. NIEUWE JUSTITIE (B. Allemeersch, P. Taelman, P. Van Orshoven & B. Vanlerberghe eds., Mortsel: Intersentia 2014).
103. Cf. R. Van Caenegem, *Reflexions on the Place of the Low Countries in European Legal History*, *in* EUROPÄISCHES RECHTSDENKEN IN GESCHICHTE UND GEGENWART. FESTSCHRIFT FÜR HELMUT COING ZUM 70. GEBURTSTAG 3, 5–6, 13 (Munich: Beck 1982).
104. Cf. R. HOLTHÖFER, BEITRÄGE ZUR JUSTIZGESCHICHTE DER NIEDERLANDE, BELGIENS UND LUXEMBURGS IM 19. UND 20. JAHRHUNDERT 149 (Frankfurt: Klostermann 1993). On Belgian law practitioners, *see* part 3 in DEUX SIECLES DE JUSTICE. ENCYCLOPEDIE HISTORIQUE DE LA JUSTICE BELGE 303–451 (M. De Koster, D. Heirbaut & X. Rousseaux eds., Bruges: die Keure 2015).

culture, but there is, at least, a Belgian attitude toward law: law has to be practical.[105] This pragmatic attitude is, in fact, a general phenomenon in Belgium.[106] For example, throughout history the country has not produced any great philosophers either.

§1.04 BELGIUM'S CONTRIBUTION TO LAW

The pragmatism of law in Belgium has not stimulated original legal thinking. It is not very practical to reinvent what can be imitated. Even so, there were a few great 'Belgian' contributions to legal development. To students of the rule of law England's *Magna Carta* is well known. Yet, it is less known that the idea of the rule of law was already present in Flemish cities in the twelfth century. When count William Clito came to power in Flanders in 1127, he guaranteed the inhabitants of his cities a right judgment of the cities' aldermen against every man and against himself. The prince is clearly subject to the laws. The 1127 city charters were no mere words. On 16 February 1128 Ivan, lord of Aalst, acted as the spokesman of the city of Ghent towards the count. Ivan rebuked the court for not respecting the privileges he had given the burghers of Ghent and other cities. To settle the matter, he proposed to have a special court convene, in which the Peers of Flanders and representatives of the clergy and the people would sit to judge over the count. If this court should find the count to be unworthy of the countship, he should have to give it up. The count did not agree to this, and Ivan and Ghent rose in revolt. William was killed in the civil war that ensued, and a new count came to power. The background of the conflict was the opinion of Ghent and other cities that there was a contractual relationship between the count and the citizens. They recognised him as their lord and he, in turn, recognised their privileges. If the count no longer respected his part of the deal by acting against the rights of the citizens, they had a right to break their contract and to fight him. This contractual conception of the relationship between ruler and subjects returns in the city charters granted by William's successor. Thereafter, the counts managed to suppress it, but it reappeared at regular times in Flemish history. In 1191 the first article of a charter for the city of Ghent stated that the citizens were only subjected to the count as long as he wanted to treat them justly and reasonably. Another resurgence of the contractual idea happened in the sixteenth century. The 1581 Act of Abjuration is reminiscent of Ivan of Aalst. By his failure to respect the rights of his subjects, Philip II of Spain had lost his right to rule the Netherlands. That the revolt against Philip was only successful for the

105. Cf. P. Godding, *Rechtspraakgeschiedenis in België: de huidige stand van het onderzoek, in* FABRICA HISTORIAE FORENSIS. HANDELINGEN VAN HET AFSCHEID VAN J. TH. DE SMIDT 47 (Leiden: Faculteit der rechtsgeleerdheid 1989); F. Ost & M. Van Hoecke, *La jurisprudence en Belgique*, 33 REVUE INTERDISCIPLINAIRE D'ÉTUDES JURIDIQUES 107, 109–111 (1994); J. Van Biervliet, *L'interprétation belge du code civil, in* 2 LE CODE CIVIL. 1804–1904. LIVRE DU CENTENAIRE 662 (Paris: Rousseau 1904); E. VAN DIEVOET, HET BURGERLIJK RECHT IN BELGIË EN NEDERLAND VAN 1800 TOT 1940. DE RECHTSBRONNEN 97 (Antwerp, De Sikkel, 1943); E. Vieujean, *Place de la doctrine dans le droit belge actuel*, 57 ANNALES DE DROIT DE LOUVAIN 23–25 (1997).

106. Cf. R. Micha & A. De Waelhens, *Du caractère des Belges*, 4 LES TEMPS MODERNES 413–442 (1949). *See also* BELGITUDE ET CRISE DE L'ÉTAT BELGE (Brussels: Publications des Facultés universitaires Saint-Louis 1989).

Northern, and not for the Southern Netherlands, should not obscure the fact that its earliest antecedents could be found in the Southern Netherlands.[107]

§1.05 CONCLUSION

A Belgian legal tradition does not exist. Before the coming of the French, there were mostly local and regional laws. Thereafter, Belgium had French laws. The weakening of French influence has not led to the development of a national legal culture, but rather of two regional legal cultures, one in Flanders, and the other in the French-speaking part of Belgium. Yet, there is one common element in the legal history of Belgium: a pragmatic attitude toward law, which has, so far, enabled its jurists and politicians to find comprises in spite of the growing rift between Dutch- and French-speaking Belgium.

§1.06 SELECTED BIBLIOGRAPHY

J. Gilissen, *La constitution belge de 1831: ses sources, son influence*, 10 Res publica 107–141 (1968).

J. Gilissen, *Belgique et Nord de la France, in Introduction bibliographique à l'histoire du droit et à l'ethnologie juridique*, Vol. C/3 (Brussels: Université libre 1970).

J. Gilissen & M. Magits, *De bronnen van het recht in de Belgische gewesten sedert de dertiende eeuw* (Antwerp: Kluwer rechtswetenschappen 1989).

P. Godding, *Le droit privé dans les Pays-Bas méridionaux du 12e au 18e siècle* (Brussels: Académie royale de Belgique 1987).

P. Godding & J. De Smidt, *Evolutie van het recht in samenhang met de instellingen, in* 4 *Algemene Geschiedenis der Nederlanden* 172–181 (Haarlem: Fibula - Van Dishoeck 1982).

D. Heirbaut, *Een beknopte geschiedenis van het sociaal, het economisch en het fiscaal recht in België* (Ghent: Academia Press 2013).

E. Holthöfer, *Belgien, in Handbuch der Quellen und Literatur der neueren Europäischen Privatrechtsgeschichte* III/1, 1070–1165 (H. Coing ed., Munich: Beck 1982) and III/3, 3277–3395 (H. Coing ed., Munich: Beck 1986).

E. Holthöfer, *Beiträge zur Justizgeschichte der Niederlande, Belgiens und Luxemburgs im 19. und 20. Jahrhundert* (Frankfurt: Klostermann 1993).

J. Monballyu, *Six Centuries of Criminal Law. History of Criminal Law in the Southern Netherlands and Belgium* (1400–2000) (Leyden: Brill 2014).

F. Ost & M. Van Hoecke, *La jurisprudence en Belgique*, 33 Revue interdisciplinaire d'études juridiques 107–137 (1994).

107. D. Heirbaut, *Galbert of Bruges on the Flemish 1127-1128 Crisis. An Early Experiment in Constitutionalism, Parliamentarism and Popular Sovereignty Inspired by Feudal Law, in* CONSTITUTIONALISM BEFORE 1789. CONSTITUTIONAL ARRANGEMENTS FROM THE HIGH MIDDLE AGES TO THE FRENCH REVOLUTION 49–59 (J. Oyrehagen-Sunde ed., Oslo: Pax Forlag 2014).

X. Rousseaux, *Crime, justice et droit: quelques réflexions sur l'historiographie récente en Belgique, in Bilans critiques et historiographiques en histoire contemporaine* 47–154 (J.-P. Nandrin ed., Brussels: Facultés Universitaires Saint-Louis 2005).

E. Spanoghe & R. Feenstra, *Honderdvijftig jaar rechtsleven in België en Nederland, 1830–1980. Preadviezen uitgebracht voor een colloquium georganiseerd door de juridische faculteiten van de universiteiten van Gent en Leiden* (Leyden: University Press 1981).

R. Van Caenegem, *Reflexions on the Place of the Low Countries in European Legal History, in Europäisches Rechtsdenken in Geschichte und Gegenwart. Festschrift für Helmut Coing zum 70. Geburtstag* 3–17 (Munich: Beck 1982).

D. Van Den Auweele, *De evolutie van het recht in het Zuiden. 12de-14de eeuw, in* 3 *Algemene Geschiedenis der Nederlanden* 145–163 (Haarlem: Fibula - Van Dishoeck 1982).

E. Van Dievoet, *Het burgerlijk recht in België en Nederland van 1800 tot 1940. De rechtsbronnen* (Antwerp, De Sikkel, 1943).

G. Van Dievoet, *De ontwikkeling van de rechtswetenschappen,* 7 *Algemene Geschiedenis der Nederlanden* 311–320 (Haarlem: Fibula - Van Dishoeck 1980).

K. Velle, *Recht en gerecht. Bibliografische inleiding tot het institutioneel onderzoek van de rechterlijke macht* (1796–1994) (Brussels: Algemeen rijksarchief en rijksarchief in de provinciën 1994).

Deux siècles de justice. Encyclopédie historique de la justice belge (M. De Koster, D. Heirbaut & X. Rousseaux eds., Bruges: die Keure 2015).

The French Code of Civil Procedure (1806) after 200 Years. The Civil Procedure Tradition in France and Abroad (D. Heirbaut, C.H. Van Rhee & M. Storme eds., Mechelen: Kluwer 2008).

Un héritage Napoléonien. Bicentenaire du Code civil en Belgique (D. Heirbaut & G. Martyn eds., Mechelen: Kluwer 2005).

CHAPTER 2

Basic Features of the Belgian Legal System

Mark Van Hoecke & Sebastiaan Vandenbogaerde

§2.01 BELGIAN LEGAL CULTURE(S)

In the nineteenth century and during the first half of the twentieth century Belgian law and legal culture have been strongly influenced by French law and legal culture. On many points (e.g., statutory interpretation, supporting reasoning in judgments) there is still an important similarity between both legal systems.

Over the last few decades a growing attention has been paid to other foreign legal systems: the Dutch, the English, the American ones and, albeit to a lesser extent, the German legal system. Occasionally other (European) legal systems are taken into account,[1] without, however, having an influence on Belgian legal culture.

For obvious linguistic reasons legal culture in the French speaking part of Belgium is still mainly influenced by the French legal culture, whereas in Flanders the Dutch and English influence became much more important than the French one. This leads to a division of Belgian legal culture into two different legal cultures: the Flemish one and the French speaking one. Even when the Belgian supreme courts[2] apply national (federal) law, a newly formulated interpretation is sometimes shown to be followed only in the community of the parties and the justices involved.[3] Thus, one can

1. During the early period of the European Communities, when only Belgium, Luxembourg, the Netherlands, France, Germany and Italy were members of the EC, it became customary in doctoral theses to compare the Belgian law with all other legal systems within the EC. Today comparison is, inevitably, limited to a few major legal systems, of which the English, the German and the French are the most prominent ones.
2. The Council of State (*Conseil d'Etat – Raad van State*) for administrative cases (*see infra* Chapter 4, §4.04 and Chapter 5, §5.02 [D]) and the Court of Cassation (*Cour de cassation – Hof van Cassatie*) for civil cases (*see infra* Chapter 5, §5.02 [B] and §5.05 [C] [3] [a]).
3. In the 1980s the Council of State annulled the decision of an examination board of Ghent University because a student, who failed for a written examination, did not get the chance to take an additional oral examination (*Bracke v. Ghent University*, Council of State 13 May 1980, 1980

expect for the future a growth of the two Belgian legal subcultures because of the federal structure of the State[4] and the autonomy of the communities and regions to legislate in important fields such as education, culture, environment. Moreover, we can also find a development, which has already commenced, by which both main linguistic communities are seen to go their separate ways beyond the level of the creation of their own rules within the limits of their constitutional legal autonomy. Interpretation of federal rules, legal doctrine, judicial style, and other elements of legal culture tend to develop partly into different directions as well. A declining knowledge of the language[5] of the other subculture already restricts the opportunity to read each other's literature and court decisions. But it also limits the possibility of reception of doctrinal legal constructs. The Dutch legal concept of '*marginale toetsing*'[6] for instance, has been adopted by Flemish legal doctrine and has taken hold in several fields of the law. However, because of lack of an adequate French word which could be considered the equivalent of '*marginale toetsing*', the concept is a lot less established in French-speaking legal doctrine and legal practice.

Nevertheless, one should not overestimate the differences in legal culture between the north and the south of the country. As regards culture in general, way of life, food habits, etc., both linguistic communities have much more in common than they have with respectively the Dutch and the French people, with whom, however, they share their language. Even though both legal communities go their own way more than in the past, they still will, for a long time, share, to a large extent, a common legal culture, the core of which will be described in broad outline in this chapter.

For legal practice and legal doctrine there are at least three levels, three domains where common (unconscious) premises constitute a 'legal culture'[7] and make legal practice and doctrine possible by constituting their framework: the levels of epistemology, methodology and ideology. At the level of epistemology one has to agree which

---

Arresten van de Raad van State 633). The Court interpreted the applicable statutory rules in the sense that every student is entitled to ask for an (additional) oral examination, when written tests are organised. As, especially in large faculties, a majority of the tests were only organised in written form, this decision caused a lot of commotion. All Flemish universities adapted their examination rules in such a way as to abide by the rule which followed from the decision of the Council of State. In French-speaking universities, however, nothing changed, although from a legal point of view there was no reason why these universities should not follow these rules (at that time those rules were still a national (federal) matter). French-speaking universities, including their law professors, considered that decision of the Council of State not to be relevant for their examination practice as it was a 'Flemish case', in which a Flemish student and a Flemish university were involved, and which had been decided by Flemish justices within the Council of State.

4. *See infra* Chapter 3, §3.09 [D].
5. Knowledge of Dutch is slightly increasing amongst French-speaking law students, but knowledge of French is considerably decreasing amongst Flemish law students.
6. A limited review by the judge of legal acts, not in view of checking their contents as such – as the persons or bodies concerned have the legal power to decide freely about it – but only in view of the question whether they did not exceed their authority, including compliance with minimum standards of reasonableness, fairness, etc.
7. For the concept of 'legal culture' *see* M. Van Hoecke & W. Warrington, *Legal Cultures, Legal Paradigms and Legal Doctrine: Towards a New Model for Comparative Law*, 47 The International and Comparative Law Quarterly 495–536, at 498 and, as regards the paradigm of a legal culture, at 513–520 (1998).

are the sources of law (where do we find valid law?). At the level of methodology one needs a common set of (workable) interpretation rules and techniques and a common argumentation theory (which types of arguments and lines of reasoning are allowed?). At the level of ideology there is a common basic world view amongst lawyers, which is determining (part of) the content of vague concepts in law (fairness, abuse of right, reasonableness, interest of the child, etc.). More specifically there is a common view on the role of law in society, on the roles of judges and of other legal professions (do, e.g., judges have to play an active role in a trial, or not?).

In the following paragraphs we will give an outline of the presuppositions of Belgian lawyers on each of these three levels. Together they form the paradigm of Belgian legal culture.

[A] Epistemological Presuppositions: The Sources of Law

Over the last two centuries law has always been considered valid to the extent that it could be based, directly or indirectly, on acts of the Belgian Parliament, including in the first place the Belgian Constitution. In the nineteenth century, when customary law still played an important role besides statutory law, this customary law was considered valid to the extent that it was implicitly or explicitly recognised by Parliament. In the second half of the twentieth century courts also started to accept unwritten 'general principles of law' as sources of law. But in most cases they were, or at least assumed to be, derived from statutory law, behind which they were considered to be implicitly present, as an unuttered starting point on which at least some specific statutory provisions had been based. Even when court decisions depart considerably from the 'will of the legislature' at the time when the statute is enacted, they will, as a rule, try to present their interpretation as a true expression of the legislature's intent.

In general, one can say that the 'official' doctrine is strictly legal positivistic: 'as (only) parliament has been democratically elected, valid law can only be derived from decisions of that parliament. The judge has to determine the scope of these acts, but he should not create law, except when he would find a gap in the law.'[8] Actually, this (limited) law making power awarded to the judge by traditional doctrine, is as such directly based on the text of Article 5 of the Judicial Code.[9] In practice, however, Belgian lawyers and especially judges tend to be more flexible and less formalistic than the appearances they are keeping up.

After the First World War, the principle of one man one vote was accepted for parliamentary elections. However, the Parliament, which voted for this important change of the Constitution, had already been elected according to this principle. From a strict legal point of view this Parliament had not been elected in a valid way, and so

8. This position has e.g., been taken in an explicit way by R. Kruithof, *Naar een 'gouvernement des juges' in het verbintenissenrecht?*, *in* HULDE AAN PROF. DR. R. KRUITHOF 70–79, at nos. 29 & 31 (Antwerp: Maklu & Brussels: Bruylant 1992).
9. This Article, previously included in the Civil Code as Article 4, reads: 'There is denial of justice when the judge refuses to decide a case under any pretext, be it the silence, the obscurity or the incompleteness of the statute.' (Article 5 Judicial Code).

the change of the Constitution was also invalid. As a consequence, everything enacted by the Parliament after 1921 would have to be considered as invalid ... However, this kind of reasoning has not been followed by a majority, and even not by a minority amongst the lawyers: this problem, albeit a very serious one within the frame of the official positivistic doctrine, has never even been discussed!

Both during the First and the Second World War it was impossible for the legislature to act in compliance with the Constitution. In practice the executive enacted statutes, without any parliamentary approval. During the First World War, there was still an assent by the King, but during the Second World War, this was not possible, as the King stayed in Belgium, as a prisoner of the Germans, whereas the executive was in exile, mainly in London. Nevertheless, after these wars, the Court of Cassation (*Cour de cassation – Hof van Cassatie*) considered all acts enacted in this way to be fully valid. The courts, including the Court of Cassation, accepted the principle of constitutional force majeure, although the Constitution does not provide any such principle.

The same official legalistic doctrine did not prevent lawyers from developing the theory of abuse of right, by which a formally valid right is put aside on moral grounds. Neither did it prevent judges from applying this theory in a generally accepted way.[10]

This pragmatic approach of Belgian lawyers sometimes leads to 'kinks' in the justification of the decision. The court decides in a way it considers desirable from a practical and moral point of view, but afterwards feels compelled to present the decision as if it followed in a strict logical way from statutory law, while in reality it does not.

[B] Methodological Presuppositions

[1] Statutory Interpretation

The maxim '*interpretatio cessat in claris*' is still part of the dominant interpretation theory in Belgium. It is regularly used as an argument in the justification of judicial decisions,[11] thus allowing the judge to disregard the whole interpretation discussion. But, on the other hand, statutory texts with an obvious 'plain meaning' are often interpreted in view of a different outcome, when the prima facie 'plain meaning' seems absurd, unjust, or inadequate in the instant case.[12]

The assumption of the rationality of the legislature is another methodological presupposition in Belgian law. When interpreting a text, lawyers, as a rule, assume that the legislature does not make mistakes, that he is always using the same coherent,

10. Accepted by the Court of Cassation since its decision of 10 September 1971, 1972 Arresten van het Hof van Cassatie 31, 1972-I Pasicrisie belge 28.
11. Since the middle of the 1970s, the Court of Cassation seems to have become reluctant in mentioning the rule explicitly, without, however, rejecting it either. *See* F. OST & M. VAN DE KERCHOVE, ENTRE LA LETTRE ET L'ESPRIT. LES DIRECTIVES D'INTERPRÉTATION EN DROIT 97 (Brussels: Bruylant 1989).
12. References: M. VAN DE KERCHOVE ET AL., L'INTERPRÉTATION EN DROIT. APPROCHE PLURIDISCIPLINAIRE (Brussels: Publications des Facultés Universitaires Saint-Louis 1978); M. VAN HOECKE, DE INTERPRETATIEVRIJHEID VAN DE RECHTER (Antwerp, Kluwer, 1979).

univocal language, that, notwithstanding the daily changes in legislation, the legal system remains a coherent whole, without antinomies or gaps. Rather than an assumption, this is a fiction that sometimes seems necessary in order to reduce the complexity of an interpretation problem. In fact, all lawyers today are aware of the incoherence of the legal system and of a lack of 'rationality' of the legislature as regards large parts of the present-day regulations. But, in interpretation practice this assumption of rationality of the legislature still plays, to a large extent unconsciously, an important role as a presupposition for the interpretation of statutes.

As regards the methods of statutory construction, the Belgian judge uses the classical methods of interpretation, without any clear hierarchy amongst them: the grammatical interpretation, the systemic one, the use of legislative materials (*travaux préparatoires – voorbereidende werken*), the historical interpretation and the teleological construction of statutes.

Methodology is used for underpinning a (desired) result, rather than as a means for 'discovering' the 'correct' interpretation. The canons of interpretation are pragmatic tools for judges when deciding cases, not rigid rules, that dictate the result of judicial reasoning.[13]

[2] Argumentation Theory

Following the French tradition, the reasons stated in Belgian judicial decisions are rather limited. This is mainly the case for the Court of Cassation.[14] This Court in fact gives hardly any reasons at all in its decisions. The correct interpretation and application of the law is simply stated.[15] Implicitly however the Court refers to the highly elaborated opinion of the Advocate-General.[16]

Offering adequate reasons for judicial decisions being a ground for appeal at the Court of Cassation (Article 149 of the Constitution), lower courts have to indicate the grounds of the decision in their judgments. According to the case law of the Court of Cassation, however, this obligation is interpreted in a rather narrow way, so that judges, for example, do not have to answer every argument invoked by the parties at the trial. Giving reasons for a judgment is considered to be formal, rather than an attempt to persuade the losing party that (s)he was wrong, which could help him or her to accept the judgment more willingly.

---

13. Justice P. Mahillon of the Court of Cassation, when analysing the construction of statutes by Belgian judges, also stated 'that courts, as a rule, proceed in a pragmatic way, thus disillusioning legal doctrine' (P. Mahillon, *La contribution du juge à l'évolution du droit des personnes*, *in* MÉLANGES OFFERTS À ROBERT LEGROS 424 (Brussels: ULB Faculté de droit 1985).
14. Reasons given in the decisions of the Council of State are much more elaborated. This can partly be explained by the fact that this court was only founded in 1946, so that it has not been directly seized by the French tradition which the Court of Cassation has followed from the very beginning.
15. This is the case even when the court changes its own jurisprudence. *See* A. Vanwelkenhuyzen, *La motivation des revirements de jurisprudence*, *in* LA MOTIVATION DES DÉCISIONS DE JUSTICE 270 (Ch. Perelman & P. Foriers eds., Brussels: Bruylant 1978), where a few examples are given.
16. A. Vanwelkenhuyzen, *La motivation des revirements de jurisprudence*, *in* LA MOTIVATION DES DÉCISIONS DE JUSTICE 278–279 (Ch. Perelman & P. Foriers eds., Brussels: Bruylant 1978).

Two types of argument prevail in Belgian case law and doctrinal legal writing: arguments of authority and arguments of consensus.

Argumentation in the first place aims at linking the decision with the authority of the legislature. Showing that the judgment follows directly from the text of the statute, or at least from the intent of the legislature, seems to be the most powerful argumentation. It is for this reason that judges will try to present their reasoning as much as possible in this way, even if it is only a façade (as we have seen above).

A second type of authority argument is a reference to a decision by a (higher) court. Although precedents do not have any binding force in the Belgian legal system, referring to a Court of Cassation decision will always be a very strong argument,[17] and in one way even stronger than the text of a statute itself. If the act only offers a text which still has to be interpreted, when applied to a concrete case, the Court of Cassation decision offers an authoritative interpretation of that act. And, at the end, this interpretation will be the valid, enforceable[18] law.

For lower courts, decisions of the court of appeal in their territorial jurisdiction, will have a similar weight. In general, the weight of judgments as authoritative arguments will follow the hierarchy of the courts: the higher the court, the more weighty the precedents will be.

Reference to doctrinal legal writing as an authoritative source will never be found in the case law of the Court of Cassation. In the motivation of other courts' judgments it may play some limited role as an argument of authority, but less than the text of the statutes or than other court decisions.

To the extent that it would not prove possible to link the decision to the will of the legislature as it appears from the act(s) or from the legislative materials, or to construe it through another type of interpretation, judges will try to link up with some kind of *consensus* amongst lawyers.

Referring to a consensus about a particular interpretation or legal solution for the type of case under consideration is a most powerful argument. Such a consensus in doctrinal legal writing, but especially in case law, is very weighty. A large consensus amongst judges of (lower) courts, as it appears from their judgments, sometimes can be considered as a stronger argument than the authority of a decision by the Court of Cassation. In fact, such a consensus amongst lower courts, on a position which is opposed to a previous decision of the Court of Cassation, is one of the scarce reasons for this Court to change its opinions.[19]

---

17. Henri De Page remarked that 'once the Court of Cassation has decided, the lower courts are almost always reconciling themselves' even if previously there were strong oppositions amongst them as regards the decided issue. *See* H. De Page, 1 Traité élémentaire de droit civil belge No. 212*bis*A, p. 307 (3d ed., Brussels: Bruylant 1962).
18. R. Kruithof has argued that although decisions of the Court of Cassation are formally not '*arrêts de règlement*', as the judge is not entitled to formulate (new) general rules in his judgments, in a material sense they really are. *See* R. Kruithof, *Naar een 'gouvernement des juges' in het verbintenissenrecht?*, *in* Hulde aan Prof. dr. R. Kruithof 57 (Antwerp: Maklu & Brussels: Bruylant 1992).
19. A. Vanwelkenhuyzen, *La motivation des revirements de jurisprudence*, *in* La motivation des décisions de justice 258–259 (Ch. Perelman & P. Foriers eds., Brussels: Bruylant 1978).

An underlying presupposition is that such a consensus amongst courts, amongst lawyers in general, is a safeguard, and maybe the only conclusive safeguard, against arbitrary judgments.

[C] Ideological Presuppositions

[1] Theory of the State: The Task of the Judge

The way of deciding cases and of interpreting statutes is strongly influenced by the judge's conception of his role as a judge. In its turn this conception is to a large extent determined by the current view amongst lawyers and in society of the task of the judge, and, more generally, of the functioning of the state.

As already mentioned above, a traditional basic assumption is the strict division of power between the legislature, the executive and the judiciary, with a very strong emphasis on the first one. In this view the potential active role of the judge is very limited. This is still the official doctrine. In practice, however, there has been an important historical shift as regards the view on the relation between the legislature and the judiciary. One of the main concerns by the end of the eighteenth century and early nineteenth century was to limit the large power of judges by statutes enacted by a (relatively) democratically elected parliament: it was obvious that the active role of the judge should and would, henceforth, be limited. A pragmatic approach has allowed judges to play a more active role when they considered it necessary, whilst still upholding the legalistic façade, although without ever usurping their position. Even if the strict legalistic borderlines have, ever since the early nineteenth century, often been crossed, there has always been a loyalty towards the general principles of the legal system. Judges may sometimes have curbed developments of the law, but they have never tried to make radical changes. Wherever they have departed from the strict wording of statutory law, they remained faithful to the aims of the law. Whenever the aim of the historical legislature has, exceptionally, not been followed, the judicial decision has been based on a current, generally shared, view in society.

On the other hand, legislative inflation, rapid changes of statutes because of a relative political instability, an actual shift of real power from Parliament to the executive, political scandals, and the like, have greatly diminished the reputation of the legislature. Today, stability, defence of the rule of law, protection of the individual against the State, implementation of the general principles of law seem to be offered mainly by the courts, instead of, if not against, the legislature and the executive. This image has been reinforced by the role, and the influence, of the European Court of Human Rights (ECtHR), the Belgian Constitutional Court (*Cour constitutionnelle – Grondwettelijk Hof*)[20] and the administrative supreme court, the Council of State

20. The Constitutional Court was established in 1983 as '*Cour d'arbitrage – Arbitragehof*', as its main task was to 'arbitrate' between the different (regional and federal) legislatures which had obtained exclusive and complementary legislative jurisdiction. Its role has been very significant since 1989, when its competence was considerably enlarged. Finally, in 2007 the name was changed into 'Constitutional Court' (*Cour constitutionnelle – Grondwettelijk Hof*).

(*Conseil d'Etat – Raad van State*),[21] and through the acceptance, by the Court of Cassation of the precedence of international treaties, ratified by the Belgian Parliament over more recently adopted statutes.[22] Nowadays the dominant view in society is no longer a fear for the arbitrary judge and a trust in the democratically functioning legislature. There is rather a distrust of politicians, and hence of Parliament and the executive, and a hope that courts will protect and enforce fundamental legal principles, when the legislature or the executive are seen to depart from them. In this spirit of the age there is a growing acceptance of a more active role of the judge. This active role often appears in a different form to a more liberal construction of statutes. Summary proceedings, for instance, have become very important, not only as a means for the rapid attainment of a temporary solution for a dispute, but, in fact, often as a solution accepted by all parties and thus definitive. The 'real' legal discussion is very often not even brought before the court, as the procedure ends, in a very large majority of the cases, with a 'temporary' injunction.

Although a more active role of the judge is more and more accepted and even expected, judges still basically stick to the traditional conception of their task: a cautious pragmatic approach, often still behind a legalistic façade.

One of the most striking materials of this façade is the presentation of the legal system as being coherent and stable over time. When the (supreme) courts are changing their decisions they generally hide the change and try to give an impression of continuity.[23] Starting from the assumption of the rationality of the legislature, judges consider it to be their task to interpret the law in such a way as to be as coherent as possible.[24]

[2] World View of the Belgian Judge

It is not only when interpreting statutes that the personal world view of the judge may influence his judgment. This is also the case when judges are interpreting and evaluating facts and the evidence submitted. Most obviously the world view of the judge plays a decisive role when applying vague concepts, such as 'the interest of the child', 'good faith', 'common decency', 'wrong', 'reasonable', or when filling gaps in the law.

Empirical research has shown that this does not lead to strongly divergent decisions, depending on the personal opinion of the judges concerned, as one could

21. This Court has the power to annul rules enacted by the executive.
22. *Fromagerie Franco-Suisse Le Ski v. Belgische Staat*, Court of Cassation 27 May 1971, 1971 Arresten van het Hof van Cassatie 959, 1971 JOURNAL DES TRIBUNAUX 460.
23. A. Vanwelkenhuyzen, *La motivation des revirements de jurisprudence*, *in* LA MOTIVATION DES DÉCISIONS DE JUSTICE 252–253, 263, 270–277 and 286 (Ch. Perelman & P. Foriers eds., Brussels: Bruylant 1978).
24. F. OST & M. VAN DE KERCHOVE, ENTRE LA LETTRE ET L'ESPRIT. LES DIRECTIVES D'INTERPRÉTATION EN DROIT 83–85 (Brussels: Bruylant 1989).

expect. On the contrary, there seems to be a striking homogeneity in the world views of the judges.[25]

Judges tend to be rather conservative, as lawyers mostly are. In general, however, they seem to follow developments in society, as it appears from the case law on divorce, concubinage, the relationship between parents and children, the position of women within marriage, the concept of 'common decency'.[26] In 'adapting' the content of concepts following changes in society, the judges indeed seem to express a general 'legal awareness'. It is indeed striking that the legislature never reacted to such developments except by adapting the statute to the judicial developments.[27]

An increased 'moral' approach to the law can be noticed: over the last decades courts have accepted the protection of 'abuse of right' as a general principle of law.[28] The duty to act according to 'good faith', which only finds a statutory application as regards the performance of contracts, is now considered to be an unwritten general principle of law.[29] The judiciary has limited the discretionary power of the authorities by introducing the principle of reasonableness.[30] Since 1989, statutes in violation of constitutional principles of equality[31] can be annulled by the Constitutional Court.

Nevertheless, courts have never, or rarely[32] been criticised for applying their own world view, even against the wording of statutes. The main reason for the general acceptance of this case law is the cautious manner in which judges have applied their moral views. It is only when behaviour, which apparently seems to be legal, *clearly*

---

25. *See* M. Van Hoecke, Mens- en maatschappijbeeld van de rechter (Ghent: RUG Seminarie voor Privaatrechtelijk Procesrecht 1975), presenting the results of an analysis of all civil judgments of the Ghent Court of Appeal in the year 1972, and M. Van Hoecke, *Mens- en maatschappijbeeld van de vrederechter, in* Vrederechter: Openbare Dienst 123–178 (J. Broekman et al. eds., Bruges: die Keure 1989), containing an analysis of the judgments of the justices of the peace, published in the journal of the association of the justices of the peace (*Journal des Juges de Paix – Tijdschrift van de Vrederechters*) between 1986 and 1989; E. Verdonck, Mens- en maatschappijbeeld van de vrederechter (unpublished master's dissertation Ghent University Faculty of Law 2010).
26. For example: The negative attitude towards divorce and the traditional view on the roles of husband and wife as they appeared from the Ghent court decisions in 1972 (M. Van Hoecke, Mens- en maatschappijbeeld van de rechter (Ghent: RUG Seminarie voor Privaatrechtelijk Procesrecht 1975)) have been seen to have considerably diminished nowadays, if not, to have disappeared. By the end of the 1970s courts in Belgium have considered that the criminal act of rape is even possible within a marriage (first published case: Court of Appeal of Brussels 21 June 1979, 1980 Revue trimestrielle de droit familial 159). The legislature followed this evolution and changed the law in 1989.
27. M. Van Hoecke, *Naar een theorie van de algemene rechtsbeginselen, in* Algemene Rechtsbeginselen 400–401, No. 16 (M. Van Hoecke ed., Antwerp: Kluwer Rechtswetenschappen 1991).
28. Court of Cassation 10 September 1971, 1972 Arresten van het Hof van Cassatie 31, 1972-I Pasicrisie belge 28; A. Van Oevelen, *Algemene rechtsbeginselen in het verbintenissen- en contractenrecht, in* Algemene Rechtsbeginselen 142–146 (M. Van Hoecke ed., Antwerp: Kluwer Rechtswetenschappen 1991).
29. P. Van Ommeslaghe, *L'exécution de bonne foi, principe général de droit?*, 1987 Revue générale de droit civil belge 101–110.
30. F. Debaedts, *Algemene rechtsbeginselen in het administratief recht, in* Algemene Rechtsbeginselen 256–258 (M. Van Hoecke ed., Antwerp: Kluwer Rechtswetenschappen 1991).
31. Title II of the Belgian Constitution (Articles 8–32 on the rights and freedoms of the Belgians), on Articles 170 and 172 (legality and equality of taxes) and Article 191 Constitution. Article 142 Constitution.
32. *See* e.g., R. Kruithof, *Naar een 'gouvernement des juges' in het verbintenissenrecht?, in* Hulde aan Prof. dr. R. Kruithof 70–79 (Antwerp: Maklu & Brussels: Bruylant 1992).

conflicts with generally accepted moral principles, that these moral rules are applied and that a black letter interpretation is disregarded.

§2.02 RECOGNISED SOURCES OF LAW

[A] Internal Sources of Law

Truly *binding* sources of law are virtually only the Constitution and legislation issued by bodies with a legislative competence. However, other sources such as court decisions or doctrinal writings of legal scholars may have a lot of authority and a strong influence on the way law is perceived and interpreted in legal practice.

[1] Legislation

Belgium has a written Constitution since 1831. This document, with its subsequent amendments, is the highest legal rule in the internal legal order. It lays down: (a) the principal functions of, and the interaction between the legislative, the executive and the judicial branches of government; (b) the general principles of the federal system; and (c) fundamental rights and freedoms protecting the individual from abuse of power by the government and, since 1994, socio-economic fundamental rights.

The constitutional rules on the federal system are further elaborated in so-called special acts, these are statutes that can only be adopted by the federal legislature in compliance with a qualified (linguistic) majority requirement.

Ordinary statutes - here called 'acts' (*lois* - *wetten* at the federal level, *décrets* - *decreten* at the level of the communities and of the Walloon and Flemish Regions, and *ordonnances* - *ordonnanties* at the level of Brussels-Capital Region) - all have equal force of law throughout the territory over which the respective legislatures have jurisdiction, insofar as they are enacted within the allocation of powers provided under the Constitution and the special acts. It is an important feature of the Belgian federal system that there is no hierarchy between national or federal statutes and the statutory instruments enacted by the communities and the regions. The Constitutional Court is entrusted with the power to control whether the federal, regional or community acts violate, either *ratione loci*, or *ratione materiae*, this allocation of powers. Moreover, the Constitutional Court has the power to annul, to declare unconstitutional and suspend federal, regional and community acts infringing on Title II of the Constitution (Articles 8–32 on the rights and freedoms of the Belgians), on Articles 170 and 172 (legality and equality of taxes) and Article 191 (protection of foreign nationals), on the power-defining rules between those authorities, provided for in the Constitution and in statutes on institutional reform and on Article 143, § 1, of the Constitution (the principle of federal loyalty).

The ordinary courts always have refused to review the constitutionality of statutory rules, arguing that the legislature at the national and regional levels itself, and not the courts should ensure that legislation is not unconstitutional.[33] If the meaning of a legislative act is unclear, the courts are guided in their interpretation by the presumption of constitutionality, i.e., they may assume that it was not the intention of the legislature to violate the Constitution.[34]

Legislative acts are implemented by the executive in the form of royal decrees (*arrêtés royals – koninklijke besluiten*) and for matters of secondary importance, ministerial decrees and decrees of the state secretaries (*arrêtés ministériels – ministeriële besluiten*) at the national level, and by regulations and orders of the regional governments (called *Executives – Exécutifs – Executieven* until 1993) at the level of the communities and regions. Subordinate authorities may enact provincial and municipal regulations and orders (*règlements provinciales & municipales – provinciale & gemeentelijke reglementen* or *verordeningen*) in all matters of provincial or municipal interest.

All these administrative regulations and orders are subject to the principle of legality, which means that these administrative authorities may only act insofar as they are empowered to do so by the Constitution or federal, regional or community statute. By virtue of Article 159 of the Constitution, the ordinary courts must refuse the application of administrative acts violating the higher legal rules. Moreover, the Administration Section of the Council of State is empowered to annul regulations and orders on the same grounds.

In case of conflicting rules of different subordinate authorities, the local autonomy and the respective powers *ratione materiae* are to be taken into account. In this way a provincial regulation does not automatically prevail over a municipal regulation.[35] In any case, this local autonomy represents less than it suggests, as the acts of the local authorities are subject to administrative oversight by the higher authorities, which review not only its legality, but also its merits.

[2] Case Law

Precedents in case law do not have any legally binding force. There are only two exceptions to this rule.

The first case in which a court decision is binding is a *second decision* in one and the same case by the Court of Cassation after a second appeal to this court *on the same legal grounds*. In this case, and this case alone, the lower court is bound by the interpretation and application of the law as made by the Court of Cassation for giving the final decision *in that same case*. The Court of Cassation, indeed, does not decide the case under consideration as such, it only checks whether the law and its interpretation

33. The law provides for one exception in regard of statutes issued by the Brussels-Capital Region (*ordonnances – ordonnanties*). They are, contrary to federal statutes and statutes of the communities and other regions, subject to a limited judicial review by the ordinary courts. Moreover they are, in certain cases, subject to limited administrative oversight by the federal authorities in order to protect Brussels' international role and its function as a capital.
34. *Waleffe*, Court of Cassation 20 April 1950, 1950-I Pasicrisie belge 560.
35. A. Alen & B. Tilleman, Treatise on Belgian Constitutional Law 47 (Deventer: Kluwer Law and Taxation Publishers 1992).

have been correctly applied by lower court. After a successful appeal in cassation, another lower court rules the final decision.

This is also true for the second case: administrative tribunals and commissions to which a case is referred for final decision after the annulment of an earlier decision in the same case by the Council of State are bound by the decision of Belgium's highest administrative court insofar as it interprets and applies the law. Contrary to the first case, already the first decision of the Council of State has binding force for the administrative tribunal to which the case is referred.

In practice, decisions of the highest courts do have a strong moral authority, especially when confirmed repeatedly over the years.

[3] Customary Law and General Principles of Law

Customary law is also a binding source of law, but, today, it plays only a very marginal role, as almost every aspect of social life is nowadays ruled by some form of legislation at a local, regional, federal or European level. Nowadays, examples of customary law may still be found in constitutional law, such as the limitation of the powers of an outgoing Government to the conduct of the 'current affairs', and the rule of secrecy governing the relations between the King and his Ministers.

Over the last few decades courts have accepted a new legally binding source of law, notably the unwritten general principles of law (*principes généraux du droit – algemene rechtsbeginselen*). Although these principles are found and worded by courts (which do not have the power, or even the right, to impose general rules), a breach of such a principle has been accepted by the Court of Cassation as a reason for annulment of a judicial decision. Such general principles of law are mostly derived from existing elements of the legal system. As it has been the case in many European countries, the general principle of good faith, for instance, has been derived from the statutory obligation that performance of a contract has to be in accordance with good faith (Article 1134 of the Belgian Civil Code). But, sometimes there is no such statutory support to be found for an unwritten general principle of law. This, for instance, is the case with the reasonableness principle applied to the use of discretionary powers by authorities. In the last case unwritten general principles have a more limited scope and are used for correcting unreasonable or inequitable effects of a strict application of legislative rules, whereas the former are used as guiding principles, comparable to those laid down in legislation.

Equity also is generally recognised as a source of law. However, its role is very marginal, for the same reason that customary law plays an extremely limited role in the current Belgian legal system: an inflation of regulation by public authorities. Moreover, the role of 'equity' has also to a large extent been taken over by several unwritten general principles of law, most notably the 'abuse of right principle'.

[4] Legal Doctrine

Doctrinal writings of authors play an important role in the creation and the development of law. But, they are only an indirect source of law, as new interpretations and theories proposed by legal writers have to be accepted by courts first, before they will be considered to be positive law. However, in practice, in order to have knowledge of Belgian law, one will start looking for scholarly writings, as they offer a coherent description of the content of the 'main' legal sources (applicable legislation and relevant court decisions). From the point of view of information, legal writing then is the most important source for finding the law.

[B] Influence of European and International Law

[1] The Supremacy of International Law

The Belgian Constitution remains silent on the relationship between international and domestic law. Before 1971 Belgian judges advocated a dualistic vision, stating that the international and national levels are two separate legal systems. Following this theory, a legal rule in an international treaty only became part of the internal, national legal system if it was incorporated or implemented into national law. In the hierarchy of norms, a treaty had the same legal force as an act of Parliament: pursuant to the principle of *lex posterior derogat priori* the treaty prevailed over earlier statutes, but not over acts of Parliament adopted and entered into force after the incorporation of the said treaty into the national legal order.

In the *Le Ski* case of 1971 the Court of Cassation left its former dualistic approach, and adhered to a monistic vision.[36] Ever since, international and domestic law are considered to form a unity. Once Parliament has given its consent to an international treaty, it becomes part of the unitary legal order. There is no further need for incorporating acts. If, moreover, the provisions of such treaty are sufficiently clear and complete to generate all of their own rights and duties for individuals, in the sense that no additional national implementing regulations are required, then these provisions are self-executing, and they prevail over former and later acts of Parliaments. Ordinary courts confronted with national legislation containing provisions inconsistent with self-executing treaties, must declare these laws inoperative.

This prevalence of self-executing international legal norms over domestic law is particularly important in the field of human rights and European Union (EU) Law.

[2] Human Rights Treaties

The Belgian courts hold most of the provisions of the European Convention for the Protection of Human Rights and Fundamental Freedoms (ECHR), its Protocols and the

36. *See Fromagerie Franco-Suisse Le Ski v. Belgische Staat*, Court of Cassation 27 May 1971, 1971 Arresten van het Hof van Cassatie 959, 1971 JOURNAL DES TRIBUNAUX 460.

International Covenant on Civil and Political Rights to be self-executing. Citizens may therefore directly invoke the provisions of these treaties before the courts, even if this means that acts of the Parliament are to be set aside.

This is not so obvious as it seems. As we have seen, the ordinary courts traditionally refrain from reviewing the constitutionality of statutes, and therefore do not verify whether the acts of the Parliament contradict the fundamental rights provisions in the Constitution. Nevertheless, since the *Le Ski* decision, they do control the conformity of such acts with the provisions of the international human rights treaties mentioned above.

Moreover, the Constitutional Court, when exercising its judicial review of federal, regional or community statutes, may link the constitutional principles of equality and non-discrimination to the human rights as they are formulated, not only by the Constitution itself, but also by the self-executing human rights treaties. Thus, it may annul a legislative act for reason of unconstitutionality, if such law contains a provision that introduces an unjustified unequal treatment of citizens (Article 10 of the Belgian Constitution) in the way they may exercise their freedom of association (Article 11 of the ECHR).

As a result the impact of the human rights treaties, and more in particular the ECHR, on the legal developments in Belgium is significant in several branches of law, especially family law and criminal procedure law (*see* the respective chapters in this book).

[3] European Law

The legal order of the EU is a very particular international legal system, as the basic EU Treaties establish institutions that are empowered to create in an autonomous way rules that are binding in the territories of all of the Member States. European law was superimposed on the domestic legal systems of the Member States. One of these autonomous institutions, the European Court of Justice (ECJ), considered that a supranational legal order would be meaningless and lose its uniformity, if it could be set aside by domestic norms of the Member States.[37] This reasoning was also accepted by the Court of Cassation in its leading *Le Ski* ruling, in which it recognised the direct applicability and the self-executing character of Article 12 of the EC Treaty (now Article 18 of the Treaty on the Functioning of the European Union (TFEU)), and the supremacy thereof in relation to domestic norms, even of a later date.

Secondary community law, i.e., the norms adopted and promulgated by these autonomous institutions within the powers granted to them by the EU Treaties, also prevails over domestic law. This clearly is the case for EU regulations, which are by definition directly applicable in the Member States (Article 288 of the TFEU), which means that they belong automatically to the (highest) norms of the internal legal order

37. *Costa v. E.N.E.L.*, ECJ case 6/64, 1964 *ECR* 1199 (Judgment of 15 July 1964).

of the Member States without any need for implementation into domestic law.[38] If the provisions of a regulation are sufficiently clear and determined, and do not leave any margin of appreciation to the national authorities, they may be invoked by natural and legal persons, not just against the state, but also against other persons.

European directives are not directly applicable, but must be implemented into national law within a certain time period set by the directive itself. Still directives may contain provisions that fulfil all conditions for being self-executing. If the period for implementation has lapsed, and a Member State has failed to take the necessary measures for reaching the aim set by the directive, persons may invoke the self-executing provisions against the negligent Member State, but not against other persons. Moreover the Member State may be held liable for damages caused to persons as a result of this untimely or incorrect implementation.[39]

[4] International Law Versus the Constitution

There is a general consensus that the Constitutional Court has the power to control the so-called extrinsic constitutionality, i.e., the power of the respective authorities to give consent to a treaty. The Constitutional Court is indeed empowered to annul an act expressing the consent of Parliament to a treaty, if this act violates the division of competences between the federal State, the regions and/or the communities.

Moreover the Constitutional Court seems to consider that it is also empowered to control the intrinsic constitutionality, i.e., to control whether the contents of a treaty conform to the constitutional principles the safeguarding of which is entrusted to that Court (principles of equality, non-discrimination, and freedom of education). The Court argues that, if the constitutioner forbade the legislature to adopt internal acts that violate the Constitution, he may not be presumed to have allowed the legislature to violate the Constitution in an indirect way, through giving consent to an international treaty. Moreover, there is no rule of international law granting states the power to conclude a treaty contravening their respective constitutions. Still, the Constitutional Court concedes that such control must be exercised in a reserved manner, as a treaty is not just a one-sided act of sovereignty, but also generates legal consequences outside the internal legal order.[40]

The Constitutional Court has not yet been confronted with a conflict between the Constitution and a norm of primary or secondary EU law. The Administration Section of the Council of State, on the other hand, seems to have accepted the prevalence of EU norms, as they are interpreted by the ECJ (in this concrete case through application of an evolutionary construction method), over norms contained in the Belgian Constitution. In two cases on the access to the Belgian civil service for nationals of EU Member

38. In fact the formal reception of a regulation into the internal legal order is unacceptable, as this would lead to misunderstandings as to the legal nature of these norms and the date of their entry into force: *Commission v. Italy*, ECJ case 39/72, 1973 *ECR* 101 (Judgment of 7 February 1973).
39. *Francovich a.o.*, ECJ joint cases C-6/90 & C-9/90, 1991 *ECR* I-5357 (Judgment of 19 November 1991).
40. Court of Arbitration No. 26/91 of 16 October 1991, Belgisch Staatsblad, 23 November 1991; Court of Arbitration No. 12/94 of 3 February 1994, Belgisch Staatsblad, 11 March 1994.

States, the Council of State considered that 'from the Belgian constitutional point of view, the authority of the interpretation given to the Treaty of Rome by the Court of Justice is based on Article 34 of the Constitution, even if this interpretation would lead to the setting out of force of a part of articles 8 and 10 of the Constitution'.[41] Article 34 was introduced into the Constitution in 1970 to take away all doubts about the constitutionality of the EU Treaties. As these Treaties imply a transfer of sovereignty to supranational bodies, and Article 33 of the Constitution considers the nation and its representatives as the exclusive holders of sovereignty, the constitutioner felt the need to include a provision into the Constitution (Article 34) expressly stating that the exercise of certain powers may be attributed by a treaty or an act to institutions of international public law. No doubt this Article 34 of the Constitution is a major argument in favour of the primacy of EU Law over the Belgian Constitution.

§2.03 FINDING THE LAW[42]

The last decade digitisation has altered the way lawyers find legal information. Reference databases are no longer sufficient for the legal practitioner who, nowadays, demands online access to the full text of the document, irrespectively whether it is legislation, case law or doctrine.

[A] Bibliographical Works

Printed bibliographical works appeared very late in Belgium's history and lost their importance for legal practice ever since digitalisation took over during the 2000s. Technological evolutions have had inevitably consequences on how lawyers look for references to the traditional sources of Belgian law. During the 1990s, CD-ROMs were a commonly used medium for catalogues, but nowadays electronic databases are searched online. During their training, law students develop skills to use online databases such as *Jur@*, *Juridat* and *Jurisquare*. All are indispensable for the legal practitioner.

Juridat[43] is the online portal site of the Belgian judiciary. It can be used to find legislation as it is in force today, and it contains a growing body of case law. Printed bibliographical reference works are a relic of the past. The *Recueil annuel de jurisprudence belge* changed its name to Projects such as *Judit* and *R.A.J.B.i.* (*Recueil annuel de jurisprudence belge informatisé*), both available on CD-ROM, became also outdated. *Judit* was a project ignited by Kluwer Legal Publishing and contained references to legal acts, case law and doctrinal writings dating from 1980. It was in fact a cumulative

41. Council of State No. 62.922 of 5 November 1996, 1997 JOURNAL DES TRIBUNAUX 254, with case note by R. Ergec (*see also* case No. 62.920 of the same date).
42. *See* e.g., Ch.F. Verbeke, *Belgian Law: Bibliographic Guide to Reference Materials, 1830–1990*, 20-2 INTERNATIONAL JOURNAL OF LEGAL INFORMATION 133–154 (1992); A. DE THEUX & I. KOVALOVSZKY, PRÉCIS DE MÉTHODOLOGIE JURIDIQUE. LES SOURCES DOCUMENTAIRES DU DROIT (Brussels: Publications des Facultés universitaires Saint-Louis 2000); GUIDE DES CITATIONS, RÉFÉRENCES ET ABBRÉVIATIONS JURIDIQUES (P. Vandernoot ed., Waterloo: Kluwer 2010).
43. *See* www.juridat.be.

compilation of two traditional bibliographical publications, the monthly journal *Tijdschrift Rechtsdocumentatie – Information et documentation juridiques*. *Judit* is now embedded in the *Jur@*-database. Another publishing house, namely Larcier, established the *R.A.J.B.i.* in 1978. It did only contain references to case law and a selection of doctrinal writings, not to legislation. Today that database is embedded in the *Strad@ Lex* database,[44] together with the digital version of the Codes Larcier.

A third important online platform is *Jurisquare*,[45] which offers subscribers journals in full text. It is the result of three cooperating publishing houses: die Keure, Bruylant and Intersentia. This database is fully integrated with the database *Jur@*[46] and *Strad@*, which means it is the most complete full text database in Belgium.

Other traditional law bibliographies are the *Répertoire décennal de la Jurisprudence Belge* (an extremely useful instrument for finding references to case law and legal doctrine from 1814 to 1975), the *Répertoire bibliographique du droit belge* (with references to Belgian legal doctrine from 1919 to 1970) and the *Doctrine juridique belge*, which appears as a yearbook since 1986 and contains references to legal doctrine, including comments under published case law. However, today these reference works seem to have lost their importance.

[B] Where to Find Legislation

The bilingual *Moniteur belge – Belgisch Staatsblad* is the official record of Belgium's legislation and regulation. Since 1 June 1997 it is accessible for everyone on an official website.[47] Since 2005 the *Moniteur belge – Belgisch Staatsblad* is exclusively published online. However, four printed copies can still be found on four public places: the Royal Library of Belgium, the Department of Justice, the National Archives and the *Moniteur belge – Belgisch Staatsblad*. In addition, one copy is kept on microfilm.

All acts and decrees enacted by the national legislature or executive, or the acts and regulations of the Brussels-Capital Region are published in French and Dutch, both being equally authentic versions. This means that, the case arising, differences between the Dutch and French texts must be solved according to the intention of the legislature, which is to be determined according to the usual construction methods and without giving preference to one of both texts.

Normative acts adopted by the legislative and executive bodies of the communities and regions, except for those of the Brussels-Capital Region, are unilingual. Their official publication is always accompanied with a non-authentic translation into one or two of the other national languages.[48]

Although the *Moniteur belge – Belgisch Staatsblad* provides the only official version of a normative act, it is certainly not the best instrument to find a specific law.

44. *See* www.stradalex.be.
45. *See* www.jurisquare.be.
46. *See* www.jura.be.
47. *See* www.staatsblad.be (in Dutch) and www.moniteur.be (in French).
48. Statutes and decrees of the Flemish Community and Region (French Community) are published in Dutch (French) with a translation into French (Dutch); statutes and decrees enacted by the Walloon Region (German Community) are published in French (German) with a translation into

If the date of promulgation of the legal act is known but not the date of publication, then the basically chronological collections, such as *Omnilegie* (bilingual, since 1952) and *Pasinomie* (in French since 1833, but containing texts retrospectively to 1788), may be helpful. However, the easiest way to find a specific piece of legislation, is using the search engine on www.staatsblad.be, or using the collection of coordinated legislation as it is in force, including most of its recent history, on the site of the federal Justice Department,[49] or the sites for regional legislation.[50]

In all other cases one should resort to one of the many privately coordinated collections of laws, of which the most important and complete ones are the *Tweetalige Wetboeken Story-Scientia* (*TWS*) and the *Codes Larcier*. Both have the ambition to cover most, if not all, branches of law. The former is a loose-leaf bilingual publication, divided according to the different branches of law, and containing within each branch first the official code (if any), then the specific statutes and regulations in chronological order, and finally the international treaties. *TWS* is also available on CD-ROM (TWS-CD). The *Codes Larcier* are bound, and exist in separate French (5 volumes) and Dutch (7 volumes) versions. They are also divided according to the branches of law; within each branch first the official code is published (if any), and then all specific laws and regulations are subsumed under topical entries which are set in alphabetical order. It is updated by supplemental volumes. Both *TWS* and *Codes Larcier* have very useful analytical and chronological tables. Apart from these two collections of laws, there are many pocket publications of laws, or collections of law in specialised law fields (e.g., *Medialex* for media law).

For both Houses of the federal Parliament, and for all regional and community parliaments, separately the *Parliamentary Papers* include three kind of publications: a first one reporting the parliamentary debates, discussions and votes in the respective assemblies (e.g., *Annales du Sénat de Belgique – Handelingen van de Belgische Senaat*), a second one containing the record of parliamentary questions and answers (*Bulletin des questions et réponses – Bulletin van Vragen en Antwoorden*), and a third one containing all documents used in the legislative process, such as bills, proposed amendments, the record of discussions within the parliamentary commission, the advice formulated by the Legislation Section of the Council of State (e.g., *Documents du Sénat – Stukken van de Senaat*). There is a growing tendency to make these publications also available on Internet.[51]

Dutch and German (Dutch and French). Moreover, the statutes and decrees enacted by the authorities of the German Community are published in German in the *Memorial des Rates der deutschsprachigen Gemeinschaft*.

49. *See* www.ejustice.just.fgov.be/cgi_wet/wet.pl.

50. For Flemish legislation, *see* www.codex.vlaanderen.be, for Walloon legislation, *see* https://wallex.wallonie.be, and for legislation of the Brussels-Capital Region, *see* http://be.brussels/.

51. For the national federal Parliament, *see* www.senaat.be and www.dekamer.be. Except for an introduction in English, all documents are exclusively available in French and Dutch. For the Flemish Region, *see* www.vlaamsparlement.be, for the Walloon Region, *see* www.parlement.wallonie.be, and for the Brussels-Capital Region, *see* www.parlbruparl.irisnet.be and www.weblex.irisnet.be.

[C] Where to Find Case Law

In Belgium all judgments are - in principle - read in public to ensure that the administration of justice is accessible and open to public scrutiny. The government offers all judges the opportunity to upload their verdict in an official database.[52] Some judges do it systematically, whereas others forget or even neglect to do so. Consequently, some courts might be better represented than others, simply because the magistrate does not use the upload option.

Some courts are legally obliged to make their judgments accessible for the general public. For instance, all judgments of the Constitutional Court are published in the *Moniteur belge - Belgisch Staatsblad* and can be consulted online.[53] The digital version of Judgments of the Court of Cassation is accessible through the website of the Justice Department[54] (in anticipation of the new website of the Court of Cassation).[55] The cassation appeal and that of the Constitutional Court may also be consulted via *Juridat*. The judgments of the Council of State annulling or suspending executive or local regulations are communicated to the public in extract at the same place where these regulations were published (for instance in the *Moniteur belge - Belgisch Staatsblad* for royal decrees, by posting at the outside of the town hall for municipal regulations).[56] Otherwise there is no legal obligation to publish court decisions.[57] Therefore, only a tiny part of case law is accessible to the public.

However, the highest courts do have their own periodicals (*Arrêts Cour Constitutionnelle - Arresten Grondwettelijk Hof*; *Bulletin des arrêts de la Cour de cassation - Arresten van het Hof van Cassatie*; and *Recueil des arrêts du Conseil d'Etat - Verzameling der Arresten van de Raad van State*), and many of their decisions are published on their websites.[58] A sheer endless list of legal journals also publish case law, often accompanied by critical comments by legal scholars.[59] They may be either general, in the sense that they cover any branch of law and any jurisdiction (*Journal des tribunaux, Rechtskundig Weekblad, Nieuw Juridisch Weekblad, Revue critique de jurisprudence belge*), or specific as to the territory (e.g., *Revue de jurisprudence de Liège, Mons et Bruxelles, Rechtspraak Antwerpen Brussel Gent*), the jurisdiction (e.g., *Journal des tribunaux du travail*) or the branch of law (such as *Tijdschrift voor Belgisch Burgerlijk Recht - Revue générale de droit civil belge*) covered. Finally, special mention

---

52. *See* www.juridat.be.
53. *See* www.const-court.be; www.staatsblad.be; www.moniteur.be.
54. *See* http://justitie.belgium.be.
55. *See* www.cass.be.
56. All judgments of the Council of State will become available in full text on the internet and CD-ROM (Article 28 Coordinated Act on the Council of State, as amended on 4 August 1996; Royal Decree of 7 July 1997). The website address is www.raadvst-consetat.be.
57. Unless otherwise provided by law (e.g., extracts of judgments declaring an enterprise bankrupt are to be published in the Moniteur belge - Belgisch Staatsblad) or ordered as an additional sanction by the judge.
58. For the Constitutional Court, *see* www.const-court.be, for the Court of Cassation, *see* www.cassonline.be, and for the Council of State, *see* www.raadvst-consetat.be.
59. S. Vandenbogaerde, Vectoren van het recht. Geschiedenis van de Belgische juridische tijdschriften (PhD dissertation Ghent University 2014).

should be made of the *Pasicrisie belge*, an impressive collection of case law in all branches of law from 1791 to date.

[D] Where to Find Legal Doctrinal Writings

First and foremost, one can find legal doctrine in the aforementioned law journals which, determined by their field of interest, publish (scholarly) articles on general or specific topics of legal practice and theory. Many law journals are bilingual, others are unilingual (Dutch or French). Apart from those journals already mentioned, reference should be made – just to name a small selection – in the field of public law to *Tijdschrift voor Bestuurswetenschappen en Publiek Recht*; in the field of private law to *Tijdschrift voor Privaatrecht*; in the field of social security and labour law to *Revue de droit social – Tijdschrift voor Sociaal Recht*; in the field of commercial law to *Revue de droit commercial belge – Tijdschrift voor Belgisch Handelsrecht*; in the field of criminal law to *Panopticon* and *Revue de droit pénal et de criminologie*; in the field of intellectual property and media law to *Intellectuele Rechten – Droit intellectuel*, *L'ingénieur-Conseil* and *Auteurs & Media*; etc.[60]

Apart from the articles in law journals, especially francophone legal doctrine sometimes has taken the form of legal encyclopaedias, with the (impossible) ambition to cover all branches of law. The most important ones are *Les Pandectes belges* (1878–1933, 151 volumes!), *Les Novelles* (1931 to date) and *Répertoire pratique du droit belge* (1930–1961, since then eight supplements). These monumental works, especially the latter two, were for a long time important tools in Belgian law, but today *Les Pandectes* has lost its value.

Thousands of manuals, monographs, doctoral dissertations, collections, *libri amicorum*, etc. complete the picture.[61]

§2.04 BRANCHES OF LAW

In Belgian doctrinal writings the branches of law are usually subsumed into two broad categories, *public law* and *private law*. Whereas the latter regulates the legal relationships among citizens, the former focuses on the relationship between these citizens and the government, on the internal organisation of the State, and on the legal relations between states (i.e., international public law). At first sight, this basic division seems to have a mere academic, or heuristic nature. Moreover, it is subject to modifications and nuances. As in the modern welfare state the authorities intervene in one way or another in nearly every aspect of social and economic life, those branches of law that are the typical products of this tendency, and therefore have developed in an explosive

60. For a more or less complete list of law journals, *see* JURIDISCHE VERWIJZINGEN & AFKORTINGEN (5th ed., Antwerp: Kluwer rechtswetenschappen 2015).
61. C. MALLIET, ELEMENTAIRE BIBLIOGRAFIE BELGISCH RECHT (Elementary Bibliography of Belgian Law), available on the internet, with a list of English publications on Belgian law at www.rechtgenoot.be.

manner after the Second World War, all have a mixed public/private character: social security law, environmental law, media and entertainment law, etc.

As a general rule it is accepted that not the identity of parties, but the character of their relationship determines the nature of the applicable legal norm. If the State, a region, a province or a municipality purchases a building to house its administration, this official body acts as a private person; it stands in a horizontal relationship with the seller, to which private law rules apply. If the same authority expropriates a private person in order to reach the same purpose, it uses its vertical monopoly of force, which implies the application of public law rules.

National public law consists of:

- *constitutional law*, determining the organisation and functioning of the State, and the fundamental rights and liberties of the citizens. It may be found mainly in the Constitution and a number of special acts;
- *administrative law* regulates, in numerous acts of Parliament, royal and ministerial decrees, provincial and municipal regulations, etc., the functioning of the executive branch of government, the administration (including expropriation, environmental planning, etc.);
- *tax law*, mainly fixed in a number of tax codes, defines how the income of the authorities is established and collected;
- *criminal law* and *criminal procedure* are mainly laid down in the 1867 Penal Code and 1808 Code of Criminal Procedure.

Private law embraces the following branches of law:

- *civil law*, i.e., the set of rules regulating the civil status of persons (name, domicile, legal capacity) and goods (ownership, mortgage, etc.), family law, the relationship between parents and children, patrimonial law, inheritance law, contracts, torts, etc. Many of these rules are fixed in the Napoleonic Civil Code of 1804 (amended on numerous occasions since then);
- *commercial law*, regulating the status of merchants and commercial activities. It is based on the 1807 Commercial Code and a great number of specific acts. Today economic law is regulated by the 2013 Code of Economic Law, which encompasses aspects of competition law, consumer law and the like;
- *social law*, including social security law and labour law.

The division between these three branches of private law is not of a mere academic nature, as it determines also the structure of the courts. The courts of first instance have a general jurisdiction as to civil disputes exceeding EUR 2,500. Disputes among traders, relating to matters deemed to be commercial by law, as well as disputes involving certain matters of corporate law and commercial law (bankruptcy, bills of exchange, promissory notes) and are decided upon by commercial courts, at least when the claim exceeds the same amount. Individual labour disputes and certain claims related to social security benefits are submitted to the labour courts; appeals against their judgments are brought before a proper labour court of appeal.

Civil procedure law determines the structure and powers of all these courts, including the courts of appeal and the Court of Cassation deciding in civil matters, as well as the procedure before these courts. These rules are mainly laid out by the 1967 Judicial Code, as adapted in later years.

§2.05 LEGAL EDUCATION AND LEGAL PROFESSIONS

[A] Legal Education

Studying law in Belgium normally takes five years. Students generally start at the age of 18 or 19 years, after having finished secondary school. There is no selection procedure before the entrance in law school. In practice, however, the examinations at the end of the first year function as a selection, as, at the average, only 40% of the students succeeds in this first year and almost half of the group which starts law school never will graduate.

There is, since the 1990s, a different statutory regulation of university studies for Flemish and francophone universities, but roughly both the curriculum and the general organisation of the law studies are comparable.

In 2004 the European bachelor-master organisation of university degrees has been introduced. Before, the first two years (*candidatures – kandidaturen*) contained non-legal disciplines up to half of the courses, such as economics, sociology, psychology, but most notably history and philosophy. From the third till the fifth year (*licences – licenties*) almost only positive law subjects were taught. As from 2004 this 2 + 3 structure has been reversed into a 3 + 2 one. As it is assumed that a bachelor degree should not only prepare for the master studies but should also offer perspectives on the labour market, it has led the law schools to offer a full legal education at bachelor level, whereas the master studies are just deepening the knowledge of the students in some fields of the law. Compared to the UK, for instance, many more subjects are offered (about ten courses a year) and most of the courses are compulsory at bachelor level. More optional courses are offered at master level.

At the bachelor level, the teaching is generally not interactive but *ex cathedra* and most courses end with an oral or written examination at the end of the semester (or the year, in case of reassessment). For optional courses the evaluation is more often done on the basis of a paper, written by the student in the course of the academic year. At the master level, when courses are more elective and therefore students are taught in smaller groups, more interactive teaching methods are used.

[B] Legal Professions

The basic master of laws degree gives direct access to most legal professions.

[1] Advocates

In order to defend a case in court one has to be a member of the bar. In order to be accepted as a trainee attorney (*avocat stagiaire – advocaat-stagiair*) one needs an elder attorney who accepts to be a supervisor of the trainee during the next three years and to pay at least the minimum salary. Until today, there are twenty-six independently functioning bars in Belgium, with their own rules and practices. They are organised at the level of the 'gerechtelijk arrondissement', which is the territory for which a court of first instance has competence. In 2014, these conscriptions were reorganised and reduced to twelve, which also has its consequences for the bar associations, which will have to follow this evolution.

In Brussels there is a francophone bar and a Flemish bar.

After three years of apprenticeship and fulfilment of the local requirements, including sometimes examinations, one may be accepted as a full attorney. In practice a trainee attorney can act before court as a full attorney. The only exception to this rule, the prohibition to plead before the supreme administrative court, the Council of State, was declared unconstitutional by the Constitutional Court.[62]

Every attorney may take cases for any court in Belgium, except non-penal cases in the Court of Cassation, for which one has to be represented by one of the sixteen appointed 'advocates at the Court of Cassation'.[63]

Generally speaking only attorneys are entitled to defend a client before courts.

[2] Notaries

In order to become a notary one has to obtain a basic law degree and an additional diploma of '*master en notariat*' or '*master in het notariaat*' after one year of full time academic studies. Once the degree obtained, one has to do an apprenticeship of three years as a 'candidate notary' with a notary. After having fulfilled these requirements one may be appointed as a notary, if there is a vacancy. The number of notaries is limited (1,519 notaries in 2014) and only the Minister of Justice can appoint one. A majority of notaries works alone whereas only a minority is associated with colleagues (in total there are 1,164 offices).

Acting by a notary is compulsory for all conveyancing of rights in rem on real estate and for concluding a matrimonial contract. Notaries also often act for drafting last wills.[64]

62. The only exception to this rule, the prohibition to plead before the supreme administrative court, the Council of State, was declared unconstitutional by the Constitutional Court (Court of Arbitration No. 55/98 of 20 May 1998.
63. *See* www.advocass.be.
64. Practical information, offered by the *Royal Federation of Belgian Notaries* is available on www.notaris.be (in Dutch) and www.notaire.be (in French) and in English on www.notaire.be/other-languages/english-1.

[3] Judges and Public Prosecutors

In order to become a judge or a public prosecutor one has to pass an examination, organised by the High Council of Justice (*Conseil Supérieur de la Justice – Hoge Raad voor de Justitie*) which also plays a key role in the appointment of a judge. Appointments of judges and public prosecutors are made upon a vacancy by the Minister of Justice. The position is for life. A career change can only be made when a new vacancy arises.

CHAPTER 3
Constitutional Law

Francis Delpérée

§3.01 THE CONSTITUTION

Constitutional law is the law of the Constitution. It is the law which, to give the State its main characteristics and the citizens their fundamental rights, materialises in a written and formal document which is adopted according to a rigid procedure by a large political majority. Other legal instruments necessarily complete the Constitution: different categories of statutes, decrees and orders, as well as regulations which are designed to implement them. On the other hand, legal decisions contribute to clarify the meaning of the constitutional provisions and to modify the interpretation of the texts to take into account the political, economic and social evolution. Important but limited doctrinal works also try to build from these materials a legal system which is as coherent as possible.

Still, the Constitution remains the legal reference document. 'All the Constitution, nothing but the Constitution ...', as Dean G. Vedel used to say.[1] In a state where the rule of law prevails, constitutional law can only develop and be useful from the drafting, the revision and the interpretation of the Constitution.

§3.02 HISTORY

The Belgian Constitution dates back to 7 February 1831. It was written and deliberated upon very quickly.

It was indeed on 4 October 1830 that the 'Provisional Government' proclaimed the independence of Belgium. It ordered that a draft constitution be written 'as soon as

1. G. Vedel, *Souveraineté et supraconstitutionnalité,* in: *La souvernaineté,* 67 POUVOIRS. REVUE FRANÇAISE D'ÉTUDES CONSTITUTIONNELLES ET POLITIQUES 79 (1993).

possible'. It entrusted a fourteen-member Commission with the preparation of this document. It convened at the same time the National Congress to examine the draft, to amend it if necessary, and to make the definitive Constitution 'enforceable all over Belgium'.

The Commission worked from 12 to 16 October 1830, that is to say a total of five days. The draft written by Devaux and Nothomb was approved by the Commission, apparently without any substantial modifications and then given as a draft to the Provisional Government on 27 October 1830.[2]

The final text was approved on 7 February 1831: 'The discussions lasted for two months: December 1830 to January 1831.'[3]

In short, the original Constitution of Belgium was prepared in a few days and adopted in a few weeks. Most constitutional provisions did not give rise to any discussion. Members of the National Congress more or less unanimously agreed on the draft prepared by the Commission. The attention was focused on only three issues: the choice of a king, the nomination of senators, and the system of freedoms – in particular, of religions and education.

In addition to the actual Constitution, which was proclaimed 'in the name of the Belgian people', the National Congress adopted two 'decrees'. The first one declared the independence of the Belgian people (18 November 1830), the other one excluded forever the members of the d'Orange-Nassau family from all powers in Belgium (24 November 1830). It is generally considered that both 'decrees' have constitutional force.

§3.03 SOURCES

The Belgian Constitution was mainly based on three documents: the French Constitution of 1791, the Dutch Fundamental Law of 1815, and the July Charter of Monarchy.[4]

The Belgian Constitution drew its inspiration from the French Constitution of 1791 by establishing the rule of ministerial countersignature and by drawing from this procedure the principle of ministerial responsibility. As Mirkine-Guetzevitch underlines, the Belgian Constitution sets up a 'type of parliamentary monarchy with a limited power for the king and defined the decisive role of Parliament, not only for the legislation but also in the choice of the government, that is to say in the government itself. The parliament which governs is the big conquest of 1830',[5] or, in any case, the parliament which controls those who govern.

The Belgian Constitution took from the Dutch Fundamental Law a set of technical provisions on the organisation of courts and on the system of public finance.

2. J. Gilissen, *La Constitution belge de 1831: ses sources, son influence*, 1968 Res Publica No. special, 13. Paraphrased translation.
3. J. Gilissen, *ibid. See* E. Huyttens, Discussions du Congrès national, Vol. I-V (Brussels: Wahlen, A. 1844).
4. *See* for this the still actual study by E. Descamps, La mosaïque constitutionnelle. Essai sur les sources du texte de la Constitution belge (Louvain, 1891).
5. 2 Annales de l'institut de droit comparé 95 (1936).

The Belgian Constitution mostly drew its inspiration from the Charter accepted by Louis-Philippe on 14 August 1830. The constitutional text listed the freedoms. It set up a hereditary monarchy and endeavoured to limit the attributions of the king. However, it was much different from the July Charter of Monarchy on one main point: it is not subject to any transaction between the National Congress and the king. This was determined by historical circumstances. The first king, Prince Leopold von Sachsen-Coburg und Gotha, only came to the throne on 21 July 1831. At that time, he took the oath of respecting a Constitution which had been written without his participation as it had been adopted as early as 7 February 1831.

Leopold I, in accepting the Belgian Crown on 20 April 1831, was right when he said to the members of the National Congress who met him on that occasion in London: 'Gentlemen, you have been hard with the kingship who was not there to defend itself'.[6]

§3.04 INFLUENCES

The Constitution of 7 February 1831 has had a determining influence on the constitutions of the nineteenth century. It was seen as the prototype of the constitutions of liberal states. Several states were directly inspired by its provisions for the definition of their freedoms as well as the organisation of their powers. It is not an exaggeration to say that Belgium was an example to a number of nation-states that adopted a constitution based on grounds of political liberalism. In particular those that became independent from 1848 onwards.

L. Luzzatti, a famous Italian statesman, wrote in 1917: 'Belgium has tried to solve one of the most difficult problems of modern times, the one of conciliating safe and stable guarantees of freedom with the representative monarchy. Anglo-Saxons call it small England. How could one pay a more beautiful tribute?'

As to the Belgian Constitution, it has been, in time, subject to influences from more recent constitutions. It draws its inspiration from them, for instance, to reflect the phenomenon of European integration, to define the respective role of sources of national law, community law and international law, and to establish some forms of rationalised parliamentary government.

§3.05 INTERPRETATION

The Belgian Constitution was once considered as a purely political instrument.[7] It is said to contain a set of rules which are meant to determine the aims of political action. What is more, it contains rules relating to the organisation and the running of the main public authorities. Because of this, it appears as one of the major elements of the organisation of the Belgian political system.

6. A. Molitor, *Réflexions sur la fonction royale*, *in* NOUS, ROI DES BELGES. 150 ANS DE MONARCHIE CONSTITUTIONNELLE 14 (Brussels: Crédit communal, 1981); F. Delpérée & B. Dupret, *Le roi des Belges*, 78 POUVOIRS. REVUE FRANÇAISE D'ÉTUDES CONSTITUTIONNELLES ET POLITIQUES 43 (1996).
7. A. MAST, OVERZICHT VAN HET BELGISCH GRONDWETTELIJK RECHT 80 (8th ed., Ghent: Story-Scientia 1975).

At the basis of such an analysis, it is easy to consider the Constitution as one element among many of the political system. Violations of the Constitution and processes which could be implemented to censure abuses are not particularly taken into consideration. Legislators do not try to consider all the institutional realities or activities 'in the eyes of the Constitution'[8] But simply, they also take note of the political realities. The reason for such developments has been a source of worry.

However, this is not the dominant point of view. On the contrary, the Belgian Constitution is more generally considered as a legal rule - and, indeed, the primary legal rule. Its provisions are supposed to be applicable to all those who are governed and those in power. They impose respect in all circumstances. In this way they allow and even require, controls and censures - in particular through the institution of the constitutional justice. In particular, we have to emphasise the fact that right from the beginning, public freedoms have been considered as constitutional rules - and not as a preamble or a declaration of rights (Title II: Belgians and their rights). One did not have to wait until the writing of international documents, in particular after the Second World War, to provide Belgians and foreigners living in Belgium (Article 191 of the Constitution) with a corpus of rights and freedoms, in the classical meaning of the expression.

Of course, the Belgian Constitution is an old constitution.[9] Most of the initial provisions are still applicable or have only been modified on certain points. Its old character gives interpreters of the Constitution a particular task: to interpret provisions, not only by taking into consideration unavoidable technical and scientific progress, but also by adapting, cautiously, to new political, economic and social realities and by integrating these provisions in a society which is universalising.[10]

How will this adaptation be realised? The constitution establishes primary law. Other legal instruments, such as statutes and regulations, create complementary law. But, between the two of them, there might be some space for an intermediary law which interpreters of the Constitution have to update.[11]

First, one has to take into account the principles of constitutional law, those which rule its development and explain its structure. The notion of 'democratic society', to use the language of the ECHR, is not expressed, for instance, in the provisions of the Constitution. But it is not an exaggeration to say that it goes beyond that point.

One must also consider the unwritten rules of constitutional law, those which appear between the lines of the original text, which have not been written as such but which complete, on essential points, the provisions of other formalised rules.

8. F. Delpérée, *Au regard de la Constitution*, *in* REGARDS CROISÉS SUR LA COUR D'ARBITRAGE 9 (F. Delpérée, A. Rasson-Roland & M. Verdussen eds., Brussels: Bruylant 1995).
9. The Belgian Constitution, it must be pointed out, has come into force without any revolts, uprising or civil war in 185 years.
10. *See* W.J. GANSHOF VAN DER MEERSCH, POUVOIR DE FAIT ET RÈGLES DE DROIT (Brussels: Librairie encyclopédique 1957).
11. F. Delpérée, *Complementary Sources to Old Constitutional Texts*, *in* CONSTITUTIONAL JUSTICE UNDER OLD CONSTITUTIONS (E. Smith ed., Oslo 1992).

Therefore, the joint reference to the monarchy and the ministerial responsibility induces a set of rules on the respective behaviours of the king and the ministers.

We finally have to examine the adjacent rules of constitutional law, an analogical interpretation of which allows to disclose progressively. The Constitution proclaims the principle of 'equality of the Belgians before the law'. It provides examples: equality for the granting of political mandates, equality for the access to public tasks, equality on offices, equality on access to justice. Beyond these examples, we can see other implementations of constitutional rules of equality and non-discrimination, for instance, the one which has to prevail between ideological and philosophical tendencies (Article 11 of the Constitution).

The task of constitutional interpretation finds herewith its guidelines, as well as its limits.[12]

§3.06 THE REVISION PROCEDURE

The Belgian Constitution is a highly rigid constitution. It tries to preserve the balance on the basis of which the Belgian State has been created and organised for more than 185 years.

The revision procedure contains three distinct stages. First, the federal legislature writes a declaration for the revision of the Constitution. Then, the Parliament is dissolved and new elections are held to form a new legislature, which will have constitutional powers. In the third phase, the actual revision starts. It is performed by constituent chambers, approved by a qualified majority of two-thirds of votes casted with two-thirds of the members present, and is then approved by the King.[13]

One can wonder whether the revision procedure, such as it is provided for in Article 195 of the Constitution, is not excessively heavy, at least in three regards.

First of all, the three stages: initiative, dissolution and revision of the constitutional work contribute to make the proceedings longer.

Then the setting up of a second stage characterised by the dissolution of Parliament compromises the normal functioning of the parliamentary action. Anticipated elections will not necessarily lead to the same majority in the assemblies. This can also affect the pursuit of governmental action.

The succession of different majorities can jeopardise the revision. The preconstituent Chambers make decisions by an absolute majority and the constituent

12. F. Delpérée, *La vie de la Constitution*, 1980 ANNALES DE DROIT DE LOUVAIN 123; F. Delpérée, *La Constitution belge et son interprétation*, *in* L'INTERPRÉTATION PAR LE JUGE DES RÈGLES ÉCRITES 151 (Paris: Travaux des journées louisianaises de l'Association Henri Capitant); F. Delpérée, *Le bon usage de la Constitution*, 1993 ANNALES DE DROIT DE LOUVAIN 27.
13. A. Alen & F. Meerschaut, *De impliciete herziening van de Grondwet*, *in* 1 PRÉSENCE DU DROIT PUBLIC ET DES DROITS DE L'HOMME – MELANGES OFFERTS A JACQUES VELU (Brussels: Bruylant 1992); H. Simonart, *La révision de la Constitution*, *in* LA BELGIQUE FÉDÉRALE (F. Delpérée ed., Brussels: Bruylant 1994); LA PROCÉDURE DE RÉVISION DE LA CONSTITUTION (F. Delpérée ed., Brussels: Bruylant 2003).

Chambers by a qualified majority. The elections which take place before any constitutional revision can result in depriving the government of the qualified majority which is necessary for it to be effective.

One should also wonder if the constitutional revision process is adapted to the federal structures of the State. Qualified majorities which are required to modify a constitutional text actually allow involvement of the communities and the regions in the process of constitutional amendment. Is it not necessary to ensure in this field a more formalised collaboration between the State and particular political collectivities, especially where the envisaged revision aims at sharing the attributions or the means between them?[14] A modification of Article 195 of the Constitution could, for instance, be recommended. New constitutional texts should be adopted, not only by a majority of two-thirds of the members of Parliament, but also by an absolute majority of the votes in the French and Flemish linguistic groups of each of the Chambers.

§3.07 THE FIRST CONSTITUTIONAL REVISIONS

In approximately a century and a half, the Belgian Constitution has only been subject to minor revisions – in 1893 and in 1920–1921. At that time, the aim was to modify the electoral system[15] – first by bringing to an end the suffrage on the basis of property qualification and by introducing the universal suffrage with the reservation of the plural vote, then by setting up the actual universal suffrage at the end of the First World War. It has to be underlined that a particular provision of the Constitution allowed the legislature to postpone the implementation of this measure to the female electorate for nearly thirty years.

Article 195 of the Constitution is regularly listed in the list of articles to be revised. To date, it has not been altered, except to state that 'the constituent Houses may adapt the numbering of articles and subdivisions of articles of the Constitution... into titles, chapters and sections' and thus ensure coordination of the constitutional text (Article 198). This operation, together with a new numbering, was completed on 17 February 1994.

Insertion of Article 195 in the list of revisable provisions enabled the listing of a long transitional provision, which authorised the houses elected on 13 June 2010 to alter, during the legislature and with a two-thirds majority, articles that were not included in the initial declaration. This operation was not criticised by the Venice

---

14. F. Delpérée, *Le processus de modification de la Constitution belge*, 14 REVUE PARLEMENTAIRE CANADIENNE 20 (1991).
15. J. BARTHELEMY, L'ORGANISATION DU SUFFRAGE ET L'EXPÉRIENCE BELGE (Paris, Girard et Brière); F. Delpérée, *Principe d'égalité et droit de suffrage*, *in* 1989 ANNUAIRE INTERNATIONAL DE JUSTICE CONSTITUTIONNELLE 221; F. Delpérée & D. Renders, *Belgique*, *in* LES RÉGIMES ÉLECTORAUX DES PAYS DE L'UNION EUROPÉENNE 77 (A. Pantelis & St. Koutsoubinas eds., London: Esperia Publications 1998); L. DUPRIEZ, L'ORGANISATION DU SUFFRAGE UNIVERSEL EN BELGIQUE. VOTE PLURAL, VOTE OBLIGATOIRE, REPRÉSENTATION PROPORTIONNELLE (Paris: Larose 1901); I. Stengers, *Histoire de la législation électorale en Belgique*, *in* STRATÉGIES POLITIQUES ET RÉFORME ÉLECTORALE: AUX ORIGINES DES MODES DE SCRUTIN AUX XIXEME ET XXEME SIÈCLES 76 (Baden-Baden: Nomos 1990).

Commission and was completed on 6 January 2014. Since then, the transitional provision has become irrelevant.

Another major electoral change took place in 1893, the giving up by Belgium of the system of election on a majority basis which was used since its independence. The Constitution now requires the use of proportional representation in ways 'determined by statute'. By implementing the D'Hondt system, the election law chooses a proportional representation 'pure and simple', according to the technique of 'the strongest average'. The parliamentary system was corrected at the same time. Both assemblies, the Chamber of Representatives and the Senate, were placed on an equal footing. Neither priority in time nor political primacy of one over the other was settled. Any specialisation of tasks was also put aside.

The status of the Senate was reorganised at the same time.[16] The representativeness of the upper chamber was improved. Apart from the requirement of age (40 years), the conditions of eligibility are now similar in both chambers. The legitimacy of the Senate was also consolidated: an egalitarian two-chamber system prevailed with a few minor exceptions.

An important difference remained. If the Chamber of Representatives was appointed only through the direct election process, the Senate was, for its part, constituted by senators who were directly elected, by provincial senators, by co-opted senators and, if necessary, by the children of the king.

§3.08 MORE RECENT CONSTITUTIONAL REVISIONS

Minor revisions were made to the Constitution in 1967, 1968 and 1969. As late as 1970, the Constitution underwent radical alterations which led to the progressive transformation from a unitary structure into a federal-type state.[17] This was the aim of the constitutional revisions of December 1970, July 1980, July 1988, June 1989, May 1993 and January 2014.[18]

From then on, a regional system of government was added to the central system of government. It comprised the regions of Wallonia, Flanders and Brussels.[19] Each one of these political collectivities consists of elected assemblies and of a responsible executive. The rules of the parliamentary system apply with some reservations: the assembly can dismiss the executive which it has elected with a constructive vote of defiance; the regional government cannot, for its part, dissolve the assembly.

Each region takes the place of the State for the definition of policies and the management of regional matters: national and regional development of the territory, urbanisation, environment, transport, communication and economics.

16. Ch. Goossens, *Le bicaméralisme en Belgique et son évolution, in* 2 Liber amoricum F. Dumon 796 (Antwerp: Kluwer); J. Stengers, *Les caractères généraux de l'évolution du Sénat depuis 1831, in* La réforme du Sénat 13 (Brussels: Bruylant 1990).
17. F. Delpérée, *Belgique, in* Dictionnaire constitutionnel 73 (O. Duhamel & Y. Meny eds., Paris: P.U.F. 1992).
18. *See* R. Ergec, *Un État fédéral en gestation: Les réformes institutionnelles belges de 1988–1989,* 1991 Revue du droit public et de la science politique 1593.
19. La Région de Bruxelles-Capitale (F. Delpérée ed., Brussels: Bruylant 1989).

In addition to the double system of central and regional government, there is the community system of government. It is organised around three political collectivities: the French, Flemish and German communities. If the German Community is a territorial community, the other two cannot be considered as such. Indeed, they intervene in areas which are defined without precise geographical references: people from Brussels are linked to the French and Flemish communities according to the institutions of each of them on which they depend.

Each community takes the place of the State for creating policies and the management of community matters, such as education, culture, broadcasting and television, protection of the youth, and preventive medicine.

The revision of 5 May 1993[20] led to the explicit inclusion in Article 1 of the Constitution that 'Belgium is a federal state which is composed of communities and regions'.[21] It also induces a restructuring of the institutions of the federal State and a reorganisation of some rules regarding the running of the federate authorities.[22]

Multiple amendments brought to the initial text led the adoption, on 1 February 1994, of a coordinated and renumbered Constitution.[23]

§3.09 BASIC CONSTITUTIONAL DATA

[A] Rights and Freedoms

The originality of Belgian constitutional law is that it has never been a purely institutional law. As early as 1831 the Constitution began with the declaration of rights and freedoms which are granted to Belgians. Therefore the emphasis is placed on the protection of citizens as a result of their constitutional status.

The Constitution proclaims the standard political rights, those which define the citizenship and which are, in principle, reserved to nationals: voting, eligibility and access to public employments. It also lists the main freedoms, such as freedom of opinion, press, religion, gathering, demonstration, association and education, and provides that no preventive measure may restrain their implementation.

At the same time, the Constitution contains the measures which ensure the effectiveness of this legal system. In the event of incidental control, it is up to the courts, as well as the Council of State (*Conseil d'Etat – Raad van State*), to refuse the application of national and local regulations which would be contrary to provisions of the Constitution. When examining the case of a direct action for abuse of power, the administrative judge is, moreover, able to suspend and annul such acts for the same reason.

20. La Constitution fédérale du 5 mai 1993 (F. Delpérée ed., Brussels: Bruylant 1993).
21. F. Delpérée, *La Belgique est un État fédéral*, 1993 Journal des tribunaux 637.
22. La Belgique fédérale (F. Delpérée ed., Brussels: Bruylant 1994).
23. H. Simonart, *La coordination de la Constitution belge*, 1995 Revue belge de droit constitutionnel 133; F. Tulkens, *L'accessibilité du texte constitutionnel: l'enjeu de la renumérotation*, 1994 Administration publique (Trimestriel): Revue du droit public et des sciences administratives 115; F. Delpérée, *Constitution et codification*, *in* L'État de droit – Mélanges en l'honneur de Guy Braibant 135 (Paris: Dalloz 1996).

Since 1994, the Constitution lists economic, social and cultural rights from which the citizen has already benefitted through international instruments by which Belgium is bound and, in particular, the UN covenants.[24] It gives them an eminent objective: to give to each citizen 'the right to have a life conform with human dignity'.[25] At the same time, specific rights, such as the right to have access to administrative documents, to consult them and to get a copy of them, are also guaranteed.[26]

[B] Separation of Powers

As far as the organisation of public powers is concerned, the Belgian Constitution was inspired by Montesquieu. In contrast with foreign constitutions, it does not expressly claim the principle of separation of powers. However, it makes it one of the underpinnings of the organisation of public powers, at least at the level of the federal authorities.[27]

The principles seem to be clear. Different governmental functions are identified. They are attributed to different branches of government. Legislative power is exercised jointly by the King and both Chambers of Parliament. Executive power is also exerted by the King and judicial power goes to the judiciary. Nevertheless, the separation of powers is not absolute. There is an interdependence - and even a collaboration - among public authorities. The parliamentary system - which is rationalised[28] since 1993 through the technique of constructive motion of defiance - reflects this preoccupation.

The government plays a key role in these cooperative mechanisms. It assumes, together with the King, the functions of direction and administration. It actively contributes to the enactment of laws. It insures the implementation of the decisions of justice.

Amongst the three branches of government, the judiciary - which is also the most federal power, since it has no equivalent power within the federated collectivities - has an interest in appearing as the most 'distinct, the most autonomous and the most

24. J. Velu, *La protection juridictionnelle des droits de l'homme au niveau interne et au niveau international, in* LE NOUVEAU DROIT CONSTITUTIONNEL 259 (Brussels: Bruylant 1987); Chambers of Representatives, Commission of revision of the Constitution, of institutional reforms and of solving of the conflicts, L'inscription des droits économiques et sociaux dans la Constitution (Brussels 1989).
25. G. Haarscher, *Le droit de mener une vie conforme à la dignité humaine, in* LES DROITS ÉCONOMIQUES, SOCIAUX ET CULTURELS 134 (R. Ergec ed., Brussels: Bruylant 1995).
26. C. de Terwagne, *L'accès du public à l'information détenue par l'administration*, 1996 REVUE BELGE DE DROIT CONSTITUTIONNEL 107.
27. F. Delpérée, *La séparation des pouvoirs aujourd'hui*, 1990 ADMINISTRATION PUBLIQUE (TRIMESTRIEL): REVUE DU DROIT PUBLIC ET DES SCIENCES ADMINISTRATIVES 126; E. Liekendael, *La séparation des pouvoirs à l'aube du troisième millénaire*, 1997 JOURNAL DES TRIBUNAUX 553; A. Vanwelkenhuyzen, *La séparation des pouvoirs (1831–1981), in* DE GRONDWET HONDERDVIJFTIG JAAR 69 (Brussels: Bruylant 1981).
28. Ph. Lauvaux, PARLEMENTARISME RATIONALISÉ ET STABILITÉ DU POUVOIR EXÉCUTIF: QUELQUES ASPECTS DE LA RÉFORME D'ÉTAT CONFRONTÉS AUX EXPÉRIENCES ÉTRANGÈRES (Brussels: Bruylant 1988).

independent'.[29] Justice has to be done without undergoing pressure from the other branches of government. It also has to resist the pressure from the public opinion.

[C] The Imperfect Two-Chamber System

Until 1993, federal law was made by the two legislative chambers of the federal Parliament and the King, in other words the Government. Belgium was one of the few states to have an integral bicameral parliamentary system. The federal Parliament was composed of two assemblies which were the governmental action.

Since 1993, the bicameral system has become unequal. The Senate no longer plays a role in exercising the budgetary function. It no longer supervises the government's political and administrative action. It only plays a secondary role in the legislative function.

In 2014, this shift continued. The Senate has become a chamber of reflection or a forum of political discussion. It is no longer a truly legislative chamber, according to the primary meaning of the expression. If it is able, if it has the means, the Senate can put together, for the government or the Chamber of Representatives, a number of dossiers, which these authorities will have to see through to completion.

[D] The Establishment of a Federal System

The separation of powers is not only ensured on a vertical basis but also on a horizontal one. Not only the legislative function but also the governmental and administrative functions have been dismantled. Several legislatures and several executives are now active. The sharing of powers becomes a reality according to complex rules, which take into account the distribution of competences, as well as a sharing of geographical jurisdiction.[30]

The federated entities, that is the communities and regions, have jurisdiction only by devolution; residual powers belong to the federal State. Certainly, the Constitution contemplates the future transfer of the residual powers to the federated entities. However, in order for that to happen, there would have to be a constitutional accord, and this is not foreseeable at present. As the Constitutional Court (*Cour constitutionnelle – Grondwettelijk Hof*) has said, this rule is therefore of no effect.[31]

In their respective fields of jurisdiction, the federated entities have autonomous powers. They may accordingly pursue 'distinct policies'. The result could be differences in treatment among citizens. Such differences cannot be considered per se to be contrary to the federal principle of the equality of Belgians before the law. Again according to the Constitutional Court, 'Autonomy would be meaningless if the mere fact that there were differences in treatment among the persons to whom rules in

29. A. Alen, *Séparation ou collaboration des pouvoirs*, 1990 ADMINISTRATION PUBLIQUE (TRIMESTRIEL): REVUE DU DROIT PUBLIC ET DES SCIENCES ADMINISTRATIVES 223.
30. For a detailed description of this system, F. DELPÉRÉE & S. DEPRÉ, LE SYSTÈME CONSTITUTIONNEL DE LA BELGIQUE.
31. *See* Court of Arbitration No. 76/98.

respect of the same subject matter apply in the various communities and regions were held to be contrary … (to) the Constitution.'[32]

A few rules govern the sharing of powers in this federal system:

- The federal statutes (*loi* - *wet*) and the community and regional statutes (*décret* - *decreet*) have identical value. Perfectly identical, to be precise. A federal act is the same as a regional act or a community act. This is not open to any discussion. It is written, in full, in the Constitution.
- In theory, federal law cannot intervene in the fields of competence of the communities or regions. Competences are considered exclusive. Different than in other federal states, there are no concurrent competences.
- Conversely, community or regional law cannot intervene in the field of federal jurisdiction. The exclusivity operates in both directions.
- A Constitutional Court, formerly called the 'Court of Arbitration', makes sure that the federal State, the communities and regions stay within their field of legislative competences. If necessary, the Court can annul any improper interventions by any of these statutory instruments.

In addition to the subject matter jurisdiction that has explicitly been devolved to the communities and regions, they have also implied subject matter jurisdiction. In some cases, they may legislate in relation to subjects of federal jurisdiction. It would not be wrong to say that Belgian law makes moderate use of implied subject matter jurisdiction. It is recognised, but clearly with caution and only in limited circumstances. At least three prerequisites must be met:[33]

- the legislation enacted must really be necessary to the exercise of an explicit subject matter jurisdiction of the community or region;
- the subject matter must be amenable to different application from region to region; and
- the intrusion of the federated authorities into the federal field must be only marginal.

Belgian federalism mirrors the experiences of federal states all around the world, especially in Europe. However, it presents some original characteristics which set it apart.

Federal states tend to be created by association - a method expressed by the motto '*e pluribus unum*'. Conversely, federal Belgium is being created by disassociation. It is a unitary state that is gradually turning itself into a federal state. This means that this State is transferring more and more competences, and is also transferring more and more budgetary means, to the communities and regions. In brief, the Belgian State is stripping and impoverishing itself. This raises a rather worrying question. Just where will the process of disassociation end? Is the disassociation not paving the way for

32. *See* Court of Arbitration No. 83/98.
33. *See* Court of Arbitration No. 95/98.

disunion or division? Is federalism just an intermediate step on the path towards the emergence of three new independent states in the heart of the EU?

The other federal states are multipolar states: the United States of America contains fifty federated entities, Switzerland twenty-six, federal Germany sixteen, Canada ten (not including the North-West Territories), and so on. As for federal Belgium, it is in essence bipolar. We are two: the north and the south. The federal Council of Ministers, which together with the King forms the federal executive, contains seven French-speaking and seven Dutch-speaking ministers; the Constitutional Court contains six French-speaking judges and six Dutch-speaking judges; the federal parliamentarians are divided into two language groups. This situation has serious consequences. Bipolar federalism is not a federalism of cooperation. It is more a federalism of confrontation, competition and even of conflict. Belgians spend a great deal of time solving (or trying to solve) a number of political conflicts, at the end of which no political authority wants to be a loser. It can be hard to find 'win-win' solutions.

The other federal states are, in general, organised around a simple structure. There is a first level, that of the federal State. There is a second level, comprising the federated entities. They are called 'states', *Länder*, cantons, regions, and so on. Yet these federated authorities are all of the same kind: they have identical competences and have similar means. However, federal Belgium practices a layered federalism. At the federated level, there is no single type of authority, but there are two. There are three communities – which match linguistic and cultural concerns – and there are three regions – which match economic and social concerns. This may seem surprising. But, when all is said and done, we experience the same realities at European level: the EU of twenty-seven is not the Eurogroup, nor is it the Schengen Area ... There are European policies with a variable geometry.

To further complicate this presentation of the institutions, the two federated entities that are present in the northern geographical area of the country, the Flemish Community and the Flemish Region, decided to merge their institutions, administrations and budgets. The same movement has not yet happened in the southern geographical area of the country, where the Walloon Region and the French Community are present.

Within the territory of Brussels, three federated collectivities – the French Community and the Flemish Community and the Brussels-Capital Region – assume responsibility. These tangled situations result from the small size of the national territory and from the distribution of the population in several linguistic groups. They also show the preoccupation of the public authorities to give an 'as concrete as possible' solution to the problems that the citizens have to face in their daily life.

Within each community and each region, there is an executive in the form of a council of ministers, a parliament, and an administration – but there is no real network of judicial courts. This institutional system is, broadly speaking, modelled on the one that exists at the federal level. But there is an exception to this. During a five-year session, the parliaments of the communities and regions cannot be dissolved. There are no impromptu community or regional elections.

[E] Political Decentralisation

The Belgian Constitution enumerates, among the powers that it establishes, the 'municipalities and provinces'. It defines the principles of their organisation by prescribing *inter alia* that the local assemblies will be directly elected every six years. It also specifies the controls which can affect the action of the local powers and in this regard set supervision controls to prevent the law from being violated or the public interest from being affected. The federal organisation of the State is not without influence on the implementation of the principles of the political decentralisation.

The Special Act of 13 July 2001 transferred various competences to the regions and communities. It came into force on 1 January 2002. Now, the rules on the 'composition, organisation, competence and functioning of the municipal institutions' are established by regional statute. All areas have been regionalised. This applies to all the kingdom's municipalities: small and large, urban and rural, including the municipalities within the Brussels-Capital Region, peripheral municipalities, municipalities with a special status, and so on. So it follows that, subject to several principles set down in Article 162, paragraph 2, of the Constitution – such as the principle of the direct election of municipal councillors – each region may establish a separate status for local authorities that are part of its territory.

§3.10 THE CONSTITUTION AND THE EUROPEAN INTEGRATION

In 1970, so fifteen years after the appearance of the first steps towards European integration, Belgium modified its Constitution and introduced a 'general clause of integration'. It states that the 'execution of specified powers' could by a treaty or a statute be entrusted 'to institutions of public international law'. This constitutional clause allows important transfers of competence – especially with the European treaties of Maastricht and Amsterdam – in fields of economic or financial policy. However, it raises major constitutional problems. For example, constitutional problems arise when European treaties not only consider the transfer of a national or federal subject matter to the European institutions, but also turn their attention to solving questions of internal organisation of the Belgian State or of its political collectivities, notably by defining the conditions of the municipal electorate. It is also the case when European treaties do not only consider the transfer of a national matter to the European order but also turn their attention to handling questions of federal competence. In order to avoid conflicts within the internal Belgian order, it is made clear that the communities and the regions have to approve such treaties.

European primary law is part of the treaties – which are characterised as mixed. They must be approved by the federal Chamber of Representatives and the federal executive but also by each of the regional parliaments (Article 167, paragraphs 2, 3 and 4 of the Constitution), as well as their respective council of ministers. If just one refuses to give approval, the procedure will be blocked. A blockage at regional level has been seen to occur for reasons that have nothing to do with the content of the treaty, yet for reasons to do with internal political conflicts.

Secondary European law – regulations, directives and decisions – is not subject to approval procedures at the domestic level. However, there is room for advance consultations. These are held at government level. Note that, once again, the word 'government' should be understood in the plural in Belgium.

It should be pointed out that there are three procedural rules in this area. They were established in the Cooperation Agreement of 8 March 1994. The first is the rotating rule, with just one presence, one signature carrying a single engagement. Yet this is not always the same. There is a carefully orchestrated rota. The second rule concerns prior consultation. The accredited person only represents the specific authority from which they come. This person is supposed to speak for all Belgian partners. The overall position is decided in the Interministerial Commission for Foreign Policy. The third rule concerns consensus. In the absence of an agreement between the partners, Belgium is bound to abstain.

§3.11 REORIENTATION OF THE CONSTITUTION

Without actually being revised, the Belgian Constitution has undergone some reorientation following the adoption of particular types of statutes which it allowed to be established.

Acts voted by a qualified majority led in the nineteenth century to modifying the scope of the census; in the twentieth century they allowed votes for women.

Since 1970 so-called special acts led to the development of the main constitutional provisions. Thus, the provisions of the Constitution which prescribe the organisation of the communities and regions are achieved by special acts of institutional reforms, as well as by a Special Finance Act of the communities and regions.

Special acts extended and updated the constitutional operation. From a formal point of view, these are statutes accomplished by the legislative power and are actually bound to respect the Constitution. From a material point of view, these are legal instruments which give constitutional principles their effective meaning.

§3.12 CONSTITUTIONAL JUSTICE

The establishment of a federal state – that is to say of a state within which distinct legislatures are able to establish rules of the same legal force – has led to the establishment of the Constitutional Court (formerly *Cour d'arbitrage – Arbitragehof*).[34] Since 1984 it has dealt with appeals introduced against federal, regional and community acts.[35] It provides a preliminary ruling, if requested by a court, a tribunal or a judge.[36] If it has to deal with an 'objective action' (*recours objectif*), it has the ability to

34. *See also infra* Chapter 5, §5.02 [E].
35. On the distinction between these different norms, *see* F. Delpérée, *La Constitution, la loi, le décret et l'ordonnance*, 1990 JOURNAL DES TRIBUNAUX 107.
36. A. Rasson-Roland, *Les questions préjudicielles*, *in* LA SAISINE DU JUGE (F. Delpérée & P. Foucher eds., Brussels: Bruylant 1998).

suspend and annul the challenged norm. Since 1989, any physical or legal person having a sufficient interest[37] can submit a constitutional challenge to the Court.

The Court has a specialised constitutional jurisdiction.[38] Its task is to verify that the normative instruments challenged before it conform with the provisions listed in the Constitution. These are the provisions which enunciate the rules of equality and non-discrimination (Articles 10 and 11 of the Constitution), which list the general principles for the organisation of education (Article 24 of the Constitution) or which set the sharing of powers between the State, the communities and the regions.[39] Moreover, the Constitutional Court also has the power to rule on the infringement, by a rule with force of law, of fundamental rights and freedoms guaranteed by Title II of the Constitution (Articles 8–32) and by Articles 143 paragraph 1 (principle of federal loyalty), 170 (principle of legality in tax matters), 172 (principle of equality in tax matters) and 191 (protection of foreign nationals) of the Constitution.

The Court, however, has not hesitated in developing daring case law to establish the broadest possible constitutional review. Through its jurisdiction regarding the conflict of competences, it now has sole federal constitutional control. Through the control of violations of the principle of equality and of non-discrimination – not forgetting the principles and the rules in the specific area of education – it ensures for itself quite a large field of analysis and of censorship. One can wonder which provision of the Constitution, when it is read out of context or when it is joined to either a rule of sharing of competences (in either Articles 10, 11 or 24 of the Constitution), could not, even in a marginal way, justify an examination of the constitutionality by the Court.

In this way, the control of constitutionality of laws and instruments of equivalent value crystallises the large, if not global phenomenon of constitutionalisation of the legal order. For nearly twenty years, Belgium has been part of the 'club of the constitutionally developed states'.[40] This evolution has not been easy. Clear reluctance has appeared within the political spheres and within the judiciary, as well as within academic circles. This era is mainly in the past. There is still rear-guard action. There are still attempts to ignore this evolution, notably in the European and international order. There is still a large degree of ignorance. However, the institution of constitutional justice is well established. The jurisprudence which it builds up has been accepted without too much reluctance.[41] It constitutes, from this standpoint, an important source of Belgian constitutional Jaw.[42] It clarifies it and gives it a calming

37. LE RECOURS DES PARTICULIERS DEVANT LE JUGE CONSTITUTIONNEL (F. Delpérée ed., Paris: Economica & Brussels: Bruylant 1991).
38. F. DELPÉRÉE & A. RASSON-ROLAND, LA COUR D'ARBITRAGE (Brussels: Larcier 1997).
39. LA COUR D'ARBITRAGE. ACTUALITÉ ET PERSPECTIVES (F. Delpérée ed., Brussels: Bruylant 1988).
40. F. Delpérée & A. Rasson-Roland, *La Cour d'arbitrage belge*, 1988 ANNUAIRE INTERNATIONAL DE JUSTICE CONSTITUTIONNELLE 67.
41. *See* our annual articles in Annuaire international de justice constitutionnelle and in the Revue belge de droit constitutionnel. *Adde*: J. SAROT, P. VANDERNOOT, E. PEREMANS & B. PATY, DIX ANS DE JURISPRUDENCE DE LA COUR D'ARBITRAGE (5 AVRIL 1985 – 31 AOUT 1995) (Brussels: Bruylant 1995).
42. J. SAROT, P. VANDERNOOT & E. PEREMANS, LA JURISPRUDENCE DE LA COUR D'ARBITRAGE (Brussels: Bruylant 1989, 1991 & 1992).

interpretation. Sometimes it even provides the revision of the Constitution on essential points.[43]

§3.13 REVISIONS TO COME

The pace at which constitutional revisions have taken place for more than twenty years, raises questions as to the ability of the Belgian political system to transform itself in a positive way and to organise a viable federal state.

Beyond technical discussions on the organisation of the institutions and processes, there is also the question of the existence of the State which arises in constitutional discussions.

One point is clear. If Belgians are able to conceive at the same time autonomous methods of management for the federated matters, and joined methods of management for the federal ones, they will show their ability to adapt the provisions of an old constitution to the political and economic realities of the contemporary society. This is not beyond their reach.

§3.14 SELECTED BIBLIOGRAPHY

Ch. Behrendt & F. Bouhon, *Introduction à la Théorie générale de l'État. Manuel* (Brussels: Larcier 2009).

F. Delpérée, *Le droit constitutionnel de la Belgique* (Brussels: Bruylant, Paris: LGDJ, 2000).

M. Pâques, *Droit public élémentaire en quinze leçons* (Brussels: Larcier, 2005).

M. Uyttendaele, *Précis de droit constitutionnel belge – Regards sur un système institutionnel paradoxal* (3d ed., Brussels: Bruylant 2005).

M. Uyttendaele & M. Verdussen, *Dictionnaire de la Sixième Réforme de l'Etat* (Brussels: Larcier 2015).

J. Vande Lanotte & G. Goedertier, *Handboek Belgisch publiekrecht* (5th ed., Bruges: die Keure 2007).

43. F. Delpérée, *Crise du juge et contentieux constitutionnel en droit belge*, *in* LA CRISE DU JUGE 54 (J. Lenoble ed., Paris: LGDJ 1990).

CHAPTER 4

Administrative Law

Robert Andersen & David Renders

§4.01 INTRODUCTION

Administrative law can be defined as a set of legal rules and principles which aim to regulate the organisation, the functioning and the control of the executive. The definition is broader than the one traditionally used in Belgian law. Indeed, some essential legal rules and principles are usually considered as part of constitutional law. In such a narrow conception, administrative law appears, rather, as a kind of subsidiary sector of law. It can be considered as a process of deepening of these broad rules and principles that can be found in the Constitution. While this distinction between constitutional and administrative law can be justified from a strictly didactic standpoint, it does not correspond with reality. Indeed, it is absolutely impossible to divide the whole set.

In Belgium, as in other countries, the principle of three separate powers of government – the legislative, the executive and the judiciary – is applicable. Such a separation is not absolutely complete in Belgium. The executive branch, for instance, whose essential task is to govern and administrate, also shares part of the legislative function, which consists in enacting general and abstract rules. It also shares part of the judicial function, whose aim is to settle individual disputes on the basis of legal rules.

Belgium is an '*État de droit*' (*Rechtsstaat*). The executive has to abide by the law, as do the two other branches of government. Such a concept, which is partly similar to the English 'rule of law', means that there are fixed general rules which both citizens and the government have to live by. By law, we mean here not only the hierarchically organised set of national rules (Constitution, statutes, regulations enacted by the various executive authorities, regulations enacted by local government, etc.) but also treaties and other acts of international law with (in principle) direct effects.

This sector of law is not confined to written sources but also includes general principles of administrative law that are not all contained in the Constitution. Some of these are established by administrative courts, mainly the Council of State (*Section du contentieux administratif du Conseil d'État – Afdeling bestuursrechtspraak van de Raad van State*). The obligation of complying with the law may be seen as a brake against a would-be arbitrary administration. It is, however, not a complete restraint. If sometimes the executive has a bound power of decision (*compétence liée – gebonden bevoegdheid*) – its decisions are in a way automatic –, one must observe that usually it has a wide discretionary power of decision (*compétence discrétionnaire – discretionaire bevoegdheid*). The executive is thus legally entitled to decide whether or not it has to intervene and, if so, to choose among all the possible measures, which will be the most appropriate to achieve the objective in the general interest.

In practice, it is important to underline that the difference between bound powers of decision and discretionary powers of decision is not absolute. A single decision can be composed of elements related to bound powers of decision and others to discretionary powers. The wide room for manoeuvre which is given to the executive has led the courts to develop a certain number of tools in order to reconcile the necessity of quick and efficient administrative action with that of a minimal protection for citizens.

The executive is essentially the government, consisting of the council of ministers. To be more precise in a federal state such as Belgium, it is essentially the federal Council of Ministers and the various councils of ministers of the federated entities. These governments would not have any influence at all if they did not have at their disposal an infrastructure and an administrative organisation in order to perform their own tasks. All those tasks could not, of course, be executed by the few individuals who work closely with each minister.

§4.02 THE ADMINISTRATIVE ORGANISATION

Both at the federal level and the level of the federated entities – 'communities' and 'regions' – there are various departments. Unsurprisingly, each of them is headed by a minister who is in charge of the management and who is also responsible for the whole staff of the department. The executive decides to create and suppress departments according to the evolving requirements of community life. Their number, as well as the distribution of the tasks between them, is relatively stable. Their main task consists in preparing and executing governmental decisions especially those taken or initiated by the minister who is responsible for the department. Each department has its own civil servants and budget but does not possess legal personality. The latter is only granted to the State (i.e., the central or federal entity), the three communities and the three regions.

Although the structure of a department has become more complex, it keeps, to a large extent, its very hierarchical character. It is true that, for practical reasons, the department is composed of external services created besides its central services. Such a phenomenon, however, does not affect its hierarchical structure. The decision centre of the department is located at the central office where most important decisions have to be adopted.

The governments, assisted by the members of the minister's staff and the civil servants working for the departments, do not have the sole power of decision. Although they have to ensure that the general interest is protected, as political bodies accountable to the parliamentary assemblies, they also have to take into account the principle of provincial and municipal autonomy provided for by the Constitution. Indeed, political organisations exist at the local level. This is the application of 'territorial decentralisation' (*décentralisation territoriale – territoriale decentralisatie*). Those local authorities have their own bodies and are responsible for the management of local affairs under a system of self-government. Their autonomy is, however, not absolute. According to the constitutional repartition of competencies, regional legislation has to set up uniformly the rules of organisation and functioning of these authorities. One of the tasks of the legislature, for instance, is to determine either positively or negatively the extent of the concept of provincial or municipal interest. Such principles are thus essentially changeable concepts.

Autonomy does not mean independence. Within the limits of local interest, these political authorities are submitted to a system of supervision by a higher authority (*contrôle de tutelle – administratief toezicht*), which, at present, is usually organised and performed by the regions. This supervision aims to ensure that acts of provinces and communes are adopted without any breach of both the law and the general interest.

Provinces and communes are not only competent to rule all matters of provincial or municipal interest. They are also required by federal State, as well as by federated entities, to carry out the implementation at local level of some missions of general interest.

Such diversity also appears from a purely organisational point of view. Apart from collegial bodies, which result directly or indirectly from elections organised on the basis of universal suffrage (*conseil communal – gemeenteraad* and *collège communal – gemeentecollege* for the municipality, *conseil provincial – provincieraad* and *collège provincial – provinciecollege* for the province), these are also some individualised functions. The first example is the mayor (*bourgmestre – burgemeester*) who is appointed by the regional government, theoretically, from amongst the members of the municipal council (*conseil communal – gemeenteraad*). He performs his tasks both as the first authority of the municipality and as an agent of the central authorities. Another example is the provincial governor (*gouverneur de province – provinciale gouverneur*), who is appointed and can be dismissed *ad nutum* by the regional government. Most of his functions are related to his quality as governmental agent (*commissaire du gouvernement – regeringscommissaris*).

The federal State, communities, regions, provinces and communes are all political authorities charged with acting in the global interest of their members. It is also necessary to create other public services in order to satisfy certain specific needs and to give them some autonomy in order to perform these tasks. This is a phenomenon known as 'functional decentralisation' (*décentralisation par services – functionele of dienstgewijze decentralisatie*) appearing at the federal level, as well as at the level of the federated entities, – the three communities and the three regions – and operating both centrally and locally. Those public services exist in many different areas.

Some of them are created by a unilateral act. Others stem from an association. Regarding the former, there is a traditional distinction between *régies* (*regieën*) and public establishments (*établissements publics – openbare instellingen*). A *régie* can be considered as a kind of appendix to a governmental department. Although they are legal persons and can therefore benefit from legal autonomy and avoid a series of constraints, the *régies* do not have any organisational and managerial autonomy since they have to respect the hierarchical power of the relevant minister.

Organisational and managerial autonomy is the main characteristic of the *établissement public*. This autonomy, although considerable, is not absolute. There are many different *établissements publics* but for any of them, the creating authority maintains a power of control over its acts. This control is mainly exercised through specific governmental agents called '*commissaires du gouvernement*' (*regeringscommissarissen*). They have to check whether the *établissement public* respects the law and the general interest.

At the municipal level, there is a uniform model for creating some kind of the *établissement public*. This is the case for local social assistance centres (*centres publics d'action sociale – openbare centra voor maatschappelijk welzijn*) and parochial associations (*fabriques d'église – kerkfabrieken*), which are respectively organised and controlled by the communities and the regions. Such a uniform model does not exist as regards the creation of *établissements publics* either by the federal State or by the federated entities. Each legislature has the power to create, if necessary, *établissement public* within its sphere of competences and to lay down its rules of organisation, functioning and supervision.

The above-mentioned associations can be constituted either exclusively by public authorities or jointly by public authorities and private actors. In the latter case, associations are usually known as mixed economic societies (*sociétés d'économie mixte – gemengde ondernemingen*). It is often very difficult to determine whether such a body is a public authority or not. There is no absolute criterion capable of giving a sharp and definitive answer to the question. In this respect, courts have elaborated an empirical and pragmatic theory called '*théorie du faisceau d'indices*' whose aim is to find a body of elements identifying the public character of the association.

These associations often take very different legal shapes. Sometimes they are civil companies with a commercial form, sometimes commercial companies and sometimes non-profit associations. Legislative acts allowing the constitution of such associations often authorise derogation from ordinary company or association law in order to help the association to perform its specific missions of public service in the best way possible.

Such a phenomenon of association can also be observed at the local level. The Constitution itself allows the possible association or creation of closer relations between several municipalities or provinces on the basis of the conditions to be established by the regional legislature (Article 162 of the Constitution).

There is a final distinction worth underlining. A public service governed by a public authority is known as 'organic public service'. It is, however, also possible for a public authority to ask a private actor to manage a public service while continuing to control the situation. In such a case, a contract called 'concession' (*concession de service public – concessie van openbare dienst*) is entered into by the public authority and the private body providing the service.

The wave of privatisations within the Member States of the EU has given a major renewal to the '*concession de service public*'. Public companies have been, one way or another, partly or completely privatised, whether with or without a right of control for the public authorities.

On the other hand, private companies may themselves, for essentially social reasons, be partly or completely taken over by the public authorities while remaining subject to ordinary law.

In addition to the traditional administration invested with a power of decision, there is also an advisory administration. The latter is usually composed of collegial bodies and is omnipresent. Its missions are varied. In some cases, it has to coordinate administrative activities trying to prevent many decision centres from acting in opposite directions. In other cases, the advisory administration acts as an expert advising the authority on the technical aspects of the decision to be adopted.

It may also demonstrate a willingness to allow the democratisation of the administration, trying through various means to involve the citizens in the administrative decision-making process. It is obvious that these different functions are not mutually exclusive and can be exercised simultaneously.

This overview of administrative institutions would be incomplete if one did not talk about independent administrative authorities. This entity derives from French administrative law and can be defined as a private person or a commission to whom a legislative act gives both the right to exercise several missions of general interest within a particular sector and a specific status making it independent. Such authorities can separately or altogether hold regulatory, executive or repressive missions, as well as the function of preventing and settling conflicts.

§4.03 ADMINISTRATIVE ACTION

[A] The Regime of Administrative Acts

The collection of bodies described in the previous section makes up a large and varied administrative machinery which produces a broad range of administrative activity. The action of the administration is unilateral in nature. Through orders and commands, the relevant authority unilaterally imposes its will on the citizens. In order to be able do so, several privileges derogating from generally applicable law have been conferred on the administration. The first one is called '*privilège du préalable*' (*vermoeden van wettigheid*). It allows the administration to issue itself the enforceable instrument it needs in order to fulfil its missions. This instrument benefits from a presumption of legality until evidence to the contrary has been shown. Apart from a few exceptions, this privilege has a broad scope.

That is not the case for the second privilege, the '*privilège de l'exécution d'office*' (*voorrecht van de ambtshalve uitvoering*), which permits the authority to enforce acts it has itself adopted. It is therefore empowered to force the reluctant citizen to obey.

The authority can force the disobedient citizen to act under duress, with the possible use of police force, without having to obtain preliminary authorisation from the courts. This substantial privilege only exists, in the absence of specific legal rules, in emergencies and when the measure is necessary and proportional to the requirements of the general interest. In more and more situations, the authority may impose sanctions on citizens who fail to respect the order given. Besides the criminal penalties imposed by the courts, there are also administrative penalties. Unsurprisingly, many problems arise regarding the connections between these two systems of sanction.

Unilateral legal act, which is the most traditional method used by the administration to make use of the *imperium* (*gezag*), plays a key role within administrative law. Unlike other countries, Belgium has no codified non-contentious administrative procedures. The theory of unilateral administrative act has developed in the doctrinal writings. Such a theory consists in analysing the different elements of these acts, as well as in studying the principles used as references for their elaboration. The case law of the Council of State has provided legal commentators with the materials required to elaborate their theory. Increasing importance is conferred on the process of decision-making itself, i.e., to all the steps preceding the adoption of the decision.

A significant contribution to this shift in emphasis comes from the phenomenon of participation and administrative democratisation, which allows citizens, acting either individually or as representatives of various interest groups, to be involved in the adoption of the decision.

Notwithstanding the absence of any express textual basis in the Constitution or in legislation, the Council of State has elaborated a number of principles of 'good governance' (*principes de bonne administration – algemene beginselen van behoorlijk bestuur*), which must be respected by the administration when taking its decisions. The administration must prepare the decision with care so as to act with optimal knowledge of the situation. It may be required to listen to the opinion of citizens concerned by the planned decision or to call for an expert, etc. The principles of respect for rights of the defendant and cross-examination have also been highly developed.

The study of the administrative decision itself is of course also very important. A typology of unilateral administrative act has been established. The *summa divisio*, i.e., the major classification, distinguishes between individual administrative decisions and regulations. There is another major distinction between explicit and implicit decisions, the latter raising the issue of the meaning to be given to the silence of the administration.

Whatever the act, it has to be taken by a competent authority. Competence is traditionally studied from a triple point of view: the author of the act must be competent *ratione materiae*, *ratione loci* and *ratione temporis*.

Regarding the *ratione materiae* competence, one must recall that the executive partly holds the legislative function. The king at the federal national level, as well as community and regional governments at the level of the federated entities, are invested with the duty to implement legislative acts (*lois – wetten*, *décrets – decreten* and *ordonnances – ordonanties*) enacted by the legislative branch.

Within certain limits, they are sometimes allowed to take general measures having a broader scope than purely implementing measures.

Finally, in some fields, the Constitution offers them an autonomous power to enact general measures. This is, for instance, the case with the organisation of their own services, including the adoption of the legal 'status' of their civil servants.

Other authorities also have a rule-making power, either directly conferred by the Constitution (provinces and municipalities, for instance) or granted by statute (some *organismes d'intérêt public – instellingen van openbaar nut*, for instance).

There is a general principle of attributed character of competences; they have to be exercised by those to which they have been attributed. A strict application of this principle would, however, paralyse administrative action. Therefore, many acts use an attribution of competences to allow the appointed authority to delegate part of these competences. Such delegation, however, may never deprive the authority from its essential attributions.

There are also territorial restrictions to the competence (*ratione loci* competences), notably where acts of federated entities and local authorities are concerned.

Finally, one has to mention time restrictions (*ratione temporis* competence). Authorities deriving their power from an election are specifically concerned by these restrictions since their competences are normally limited to the length of their mandate.

In most cases, the administrative act is in written form with a certain number of elements, two of which merit greater attention. The first is the signature, the presence of which is the basic condition for the act's existence. It also serves to establish the identity of the author of the act and therefore helps to determine whether he is legally competent to enact it. The signature is the best application of the adage '*forma dat esse rei*'; content and form join to make one only.

The second major element is the formal duty to motivate the act. The Act of 29 July 1991 related to formal motivation of administrative acts sets up as a basic principle the requirement that any individual administrative decision mention the practical and legal motives or grounds, which have been used as basis for its adoption. The motivation has to be adequate. Vague sentences and clichés are treated as a lack of formal reasoning.

Such a principle is based on several factors. First and foremost, it is intended to make decisions as clear and understandable as possible for their addressees. Once these know the reasons for the act, they are in a better position to decide whether they can bring an action against the administrative act. The reasoning thus plays a kind of inhibiting role as far as claims against administrative acts are concerned. Another benefit of the principle is that it forces the author of the act to take more care before enacting it. In this way, formal reasoning is a protection against the arbitrary exercise of power. Finally, formal reasoning facilitates the review of decisions. Such review is indeed limited to the reasons and grounds mentioned in the decision.

The principle is, however, not absolute. Derogations are allowed when disclosure of the motives or grounds of the decision endangers the external security of the State, public order, the fundamental right of privacy or when this disclosure may violate the rules regarding professional secrecy. Urgency may, however, not be invoked in order to try to avoid the duty to motivate. Under current Belgian law, general (i.e., non-individual) administrative acts, regulations, do not have to be formally motivated, except a few of them, notably in urban and environmental law.

The above-mentioned Act of 29 July 1991 gives to citizens a minimal protection in this respect. A higher degree of protection may be offered by other, specific statutes.

There is a traditional distinction between external and internal motivation of administrative acts. Besides the obligation to offer formal motivation for individual administrative decisions, another principle forces the administration to take its decisions only if they are based on grounds that can justify them both from a legal and from a practical point of view. Administrative authorities do not hold the competences in their own interest but for the general interest. They perform what is called 'abuse of power' (*détournement de pouvoir – machtafwending*) if they make use of their powers for a purpose other than the official one. The administration has satisfied its duty to offer formal motivation only if these practical and legal grounds have been indicated in the act. However, such grounds might be incorrect. The problem thus arises at the level of internal motivation. Regarding general (non-individual) acts or regulations, the grounds do not have to be indicated in the act itself but they have to exist and to be adequate. There is no act without correct grounds.

To be obligatory for the citizens, it is not sufficient that an administrative act has been correctly enacted. There is another duty of publicity. Such publicity takes different forms and often has a varying degree of intensity according to the individual or general character of the act.

It is also important to observe that Article 32 of the Belgian Constitution gives any citizen the right to access any administrative document and to get a copy of it, except where otherwise provided for by an act of Parliament. Such a system has been implemented by the legislatures. A distinction is traditionally made between active and passive publicity. The latter forces the administration to provide citizens with a certain amount of information. One can mention, for instance, the obligation to indicate on any individual administrative act the eventual possibilities of appeal. In the absence of such notification, the limitation period for bringing an action does not run. Active publicity covers the information expressly required by the citizens. Except for documents containing some private information, the citizen does not have to show any interest to obtain such information.

While restrictions may be placed upon the right of access to administrative documents, it is important to underline that such restrictions are exceptions and that, as with any exception, they are strictly interpreted. The basic principle is and must be that of unrestricted access to administrative documents.

According to a general principle of law, administrative acts may not be retroactive. This principle is, however, not absolute. It is possible for the legislature to derogate from the principle. Furthermore, the supreme administrative court, the Council of State, has also limited its application. Among these limitations, it is worth noting the theory of withdrawal of act (*théorie du retrait d'acte – de leer inzake intrekking van een administratieve rechtshandeling*), enabling the author of an illegal individual act to withdraw it within certain time limits in order to prevent its annulment by administrative courts.

Public authorities must be able to adapt their action according to the evolving requirements of the general interest. This imperatively justifies the existence of the principle of mutability of administrative acts. The intensity of this principle varies according to the act's individual or general character.

Where regulations are concerned, the principle is absolute. The author of a general act must be able to modify it for the future, at any time, without any right for its addressees to require its maintenance, without prejudice to transitional provisions in the event that circumstances arise. Moreover, there is no possibility for the administration, either unilaterally or conventionally, to reject this principle except where specifically authorised by statute.

As far as decisions are concerned, the situation is more complex. Such individual acts may create rights. In this case, they may only be modified for the future and according to legally established conditions.

It has been observed that the administrative authorities usually function by means of unilateral acts. Sometimes, however, contracts may also be used. Under the influence of French administrative law, most Belgian administrative authorities make a distinction between contracts of the administration (*contrats de l'administration – door de administratie gesloten burgerrechtelijke contracten*) and administrative contracts (*contrats administratifs – administratieve contracten*). While the former resemble private law contracts, the latter are quite distinct. Their particular regime is explained not only by the existence of specific statutes in this area but also by their status within case law and legal commentary, and can be best observed in the sphere of public procurements.

[B] The Status of Civil Servants and Other Public Employees

Administrative action involves the use of human resources. Government relies on civil servants and other public employees. Usually, the situation of civil servants is characterised by the existence of a 'status' (*statut – statuut* or *rechtspositieregeling*). As a result, their legal situation is completely organised by the competent authority on a unilateral basis, through general and abstract rules that can be modified at any time in the higher interest of the service.

There is no unique status for the personnel of all public authorities. There are rather 'statuses', each taking into account the specificities and particularities existing within the civil service. Communities and regions, for instance, are largely autonomous in the organisation of the status of their civil servants. In order to establish a certain uniformity, a Royal Decree of 22 December 2000 fixed the general principles governing the administrative and pecuniary status of civil servants. It was directly applicable to the communities' and regions' civil services, as well as to the administrative agencies (*organismes publics – openbare instellingen*) that depend on them, with the exception of education staff. The sixth Reform of the State, adopted in 2014, abrogated the legal basis of this Royal Decree.

The 'status' only exists in the public sector. There is no equivalent system in the private sector, where employment relationships are essentially organised on the basis of employment contracts. In the public sector, it is also possible to employ staff on a contractual basis but such a possibility is, at present, often restricted to specific, limited situations, such as, for example, performing highly specialised tasks or replacing temporarily absent staff.

Civil servants under status have to be recruited and selected on the basis of competitive entrance examination, which is open both to Belgian citizens and to nationals of other EU Member States. It is possible to refuse to employ the latter but only for public functions involving a direct or indirect participation of the public power. Similar exclusions may arise in relation to functions which aim at safeguarding the general interest of the State and other authorities. Such jobs require the existence of a particular relationship of solidarity with the State, as well as a reciprocity of fundamental rights and duties, which is the very basis of the relationship created by nationality.

Definite appointment is usually made after a probation period. The civil servant performs his tasks immediately after having been appointed but the official assumption of the office only takes place after having taken the oath provided for by the *Décret* of 20 July 1831. Such an oath has to be taken by all citizens responsible for any public employment or service. After appointment, the civil servant is supposed to continue his career within his original service. There is, however, a significant trend in favour of a de-compartmentalisation between the different administrations and between the different services within one single administration. In this respect, there are means to encourage civil servants' voluntary mobility and, if necessary, to impose mobility.

A promotion requires the presence of a vacancy. It also requires several conditions regarding the civil servant: seniority, favourable evaluation, success in suitability tests, good results in a competitive examination, etc.

Except for the competitive examination, where the promotions depend on the ranking, the candidates are usually selected on the basis of the grading criteria. In practice, the system of evaluation seems to have failed, most civil servants usually getting the same mark, 'very good'. Such a phenomenon is known as '*déviance du statut*'. Promotions, at least at the highest ranks, were in practice based on purely political factors. In order to achieve the long-standing goal of a depoliticised civil service, there has been, in most administrations, a reform of the system of assessment called '*évaluation*'. This has occurred both in central and local administrations.

Being a civil servant implies a certain number of rights but also certain duties, such as the duty of loyalty or the obligation of neutrality. If they fail to comply with these duties, civil servants may be submitted to disciplinary proceedings. Despite some similarities, disciplinary law is quite different from criminal law, and therefore appears as an autonomous sector of law.

Finally, it is important to mention the legislation regarding the languages to be used in administrative matters. In a multilingual country such as Belgium, these rules regulate the use of languages both within the administrative services and in the relations between those services and the citizens.

[C] Public Property

In order to fulfil its tasks, the administration not only needs human resources but also goods and materials. Some of these are subject to a particular public property regime (*régime de domanialité publique – domeingoederen of goederen van het openbaar domein*). Although there is some dispute between civil lawyers and administrative lawyers regarding its specific content, the public property regime is generally considered to be applicable to goods that are immediately accessible to the public, as well as to goods allocated to a public service. In the latter case, these goods have to be exclusively or essentially adapted to the functioning of the particular public service to which they are related, either by virtue of their own nature or of particular adjustments, in order to be irreplaceable.

This allocation explains why the public property regime contains some special legal privileges. Public goods are, as a result, untransferable and imprescriptible; in principle, they are also undistrainable. While conserving these general principles, Article 1412*bis* of the Judicial Code, inserted by an Act of 30 June 1994, has contributed to ending many abuses. It is now possible for creditors of public entities to attach or distrain the goods mentioned on a list established by public authorities. If such a list has not been adopted or is not satisfactory, the creditor will be allowed to attach or distrain the goods which do not appear to be obviously necessary for the public authority to fulfil its general interest tasks or to ensure the continuity of the public service. In the latter case, the public authority subject to an order of attachment or distraint may propose the replacement of the attached or distrained goods by other goods.

The public authority can authorise some private uses of goods which are part of its public property, subject to one condition. These uses must be compatible with the particular purpose or function of these goods. Such private uses can be authorised either by unilateral decision (*autorisations domaniales – vergunningen*) or by contract (*concessions domaniales – concessies van het openbaar domein*).

Other goods are part of the public entity's private property (*domaine privé*) and as such are, in the main, subject to the general civil property law regime, and can be attached or distrained subject to the conditions of the above-mentioned Article 1412*bis* of Judicial Code.

Administrative law not only deals with the legal situation of the administration's goods but also with the administrative system related to private property. Indeed, in the general interest, private property can be restricted with a varying degree of intensity. The most significant restriction is the State's eminent domain or power of expropriation (*expropriation pour cause d'utilité publique – onteigening ten algemene nutte*). The exercise of this power involves not merely the limitation of the right of property but a real deprivation of it. Such a serious restraint may only be justified on the grounds of public purpose. It has to occur following the conditions provided for by statute, and requires a fair and preliminary compensation (Article 16 of the Constitution). This mechanism only concerns real property and leads to a transfer of property to the appropriating authority.

'Réquisition' (*opeising*) is another prerogative specific to public law and different from ordinary civil law. It allows the authority, in exceptional circumstances, to commandeer all it needs in order to achieve the aim of general interest that justifies the requisition. It includes not only human resources but also properties, whether personal or real. The main difference with expropriation or compulsory purchase in the public interest is that there is no fair and preliminary compensation. This is why it would be unconstitutional to make a requisition of a building, which implies a transfer of property.

The public interest easements (*servitudes d'utilité publique – erfdienstbaarheden van algemeen nut*) do not lead to a deprivation of real property. The right of property is limited in its exercise but does not disappear. As a result, the *'servitude d'utilité publique'* traditionally does not confer the right to compensation. Frequently, however, when the limitation creates a particularly heavy burden, the legislature sets up a specific system of compensation. The indemnity is then usually only partial. Recently, the case law of the Belgian supreme courts evolved. It establishes that an indemnity is due in order to compensate the excessive burden generated by the public interest easement if it exceeds the one that everyone must bear in the collective interest.

§4.04 THE CONTROL MECHANISMS OF THE ADMINISTRATIVE ACTION

Many control mechanisms are set up in order to ensure the respect of legality. Some of them operate inside the administrative structure and could be described as incorporated within it. Some controls are performed on the initiative of the controller. These include the controls related to the hierarchical structure within the administration, as well as the supervision by a higher authority in the system of decentralisation. Other controls are initiated after a claim by a citizen. In this case, the initial decision may be subject to review by several administrative authorities. They may sometimes set aside the initial decision. They can also be entitled to modify the initial decision or to replace it with their own decision.

External controls also exist. The executive, i.e., the collection of all administrative authorities, is subject to the control of the two other branches of government. Parliamentary assemblies exercise a political control over governmental action, and thus over administrative action. Without trying to describe completely the different instruments of political control in Belgian public law, it is interesting to note some instruments of control such as the introduction of an ombudsman, both at the federal level and that of the federated entities.

Finally, there is judicial review of administrative acts by courts. Civil courts belonging to the judicial branch of government have exclusive jurisdiction over claims related to what are referred to as 'civil rights', as opposed to 'political rights'. An important category of civil rights disputes regards the crucial question of the liability of public powers, included the liability of the administration or one of its politicians or civil servants considered individually.

In Belgian law, indeed, the liability of public authorities can be invoked on the same basis as that of private persons. Both can be ruled on by civil courts and are subject to the same system of civil liability provided for by Articles 1382 et seq. of the Civil Code. Neither executive nor administrative authorities hold any immunity or exception with regards to ordinary law.

Some particularities may, however, be mentioned in a system that has seen, until recently, many developments. Any act of the administration may lead to its liability if it is wrongful. The fault lies in any failure, even if minor, to respect a particular obligation provided for by a specific rule of law or by a general principle of law or, in the absence of such an obligation, in any error of behaviour judged by reference to the attitude that would be taken by a sufficiently conscientious and diligent authority placed in the same situation.

Except where the public authority is liable because of an anonymous fault of the service, it is usually liable because of a wrong of one or several of its personnel. The conditions for such liability originally varied on the basis of whether the member of staff has the quality of 'organ' (*organe – orgaan*), which requires that he or she holds or exercises part of the *imperium* of the public entity, or that of 'subordinate' (*préposé – aangestelde*), which does not imply such a power. However, the Act of the 10 February 2003 terminated this distinction. From then on, the public servant engaged under a status is civilly liable in case of fraud, gross fault and repetitive minor fault committed in the performance of his or her duties. The same regime is applicable to a member of the contract staff who falls within the scope of the Employment Contracts Act of 3 July 1978, whose content in this regard is almost identical to the Act of the 10 February 2003 applicable to non-contractual staff in the public sector.

If we consider the situation from the victim's standpoint, he has the choice to claim against either the authority, or the employee, organ or subordinate, or both.

Civil courts belonging to the judiciary also have jurisdiction over disputes relating to political rights. However, for such claims, the Constitution allows the legislature to create administrative courts, which do not belong to the judicial branch of government. This, of course, has been done, notably regarding to entry, stay, permanent residence and removal of aliens, with the creation of a council for disputes regarding aliens (*Conseil du contentieux des étrangers – Raad voor vreemdelingen betwistingen*).

As far as annulment of administrative acts (*contentieux objectif – objectief contentieux*) is concerned, the highest administrative court, the Council of State has general jurisdiction to annul both individual acts (decisions) and general acts (regulations) enacted by all administrative authorities.[1] Since 1989, or more broadly 1991, it has also been possible for the Council of State to decide to suspend an act until it has ruled upon the request for annulment.

An Act of 20 January 2014 gives to the Council of State a range of tools – either new or revised – allowing it to model, one way or another, the annulment it decides. We notably note the maintenance of the effects of the annulled act, either general or

1. *See also infra* Chapter 5, §5.02 [D].

individual, the injunction to the administration and the substitution of the annulled act by the judgment delivered.

Another Act, also adopted at the beginning of 2014, gives the Council of State jurisdiction over civil consequences of its decision to rule an administrative act unlawful (*contentieux de l'indemnité réparatrice – schadevergoeding tot herstel*). At the choice of the citizen demanding the annulment of an administrative act, he can either claim full compensation for the loss he suffered before the civil courts of the judiciary based on general civil liability law, in which case he has to prove that the administration committed a fault, or he can claim a reasonable compensation based on this administrative principle before the Council of State, in which case the unlawfulness of the act suffices so no fault of the administration has to be shown, but in which case only partial compensation could be awarded if private or public interests related to the case so require.

Since birth, the Council of State has been, in principle, the court of administrative cassation. Indeed, most of the judgments of other administrative courts can be annulled by the highest administrative court. It is notably the case of the judgments delivered by the *Conseil du contentieux des étrangers* (*Raad voor Vreemdelingen betwistingen*), above mentioned, which is charged with deciding on the cases related to entry, stay, permanent residence and removal of aliens.

Even if it is, at present, a minor legal reality, we can mention that the mediation of administrative litigation is possible but still not explicitly set up by the law. As for arbitration in public law, it is explicitly organised by the Judicial Code about contracts litigation.

The simultaneous existence of civil courts, belonging to the judicial branch of government, and administrative courts, belonging to the legislative or executive branch of government, naturally gives rise to conflicts of jurisdiction. The Constitution provides that such problems have to be settled by the Court of Cassation (*Cour de cassation – Hof van Cassatie*), the supreme civil court belonging to the judicial branch.

§4.05 CONCLUSION

This brief outline of Belgian administrative law may leave the foreign reader with a feeling of complexity. It is hardly surprising that such complexity exists in all contemporary societies where the State is answerable for the various needs and expectations of citizens. It is also the inescapable result of the need to reconcile administrative efficiency and protection of citizens' fundamental rights.

§4.06 SELECTED BIBLIOGRAPHY

D. Batsele, T. Mortier & M. Scarcez, *Algemeen administratief recht* (Brussels: Bruylant 2012).

D. Batsele & M. Scarcez, *Abrégé de droit administratif* (Brussels: Larcier 2015).

Ph. Bouvier, R. Born, B. Cuvelier & F. Piret, *Eléments de droit administratif* (2nd ed., Brussels: Larcier 2013).

A. Buttgenbach, *Manuel de droit administratif*, Première partie, *Théorie générale du droit administratif belge* (3d ed., Brussels: Larcier, 1966).

C. Cambier, *Droit administratif* (Brussels: Larcier 1968).

J. Dembour, *Droit administratif* (3d ed., La Haye: M. Nijhof 1978).

M.-A. Flamme, *Droit administratif* (Brussels: Bruylant 1989).

P. Goffaux, *Dictionnaire de droit administratif* (2nd ed., Brussels: Bruylant 2016).

M. Leroy, *Contentieux administratif* (5th ed., Limal: Anthemis 2011).

P. Lewalle & L. Donnay, *Contentieux administratif* (2nd ed., Brussels: Larcier 2008).

A. Mast, J. Dujardin, M. Van Damme & J. Vande Lanotte, *Overzicht van het administratief recht* (18th ed., Antwerp: Kluwer 2009).

D. Renders et al., 3 *Droit administratif, Le contrôle de l'administration* (Brussels: Larcier 2010).

D. Renders, *Droit administratif général* (2nd ed., Brussels: Bruylant 2017).

J. Salmon, J. Jaumotte & E. Thiebaut, *Le Conseil d'Etat de Belgique* (Brussels: Bruylant, 2012).

J. Vande Lanotte, G. Goedertier, Y. Haeck, J. Goossens & T. De Pelsemaeker, *Belgisch publiekrecht* (Bruges: die Keure 2015).

CHAPTER 5

The Judicial System and Civil Procedure

Piet Taelman & Claudia Van Severen

§5.01 GENERAL INTRODUCTION

[A] The Belgian Civil Justice System: A Brief Historical Perspective

[1] The Belgian Judicial Code of 1967

The Belgian civil justice system has its roots in the French Code of Civil Procedure (*Code de procédure civile*) of 1806. Whereas the 1806 French Code lost its position as central point of reference in the international procedural debate by the end of the nineteenth century, the Code remained in force in Belgium for a long period of time. It was not until 1967 that a fundamental judicial reform was realised, with the promulgation of the Judicial Code (*Code judiciaire - Gerechtelijk Wetboek*), which gradually came into force between 1967 and 1970. The objective of its founding fathers - Charles Van Reepinghen, Royal Commissioner for Judicial Reform, and his successor, Ernest Krings - was to make justice quicker, less expensive and less cumbersome. In view of the ongoing problem of judicial backlog, it appears that this goal has not been achieved. The most sweeping innovation of the Judicial Code was that, finally, the rules of civil procedure were described in one single code. Until then, those rules were scattered over hundreds of statutes. Additionally, the Judicial Code introduced a common procedural model that is, in principle, applicable to all ordinary (civil) courts in each instance.[1] Further on, the Judicial Code is undeniably a product of the liberal thinking at the time of its promulgation. It is exactly this liberal attitude that is currently recognised as one of the major flaws in the Belgian procedural model. The liberal

1. Over the years, however, some topics have become heavily crisscrossed with complex and deviating rules in specific separate statutes that are not incorporated in the Judicial Code.

regime as to the extension of the scope of the case on appeal, for example, which does not preclude the introduction of new claims which have not been submitted in first instance, is said to have resulted in first instance proceedings not being taken seriously. Also, the liberal attitude towards the timetable of the proceedings is considered as an important cause of the currently existing judicial backlog.

[2] Numerous and Significant (Ongoing) Amendments

Since its entry into force some fifty years ago, the Judicial Code has been amended several times.

In an attempt to reduce the backlog of cases, the judicial procedure has undergone a great number of changes. Important reforms regarding the time management of cases were implemented by the Act of 3 August 1992[2] and the Act of 26 April 2007.[3] The latter act intended to create a more powerful, so-called active judge, who has (more) control over the timetable and progress of proceedings, thus embedding the idea that the judge has to see to the orderly evolution of the proceedings in order to ensure that a judgment is rendered within a reasonable delay.

The optimisation of the proper organisation and functioning of the judiciary is also an ongoing priority of the Belgian legislature. Several significant measures were taken in the wake of the case (and escape) of Dutroux in 1998.[4] The so-called Octopus Agreement of 24 May 1998[5] laid the basis for a comprehensive and far-reaching reform of the judiciary. In November 1998, Article 151 of the Belgian Constitution was amended with a view to anchor the principle of judicial independence constitutionally,[6] as well as to establish the High Council of Justice (*Conseil supérieur de la Justice - Hoge Raad voor de Justitie*), an external body for controlling the proper functioning of the judiciary, which also has certain powers in relation to the nomination, evaluation and training of members of the judiciary.[7]

During the term of the Di Rupo Government,[8] the structure of the judiciary was given a major make-over on three fronts. First of all, the number of judicial districts was reduced from twenty-seven to twelve. Second, the mobility of the judges and court staff within districts was enhanced, which should make it possible to deploy them according to the districts' needs, taking into account the districts' workload and the judges'

2. Moniteur belge - Belgisch Staatsblad, 31 August 1992.
3. Moniteur belge - Belgisch Staatsblad, 12 June 2007.
4. In the mid-1990s, six young Belgian girls were kidnapped, four of whom were murdered. The atrocities were committed by a man named Marc Dutroux. A number of shortcomings in the Dutroux case caused widespread discontent with the country's justice system and the functioning of its law enforcement agencies in Belgium. The reform of the justice system was catapulted up the political agenda in April 1998 when Dutroux, while being transferred to a court house without handcuffs, managed to escape (but was caught a few hours later).
5. The term 'octopus' refers to the fact that eight political parties (all government coalition parties and all opposition parties except for the extreme right-wing party) concluded the agreement.
6. Up until then, the principle of judicial independence - a cornerstone of every democratic state - was an unwritten norm in Belgium.
7. *See infra* §5.02 [C] and §5.03 [A] [1].
8. December 2011-October 2014.

specialisation. These first two pillars were mainly aimed at reducing judicial backlog as well as achieving better service through specialisation. Third, the judiciary was given greater autonomy as to its management. A shift of responsibility regarding budgets and deployment of staff should allow to achieve better judicial management and more efficiency regarding the use of public means.[9] Different sources, however, criticise the legislature for having unrealistic expectations of the judiciary, which is now being burdened with the difficult task to restore public trust in the justice system on the one hand,[10] while reducing the available budget on the other hand.[11]

In a new attempt to resolve the backlog of cases, the current Minister of Justice of the Michel Government[12] has committed himself to do everything in his power to ensure that all ordinary (civil) courts in each instance will render judgment within one year after the initiation of proceedings. This is a very ambitious promise, taking into account the fact that the current average lead time for civil cases on appeal amounts to two and a half years.[13] In his plan for justice entitled 'More Efficiency for More Justice',[14] a series of measures is announced which aim to improve the proper administration and functioning of the judiciary, as well as the efficiency of the procedural rules, without making any concessions in terms of quality. In other words, the goal is to assure 'reasonable justice in a reasonable delay at a reasonable cost'. In particular, it is the Minister's ambition to reduce the number of cases on appeal and to stimulate the proper treatment of cases at the first instance level. With reference to the courts' heavy workload, the Minister also announced measures to stimulate out-of-court dispute resolution. One of these measures is the implementation of an extrajudicial order for payment procedure for the recovery of unchallenged claims.[15] Furthermore, the Minister is putting his efforts towards the digitalisation of the judiciary, in which area only very limited progress has been made in the past decades. Concrete

9. To this end, the legislature created two new managing bodies, which are responsible for the central management of the operating means allocated to the bench (Management Committee of the Courts) and the public prosecutor's office (Management Committee of the Public Prosecutor). In time, the respective committees and the Minister of Justice will conclude management contracts, establishing commitments and objectives for the judiciary and the resources made available for this. The committees will in turn distribute the allocated resources between the different entities of the judiciary.
10. A survey carried out by the High Council of Justice in 2014 indicates that 61% of the Belgian citizens has confidence in the Belgian justice system. This is undoubtedly a step forward in comparison with the results of 2002 (41%), but there is still room for further improvement. *See* www.hrj.be/en/content/barometer (accessed 15 July 2016).
11. Recent European research has demonstrated that the Belgian justice system faces a budgetary deficit: the budgetary effort for justice only represents a tiny 0.7% of Belgium's annual public expenditure, whereas the European average is 2.2%. *See* European Commission for the Efficiency of Justice (CEPEJ), *Report on 'European judicial systems – Edition 2014 (2012 data): efficiency and quality of justice'* 24, Figure 2.2, www.coe.int/t/dghl/cooperation/cepej/evaluation/2014/Rapport_2014_en.pdf (accessed 15 July 2016).
12. Since October 2014.
13. Moreover, simulations for the implications of the attempted cutting on staff costs have indicated that the average lead time over the period 2015–2019 will increase with six months.
14. *See* http://justitie.belgium.be/sites/default/files/downloads/Plan%20justitie_18maart_NL.pdf (Dutch) – https://cdn.nimbu.io/s/1jn2gqe/assets/Plan_Justice_18mars_FR.pdf (French) (accessed 15 July 2016).
15. *See infra* §5.05 [B] [4].

steps towards implementing these objectives are being taken with the series of so-called Potpourri Acts.

[B] Delimitation of the Subject Matter

Procedural law is the area of law that deals with the organisation and administration of justice, i.e., the settling of disputes by a judicial body. Within the general area of procedural law, a distinction can be made between procedures dealing with so-called subjective rights, procedures of an objective nature, disciplinary procedures and criminal procedures.

The ordinary courts, i.e., the courts that are part of the judicial branch of government, have exclusive jurisdiction to settle all matters pertaining to 'civil rights'.[16] They also have jurisdiction, albeit not exclusively, to settle disputes over 'political rights'.[17] Disputes about civil and political rights, together forming the subjective rights, centre around a legal subject's right to demand a specific attitude from another legal subject. This illustrates the difference with disputes of an objective nature, which are not concerned with the subjective rights of a legal subject, but instead concern the validity of acts emanating from an administrative authority, and which belong to the exclusive jurisdiction of the administrative courts.[18]

Apart from a general overview of the structure of the Belgian judiciary (§5.02 [A] & [B]) as well as a brief introduction to the organisation and functioning of the Council of State (§5.02 [D]) and the Constitutional Court (§5.02 [E]), this chapter will deal exclusively with the rules of civil procedure, which can be defined as the procedural rules governing disputes over subjective rights before the ordinary civil courts belonging to the judiciary, thus excluding procedures of an objective nature, disciplinary procedures and criminal procedures. Nevertheless, the rules of civil procedure (i.e., the Judicial Code) are in principle applicable to these other types of procedure, without prejudice however to any special rules or general principles of law which derogate from the general rules of the Judicial Code and of which the application would be irreconcilable with those rules.[19]

[C] Principles Governing the Proper Administration of Justice

[1] Access to Justice

The right to bring a dispute before a court is a fundamental right recognised under national, as well as international law. It has, *inter alia*, been derived by the European Court of Human Rights (ECtHR) from Article 6.1 of the ECHR.[20]

16. Article 144, para. 1, Constitution. However, pursuant to Article 144, para. 2, Constitution, the legislature may authorise administrative courts to decide upon the (private) civil law consequences of their decisions. *See also supra* Chapter 4, §4.04 and *infra* Chapter 11, §11.03 [D] [1] [a].
17. Article 145 Constitution.
18. *See supra* Chapter 4, §4.04.
19. Article 2 Judicial Code.
20. *Stanley Golder/United Kingdom*, ECtHR No. 4451/70 of 21 February 1975, §36.

This fundamental right consists of two components. First of all, there is the right of access to a court, meaning that for each dispute concerning civil rights, a possibility of recourse to a court – established by law[21] – should be provided. As a result, the State should establish a system of legal aid for those with limited resources.[22] Second, the right of recourse to judicial remedies requires a minimal jurisdiction on behalf of the judge.[23] Regarding purely private matters, the courts should be able to determine with full jurisdiction the rights and duties of the parties.

The 'right to a court' is, however, not an absolute right. It may be subject to legitimate and proportional limitations.[24]

[2] Fair Trial

The right to a fair trial, as safeguarded by Article 6.1 of the ECHR, includes the right to an adversary treatment of the case before an independent and impartial judge within a reasonable delay.

The right to an adversary treatment of the case implies that each party must be afforded a reasonable opportunity to present his case – including his evidence[25] – under conditions that do not place him at a substantial disadvantage *vis-à-vis* his opponent.[26] It is often named together with the right to equality of arms, another long established element of fairness, in the sense of a 'fair balance' between the parties.[27]

The right to an independent judge, as safeguarded by Article 151 of the Constitution, implies that the judge should be able to render judgment according to his conscience, independently of any outside influence and without being accountable to the government or other forces. The independence of the judge is guaranteed by his appointment for life, the existence of incompatibilities, and the objective nature of the conditions for appointment to the courts.[28]

The right to an impartial judge implies that the judge must act with an open mind, free of bias and without prejudice to any of the parties or their dispute. Additionally,

---

21. Article 146 Constitution stipulates that no court or any other entity capable of rendering judgment may be established other than by statute.
22. *Airey/Ireland*, ECtHR No. 6289/73 of 9 October 1979, §§20–28. *See infra* §5.05 [A].
23. *Sigma Radio Television Ltd./Cyprus*, ECtHR No. 32181/04 and 35122/05 of 21 July 2011, §157; *Obermeier/Austria*, ECtHR No. 11761/85 of 28 June 1990, §70.
24. Legitimate restrictions to the right of access to justice are legal certainty, a proper functioning of the judiciary and measures which aim at reducing the courts' workload. The requirement that the limitations must be proportional means that they must not restrict or reduce the access left to the individual in such a way or to such an extent that the very essence of the right is impaired (*Stanev/Bulgary*, ECtHR No. 36760/06 of 17 January 2012, §§230 & 241; *Brualla Gómez de la Torre/Spain*, ECtHR No. 26737/95 of 19 December 1997, §33; *de Geouffre de la Pradelle/France*, ECtHR No. 12964/87 of 16 December 1992, §28).
25. *K.D.B./Netherlands*, ECtHR No. 80/1997/864/1075 of 27 March 1998, §44; *Mantovanelli/France*, ECtHR No. 21497/93 of 18 March 1997, §33; *Vermeulen/Belgium*, ECtHR No. 19075/91 of 20 February 1996, §33.
26. *Kress/France*, ECtHR No. 39594/98 of 7 June 2001, §§72–76; *Dombo Beheer B.V./Netherlands*, ECtHR No. 14448/88 of 27 October 1993, §33.
27. *Nideröst-Huber/Switzerland*, ECtHR No. 18990/91 of 18 February 1997, §23.
28. *See infra* §5.03 [A] [1].

the judge's behaviour should be free of any sign or appearance of partiality: 'Justice must not only be done, but also seen to be done.'[29]

The right to a treatment of the case within a reasonable delay must be assessed on a case-by-case basis, taking into account all the relevant factors in each individual case.[30] It requires that a careful balance is struck between the interest of the parties in obtaining a decision as soon as possible and the requirement to comply with the fundamental principles of due process.

Another aspect of the right to a fair trial is the right to a reasoned decision. Article 149 of the Constitution requires the court to state the reasons on which its decision is based, in order to avoid any sign of unfairness and to enable review by a higher court. Article 149 of the Constitution should be regarded as a merely formal obligation; it can be considered to be complied with if the court has indicated the (legal and factual) reasons founding its decision, irrespective of the legal validity of these reasons.[31] On the other hand, the fact that the (substance of the) decision seems legally justified may still constitute a violation of Article 149 of the Constitution if the court failed to answer to all pleas and arguments raised by the parties.[32]

[3] Party Autonomy Versus Role of the Judge

Belgian civil procedure is guided by the principle of party autonomy, which means that the parties set the limits of the dispute. The parties decide if and when proceedings are initiated (and ended), as well as what their object will be[33] and who will be involved therein.[34] Within these limits, the court decides the case. This does not entail, however, as traditionally argued, that the judge is a mere passive observer, who just sits back and enjoys the show. The judge plays an active role on various fronts. First of all, the judge is entrusted with and responsible for controlling and managing the orderly conduct of proceedings. He has a case management responsibility, meaning that he must ensure that matters are properly focused, procedural rules respected, expenses kept in check and progress maintained or even accelerated. Second, the judge has to be active with regard to the administration of evidence.[35] Furthermore, the judge must invoke *sua sponte* all rules of (substantive and procedural) law which are considered to be of public policy. Finally, the court must resolve the dispute according to the rules that are applicable to the case, meaning that it must examine, on its own initiative, the legal nature of the facts presented to it by the parties, irrespective of their legal qualification

29. *De Cubber/Belgium*, ECtHR No. 9186/80 of 26 October 1984, §26.
30. Court of Cassation 30 June 2000, C.98.0484.N; Court of Cassation 5 May 1987, AR 1059, 1986–1987 Arresten van het Hof van Cassatie 1165, 1987 Pasicrisie belge 1029.
31. Court of Cassation 14 January 1997, P.97.0005.N; Court of Cassation 3 January 1995, P.93.1560.N.
32. Court of Cassation 5 October 1998, S.98.0032.N.
33. Article 1138, 2°, Judicial Code stipulates that the judge cannot grant a claim that was not expressed, nor can he grant more than was claimed. Conversely, Article 1138, 3°, Judicial Code requires the judge to render judgment on each of the claims presented by the parties.
34. Article 811 Judicial Code prohibits the judge from ordering *ex officio* that third parties be joined in the proceedings.
35. *See infra* §5.06 [C].

by the parties. As such, the court is obliged to complete and/or substitute the legal argumentation of the parties, provided that it does not raise a dispute that has not been raised by the parties, that it only relies on information properly submitted to it by the parties and that it respects the rights of defence. The latter means, *inter alia*, that the court must give the parties the opportunity to give their point of view on the legal grounds advanced by it.

§5.02 STRUCTURE OF THE JUDICIARY

[A] Introduction

The organisation of the court system has remained a federal matter. Article 40, paragraph 1, of the Constitution stipulates that the judicial power is exercised by the ordinary courts, which constitute the judiciary, i.e., the judicial branch of government. The judicial function, however, is not exclusively exercised by the judiciary, but also by other bodies such as administrative courts and the Constitutional Court. These courts are not part of the judicial branch of government.

Figure 5.1 Structure of the Belgian Court System

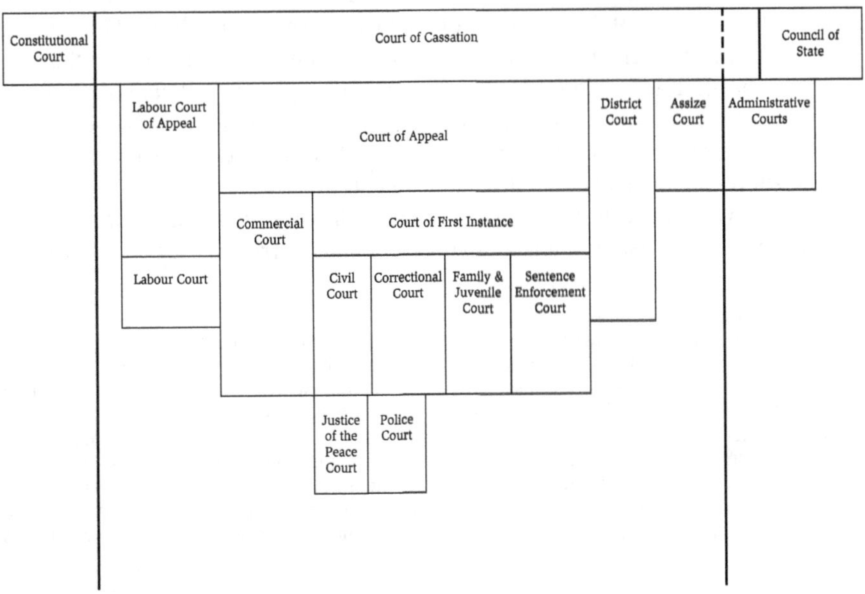

[B] Organisation and Composition of the Different Courts

The judicial organisation rests on a division of the national territory into several areas.

The sub-districts or cantons (*canton* – *kanton*) are the smallest geographical subdivision, of which there are currently 187.[36] There is one justice of the peace court (*justice de paix* – *vredegerecht*) in each sub-district, which consists of a single courtroom, presided by a single judge.

The sub-districts are grouped into judicial districts (*arrondissement*), of which there are currently twelve. The districts' borders correspond mainly with the borders of the provinces Antwerp, Limburg, Walloon Brabant, East Flanders, West Flanders, Luxembourg, Liège, Namur and Hainaut. There are, however, separate districts for Brussels, Louvain and Eupen. In principle,[37] each district encompasses one police court (*tribunal de police* – *politierechtbank*) and one court of first instance (*tribunal de première instance* – *rechtbank van eerste aanleg*). It also accommodates a district court (*tribunal d'arrondissement* – *arrondissementsrechtbank*), which is not a permanent court, but only convenes in case of certain jurisdictional disputes.[38]

The police court is a single-judge court, but may consist of several divisions, called 'chambers'.

The court of first instance is divided into three sections: the civil court (*tribunal civil* – *burgerlijke rechtbank*), the family and juvenile court (*tribunal de la famille et de la jeunesse* – *familie- en jeugdrechtbank*) and the criminal court (*tribunal correctionel* – *correctionele rechtbank*).[39] Each of these sections is composed of one or more chambers presided by one or three judges.[40] Cases relating to civil matters are in principle handled by a single judge.[41] The family and juvenile court is a newly established section within the court of first instance (operational since 1 September 2014),[42] which comprises of juvenile chambers (juvenile court), family chambers and, within the latter, chambers for amicable settlement (*chambre de règlement à l'amiable* – *kamer voor minnelijke schikking*) (family court). Finally, every court of first instance has one or more judges of attachments (*juge des saisies* – *beslagrechter*),[43] dealing with the enforcement of judgments and pre-trial attachments.

Until 1 April 2014, there were twenty-seven districts, which had each a police court, a court of first instance, a labour court (*tribunal de travail* – *arbeidsrechtbank*)

36. Article 1 Judicial Code Supplement.
37. An exception is made for Brussels, Mons and Eupen. As to Brussels, note that the scale operation of the districts was crisscrossed with the reform of the judicial district of Brussels by the Act of 19 July 2012 (Moniteur belge – Belgisch Staatsblad, 22 August 2012 (ed. 1)), which entered into force on 31 March 2014. The reform of the judicial district of Brussels entailed that some courts (court of first instance, commercial court, labour court and district court) were 'duplicated' in the sense that both a Dutch-speaking and a French-speaking court were installed, each competent for the entire judicial district of Brussels. In principle, cases are allocated between the Dutch- and French-speaking courts according to the previously existing rules regarding the allocation of cases between the former Dutch- and French-language chambers of the Brussels courts.
38. *See infra* §5.04 [A] [3].
39. Article 76, §1, Judicial Code. Courts of first instance located in the same city where a court of appeal is vested also have a fourth section which has jurisdiction over the enforcement of criminal penalties, e.g., parole issues. This section is called the sentence enforcement court (*tribunal de l'application des peines* – *strafuitvoeringsrechtbank*).
40. Article 78, para. 1, Judicial Code.
41. Articles 91 and 92, §1/1, Judicial Code.
42. Before 1 September 2014, there was only a separate juvenile court.
43. Article 79, para. 1, Judicial Code.

and a commercial court (*tribunal de commerce – rechtbank van koophandel*). As part of the 2014 reform, the number of districts was reduced from twenty-seven to twelve. Furthermore, the labour courts and commercial courts are now organised at the level of the courts of appeal, which is called the 'judicial area' (*resort – rechtsgebied*) and of which there are five: Antwerp, Brussels, Ghent, Liège and Mons.[44] The former locations of these courts (in the twenty-seven judicial districts), however, are maintained as local divisions of these five centralised courts where hearings are held, in order to preserve the proximity of justice.[45]

The labour court is composed of several chambers. Normally, each chamber is presided by one professional judge, assisted by two (exceptionally four) lay judges, one from the side of the employers and one from the side of the employees or the self-employed, depending on the litigating parties.[46]

The commercial court consists of several chambers, presided by one professional judge and two (assisting) lay judges, the latter being appointed on the recommendation of various associations representing commerce and industry.[47]

Courts of appeal (*cour d'appel – hof van beroep*) and labour courts of appeal (*cour du travail – arbeidshof*) are organised on the level of each of the five judicial areas. In the court of appeal there are chambers for civil matters, chambers for juvenile matters, chambers for family matters (and within the latter, chambers for amicable settlement) and chambers for criminal matters.[48] Every chamber is presided over by one or three judges.[49] Cases relating to civil law matters are in principle dealt with by a single judge on appeal.[50] The labour court of appeal is composed of professional and lay judges on appeal, similarly to the labour court.[51]

Finally, on top of the pyramid, there is the Court of Cassation (*Cour de cassation – Hof van Cassatie*), Belgium's supreme court of the judiciary, located in Brussels.[52] There are three chambers: one for civil cases, one for labour cases and one for criminal cases.[53] Each chamber consists of a Dutch- and French-speaking department.

44. Article 156 Constitution and Article 5 Judicial Code Supplement.
45. The idea is that each local division offers the 'basic judicial services', whereas the cases that require more specialised skills or knowledge are assigned to one of the divisions for the whole district or area. The allocation of cases to the divisions is laid down in a 'case allocation regulation' per judicial district or area (Article 186 Judicial Code).
46. Articles 81 and 197–202 Judicial Code.
47. Articles 84 and 203–205 Judicial Code. *See infra* Chapter 12, §12.03 [B].
48. Article 101, §1, para. 1, Judicial Code.
49. Article 101, §2, para. 2, Judicial Code.
50. Article 109*bis*, §3, Judicial Code.
51. Article 104 Judicial Code.
52. Article 147, para. 1, Constitution.
53. Article 133 Judicial Code.

Figure 5.2 Structure of the Belgian Judiciary (Ordinary Courts)

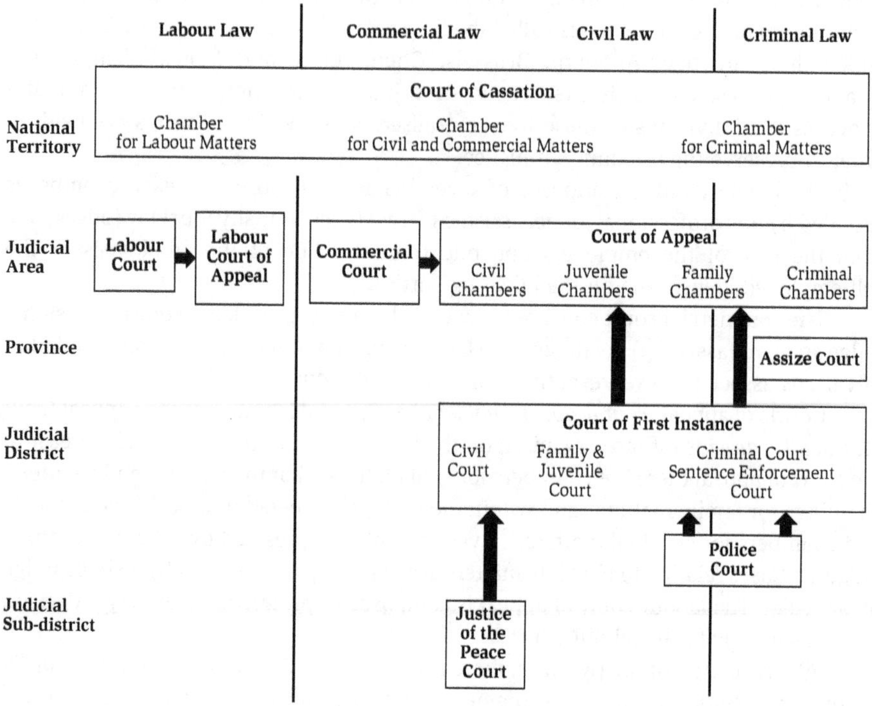

[C] High Council of Justice

The High Council of Justice does neither belong to the judiciary, nor to the other branches of government. It is an institution *sui generis* that serves as an intermediary, or a bridge, between the judiciary on the one hand and the legislature and executive on the other hand. Its constitutional foundations are laid down in Article 151 of the Constitution, while detailed rules on its composition and functions are elaborated in Articles 259*bis*/1–22 of the Judicial Code.

The High Council consists of two joint committees – a Dutch-speaking and a French-speaking committee – which are comprised of eleven judges and eleven non-judges.[54] The judges are elected by their peers; the non-judges are appointed by the federal Senate.[55] Two commissions are assembled from among each committee: a

54. Article 259*bis*/1, §1, Judicial Code.
55. Article 259*bis*/2, §§1–2, Judicial Code.

Nomination and Appointment Commission[56] and an Advisory and Investigation Commission.[57] These commissions are equally composed of judges and non-judges. In a number of cases, the respective Dutch-speaking and French-speaking commissions have to act together, in which case they are referred to as the Joint Nomination and Appointment Commission[58] and the Joint Advisory and Investigation Commission.[59]

The nomination and appointment commissions have certain powers in relation to the nomination, appointment, evaluation and (initial and in-service) training[60] of members of the judiciary.[61] The advisory and investigation commissions' primary task is to prepare (non-binding) recommendations and opinions regarding the general functioning of the judiciary,[62] as well as to investigate complaints in this respect.[63]

[D] Council of State

The Council of State (*Conseil d'Etat – Raad van State*) is the highest (i.e., supreme) administrative court in Belgium.[64] As such, it is not a part of the judiciary, the judicial branch of government. It encompasses, within a single institution, both an advisory body (the Legislative Section) and an adjudicating body (the Administrative Section). The Legislative Section delivers legal advisory opinions on draft statutory texts. Although these opinions are not binding upon the authorities requesting the advice, in practice they have great moral authority. The Council also has a judicial role, offering legal recourse to citizens being wronged by government actions. For this purpose, the Administrative Section is given the power to suspend and annul (individual and legislative) administrative acts, i.e., acts performed by an administrative authority. It is also authorised to review and, as the case may be, suspend and/or annul decisions rendered by a lower-ranking administrative court. In the latter case, the Administrative Section of the Council of State functions as an administrative court of cassation, and thus as a supreme court.

The Council's constitutional foundations are laid down in Article 160 of the Constitution, while detailed rules on its composition, authority and functioning are elaborated in the (repeatedly amended) Coordinated Act on the Council of State.[65]

56. Article 259*bis*/8 Judicial Code.
57. Article 259*bis*/11 Judicial Code.
58. Article 259*bis*/9–10 Judicial Code.
59. Article 259*bis*/12–14 Judicial Code.
60. Since 2009, a new independent body – the Institute for Judicial Training (*Institut de Formation Judiciaire – Instituut voor Gerechtelijke Opleiding*) – is charged with the implementation of the training programmes.
61. Article 259*bis*/9 Judicial Code. *See infra* §5.03 [A] [1].
62. Article 259*bis*/12 Judicial Code.
63. Article 259*bis*/15–16 Judicial Code. On the understanding, however, that the High Council cannot interfere in the handling of a particular (court) case.
64. *See also supra* Chapter 4, §4.04.
65. Royal Decree of 12 January 1973.

[E] Constitutional Court

Traditionally, the Belgian judiciary has held the position that it does not have the power to review the validity of statutes under the Constitution. This power of judicial review rests exclusively with the Constitutional Court, which is not part of the judiciary, the judicial branch of government.[66]

The Constitutional Court owes its existence to the transformation of the Belgian State from a unitary state into a federal state. Major reforms since 1970 have resulted in the establishment of a federal state within which the legislative power is divided between the federation and the federated entities according to a system in which each legislative body has exclusive powers. The statutes of the federation and of the federated entities, the regions and communities, have the same force of law.[67] The division of the legislative power between different legislatures brought with it the risk of conflicts of legislative jurisdiction. In this context, the constitutional legislature of 1980 decided to establish a new adjudicative body, the Court of Arbitration (*Cour d'arbitrage – Arbitragehof*), which was entrusted with the task of demarcating the boundaries of each authority's legislative power. For this purpose, it was given the power to nullify any statutes, whether federal or regional, promulgated in breach of the division of legislative jurisdiction that has been established by or in pursuance of the Constitution.

Since then, however, the jurisdiction of the Court has been gradually extended to include the review of federal and regional statutes on their compliance with other articles of the Constitution.[68] Accordingly, the name of the Court of Arbitration was changed into Constitutional Court (*Cour constitutionnelle – Grondwettelijk Hof*) in 2007.

There are two ways in which a case can be brought before the Constitutional Court: in the form of an action for annulment, which may be instituted by certain government authorities, as well as by any (natural or legal) person declaring a justifiable interest, or in the form of a preliminary question referred by another court (if a question comes up in a court regarding the compatibility of federal or regional statutes with the Constitution, that court must in principle address a preliminary question to the Constitutional Court).

The Court's constitutional foundations are laid down in Article 142 of the Constitution, while detailed rules on its organisation, functioning, procedure as well as the effects of its judgments are elaborated in the (repeatedly amended) Special Act of 6 January 1989.[69]

66. *See also supra* Chapter 3, §3.12.
67. *See supra* Chapter 3, §3.09 [D].
68. To date, the Court's competence has been extended to Section II of the Constitution, which relates to rights and freedoms (Articles 8–32), as well as to Article 143, §1 (the principle of federal loyalty), Article 170 (the legality principle in tax matters), Article 172 (the equality principle in tax matters) and Article 191 (the protection of foreign nationals) of the Constitution.
69. An (unofficial) English version of these texts is available on the Constitutional Court's website under the heading 'Basic Texts', at www.const-court.be (accessed 15 July 2016).

§5.03 PARTICIPANTS IN THE JUDICIAL SYSTEM

[A] Members of the Judiciary

[1] Judges

[a] Nomination and Appointment

Until the 1990s the criteria for the appointment of judges were rather opaque. It was not transparent whether access to the position of judge was based solely on the qualifications and merits of the candidate. Greater objectivity and transparency in the appointment of judges was realised as part of the Octopus Reform of 1998.[70] One of the central points of this reform was the elimination of the so-called political appointments whereby, next to capacity and suitability to carry out the office, political support from the governing political parties was indispensable to be appointed as a magistrate. To this end, Article 151 of the Constitution was amended, which now stipulates that judges are appointed by the King pursuant to their reasoned nomination by the respective Nomination and Appointment Commission of the High Council of Justice, by a majority of two-thirds in accordance with the terms specified by the law and after evaluation of their qualifications and aptitude. The nomination can be rejected only in the manner specified by law and with adequate justification.

There are three alternative ways of entering the judiciary: (1) the judicial traineeship; (2) the professional aptitude exam; and (3) the oral evaluation exam. The first way of access is designed for candidates with little working experience. It includes a judicial traineeship, which may be commenced only after the candidate has passed a competitive entrance exam. The second way of access is intended for candidates with a larger professional experience. In addition to a required number of years of working experience, candidates need to pass the 'professional aptitude exam', giving immediate access to a vacancy. The third way of access includes the successful completion of an oral evaluation exam, also giving instant access to a vacancy, which is reserved to candidates who have acquired many years of professional experience.

The nomination and appointment commissions of the High Council of Justice are responsible for the preparation and organisation of the exams, as well as the nomination for appointment of candidates for a vacancy for a position of judge.

[b] Incompatibilities

The Judicial Code provides for a series of incompatibilities, aimed at safeguarding the impartiality and independence of judges.[71] Most incompatibilities relate to the simultaneous exercise of the judicial function and certain other offices and professions. Other rules provide for incompatibilities in case of kinship. In addition to compliance

---

70. *See supra* §5.01 [A].
71. Articles 292–304 Judicial Code. *See also* Article 155 Constitution.

with the rules on incompatibilities, judges must refrain from dealing with a case as soon as there can be reasonable doubt about their independence or impartiality, in the absence of which their authority can be challenged[72] or they can be withdrawn from the case.[73]

[c] Evaluation and Discipline

Judges are subject to an evaluation.[74] This evaluation entails a periodic internal quality assessment with respect to the way in which the office is exercised, but cannot relate to the (quality of the) content of a court decision.[75]

No judge can be deprived of his office or suspended otherwise than by way of a (disciplinary) court decision.[76] Judges who neglect their duties or harm the dignity of their office through their behaviour may be subject to disciplinary sanctions.[77] The disciplinary rules for members of the judiciary[78] have been changed considerably by the Act of 15 July 2013.[79] The new rules should make disciplinary proceedings quicker, simpler and more transparent and, above all, they should guarantee (more so than before) the independence and impartiality of the disciplinary authorities.

[d] End of Functions

Although Article 152, paragraph 1, of the Constitution provides that judges are appointed for life, retirement is mandatory at the age of sixty-seven.[80] Judges approaching their retirement age may, however, at their own request, be authorised by the King to continue exercising their office until they have reached the age of seventy.[81] Retired judges may also be appointed as substitute judge at their own request.[82]

[e] Interest Groups and Networks

There exist several national organisations that promote the collective interests of (part of) the Belgian magistracy, of which the most important one is the Advisory Council for

72. Articles 828–842 Judicial Code.
73. Articles 648–659 Judicial Code.
74. Article 151, §6, para. 1, Constitution.
75. Articles 259*novies–undecies* Judicial Code. The evaluation criteria and their weightings are set by the King, upon a proposal from the High Council of Justice (Article 259*nonies*, §1, para. 6, Judicial Code).
76. Article 152, para. 2, Constitution.
77. Articles 404–423 Judicial Code.
78. Which are not only applicable to judges, but also to court clerks and officers of the public prosecutor's office.
79. Moniteur belge – Belgisch Staatsblad, 25 July 2013.
80. Article 383, §1, para. 3, Judicial Code. The age limit for judges and officers of the public prosecutor's office in the Court of Cassation is seventy (Article 383, §1, para. 2, Judicial Code).
81. Article 383*ter* Judicial Code. The age limit for judges and officers of the public prosecutor's office in the Court of Cassation is set at seventy-three.
82. Retired judges who have been appointed as substitute judge may even continue exercising this office after the age of seventy as far as it is considered useful for the requirements of the service (Article 383, §2, Judicial Code).

the Magistracy (*Conseil consultatif de la magistrature – Adviesraad van de magistratuur*). The Council's members represent all branches of the judiciary and are elected by their peers. The Council's mission is to give advisory opinions to the Minister of Justice, the federal Parliament, i.e., the Chamber of Representatives and the Senate, and to consult with them, on topics relating to the status, rights and duties, as well as the working conditions of judges and officers of the public prosecutor's office.

Another important (European) initiative is the European Judicial Network in civil and commercial matters, which facilitates relations between the national judicial authorities of the respective Member States through a network of national contact points, thereby furthering cooperation in cross-border cases.[83]

[2] Court Registries

Every court has a registry (*greffe – griffie*), which serves as the court's secretariat and is headed by a chief registrar (*greffier en chef – hoofdgriffier*).[84] The court registrars are members of the judiciary; they fulfil a judicial function, but have no adjudicating authority. They assist the judges in the exercise of their office. In principle, a court registrar must be present at every hearing.[85] The registrar acts as an independent and impartial observer; he takes minutes of the hearing and ensures that the applicable rules are complied with.

[B] Public Prosecutors

In Belgium, a distinction is made between 'sitting magistrates', who adjudicate the cases that are brought before them and who are judges, and 'standing magistrates',[86] who serve in the public prosecutor's office (*ministère public – openbaar ministerie*). There is a public prosecutor's office within each court, except for the justice of the peace court. The public prosecutor's legal status differs from the judiciary. Officials of the public prosecutor's office are not appointed for life, but can be dismissed.[87] Further on, they are subject to the supervision of the Minister of Justice, who has the right to order the public prosecutor's office to take action in a certain case. Nevertheless, they also enjoy a constitutionally guaranteed independence.[88] They are also independent *vis-à-vis* the sitting judge.

The public prosecutor's office fulfils a number of tasks in both criminal and civil cases. Its most important task in civil cases is to act as an advisor to the court in the circumstances provided for by law or whenever it considers its advice to be useful.[89]

83. *See* https://e-justice.europa.eu/content_about_the_network-431-en.do (accessed 15 July 2016).
84. Article 157 Judicial Code.
85. Article 168 Judicial Code.
86. So named because they stand up when addressing the court.
87. Article 153 Constitution.
88. Article 151, §1, para. 1, Constitution.
89. Articles 138*bis juncto* Articles 764–768 Judicial Code.

The advice is, however, not binding on the court and the judge is not obliged to respond to it.

[C] Attorneys

[1] Legal Status, Role and Duties

Attorneys are professionally engaged in the defence of private interests. At all times and under all circumstances, they are at the service of parties seeking justice. This mission statement includes legal counselling and legal representation in court. Attorneys have the right to plead and represent their client before all ordinary civil courts, without the need of a specific power of attorney.[90] The mere declaration of acting on behalf of their client serves as a presumption of lawful representation.[91] As with any mandate, mistakes or negligence of the attorney, which fell within the limits of the representation, are considered to be the mistakes or negligence of the principal, i.e., the client, and cannot give rise to force majeure.[92]

As legal representation is not compulsory in Belgium, parties have the right to choose to appear and plead in person, without a legal representative.[93] Only in exceptional circumstances, proceedings may not be initiated without the intervention of a (specialised) attorney.[94] In principle, only attorneys have the right to speak on behalf of the parties in court.[95]

[2] Remuneration and Fee Agreements

With the exception of attorneys taking on (state-funded) *pro bono* cases, attorneys are paid by their clients, irrespective of the outcome of the proceedings.[96] The 'winning' party, however, may recover (part of) his attorney's fees from the 'losing' party. The compensation for attorney's fees and expenses is limited to a fixed lump sum

90. Article 440, para. 2, Judicial Code.
91. The Judicial Code provides for a special procedure enabling parties to rebut that presumption (Articles 848–850).
92. Court of Cassation 3 May 2011, P.10.1865.N; Court of Cassation 27 April 2010, P.10.0512.N; cf. Court of Cassation 9 November 2011, P.11.1027.F.
93. If a party is unable to present its arguments in a calm and clear manner to the court, the judge may interrupt the pleadings and ask that the party presents its case through a legal representative (Article 758, para. 2, Judicial Code).
94. For instance, in civil matters, only attorneys who are admitted to practice before the Court of Cassation may plead and represent their clients before this supreme court (Article 478 *juncto* Article 1080 Judicial Code). Their number is limited to twenty. They are appointed by the King upon recommendation of an Advisory Commission (Articles 478*bis*–478*ter* Judicial Code). They are neither employees of the Court of Cassation, nor are they part of it. They serve as a filter, ensuring the high quality standard of the cassation appeals.
95. In some (lower) courts, parties may be assisted or represented by their spouse or close relatives. In the labour courts, parties may be assisted or represented by a representative of a trade union (Article 728, §§2–3, Judicial Code).
96. As of 1 January 2014, attorneys are subject to VAT, so parties are also charged with the VAT (at a rate of 21%) owed on the attorney's fees.

indemnification (*indemnité de procedure – rechtsplegingsvergoeding*), which is awarded by the court to the prevailing party.[97]

Article 446*ter* of the Judicial Code prohibits contingency fee based agreements. This prohibition must be interpreted narrowly to target only such arrangements whereby the very existence of any kind of fee is made dependent upon the outcome of the litigation ('no cure, no pay') and whereby, if the case is won, the calculation of the fee is based exclusively on the level of damages awarded. The reason for this prohibition is that such agreements affect the attorney's independence in the handling of the case because he acquires a personal interest in its outcome.

[3] Organisation of the Profession

Every attorney must be member of a local bar (*Ordre des Avocats – Orde van Advocaten*). Every bar elects a bar council (*Conseil de l'Ordre – Raad van de Orde*) and a president (*bâtonnier – stafhouder*) from among its members for a term of one year. The bar council is responsible for the general management of the bar, which includes, *inter alia*, the organisation of the legal aid system in its territory. The president is responsible for the day-to-day management of the bar. He also considers complaints about the attorneys of his bar.[98]

All local bars of the Dutch-speaking community are grouped into the Flemish Bar Association (*Orde van Vlaamse Balies*), whereas the French and German Bar Association (*Kammer der französischsprachigen und deutschsprachigen Rechtsanwaltschaften – Ordre des barreaux francophones et germanophone)* encompasses the French- and German-speaking local bars. The role of the respective associations is to promote the collective interests of its members, as well as to issue regulations regarding the legal profession (including disciplinary and deontological rules), which are binding upon its members.

[D] Bailiffs

[1] Legal Status, Role and Duties

Bailiffs (*huissier de justice – gerechtsdeurwaarder*) are public officials, who alone have the authority to carry out the service of writs of summons, as well as the enforcement of judgments, court orders or other enforceable titles (including the seizure of property).[99] Their office is said to be mandatory, i.e., they are obligated to deliver their services when requested, unless there are legal reasons not to do so. Bailiffs may only act within the judicial district in which they are appointed by the King.[100]

---

97. *See infra* §5.05 [A].
98. Disciplinary sanctions are imposed by the Disciplinary Board (Articles 456–477 Judicial Code).
99. Article 519, §1, para. 1, Judicial Code.
100. Article 516 Judicial Code.

The legal status of the bailiffs was changed considerably by the Act of 7 January 2014,[101] which aimed at attaining greater objectivity as to their appointment,[102] as well as their disciplinary system.[103]

[2] Organisation of the Profession

There is a Bailiff's District Chamber (*chambre d'arrondissement des huissiers de justice – arrondissementskamer van gerechtsdeurwaarders*) in every judicial district,[104] which is composed of the bailiffs of the respective districts. The Chamber is managed by a Council,[105] which is responsible for the maintenance of good order and discipline among its members.[106]

There is also a Belgian National Association of Bailiffs (*Chambre nationale des huissiers de justice de Belgique – Nationale Kamer van Gerechtsdeurwaarders*), which is a national representative organisation that promotes and defends the collective interests of the bailiffs.

§5.04 JURISDICTION

[A] Domestic Jurisdiction

[1] Subject Matter Jurisdiction

[a] General Principles

[i] General, Specific and Exclusive Jurisdiction

The courts' subject matter jurisdiction is dependent on four factors: the nature of the claim, its (economic) value,[107] its urgency and the legal status of the parties involved.[108] Most courts have a general jurisdiction, in addition to some specific or exclusive competences. Whereas the value of the claim is decisive with regard to a court's general jurisdiction, the specific and exclusive competences are mainly determined by the nature of the claim. The urgency of the claim is only relevant with regard to summary proceedings. The parties' legal status is an element of the commercial court's general competence.

101. Moniteur belge – Belgisch Staatsblad, 22 January 2014.
102. Articles 510–515 Judicial Code.
103. Articles 533–548 Judicial Code.
104. Article 549, §1, Judicial Code. There is, however, a joint chamber for the districts of Verviers and Eupen.
105. Article 551 Judicial Code.
106. Article 552 Judicial Code.
107. Which is determined in accordance with Articles 557–562 Judicial Code.
108. Article 9 Judicial Code.

[ii] Functionality: Specialisation – Public Policy

The distribution of powers between the courts is functional. Its goal is to safeguard the sound administration of justice, by ensuring that disputes are adjudicated by their 'natural judge', i.e., a judge who has the expertise and know-how required to deal with the case. The judiciary's pyramidal structure is inherently characterised by specialisation: each court has jurisdiction over specific types of cases. Over the years, the courts have been assigned additional specific competences. Reasons relating to substantive law, as well as reasons of expertise or location of the court are at the root of these additional competence allocations. In some cases, however, the allocation of jurisdiction has been nothing more than an arbitrary shift of caseload, thereby compromising the intended specialisation and transparency of the rules of jurisdiction.

The subject matter jurisdiction of the courts is a matter of public policy. Any deviating agreements between the parties are to be considered null and void. The court's lack of jurisdiction may be raised at any moment in the course of the proceedings, either on the court's own motion or at the initiative of the parties. It is also a ground for appeal and further appeal.

[b] Overview of the Jurisdiction of the Different Courts

[i] First Instance Courts

The justice of the peace court is a small claims court. It has general jurisdiction over all claims that do not exceed EUR 2,500,[109] provided these claims do not belong to the specific or exclusive jurisdiction of another court. The justice of the peace court is also regarded as a proximity court, due to its accessibility and informal atmosphere. Therefore, it has a specific jurisdiction over certain disputes, irrespective of the amount of the claim,[110] such as disputes regarding immovable property (such as lease and the use and administration of jointly owned property) and neighbour disputes.

The police court is a traffic court. In addition to its traditional criminal jurisdiction regarding traffic offences, it has been provided with exclusive jurisdiction in civil matters for all compensatory claims, irrespective of their value, relating to traffic accidents.[111] It also has a specific jurisdiction with regard to certain matters, such as the hearing of appeals against municipal administrative sanctions.[112]

The court of first instance consists of two branches which deal with civil matters: the civil court and the family and juvenile court.[113] The civil court has the power to

109. Article 590 Judicial Code.
110. Articles 591 and 594 Judicial Code.
111. Article 601*bis* Judicial Code.
112. Article 601*ter* Judicial Code.
113. With the understanding that the criminal court is competent to rule over the civil law consequences of the criminal offence in question.

adjudicate all civil claims, except for the ones that pertain to the exclusive jurisdiction of another court or that are to be brought directly before the court of appeal or the Court of Cassation. Therefore, the civil court is said to dispose of a full general jurisdiction (*plénitude de jurisdiction – volheid van bevoegdheid*).[114] The juvenile court handles juvenile matters.[115] The family court has a specific jurisdiction over family-related disputes in the broadest sense, regardless of the value of the claim.[116] Every court of first instance also accommodates one or more judges of attachments, who have exclusive jurisdiction over attachments for sale and preliminary seizures.[117]

The commercial court has general jurisdiction to adjudicate all disputes between 'undertakings' – defined as entities durably pursuing an economic goal – in relation to an action that was performed in pursuance of that goal, irrespective of the monetary value of the claim.[118] It also has exclusive jurisdiction over insolvency proceedings for enterprises, such as bankruptcy and judicial reorganisation.

The labour court has specific jurisdiction with regard to matters of (individual) labour law and social security law, regardless of the value of the claim.[119] It has also been provided with jurisdiction over a specific type of insolvency proceedings, namely the collective debt settlement procedure (*règlement collectif de dettes – collectieve schuldenregeling*).[120]

[ii] Appellate Courts and Court of Cassation

The courts of appeal have jurisdiction to hear appeals against judgments rendered in first instance by the courts of first instance and by the commercial courts.[121] The labour court of appeal hears appeals against judgments rendered in first instance by the labour courts.[122] Decisions rendered in first instance by the justice of the peace courts and police courts are to be appealed, however, before the court of first instance.[123]

The Court of Cassation is Belgium's supreme court. It has jurisdiction over further appeals, i.e., appeals against judgments rendered in last instance.[124] It also deals with

114. Article 568, para. 1, Judicial Code. The full general jurisdiction of the civil court is limited, however, by the possibility for the defendant to dispute the jurisdiction of the civil court and request that the case be referred to the court which has the general or specific jurisdiction over the case. This request must be made in the first pleadings (Article 568, para. 2, Judicial Code).
115. Within the meaning of the Act of 8 April 1965 on the protection of youth (Moniteur belge – Belgisch Staatsblad, 15 April 1965).
116. Article 572*bis* Judicial Code.
117. Article 1395 Judicial Code.
118. Article 573, para. 1, 1°, Judicial Code. *See infra* Chapter 12, §12.03 [B].
119. Articles 578–583 Judicial Code.
120. Article 578, 14°, Judicial Code. This procedure gives over-indebted private individuals the opportunity to reorganise their finances and re-establish their economic capability under the supervision of a court-appointed debt mediator. The procedure is described in Articles 1675/2–19 Judicial Code.
121. Article 602, 1° & 2°, Judicial Code.
122. Article 607 Judicial Code.
123. Article 577 Judicial Code.
124. Article 608 Judicial Code.

certain specific procedures, such as conflicts of attribution (i.e., jurisdictional conflicts between the ordinary and administrative courts), requests for annulment of regulations of the bar associations and the removal of a judge from a case.[125]

[2] Venue (Territorial Jurisdiction)

[a] General (Default) Rules

Every court's power to adjudicate disputes is limited by the boundaries of the area which has been conferred to it by law.[126] Hence, the plaintiff must not only determine which is the materially competent court, but he must also identify that court's location.

In principle, the rules governing the courts' territorial jurisdiction are supplementary rules of law, meaning that they can be overridden by contract. In the absence of such forum selection agreement, the plaintiff has the choice to initiate his claim before the court of: (1) the domicile of the defendant or one of them, if there are multiple defendants; (2) the place where the disputed contract has been concluded or has been or must be performed; (3) the place which has been chosen for the performance of the contract; or (4) the place where the bailiff has served the writ of summons in the event that the defendant does not have a known domicile in Belgium or abroad.[127]

[b] Specific (Mandatory and Public Policy) Rules

In some cases, however, the court's territorial jurisdiction is governed by mandatory rules of law.[128] In this event, the parties can still conclude an agreement with respect to the competent court, but only after the dispute has arisen.[129] Only in exceptional cases, the court's territorial jurisdiction is a matter of public policy, in which event the parties may not under any circumstances choose their own forum (and the judge must examine his jurisdiction on his own motion).[130]

[3] (Resolution of) Jurisdiction Conflicts

Conflicts over jurisdiction are time-consuming and are therefore to be resolved as quickly as possible. The Belgian civil justice system provides for a special non-permanent court, namely the district court, which has as its only task to resolve jurisdiction conflicts. The district court is composed of four members[131] and only

125. Articles 609–615 Judicial Code.
126. Articles 10 and 622 Judicial Code.
127. Article 624 Judicial Code.
128. Articles 627–629*quater* Judicial Code.
129. Whereas the default rules can be overridden prior to the arising of any dispute.
130. Articles 631–633*decies* Judicial Code.
131. Articles 74–75*bis* Judicial Code.

convenes when it is asked to rule about a jurisdiction conflict. Its decisions are not appealable.[132]

A court's jurisdiction may be challenged by one of the parties or by the court on its own motion. The latter is only possible if the relevant jurisdiction rule is a matter of public policy. If the jurisdiction issue is raised by the court on its own motion, the issue is referred to the district court.[133] The district court's decision is binding on the court to which the case is remanded. The same applies if the jurisdiction issue is raised by one of the parties, provided that the opposite party requests that the issue is referred to the district court. In all other cases, e.g., in the absence of any response from the opposite party, the jurisdiction issue is settled by the court itself which shall, if necessary, refer the case to the competent court.[134]

If a jurisdiction issue is raised at the appellate level, the court of appeal (or labour court of appeal) itself will decide upon the issue and, as the case may be, refer the case to the competent appellate court.[135]

[B] International Jurisdiction

Whether or not the Belgian courts have jurisdiction over a cross-border dispute is determined by the *lex fori* (i.e., the laws of the jurisdiction where the legal action is brought), which consists of treaties, regulations and national (private international) rules of law.

Roughly speaking,[136] the rules of international jurisdiction may be governed by: (1) EU regulations, of which the most important one in this area is Regulation No. 1215/2012 of 12 December 2012 on Jurisdiction and the Recognition and Enforcement of Judgments in Civil and Commercial Matters[137] (the so-called Brussels I*bis*-Regulation, which is a recast of the Brussels I-Regulation (EC) No. 44/2011 of 22 December 2000[138]);[139] (2) bilateral and international treaties, which have lost most of their importance due to the introduction of the aforementioned European instruments; or (3) the Belgian Code of Private International Law,[140] for cases in which neither the EU regulations nor any other international instruments do apply.

---

132. Article 642 Judicial Code.
133. Article 640 Judicial Code.
134. Article 639 Judicial Code.
135. Article 643 Judicial Code.
136. For a more detailed account, *see infra* Chapter 16, §16.03.
137. Official Journal L351/1 of 2012. The general rule is that jurisdiction is conferred upon the courts of the Member State in which the defendant is domiciled, regardless of his nationality.
138. Official Journal L12/1 of 2001.
139. For some areas, specific EU regulations have been issued. To name but one: Regulation No. 4/2009 of 18 December 2008 on Jurisdiction, Applicable Law, Recognition and Enforcement of Decisions and Cooperation in Matters relating to Maintenance Obligations (Official Journal L7/1 of 2009).
140. The general rule is that the Belgian courts have jurisdiction if the defendant has his domicile or habitual place of residence in Belgium at the time of the initiation of the proceedings.

§5.05 PROCEEDINGS

[A] Access to Justice: Legal Aid, Legal Assistance and Legal Costs

[1] Legal Aid and Legal Assistance

The Belgian justice system provides for several mechanisms available to people who do not have the resources needed to cover the costs of litigation. These mechanisms are available to both claimants and defendants.

Legal aid means that a person with limited resources is (entirely or partially) exempt from the payment of certain litigation costs (with the exception of attorneys' fees), such as the various court fees, costs for the intervention of public officials such as bailiffs, and expenses concerning investigation measures. The request for legal aid has to be made to the court that is competent to rule on the merits of the case.[141]

Legal assistance means, *inter alia*, that a person with limited resources and in need for legal counsel is appointed an attorney whose services are paid (in full or in part)[142] by the Belgian State. The application for legal assistance has to be made to one of the bureaus for legal assistance, which are established within every local bar under the auspices of the respective bar councils. In principle, all Belgian attorneys have an ethical duty to take on some *pro bono* cases. For trainee-attorneys, it is mandatory as part of their training.

[2] Legal Costs

The court determines in every final judgment the litigation costs as well as the party who has to bear them, generally the party losing the case.[143] Special attention should be paid to the compensation for attorneys' fees and expenses, which is a fixed lump sum allowance awarded by the court to the winning party who was represented by an attorney during the proceedings.[144] The amount of the compensation depends on the monetary value of the claim.[145] No party can be obliged to pay additional compensation for the attorney's intervention of the opposite party above the lump sum allowance awarded by the court.

141. Within every court there is a bureau for legal aid, i.e., a special chamber presided by a single judge, that decides on the requests for legal aid. In the justice of the peace court and police court, however, where there is no such bureau, it is the judge himself who decides whether or not to grant the request.
142. People whose resources are above a certain threshold are asked to pay a small non-refundable contribution.
143. Article 1017, para. 1, Judicial Code.
144. Article 1022 Judicial Code.
145. The amounts are determined in a Royal Decree of 26 October 2007 (Moniteur belge – Belgisch Staatsblad, 9 November 2007).

[B] Proceedings in First Instance

[1] Pre-trial Settlement

Before initiating formal proceedings, one party may invite the other to a settlement procedure before the judge.[146] The judge will then try to achieve an amicable settlement by assisting the parties towards an agreement. If a settlement is reached, the judge shall incorporate the details of the settlement in a formal statement, which is binding on the parties and can be enforced against them in the event of non-compliance. If the conciliation attempt fails (or one of the parties does not show up), the judge does not have the power to adjudicate the dispute. Any party, however, has the right to initiate formal proceedings after a failed attempt at conciliation. The pre-trial reconciliation attempt is voluntary, unless it is required by statute.[147] In addition, if the parties reach a settlement in the course of court proceedings, they may always ask the judge to take notice of that agreement, in which case he will render a 'settlement judgment'.[148] In any event, the judge merely acts as a notary, taking notice of the parties' agreement. He does not interfere in, or rule on, the content or fairness of the settlement, unless rules of public policy are violated.

[2] Ordinary Proceedings

[a] Initiation of Proceedings

[i] Language

Belgium has three official languages: Dutch, French and German. The language of civil proceedings is, in principle, determined by the language of the court before which the claim is to be initiated. The courts are, in principle, unilingual. Whether proceedings are conducted in Dutch, French or German is subject to the rules laid down in the Act of 15 June 1935 on the Use of Languages in Judicial Matters.[149] Proceedings before courts situated in a unilingual region are usually conducted in the language of that region. Put simply, proceedings in the southern region of Belgium (Wallonia) are in French, whereas those in the northern region (Flanders) are in Dutch. Proceedings before courts situated in the German-speaking community (the district of Eupen, within Wallonia) are conducted in German. A special regime applies to Brussels, where the rules governing the use of languages will not only determine the language of the proceedings but also the competent court.

146. Articles 731-733 Judicial Code.
147. In land rent cases, for instance, the claimant is obliged to undertake a pre-trial settlement attempt before the judge prior to the initiation of formal proceedings (Article 1345 Judicial Code).
148. Article 1043 Judicial Code.
149. Moniteur belge – Belgisch Staatsblad, 22 June 1935.

[ii] Notice to Appear Before Court

The most common way to initiate civil proceedings is by way of a writ of summons, i.e., an official document that is served on the defendant by a bailiff at the request of the claimant.[150] In some cases, proceedings may be initiated by means of a petition, which is a written request directly addressed to the court by the plaintiff (or his legal counsel) which is subsequently notified to the defendant by the court registrar.[151] Apart from its form, the petition has the same legal effects as the writ of summons, but it is a more informal and less expensive manner to launch legal proceedings. In any event, the defendant is granted a minimum period of eight days between the day of the service or notification of the act instituting the proceedings and the day of the preliminary hearing, in order to allow him to prepare his defence and consult an attorney.[152] If both parties agree on presenting their dispute to the court, they may file a joint petition declaring their voluntary appearance.[153]

[iii] Registration by the Court

After the payment of an enrolment fee, the court registrar will register the case on the court's docket. This is a register in which all cases submitted to the court are registered under a serial number, thus identifying the case.[154]

[b] Progress of Proceedings

[i] Adversary Proceedings

Preliminary Hearing

The preliminary hearing, the date of which is determined in the act instituting the proceedings, can be considered as a first case management hearing where the judge will decide on the further course of the case. Two categories of cases can be distinguished: cases that only require short hearings (these are immediately resolved at the preliminary hearing or at a hearing at a nearby date)[155] and more complex cases. The latter are generally handled in accordance with a procedural calendar, which is either agreed upon by the parties or, in the absence of such agreement, imposed by the judge.[156] The procedural calendar fixes the deadlines that need to be respected by the

150. Article 700 *juncto* Article 43 Judicial Code.
151. Articles 1034*bis*–1034*sexies* Judicial Code.
152. This period may be shortened by the court in case of urgency (Article 708 Judicial Code); it may be extended if the defendant has no (elected) place of residence or domicile in Belgium (Article 709 *juncto* Article 55 Judicial Code).
153. Article 706 Judicial Code.
154. Articles 711 et seq. Judicial Code.
155. Article 735 Judicial Code.
156. Articles 747–748 Judicial Code.

parties with regard to the filing and exchange of their written pleadings and supporting documents.[157] It also provides for the trial date, which is determined by the judge.

In principle, parties are required to appear in person or through their legal representative at the preliminary hearing.[158]

Exchange of Written Pleadings and Supporting Documents

Parties must set out their claims and defences, as well as the (numbered) arguments in support thereof, in written pleadings.[159] The last written pleadings of each party are deemed to replace all previous pleadings; hence, they must be comprehensive and contain all claims, defences and arguments the parties maintain and submit to the court for decision.[160] This should facilitate the task of the judge, because he is only held to decide on claims, defences and arguments which have been presented by the parties in their last pleadings.[161]

Unlike before, the time limits for the filing of the pleadings (as laid down in the procedural calendar) are mandatory. Pleadings filed after the expiration of the deadlines, will be disregarded by the court.[162]

In addition, parties must communicate to each other all documents on which they rely. Failure to disclose will result in a stay of the proceedings.[163]

Trial

On the trial date, the case will be presented orally to the court. Parties may plead in person or through their legal representative. In practice, however, the oral pleadings are mostly done by attorneys.[164] Generally, the claimant presents his oral arguments and evidence first, followed by the defendant's oral arguments and evidence. The parties may also agree to replace the traditional pleadings with an interactive debate, which is presided over by the judge.[165] The importance of the oral pleadings should not be exaggerated, as the court is not held to answer claims and arguments which have only been put forward at the occasion of the oral pleadings. Apart from the exceptions

---

157. The procedural calendar is determined by the agenda of the court, in the sense that the parties' deadlines are fixed in accordance with the earliest date on which the hearing of the case can take place.
158. Article 728, §1, Judicial Code.
159. Which must meet the formal and substantive requirements of Articles 743–744 Judicial Code. As part of a recent reform of the Judicial Code, written pleadings now need to be drafted in accordance with a predetermined structure. If not, the court is not held to respond to the pleadings.
160. Article 748*bis* Judicial Code.
161. According to the Court of Cassation, the judge is even forbidden from deciding on claims or defences that were expressed in previous pleadings, but not reiterated in the last pleadings (Court of Cassation 8 March 2013, C.11.0477.N).
162. Unless parties mutually agree that the late pleadings are not to be excluded from the proceedings (Article 748, §1, Judicial Code).
163. Article 736 Judicial Code.
164. An exception to this is the justice of the peace court, where *pro se* litigants are common.
165. Article 756*ter* Judicial Code.

provided for by law, the hearings are open to the public.[166] There is no jury trial in civil cases.

Oral pleadings are not a must. The parties (or their counsels) may agree to a purely written procedure whereby the judge will decide the case on the basis of the written pleadings and supporting documents.[167]

Deliberation and Judgment

After the closing of the hearings and, as the case may be, the delivery of the opinion of the public prosecutor's office,[168] the court takes the case into deliberation. A written judgment should normally be rendered within one month,[169] but in practice this may take longer.[170] As long as the judgment has not been rendered, the parties may request the court to reopen the proceedings upon discovery of a new fact or document that is essential to the case.[171] The court may also ex officio decide to reopen the proceedings, for instance if it has additional queries that were not answered in the parties' written and oral pleadings.[172] Moreover, it is under an obligation to do so if it considers dismissing the claim on the basis of a legal reason that has not been addressed by any of the parties.[173]

Res Judicata

The authority of res judicata is an inherent feature of final judicial decisions, meaning that what has been decided, cannot be questioned anymore. On the one hand, it indicates that the judgment is conclusive as to the rights and obligations of the parties; on the other hand, it prevents any subsequent action by the same parties regarding the same claim.[174] The plea of res judicata must be entered by the defendant. The judge is prohibited from raising the issue on his own motion.[175] The plea will be granted if it is clear that both actions are identical, meaning that they concern the same parties (acting in the same capacity), the same subject and the same (factual) cause.[176]

If the time for initiating ordinary legal remedies - opposition and appeal[177] - has elapsed, the decision acquires the force of res judicata.[178] This implies that it is definite and can only be challenged through extraordinary judicial means.[179]

166. Article 148 Constitution and Article 757 Judicial Code.
167. Article 755 Judicial Code.
168. *See supra* §5.03 [B].
169. Article 770, §1, para. 1, Judicial Code.
170. If the judge has not rendered judgment within six months, the case can be withdrawn from him (Article 652 Judicial Code).
171. Articles 772–773 Judicial Code.
172. Article 774, para. 1, Judicial Code.
173. Article 774, para. 2, Judicial Code.
174. Article 25 Judicial Code.
175. Article 27 Judicial Code.
176. Article 23 Judicial Code.
177. *See infra* §5.05 [C] [2].
178. Article 28 Judicial Code.
179. *See infra* §5.05 [C] [3].

Notice and Service of the Judgment

In all cases, the court registry sends an unsigned (free) copy of the judgment by ordinary mail to each of the parties or their counsel.[180] This notice is given for information purposes only and does neither make the judgment enforceable against either party, nor does it trigger the running of the term of appeal (or any other appellate remedy).

In most cases, if a party wants a judgment to be enforceable against the other party, it needs to be served on that other party.[181] This means that the party wanting the judgment to be enforced must request the court registry to deliver a copy thereof with an order for enforcement[182] and request the bailiff to serve the judgment on his opponent(s). Normally, the service of the judgment constitutes the starting point of the term of appeal (and other appellate remedies).[183]

[ii] Default Proceedings

Conditions for Rendering a Judgment by Default

A judgment can only be rendered by default when one of the parties does not appear at the preliminary hearing and the other party asks a default judgment to be pronounced.[184] The judge cannot, under any circumstances, deliver a default judgment ex officio. The party who is present at the hearing can also request the judge to adjourn the case. In this event, the court registry will notify the defaulting party of the date of the second hearing upon receipt of a written request in this respect from the other party.[185] If the defaulting party is absent again at the second hearing, the other party may request that a default judgment is rendered.[186]

When none of the parties appear at the preliminary hearing or the party appearing does not request a default judgment or the (re-)summoning of the defaulting party, the judge will have to impose a procedural calendar and fix a trial date, in which case the (future) judgment will be deemed to have been rendered after adversarial proceedings.[187]

If a party was present at the preliminary hearing but did not appear later at the trial date or a later hearing, a default judgment can be pronounced against that party,[188] unless the absent party has already submitted written pleadings.[189]

180. Article 792, para. 1, Judicial Code.
181. Article 1495, para. 1, Judicial Code.
182. Article 1386 Judicial Code.
183. In some exceptional cases, however, the Code requires the court registry to notify the decision to the parties by 'judicial mail' (a special type of registered letter with acknowledgement of receipt), in which case this notification is the starting point of the term of appeal (for both parties) (Article 792, paras 2 & 3, *juncto* Articles 46, §2, and 57 Judicial Code).
184. Article 802 Judicial Code.
185. Article 803 Judicial Code.
186. Article 804, para. 1, Judicial Code.
187. Article 747, §2, para. 6, Judicial Code.
188. Article 804, para. 1, Judicial Code.
189. Article 804, para. 2, Judicial Code.

Assessment of the Judge in Default Proceedings

Although the wording of Article 806 of the Judicial Code – 'the judge shall honour the claims or defences of the party that is present, unless the proceedings, those claims or defences violate rules of public policy' – seems to suggest only a very narrow task for the judge in the event of default by one of the parties, most Belgian courts and legal scholars attribute a broader task to him. Before rendering a judgment by default, the judge must first verify whether the defaulting party was duly summoned or notified of the hearing. Second, the judge must verify whether he has jurisdiction over the case. As to the merits of the case, the judge must at least verify whether the claim does not violate any rules of public policy. Moreover, for the purposes of Article 806 of the Judicial Code, the concept of 'public policy' is to be interpreted flexibly and evolving. This means, for example, that the judge is authorised to undermine (or tone down) manifestly unfounded or plainly disproportionate claims or excessive interest demands of the party that is present.

[3] Summary Proceedings

The presidents of the courts of first instance, labour courts and commercial courts may provisionally rule on urgent matters which fall within the normal scope of their jurisdiction. The procedure is laid down in Article 584 *juncto* Articles 1035–1041 of the Judicial Code. There are two basic conditions. First of all, the request has to be urgent, meaning that an immediate decision is desirable to prevent (further) harm or serious discomfort.[190] Second, the president can only order interim measures, meaning that he can only act on a temporary basis and cannot decide on (nor cause any prejudice to) the merits of the case.[191] This also means that the court hearing the main action is not bound by the findings of the president.

In principle, interim proceedings are adversarial proceedings. However, in very urgent cases, a party may apply to the president unilaterally (by using a unilateral or *ex parte* petition).[192] This exceptional procedure – in which the opponent is not involved and not even summoned – can only be used in case of absolute necessity, which means that the requested provisional measure is of such urgency and/or nature that it would be harmful for the plaintiff to rely on the ordinary (adversarial) summary proceedings.

In addition, *any* judge is authorised to order provisional measures in relation to the dispute in the main proceedings (such as investigation measures or measures aimed at the provisional settlement of the parties' dispute).[193] This procedure, which can be used at any stage of the proceedings, is initiated informally by the filing of a

190. Court of Cassation 23 September 2011, C.10.0279.F; Court of Cassation 11 May 1990, AR 7089, 1989–1990 Arresten van het Hof van Cassatie 1175, 1990 Pasicrisie belge 1050; Court of Cassation 21 May 1987, AR 7613, 1986–1987 Arresten van het Hof van Cassatie 1287, 1987 Pasicrisie belge 1160.
191. Article 1039, para. 1, Judicial Code.
192. Article 584, para. 4, *juncto* Articles 1025–1034 Judicial Code.
193. Article 19, para. 3, Judicial Code.

simple written request with the court's registry. Contrary to summary proceedings, urgency is not required.

[4] Ex Parte Proceedings

As they undermine the adversarial principle, *ex parte* proceedings - whereby the opposite party is not involved in the proceedings and not even informed thereof - are available only in cases expressly provided for by statute. The procedure is laid down in Articles 1025–1034 of the Judicial Code. The unilateral petition must be filed with the court's registry by an attorney, who serves as a filter by ensuring that these kinds of proceedings are used with caution. A particular legal remedy is available to the third party against whom the decision is directed, namely third-party opposition.[194]

In practice, the preliminary seizure is an important type of *ex parte* proceeding. Similar to freezing injunctions in common law, the preliminary seizure could be described as the blocking of a debtor's assets without prior notice. It prevents the debtor from disposing freely over his assets. Normally, the preliminary seizure requires the permission of the judge of attachments, which is requested by means of a unilateral petition.

Another particular type of *ex parte* procedure is the summary order for payment procedure,[195] which was introduced in 1967, at the same time of the promulgation of the Judicial Code, in order to provide for a quick and simple procedure for the collection of small and *prima facie* uncontested monetary claims. In practice, however, the procedure turned out to be burdensome, inefficient, costly and therefore not frequently used by creditors to obtain relief in small and simple matters. A comprehensive reform of the summary order for payment procedure has not been realised so far. Recently, however, a completely new administrative recovery procedure for uncontested claims was introduced.[196] The scope of the new procedure is limited to uncontested (national and cross-border) claims between businesses ('B2B') relating to the payment of a sum of money, irrespective of the amount of the claim. In order to surround the out-of-court procedure with necessary guarantees (such as expertise and independence), a key role is allocated to the bailiffs and the National Chamber of Bailiffs.

[5] Collective Redress Proceedings

As of 1 September 2014, a collective mass claims settlement procedure has been made available in consumer law disputes. The procedure is laid down in the Code of Economic Law. It allows a class representative to introduce an action for collective redress where a group of consumers has suffered harm resulting from a company's breach of contract or violation of certain specified statutory provisions and EU

194. *See infra* §5.05 [C] [3] [b].
195. Articles 1338–1344 Judicial Code.
196. Articles 1394/20–27 Judicial Code.

regulations relating to consumer protection.[197] A notable feature of the procedure is that the interests of the individual consumers - who are not involved as parties in the procedure as such - are represented by a class representative.[198] Only consumer associations and authorised non-profit organisations with articles of association specifying a purpose corresponding with the collective harm, have standing to bring a class action.[199] Furthermore, it is required that the class action appears to be more effective than (or superior to) an individual civil action.[200] The courts of Brussels have exclusive jurisdiction (for the whole country) over consumer class actions.[201]

[C] Review Proceedings

[1] In General

The Judicial Code distinguishes between ordinary and extraordinary appellate remedies.[202] The ordinary remedies are opposition (*opposition – verzet*) and (ordinary) appeal (*appel – hoger beroep*). The extraordinary remedies comprise the petition for cassation (*pourvoi en cassation – voorziening in cassatie*), third-party opposition (*tiers opposition – derdenverzet*), revocation of *res judicata* (*requête civile – herroeping van het gewijsde*), redress against the judge (*prise à partie – verhaal op de rechter*) and repeal (*rétractation – herziening*). The essential distinguishing feature is that, in principle, all decisions are susceptible to the application of ordinary appellate remedies,[203] whereas extraordinary remedies are only available if they are expressly provided for by statute.

197. Articles XVII.36, 1° and XVII.37 Code of Economic Law.
198. The (positive or negative) outcome of the procedure, however, will be binding on the individual consumers who have expressly made known their desire to be part of the class action (opt-in system) or have not expressly made known their desire to be excluded (opt-out system). In principle, the competent Belgian court can freely choose between an opt-in or opt-out system, thereby taking into account the underlying facts and claims of the case (Articles XVII.38, §1, and XVII.43, §2, 3°, Code of Economic Law).
199. Article XVII.39 Code of Economic Law. Note that the Constitutional Court annulled this provision, insofar as it does not provide that representative bodies from Member States of the European Union and the European Economic Area that meet the requirements set forth in para. 4 of the Commission Recommendation 2013/396/EU of 11 June 2013 on Common Principles for Injunctive and Compensatory Collective Redress Mechanisms in the Member States concerning Violations of Rights Granted under Union Law (Official Journal L201/60 of 2013) may act as group representative (Constitutional Court No. 41/2016 of 17 March 2016).
200. Article XVII.36, 3°, Code of Economic Law.
201. Article XVII.35 Code of Economic Law.
202. Article 21 Judicial Code.
203. The right to appeal is, however, not constitutionally guaranteed, nor does it amount to a general principle of due process in civil matters (ECtHR 23 July 1968, 'Belgian linguistics case', §9: the Court held that Article 6 ECHR does not require any right of appeal, but if there is an appeal, the guarantees of said Article 6 apply; *see also* Constitutional Court No. 96/2016 of 16 June 2016, §B.6.1 and Court of Cassation 21 January 1983, AR 3621, 1982–1983 Arresten van het Hof van Cassatie 675, 1983 Pasicrisie belge 594).

In principle, the procedural rules governing the first instance proceedings also apply at the appellate level, without prejudice, however, to any special rules that derogate from the general procedural rules.[204]

[2] Ordinary Appellate Remedies

[a] Opposition[205]

[i] Admissibility

Opposition is only available to persons who were summoned to appear as a party in the proceedings but defaulted and are aggrieved by the default judgment.

As a general rule, each judgment rendered *in absentia* can be opposed by the party who defaulted.[206] The possibility to lodge opposition against a default judgment is a right of the defaulting party, irrespective of the reason of the default (and without prior leave by a court or other authority being required). Nevertheless, a statutory provision can provide that opposition is not possible against a certain decision, such as decisions which are deemed to have been rendered after a trial.[207] Some decisions are not susceptible to the application of any ordinary appellate remedies, such as decisions regarding the administration of the trial, for instance decisions fixing the procedural calendar and trial date,[208] or decisions ordering certain investigation measures, such as decisions ordering a judicial site inspection[209] or appearance of the parties before the judge in person.[210]

Unlike the (ordinary) appeal, no statutory threshold must be met in order to lodge opposition.

Opposition can be lodged as soon as the default judgment has been rendered, even if it has not yet been served on the defaulting party. The term for lodging the opposition is generally one month from the date of service (or notification) of the judgment. This is a peremptory time limit that is provided for by statute under penalty of inadmissibility, which must be pronounced by the court *sua sponte*.[211]

204. Article 1042 Judicial Code.
205. Articles 1047–1049 Judicial Code.
206. Article 1047 Judicial Code.
207. Articles 747, §2, para. 6, 748, §2, para. 6, 804, para. 2, and 1113, para. 1, Judicial Code.
208. Articles 747, §2, para. 4, and 748, §2, para. 5, *juncto* Article 1046 Judicial Code.
209. Articles 1007–1008 Judicial Code.
210. Articles 992 and 996 Judicial Code.
211. Article 860, para. 2, *juncto* Article 865 Judicial Code. There are a few exceptional circumstances in which the time limit is prolonged (e.g., in favour of the party who has no place of residence or domicile in Belgium) or suspended (e.g., due to the death of a party or force majeure). In addition, when the time limit begins and ends during the judicial holidays (1 July–31 August), it is (automatically) extended until the fifteenth day of the new judicial year (15 September) (Article 50, para. 2, Judicial Code).

The opposition is lodged before the same court that delivered the default judgment[212] by service of a writ of summons upon the other party.[213]

If the party who has lodged the opposition defaults again, no opposition is allowed against the second default judgment.[214]

[ii] Scope of Review

Opposition allows the defaulting party to re-submit the case in its entirety to the scrutiny of the same court that delivered the opposed default judgment. The court that has to decide upon the opposition can review and re-litigate upon both facts and legal assessments. The scope of the court's review is defined by the litigating parties, meaning that the court cannot re-litigate on points at issue that are not challenged in the notice of opposition. The opposition has a relative effect, meaning that it cannot have adverse effects for the party that lodges the opposition. This relative effect does not prevent, however, the extension or amendment of the original claim.

[iii] Consequences for (Provisional) Enforcement

As a general rule, the lodging of opposition entails a stay of the enforcement of the default judgment,[215] unless the court has authorised the (provisional) enforcement thereof or the law expressly provides for an exception to this rule. With regard to default judgments concerning the conviction of the defaulting party to pay a sum of money, both the effective lodging of opposition, as well as the fact that the time limit to lodge opposition has not yet expired suspends the ability to enforce the default judgment, unless the court has authorised the provisional enforcement thereof.[216]

[b] Appeal[217]

[i] Admissibility

As a general rule, each judgment rendered in first instance (whether it is an interlocutory judgment, a judgment before adjudicating, a standard final judgment or a default judgment) may be subject to appeal, without prior leave by a court or other authority being required.[218] However, a statutory provision can provide that a certain decision is not appealable, such as decisions concerning the administration of the trial (i.e.,

212. Article 1047, para. 2, Judicial Code.
213. Article 1047, para. 2, Judicial Code. This formality may be abolished if all of the parties agree to appear voluntarily before the court (Article 1047, para. 3, *juncto* Article 706 Judicial Code). In some cases, opposition may be lodged by means of a petition.
214. Article 1049 Judicial Code.
215. Article 1397, para. 1, Judicial Code.
216. Article 1495, para. 2, Judicial Code.
217. Articles 1050–1072 Judicial Code.
218. Article 616 Judicial Code.

administrative measures ordered by the court with respect to the progress of proceedings) or judgments rendered by the district court.[219]

A statutory provision can also determine that a court decision is not appealable because judgment is delivered 'at first and final instance'. In this type of case, only extraordinary appellate remedies, such as a procedure before the Court of Cassation, are available. This is the case if the amount in dispute does not exceed the threshold laid down in Article 617 of the Judicial Code:[220] EUR 2,500 for judgments of the courts of first instance and the commercial courts, EUR 1,860 for judgments of the justice of the peace courts and the police courts (in civil disputes). The judgments of the labour courts, however, are always open to appeal, regardless of the monetary value of the claim.[221]

In principle, an appeal can be filed as soon as the judgment has been rendered, even if it has not yet been served.[222] In some cases, a certain waiting period has to be observed before a judgment can be appealed. Appeal against an interlocutory judgment deciding upon the competence of the court is not immediately possible, and can only be lodged together with the appeal against a decision on the admissibility or on the merits of the case.[223] The term for lodging an appeal is generally one month from the date of service (or notification) of the judgment.[224] The term of appeal is a peremptory time limit and is provided for by statute under penalty of inadmissibility, which must be pronounced by the court *sua sponte*.[225] Cross appeals (*appel incident – incidenteel beroep*) can be lodged 'at all times', meaning until the hearings are closed, provided that the principal appeal was filed in time.[226]

Appeal is only available to persons who were a party (or represented by a party) in the first instance proceedings. Appeal is not possible by third parties, not even if they are aggrieved by the judgment; only third-party opposition is available to them.[227] The respondent on appeal must also have been a party in the first instance proceedings and must have been the opponent of the appellant. The latter condition is fulfilled when the first instance judgment creates an obligation for the appellant towards that party. A cross appeal can only be filed by a party against whom a (principal or other cross) appeal is already pending. A cross appeal can be filed against all parties involved in the case before the appellate judge.[228]

---

219. Article 642 Judicial Code.
220. The monetary value of the claim is determined in accordance with Articles 618–621 *juncto* Articles 557–562 Judicial Code.
221. Article 617, para. 2, Judicial Code.
222. Article 1050, para. 1, Judicial Code.
223. Article 1050, para. 2, *juncto* Article 19, para. 1, Judicial Code. As part of a recent reform of the Judicial Code, decisions before adjudicating (e.g., decisions ordering investigation measures or measures aimed at the provisional settlement of the parties' dispute) rendered after 1 November 2015 are subject to the same rule, unless the judge decides otherwise (Article 1050, para. 2, Judicial Code).
224. Article 1051, para. 1, Judicial Code.
225. Article 860, para. 2, *juncto* Article 865 Judicial Code. Only exceptional circumstances may result in an extension or suspension of the time limit (*see supra* §5.05 [C] [2] [b]).
226. Article 1054 Judicial Code.
227. *See infra* §5.05 [C] [3] [b].
228. Article 1054, para. 1, Judicial Code.

Appeal is only available to parties in the first instance proceedings who are aggrieved by the first instance judgment. This means that the appellant must have a legitimate interest in bringing the case before the appellate court.

The notice of appeal can take on various forms[229] and must contain certain information,[230] such as the grounds for the appeal, being the grievances, complaints and reproaches of the appellant with respect to the contested judgment. The statement of the grounds of appeal may be brief, but a simple referral to the pleadings of the appellant filed during the first instance proceedings is not sufficient.

[ii] Scope of Review

Ordinary appeal submits the case to the scrutiny of a higher court, which can review and re-litigate both the facts and the legal assessments. The appellate court cannot restrict its review to questions of law, but must itself (re-)decide the case on the merits, including finding the facts in dispute. In principle, the appeal brings the whole case before the appellate court for a new and independent adjudication. All (factual and legal) issues that have not yet been decided by the first instance court are transferred to the appellate court. The case is not remanded to the first instance court. The appeal is thus said to have a 'devolutive effect'.[231] Even the appeal against a mere interlocutory judgment brings the entire dispute before the appellate court.[232] This is, however, without prejudice to the fact that the parties can restrict the scope of the appeal to designated issues (which is expressed by the Latin phrase '*tantum devolutum, quantum appellatum*').[233] The appeal also has a relative effect, meaning that it cannot have adverse effects for the party who lodges the appeal. The position of such party may only become worse at the appellate level if the other party has lodged a cross appeal.

[iii] Consequences for (Provisional) Enforcement

Until recently, the general rule was that lodging an appeal imposed a complete stay of execution of the first instance judgment, unless the first instance court authorised the (provisional) enforcement of the judgment notwithstanding an appeal. This feature of appeal proceedings was often perceived as frustrating, leading to abusive appeals only aimed at delaying the execution of the judgment. Therefore, the rule has recently been reversed. Lodging an appeal no longer stays the (provisional) execution of the

229. Article 1056 Judicial Code.
230. Article 1057 Judicial Code.
231. Article 1068, para. 1, Judicial Code.
232. There is only one exception to this rule: when the first judge has ordered an investigation measure and this decision is – even partially – affirmed, the appellate court must remand the case to the first instance judge. If the appellate court reverses the decision ordering the investigation measure, it will deliver judgment with regard to the entire case (Article 1068, para. 2, Judicial Code).
233. Free translation: 'as much is brought up on appeal as has been appealed from'.

judgment under appeal. This is only different if the first instance judge expressly ordered a deviation from this rule in a well-reasoned decision or if a statute expressly provides for an exception to the rule.[234]

[3] Extraordinary Appellate Remedies

[a] Appeal to the Court of Cassation[235]

[i] Admissibility

The Belgian judicial system provides for a further 'ultimate' recourse against judgments rendered in last instance, i.e., the petition for cassation which is to be filed before the Court of Cassation.

The petition for cassation can be filed only against judgments delivered in last instance, i.e., judgments against which it is no longer (or has never been) possible to lodge an (ordinary) appeal on points of fact and law.[236] The petitioner is not required to obtain prior leave by a court or other authority. The petition may be filed only on the grounds of violation of the law or violation of substantial procedural formalities. The petition must specify in which way and to what extent the judgment against which it is filed is not in accordance with the law. It must also precisely indicate the allegedly violated statutory provisions.[237]

The petition must be signed by an attorney admitted to practice before the Court of Cassation. A petition that is not signed by such a specialised attorney will be declared inadmissible. It is usual, before initiating cassation proceedings, to consult an attorney admitted to practice before the Court of Cassation about the chances for success of the remedy. In case of a negative advice, the intention to lodge an appeal before the Court of Cassation is mostly abandoned. However, in case a party persists in its intention, he can order an attorney before the Court of Cassation to initiate proceedings.

The petition for cassation has to be filed within three months from the date of service (or notification) of the contested judgment.[238] This term is a peremptory time limit and is provided for by statute under penalty of inadmissibility.

[ii] Scope of Review

The petition for cassation is not a second appeal or third instance procedure, but a review procedure that aims at reviewing only whether the judgment against which the petition for cassation is made is rendered in accordance with the law and the applicable

234. Article 1397, para. 2, Judicial Code.
235. Articles 1073–1121 Judicial Code.
236. Article 608 Judicial Code.
237. Article 1080 Judicial Code.
238. Article 1073 Judicial Code.

formal requirements. In other words, the Court of Cassation does not rule on the facts but only on questions of law.

The scope of review by the Court of Cassation in civil cases is set by the petitioner only. The Court has no jurisdiction regarding points of law which are not included in the petition for cassation, not even if it is apparent that the judgment against which the petition is filed contains (other) violations of the law or general principles of law.

When the petition for cassation is dismissed, the judgment against which the petition was made (including its res judicata) is preserved. If the petition is granted, the Court of Cassation quashes the judgment, in whole or in part. If the substance of the case has to be reconsidered, the case is remanded to a court of the same level as the one that rendered the quashed judgment.[239] In re-deciding the case, this court is not bound by the decision of the Court of Cassation, except when there are two subsequent cassation decisions in the same case on the same point of law.[240] In practice, however, the decisions of the Court of Cassation have a decisive influence on the creation of case law. The lower courts usually follow precedents set by the Court of Cassation and the Court of Cassation only exceptionally overrules its own precedents.

[iii] Consequences for Enforcement

In civil cases, the filing of a petition for cassation does not entail a stay of the enforcement of the contested judgment, unless a statutory provision expressly provides otherwise.[241]

[b] Third-Party Opposition[242]

Third-party opposition is only available to persons whose rights are adversely affected by a judgment rendered pursuant to proceedings to which they were not a party.[243] All judgments may be subject to third-party opposition, except for decisions of the Court of Cassation.[244] Third-party opposition has to be brought before the judge who rendered the contested judgment[245] within three months from the date of the service of the judgment on the third party.[246] If the remedy is successful, the judge shall annul the judgment, but only *vis-à-vis* the third party. In principle, the annulment does not affect the (res judicata of the) judgment between the original parties to the case.[247]

239. Article 1110 Judicial Code.
240. Article 1120 Judicial Code.
241. Article 1118 Judicial Code.
242. Articles 1122–1131 Judicial Code.
243. Article 1122 Judicial Code.
244. Article 1123 Judicial Code.
245. By serving a writ of summons upon all the parties in the original action (Article 1125, para. 1, Judicial Code).
246. Article 1129 Judicial Code.
247. Article 1130, para. 1, Judicial Code.

[c] *Revocation of Res Judicata*[248]

This extraordinary legal remedy is subject to very strict conditions. The grounds on the basis of which a party may request the revocation of a judgment's res judicata are listed exhaustively in Article 1133 of the Judicial Code and relate, *inter alia*, to situations where the judgment is vitiated by fraud or withholding of evidence by one of the parties or false testimonies of witnesses or court-appointed experts. The request is introduced by means of a petition, which must be signed by three attorneys, two of whom must have been members of the bar for at least twenty years.[249] The petition is served with a writ of summons to appear before the court that rendered the judgment. It must be brought within six months after discovery of the facts on which the request for revocation is based.[250]

[d] *Redress Against the Judge*[251]

In a limited number of cases, a party may file a direct civil liability claim against the judge (or the public prosecution service). Article 1140 of the Judicial Code provides for an exhaustive list of circumstances where such action against a judge can be undertaken (e.g., if the judge committed fraud or refused to render judgment). The claim has to be brought before the Court of Cassation.[252] If the claim is found to be grounded, the Court can either annul the judgment (if any) or order the judge to pay damages.[253]

[e] *Repeal*[254]

The repeal is a legal remedy that can be applied against judgments that are based on a statutory or regulatory provision which has subsequently been nullified by the Constitutional Court.[255] The action is brought before the court that rendered the judgment. This court may, within the limits of the repeal, pronounce a new judgment based on a different legal ground.

§5.06 EVIDENCE

[A] Burden of Proof and Admissibility of Evidence

The basic (procedural) rule regarding the burden of proof in civil cases is laid down in Article 870 of the Judicial Code: every party has the burden to adduce evidence for his

248. Articles 1132–1139 Judicial Code.
249. Article 1134 Judicial Code.
250. Article 1136 Judicial Code.
251. Articles 1140–1147 Judicial Code.
252. Article 1143 Judicial Code.
253. Article 1147 Judicial Code.
254. The rules regarding the repeal are laid down in Article 16 of the Special Act of 6 January 1989 on the Constitutional Court.
255. *See supra* §5.02 [E].

allegations. In other words, each party has to prove his claim. Contrary to for example American law,[256] Belgian law does not provide for different standards of proof.

Only facts in dispute need to be proved. Facts of general knowledge must not be proved. Foreign law is regarded as a question of law, not as a matter of fact to be proven.[257] The judge has to decide the case on the basis of the rules of evidence applicable to the type of action concerned.[258] The action will either be civil or commercial. The law of evidence in civil matters is described in Articles 1315 et seq. of the Civil Code. It is a closed system with tightly regulated forms of evidence ruled by a strict hierarchy. The law of evidence in commercial law is described in Article 25 of the Commercial Code. It is an open system with open forms of evidence.[259]

The rules regarding evidence are in principle supplementary rules, meaning that the parties may validly derogate from those rules by mutual agreement.

[B] Discovery and Disclosure

Since Belgium has a civil law tradition, rules regarding evidence are not as elaborate as in most common law countries. There is no formal pre-trial discovery in civil proceedings, nor does the Judicial Code contain any specific rules as to the preservation of evidence.[260]

With respect to disclosure, each party must disclose and allow inspection of all documents on which they wish to rely. Failure to disclose will result in a stay of the proceedings.[261] Despite the fact that there is no obligation to submit evidence which might adversely affect one's case (or support the opponent's case), the fair-play principle requires parties to collaborate in good faith in the delivery and gathering of evidence.

[C] Administration of Evidence

As far as the administration of evidence goes, the judge is the master of the proceedings. If the parties fail to produce (sufficient) evidence allowing to grant or reject the claim, it is up to the judge to order any additional investigation measure which may provide him with more certainty as to the substance of the claim.[262] The most important techniques on the delivery and gathering of evidence are the following.

256. Where there are different standards of proof in different circumstances (e.g., 'preponderance of the evidence' and 'clear and convincing evidence').
257. Court of Cassation 9 October 1980, AR 6142, 1980–1981 Arresten van het Hof van Cassatie 142, 1981 Pasicrisie belge 159. *See also* Article 15 Code of Private International Law.
258. Article 876 Judicial Code.
259. *See infra* Chapter 12, §12.02 [A].
260. If urgency or the necessity of a 'surprise' effect (e.g., in order to prevent the destruction, spoliation or alteration of evidence) can be demonstrated, one may seek an injunction to preserve evidence before the president of the court. *See supra* §5.05 [B] [4].
261. Article 736 Judicial Code.
262. With due regard to the principle of subsidiarity (Article 875*bis* Judicial Code), meaning that the judge must choose the quickest, cheapest and most simple method of inquiry, taking into account the economic value of the claim.

[1] Forced Production of Documents[263]

The judge can order a party, or even a third party, to submit certain documents which could constitute proof of certain facts relevant to the outcome of the case. The forced production of documentary evidence may only be ordered if there are serious, precise and concurring reasons to believe that the person concerned is in possession thereof.

[2] Testimony of Witnesses[264]

The judge can order a witness testimony if a party proposes to establish certain specific and relevant facts by means of a witness. The judge may also order a witness testimony ex officio. Witnesses are obliged to testify, unless they have a justified reason (e.g., professional secrecy) not to do so. The witness examination is conducted under oath; false testimony constitutes a punishable offence.[265] Contrary to for example the English system of trial, the witness is interrogated by the judge. There is no cross-examination by the parties (or their counsel). Nevertheless, parties can request the judge to ask certain questions to the witness that may clarify or complete the latter's testimony.

[3] Testimony by the Parties Themselves[266]

Usually, parties do not appear in person at court hearings in civil or commercial cases, but are mostly represented by their counsel. The judge can, however, even on his own initiative, order the parties (or one of them) to appear in court with a view to an oral examination. Said examination is not conducted under oath, so prosecution for perjury is not possible.

[4] Expert Evidence[267]

Contrary to other (such as common law) systems, Belgian courts mostly rely on court-appointed experts. Parties can present their own expert evidence, but this is not considered to be objective. Therefore, in most cases where there is a technical dispute, the court will appoint an expert. The expert's mission is limited to the delivery of an independent and impartial advice on technical issues. The court cannot request the expert to render legal advice as to the merits of the case.[268] Accordingly, the court is not

263. Articles 877–882 Judicial Code.
264. Articles 915–961 Judicial Code. *See also* Articles 961/1-3 Judicial Code, which provide for the submission of written testimonies as a means of evidence.
265. Article 220 Penal Code.
266. Articles 992–1004 Judicial Code. Special rules apply regarding the hearing of minors (Articles 1004/1-2 Judicial Code). *See infra* Chapter 7, §7.03 [D].
267. Articles 962–991*bis* Judicial Code.
268. Article 11, para. 1, Judicial Code.

bound by the expert findings, which may be contested by the parties (although, in practice, the court will mostly attach great importance to the expert report provided that it has been drafted regularly). An important feature of the expert investigation is its adversarial nature. This means that the expert must give the parties the opportunity to present their arguments before the filing of the expert report with the court.

[5] On-Site Inspection by the Judge[269]

The judge can order an official visit to the scene and thereby perform certain fact finding operations. The justice of the peace, for instance, frequently resorts to this measure in rental damage cases.

§5.07 ENFORCEMENT OF JUDGMENTS

[A] Enforcement of Domestic Judgments

[1] General

The losing party is expected to satisfy or comply voluntarily with a judgment that is (provisionally) enforceable, but if he fails to do so, the prevailing party may have it enforced on him. If the obligation of the losing party relates to the delivery of a good or the payment of a sum of money, the prevailing party may proceed to the attachment of the losing party's (movable and/or immovable) property. The attachment may also relate to amounts or goods owed by a third party (for instance the debtor's employer) to the debtor.

[2] Leading Role for the Bailiff

The enforcement of judgments requires the intervention of a bailiff on two fronts. First of all, a judgment can only be enforced after it has been served on the debtor by a bailiff.[270] This is to ensure that the debtor is fully aware of the judgment and the fact that the opposite party pursues its enforcement.[271] Further on, the seizure itself is also performed by a bailiff at the request of the creditor. The seizure must be preceded by a formal order of payment served on the debtor.[272] This order is intended as a last warning and last opportunity for the debtor to comply with the judgment voluntarily. If the debtor fails to do so, the bailiff will proceed with the seizure and subsequent (public) sale of the goods of the debtor.

---

269. Articles 1007–1016 Judicial Code.
270. Article 1495, para. 1, Judicial Code.
271. The service of the judgment also triggers the running of the statutory time limit for seeking review (*see supra* §5.05 [B] [2] [b]).
272. The judgment and the payment order are usually served together at the same time.

[3] *Role of the Judge of Attachments*

In principle, enforcement measures in execution of a judgment (or other enforceable title) do not require the prior authorisation or intervention of the judge of attachments (or any other judge). However, any party may bring an action before this specialised judge if a dispute arises in relation to the execution.[273]

[4] *Consignment*

The debtor, who has lodged an appeal or opposition against the judgment of which the (provisional) enforcement is sought, has the right to prevent or release the seizure of his assets by depositing an amount sufficient to cover the debt in principal, interest and charges, at the Deposit and Consignation Office (or with a sequestrator appointed for this purpose or with the bailiff acting on behalf of the creditor), unless this right has been explicitly excluded by the judge.[274] This consignment is to be considered as a conditional payment of the debt.

[5] *Unseizable Amounts and Property*

Article 1408 of the Judicial Code contains a list of goods which cannot be seized from the debtor. In essence, they are goods and utensils necessary for everyday life and employment. Due to evolving social and economic circumstances, however, the list has become rather outdated. Pursuant to Article 1409 of the Judicial Code the amount of income from employment which may be seized is subject to certain limitations (which are indexed annually).[275] Articles 1412*bis–quinquies* of the Judicial Code also provide for a particular enforcement immunity in favour of goods belonging to government entities and foreign states.

[6] *Publicity*

As of 31 January 2011, all reports in respect of seizure are centralised in a digital database, the so-called Central Database of Reports concerning Attachments.[276] Up until then, seizure reports were only collected and retained in hard copy at the courts' registries. Hence, a trip to the court was required in order to have access to seizure information. Moreover, as seizure reports were held per local court, a change of the debtor's address was sufficient to enable him to 'start over' with a spotless seizure record. The Central Database responds to these deficiencies. Further on, it allows

273. Article 1395 *juncto* Article 1498 Judicial Code.
274. Articles 1403–1407*bis* Judicial Code.
275. These limitations do not apply, however, to maintenance creditors, who are said to have a 'super-privilege' in respect of maintenance claims (Article 1412 Judicial Code).
276. Articles 1389*bis*/1–18 and 1390–1391 Judicial Code.

preventing attachment against debtors whose property has already been seized, with all the unnecessary expenses that entails.

[7] Non-compliance Penalties

In principle, each creditor has a right to restitution in kind. However, the obligation of the debtor which consists of the duty to perform or refrain from a certain action cannot be enforced by institutionalised force. To solve this problem, the creditor could request the court for authorisation for having the action performed by a third party at the expense of the debtor, but this does not often happen in practice. It is more common that the creditor requests the court to impose a non-compliance penalty (*astreinte – dwangsom*) to be paid in the event that the debtor does not voluntarily comply with the judgment.[277] The penalty is an additional conviction, serving as an incentive for the debtor to execute his main conviction. The court can impose a periodical penalty (due per time unit or per established breach) or a lump sum (which is due at once). The court cannot impose a non-compliance penalty on its own initiative, but it may ex officio raise or lower the amount requested by a party, depending on what it considers being appropriate under the circumstances. The penalty is collected by the party to whom it has been granted. It can be requested in all cases, except where the main claim relates to the performance of a labour contract or the payment of a sum of money.

[B] Recognition and Enforcement of Foreign Judgments[278]

Roughly speaking, the recognition and enforcement of a foreign court's decision may be governed by: (1) EU regulations, of which the most important one in this area[279] is the Brussels I-Regulation No. 44/2011 of 22 December 2000,[280] which was recast by the Brussels *Ibis*-Regulation No. 1215/2012 of 12 December 2012;[281] (2) international and bilateral treaties;[282] or (3) the Belgian Code of Private International Law of 2004, applicable in cases for which there is no regulation or treaty between Belgium and the state where the judgment was given.

These instruments generally provide for an automatic (*de plano*) recognition of foreign judgments – meaning that a foreign judgment has the same legal effects in

277. The rules regarding the non-compliance penalty, which are laid down in Articles 1385*bis* et seq. Judicial Code, originate from the Benelux Convention of 26 November 1973 on the Uniform Law on Non-Compliance Penalties. Accordingly, the case law of the Benelux Court of Justice is of utmost importance for the application and interpretation of the rules.
278. *See also infra* Chapter 16, §16.06.
279. For some areas, specific EU regulations have been issued. To name but one: Regulation No. 2201/2003 of 27 November 2003 concerning Jurisdiction and the Recognition and Enforcement of Judgments in Matrimonial Matters and the Matters of Parental Responsibility (Official Journal L338/1 of 2003).
280. Official Journal L12/1 of 2001.
281. Official Journal L351/1 of 2012.
282. For instance, the Lugano Convention of 21 December 2007 (Official Journal L339/3 of 2007) regarding the Recognition and Enforcement of Judgments in Civil and Commercial Matters given in Iceland, Norway and Switzerland.

Belgium as in the state where it was rendered – without there being a need for a special (preliminary) procedure before the Belgian courts.

On the other hand, the enforcement of a foreign judgment generally requires the assistance of the Belgian courts, to which an application must be made for the granting of a declaration of enforceability ('exequatur'). The Code of Private International Law, for instance, provides for an (*ex parte*) exequatur procedure, which is to be initiated before the competent court of first instance.[283] The Brussels I-Regulation also provides for an (*ex parte*) exequatur procedure, but the formalities are simplified, thus allowing the swift enforcement of a judgment rendered by a court in another Member State. The new Brussels I*bis*-Regulation, which is only applicable to proceedings initiated on or after 10 January 2015, has even abolished the need for an exequatur. This implies that a judgment given in a Member State shall be enforceable in another Member State without any special procedure or declaration of enforceability being required. The creditor only needs to obtain a 'certificate' in the Member State in which the judgment is rendered (certifying that the judgment is enforceable in that Member State), which is to be served on the debtor, together with the judgment. Other European instruments which provide for enforcement without exequatur are the European Enforcement Order for Uncontested Claims,[284] the European Small Claims Procedure[285] and the European Order for Payment Procedure.[286] These instruments, however, have not enjoyed great success in Belgium.

While the recognition or enforcement of a foreign judgment does not imply under any circumstances a review of its merits, the Belgian courts may refuse such recognition or enforcement if the foreign judgment infringes upon one or more of the grounds for refusal, as defined in the applicable legal instrument (for instance if the result of such recognition or enforcement is manifestly incompatible with Belgian (international) public policy).[287]

§5.08 ARBITRATION

[A] UNCITRAL Model Law

Parties may grant the power of adjudication to an arbitration tribunal, provided that the dispute is susceptible to settlement. The rules on arbitration, which are incorporated in the Judicial Code,[288] are largely inspired on the UNCITRAL Model Law. They apply equally to both national and international arbitration. Most of the rules are of a

283. Article 23 Code of Private International Law *juncto* Article 570 Judicial Code.
284. Official Journal L143/15 of 2004.
285. Official Journal L199/1 of 2007.
286. Official Journal L399/1 of 2006.
287. *See*, for instance, the refusal grounds listed in Article 45 Brussels I*bis*-Regulation and Article 25 Code of Private International Law.
288. Part VI ('Arbitration') of the Judicial Code (Articles 1676–1723). An (unofficial) English version is available at www.cepani.be/en/arbitration/belgian-judicial-code-provisions (accessed 15 July 2016).

supplementary nature, meaning that parties are free to deviate from them in the arbitration agreement.[289]

[B] Arbitration Procedure

Both the composition of the arbitration tribunal and the procedural rules to be followed by that tribunal may be freely agreed upon by the parties, with the understanding that the guarantee of due process may not be compromised. The only statutory requirement is that the arbitration tribunal must be composed of an odd number of arbitrators.[290]

The arbitration tribunal decides the dispute in accordance with the rules of law chosen by the parties. Failing any designation by the parties, the tribunal shall apply the law determined by the rules of private international law which it considers applicable.[291]

[C] Arbitral Award

An arbitral award is binding upon the parties and can serve as the basis for a preliminary attachment, but it is not an enforceable instrument in itself. The award can only be enforced after it has been given executive force (exequatur) by the court of first instance.[292]

Appeal against an arbitral award is only possible if the parties have provided for that possibility in the arbitration agreement.[293] Parties may also, in a limited number of cases, challenge the arbitral award through an annulment procedure before the court of first instance, provided that the award can no longer be challenged before the arbitrators.[294]

§5.09 MEDIATION

Every dispute that is susceptible to settlement may be submitted to mediation. Mediation leaves the control of the outcome of the dispute with the parties. Contrary to a judge, a mediator does not impose a solution, but assists the parties in communicating with each other so they can try to settle the dispute themselves. The rules on mediation form an integral part of the Judicial Code.[295]

Parties are, in all circumstances, free to choose for mediation, as well as to end it (without prejudice). The distinction in the Judicial Code between what is called

289. The arbitration agreement must not be made in writing, but the burden of proof of its existence lies with the party who wants to rely on it (Article 1681 Judicial Code).
290. A sole arbitrator is allowed (Article 1684, §1, Judicial Code).
291. Article 1710, §2, Judicial Code.
292. Articles 1719–1721 Judicial Code.
293. Article 1716 Judicial Code.
294. Article 1717 Judicial Code.
295. Part VII ('Mediation') of the Judicial Code (Articles 1724–1737). An (unofficial) English version is available at http://www.cepani.be/en/mediation/belgian-legislation (accessed 15 July 2016).

'voluntary' mediation[296] and 'judicial' mediation[297] is therefore poorly chosen, as it suggests that judicial mediation without the voluntary consent of the parties is possible, which is actually not the case. Judicial mediation means that the mediation is ordered by the judge in the framework of pending court proceedings but with the consent of the parties, whereas voluntary mediation implies that the choice for mediation is made without any involvement of a judge.

If parties agree to mediation, a mediation protocol must be drafted. It constitutes the framework in which the parties, with the assistance of the mediator, mutually determine the rules for the conduct of the mediation, and acts as a contract between them.[298]

Successful mediation results in a settlement agreement, which is laid down in a document dated and signed by the parties and the mediator. The parties (or one of them) may ask the competent state court[299] to homologate the settlement agreement, making it enforceable as a 'regular' judgment. Homologation can only be granted if parties have concluded a mediation protocol (which fulfils the statutory requirements) and if the mediation was conducted by an accredited mediator. The substantive grounds for refusal of homologation are limited. Homologation may be refused only if the settlement agreement is contrary to public policy or, in the case of a mediation in family matters, if the agreement is against the interests of underage children.[300]

There is a Federal Mediation Commission, with as its main mission to supervise the development and quality of the mediation procedures and mediators. As such, it is charged with, *inter alia*, the accreditation of mediators.

§5.10 SELECTED BIBLIOGRAPHY

B. Allemeersch, *Taakverdeling in het burgerlijk proces* (Antwerp: Intersentia 2007).

K. Broeckx, *Het recht op hoger beroep en het beginsel van de dubbele aanleg in het civiele geding* (Antwerp: Maklu 1995).

G. de Leval, *Eléments de procédure civile* (Brussels: Larcier 2005).

E. Dirix & K. Broeckx, *Beslag* (Algemene Praktische Rechtsverzameling, Mechelen: Kluwer 2010).

A. Fettweis, *Manuel de procédure civile* (Liège: Fac. Droit Liège 1987).

J. Laenens, D. Scheers, P. Thiriar, S. Rutten & B. Vanlerberghe, *Handboek gerechtelijk recht* (Antwerp: Intersentia 2016).

M. Piers & D. De Meulemeester, *A New Arbitration Law in Belgium: UNCITRAL Enters the Scene*, 25 The American Review of International Arbitration 63–83 (2014).

P. Taelman, *Het gezag van het rechterlijk gewijsde: Een begrippenstudie* (Diegem: Kluwer 2001).

296. Articles 1730–1733 Judicial Code.
297. Articles 1734–1737 Judicial Code.
298. Article 1731 Judicial Code.
299. That is the court that would have had jurisdiction if the dispute had been submitted to it without mediation taking place.
300. Articles 1733, para. 2, and 1736, para. 4, Judicial Code.

P. Taelman & S. Voet, *Mediation in Belgium: A Long and Winding Road*, *in New Developments in Civil and Commercial Mediation* 89–112 (C. Esplugues & L. Marquis eds., Heidelberg: Springer 2015).

Droit judiciaire, Vol. I, *Institutions judiciaires et éléments de compétence* (G. de Leval & F. Georges eds., Brussels: Larcier 2014).

Droit judiciaire, Vol. II, *Manuel de procédure civile* (G. de Leval ed., Brussels: Larcier 2015).

CHAPTER 6

Criminal Law

Joëlle Rozie

§6.01 THE BELGIAN PENAL CODE

When Belgium became independent in 1830, the French Penal Code was the applicable law.

Minister Haussy appointed a commission in 1848 charged with the profound reform of criminal law and the framing of a draft of a new penal code. Haus and Nypels in particular were the leading figures of the reform commission. Parliament started discussions on the document drafted by this commission in 1851. The Belgian Penal Code (*Code pénal – Strafwetboek*) came into force in 1867. The remarkable bills and explanatory statements of Haus and the legislative history are extremely important for the doctrine. They were coordinated by Nypels.[1]

The Penal Code of 1867 is permeated by the principles of the classical school. The Penal Code contains two books. The first book concerns the offences (*infractions – misdrijven*) and their punishment in general. It contains the general principles relating to the penalisation and the punishment of all the offences, as defined in the second book and in the separate statutes, which apply except when divergent provisions are provided for specific cases,[2] except for the application of Article 100 of the Penal Code and divergent provisions.

This book contains ten chapters (Articles 1–99) plus Articles 100 and 100*bis*:

- I. Offences (*infractions – misdrijven*)
- II. Punishments (*peines – straffen*)

1. NYPELS, LÉGISLATION CRIMINELLE DE BELGIQUE, 4 volumes (Brussels 1867–1870).
2. Article 100 Penal Code.

- III. Other judgments which can be passed because of felonies (*crimes – misdaden*), misdemeanours (*délits – wanbedrijven*) and contraventions (*contraventions – overtredingen*)
- IV. Attempt to commit a felony or misdemeanour (*tentative – poging*)
- V. Recidivism (*récidive – herhaling*)
- VI. Concurrence (*concours – samenloop*)
- VII. Participation of several persons in a felony or misdemeanour (*participation – deelneming*)
- VIII. Grounds of justification and grounds of excuse (*causes de justification et d'excuse – rechtvaardigings- en verschoningsgronden*)
- IX. Extenuating circumstances (*circonstances atténuantes – verzachtende omstandigheden*)
- X. Extinction of punishments (*extinction des peines – tenietgaan van de straffen*).

The second book lists the offences and their punishments in particular. It contains ten titles, the first nine relate to felonies and misdemeanours and the last to contraventions.

The Penal Code, which has not been fundamentally modified since 1867, is at present the object of a global reform. The two members of the reform commission are Damien Vandermeersch and Joëlle Rozie.[3]

§6.02 CRIMINAL LAW

[A] Principle of Legality

Article 15 of the International Covenant on Civil and Political Rights and Article 7 of the ECHR provide that no one shall be held guilty of any criminal offence on account of any act or omission which did not constitute a criminal offence, under national or international law, at the time it was committed. Article 12, paragraph 2, and Article 14 of the Belgian Constitution provide that no one shall be prosecuted except in the situations provided by statute and that no punishment shall be introduced and applied save by virtue of a statute. These international provisions and constitutional rules establish the principle of legality, which lies at the root of Belgian criminal law, of the penalisations and the punishments. Article 2, paragraph 1, of the Penal Code contains an affirmation of the principle of legality:

> No offence shall be punished with punishments which were not applicable at the time the criminal offence was committed.

[B] Application of Criminal Law *Ratione Temporis*

Criminal law is modified or abrogated as a reaction to the evolution of the social or economic situation, of the ethical conceptions and of the changing characteristics of

3. Ministerial Decree of 30 October 2015, Moniteur belge – Belgisch Staatsblad, 29 December 2015.

delinquency itself. As a consequence, new offences are introduced, existing penalisations are abrogated, the punishments are tightened or relaxed, and existing offences are adapted to new situations.

Which law must be applied? That is the question of the conflict of criminal laws *ratione temporis*.

Article 2 of the Penal Code states:

> No offence shall be punished with punishments that were not applicable at the time the criminal offence was committed. In case the punishment applicable at the time of sentencing is different from the punishment that was in effect at the time the criminal offence was committed, the most lenient shall be applied.

This article contains a general principle of non-retroactivity of criminal law and an exception to this rule, providing retroactivity of the more lenient criminal law. The wording of Article 2 of the Penal Code only refers to the situation in which the punishment at the time of sentencing is different, but it is generally accepted that this rule concerns the punishment, as well as the penalisation.

The *rule of non-retroactivity* is an application of the principle of legality, under which no one shall be punished for an act that was not prohibited at the time it was committed, nor shall a heavier punishment be imposed than the one that was applicable at the time the criminal offence was committed.

The *retroactivity of the more lenient law* implies that a new statute has retroactive effect in case it is more lenient than the one which was in force when the offence was committed, either because the punishment is less severe or because an act is no longer prohibited. This concept is founded on grounds of justice and humanitarian reflections.

[C] Application of Criminal Law *Ratione Loci*

Apart from the principles of legality and the rule of non-retroactivity it is also required that the criminal law is binding at the place where the offence is committed.

Article 3 of the Penal Code states the principle of territoriality: Belgian criminal law is only applicable to all offences committed on Belgian territory, by whomever they are committed, save the exceptions provided by national statute or international treaties. Article 4 of the Penal Code derogates from this principle. It extends the scope of application of Belgian criminal law to offences committed abroad by whomever they are committed - Belgians or foreigners - but only in the situations and on the conditions provided by statute.

[D] Application of Criminal Law *Ratione Personae*

All Belgians are equal before the law.[4]

On the other hand, the principle of territoriality implies that the provisions of Belgian law are also applied to foreigners who commit offences in Belgium.

4. Article 10 Constitution.

Article 13 of the Constitution provides also that no one can be withdrawn from a judge that is granted by law. Nevertheless there are immunities deriving from the Constitution, statutes, international usages and treaties. These immunities concern criminal law and criminal procedure, as well as constitutional law and international public law.

Immunity is granted to the King, members of parliaments, the foreign heads of state and the diplomatic, consular and international officials.

§6.03 THE OFFENCE

[A] Elements of the Offence

Every offence (*misdrijf – infraction*) has two parts. The prerequisites for the existence of a criminal offence are a material and a moral element.

[1] Material Element

The criminal statute describes the contents of the material element. Sometimes mention of the juridical name of the offence, whereof the elements are normally well known, is sufficient.[5] Sometimes the statute enumerates the elements of the criminal conduct, but no juridical name is given for the offence.[6] Sometimes the statute gives the constituent elements of the offence plus a juridical qualification.[7]

The offences may be distinguished as offences of commission or of omission, depending on whether the prohibited conduct is an act or an omission. The fraudulent organisation of insolvency[8] usually supposes positive actions (embezzlement of goods), but the offence could also be defined in terms of abstinence (refusal to raise wages). This is called an offence of commission by omission.

[2] Moral Element

The Penal Code gives no general definition of the moral element, and the practice of the Court of Cassation is not clear.

There are two theories in the doctrinal literature.

[a] Classical Theory

The common classical doctrine distinguishes two types of guilt: *intent* (defined in many variants) and *negligence*.

5. For instance Article 372 Penal Code: indecent assault.
6. For instance Articles 508*bis* and 508*ter* Penal Code: the so-called swindle (*grivèlerie – afzetterij*).
7. For instance Articles 393–394 Penal Code: homicide and murder (*homicide et meurtre – doodslag en moord*); Article 461 Penal Code: theft (*vol – diefstal*).
8. Article 490*bis* Penal Code.

In an intentional offence the moral element consists of the goal-directed aim to develop a conduct (act or omission) which is prohibited or commanded by law.[9] An offence of negligence or an unintentional offence requires that the offender accepts the act or the omission, but not its consequences, even if he was able to foresee or had foreseen them.[10]

Besides the intentional and unintentional offences there is also a third category of offences for which no intent or negligence is required, as it is sufficient that the offence was materially committed. It concerns mainly the contraventions and some misdemeanours embodied in separate statutes (e.g., in matters of social or environmental law), the so-called contraventional misdemeanours or material offences.

[b] Theory of Legros

According to Legros[11] only a violation of the criminal law is required, a guilt by transgression of the law, when the law does not define the moral element. However, the perpetrator of such offences could appeal to a mistake of fact or law, or to duress in order to escape from punishment. He further rejects the notion 'general intent' (*dol général – algemeen opzet*).

According to him this concept has only a negative content. The notion 'knowingly' concerns the absence of a mistake of fact or law, and the term 'willingly' implies that the offender did not act under duress. He thus points out that the supposedly required general intent merely corresponds to the absence of a ground of exemption of guilt (*cause d'exemption de culpabilité – schuldontheffingsgrond*). Legros proposes substituting the notion 'guilt by transgression of the law' for the term 'general intent'.

[B] Classification of Offences

[1] Tripartite Classification

The Penal Code distinguishes three types of offences: felonies, misdemeanours and contraventions.[12]

Felonies (*crimes – misdaden*) are offences carrying a criminal punishment (*peine criminelle – criminele straf*). Misdemeanours (*délits – wanbedrijven*) are offences carrying a correctional punishment (*peine correctionnelle – correctionele straf*). Contraventions (*contraventions – overtredingen*) are offences carrying a police punishment (*peine de police – politiestraf*).

The relevant criterion for the classification of offences is in the first place the punishment they carry. But this so-called legal tripartite classification has a provisional character.

9. For example Article 398 Penal Code: causing grievous bodily harm with intent.
10. For example Article 418 Penal Code: unlawful wounding.
11. R. Legros, L'élément moral dans les infractions (Liège: Sirey-Desoer 1952).
12. Article 1 Penal Code.

The nature of the offence can indeed be changed during the procedure, as well as by virtue of a definitive sentence of the court. Despite the words of Article 1 of the Penal Code it is the punishment that is inflicted by virtue of an irrevocable sentence that determines the nature of the offence. Aggravating circumstances could alter the nature of an offence. Circumstances which have a mitigating effect such as extenuating circumstances or mitigating grounds of excuse, could also change the classification of an offence.

[2] Other Classifications

Besides the legal tripartite classification of offences there are also some doctrinal classifications based on various criteria such as the intrinsic nature of the offence or its material execution.

[a] Classification Based on the Intrinsic Nature of the Offence

[i] Political Offences

The Court of Cassation distinguishes two kinds of political offences: the objective and the miscellaneous political offences. This differentiation is based on two doctrinal theories.

The first considers the nature of the offence itself as decisive (objective theory) and the second believes the offender's motive is significant (subjective theory).

Objective political offences are directly and exclusively directed against the interior political system, for example, against the organisation or the working of the branches of government, the political institutions including the citizen's rights, or against the external political order.

On the other hand, *miscellaneous political offences* acquire a political character because of the offender's motive and because they directly attack the political system. This is the case with the offence of forgery in public or private deeds with the intent to falsely achieve the recognition of one's suffrage.[13]

The prerequisites for the miscellaneous political offences are that the offender must have the specific intent to make an assault on the political order, and the conduct must directly and immediately result in (potential) political harm.

[ii] Offences Committed by Means of the Press

The liberty of the press is curtailed by the prohibition to use this form of freedom of speech to commit offences.

An offence committed by means of the press is a common offence distinguishable from the other offences because of its mode of execution. The punishable expression of

13. Article 196 Penal Code.

an idea or opinion in printed and published writings constitutes an offence committed by means of the press. The punishable thought, to which a real publicity is given, must be uttered by means of the press.

[b] Classification Based on the Material Execution of the Offence

[i] Terminable and Permanent Offences

A terminable (*instantanée – aflopend*) or momentary offence, as described by law, is an offence that is accomplished at a certain moment by one simple fact, such as intentional and unintentional wounding, fraudulent organisation of the insolvency, concealment or bigamy.

A permanent (*continue – voortdurend*) offence implies an uninterrupted and continuous punishable situation, for example abandonment of family,[14] desertion,[15] and maintenance of a construction without permission.[16]

[ii] Singular and Continuous (or Collective) Offences

A singular (*simple – enkelvoudig*) offence consists in one simple act or omission which can be terminable or permanent (e.g., theft, abandonment of family).

A continuous (*continuée – voortgezet*) or collective (*collective – collectief*) offence is an offence which consists of several similar (a continuous offence) or different (a collective offence) punishable conducts. These punishable conducts together constitute one offence because of the unity of intent present in the person of the offender, for example, the removal of several objects by thefts committed on several occasions is a continuous offence; the theft of cheques, forgery by signing cheques with a false name, and swindle of money and goods by means of the false cheques constitute a collective offence.

The qualification of offences as a permanent, a continuous or a collective offence is extremely important for the punishment, the prescription of the prosecution, and the application of the criminal law *ratione temporis* and *ratione loci*.

[C] Aggravating Circumstances

The judge adjusts the punishment to the concrete seriousness of the offence and to the offender's personality based on all sorts of factual circumstances unspecified by law. If there are extenuating circumstances, the judge will pronounce a punishment closer to the legal minimum or even below it, or may grant suspension or delay. On the other hand, if there are aggravating circumstances (criminal antecedents, harm caused,

14. Article 391*bis* Penal Code.
15. Article 43 Military Penal Code.
16. Article 64 Territorial Planning and Urbanisation Act of 29 March 1962.

extraordinary reprehensible character of the offence), the judge will pronounce a punishment that is closer to the legal maximum, and this maximum may not be exceeded.

Besides factual elements, there also are legal aggravating circumstances: these are circumstances provided by law, and they constitute additional elements of a distinct, more serious offence. They automatically result in a specific aggravation of the punishment.

[D] Punishable Attempt

An offence is only committed if all the elements of the punishable conduct are united. Attempts to commit an offence, however, can also be punishable.

According to Article 51 of the Penal Code, a punishable attempt of an offence requires three elements: criminal intent, a beginning of execution of the offence, and the non-completion of the offence for a cause other than the offender's decision.

[1] Intent

The offender must have been resolved to commit the offence. His decision to engage in the conduct in question must be definite, even though the offence was not completed because of unforeseen obstacles over which the offender had no control.

[2] Beginning of Execution

Just preparatory acts are not enough to constitute a punishable attempt. Theoretically, the differentiation between preparatory acts and acts constituting elements of the offence is still a matter of some controversy. According to the objective doctrine there needs to be a commencement of one of the prerequisites of the punishable offence. According to the subjectivists a person is deemed to have begun a criminal attempt when, circumstances of time and place considered, he has shown himself psychologically able to commit the offence. The court practices have opted for a mixed objective-subjective system. The limit between preparatory acts and the beginning of execution should be drawn when it can be ascertained that an offender tends to commit the offence, all circumstances considered.

[3] Non-completion

The absence of voluntary withdrawal is a specific element of the punishable attempt. Pursuant to considerations of criminal policy an offender who has commenced committing an offence shall not be punished for it if he voluntary desists before he has completed all the constituent elements or prevents the completion of the offence. The reasons for aborting the offence are irrelevant (repentance, fear of the consequences, etc. ...), but the withdrawal must result from an action of the will.[17]

[E] Grounds of Justification

[1] General Notion

An act containing all the constituent elements of an offence is in principle unlawful. Grounds of justification are circumstances, recognised by law, that eliminate the *unlawfulness* of the act. Grounds of justification have a general scope: they apply to all offences.

[2] The Different Grounds of Justification

[a] Order of Law and Command of Authority

According to Article 70 of the Penal Code, 'there is no offence when the act is provided by law and commanded by the authority'.

'There is no offence...' means that the act is not unlawful. For instance, if a locksmith bursts a door for a house search by the police, there is no infringement of Article 545 of the Penal Code nor of Article 439 of the Penal Code.

The term 'law' needs to be understood in the larger sense of the word: it is not limited to rules imposed by statute.

The notions 'provided by law' imply the order of law, as well as the explicit permission by law[18] or the implicit permission by law (e.g., medical acts covered by the definition of indecent assault or inflicting grievous bodily harm, or unlawful wounding caused by sporting activities). 'Commanded by the authority' means that the command needs to be given in accordance with the law and that it needs to emanate from a legal public authority that acts within its competence.

[b] Legitimate Defence

There is no felony or misdemeanour if the homicide or the inflicting of grievous bodily harm is dictated by the immediate necessity of legal self-defence and defence of others.[19]

Article 417 of the Penal Code mentions two different cases of legitimate defence. They concern the repelling of attacks against property involving assault or serious menaces directed against persons. Legitimate defence implies several prerequisites: the attack must be directed against persons, it must be unlawful, it must be serious and actual, and the defence must be necessary and proportionate.

17. Article 51 Penal Code.
18. Article 458 Penal Code.
19. Article 416 Penal Code.

[c] *State of Necessity*

Necessity is not provided by statute, but it is recognised as a ground of justification by literature and applied by the courts.

The state of necessity implies that the commission of an offence is not unlawful if it is committed to avert a serious and imminent danger to a legally protected interest, which cannot otherwise be averted and if the interest protected by the offender clearly outweighs the interest harmed by his conduct.

§6.04 THE OFFENDER

[A] Grounds of Exemption of Guilt

[1] *General Principles*

The court has to decide in the first place whether an offence was committed. At this level the grounds of justification, which take away the unlawfulness, come into play. Subsequently it has to be ascertained whether there is a ground of exemption of guilt, also called subjective ground of justification according to the classical doctrine. Such grounds do not justify the offence itself, as the punishability of the fact is left intact. Grounds of exemption of guilt are circumstances provided by statute or law that take away the blameworthiness, the culpability or the guilt. Even if the situation remains unlawful, the offender may not be blamed for it.

These subjective grounds of exemption of guilt only count in regard to this particular person. The objective grounds of justification, on the other hand, extend to all the participants whose participation falls within the scope of the justified situation.

The two recognised grounds of exemption of guilt are duress and mistake.

[2] *Different Grounds of Exemption of Guilt*

[a] *Duress*

Article 71 of the Penal Code provides that there is no offence when the accused (*accusé – beschuldigde*) or the defendant (*prévenu – beklaagde*) was forced by a power, which he could not have resist.

The conditions are an external duress, the elimination of the free will and absence of negligence or fault.

The force, which the offender could not resist, can be a physical duress, as well as a superior psychological force.

Physical duress or material circumstances beyond one's control result from external, irresistible material powers, which force a person to commit an act prohibited by criminal law or to omit an act commanded by law. The majority of the cases relates to traffic accidents caused by sudden frost or storm, or by the unforeseeable state of health of the driver.

Psychological duress or moral circumstances beyond one's control presume that the offender, at the moment of the punishable conduct, was in a predicament through which he could not exercise his free will. It concerns cases where the offender through external circumstances is abnormally coerced in his freedom to choose, as a result of which he cannot be expected to act in conformity of the norm. Duress can arise when the offender was threatened that if he did not commit the offence, he or someone close to him would be killed or seriously injured.

[b] Mistake and Ignorance

Mistake or ignorance form a ground of exemption of guilt that is not defined by law. Mistake requires a misunderstanding by the offender about the punishability of his conduct, either because he was mistaken about the lawfulness of the fact (mistake of law: *erreur de droit – rechtsdwaling*), or because he was unaware of the facts themselves (mistake of fact: *erreur de fait – feitelijke dwaling*). Ignorance supposes the absence by the actor of each insight into the punishability of his conduct. Ignorance relates to the law, as well as to the factual circumstances.

Even if it was invincible, a mistake of law was originally not taken into account, the assumption being that everyone is supposed to know the law. But since the last few decades, mistake is generally accepted as ground of exemption of guilt.

Mistake and ignorance are only considered to be grounds of exemption of guilt if they are invincible. That implies that the accused acted in the same way a normal and reasonable person would have done in the same circumstances.

[B] Grounds of Irresponsibility

[1] General Notions

Culpability (*imputabilité – toerekingsvatbaarheid*) refers to the extent that the offender has the mental capacities and insight to be held responsible for his own behaviour. Grounds of irresponsibility can be invoked by mentally ill persons and minors. If successful, no punishments shall be inflicted, but protective measures will be imposed (*mesures de sûreté – beveiligingsmaatregelen*).

[2] The Different Grounds of Irresponsibility

[a] Mentally Ill

The regime of the mentally ill was originally organised by the Act of 9 April 1930, which was influenced by positivism. This Act related to the accused, who was either in state of insanity (*démence – krankzinnigheid*), a serious state of mental disorder (*déséquilibre mental – geestesstoornis*) or mental retardation (*débilité mental – zwakzinnigheid*) which makes him unsuitable to control his actions (Article 1). This Act has recently been modified by the Act of 5 May 2014 (modified by the Act of 4 May 2016).

The court now has to determine whether the mentally unbalanced person (*déséquilibré mental – geestesgestoorde*) has committed the felony or misdemeanour in the same manner as a normal suspect would have.

The psychiatric state of the offender at the time of the trial is then evaluated by the court: it examines whether the offender is in the state as described by the law. If so, the punishment is replaced by internment, which is not a punishment but a protective measure. The internment is imposed for an indefinite period, because one cannot foresee how long the mental illness will last and how long an internee will remain socially dangerous. The Act of 4 May 2016 has limited the scope of application of the internment to the felonies and misdemeanours affecting or threatening the physical and psychological integrity of third parties.

The chamber for the protection of society (*chambre de protection sociale – kamer voor de bescherming van de maatschappij*), a separate entity within the sentence enforcement court (*juge de l'application des peines & tribunal de l'application des peines – strafuitvoeringrechter & strafuitvoeringsrechtbank*), decides on the modalities of execution and the duration of the internment.

[b] Minors

The regime for minors is provided on the one hand by the Federal Act of 8 April 1965, which is influenced by the ideas of social defence (*défense sociale – sociaal verweer*), and on the other hand by community statutes, which have jurisdiction because of the federal structure of Belgium.

According to Article 37 of this federal Act, the juvenile court can choose among a number of measures and apply the one which specifically fits the personality of the minor and which is able to facilitate his rehabilitation.

The juvenile court can reprimand the minor, place the minor under the supervision of the competent social service, place the minor under the foster care of a reliable person, place him in a suitable institution, place the minor under the care of a public institution for observation and education under supervision, or impose a measure which serves an educational and social function.

According to Article 57*bis* of the Act, the juvenile court can waive jurisdiction (*dessaisissement – uit handen geven*) when a measure of custody (*garde – bewaring*), guarding (*préservation – behoeding*) or education (*éducation – opvoeding*) is inappropriate. Thus the case is sent to the public prosecutor so as to allow prosecution in adult criminal court.

A waiver of jurisdiction is only possible if the minor has committed an act in itself constituting an offence (*fait qualifié infraction – een als misdrijf omschreven feit*), the minor was older than sixteen years at the time of the offence, and the juvenile court, after a social and medical-psychological examination, considers a measure of custody, guarding or education not appropriate. The juvenile court must specifically motivate its decision.

[C] Absolute Grounds of Excuse

Because of considerations of opportunity or criminal policy the legislature has ruled that in certain cases a lower or even no punishment is required, even if the accused has committed the offence for which he can be blamed. Absolute grounds of excuse (*causes d'excuse absolutoires – strafuitsluitende verschoningsgronden*) are circumstances provided by statute for specific offences that, once the court has established their presence, reduce or take away the punishment *ipso jure*.

The different absolute grounds of excuse are:

- consanguinity and affinity, especially relating to offences against property, such as theft, breach of confidence, swindle;[20]
- reporting to the authority, especially relating to offences concerning drugs, hormones and association of malefactors.

The potentially existing grounds of justification - which take away the unlawfulness (*illicéité – wederrechtelijkheid*) - and grounds of exemption of guilt - which take away the culpability (*culpabilité – verwijtbaarheid*) - have to be considered and rejected before the court can look into these potentially applicable absolving grounds, which only determine the punishableness (*punissabilité – strafwaardigheid*). As absolute grounds of excuse do not affect the unlawfulness of the behaviour, nor the culpability of the offender, their presence does not exclude an eventual finding of civil liability of the offender towards the victim of the offence.

[D] Punishable Participation

[1] General Concepts

The legislature usually thinks in terms of one offender-one offence. But in many cases more than one person is involved in the commission of an offence. This is the question of the punishable participation. Punishable participation implies that someone knowingly and willingly takes part in a felony or a misdemeanour in a way provided by law. Thus, a punishable participation requires three components: the person needs to take part in a felony or a misdemeanour as defined by law, the participation needs to take place in a way provided by law, and there must be an intent to commit a felony or a misdemeanour.

[2] Legal Ways of Participation

Those who have played an essential or indispensable role in the commission of an offence, are called co-perpetrators (*coauteurs – mededaders*).[21] Accomplices (*complices – medeplichtigen*) are those who play a secondary part in the commission of an

20. Article 462 Penal Code.
21. Article 66 Penal Code.

offence.[22] The executors, the direct contributors to the execution and the persons who render indispensable aid and assistance, are the perpetrators and co-perpetrators. Accomplices are those who give instructions, willingly procure weapons, instruments or other means or those who render useful aid and assistance.

The co-perpetrators in a felony or a misdemeanour are subject to the same punishment as the perpetrators. Thus they are subject to the full punishment of the offence. Accomplices to a felony are exposed to lesser punishment than the perpetrators.[23] The same rule applies to the attempt of a felony.[24] Accomplices to a misdemeanour incur a punishment of maximum two-thirds of the full punishment, which can be imposed on perpetrators of a misdemeanour.[25]

[E] Criminal Liability of Legal Persons

Criminal law has traditionally assumed that only a natural person can be punished. The criminal responsibility for the offence committed by a legal person (*personne morale – rechtspersoon*) was vested in the natural person(s) that have acted for the incorporated entity. In case of offences of omission, the natural person who had to act on account of the legal person but neglected to do so, was held criminally responsible.

These rules have changed (Act of 4 May 1999). A legal person can now also be punished. All offences are possible, but the law requires that the offence can be imputed to the legal person.

§6.05 PUNISHMENTS AND OTHER CONSEQUENCES OF THE OFFENCE

[A] General Principles

Punishment is usually defined as a harm provided by law and imposed by the judiciary for the committed offence.

Legally there are three main categories of punishments: criminal, correctional and police punishments.

According to Article 7 of the Penal Code the punishments for offences are:

- in criminal cases: reclusion (*réclusion – opsluiting*) and detention (*détention – hechtenis*);
- in correctional and police cases: imprisonment (*emprisonnement – gevangenisstraf*), community service (*peine de travail – werkstraf*) and autonomous probation (*peine de probation autonome – autonome probatiestraf*);
- in criminal and correctional cases: deprivation of certain political and civil rights (*interdiction de certains droits politiques et civils – ontzetting van bepaalde burgerlijke en politieke rechten*) and the prolonged detention at

22. Article 67 Penal Code.
23. Articles 80 and 81 Penal Code.
24. Article 52 Penal Code.
25. Article 69 Penal Code.

the disposal of the sentence enforcement court (*mise à la disposition du tribunal de l'application des peines – terbeschikkingstelling van de strafuitvoeringsrechtbank*);
- in correctional cases: electronic monitoring (*peine de surveillance électronique – straf onder elektronisch toezicht*);
- in criminal, correctional and police cases: fine (*amende – geldboete*) and confiscation (*confiscation – verbeurdverklaring*).

[B] The Different Punishments

[1] Principal Punishments

[a] Incarceration

As discussed above, reclusion is the punishment involving incarceration for felonies of the Penal Code. Unless a statute authorises a life sentence, reclusion is for a limited term (five to ten years, ten to fifteen years, fifteen to twenty years, twenty to thirty years, thirty to forty years).[26]

Detention is a special punishment involving incarceration for political offences. Detention is for a limited term (five to ten years, ten to fifteen years, fifteen to twenty years, twenty to thirty years, thirty to forty years) or for life.[27]

The duration of a correctional imprisonment is from eight days to five years, save the exceptions provided by law.[28] This is the case for material concurrence of offences (i.e., the offences committed by different acts),[29] for recidivism,[30] and correctionalisation.[31]

[b] Electronic Monitoring

Electronic monitoring does not involve an incarceration, only a restriction of freedom. The convict receives a mandatory daily schedule which only allows him or her to leave his or her residence or place of stay for necessary relocations and absences. The presence at the residence or place of stay is monitored by electronic surveillance.

The duration of electronic monitoring is from one month to one year.[32]

26. Articles 8–9 Penal Code.
27. Articles 10–11 Penal Code.
28. Article 25 Penal Code.
29. Articles 59–60 Penal Code.
30. Articles 56–57 Penal Code.
31. Article 25 Penal Code: up to forty years.
32. Article 37*ter* Penal Code.

[c] Community Service

Community service is based on the idea of restorative justice. The harm inflicted upon society will be compensated in a symbolic way by doing unpaid work. The convicted person performs the community service alongside his possible educational or professional activities during his spare time.

The duration of community service is from twenty hours to three hundred hours.[33]

[d] Autonomous Probation

Autonomous probation requires the offender to comply with specific conditions, determined by a criminal sentencing judge, for a certain period of time.

The duration of autonomous probation is from six months to two years.[34]

[e] Fine

A fine is a pecuniary punishment which is collected for the benefit of the State.[35] If imposed separately, the fine is a principal punishment. If it is combined with a punishment involving incarceration, it is an additional punishment. The fine as a principal punishment is a police punishment if its amount ranges from EUR 1–25. It is a correctional or criminal punishment if the fine amounts to EUR 26 or more. In criminal cases, however, the fine is never a principal punishment.

Because of inflation the amounts of the fines provided in the Penal Code and in other criminal statutes have to be multiplied by a coefficient. The coefficient is currently 6.[36]

[2] Additional Punishments

[a] Special Confiscation or Forfeiture

If a person has obtained something through the commission of an office, the court shall order its forfeiture (*confiscation – verbeurdverklaring*). The right of property of forfeited items is made over to the State or to interested third parties.

Forfeiture is not limited to the object or product of a criminal offence in the narrow sense of the word (*productum sceleris*), but pertains also to any advantage

33. Article 37*quinquies* Penal Code.
34. Article 37*octies* Penal Code.
35. Article 38, para. 3, Penal Code.
36. Act of 5 March 1952, as amended by the Act of 28 December 2011. The coefficient will probably be increased in 2017 (x8).

which the offender has gained because of the offence (*lucre sceleris*), to the objects that have been used for the commission of the offence, and to the criminal assets.[37]

[b] *Deprivation of Civil and Political Rights*

This concerns the right to hold public office, to stand for election, to carry marks of honour, to be a juror or an expert, to testify, or to be legal guardian or a trustee.[38]

[c] *Prolonged Detention at the Disposal of the Sentence Enforcement Court*

The prolonged detention at the disposal of the sentence enforcement court is an additional punishment that must or may be pronounced in the cases provided by statute, in order to protect society against people who commit certain serious offences that affect the integrity of persons. The punishment begins after the custodial sentence has been completed or, in cases of early release, on the day the convict finally has been released, taking into account the trial period.

[d] *Other Additional Punishments*

Other additional punishments are:

- endorsement of a driving licence;
- prohibition to exercise a certain profession and closing down of the business;
- publication of the judgment.

[C] Determination of Punishment

All offences defined in criminal law carry scales of punishment. The punishment can be aggravated or mitigated. Sometimes the relative legal provisions have an mandatory character (the so-called statutory punishment determination), and sometimes they are facultative (the so-called judicial punishment determination).

Mitigating circumstances, extenuating circumstances, recidivism, ideal concurrence of multiple offences (i.e., several offences are committed by the same act; *concours idéal – eendaadse samenloop*) and material concurrence of offences (i.e., different offences are committed by different acts; *concours matériel – meerdaadse samenloop*) are elements that determine the height of the punishment.

37. Article 42 Penal Code. The last mentioned has been added by Act of 17 July 1990 under the influence of international treaties and resolutions.
38. Article 31 Penal Code.

The criminal judge will be obliged to restrict punishment if there are mitigating circumstances.[39] The judge can decide (it is facultative) to take into account whether there are extenuating circumstances.[40]

In case of recidivism the judge is usually free to aggravate the punishment.[41] In fixing the level of punishment, the judge takes into account whether there is an ideal concurrence of multiple offences,[42] but relating to the material concurrence of offences his competence is more limited.[43]

The punishment imposed on an offender may also be influenced by considerations pertaining the personality of the defendant. In addition, there is a large scale of modalities of punishment.

The Delay, Suspension and Probation Act of 29 June 1964 was aimed at individualising the punishment and rehabilitating the offenders. This Act gives the judge many possibilities in determining the punishment: probationary suspension of sentence and probationary delay of execution, or an effective punishment without delay can be imposed.

[D] Sentence Enforcement

[1] General Principles

Because it is an executive matter, the courts, belonging to the judiciary, cannot interfere in the enforcement of sentences in Belgium.

The executive character of the enforcement of sentences is consistent with the concept of classical criminal law. The punishment must be proportionate to the degree of guilt of the offender. Also a moral improvement of the offender must be achieved. This concept implies that the province of criminal law ends as soon as a judgment is passed.

The enforcement of prison sentences now lies within the competence of the sentence enforcement court (*juge de l'application des peines & tribunal de l'application des peines – strafuitvoeringrechter & strafuitvoeringsrechtbank*), but the executive still takes important decisions relating the nature and the duration of the incarceration (Act of 17 May 2006). The legal status of the prisoners is a very important point too nowadays (Act of 12 January 2005).

New questions have arisen about the necessity of the courts' interference in the execution of sentences. In order to redress more or less the legal vacuum, there is a special procedure in matters of particular urgency (*référé – kort geding*).

39. Article 78 Penal Code.
40. Articles 79–85 Penal Code.
41. Articles 54–57 Penal Code.
42. Article 65 Penal Code.
43. Articles 58–64 Penal Code.

[2] Modalities of Execution

Compared to other regimes around the world, it can be said that the execution of prison sentences in Belgium tends to be rather liberal. The Act of 12 January 2005 prescribes for instance the regime of prisoners relating their treatment, the correspondence, the visits, the labour and the discipline.

The victim is becoming more and more important at the stage of sentence enforcement. The victim can be heard and conditions could be imposed on the offender in the interest of the victim.[44]

According to Article 110 of the Constitution and Article 87 of the Penal Code, the King, as president of the executive branch, is empowered to grant pardons. A pardon may set aside, reduce or make more lenient a (principal or additional) punishment.

The prescription of punishment implies that punishments shall be set aside when periods indicated by statute elapse. This is not the same as the prescription of prosecution, i.e., that the prosecution shall be dismissed upon the lapse of the periods stated in the statute.

Pardon and prescription only relate to the execution of the punishment. The conviction itself and its consequences are not affected.

[E] Extinction of Punishments

The cause of extinction of punishments (*extinction des peines – verval van de straffen*) is normally their execution. Amnesty (*amnistie – amnestie*), rehabilitation (*réhabilitation – herstel in eer en rechten*) and effacing (*effacement – uitwissing*) will also result in the extinction of the punishment.

The Constitution does not regulate amnesty as a right. The legislature is empowered to grant amnesties by virtue of the general principle that it is allowed to do everything that has not been forbidden by the Constitution or has not been transferred to another branch of government. Amnesty implies that there is no offence anymore. The amnesty statute prevents prosecutions, nullifies passed sentences and stops the execution of punishments. The underlying motives are mostly politically coloured. In this way offences which are committed in dark circumstances such as war and general strike can be forgotten.

Rehabilitation implies the abolition for the future of all the criminal consequences of a conviction. The decision of rehabilitation is made by the Chamber of Accusation (*chambre des mises en accusation – kamer van inbeschuldigingstelling*),[45] as distinct from the effacing of convictions, which takes place automatically.

The effacing of convictions implies the nullification for the future of convictions to police punishments. After a lapse of three years from the sentence, those convictions are automatically effaced.

44. Act of 17 May 2006.
45. Article 621 Code of Criminal Procedure.

§6.06 SELECTED BIBLIOGRAPHY

A. De Nauw & F. Deruyck, *Overzicht van het Belgisch algemeen strafrecht* (Bruges: die Keure 2015).

L. Dupont & R. Verstraeten, *Handboek Belgisch strafrecht* (Leuven: Acco 1990).

P.E. Trousse, *Les principes généraux du droit pénal positif belge, in Les Novelles, Droit pénal* (2 vol., 1956 & 1962).

C. Van den Wyngaert, B. De Smet & S. Vandromme, *Strafrecht en strafprocesrecht in hoofdlijnen* (Antwerp: Maklu 2014).

D. Vandermeersch, *Éléments de droit pénal et de procédure pénale* (Brussels: La Charte 2015).

C.J. Vanhoudt & W. Calewaert, *Belgisch strafrecht* (Ghent: Story-Scientia 1976).

CHAPTER 7

Family Law

Patrick Senaeve

§7.01 GENERAL DESCRIPTION OF FAMILY LAW

[A] The Legislation

Belgian civil law in general and the Belgian law of persons and the family in particular have as their primary source the Belgian Civil Code, which had its formal origin in the French Napoleonic Civil Code of 1804.

For decades, texts of the Civil Code in general and those regarding the law of persons and the family in particular were changed very little. It can be said that the Belgians remained more faithful to the Code of the occupiers – for that was what the French were between 1795 and 1814 – than the occupiers themselves.

Since the end of the 1950s, the amendments in the field of the law of persons and the family have become more frequent and more radical. In recent years, we have gained legislative momentum.

A review is given below of the most important comprehensive and radical reforms that have taken place in Belgium over the last five decades:

- An Act of 21 March 1969 completely changed adoption law. Two forms of adoption were introduced (now called 'simple adoption' and 'full adoption'), and adoption was made an institution for child protection. Later, adoption law was again amended, though less radically and only partially, by an Act of 27 April 1987.
- After the principle of legal equality of men and women in marriage was formulated in an Act of 30 April 1958, an Act of 14 July 1976 implemented this principle of equality on all levels of marriage law. The marriage property law was completely reformed and modernised, and the content of the rights and obligations of spouses was adapted with, on the one hand, guarantees for

minimal autonomy of the spouses but, on the other hand, a strengthening of the solidarity of the legitimate family. The intervention of a judge in crisis situations in the family was also strengthened considerably.
- An Act of 14 May 1981 changed the right of inheritance of the surviving spouse, resulting in a reinforcing of his or her position of succession in the estate of the deceased spouse.
- An Act of 31 March 1987 radically tackled the law of affiliation, which up to that time had remained that of the Napoleonic Code with minor changes. This led to an egalitarian law of affiliation and to its liberalisation and modernisation, in the light of the evolving ideas and the scientific advances in the methods of proof.
- By various successive amendments (an Act of 8 April 1965 on the protection of youth, an Act of 1 July 1974 on parental authority, an Act of 31 March 1987 changing the law of affiliation), the matter of parental authority was comprehensively and profoundly reformed: the equality of the father and the mother was then implemented completely; parental authority was regulated uniformly for children born in and out of wedlock; and it was entirely converted in its content from an instrument of power into an institution whose purpose was to serve the interests of the child alone and to require parents to exercise their parental obligations properly. An Act of 13 April 1995 introduced the principle of joint custody.
- By an act passed by Federal Parliament in January 1990, the age of majority was reduced from 21 to 18 years old, with consequences in all kinds of areas, such as child-protection law and the marriage of young people.
- An Act of 27 April 2007 profoundly modified divorce law. Divorce on the grounds of fault has been abolished and replaced by divorce on the grounds of the irretrievable breakdown of the marriage, and divorce by mutual consent has been simplified.
- An Act of 30 July 2013 instituted a family court. This new court was granted jurisdiction for all proceedings related to family law, which formerly had been spread over four different courts.
- An Act of 5 May 2014 on the parenthood of the co-mother created a third legal category of parents, that is the *co-mother*, with the same rights and duties as mothers and fathers.

As a general characteristic of all these reforms, it must be noted that they result from a compromise, which is inevitable in a pluralistic society with ideologically strongly divided population groups. Because of these compromises, the recent statutes in family law are usually very complicated.

[B] Treaty Law

Since the end of the 1970s, a very important influence on Belgian family law has been exercised by international treaties, particularly the (ECHR) (Rome 4 November 1950), as well as by international case law and, more specifically, by the case law of the

European Court for Human Rights (ECtHR) in Strasbourg. Of great importance has been the *Marckx* judgment of the Strasbourg Court of 13 June 1979, which has become well known. For Belgium, this meant an obligation under international law to replace the specifications of the law on affiliation and inheritance of extramarital children that were criticised by the Court, by legislation that would be in harmony with the ECHR. The influence of the ECHR and the rulings of Strasbourg has also been felt in other areas of family law.

Recently we met with the influence of the 1989 UN Convention on the Rights of the Child, which has been ratified by Belgium at the end of 1991.

[C] Case Law

Case law plays an important role in the development of Belgian family law. It has filled gaps in statutory law (for instance regarding rights of personality) and supplemented the Code where it had been intentionally silent (such as regarding the cohabitation of unmarried couples). With regard to the many recent statutes, case law has been obliged to remedy the vagueness and incompleteness of family law dispositions.

On the whole, Belgian case law in the area of family law has played a markedly conservative role in the past. The most typical expression of this was the condemnation by the Court of Cassation of unmarried couples living together, which was considered illicit.

During the last decade, a marked evolution is observable.

The Constitutional Court also plays an important role in the evolution of Belgian family law, since the Special Act of 6 January 1989 gave the Court jurisdiction to review the constitutionality of statutes under the principle of equality and non-discrimination (Articles 10 and 11 of the Constitution). Since the Special Act of 9 March 2003 extended the jurisdiction of the Constitutional Court to all provisions of Section II of the Constitution, which relate to rights and freedoms (Articles 8–32 of the Constitution), the role of the Constitutional Court in the field of family law has become even more substantial, especially in the field of affiliation law.

§7.02 AFFILIATION

[A] Short History

In the *Marckx* judgment of 13 June 1979, Belgium was condemned by the ECtHR because of the conflict of its previous legislation regarding ex-nuptial children with stipulations of the ECHR, namely, Article 8 (right to respect for family life), Article 14 (prohibition of discrimination) and Article 1 of the first Appended Protocol (guarantee of the peaceful enjoyment of possessions).

On three points, the previous Belgian law was judged not to conform with the ECHR:

- The rule that obliged an unmarried mother to recognise her child so that the affiliation could be legally established.
- The rule that the child had, in principle, no relational link with the family of his/her mother, even after recognition by the mother.
- The inferior right of inheritance of the ex-nuptial child under the previous law, which was considered by the Court to be discriminatory.

The condemnation of Belgium by the Strasbourg court imposed an obligation under international law on Parliament to change the legal stipulations considered by the Court to be in conflict with the ECHR. This was finally done by the Act of 31 March 1987.

As regards the content, the most important conclusion to be derived from the *Marckx* judgment is that, on the basis of the evolutionary and teleological interpretation method applied by the Strasbourg Court, Article 8 of the ECHR concerning the law on the respect due to the family life also offered protection as regards the civil rights status of the person. This constitutes an entirely different legal interpretation than was intended by 'family life' in the drafting of the Convention in 1950.

By the Act of 31 March 1987, Belgian affiliation law was radically reformed. The major effects of this change were:

- *Equalisation*: discrimination between children on the basis of their birth was largely removed, even with regard to terminology.
- *Liberalisation*: obsolete restrictions on the establishment and on the contestation of affiliation relationships were repealed or at least liberalised.
- *Modernisation*: affiliation law was adapted to artificial means of conception and to scientific advances in the proof of genetic parenthood.

After the Constitutional Court had held that several provisions of the 1987 Affiliation Act violated the constitutional rules on equality and non-discrimination (Articles 10 and 11 of the Constitution), a new major reform of affiliation law was implemented by the Act of 1 July 2006 (in force since 1 July 2007).

[B] Maternal Affiliation

Present affiliation law has a *unified system* regarding the establishment of maternal affiliation for all children, irrespective of whether they are born in or out of wedlock.

There are three ways to establish maternal affiliation and they are applied in this order: the birth certificate, recognition and judicial investigation of maternity.

[1] Birth Certificate

The primary way of establishment of affiliation on the mother's side is the birth certificate (*acte de naissance – akte van geboorte*) of the child with the indication of the woman who brought him/her into the world.[1] In this way, maternal affiliation automatically comes into being on the granting of the birth certificate. It applies retroactively to the birth.

Thus, in Belgian law, the adage *mater semper certa est* is confirmed.[2]

For a good understanding of the implications of this, we must refer to the rule that the birth certificate must necessarily contain the family name, first names and the residence of the woman to whom the child is born.[3] The combination of this rule of birth registration with the affiliation rule means that, at a birth on Belgian territory, the maternal affiliation of a child will be established on the basis of the birth certificate except in the very rare case of a child being born of an unknown mother.

Strictly speaking, still another component is required for the establishment of the maternal affiliation in addition to the birth certificate with indication of the name of the mother. That is the identification of the person whose affiliation is questioned as the child to whom the woman, according to the birth certificate, gave birth. This second component can, if necessary (i.e., in the absence of 'possession of status', i.e., public occupation of the position of the child of a person, irrespective of the legal status) be demonstrated as a fact with all legal means.

If the child has possession of status with respect to its mother that concurs with the birth certificate, then its maternal affiliation cannot be contested.[4] This means that, even if one child is exchanged for another, and also in the case of supposition of a child with a mother who did not give birth, the maternal affiliation established by the possession of status is afterwards not subject to contestation.

If there is no possession of status with respect to the woman whose name is given in the birth certificate, an action contesting the maternal affiliation is, in principle, possible. It must be proven that there is no concurrence between the status of the child (as it flows from the birth certificate) and the birth of the child from this woman.

On the mother's side, the genetic relationship between parent and child as such is not relevant for contesting the affiliation. Only the fact of being born of a particular woman is relevant. With the evolution of medical fertilisation technology, however, the two may not necessarily coincide, for example in the case of egg donation or embryo donation.

The action contesting maternity is a reserved legal action: only the legal father, the biological mother, the child and the legal mother can institute the action.[5] The action lapses upon the expiration of one year from the discovery by the plaintiff of the untrue character of the established motherhood.

1. Article 312, §1, Civil Code.
2. *See also* the *Marckx* judgment, para. 41.
3. Article 57, 2°, Civil Code.
4. Article 312, §3, Civil Code.
5. Article 312, §2, Civil Code.

[2] Recognition

In the very exceptional case where the maternal affiliation is not ascertained on the basis of the birth certificate, and only in that case, it can be established by a voluntary recognition (*reconnaissance – erkenning*) of the child by the mother.[6]

Maternal recognition is a unilateral legal act proceeding from the woman who intends to establish an affiliation relationship with respect to a child.

The recognition of maternity is impermissible if the recognition would show that a marriage impediment exists between the mother and the father for which no exemption can be granted.[7]

The recognition must be done in a certified document executed either before the officer of civil status or before a notary. This document, however, may not be a will.[8]

In the event of recognition by a married woman of a child that was born during her marriage, her husband must be notified of this recognition. The sanction on the non-fulfilment of this additional formality is only the *non-opposability* of the recognition to her husband and to the children born in wedlock.[9]

In the event the child has possession of status with respect to its mother that concurs with the act of recognition, then his maternal affiliation cannot be contested, even if the recognition is fraudulent,[10] except in the case of an absence of *consensus ad idem*. This means that even in the case of surrogate motherhood, where the surrogate mother delivered the child anonymously in a foreign country and the child is recognised by the woman who wishes to have the child, this recognition may no longer be contested as soon as continual and permanent possession of status with respect to that woman has been formed.

If there is no possession of status with respect to the woman who recognised the child, an action contesting the maternal affiliation is possible in principle.

There are two totally different grounds for contesting a recognition:

- lack of *consensus ad idem* on the part of the recogniser; and
- lack of concurrence between the status of the child (as it flows from the act of recognition) and the birth of the child from this woman.

Only the legal father, the child and the woman who claims to be the mother can introduce an action contesting the maternal recognition.[11] The recognising woman herself can never plead her own fraud: she can only contest her recognition on the basis of a lack of her *consensus ad idem*.[12]

The action of the legal father must be instituted within one year from the discovery of the untrue character of the maternal recognition. The woman who claims to be the mother can institute the action within one year from the discovery that she is

6. Article 313, §1, Civil Code.
7. Article 313, §2, Civil Code.
8. Article 327 Civil Code.
9. Article 313, §3, Civil Code.
10. Article 330, §1, para. 2, Civil Code.
11. Article 330, §1, para. 1, Civil Code.
12. Article 330, §1, para. 2, Civil Code.

the mother, that is from the birth.[13] In the case her action is successful, the maternal affiliation of the child is automatically established towards her.[14]

[3] Investigation of Maternity

The third and last way of establishing maternal affiliation is judicial establishment on the basis of an action for investigation of maternity (*recherche de maternité – onderzoek naar het moederschap*).

Two categories of children can become subject to an investigation of maternity:[15]

- children who have no legally established maternal affiliation; and
- children whose maternal affiliation is established on the basis of their birth certificate but who have no concurring possession of status.

With regard to the latter category of children, for whom another status is claimed than that which resulted from the birth certificate, there need be no prior procedure contesting the established maternal affiliation.

Even regarding these categories of children, the investigation of maternity is impermissible if it appears from the claimed maternal affiliation that a marriage impediment exists between the mother and the father for which no dispensation could be obtained.[16]

For the action to be declared to have merit, proof must be provided in two areas: that the alleged mother gave birth to a child and that there is concurrence between the child involved and the child to whom this woman gave birth.[17]

There are two methods of proof prescribed by the law:

- the possession of status the child has with respect to the alleged mother:[18] this applies only as a supposition *juris tantum* of the affiliation relationship;
- direct proof of the delivery of a child and of the identity, to be provided with all the legal means.[19]

Only the child itself (and after its death, its descendants) and its father can introduce this legal action.[20] The action has to be introduced against the alleged mother.

This action also lapses after expiration of thirty years from the day on which the status which the child claims has been denied, thus from birth.[21] It is a limitation period that is suspended with respect to the child itself during its minority.[22]

13. Article 330, §1, para. 4, Civil Code.
14. Article 330, §3, Civil Code.
15. Article 314, para. 1, Civil Code.
16. Article 314, para. 2, Civil Code.
17. Article 314, para. 3, Civil Code.
18. Article 314, para. 4, Civil Code.
19. Article 314, para. 5, Civil Code.
20. Article 332*ter*, paras 1 and 2, Civil Code.
21. Article 331*ter*, para. 1, Civil Code.
22. Article 2252, Civil Code.

[C] Paternal Affiliation

Belgian law uses a fundamentally different way to establish paternity depending on whether the child is born in wedlock or out of wedlock.

[1] Paternal Affiliation Within Marriage

[a] Establishment of Paternity

Paternal affiliation in marriage is established on the basis of the rule *pater est quem nuptiae demonstrant*: the father is he whom the marriage points out.[23] This is a rule whereby the paternity is compulsorily and automatically attributed to the husband of the mother. Incorrectly, one often speaks of a 'presumption' of paternity.

For the application of this paternity rule, two fundamental requirements must be fulfilled:

- the mother of the child must be married; and
- the maternal affiliation of the child must be ascertained. The manner of establishment of the maternal affiliation is not relevant for the application of the paternity rule.

The *pater est* rule is applicable for all children who are born at the earliest on the day of the marriage of their mother and at the latest the 300th day after the dissolution (or the annulment) of her marriage. It suffices that the mother was married for at least one day of the legal period of her pregnancy.

However, this paternity rule does not apply if the child was born:

- more than 300 days after a judgment by the family court authorising the parents to reside separately and less than 180 days after the date on which this decision expired or the parents reunited;
- more than 300 days after the confirmation by the family court of an agreement between the parties to reside separately, or after the authorisation by the family court to reside separately during the divorce proceedings;
- more than 300 days after the submission date of the petition for divorce by mutual consent;
- more than 300 days after the date on which the spouses registered at different addresses according to the population register, the aliens register or the waiting list, as long as they have not subsequently been re-registered at the same address.[24]

These exceptions do not apply if the spouses made a common statement at the time of birth.

23. Article 315 Civil Code.
24. Article 316*bis* Civil Code.

If the birth takes place no more than 300 days after the dissolution (or annulment) of the previous marriage of the mother and after the conclusion of a subsequent marriage, a simple application of the paternity rule would involve the attribution of paternity to two men. The law resolves this paternity conflict by considering the child to be exclusively the child of the new husband.[25] This attribution of paternity to the new husband, however, is not absolute: the rule contains the reservation of the contesting of this paternity proceeding from the ordinary parties of the action contesting paternity and, moreover, from the previous husband. By granting this action, not only the paternity of the new husband is retroactively dissolved, but the paternity is also retroactively granted to the previous husband.[26]

[b] *Contestation of Paternity*

In the case of conception of a child with semen from another man than the husband by means of artificial insemination or another method, the action for contesting paternity is excluded under the following cumulative conditions:

- the husband gave his consent for this act;
- he thereby intended to conceive a child with his wife;
- the conception of the child can be the result of the act to which the husband agreed.

This ground of inadmissibility can be invoked against *each* party of the action contesting paternity (husband, mother and child).

The action contesting paternity is a reserved legal action. Only the husband, the mother, the child, the man who claims the fatherhood (i.e., the biological father) and the woman who claims the co-motherhood, can institute the action.[27]

The action of the *husband* must be instituted within one year after the discovery of the fact that he is not the biological father.[28] This is a strict time limit. If the husband dies before the birth or after the birth but within the time limit to institute the action, the action is transferred to his blood relatives in the direct line, who have a [new] period of one year to institute the action.[29]

The action of the *mother* is also subject to a strict time limit of one year, which, however, necessarily begins at the birth of the child.[30] The mother's action is not transferable to others upon her death.

The *child* also has the right of action, and this in all cases (thus irrespective of the situation between the parents): also if the parents have been living together up till now. The right of action of the child is, however, subject to a special strict time limit. Its right of action occurs only on its 12th birthday and lapses on its 22nd birthday. However, the

25. Article 317, para. 1, Civil Code.
26. Article 317, para. 2, Civil Code.
27. Article 318, §1, Civil Code.
28. Article 318, §2, para. 1, Civil Code.
29. Article 318, §2, para. 2, Civil Code.
30. Article 332, para. 4, Civil Code.

child disposes of an additional time limit of one year after the discovery of the fact that its legal father is not its biological father.[31] The Constitutional Court has held these short time limits to violate the constitutional rules on equality and non-discrimination (Articles 10 and 11 of the Constitution) and the right to private and family life (Article 22 of the Constitution).[32] The child's action is also not transferred to others upon its death.

The *man who claims the fatherhood* must institute his action within one year after the discovery that he is the biological father of the child.[33] He is allowed to institute the action before the birth of the child.[34]

The *woman who claims the co-motherhood* must institute her action within one year after the discovery that she had consented with the conception of the child and the conception of the child can be the result of it.

According to the statutory provision the action is inadmissible when the child has '*possession of status*' with respect to his father that concurs with the legal fatherhood, in other words enjoys de facto status in relation to this man.[35] However, the Constitutional Court holds that, as an absolute bar to admissibility, the de facto enjoyment of status towards the legal father is incompatible with the right to respect for private life as guaranteed by Article 22 of the Constitution.[36]

In all cases, the plaintiff in paternity contestation can challenge the paternity of the husband by providing proof of the absence of a genetic bond between the husband and the child. This is a *general* form of paternity contestation. Its application is not determined by a *numerus clausus* system of cases. It must be proven that the husband cannot be the father of the child. This proof can be established by all legal means.[37]

Actually, this proof can be placed on two levels:

- *indirect* proof: proof of a lack of sexual intercourse between the husband and the mother at the time of procreation; and
- *direct* proof: proof of the lack of a genetic bond between the husband and the child by means of medico-biological techniques (male sterility, blood examination, genetic fingerprint, etc.).

In addition, the man who claims the fatherhood must prove that he actually is the biological father of the child,[38] and the woman who claims the co-motherhood must prove that she had consented with the conception of the child and the conception of the child can be the result of it.[39]

31. Article 318, §2, para. 1, Civil Code.
32. Constitutional Court No. 96/2011 of 31 May 2011 and No. 18/2016 of 3 February 2016.
33. Article 318, §2, para. 1, Civil Code.
34. Article 328*bis*, para. 1, Civil Code.
35. Article 318, §1, *in initio*, Civil Code.
36. Constitutional Court No. 20/2011 of 3 February 2011, No. 105/2013 of 9 July 2013, No. 147/2013 of 7 November 2013, and No. 18/2016 of 3 February 2016.
37. Article 318, §3, para. 1, Civil Code.
38. Article 318, §5, Civil Code.
39. Article 318, §6, Civil Code.

[2] *Paternal Affiliation Out of Wedlock*

For the establishment of paternal affiliation outside of wedlock, Belgian law knows no rule similar to the paternity rule that applies in wedlock. The establishment of paternity can be done in two ways: recognition and judicial investigation of paternity.

[a] *Recognition*

[i] Establishment of Affiliation

Upon recognition of a child by the father, his genetic paternity need not be demonstrated. Thus, recognitions as a favour (*ex gratia*) that do not correspond to the genetic truth, are legally possible.

In principle, all children whose paternal affiliation is not or is no longer established on the basis of the paternity rule can be the subject of recognition.

Thus, this includes children born to an unmarried woman as well as children born to a married woman after a successful paternity contestation. The adulterous character *a matre* of the affiliation relationship as such poses no problem. Also children who have already been recognised by another man come into consideration for paternal recognition. In this case, however, the second recognition has no effect as long as the first has not been annulled.[40]

There is an exception to the general rule. The recognition of paternity is inadmissible if it would appear from this recognition that a marriage impediment exists between the mother and the father for which no dispensation can be obtained.[41] Thus, recognition is prohibited of children conceived in *incest*.

The recognition is not subject to any time limit. Recognition of adults is also possible.

As for maternal recognition, this too must be done with an authentic deed executed either before the officer of civil status or before a notary, but with exclusion of a will.[42]

If a married man recognises a child that has been conceived with another woman than his wife before or during his marriage, his wife (or husband in the case of a same-sex marriage) must be notified of the act of recognition.[43]

While the maternal recognition is a unilateral legal act, this is not at all the case with paternal recognition. For the validity of the recognition by a man, the prior consent of the child and/or of the mother is required in most cases, since the 1987 reform.

The rules since then distinguish three cases.

40. Article 329, para. 2, Civil Code.
41. Article 321, Civil Code.
42. Article 327, Civil Code.
43. Article 319*bis*, Civil Code.

First, in the case of recognition by a man of a child that has attained the age of majority (i.e., at least 18 years old) or that is emancipated,[44] the child itself must consent to the recognition.[45] The child does not need to justify its refusal, and the aspirant-recogniser has no right to challenge this refusal in court. Thus, majority or the emancipation gives a person a *veto right* over late paternal recognitions.

Second, in the case of recognition of a non-emancipated minor child whose mother is alive and able to express her will, the prior consent of the mother is required in all cases.[46] Moreover, the consent of the child itself is also required as soon as it has reached the age of 12. In both cases, however, the man who wants to recognise can challenge a refusal before the family court. The judge has the parties summoned in chambers and tries to bring them to agreement. *Either*, the family court receives the necessary consent, *or*, if this effort fails, it has to decide on the case. There are again two possibilities:

- It is proven (by the mother and/or the child of 12 years of age or older) that the aspirant-recogniser is not the biological father of the child. In this case, the family court rejects the petition for recognition.
- It is not proven that the genetic relationship is lacking. In that case, the court has to decide whether or not the petition for recognition can be granted on the basis of the criterion of the *interests of the child*. The request must be granted unless it is proven (by the mother and/or the child) that the recognition would conflict with the interests of the child.

Third, in the case of a non-emancipated minor child without mother or whose mother is not able to express her will, the officer of civil status who received the recognition or the recogniser himself must ensure that the legal representative of the child is informed as well as the child itself if it has reached the age of 12 years old.[47] They can claim the nullification of the recognition within six months on two grounds:

- if the legal representative and/or the child of 12 years of age or older proves that the recogniser is not the genetic father, the court nullifies the recognition;
- if this proof is not delivered, the court pronounces on the basis of the criterion of the *interests of the child*.

[ii] Contestation of the Recognition

If the child has possession of status with respect to his father that concurs with the act of recognition, then – according to the statutory provision[48] – the action for contestation is inadmissible. However, the Constitutional Court holds that, as an absolute bar

44. Emancipation of a minor is possible from the age of 15 years (Article 477 Civil Code).
45. Article 319, §2, Civil Code.
46. Article 319, §3, Civil Code.
47. Article 329*bis*, §3, Civil Code.
48. Article 330, §1, *in initio*, Civil Code.

to admissibility, the de facto enjoyment of status towards the recogniser is incompatible with the right to respect for private life as guaranteed by Article 22 of the Constitution.[49]

Only the mother, the child, the man who claims to be the father and the woman who claims the co-motherhood can introduce an action contesting the paternal recognition.[50] The recognising man himself can never plead his own fraud: he can only contest his own earlier recognition on the basis of a lack of his *consensus ad idem*.[51] Nevertheless, the law provides for exceptions by denying the following persons the right to contest:[52]

- the mother, both if she gave her prior approval of the recognition and if she was a party in the procedure for substituting authorisation; and
- the child who was at least 12 years old at the time of the recognition, both if it gave its prior consent to the recognition and if it was a party in the procedure for substituting authorisation; the child who was not 12 years old at the time of the recognition, on the other hand, can contest the recognition later on.

Exceptionally, the mother and the child can still act if their consent lacked *consensus ad idem*.

The action of the mother must be instituted within one year from the discovery of the untrue character of the paternal recognition. The man who claims to be the biological father can institute the action within one year from the discovery that he is the father, and the woman who claims the co-motherhood within one year from the discovery that she had consented with the conception of the child and the conception of the child can be the result of it.[53]

The right of action of the child is subject to a special strict time limit. Its right of action occurs only on its 12th birthday and lapses on its 22nd birthday. However, the child disposes of an additional time limit of one year after the discovery of the fact that the recognising man is not its biological father.[54] The Constitutional Court holds also in this case that with regard to the child these short time limits violate the constitutional rules on equality and non-discrimination (Articles 10 and 11 of the Constitution) and the right to private and family life (Article 22 of the Constitution).[55]

In the case the action of the biological father is successful, the paternal affiliation of the child is automatically attributed to him.[56]

49. Constitutional Court No. 29/2013 of 7 March 2013, No. 96/2013 of 9 July 2013, No. 127/2014 of 19 September 2014, No. 139/2014 of 25 September 2014 - 1st part, No. 35/2015 of 12 March 2015, and No. 168/2015 of 26 November 2015.
50. Article 330, §1, para. 1, Civil Code.
51. Article 330, §1, para. 2, Civil Code.
52. Article 330, §1, para. 2, Civil Code.
53. Article 330, §1, para. 4, Civil Code.
54. Article 330, §1, para. 4, Civil Code.
55. Constitutional Court No. 77/2016 of 25 May 2016.
56. Article 330, §3, Civil Code.

[b] *Establishing Paternal Affiliation Based on an Investigation*

The second and last way of establishing paternal affiliation outside marriage is judicial establishment on the basis of an action for investigation of paternity (*recherche de paternité – onderzoek naar het vaderschap*). It must be emphasised that the effect of such a judicial paternity investigation is exactly the same as that of a recognition, that is, in general, to establish a full and complete relationship between father and child, with all the ordinary consequences of an established relationship.

Only those children whose paternal affiliation is not or is no longer established can be subject to an investigation of paternity.[57] Thus, this includes children for whom the paternity rule does not apply or for whom the paternity of the husband has been successfully contested and who also have not been the object of a paternal recognition or with respect to whom the paternal recognition has been successfully contested.

According to the statutory provision investigation of paternity is inadmissible if it would demonstrate that a marriage impediment exists between the mother and the father for which no dispensation can be granted.[58] However, the Constitutional Court holds that this provision violates the constitutional rules on equality and non-discrimination (Articles 10 and 11 of the Constitution) insofar it makes it impossible for the judge to declare the action to have merit even if he considers that the establishment of the paternal affiliation is in line with the interests of the child.[59]

For the claim to be declared to have merit, proof must be provided of the genetic paternity of the defending man. There are three possibilities of proof prescribed by the rules:

- The possession of status that the child has with respect to the alleged father,[60] but this applies only as a presumption *juris tantum* of the genetic relationship.
- Sexual intercourse between the alleged father and the mother during the legal period of the conception.[61] This, too, applies only as a presumption *juris tantum* of the genetic relationship. Moreover, the defendant can object against this presumption by proving that there are serious doubts about the causal relationship between the proven sexual intercourse and the assumed genetic paternity (e.g., by means of the *exceptio plurium concubentium*).
- Direct proof of the genetic relationship can be provided by all legal means (blood examination, genetic fingerprint, etc.).[62]

This legal action is open only for the child (and after its death, its descendants), for the mother and for the biological father.[63]

57. Article 322, para. 1, Civil Code.
58. Article 325, Civil Code.
59. Constitutional Court No. 103/2012 of 9 August 2012.
60. Article 324, para. 1, Civil Code.
61. Article 324, para. 3, Civil Code.
62. Article 324, para. 2, Civil Code.
63. Article 332*ter*, paras 1 & 2, Civil Code.

In analogy to the rule regarding paternal recognition (*see* above), there is a possibility of a right of veto or of notification of objections for the mother and/or the child.[64]

[D] Co-motherhood

The Act of 5 May 2014 on the parenthood of the co-mother created in Belgian law a third legal type of parent, that is, the '*co-mother*'. The Act, inserting new rules in the Civil Code, regulates the establishment of co-motherhood of the woman who either is married to the mother at the time of the birth (or who was married to her less than 300 days before birth), who voluntarily recognises the child, or whose co-motherhood is judicially determined. According to this new system co-mothers can establish affiliation with their child without having to proceed to adoption.

The rules on establishment and contestation of the affiliation with regard to the co-mother are similar to those with regard to the father. Legal co-motherhood is automatically attributed on the basis of the same-sex marriage of the mother.[65] If the co-motherhood is not or is no longer established on the basis of the marriage of the mother, the co-mother can recognise the child of her female partner.[66] Finally, the affiliation towards the co-mother can be established on the basis of an action for investigation of co-motherhood.[67]

[E] Rules Common to All Affiliation Actions

[1] Orders for Investigatory Measures

Since all legal means may be applied as proof in affiliation disputes, the court, to resolve the dispute submitted to it, can order blood tests or any other investigation by means of an approved scientific method. As in ordinary law, in order to obtain the proof of the blood relationship or the lack thereof in the affiliation dispute before it, the court can order these investigatory measures by virtue of its office.[68]

[2] The Effect of Judgment in Affiliation Disputes

The judgment awarded in an action for the establishment or contestation of affiliation takes effect when it becomes final: at that time, the affiliation relationship is established or cancelled, with retroactive effect to the birth. As in other judgments regarding actions of status, the enacting terms of the judgment whereby an action regarding affiliation is granted must be entered in the register of civil status. The transcription is done on the order of the public prosecutor.[69] The entry in the register of civil status,

64. Article 332*quinquies*, §§1 & 2, Civil Code.
65. Article 325/2 Civil Code.
66. Article 325/4 Civil Code.
67. Article 325/8 Civil Code.
68. Article 331*octies* Civil Code.
69. Article 333, §2, Civil Code.

however, is an administrative formality: non-compliance has no consequences for the effect of the judicial ruling.

[F] Action for Support Against the Procreator

Belgian law knows a *duality* of actions for the benefit of the child conceived out of wedlock against the procreator who does not voluntarily recognise the child: in addition to the investigation of paternity, which is intended to establish the affiliation relationship with all its legal consequences, there exists also a direct action against the procreator that is intended exclusively to have the court order him to pay child support (the so-called *Zahlvaterschaft*).

This is purely a support action and in no sense intends the legal establishment of an affiliation relationship. For a support action against the procreator, only those children are eligible for whom the paternal affiliation is not or is no longer established. Thus, these are children who do not come under the paternity rule or with respect to whom the paternity of the husband has been successfully contested, and who also have not been the object of a paternal recognition or with respect to whom the paternal recognition has been successfully contested.

The child whose maternal affiliation is already established can undertake an action for support against the procreator even though there is a marriage impediment between him and the mother. On the other hand, the child whose paternal affiliation is established on the basis of the paternity rule can never undertake an action for support against the procreator, even though there is no possession of status with respect to the legal father.

For the action to be declared to have merit, proof must be delivered of fertile sexual relations between the defendant and the mother during the legal period of conception. Here, it is not the genetic relationship *as such* that forms the basis of the action. On the other hand, sexual intercourse in and of itself is also not the basis of this action: only *fertile* sexual intercourse can be considered as the basis.

In contrast to affiliation actions, this action for support may be initiated only by the child.[70] As a rule, the child will be a minor at the time of the institution of the claim. Therefore, it will have to be represented in accordance with the general legal rules, by its legal representative (generally its mother).

This action for support is not subject to the general time limit from affiliation law, as it is not an affiliation action.

The actual consequence of a successful action is that the procreator is ordered to pay support for maintenance, raising and education of the child he has procreated.[71] As regards content, the support obligation of the procreator is exactly the same as that of the parents. Thus, the obligation does not necessarily terminate when the child comes of age but continues further if at that moment the education of the child is not completed.

70. Article 337, §1, Civil Code.
71. Article 336 Civil Code.

The support obligation of the procreator terminates if afterwards paternal affiliation is established with respect to another man.

Although condemning the procreator to pay child support does not in itself establish paternal affiliation, it has the same effect as the establishment of paternity as regards marriage impediments due to relationship by blood or marriage.[72]

Having been ordered to pay child support as such gives the procreator no claim to have personal contact with the child. However, personal contact can be obtained on the basis of the special relationship of affection he could maintain with the child.[73]

§7.03 PARENTAL AUTHORITY OVER JUVENILES

[A] Introduction

Belgian law still uses the term 'parental authority' and not the term 'parental responsibilities' used in the Council of Europe 1984 Recommendation No. R(84) 4 on Parental Responsibilities.

A typical feature of Belgian law is that, in its regime of parental authority, it makes no distinction whatsoever between children born in and out of wedlock. The only important element is that the affiliation of the child has been legally established (*see* above).

A second typical feature of Belgian law is the fundamental distinction between, on the one hand, the *entitlement* to be competent to have authority over the person of the child and the management of his property (in French: *l'attribution de l'autorité parentale*) and on the other hand, the ability to *exercise* of this authority (in French: *l'exercice de l'autorité parentale*). For a juvenile that has two parents, each of these parents holds these rights, whatever the underlying relationship between the two parents may be. However, being competent to have parental authority does not necessarily include the ability to exercise these powers.

A third feature of the Belgian law relating to parental authority is that it makes a differentiation in the exercise of parental authority by two living parents, depending upon whether or not they cohabit. The determining distinction in the legal regime of parental authority is thus not whether the parents are married to each other, but rather whether or not the parents cohabit, be they married or unmarried.

[B] Cohabiting Parents

[1] Contents of the Rule: Joint Exercise

If the juvenile has two parents who cohabit, these parents stand on a footing of complete equality in the exercise of parental authority. This equality is apparent

72. Article 341 Civil Code.
73. Article 375*bis* Civil Code.

through the system of joint exercise by the mother and father (or by the mother and the co-mother) of their powers.

This basis system in the exercise of parental authority can be described as a system of 'co-parenting', although the Civil Code itself does not use this term.

The principle of co-parenting was above all the result of the wish of the Belgian legislature to promote greater parental responsibility for the child. The essence of co-parenting is the continuing involvement of both parents in all aspects of the raising of their children.

[2] Scope of Application of the Rule

The rule of joint exercise affects all aspects of authority over a person and the management of property of the children:

- as for the juvenile in persona: the right to have physical custody, the right of care, the right to make fundamental choices relating to the child including decisions concerning medical treatment and surgical operations; it covers, therefore, both arrangements and decisions which can be counted as falling within the day-to-day raising of the child as well as more far-reaching arrangements and decisions;
- as for the property of the child: acting as a custodian, receiving income and providing a receipt, renting real property for a maximum term of nine years, etc;
- representing the child in all legal matters (e.g., applying for a loan in the name of the juvenile, sale of real and personal property), as well as in legal proceedings.

The only parental powers which do not fall within this rule, are those affecting the status in persona of the child: for example giving consent to the marriage of the juvenile or giving consent to his adoption. To these matters, separate rules are applied.

[3] The Presumption of Consent of the Other Parent

Joint exercise of powers over the person and property of a child is a good principle, but poses a great number of problems when applied in practice. In the course of normal day-to-day transactions it is indeed impractical that every act in the area of authority over the person or management of the property of a juvenile would on each occasion require the intervention of both parents. On the other hand, there may be a concern that under a system of joint exercise, third parties dealing with a juvenile would systematically require the intervention of both parents, excluding the risk of invalidity.

For this reason, Belgian law provides that for third parties acting in good faith, each parent acting individually, shall be deemed to act with the consent of the other parent. This amounts to a presumption of parental unanimity. This presumption, using an ordinary rule of evidence, is aimed at providing a legal basis for the individual acts of each parent, whereby third parties are also reassured. This is a presumption which can be invoked by any third party acting in good faith. The term 'third party' must be broadly interpreted: both private persons (such as a school head, physician, bank manager, notary) and government bodies are included.

The presumption obviously does not apply in the relationship between the parents themselves. One parent is only entitled to act individually if he has checked in advance that the other parent agrees. A matter undertaken by an individual parent without the agreement of the other parent is, in the relationship between the parents, never held to be valid.

Under French law, the presumption of consent by the other parent is limited to what is called 'usual matters'. This limitation has not been carried over into the Belgian law: this presumption applies to all matters connected with the authority over the person and the management of property, without any distinction as to whether or not it is a 'usual' matter. Therefore, the presumption also applies to important matters which (may) have a decisive influence on the future of the child (for instance arrange for the child to change school).

This is merely a rebuttable presumption which only applies insofar as the good faith of the third party, that has had dealings with one of the parents or has received the decision of one of the parents, is established.

A third party is deemed to be acting in good faith in so far as he had no knowledge and could not reasonably have had knowledge of the fact that the other parent had not given his or her consent to the arrangements made by the acting parent. This amounts to the application of the test of the general standard of care.[74]

In case the third party had knowledge or could reasonably have had knowledge of the disagreement between the parents, either directly by express notice of his or her contradictory opinion by the other parent to the third party (for instance the parent who notifies the school authorities of his differing opinion over the registration of the child), or by a contradictory act by the other parent (such as the parent who has registered his or her child for another course of study), or indirectly, for example, by a similar disagreement between the parents in the past, then the third party can no longer invoke this legal presumption. A dealing or decision that has been taken in these circumstances is also not legally valid in the relationship with these third parties. This system, therefore, has the result that one parent is in no way bound by the dealings or decisions of the other parent to which he has not indicated his or her agreement, and the third party brings its responsibility into question by only dealing with one parent although it knew (for instance because the other parent had notified) or could have known that the other parent was not in agreement.

In such a case the parties involved must apply to the court for a judgment.

This rule in favour of bona fide third parties, that cannot be deemed to have been aware of any disagreements between the parents, increases legal certainty.

74. *See infra* Chapter 11, §11.03 [A] [1] [a] [i].

[4] Case Before the Court

[a] Breaking a Deadlock

In the event that the parents, who must jointly take a decision or make arrangements, cannot reach agreement, one of them can bring the case before the family court.

The Belgian legislature sees this call upon the judge as a possibility to break the deadlock should the parents be unable to reach a mutual agreement. Indeed, under a regime of joint exercise of parental authority, neither of the two parents is entitled to make arrangements or to take decisions single-handedly and thus confront the other parent with a *fait accompli*.

In the event that the parents cannot reach an agreement, the family court can decide in the following ways:

- either give consent to one of the parents to, unilaterally, make one or several clearly described arrangements (or take decisions); or
- continue to leave the joint exercise of parental authority for all arrangements and decisions in the hands of both parents.

Equally, the family court may not only empower one of the parents to act unilaterally, but may also decide upon one concrete difference between the parents. Thus the judge can take a specific decision, when there is a lack of consensus between the parents with regard to, for example, the choice of school, both in the case where one of the parents has unilaterally – and thus in breach of the law – taken a decision or made arrangements and in the case where this has not yet happened.

The only thing the court cannot do in the case of cohabiting parents is to give the complete exercise of parental authority exclusively to one of the parents. Although the Code does not expressly indicate the criterion on which the family court should base its decision, it is clear that the only criterion, which the court may apply, is the *interests of the child*.

[b] Challenging Unilateral Acts of a Parent

It can happen that one parent unilaterally makes an arrangement or takes a decision (for instance registers the child in a particular school or for a particular course of study), and thereby confronts the other parent with a *fait accompli*. Also in this circumstance, the other parent who is not in agreement with what has happened, may turn to the family court.

The judgment which the family court must then make is often extremely delicate, particularly when the position or standpoint of each of both parents seems sound. Thus, in the case where one parent has acted unilaterally (e.g., has arranged for the child to change school), the judge must first establish whether the other parent was agreeable to this decision or arrangement. If this was not the case, then the acting parent has made an arrangement which exceeded his or her powers and thus was irregular, and therefore the judge must hold that this arrangement or decision was *null and void* (*de nul effet*).

Further the judge must establish whether or not this unilateral arrangement or decision was in the interests of the child. If it was in the interests of the child, then the judge must resume this decision for the future.

Thus it seems that a parent acting unilaterally, who knowingly and intentionally makes arrangements in breach of the rule of joint exercise of parental authority takes little or no risk if he or she is certain that what he or she is unilaterally doing, would be deemed to be in the interests of the child.

Should the court come to the opposite conclusion - that the unilaterally made arrangements were not in the interests of the child - then it must alter the irregular decision (for instance hold that the unilateral decision to change school is null and void and certify that the child remains registered in its previous school).

[C] Non-cohabiting Parents

[1] General System

If the parents are not cohabiting, Belgian law also uses as its starting position the system of *joint* exercise of the powers by both parents. This system stems from the desire of the Belgian legislature to make both parents be responsible after separation or divorce.

This rule implies that even if the parents do not cohabit, in principle they together exercise the authority over the person and the management of property of their child. It is irrelevant whether the non-cohabiting parents are married to one another.

The joint exercise of parental authority by non-cohabiting parents is subject to exactly the same system as the joint exercise of parental authority by cohabiting parents. Thus, also for non-cohabiting parents, the presumption of consent of the other parent in unilateral acts applies, both in usual and unusual arrangements. The court may also here give one of the parents the right to act in one or several well defined arrangements, and also here each parent has the right to tum to the family court in the event of dispute.

When the parents do not cohabit and the basis system of joint exercise of parental authority applies, then the parents must find a residence arrangement, in other words an arrangement covering where and for which periods the child shall reside. Through the arrangements made for the residence of the child, the each parent's right to personal contact is materialised.

All possible formulas are imaginable here, going from the pure joint physical custody or alternating residence, which means that the child alternates between each of his parents for (approximately) equal periods of time, to an arrangement whereby the child stays permanently at one of the parents' homes, except for every other weekend and half of the holiday periods (or even less) with the other parent.

If the parents are unable to reach an agreement on the residence of their child, each of them may bring the case before the family court. The judge must examine, as a matter of priority, the possibility of joint physical custody if one of the parents demands so. The law does not require the judge to impose a joint physical custody at the request of one parent, but only to examine, as a matter of priority, the possibility thereof. The family court decides taking into account the concrete circumstances of the case and the interests of the child and of the parents.[75] Since the new regime came into effect (2006) there has been a major shift in the attitude of the Belgian courts in favour of joint physical custody, particularly for children between 3 and 12 years.

Insofar as no alternating residence has been agreed or imposed, there is use of the terms 'main residence' (*hébergement principal*) at the home of one parent and the 'secondary residence' (*hébergement secondaire*) at the home of the other parent.

[2] Exceptional System

If there is no adequate consensus between the parents, the joint exercise of parental authority over the person (and the management of property) of the juvenile has little chance of success.

[a] The System of Exclusive Exercise

If one of the non-cohabiting parents wishes to refute the applicable system of joint exercise, then he or she may bring the case before the family court in order to seek an order for exclusive exercise of parental authority.

If, before the court, it indeed appears that the parents are not in agreement over several important aspects of raising the child, then the judge can entrust the exercise of parental authority over the person and the management of property exclusively to one of the parents.

The aspects deemed important in raising the child are expressly summed up in the Code: where the child will reside, important health decisions, education, the nurturing and leisure of the child, religious education or philosophical choices affecting the child. This list is in no way exhaustive.

Only if the parents have not reached agreement in at least one of the important aspects of raising the child, can the judge transfer from joint exercise to exclusive exercise. If there is in fact no lack of agreement in raising the child but one of the parents as a matter of principle wishes to end joint exercise of parental authority, then according to the statutory text, there is no option for the court to switch to a system of exclusive exercise.

The Code states that the judge can entrust exclusive exercise to one of the parents if there is a lack of agreement between the parents, which implies that he is not under a duty to do so, and thus, even in the case where there is no full consensus between the parents over all the important aspects in the raising of the child, the judge can decide that the parents must continue to undertake joint exercise. This means, for example, that in a situation where there is absolutely no dispute over the important aspects of the

75. Article 374, §2, Civil Code.

raising of the child between the parents but now that they no longer live together, they are unable to reach agreement on the residence of the child and for this reason they are obviously both seeking exclusive exercise of parental authority, the judge may nevertheless decide to continue the joint exercise of parental authority and add to this an order deciding the residence of the child.

[b] Possibility of an 'à la Carte' System

The system of the exercise of parental authority is however no all or nothing regime: alongside the maintenance of joint exercise for all prerogatives in the authority over a person and the management of property, and the change to a system of exclusive exercise by one parent of all prerogatives in the authority over a person and the management of property, the law provides for the possibility for the judge to entrust, in principle, the exclusive exercise of authority over the person to one of the parents but at the same time to require that a number of important decisions relating to the raising of the child can only be taken with the consent of both parents.

[3] Right of Access of the Parents

On each occasion that the court must decide on the exercise of authority over the person and the management of property for non-cohabiting, it must also indicate where the child will live.

If the court chooses for exclusive exercise of authority by one of the parents, it will also indicate the manner in which the other parent can maintain personal contact with the child.

During the preparatory drafting of the Act of 13 April 1995, when dealing with the right of access of the parents, reference was made to Article 9, §3 of the International Convention on the Rights of the Child (CRC), which requires that the contracting states respect the right of the child separated from one or both parents to maintain personal contact on a regular basis, unless this is against the interests of the child.

In a regime of exclusive competence there remains a right of personal contact with the child for the parent who does not exercise parental authority. The manner in which he/she maintains this personal contact (in other words the terms of access) may be laid down by the court. The Code states that the court can only refuse the exercise of personal contact for especially serious reasons.

Thus, court practice refuses the exercise of the right of access of one parent in only the most exceptional circumstances, for example in the event of serious abandonment by the parent, or of total rejection by the child of the parental figure, which rejection has not been inspired by the attitude of the other parent.

For the father and mother, therefore, the exercise of a right of access remains quasi-automatic, and it is not dependent on a test of the criterion of the interests of the child. Only the concrete terms of the exercise of the right of access, are settled by the court on a case-by-case basis in the interests of the child.

[4] The Right of Supervision

A parent who has not been entrusted with the exercise of parental authority, nevertheless keeps the right to supervise the raising of the child.

The right includes two elements: the first is the right to directly supervise the raising of the child, the second is the right of one parent to supervise the other parent in the manner in which the latter is raising the child of the family.

An important element in Belgian law is that it recognises the right of the parent who does not exercise parental authority to obtain from the other parent and even from third parties all useful information with regard to the raising of his/her child. Thus, third parties (such as school heads and class teachers, physicians and hospitals, banks, social security services, government administrations) cannot hide behind the fact that the other parent has, through a court order, obtained the exercise of parental authority, in order to refuse to convey particular information relating to the child.

In the context of his/her right of supervision, a parent can also apply to the family court to oppose a particular decision or particular arrangement made by the other parent in the raising of the child, using the interests of the child as the criterion.

[5] The Right to Introduce a Case Before the Family Court

Only each of the parents and, exceptionally, the public prosecutor can bring a case before the family court. The minor has no capacity at all to bring a case before the courts against (one of) his parents, nor has he any possibility to have designated a curator *ad litem* to represent him.

[D] The Right of Audience of Juveniles

Under Belgian law the rules relating to the right of audience of juveniles before the courts have been introduced in 1994, implementing Article 12 of the UN Convention on the Rights of the Child. In 2008 an amendment to the Belgian Constitution has been adopted, guaranteeing that 'Each child has the right to express his or her views in all matters affecting him or her, the views of the child being given due weight in accordance with his or her age and maturity'.[76] The legislation has been thoroughly amended by an Act of 30 July 2013 organising the right of audience of juveniles before the family courts.[77]

This regime provides that juveniles from the age of 12 years have to be informed by the family court of their right of audience. If the minor reacts positively, the minor must be heard by the court. Under the age of 12 years the initiative to be heard can originate either from the family court, from the public prosecutor, from the parties or from the juvenile concerned. There is no statutory minimum age limit. The judge who receives such a request by a minor under the age of twelve is required to hear the

76. Article 22*bis*, para. 2, Constitution.
77. Article 1004/1-2 Judicial Code.

juvenile. Thus in practice children of 9, 10 and 11 years old are sometimes heard in court.

In both cases, the juvenile must always be heard by the specific judge who is trying the dispute; the judge cannot designate another person. Neither the parties themselves (usually the parents) nor their lawyers are entitled to be present during the hearing of the juvenile.

In principle the child is heard on his own. Only in very exceptional circumstances the judge may decide that the child be accompanied (for instance by a member of the family or by a trusted person or by a lawyer). However the child has no right to be assisted by a personal lawyer.

The judge or his clerk must subsequently make up an affidavit of the conversation with the child, which is added to the file of the case and is made available for inspection by the parties and their lawyers who can also obtain a copy of it. In this way, the confidentiality of the discussion between the judge and the juvenile is not guaranteed.

In accordance with Article 12.1 of the UN Convention on the Rights of the Child, the judge, after having heard the child, should give his opinion 'due weight in accordance with the age and maturity of the child'. The family court is under no duty to follow the wishes of the juvenile: the opinion of the child is not the decisive criterion for the judge, but rather the interests of the child.

The hearing of the juvenile also does not have as a consequence that the juvenile becomes a party to the dispute pending before the family court. Thus, the juvenile cannot appeal against the decision of the judge who has not taken up his point of view.

§7.04 DIVORCE

[A] Introduction

[1] Historical Evolution

While marriage could be dissolved both among the Romans and the Germans, the Roman Catholic Church introduced the idea of the complete indissolubility of marriage. In the ninth century, it succeeded in imposing its point of view. This process must be seen in the broader trend that removed marriage irrevocably from the families and made it a matter for the social authorities (in the Middle Ages, for the Church; since 1789, for the State).

Since throughout the entire *Ancien Régime* most of the problems concerning marriage came under the authority of the Church, there could be no divorce. The Church did permit separation of bed and board on the request of the husband in the case of adultery committed by his wife and on the request of the wife for various reasons (but not on the grounds of mutual consent). In addition, annulment of a marriage was not uncommon because of the large number of marriage impediments.

After the legal view of marriage had already been challenged under the Austrian Emperor Joseph II, the situation changed fundamentally during the French Revolution.

Because the contractual character of marriage was stressed at that time and the freedom of the individual was also applied to marriage, divorce was introduced. An Act of 1792 even made divorce possible in very many cases:

- divorce by mutual consent upon simple declaration before the officer of civil status;
- divorce because of culpable behaviour of one of the spouses: crime, cruelty, serious offence, adultery, condemnation to a degrading punishment, obvious immorality, abandonment of the spouse for two years;
- divorce for other reasons: mental illness, absence for five years, emigration and '*incompatibilité d'humeur et de caractère*' (incompatibility of characters). In 1794, one went still further: divorce was made possible after six months of actual separation.

The Civil Code of 1804 was clearly a reaction against the broad conceptions of divorce that prevailed in the previous period. In the Napoleonic Code, the grounds for divorce were all reduced to culpable behaviour, but divorce by mutual consent was retained, albeit with stringent regulations.

The abolition of divorce in France with the Restoration in 1816 was nothing more than the logical continuation of the reaction that began in 1804. In Belgium, however, the legislation of 1804 was retained. In France, divorce was introduced again in 1884 but without divorce by mutual consent, so that Belgium, until in the 1970s of the twentieth century, was one of the few European countries that had this form of divorce.

Until 1974, there were no fundamental changes in the Belgian legislation on divorce.

An Act of 1 July 1974 constituted the breakthrough of the principle of no-fault divorce: the spouse of a mentally-ill person could, after ten years of actual separation, obtain a divorce without mention of culpability. In general, after ten years of actual separation, a divorce could be obtained even against the will of the 'innocent' partner. In this case, the settlement remains based on the crime-and-punishment idea as regards the patrimonial consequences of the divorce. An Act of 2 December 1982 reduced the period of actual separation to five years, and an Act of 16 April 2000 reduced this period further to two years.

An Act of 27 April 2007 carried out a radical reform of the grounds for and the consequences of divorce. Since this legislative reform, there exist two kinds of divorce in Belgium: divorce on the grounds of the irretrievable breakdown of the marriage,[78] and divorce by mutual consent.[79]

[2] Statistics

In 2008, the first year under the new divorce legislation, a total of 35,366 divorce judgments were pronounced by the Belgian courts, in 2014 the number of divorce

78. Article 229 Civil Code.
79. Article 230 Civil Code.

judgments had decreased to 24,310 (*compare*: in 2008 45,613 marriages were contracted, in 2014 only 39,879).

[B] Divorce on the Grounds of the Irretrievable Breakdown of the Marriage

[1] Conditions for Obtaining a Divorce

A divorce on the grounds of the irretrievable breakdown of the marriage can be obtained in two ways: the application for divorce can be submitted jointly by both spouses, or one of the spouses can institute the action for divorce against the other spouse.

If both spouses file jointly for the divorce, the court must pronounce the divorce once their de facto separation has lasted longer than six months. If this de facto separation has lasted less than six months and the spouses wish to file a joint application for divorce, then the spouses must appear before the court a second time, following a period of reflection of three months or after six months of de facto separation, and repeat their desire to be granted a divorce.[80]

If one of the spouses institutes the action for divorce against the other spouse, different possibilities to grant the divorce can occur.

First of all the spouse can obtain the divorce by proof of the irretrievable breakdown of the marriage, which can be supplied by all legal means.[81] The marriage is deemed to have suffered an irretrievable breakdown if the continuation of the cohabitation of the spouses and the resumption thereof has become impossible as a result of this breakdown.

However, a spouse has also the possibility to obtain the divorce on the basis of a de facto separation. The marriage is deemed to have suffered an irretrievable breakdown if the application for divorce is filed by one single spouse following de facto separation of more than one year. If the de facto separation of the spouses has lasted less than a year and should a party wish to file a unilateral application, then the marriage is deemed to have suffered an irretrievable breakdown if the spouse filing the application appears before the court a second time, following a period of reflection of one year or after one year of de facto separation, and repeats his/her wish to be granted a divorce.[82]

[2] Procedure

The action for divorce on the grounds of the irretrievable breakdown of the marriage is instituted before the family court in the place where the spouses had their last common marital residence or in the place where the defendant has his/her residence.

80. Article 229, §2, Civil Code.
81. Article 229, §1, Civil Code.
82. Article 229, §3, Civil Code.

During the whole trial the spouses do not need to appear in person but can be represented by a lawyer. If one of the spouses institutes the action for divorce, the defending spouse can institute a counter action for divorce on the grounds of the irretrievable breakdown of the marriage in each stage of the proceedings.

On the request of one of the spouses the divorce judgment must be served by a bailiff upon the other spouse. The divorce takes effect and the marriage is dissolved as regards the relationship between the spouses on the day the judgment becomes final.

[3] Temporary Measures

During the divorce procedure, 'temporary measures' can be taken by the family court.[83] When the divorce between the parties becomes final, the temporary measures lapse. The measures regarding the children of the marriage (custody, visiting rights, support payments for the children), however, continue in effect after the divorce (*see* below).

Temporary measures can be taken with regard to the person, the support, and the property both of the spouses themselves and of the children of their marriage.

The most common measures are:

- Separate residences for the spouses.
- Support payments between the spouses based on the obligation to help and the obligation to contribute to the costs of the marriage. These obligations continue in effect during the divorce procedure.
- *Provisio ad litem*: this is an advance to be paid by one spouse to the other to cover the court costs arising from the divorce proceedings.
- Measures related to the children: confirming the joint custody of the parents, or granting of custody to one of the parents and of access to the other parent; ordering the other parent to pay support for the children to the parent who raises them (also for adult children).
- Measures related to the property: temporarily granting the use of the property to one of the spouses, imposition of a prohibition of alienation and of movement of the property, temporary allocation of the joint debts, appointment of a notary for the compilation of an inventory, etc.

The procedure is as in summary proceedings.

[4] Consequences of Divorce

[a] General

The marriage is dissolved as regards the relationship between the spouses on the day the divorce judgment becomes final. The ex-spouses can immediately enter into a new marriage.

83. Article 1280 Judicial Code.

The dissolution of the marriage only has an effect in the future (*ex nunc*). Only one limited exception applies to this rule: as far as the property of the spouses is concerned, the divorce works retroactively to the moment of the institution of the action for divorce, but only in the relationship between the spouses themselves, not in the relationships with respect to third parties.

The former spouses are no longer each other's legal heirs.

[b] Support after Divorce[84]

Spouses can conclude an agreement laying down any claims to a maintenance payment following divorce, the amount thereof and any possibilities for review.

In the absence of an agreement, the court can, at the request of the spouse in need, authorise a maintenance payment to be borne by the other spouse. The court is permitted to refuse the request if the respondent proves that the applicant has committed a serious fault which has made it impossible to continue living together. In no circumstances can a maintenance payment be granted to a spouse who has been found guilty of acts of physical violence committed against the other spouse.

In order to determine if the applicant is in need, two elements must be taken into account:

- the income of the applicant; and
- his/her earning potential (or capacities) – a spouse who is capable of supporting himself/herself in whole or in part by working, can be obliged to work; if he/she refuses to do so, the family court can take into account a presumed earning potential.

Where the respondent demonstrates that the applicant's state of need is the result of his/her own decision during the cohabitation of the spouses that was not motivated by the needs of the family, the court is authorised to relieve the respondent from the payment of a maintenance payment, and it may also reduce the amount thereof.

The level of the payment should, as a minimum, cover the state of need of the person entitled to the payment, but it may not be higher than one third of the net income of the person obliged to make the payment.

The duration of the payment may not be longer than the length of the marriage. This term may be extended in exceptional circumstances.

In all cases, the maintenance payment can be increased, reduced or abolished by the family court if the amount is no longer appropriate as a result of new circumstances, irrespective of the volition of the parties. Likewise the family court can adjust the payment if the division of the property after divorce results in a change in the financial position of the spouses.

84. Article 301 Civil Code.

[c] The Property of the Spouses

If the spouses were married with the system of community, the community property must be liquidated and divided after the divorce.

[d] The Relationships Between Parents and Children

In principle, divorce brings about no change in the obligations of the parents with respect to their children. The parent who does not have custody of the child is obliged to pay child support to the other parent.

If child support payments have already been imposed during the course of the divorce procedure (in the framework of the temporary measures), they remain in force after the divorce until changed by the court should the occasion arise.

In all forms of divorce, the rule is that neither of the parents loses parental authority after the divorce. Both parents continue to maintain the parental authority. Thus, also after the divorce, both parents must give their consent to the marriage or to the adoption of their minor child.

However, specific rules apply in regard to the *exercise* of a number of prerogatives of parental authority, including the right to custody. Two situations can arise:[85]

- If temporary measures have been taken during the divorce proceedings on the exercise of the parental authority and/or the custody of the child, then these measures remain in force after the divorce, unless they are changed by the family court should the occasion arise.
- If, during the divorce proceedings, no temporary measures have been taken with respect to the children, then the joint exercise of the parental authority continues to apply (*see* above).

In both cases, after the divorce, the family court can take all measures related to the children. The parent who is deprived of the custody has access to his child, unless exceptionally serious reasons so demand. He also retains the right to exercise supervision over the raising of the child.[86]

[C] Divorce by Mutual Consent[87]

[1] Requirements

A procedure for divorce by mutual consent can only be started if both of the spouses not only agree on the dissolution of their marriage but also in advance have reached a complete agreement on *all* the consequences this dissolution will have both for themselves and for their children. Failing an agreement over any single one of these points, the divorce by mutual consent cannot proceed.

85. Article 302 Civil Code.
86. Article 374, para. 4, Civil Code.
87. Articles 275–276 Civil Code and Articles 1287–1304 Judicial Code.

Agreement must be reached in advance and in writing on the following points:

- The liquidation and distribution of the community property and the mutual property claims the spouses can apply.
- The intestate inheritance rights of the one spouse in the estate of the other in the event one of the spouses should die during the divorce procedure.
- The residence of each of the spouses during the divorce procedure.
- The exercise of a number of prerogatives of parental authority, especially the right to custody, both during the trial period and after the divorce (in this form of divorce, too, both of the parents continue to have all prerogatives of parental authority after the divorce). Here, too, the right to custody can be assigned to both parents (joint custody) or to one of the parents. For the parent who does not obtain the custody, visiting rights must be settled.
- The support payments for the children that will be owed by the parent who does not raise the children to the other parent.
- The amount of possible support payments to be paid by one of the spouses to the other, during the divorce procedure and after the divorce. The spouses are only obliged to conclude an agreement about these support payments, which does not mean that support actually has to be provided. In this form of divorce, the support payments after divorce are purely contractual in character. So the spouses can agree that neither of them will have to pay any support to the other party.

[2] Procedure

The divorce procedure starts with the submission, by the spouses themselves or by their lawyer or notary, of the petition for divorce together with the agreements mentioned above.

If at the moment of the submission of the petition the de facto separation of the spouses has lasted longer than six months, the divorce proceedings pass off entirely written. The spouses do not have to appear before the judge, and neither does their lawyer or their notary. However the family court has the possibility to order the personal appearance of the spouses, for instance if it has some doubts about the agreement they made on their children.

If at the moment of the submission of the petition the spouses continue to live together, or if their de facto separation has not yet lasted six months, the spouses must appear together and in person before the court, to confirm that they want to get a divorce.

In both cases the family court may suggest the spouses modify their agreement on the minor children (*not* on the other parts of their agreement) in case it considers it to be in conflict with the interests of the children.

The court may also decide to hear the children, in accordance with the general rules relating to the right of audience of juveniles (*see* above).

During a new hearing the family court can request the spouses to change their agreement on the minor children in case this agreement is obviously contrary to the interests of the children. If the spouses refuse to modify their agreement, this can lead to the rejection of the divorce petition.

The court may only determine if the legal conditions are fulfilled, whether the spouses have agreed on all points prescribed by law, and whether this agreement does not conflict with public order or good morals. In no case may the court rule on the content of the agreement: this is left completely to the discretion of the spouses, except for the agreement on the minor children.

In the divorce judgment the agreement on the minor children (not the other parts of the agreement) is approved by the court.

[3] Consequences

All relationships between the spouses themselves and with their children are governed by the prior agreement they have concluded.

After the divorce becomes final, the ex-spouses may change their agreement in mutual consent, and this with regard to *all* of its points.

In principle it is not possible for one of the ex-spouses to obtain a change in their agreement through the court: the contractual nature of the settlement between the ex-spouses holds and absolutely excludes a change imposed by the judge. However, since the Act of 27 April 2007, their agreement about the support payments between the ex-spouses can be changed or abolished by the family court under the same circumstances as the support after divorce on the grounds of the irretrievable breakdown of the marriage.[88] This new rule is only applicable on the agreements concluded starting from 1 September 2007.

A change can also be obtained through the court on the settlement with regard to the children, in the case of new circumstances, as to the exercise of the parental authority and the residence of the child, on the basis of the best interest of the child. As to the support payments for the children, the agreement can only be modified by the judge insofar as new circumstances beyond the control of the parties have fundamentally modified the situation of the parents or that of the children.[89]

§7.05 STATUTORY SCHEME FOR COHABITATION

[A] Introduction

An Act introducing the institution of legal cohabitation into the Civil Code[90] was passed by the Belgian Parliament and signed by the King on 23 November 1998. Cohabitees can choose whether to opt for the statutory scheme.

88. Article 1288, 3°, Judicial Code.
89. Article 1288, 2°, Judicial Code.
90. Articles 1475-1479 Civil Code.

[B] The Legal Position of Cohabitees Before and Outside the Statutory Cohabitation Regime

[1] Lawfulness of Cohabitation

Traditionally cohabitation was regarded as contrary to public policy and public morals. For example, in 1953 the Court of Cassation held a gift to a cohabitee to be void.[91] According to the Court of Cassation on 21 April 1958,[92] the choice made in favour of marriage as an institution enjoying the preference of the State, obliged the legislature to deny the advantages to cohabitees which are given to married couples. On 23 June 1977 the Court of Cassation designated an unmarried cohabitation as unlawful.[93] A year later, a married woman, who had lived for more than ten years together with a man who had been killed by the defendant, was held not entitled to damages from the defendant.[94]

A change came with a decision of the Court of Cassation on 1 February 1989, in which the Court allowed a claim for damages against the defendant who had caused the death of the woman with whom the plaintiff had lived for a considerable time. The plaintiff was unmarried but the victim had been married to someone else. In the court's view, the fact that the victim's husband might complain about the cohabitation was not a reason to allow the defendant to escape liability to the plaintiff.[95] In a later case the Court of Cassation accepted that the same principle applied when the plaintiff, rather than his deceased cohabitee, was married; the adulterous character of the relationship was a private matter (about which only the deceived spouse could complain) which did not excuse the defendant tortfeasor from his liability towards the cohabitee of the deceased. The Court stressed that the plaintiff's claim was entirely lawful.[96]

This case law dealt with cohabitation in which one cohabitee was living in adultery with the other. The case law has important consequences for the less sensitive situation in which neither of the cohabitees is married; for, in these circumstances, there is no one who can assert the illegality of the relationship. After these decisions it would have been inconsistent to continue to regard cohabitation where no adultery is involved as unlawful: without any doubt at the end of the twentieth century cohabitation where no adultery is involved is no longer regarded as contrary to public morals.

[2] Cohabitation Contracts

With the changes which have taken place since 1989, which mean that cohabitation (unless adultery is involved) is neither contrary to public order (because tending to undermine marriage) nor contrary to public morals (because generally accepted to be

91. Court of Cassation 13 November 1953, 1954 Arresten van het Hof van Cassatie 167.
92. Court of Cassation 21 April 1958, 1958-I Pasicrisie belge 921.
93. Court of Cassation 23 June 1977, 1977 Arresten van het Hof van Cassatie 1098.
94. Court of Cassation 19 December 1978, 1978–1979 Rechtskundig Weekblad 1709.
95. Court of Cassation 1 February 1989, 1988–1989 Arresten van het Hof van Cassatie 645.
96. Court of Cassation 15 February 1990, 1989–1990 Arresten van het Hof van Cassatie 776.

morally wrong), a cohabitation contract is in principle valid. The option is available to same-sex couples, as well as heterosexual couples. It is not possible for the cohabitees to bind themselves by contract to live together, for such obligation treats an individual as an object.[97] For the same reason it is not possible to create a valid obligation which restricts in any way the breaking up of the relationship. It is, however, possible to create a maintenance obligation by contract.

[C] Legal Cohabitation

[1] Scope of the Rules

The provisions of the Civil Code on cohabitation only regulate the relationship between two people;[98] as was the case for all earlier Belgian legislative proposals, there is no possibility for a group of persons larger than two who are living together (for instance three unmarried sisters living together after the death of the parents) to invoke the provisions.

There are no further restrictions. Thus, the provisions may be used by relatives who are legally not able to marry one another (brother and sister, father and daughter). The cohabitees seeking official recognition may be of the same or of different sex.

It was not the intention that legal cohabitation should become a new civil status. The idea was rather to provide a pragmatic solution to the practical problem of regulating property and financial matters between the cohabitees. The fact that no status was intended to be created is expressed by the position which the new provisions occupy in the Civil Code: they are not situated in Book I, where the Law of Persons can be found, but in Book III, which deals with acquisition of property rights.

[2] Formal Requirements

Legal cohabitation is brought into being by making a written declaration of cohabitation. The written document should then be handed to the civil status registrar in the place of common residence of the cohabitees.[99]

After receiving the declaration, the civil status registrar must establish whether both cohabitees satisfy the statutory requirements for entering cohabitation. If satisfied that all requirements are complied with, the civil status registrar should make a note of the declaration in the population register.

[3] Requirements

Article 1475, §2, of the Civil Code imposes two requirements which must be satisfied in order to enter legal cohabitation: (i) neither partner must be party to a subsisting

97. Article 1128 Civil Code.
98. Article 1475, §1, Civil Code.
99. Article 1476, §1, Civil Code.

marriage or other legal cohabitation; and (ii) both partners must be competent to conclude a contract.

[4] Exclusion of the Statutory Scheme

A number of the provisions on cohabitation are mandatory. The provisions regarding the family home, the obligation to share the costs of cohabitation and the joint responsibilities for debts incurred for the common household or joint children may not be excluded or restricted by contract.[100] The remaining provisions (regarding the property relationship, inheritance and maintenance of the surviving cohabitee and adjudication of disputes) will only apply in the absence of agreement by the cohabitees to the contrary.

[5] Obligation to Share Costs of Cohabitation

The cohabitees are bound to contribute to the costs of their cohabitation in proportion to their possibilities.[101] Thus a rule traditionally applicable to married couples is now also applicable to cohabitees choosing for the statutory scheme.

[6] Responsibility for Debts

Each cohabitee is responsible, on the same footing as the other cohabitee, for such debts of the other cohabitee as are incurred for the purposes of cohabitation and for the children who are brought up by the cohabitees. But one cohabitee is not liable for debts incurred by the other cohabitee which, having regard to the resources of the cohabitees, are excessive.[102] Here, again, the traditional rule for married couples applies.

[7] Property Relationship

In the statutory scheme, each cohabitee retains all goods to which title can be evidenced, any income flowing from such goods and his earnings.[103] Property to which title cannot be evidenced by either cohabitee will belong, together with any income flowing from such property, to the cohabitees in undivided shares.

A special provision ensures that when one cohabitee dies and the survivor is an heir to the deceased, the presumption that property to which title is unclear is held in equal shares is displaced by a presumption that a gift has been made.[104] This provision is aimed at the situation in which the cohabitees are, for example, mother and daughter. If the mother dies, the daughter should not be put in a preferred position

100. Article 1477, §1, Civil Code.
101. Article 1477, §3, Civil Code.
102. Article 1477, §4, Civil Code.
103. Article 1478, para. 1, Civil Code.
104. Article 1478, para. 3, Civil Code.

vis-à-vis the mother's other descendants regarding the inheritance. Were the general rule to apply, property in the common household goods to which title cannot be evidenced should be treated as in equal undivided shares of the mother and daughter. The operation of this rule might unfairly advantage the daughter *vis-à-vis* the other offspring. Therefore, the half shares of the daughter are treated as gifts to the daughter. Accordingly, the daughter will be obliged to bring them into account when the inheritance shares are calculated.

[8] Special Regime Regarding the Family Home

The family home is subject to a special protective regime under Article 1477, §2, of the Civil Code, as is the case for married couples. According to this provision, neither partner is entitled, without the consent of the other, to dispose of the rights in their main common residence. Creating a mortgage without the consent of the other party is equally prohibited. The prohibition applies whether the disposition is for value or by way of gift. Each partner is similarly prohibited from disposing of (whether or not for value), or pawning, the household goods present in the main residence without the consent of the other partner. If the partner refuses consent without having a good reason for doing so, the partner wishing to make the disposal may apply to the family court for an order that the disposition may be made.

A rented house is similarly protected. If one of the partners has rented the house which forms their main residence, even if the tenancy commenced before the registration of the cohabitation, both cohabitees become tenants by operation of law, notwithstanding any agreement to the contrary. The notice to quit or other notifications by the landlord regarding the tenancy must be sent separately to each of the cohabitees; notifications from the tenants to the landlord must come from each cohabitees separately. The cohabitees can only rely upon the invalidity of notifications which do not comply with the above requirement, if the landlord was aware of the cohabitation of the cohabitees.

If one cohabitee acts in violation of the provisions regarding disposition of the main residence or regarding the tenancy of the main residence, the other cohabitee may ask the court to declare the transaction void. The cohabitee must approach the court within one year of the date of the transaction which is sought to be annulled. In place of declaring the transaction void, the court may award damages.

[9] Inheritance

Originally the cohabitees did not inherit from one another. However since a change of the law introduced by an Act of 28 March 2007, the surviving cohabitee is a default heir of the usufruct [or the lease] of the main common residence and the household goods, but he can be disinherited.[105]

105. Article 745*octies* Civil Code.

[10] Adjudication of Disputes Between Cohabitees

Disputes between the cohabitees may be brought to the family court, which has jurisdiction to make interim orders where necessary.[106] The court must determine the duration of its orders. Such orders lapse in any event on the day upon which the cohabitation under the statutory regime terminates.[107]

Application to the court requesting a decision in case of dispute may also be made up to three months after the termination of the cohabitation under the statutory scheme. But in such application the court can only make such orders as are urgently required in consequence of the termination of the cohabitation. The court must determine the period during which the orders are to operate, which may, in any case, not exceed one year.[108]

Disputes arising from the termination of the cohabitation after the three-month period after the date of termination has elapsed are subject to the general rules of the Judicial Code regarding procedure and competence.

[11] Termination of the Cohabitation

Termination occurs:[109]

- in the event of death of one cohabitee;
- if one of the cohabitees marries the other cohabitee or someone else;
- if the two cohabitees make a joint declaration to the civil status registrar that they wish the cohabitation to end;
- if one cohabitee makes a unilateral declaration to the civil status registrar that he or she wishes the cohabitation to terminate. In such case the civil status registrar must notify, by means of official notification via a bailiff, the other cohabitee within eight days of the termination of the cohabitation.

The termination is noted by the civil status registrar in the population register. The Civil Code does not specify what should happen if the cohabitees cease to cohabit without making use of the formal modes of termination. The cohabitation under the statutory regime only ends by force of law if one of the cohabitees contracts a marriage, or in the event of death.

[12] Maintenance

Cohabitees under the statutory scheme do not owe each other any duty to maintain after the termination of the legal cohabitation, not even when one cohabitee is in need, and quite regardless of the duration of the cohabitation.

106. Article 1479, para. 1, Civil Code.
107. Article 1479, para. 2, Civil Code.
108. Article 1479, para. 3, Civil Code.
109. Article 1476, §2, Civil Code.

§7.06 SELECTED BIBLIOGRAPHY

R. Dekkers & A. Wylleman, *Handboek burgerlijk recht*, Vol. I, *Personen- en familierecht* (3d ed., Antwerp: Intersentia 420).

H. De Page, *Traité de droit civil belge*, Vol. I, *Les personnes* (A.-Ch. Van Gysel dir., Brussels: Bruylant 2015).

Y.-H. Leleu, *Droit des personnes et des familles* (3d ed., Brussels: Larcier 2016).

Y.-H. Leleu, *Droit patrimonial des couples* (Brussels: Larcier 2015).

N. Massager, *Droit familial de l'enfance. Filiation – Autorité parentale – Hébergement* (Brussels: Bruylant 2009).

P. Senaeve & A. Bekkers, *De wet betreffende de familie- en jeugdrechtbank. Commentaar, gesystematiseerde uittreksels uit de voorbereidende werken en gecoördineerde wetteksten* (Mechelen: Wolters Kluwer 2014).

P. Senaeve, *Compendium van het personen- en familierecht* (15th ed., Leuven: Acco 2015).

F. Swennen, *Het personen- en familierecht. Identiteit en verwantschap vanuit juridisch perspectief* (4th ed., Antwerp: Intersentia 2015).

G. Verschelden, *Handboek Belgisch personen- en familierecht* (Bruges: die Keure 2016).

CHAPTER 8

Successions, Donations *Inter Vivos* and Wills

Christian De Wulf

§8.01 INTRODUCTION

In Belgium, the transmission of property in the context of family relationships is governed to a great extent by the 'Law of Succession' and the 'Law of Donations *Inter Vivos* and Wills'. The statutory rules relating to these matters are embodied in Book III, Chapters I and II, of the Belgian Civil Code.

Though the Law of Succession and the Law of Donations *inter vivos* and Wills regulate legal relations which are essentially different, in practice both branches of the law are often applied together. Thus the possibility to make a donation *inter vivos* or to make a testamentary disposition is limited by the rules of the legal portion to which some heirs are entitled (reserve portion), which accompany the law of succession. On the other hand, the heirs have to restore to the succession of the donor the donations and the legacies that were given to them by the deceased person.

§8.02 SUCCESSIONS

[A] General

[1] Statutory and Testamentary Devolution

The statutory succession, i.e., devolution and distribution in the statutory order provided for intestacy (succession *ab intestato*), determines when, how, and in what proportion the estate of the deceased devolves upon his heirs (*dévolution légale – wettelijke erfopvolging*). It indicates the different heirs-at-law, stipulates their rights and duties, and regulates, if there are several heirs, the way in which they can determine the joint possession to step out of *indivisum*.

The legal succession differs from the testamentary succession (succession *ex testamento*) (*dévolution testamentaire – testamentaire erfopvolging*). The latter is in principle determined by the terms of the last will of the testator. The testamentary succession prevails over the succession by operation of law, insofar as the rights of the forced heirs are preserved. Forced heirs are the persons whom the testator or donor cannot deprive of the portion of the estate reserved for them by law.

It occurs that both the legal devolution and the testamentary devolution are partly applicable to the same inheritance. For instance, where the deceased person has disposed of only part of his property in his will, the rest of the estate is inherited according to the rules of legal succession.

[2] When?

The inheritance devolves at the event of the death.[1] Only the natural death of the testator causes the transfer of his property. Attainder has been abolished in Belgium by Article 13 of the Constitution.

He who claims to be an heir, has to prove the death of the deceased. This evidence usually consists of an official document issued by the Registry Office.[2] In order to be able to draw up a death certificate, the registration officer needs to have proof that the person concerned has deceased. This requires recognisable mortal remains to exist. In the absence of mortal remains or if these are unrecognisable, the registration officer cannot establish the death. In such case the death can be established by a judgment pronounced by the family court.

To this end, the judge has to be presented with evidence of the person's death. In the absence of such proof, no declaratory judgment of finding of presumed death can be obtained and one has to abide by the legal provisions concerning 'absence' (*absence - afwezigheid*). In Belgium the absence causes the devolution of the succession,[3] when following an appropriate legal procedure and a decision of the family court after an absence of approximately six or eight years.[4]

[3] Goods Constituting the Succession

The succession consists of all the personal estate and real estate which belonged to the deceased at the time of his death and which do not cease on the death of the holder. Some rights (e.g., the right of usufruct, of use and habitation) are extinguished by death and consequently they no longer form part of the estate of the deceased person.

As a person's estate consists of his assets as well as his liabilities, not only the deceased's property and the rights on the assets side, but also his debts are transferred

1. Article 718 Civil Code.
2. Articles 77 & 78 Civil Code.
3. Articles 120–134 Civil Code.
4. Articles 118–121 Civil Code.

to his heirs. However, an heir is not obliged, by the mere devolution of the succession, to pay *pro parte* the deceased debts. He is only obliged to do so in the event that he accepts the succession.

When the deceased is married, it will be necessary, in order to establish the size of the succession, to verify under which property regime the deceased was married. Was the deceased married in community of goods (*communanté de biens – huwgemeenschap*) or under a separate estates arrangement (*séparation de biens – scheiding van goederen*)? One should proceed first to the settlement and partition of the dissolved community before the succession of the deceased spouse can be settled.

For spouses who did not otherwise stipulate in a marriage contract, the matrimonial regime of community property applies. This regime provided by law is in fact a joint estate of spouses comprising only the property acquired during marriage[5] otherwise than by way of gift or inheritance. The succession then essentially consists of half the communal estate and the separate property of the deceased.

The spouses can, before or during the marriage, conclude a contract according to the prescribed forms (*contract de mariage – huwelijkscontract*) in which they depart from the rules of the legal community system. They can thus widen or reduce[6] this community or, if desired, agree on a separate estates settlement.[7] In the latter case the succession of the deceased consists of the goods for which evidence has been provided that they are the separate property of the deceased.

In the case of extension of the community, for instance when the parties have stipulated a community property comprising all properties present and future, the succession of the deceased spouse consists of half of this communal estate, as specified above, to which only personal belongings can exceptionally be added.

It can be stipulated in the marriage contract that the surviving spouse is assigned a larger portion than half of the joint estate, or that the total communal estate will go to the surviving spouse. When a clause providing for the total communal estate to remain to the benefit of the surviving spouse has been agreed upon, all the communal goods are in principle withdrawn from the succession of the predeceased spouse.[8]

[4] Requirements for Entitlement to Inherit

In order to be entitled to the succession, the designated heir has to be alive at the moment of the devolution of the succession, and he must not be affected by the rules which decide on 'unworthiness' (*indignité – onwaardigheid*).

In the first place the heir must exist at the moment the succession takes place.[9] The inheritance does not go to anyone predeceasing the deceased, or anyone not yet existing at the moment of the devolution of the succession. When the order in which

5. Articles 1398–1408 Civil Code.
6. Articles 1451–1456 Civil Code.
7. Articles 1466–1469 Civil Code.
8. Articles 1464–1465 Civil Code.
9. Article 725, para. 1, Civil Code.

two or more persons have deceased cannot be determined, these persons are considered to have deceased simultaneously.[10] Therefore they cannot be entitled to each other's succession, and the succession is settled as if the person deceased simultaneously were in fact predeceased. An infant already conceived at the moment the succession devolves is considered already to exist on the condition that it is later born alive and viable.[11]

Unworthy to inherit, and as such debarred from the succession, are the persons who have been convicted for having killed the deceased or for having attempted to kill that person. The part of the unworthy heir devolves upon his descendants according to the rules of representation. By default of issue it devolves upon the other heirs.[12]

In Belgium, aliens have the right to inherit, to dispose and to acquire in the same manner as Belgian subjects.[13]

[5] The Place Where the Succession Devolves

The domicile of the deceased, at the moment of his death, determines the place where the succession devolves.[14] This place is important because it determines in a compulsory way the jurisdiction of the court *ratione loci* in all that is related to the joint tenancy and the transfer of the estate.

[6] The Prohibition to Enter into Agreements on a Succession Which Has Not Yet Devolved

It is forbidden to enter into an agreement on a succession that has not devolved yet.

Though in principle future facts or things can be the subject of an agreement, Article 1130 of the Civil Code states that one cannot renounce a succession which has not devolved yet, nor can any binding provisions be made on such a succession, even with the consent of the person whose succession it concerns.

Goods belonging to the succession of a person who is still alive cannot be sold.[15]

Neither can the presumptive heirs, before the deceased death, enter into agreements on, for instance renouncing the legal portion that must devolve on the heirs, on partition of the goods of the future succession.

[B] Heirs Entitled to the Succession

The rights of succession granted by law are classified in the following categories:

- the rights of the relatives;
- the rights of the surviving spouse;

10. Article 725, *in fine*, Civil Code.
11. Article 721 Civil Code.
12. Articles 727-729 Civil Code.
13. Article 726 Civil Code.
14. Article 110 Civil Code.
15. Article 1600 Civil Code.

- the rights of the legal cohabitant;
- the succession in the context of an adoption;
- the right of statutory reversion;
- the law of succession of the Belgian State.

The above-mentioned categories are in practice often present together, e.g., relatives come into the inheritance in concurrence with the surviving spouse. Also gifts submitted to statutory reversion, and rules regulating the adoptive succession, can be applied here.

[1] The Relatives

The law distinguishes four degrees in the order of distribution, i.e., four groups of relatives who can come into the inheritance in the following order.

[a] The Children and the Descendants

The children or their descendants inherit from their parents, grandparents and other relatives in the ascending line. They are the first to be entitled to the inheritance, and they exclude all other relatives.[16]

They inherit by distribution in equal shares per capita if they are all heirs of the first degree and if they are called to the inheritance on their own account; they succeed *per stirpes* when all or part of them have come up by right of representation[17] (*représentation – plaatsvervulling*). Thus, when a child has predeceased, the descendants of the predeceased succeed in his or her place *per stirpes*.

All the children have, in principle, equal rights in the succession of their parents or ancestors, irrespective of the fact whether they were conceived within or out of wedlock. The Belgian law makes no distinction, apart from a few exceptions, between the children born in or out of wedlock as far as their hereditary rights are concerned.[18]

The children and descendants are, as we will see further on, forced heirs entitled to a statutory reserved portion.

[b] Brothers and Sisters, Possibly Together with Parents

When someone dies without leaving descendants, it is ascertained as to whether he leaves brothers or sisters. Brothers and sisters inherit in the second order.[19] If the parents of the deceased are still alive, these join the brothers and sisters in the second order.[20]

16. Article 745, para. 1, Civil Code.
17. Article 745, para. 2, Civil Code.
18. Article 745, para. 1, Civil Code.
19. Article 750 Civil Code.
20. Article 751 Civil Code.

The portions due to the heirs of the second order are:

- if there are no living parents, the brothers and sisters receive each an equal portion of the total succession;
- if one or both parents succeed to the inheritance together with brothers and sisters, each parent receives one-fourth part of the inheritance, and the rest is divided in equal parts among the brothers and the sisters. The brothers and sisters together thus receive three-quarters of the inheritance if only one parent is alive; they receive together half the inheritance when both parents of the deceased come to the inheritance.

The parents are, as we will see further on, forced heirs entitled to a statutory reserved portion.

If there are half-brothers or half-sisters belonging to the family, these inherit in the second order together with the brothers-german and/or sisters-german and possibly with the parents. The portion due to the brothers and sisters is then divided in two parts – one for the parentage on the father's side and one for the parentage on the mother's side. Full brothers and sisters inherit in both lines; half-brothers and half-sisters inherit only in the line of the parent they descend from.[21]

The descendants of predeceased brothers and sisters and predeceased half-brothers and half-sisters represent their predeceased predecessor in law, and, if there are several, *per stirpes*.

[c] Relatives in the Ascending Line

If the deceased leaves neither issue, brothers, sisters, half-brothers or half-sisters, his inheritance descends on the third order, i.e., to the relatives in the ascending line.[22] The succession is then divided into two parts: half for the relatives in the ascending line of parentage on the father's side and half for the relatives in the ascending line of parentage on the mother's side. In case of co-motherhood, the second mother takes the place of the father. The next-of-kin in the ascending line receives, to the exclusion of all the others, the half due to his line.[23] Relatives in the ascending line inherit *per capita*.[24]

There is no representation in favour of the relatives in the ascending line; the next-of-kin in either line excludes a more distant relative.[25]

The relatives of the ascending line are, as we will see further on, heirs entitled to a statutory reserved portion.

[d] Common Collateral Relatives (Other than Brothers and Sisters)

In the absence of descendants, of brothers or sisters or descendants of these, and, of relatives in an ascending line, the inheritance is due for one half to the surviving

21. Article 752 Civil Code.
22. Article 746 Civil Code.
23. Article 746, para. 2, Civil Code.
24. Article 746, paras 2 and 3, Civil Code.
25. Article 741 Civil Code.

relatives in the one ascending line, and for the other half to the next-of-kin in the other line. In the absence of ascendants in both lines, the inheritance belongs for half to next-of-kin on the father's side and for half to the next-of-kin on the mother's side. In case of co-motherhood, the second mother takes the place of the father.

If there are collateral relatives of the same degree to whom the succession is due, they share *per capita*, except when they act by right of representation.[26]

Representation applies here for the descendants of uncles and aunts of the deceased.[27] Relatives beyond the fourth degree do not inherit, except when they are called by right of representation.[28] If in one line there are no relatives in the hereditary order, then the relatives of the other line inherit the totality of the succession.[29]

[2] The Surviving Spouse

The spouse, neither divorced nor separated from bed and board, is legally entitled to the inheritance of the deceased spouse. The surviving spouse can be entitled to a hereditary right of usufruct (*usufruit – vruchtgebruik*) and in some cases in a right of freehold (*pleine propriété – volle eigendom*).

The hereditary rights of the surviving spouse differ according to which relatives of the deceased he enters in concurrence with, and according to whether it concerns the separate estate of the deceased or the joint estate belonging to the community.

The rights of the surviving spouses in the succession of the predeceased can be summarised as follows:

- If the deceased leaves issue, adopted children, or descendants of these, the surviving spouse takes the usufruct of the whole inheritance.[30]
- If the deceased does not leave issue, the surviving spouse obtains the freehold of the part of the predeceased in the communal estate and the usufruct of his separate estate.[31]
- If the deceased does not leave any persons entitled to inherit, the surviving spouse receives the freehold of the entire succession.[32]

The surviving spouse is also an heir entitled to the statutory reserved portion, as we will explain further on.

[3] The Legal Cohabitant

Persons living together out of wedlock, are divided in Belgium into two categories: the legal cohabitants and the common cohabitants. The former are registered as legal

26. Article 753, para. 2, Civil Code.
27. Article 742 Civil Code.
28. Article 755, para. 1, Civil Code.
29. Article 755, para. 2, Civil Code.
30. Article 745*bis*, para. 1, Civil Code.
31. Article 745*bis*, para. 3, Civil Code.
32. Article 745*bis*, para. 3, Civil Code.

cohabitants by the municipal authority and have to comply with some particular legal rules.[33] The latter are not submitted to any special obligations.

The legal cohabitant inherits the usufruct of the real estate consisting the main residence of the cohabitants as well as the chattels present in it.[34] Here there is no forced heirship.

[4] The Law of Succession in the Context of an Adoption

Belgian law distinguishes two kinds of adoption (*adoption* – *adoptie*): the simple or common adoption and the full or plenary adoption. The hereditary rights differ:

- The hereditary right in the case of a full adoption is simple: the fully adopted loses his rights to succeed in his original family and acquires all the hereditary rights in the adoptive family. In the adoptive family, the plenary adopted person inherits as a biological child from his adoptive parents, as well as of the blood relatives of the adopters.[35] At the moment of the death of the fully adopted, his succession devolves on his relatives in the adoptive family and the original family is excluded.[36]
- In the case of a common adoption, the adopted conserves his hereditary rights in his original family, and acquires in the adoptive family a title to succeed to the property of the adopter alone. He cannot assert titles to succeed to the estate of the blood relatives of the adopter.[37] When the succession of the commonly adopted himself devolves, the law foresees a reversion of gifts and inherited goods, which are still present in kind, to the adoptive and the original family and a partition of the rest for one half to each of both families.[38]

[5] The Right of Legal Reversion

There exists a special hereditary right to the benefit of the relatives in the ascending line regarding the gifts made by them to descendants. These goods are, under the law of succession, reverted to the ascendant donor when the following conditions are fulfilled:

- the gift is given by an ascendant to a descendant;
- the donee has deceased without descendants;
- the given goods are still present in kind in the inheritance of the bequeathed descendant.[39]

33. Articles 1475–1479 Civil Code.
34. Article 745*octies* Civil Code.
35. Article 370, §1, para. 1, Civil Code.
36. Article 370 Civil Code.
37. Article 365 Civil Code.
38. Article 366 Civil Code.
39. Article 747 Civil Code.

This right of statutory reversion (*retour légal – wettelijke terugkeer*) is a hereditary right. The ascendant must also contribute *pro parte* towards the debts of the succession.

There is an analogous right of reversion in the adoptive succession as we already mentioned above.

[6] The Right of Succession of the Belgian State

In the absence of any successors the inheritance goes in principle to the Belgian State.[40]

Unlike the other heirs, the State does not enter by law in the possession of the hereditary goods. It has to comply with some special formalities[41] and request the writ of possession before the family court of the jurisdiction where the succession has devolved.[42]

[C] Acceptance and Renunciation of Succession

Whoever is entitled to the succession acquires the qualification of heir only when he has accepted the estate. The acceptance can be pure and simple (*acceptation pure et simple – zuivere aanvaarding*) or can be done under benefit of inventory (*cum beneficio inventarii*) (*acceptation sous bénéfice d'inventaire – aanvaarding onder voorrecht van boedelbeschrijving*). The beneficiary can also renounce the succession (*renonciation – verwerping*). Every person with a right to the succession has, in principle, freedom of choice regarding his inheritance.

Every beneficiary has, in principle, a term of thirty years to decide which attitude he will adopt.[43]

However, when creditors of the succession call on the heir to pay a debt of the deceased, this heir has to make his choice within three months and forty days of the reminder, otherwise he can be convicted, against the creditor, as an heir who accepts purely and simply.

The heir guilty of misappropriation or concealment of goods belonging to the succession loses the right to renounce or to accept under benefit of inventory. He is considered to accept purely and simply, and he cannot claim the items he misappropriated or concealed.[44]

[1] The Pure and Simple Acceptance

The acceptance is retroactive to the day the succession devolves.[45] One can accept explicitly or tacitly. An acceptance is explicit when one assumes the title or the

40. Article 768 Civil Code.
41. Article 768 Civil Code.
42. Article 770 Civil Code.
43. Article 789 Civil Code.
44. Article 792 Civil Code.
45. Article 777 Civil Code.

qualification of heir in a public instrument or in a deed under private seal. An acceptance is tacit when the heir carries out an act which necessarily implies his intention to accept, and which he would be entitled to accomplish only in the capacity of heir.[46]

In practice, acceptance is usually tacit: the heir performs an intervention in the estate from which his acceptance of the succession is presumed. For instance, he transfers his hereditary rights,[47] or he performs an act other than a conservatory act or an act of provisional administration, and from which the intention of the heir to accept the succession purely and simply can be deduced. Conservatory acts, such as affixing the seals, drawing up an inventory, and actions of provisional administration, do not as such cause the acceptance of the succession.

Whether an action can be qualified as an act of tacit acceptation or not, is a question of fact. An heir who wishes to protect his right of renunciation or acceptance under benefit of inventory, should proceed with caution when performing actions related to the goods of the succession.

The pure and simple acceptance has the consequence of the heir becoming the proprietor of the assets or of the part of the assets in accordance with the portion accruing to him in the succession. He is also obliged to pay the debts in proportion to his share of the assets. He is bound to settle the debts of the succession, if necessary, from his own property and *ultra vires hereditatis*.

Once the succession has been accepted purely and simply, one cannot reconsider his option: *semel heres, semper heres*.

[2] Renunciation

An heir wishing to relinquish the succession must, either personally or by proxy, make a statement to this end at the registrar's office of the court of first instance of the district (*greffe du tribunal de première instance – griffie van de rechtbank van eerste aanleg*) where the succession devolved or before a public notary[48] (i.e., the court of the judicial district where the testator had his domicile at the moment of his death).[49] This declaration is entered in the register of renunciations by the clerk of the court.

An heir renouncing the succession is considered to have never been an heir,[50] and thus cannot claim the assets of the succession, neither can he be bound to settle the debts. His share will come to the benefit of his descendants or his co-heirs.[51]

The creditors of a renouncing heir can have the court empower them to accept the inheritance on account of their debtor and in his stead to the amount of their claim.[52]

An heir who has renounced the succession can reconsider his decision and still accept the inheritance later on, either purely and simply or under benefit of inventory,

46. Article 778 Civil Code.
47. Article 780 Civil Code.
48. Article 784 Civil Code., Article 1185 Judicial Code.
49. Article 110 Civil Code.
50. Article 785 Civil Code.
51. Article 786 Civil Code.
52. Article 788 Civil Code.

as long as no other heirs have accepted the succession and the term of thirty years has not expired.[53]

[3] Acceptance under Benefit of Inventory

By accepting the succession under benefit of inventory, the heir avoids, on certain conditions, the merger of the estate of the succession with his own estate. In this case he is only bound to pay the debts and the liabilities of the succession to the extent of the assets descended.

An heir wishing to accept under benefit of inventory is obliged to observe a double formality. First, he or a proxy holder has to make a statement before a public notary or at the registrar's office of the court of first instance of the district where the succession devolved, i.e., the court of the judicial district where the deceased had his domicile at the moment of his death.[54] Second, this declaration has to be preceded or followed by a true and accurate inventory of the goods of the succession. This inventory has to be drawn up by a public notary.[55] Both formalities have to be complied with within three months and forty days of receiving a reminder from a creditor.

An heir who has accepted the succession under benefit of inventory, has to observe some strict rules when performing administrative acts and acts of disposal in relation to the goods of the succession. The Civil Code stipulates several obligations in this context.[56]

[D] Settlement and Partition of Succession

[1] The Right to Request Partition

Each heir has the right to oblige the other heirs to determine the joint possession and thus to settle (*liquidation – vereffening*), partition and share out the succession (*partage – verdeling*).[57] The heirs may enter into an agreement in which they arrange to defer the partition for a certain time. Such an agreement cannot be binding for more than five years. It can, however, be renewed.[58]

[2] The Methods of Partition

[a] Voluntary Partition

If all the heirs involved have legal ability and agree, the partition of the estate can be settled among them as they wish (*partage amiable – minnelijke verdeling*).[59] They can,

53. Articles 789–790 Civil Code.
54. Article 793 Civil Code.
55. Article 794 Civil Code.
56. Articles 797–809 Civil Code.
57. Article 815, para. 1, Civil Code.
58. Article 815, paras 2 & 3, Civil Code.
59. Article 819 Civil Code and Article 1205 Judicial Code.

for instance, proceed to a partition in kind, sell the goods and divide the selling price, apportion certain goods to joint sharers with payment of balances.

[b] Voluntary Partition under the Supervision of the Judge

If one of the joint owners is a minor or a disabled person, the partition is carried out by a public notary, under the presidency and with the approval of the justice of the peace.[60] The parties, the minor or disabled person being represented by his legal representative, can, in principle, distribute as they mutually agree. The court will protect the interests of the minor and can, *inter alia*, appoint an expert to advise on the composition of the parcels and the appraisement of the goods.[61] If the court withholds its approval of the partition, the parties can only continue the distribution in the form of a partition by order of the court of first instance.[62]

[c] Judicial Partition

If all the parties do not approve of the proposed distribution, the party who wishes to carry through the partition has to sue the others for partition before the court of first instance of the district where the succession has devolved (*partage judiciaire – gerechtelijke verdeling*).[63] When the court orders the partition, it refers the parties to a notary who is charged with the settlement and partition.

In the case of partition by court, the notary, the expert concerned and the court, will, as far as possible, tend to the partition in kind. By a partition in kind we mean that each parcel comprises, if possible, an equal quantity of personal estate, real estate, rights or debts of equal value and equal nature.[64] If the goods cannot be divided in kind, each joint sharer can request the public sale of the goods.

The execution of the sharing out and the partition of the succession by order of the court are mainly of the competence of the public notary appointed by the court, with the understanding that the sharing out and allotment is binding only after ratification by the court. The court settles the differences, ratifies the settlement or returns it to the notary in order to draw up a complementary list of allotment or a list of allotment in accordance with the instructions of the judge.[65]

In certain cases special laws provide a more adapted regulation than the partition by court as mentioned above. This is, *inter alia*, the case in consequence of:

- The Small Estates Act of 16 May 1900: for successions comprising real estate of which the rent of land and buildings is registered in the cadastral survey as less than EUR 1,500, a preferential right of taking over on estimation is given to the surviving spouse and certain descendants of the deceased person.

60. Article 1206 Judicial Code.
61. *Ibid.*
62. *Ibid.*
63. Article 1207 Judicial Code.
64. Article 832 Civil Code.
65. Article 1223 Judicial Code.

- The Act of 29 August 1988 concerning the Continuity of Agricultural Undertakings provides among other things a right of taking over on estimation of the agricultural undertaking by the descendants who participate in the exploitation of the undertaking.
- The right of conversion of the hereditary usufruct of the surviving spouse, who, under certain conditions, can convert his or her usufruct, either in the full property of the goods encumbered with usufruct, or in a sum of money, or in a guaranteed and index-linked life annuity.[66]

[3] *Hotch-Pot* (Collatio Bonorum)

By distributing an estate, the gifts received by the heir concerned from the deceased person have to be taken into account when establishing the assets. Article 843 of the Civil Code states that each heir entitled to an inheritance, even when he accepts under the benefit of inventory, has to bring into hotch-pot whatever he has received by donation *inter vivos*, directly or indirectly, from the deceased person (*rapport – inbreng*). The bequeathed heir may not keep the gifts nor claim the legacies, unless these have been given with an explicit exemption from restoration.[67]

The Civil Code states how this return should be done, i.e., in kind or in value, and in the latter case what value should be withheld.[68]

[4] *Action in Rescission of Partition*

Partitions can be annulled on the basis of violence and fraud.

There is also cause for annulment of the partition when a co-heir proves that he was caused prejudice for more than one-fourth.[69]

§8.03 GIFTS AND WILLS

[A] Reserved and the Freely Disposable Portions of the Estate

[1] *General*

In principle anyone who has legal capacity can freely dispose of his goods.

There is an important exception to this principle in relation to making gifts and wills, when forced heirs come to the succession. When someone leaves such privileged heirs (*héritiers réservataires – voorbehouden erfgenamen*), a certain portion of his property is not disposable in order to ensure a minimum share for these heirs entitled to the legal portion of the succession (*réserve héréditaire – voorbehouden erfdeel*).

66. Articles 745*quater* et seq. Civil Code.
67. Article 843 Civil Code.
68. Articles 858 et seq. Civil Code.
69. Article 887 Civil Code.

[2] *The Heirs and the Size of the Reserved Portion*

The following relatives can, as far as they are called by law to the succession and they accept it, assert their rights as an heir entitled to the legal portion:

- *The descendants*: the gifts, either by deed *inter vivos* or by will, may not exceed one-half of the property of the donor or the testator if he leaves one child at the moment of his death, one-third if he leaves two children, or one-fourth if he leaves three or more children.[70] At this moment[71] several changes of the law of inheritance are under preparation. The statutory reserved portion of the descendants will most likely be reduced to half of their legal portion.
- *The relatives of the ascending line*: when a donor or testator has no descendants who are entitled to the succession and when he leaves heritable relatives in the line of ascent, the legal and the disposable portion are determined as follows. The relatives in the ascending line have a right to the legal portion that equals one-fourth part for each line, i.e., the donations *inter vivos* made by deeds or the gifts made by will may not exceed half of the inheritance, if the deceased person, leaving no issue, leaves in parentage on the father's side and on the mother's side one or more relatives in the line of ascent, and three-quarters if he leaves relatives of the ascending line only in one line.[72] The relatives in the line of ascent cannot claim a legal portion on gifts made by the deceased person to his surviving spouse.[73]
- *The surviving spouse* is not entitled to the legal portion in freehold as the privileged heirs do, but to a legal portion in usufruct. This legal portion in usufruct can cover the usufruct of half the succession and includes as a minimum the usufruct of the real estate constituting, at the moment in which the succession devolved, the main residence of the family, as well as the chattels present in it.[74]

[a] *Action to Abate*

The legal portion to which the forced heir is entitled is calculated not only on the goods that are still present in the succession at the moment of death but also on the estate that would have been present if the deceased had made no gifts.

[b] *Calculation of the Estate*

A total is made of all the goods present at the death of the donor or the testator. The goods of which the deceased has disposed by donation *inter vivos* are fictitiously added

70. Article 913 Civil Code.
71. The end of the year 2015.
72. Article 915, para. 1, Civil Code.
73. Article 915, para. 2, Civil Code.
74. Article 915*bis*, §2, para. 2, Civil Code.

to this total according to their state at the time of the donation and their value at the time of the donator's death. After deducing the debts, the portion of the goods the testator could dispose of is calculated taking into account the quality of the forced heirs left by the deceased person.[75]

[c] The Abatement

If, from the above calculation, it appears that the donor or testator has disposed, by donation *inter vivos* or by will, of more than what appears to be disposable (*quotité disponible – beschikbaar aandeel*), a forced heir who is entitled to the legal portion but who cannot receive his legal share out of the goods available in the succession has a right to a reduction or an abatement of the gifts and legacies (*réduction – inkorting*).

The law states the order in which the different donees can be required to return the given goods. The claim must be instituted first against the legatees (*légataires – legatarissen*). Donations *inter vivos* are not abated as long as the value of all the goods included in the testamentary dispositions is not exhausted. When an abatement is made of the donations *inter vivos*, this is done starting with the last donation and then from the last donation on to the earlier.[76]

[B] Donations *Inter Vivos*

[1] Form

In order to protect the family and to promote legal security, Article 931 of the Civil Code states that for a donation *inter vivos* to be legal, it has to be made by a deed executed before a public notary. This notarial deed is liable to meet some special formal rules. For example, to be legal, the donation *inter vivos* has to be explicitly accepted.[77] There are exceptions to this general principle, such as the gift from hand to hand (*don-manuel – handgift*). Certain movable goods can be given by a simple transfer to the beneficiary, without a notarial deed being required. Also gifts in the shape of an indirect donation or a concealed donation can be done in a valid way without a notarial deed.

[2] Content

A donation *inter vivos* may only contain the present goods of the donor. The irrevocable character is essential. For example, the law states that the donor is not entitled to dispose of something that is included in the donation.[78]

The donation, which is in principle irrevocable, can be revoked on two legal grounds: (i) because of the non-fulfilment of the charges on the condition of which the

75. Article 922 Civil Code.
76. Article 923 Civil Code.
77. Article 932, para. 1, Civil Code.
78. Article 946 Civil Code.

donation was done;[79] or (ii) because of ingratitude of the donee towards the donor. The cases of ingratitude that can cause the revocation are limitatively stated.[80]

[C] Wills

[1] Form

To be valid, a will (*testament – testament*) must be made in one of the three forms provided by the law:

- the holograph will, which has to be written completely in the testator's own handwriting and dated and signed by him;[81]
- the 'public' will, which is dictated to a public notary who embodies the last will in a notarial deed which is submitted to very strict formal rules;[82] and
- the will in the international form, which constitutes a twofold deed: on the one hand the will drawn up by the testator, and on the other hand the declaration of the notary in accordance with the Treaty of Washington of October 1993.[83]

A joint will, which is a will made by two or more persons in the same deed, is not admissible.[84]

[2] Content

The testamentary dispositions concerning the goods of the testator included in the will are, considering the terms by and the intentions of the testator, classified in one of the three categories of legacies covered by the Civil Code: the general legacy (*legs universel – algemeen legaat*), the residuary legacy (*legs a titre universel – legaat ten algemene titel*) and the specific legacy (*legs particulier – bijzonder legaat*).[85]

The rights and duties of the legatee with respect to the continuation of possession, the rights to the profits, the obligation to contribute towards the debts, etc., differ according to the qualification of the legacy among one of these three categories.

[3] Revocability

A will is always revocable. The revocation can be done explicitly or tacitly. An explicit revocation can be made in a subsequent will or in a special deed executed before a notary.

79. Articles 953–954 Civil Code.
80. Article 955 Civil Code.
81. Article 970 Civil Code.
82. Articles 971–974 Civil Code.
83. Act of 2 February 1983.
84. Article 968 Civil Code.
85. Article 1002 Civil Code.

[D] Special Kinds of Gifts

The Belgian law provides some special rules concerning certain kinds of gifts.

[1] Fidei-Commissum

The substitution in the shape of a constitution of a trust (*substitution fidéi-commissaire – erfstelling over de hand*) is forbidden in principle. Every disposition where the donee, the testamentary heir or the legatee is charged to conserve the given goods and to restore them at his death to a third person, is null and void, even with respect to the donee, the testamentary heir or the legatee.[86]

The constitution of a *fidei-commissum* is exceptionally allowed when it concerns a disposition made by a parent in favour of his children.[87]

When the deceased person leaves no children, the constitution of a *fidei-commissum* is also allowed in favour of brothers and sisters and the children descended from them.[88] These lawful dispositions will only be valid as far as the encumbrance of the restitution is stipulated in favour of all the children of the donee or legatee, those who have already been born and those to be born, without distinction, and only the children descended from the trustee in the first degree.[89]

[2] Ascendants' Partition

The partition by the ascendants of all or part of their property among their descendants can be done by means of a special legal form called the 'ascendants' partition' (*partage d'ascendants – ouderlijke boedelverdeling*).

This legal form of procedure, which can be applied *inter vivos*, as well as by will, has certain advantages from a legal technical point of view, but it implies disadvantages as well (Articles 1075–1080 of the Civil Code).

[3] Contractual Arrangement Between Spouses

Gifts by prenuptial contract between spouses-to-be and between spouses during their marriage fall under a special regime. Between these parties it is permitted to make gifts of future goods[90] and to dispose by agreement of their future succession (*institution contractuelle – contractuele erfstelling*).

Gifts between spouses made in an antenuptial settlement are, in principle, irrevocable. On the other hand, gifts made between spouses during their marriage,

86. Article 896, para. 1, Civil Code.
87. Article 1048 Civil Code.
88. Article 1049 Civil Code.
89. *Ibid.* and Article 1050 Civil Code.
90. Articles 1081–1100 Civil Code.

other than by marriage contract, are always revocable *ad nutum*.[91] In that case the legislature assumes that there is an 'irrefutable suspicion of influence'.

During their marriage, spouses may not make any mutual and reciprocal gift by one and the same deed, neither by deed *inter vivos* (other than by marriage contract) nor by will.[92]

§8.04 SELECTED BIBLIOGRAPHY

R. Dekkers & H. Casman, 4 *Handboek van burgerlijk recht, Huwelijksstelsels. Erfrecht. Giften* (Antwerp: Intersentia 2015).

P. Delnoy, *Les libéralités et les successions* (Brussels: Larcier 2013).

E. De Wilde d'Estmael, *Les donations, in* 3 & 4 *Répertoire notarial* (Brussels: Larcier 2009).

E. De Wilde d'Estmael, Ch. Thomasset & A.-C. Van Gysel, *Les testaments (Forme), in* 3 & 8 *Répertoire notarial* (Brussels: Larcier 2006).

R. Dillemans, A. Van den Bossche & M. De Clercq, *Testamenten* (Beginselen van Belgisch privaatrecht VII, R. Dillemans & W. Van Gerven eds., Mechelen: Kluwer 2012).

Y.-H. Leleu, *Droit patrimonial des couples* (Brussels: Larcier 2015).

W. Pintens, Ch. Declerck, J. Du Mongh & K. Vanwinckelen, *Familiaal vermogensrecht* (Antwerp: Intersentia 2010).

M. Puelinckx-Coene, 1 *Erfrecht, Openvallen en toewijzen van de nalatenschap, erfovereenkomsten, reserve en inbreng* (Beginselen van Belgisch privaatrecht VI, R. Dillemans & W. Van Gerven eds., Mechelen: Kluwer 2011).

A.-C. Van Gysel, *Précis du droit des successions et des libéralités* (Brussels: Bruylant 2008).

Erfenissen, schenkingen en testamenten. Commentaar met overzicht van rechtspraak en rechtsleer (R. Barbaix, M. Coene & J. Du Mongh eds., Antwerp: Kluwer 1988).

91. Article 1096 Civil Code.
92. Article 1097 Civil Code.

CHAPTER 9

Property Law

Vincent Sagaert

§9.01 INTRODUCTION

The Belgian legal system is an ancient body of law, governed by provisions reminiscent to Roman law that are largely copied from the French mother law. This is, *anno* 2016, even more prominently the case for property law. Book II of the Belgian Civil Code (Articles 516–710*bis*) was at the moment of its introduction in 1804 identical to the one coming into force in French law.

Since 1804, these provisions have largely remained unchanged, apart from: (1) some minor changes with regard to the provisions on servitudes; and (2) a full reform of the provisions on joint ownership, mainly focused on apartment buildings.[1] On top of those rather specific reforms, several property rights have been introduced in separate statutes outside the Civil Code, such as long lease rights and building rights.[2] Finally, the Belgian legislature has implemented changes into the statutory framework with regard to property security rights. The rules with regard to mortgage ('*hypothec*') are to be found in the Mortgage Act of 16 December 1851, which has been inserted as a separate statute in the Civil Code. The rules with regard to movable property security rights have been completely changed by the Federal Act of 11 July 2013.

The stability of the statutory framework is often translated in a negative perception of these legal property rules as archaic, sometimes even anachronistic. The major part of the rules is still mostly focusing on land for agricultural purposes, not taking into account the developments of property law towards modern applications. Therefore, the Minister of Justice in 2015 has taken the initiative to reform substantive parts of the Civil Code, among which property law. However, at the time of submitting this contribution there were no concrete results of this reform exercise yet.

1. Act of 30 June 1994 and Act of 2 June 2010, inserting Articles 577-3 to 577-14 in the Civil Code.
2. Two Acts of 10 January 1824: *see infra*.

[A] The Closed System of Property Law (*Numerus Clausus*)

The traditional starting point of the narrative of Belgian property law is that the freedom of contract of the parties is seriously curtailed by its most fundamental feature, i.e., the *numerus clausus* principle.[3] This principle states that the number and substance of types of property rights are limited in the sense that parties cannot create property rights which do not correspond to the essential features of the property rights that have been created by the legislature. Belgian legal scholars regard this principle as a building stone of the property law system.

Even if the *numerus clausus* principle is deeply rooted in Belgian property law, the only possible legal ground for this principle is Article 543 of the Civil Code, as it states that 'one may have a right of ownership, or a mere right of enjoyment, or a mere servitude to be claimed on property.' The incompleteness of this enumeration is an indication of the fact that the provision is not limitative in nature: long leases and building rights are not mentioned (as these rights were only introduced afterwards), co-ownership is not mentioned either, and the property security rights and liens - which are traditionally considered as property rights in French and Belgian law - have also been omitted. This provision was meant to be a mere introductory provision, announcing generally that the substance of the property rights is dealt with in later provisions.

A list can be drawn enumerating the property rights recognised in Belgian law: ownership, joint ownership, usufruct, use and habitation, servitudes, long lease rights, building rights. Apart from these property rights, Belgian law acknowledges property security rights, which secure the payment of an obligation. Even if this does not mean that there is no space for party autonomy in property law, especially with regard to the property rights to use, the contractual freedom has less space that in the field of obligations. It can be argued that during the last decades, contractual freedom has gained importance in the field of Belgian property law.

[B] Importance of the Nature of Property Rights

The importance to denominate a subjective right as a property right is obvious. In Belgian law, as in most legal systems, property rights are said to have the classical feature of having stronger third-party effects than a personal right. This traditionally implies three aspects.

First, property rights are equipped with a right to follow their object: property rights stick to the object, whoever acquires that object. Hence, the property right can be enforced against the third-party acquirer, except if the latter can rely on third-party protection rules, such as the protection of the possessor in good faith.[4]

3. For an analysis, *see* V. Sagaert, *Het goederenrecht als open systeem van verbintenissen? Poging tot een nieuwe kwalificatie van de vermogensrechten*, 42 TIJDSCHRIFT VOOR PRIVAATRECHT 983–1086 (2005).
4. Article 2279 Civil Code (*infra*).

Second, property rights have strong force in case of insolvency. They can be enforced even if the counterparty is insolvent. For instance, the depositor may vindicate his (identifiable) assets if the depositee is declared bankrupt, the holder of a usufruct or long lessee may oppose his property right against the insolvency administrator of the bare owner.

A third feature of property rights is that they are protected by the principle of real subrogation ('tracing').[5] According to this principle, a property right can be maintained despite the loss of its original object through the transfer of the property right to the substituting asset. For instance: a secured creditor is entitled to a right of priority on the insurance claim after the destruction of the asset which originally was the object of the security right.

§9.02 TYPES OF GOODS

Without giving a general framework to the reader, Book II of the Civil Code immediately presents the distinctive categories of assets. The main (and only) distinction is between movable and immovable assets. This chapter of the Civil Code is particularly outdated. The legislature provides for a random list of examples, mostly on the level of agricultural assets. Not surprisingly, given the economic context of the early nineteenth century, the legislature of 1804 pays ample attention to immovable assets and much less to movable assets. The category of immovables, at that moment and in spite of the abolishment of the feudal regime, was indeed the most important one from a value point of view. The movable assets are the residual category, containing all assets which are not immovable.

The category of immovable assets is composed of three categories of assets:

- The 'immovables by nature': this is land and all infrastructure which has been incorporated into the ground. The notion of incorporation has been flexibilised over the years: traditionally, an asset was considered as immovable if it could not be removed without causing damage or breaking it up. However, this traditional criterion was enlarged in 1988, when the Court of Cassation ruled that the assets are also immovable if the assets are usually and durably attached to the ground or stuck in the ground.[6] The subjective intention to maintain the assets where they are standing is thus determining. Even the functionally restricted possibility to move an asset – in this case a harbour crane – does not exclude its immovable nature.[7]
- The 'immovables by destination': these are by nature movable assets that are accessory to an immovable. In order to keep the connection with the immovable, a construction by case law also considers them as immovable. The

5. V. Sagaert, Zakelijke subrogatie (Antwerp: Intersentia 2003).
6. Court of Cassation 15 September 1988, 1988–1989 Arresten van het Hof van Cassatie 60.
7. Court of Cassation 14 February 2008, 2008–2009 Rechtskundig Weekblad 456, note V. Sagaert. In this case, a huge harbour crane was considered to be immovable by incorporation. It was standing on rails, permitting a small movement of the crane alongside the wharf.

conditions for the immobilisation by destination are that: (1) the accessory movable asset and the immovable asset have the same owner; (2) the movable asset is useful for the exploitation of the immovable asset or is connected in a visible and durable manner to the immovable; and (3) the immovable asset is equipped in a manner which is appropriate to the exploitation. Textbook examples are animals in a farm or vans used for transporting raw materials or manufactured goods. Article 525 of the Civil Code gives other examples of this category.

- Incorporeal immovables: these are the incorporeal rights with an immovable object. They cover both immovable property rights and property remedies. There is one immovable personal right in Belgian property law: the right to claim the transfer of an immovable property right, in the (exceptional) case that the property rights are not transferred on the ground of mere consent between the parties.

The other main distinction between the assets is the one between corporeal and incorporeal assets. The incorporeal assets comprise receivables, limited property rights, and intellectual property rights. A special category of intangibles are universalities of goods (such as a business enterprise, financial portfolio), which 'as such' – independent from changes in its constitutive assets – can be the object of a usufruct or pledge right.

§9.03 OWNERSHIP

Article 544 of the Belgian Civil Code gives a classical anti-feudal definition of ownership, which has remained unamended since 1804: 'ownership is the right to enjoy and dispose of property in the most absolute manner, provided one does not exercise these rights in a way prohibited by statutes or regulations.' This definition makes a sharp distinction between the right of ownership and limited property rights: the right of ownership grants to the owner all powers in the property, except for those which have been transferred to third parties or which have been prohibited by law. On the contrary, limited property rights only confer limited powers upon the owner.

The three main features of ownership are: (1) its comprehensive nature; (2) exclusive nature; and (3) its perpetual nature.

The *comprehensive* nature of ownership means that this right grants the owner all powers in the property, except for those transferred to third parties or prohibited by law. It is, however, false to assume that this definition intended to render the powers of the owner absolute: Belgian legal scholars have demonstrated that the absoluteness of ownership has been emphasised at the end of the nineteenth century, but did not inspire the legislature in 1804. The 1804 definition of ownership merely aimed to distinguish ownership from the limited property rights.

Since the twentieth century, the powers of the owner have been gradually more restricted. The owner must take into account several restrictions from both private law and public law. A major private law restriction is the prohibition of abuse of rights, for example, the owner cannot exercise his ownership in a manner that is manifestly contrary to the manner in which a reasonable owner would exercise his ownership in similar circumstances.[8]

The other important restrictions on ownership exclusively focus on immovables. It concerns nuisance, which in Belgian law is conceived as a basis of strict liability: independent from any wrongful act, it is prohibited to cause any abnormal nuisance to neighbours which disrupt the balance between the ownership rights.[9] Moreover, an increasing number of public 'servitudes' burden private ownership in favour of a public interest.

Article 544 of the Civil Code enumerates three categories of powers: the power to use ('*ius utendi*'), the power to take the fruits ('*ius fruendi*'), and the power to dispose of the asset ('*ius abutendi*'). The owner is in principle entitled to do everything with his asset, except for: (1) the powers he has desisted; and (2) the restrictions imposed by law. The question whether parties can contractually exclude the transferability of property has been the object of debate for a long time. Since the last century, most case law and legal scholars acknowledge that these clauses can be valid if: (i) they are restricted in time; and (ii) they serve a lawful interest.[10]

Second, private ownership has a *perpetual* nature. According to the majority opinion in French and Belgian law, extinctive prescription does not operate for ownership: one cannot lose ownership because of non-use of ownership. Ownership is a so-called perpetual right. This does not mean that ownership is not subject to prescription: ownership cannot extinguish through non-use during thirty years, but this does not prevent the loss of ownership because of acquisitive prescription by a third party. If a third party has the possession (which meets the requirements of Article 2228 of the Civil Code) for a sufficiently long period, he will become the owner, and indirectly the previous owner will lose his ownership right.

Finally, ownership has an *exclusive* nature.[11] This feature, which is thought to be distinctive between civil law and common law ownership, prevents the full powers of an owner to be split up between an economic owner and a legal owner. However, a growing number of fiduciary ownership instruments are also refining this feature of ownership.[12]

§9.04 JOINT OWNERSHIP

As we have stated before, the rules governing joint ownership (or 'co-ownership') have been the object of fundamental amendments, which mainly focused on apartment joint

8. (i) The mere intention to cause damage to a third person; (ii) a manner which causes damage to third persons if the owner would benefit to the same degree from another exercise that does not cause any damage to third persons or to the general interest; and (iii) in such way that the damage he causes is disproportionate in relation to the benefit he gains.
9. *See infra* Chapter 11, §11.03 [B] [1] [b].
10. V. Sagaert, Goederenrecht 191–199 (Mechelen: Kluwer 2014).
11. For an extensive analysis, *see* D. Gruyaert, De exclusiviteit van eigendom (Antwerp: Intersentia 2016).
12. M.E. Storme, *Van trust gespeend? Van trusts en fiduciaire verhoudingen in het Belgisch privaatrecht*, 35 Tijdschrift voor Privaatrecht 703–820 (1998).

ownership ('condominium'). The current rules are laid down in Article 577-2–577-14 of the Civil Code. Belgian law recognises three forms of co-ownership:

- ordinary ('accidental') joint ownership (Article 577-2, §§1–8 of the Civil Code);
- mandatory co-ownership (Article 577-2, §§9–10 (general rules) and Article 577-3–577-14 (apartment joint ownership) of the Civil Code); and
- voluntary joint ownership (no general statutory framework).

[A] Ordinary ('Accidental') Joint Ownership

Ordinary ('accidental') joint ownership comes into existence due to circumstances which do not depend upon the intention of the joint owners. The most frequent example is the joint ownership among the heirs or general legatees of a deceased person. Another example is the situation in which two persons have commingled their property, for instance through their factual co-habitation for a long period, and who cannot prove their individual (exclusive) ownership of the property. In that situation, the property is deemed to be in joint ownership.

With regard to the powers of the joint owner, two levels have to be distinguished:

- Each joint owner is exclusive owner of his own share, and can therefore exercise the powers with regard to the share in the most complete manner. For instance, he is entitled to transfer his rights in the jointly owned property to a third party, except if it has been otherwise agreed between the joint owners.[13] He can also freely burden his rights with property rights, such as mortgages (for immovables) or pledges (for movables).
- An individual joint owner is not entitled to operate the administration or disposition of the property in joint ownership except with unanimous consent of all the other joint owners.[14] This means that a lease, transfer or burdening with property rights of the jointly owned asset is only possible with the unanimous consent of all joint owners. However, if one joint owner sells the property without consent of the other joint owners, the protection of the possessor in good faith will have to be taken into account. Joint owners can freely commit acts aiming at the conservation of the asset or urgent acts which tend to prevent damage to the asset.

As the creation of this type of joint ownership could not be anticipated, it is often unorganised and harmful from an economic perspective. That is the reason why the legislature has granted each joint owner the right to terminate the joint ownership by pursuing the division. This right is provided in Article 815 of the Civil Code: 'No one is obliged to remain in undivided ownership and a division may always be effected,

13. Article 577-2, §4, Civil Code.
14. Article 577-2, §6, Civil Code.

unless it was delayed by judgement or agreement'. Article 1561 of the Judicial Code grants the same right to the creditors of the joint owners.

However, the joint owners can agree that they will not terminate the joint ownership for a certain period, without exceeding five years. This period can be renewed, but such agreement is only effective in relation to third parties. There are also statutory exceptions to the possibility to effect the division.[15]

[B] Mandatory Joint Ownership

Compulsory joint ownership comes into existence if the object of the joint ownership, given its nature, cannot be divided among the parties. A typical example is a family tomb. Most frequently, the property in joint ownership is accessory to property that exclusively belongs to the joint owners. It is an application of the '*accessorium sequitur principale*' principle.[16]

A specific type of mandatory joint ownership is the 'common wall' dividing two or more parcels of land. This type is also governed by specific provisions, which are included in Articles 653 et seq. of the Civil Code.

The most important example for legal practice is the joint ownership existing within a condominium building. The rules governing *comdominium* schemes are most elaborate and detailed, and can be found in Article 577-3–577-14 of the Civil Code. They have been completely changed in 1994 and refined again in 2010. These Articles have a compulsory nature, so that party autonomy within a condominium scheme is very limited. The functioning of the scheme is rigid. First, a condominium declaration and rules have to be drawn up in which the building is split up between common areas and private apartments. The declaration and rules have to be drawn up in a notarial deed and have to be registered in the mortgage register.

Belgian law adheres to the theory of dualism and not to the monistic structure, which is used in some other European countries, such as Austria and the Netherlands. Thus, the common areas in an apartment building are in joint ownership among the owners of the flats because the use of the common areas is necessary in order to gain access to the flats, which are in exclusive ownership.

The administration of the building is in the hands of an 'association of joint owners'. The 'association of joint owners' is incorporated: it has the competence to act in legal proceedings and has its own estate, composed of money gained through the contributions of the private owners.

It applies to all buildings or complex of buildings, which consists of private parcels, in exclusive ownership, and common areas, in joint ownership.

The association of joint owners has compulsory organs. First of all, there is the general assembly, taking all the fundamental decisions and assembling each year

15. Article 3 Act of 15 May 1900 on Small Heritages.
16. For an in depth analysis of this principle in Belgian law, *see* K. SWINNEN, ACCESSORITEIT IN HET VERMOGENSRECHT (Antwerp: Intersentia 2013).

within the fourteen day period mentioned in the declaration and rules. The simple or qualified majority required for the approval of a decision, is mandatorily mentioned in Article 577-7 of the Civil Code. Moreover, the legal provisions govern in a mandatory manner the way in which the general assembly must be organised, limits the number of proxies that can be given to the same owner (three or maximum 10%), limits the number of votes of one owner to half of the total number of votes, the possibilities to sue before court in order to obtain the avoidance of a decision of the general assembly (within four months), etc.

The administrator of the association of joint owners governs the association on a day-to-day basis, and is subject to the control of the 'council of joint owners'. He also represents the association of joint owners in agreements and judicial proceedings. The powers of the administrator are listed in Article 577-8 of the Civil Code. The administrator is monitored by the council of joint owners and, on a financial level, by the commissioner of the accounting.

[C] Conventional Joint Ownership

Conventional joint ownership is the indivisibility that has come into existence pursuant to an agreement among the joint owners. Typical cases are the joint ownership of ships and the joint ownership of intellectual property rights. If two legal or natural persons purchase an asset, it will also be in conventional indivision between them both. Other examples can be found in the financial sector, such as an unincorporated collective investment fund. Conventional joint ownership is not subject to a general set of rules. Each type of conventional joint ownership is governed by a specific set of statutory provisions.[17]

There was in Belgian law a highly complicated debate going on about the question whether a joint owner can operate the division of this joint ownership. Traditionally, most legal scholars adhere to the opinion that Article 815 of the Civil Code, which provides for the possibility of division, only applies to accidental joint ownership. The Belgian Court of Cassation ruled in 2013 that Article 815 of the Civil Code does not apply to voluntary joint ownership.[18]

§9.05 USUFRUCT

The main limited property right in movables is *usufruct*, which is defined in Article 578 of the Civil Code as 'the right to enjoy property, of which another has ownership, in the same manner as the owner himself, but on condition that its substance be preserved'. So, the usufructuary has the right of '*usus*' and '*fructus*', but he does not have the right to dispose of the property.

17. For collective investment funds, *see* the Collective Investment Funds Act of 20 July 2004. For co-ownership of ships, *see* Articles 55–57 of Book II of the Commercial Code.
18. Court of Cassation 20 September 2013, 2014–2015 Rechtskundig Weekblad 618, note L. De Keyser.

An important and essential feature of usufruct is that it will ultimately end by the death of the usufructuary.[19] Usufruct conferred in favour of legal persons lasts for maximally thirty years.[20] Usufruct is thus a precarious right. From an economic point of view, this practically excludes the right of usufruct as an instrument for immovable investment schemes. This precarious nature of usufruct entails that the right of usufruct is in Belgian legal practice frequently used as a tool for estate planning, but is rarely used in project development constructions.

Usufruct can be conferred by law, by the intention of persons (will or contract)[21] and by prescription. Two important illustrations of legal usufruct are the usufruct of the surviving spouse on the estate of the deceased spouse[22] and the usufruct of the parents on the assets of their underage children.[23]

The usufructuary has the right to use the asset and to claim the fruits of the asset for the duration of his right. However, the right of the usufructuary to use an asset is subject to two restrictions:

- The usufructuary has the obligation to respect the destination of the asset, to which the object has been used by the owner. For instance, the usufructuary cannot transform a residential house into a commercial business, or he cannot even change a grass field into a corn field.
- The usufructuary has to exercise his right to use and enjoy the land in compliance with the standard of a 'bonus pater familias.' This obligation, which is not expressly mentioned in the Civil Code, prevails on the first restriction: if the owner of the assets did not make use of his assets in compliance with the standard of a 'bonus pater familias,' the usufructuary is not entitled to maintain this harmful use.

§9.06 RIGHTS OF HABITATION AND USE

The Civil Code acknowledges two types of property right which are a mere variation on the right of usufruct. A person who has the use of the fruits of a tenement may only demand what is necessary for his needs and those of his family.[24] A right of habitation can only be vested on a house. A person who has a right of habitation with regard to a house, may live there with his family, even though he was not married at the time when that right was granted to him.[25] These property rights are rather rarely used in legal practice, even if they are sometimes used as an instrument for estate planning. A

19. Article 617 Civil Code.
20. Article 619 Civil Code.
21. Article 579 Civil Code.
22. Article 745*bis* Civil Code.
23. Article 384 Civil Code.
24. Article 630 Civil Code.
25. Article 632 Civil Code.

distinctive feature of both rights is that they are '*intuitu personae*', meaning that the holder cannot assign these rights or that his creditors cannot seize them.

§9.07 SERVITUDES

[A] Contractual Servitudes

As to servitudes, French and Belgian law have remained stable since the introduction of the Civil Code in 1804. Article 637 of the French and Belgian Civil Code provides for a mandatory definition of servitudes with strict requirements: a servitude is 'a charge imposed on a real estate for the use and utility of another real estate belonging to another owner.' A servitude only allows for a limited use of the servient tenement which has to be described expressly when the servitude is created. They are different from the general rights to use a land, as it is conferred to the holder of a long lease or (to a certain extent) to the holder of the usufruct of a land. Three requirements can be set out as essential characteristics of a servitude: (1) it is a burden on a parcel of land ('servient land'); (2) in favour of another parcel of land ('dominant land'); and (3) the servient tenement and the dominant tenement have a different owner.[26] The first two characteristics deserve some clarification.

The first requirement is that it must be a burden on the servient tenement, not on its owner. The objective nature of the servitude at its passive side is equated to its negative nature. A servitude can only oblige the owner of the servient tenement to take a passive behaviour, i.e., an obligation to abstain from doing something ('*non faciendo*'), as it is expressed in Article 686 of the Civil Code. This can take two forms: either the owner of the servient tenement cannot make a specified use of his land which he would have been entitled to if the land had not been burdened, or the owner of the dominant tenement can make a specified use of the servient tenement which he would not have been entitled to make if the land had not been burdened. Positive obligations are purely contractual and do not run with the servient tenement, so in case of a sale, the new owner will normally not be bound by this obligation.

Second, a servitude must be objectively useful to the dominant tenement. In other words, the servitude must be useful to the ownership of the land as such, without taking into account the identity of the actual owner.[27] This does not exclude the servitude from being profitable for the current owner personally: the mere fact that the burden grants a personal favour to the owner of the one parcel does not defer its qualification as a servitude if the charge has a direct or indirect relationship with the use of the land. It is sufficient that the servitude gave rise to the increased value of the

26. For an extensive analysis, *see* V. Sagaert & K. Swinnen, Privaatrechtelijke erfdienstbaarheden door het oog van de 21e eeuw (Brussels: Larcier 2012).

27. H. De Page, Traité élémentaire de droit civil belge, vol. VI, No. 501 (Brussels: Bruylant, 1942); V. Sagaert, Goederenrecht No. 570 (Mechelen: Kluwer 2014). It is not required that the servitude provides an economic advantage. The advantage can also exist in the more comfortable use of the dominant tenement or in an intellectual advantage.

land, and this almost always grants at least an indirect advantage to the owner of that land.[28]

It is not always very obvious whether the passive and active side of the land burden comply with the objective nature. There remains a considerable amount of legal uncertainty with regard to the (contractual or proprietary) nature of some clauses, for instance non-competition clauses or clauses of habitual residence. These are clauses inserted in the sale of a commercial building which prohibit to the purchaser to use the building for specified commercial purposes. Some consider such a clause to be only useful to the business activities of the current owner, while others recognise an obvious link with the interest of the dominant land itself.

[B] Statutory Servitudes

The Civil Code has contractualised most of the servitudes existing in the feudal regime, but has nevertheless maintained some legal servitudes. Two of the most important legal servitudes are the right of passage ('right of way') and the servitude of 'views and windows.'

The legal servitude of way is governed by Articles 682 et seq. of the French and Belgian Civil Code. An owner whose tenements are enclaved and who has no access from the public road, or only one which is insufficient either for an agricultural, industrial or commercial purpose of his property or for carrying out operations of building or development, has a right to claim on his neighbours' tenements a passage which is sufficient in order to achieve the destination of his own tenement.[29] The owner of the burdened land is entitled to a compensation for the damage the servitude may cause.

The servitude of views and windows burdens each land, restraining the possibility to have views or windows too close to the borderline with the adjacent parcel. It is prohibited to have windows or views in a common wall,[30] and views are even restricted in a proper wall which is built close to the parcel border.[31] The reason behind these legal land burdens, although old fashioned, are obvious: to avoid that the privacy of the neighbour can be violated or that quarrels between neighbours are concluded in physical ways by throwing things from one parcel to another.

The Belgian Civil Code also allows, to a limited extent, that servitudes may come into existence on the ground of acquisitive prescription ('adverse possession'). However, only visible and continuous servitudes can come into existence through a long time (more than thirty years) possession.[32] The reason behind this restriction is twofold: on the one hand, one tries to avoid confusion between the coming into existence of a servitude and a mere tolerance of the owner of the servient land, on the other hand, the legislature aimed to protect third parties acquiring right on the servient

28. Court of Cassation 28 January 2000, 2000 Arresten van het Hof van Cassatie 76.
29. Article 682 Civil Code.
30. Article 675 Civil Code.
31. Articles 678–679 Civil Code.
32. Article 690–691 Civil Code.

tenement. The latter concern is justified as these servitudes are not registered in the mortgage register.

§9.08 *EMPHYTEUSIS* ('LONG LEASE RIGHTS')

The long lease (*emphyteusis*) is the most general property right a non-owner can have on an immovable asset. The underlying idea for its abolishment in 1804 was that this property right, because of its long duration and extensiveness, created a burden which risked to erode the land ownership. The long lease right was re-introduced by the Act of 10 January 1824 and remained unamended, even if the economic development of long lease rights as a tool for project development has been very fast and radical during the last decades.

Long lease is defined by the Belgian legislature as the 'property right to have the full use of a real estate belonging to someone else, under the obligation to pay to the latter an annual compensation in money or in proceeds or fruits.' It grants the long leaseholder a general right to use an immovable asset for a long period of time between twenty-seven years and ninety-nine years. A renewal is possible, but can only be agreed upon at the end of the initial term.

The holder of the long lease is merely subject to one restriction: he may not diminish the value of the real estate. The long leaseholder is not obliged to maintain the destination to which the real estate was affected by the ground owner. The long leaseholder can construct buildings on the real estate, without any restriction.[33]

In the last decades, long leasehold agreements have been subject to a revival. They have become fairly common in business practice because they are frequently used in leasing operations with regard to immovable assets. Moreover, it is common that public authorities realise projects of public interests in cooperation with private partners, for instance sports infrastructure, concert halls, parking spaces.

Apart from its favourable tax regime, the economic attractiveness of long leaseholds is caused by the flexibility of these rights. The parties have been awarded very large freedom to model a long lease agreement. The only two requirements they have to comply with are the limitations with regard to the duration, and the obligation to agree upon a compensation.

§9.09 *SUPERFICIES* ('BUILDING RIGHT')

Another way to burden real estate with property rights is the creation of a building right (*superficies*). A building right creates a splitting up of the ownership of immovables in horizontal perspective. A building right is the right to have buildings, works or plants on, above or under the land of another. The ownership of the land is separated from the ownership of the constructions. In other words, building rights deprive the land owner of the 'immovable accession'. The creation of a building right is a contractual deviation

33. The long leaseholder will not be entitled to any compensation for the surplus value at the end of the long lease, but parties can agree otherwise.

from the '*superficies solo cedit*' rule. It thus excludes the functioning of accession in favour of the (owner of the) land.

The legislature has enacted specific statutory rules with regard to building rights in the Act of 10 January 1824. Except for the duration of the building right, all the provisions of this Act are not mandatory. Parties can deviate contractually, and they often make use of this possibility. This is one of the reasons for the revival of building rights in the last decades.

Belgian law takes a strict approach of building rights. Building rights can only be constituted for a maximum period of fifty years.[34] According to Belgian law, each derogation from the principle of accession is to be considered as the constitution of a building right. The Court of Cassation has ruled that each waiver of accession by the land owner creates a building right. Leaving aside the tax consequences, this case law has as its main consequence that the waiver of accession by the land owner is also subject to the upper limit of fifty years.[35] In this way, Belgian case law aimed to protect the legal and physical indivisibility of ownership. This strict time constraint is the basis for many problems for real estate practitioners because it makes it impossible to create different investment schemes for different horizontal shelves of a same parcel of land.[36]

§9.10 PROPERTY SECURITY RIGHTS

[A] Property Security Rights in Movables

[1] Pledge on Corporeal Movable Goods

Under Belgian law, a pledge (*gage* – *pand*) is an agreement whereby a person (whether the debtor, or a third party acting for the account of the debtor) hands over (effectively delivers) to its creditor (or to an agreed third party) an asset in order to secure performance of one or more of its obligations. The purpose of a pledge is to grant a creditor a security interest in one or more movable (tangible or intangible) asset(s), as a result of which the creditor, in the event of enforcement of the pledged asset by way of realisation (sale) or appropriation, is granted a priority right either on the proceeds of the sale of the pledged asset (in the event of realisation) or on the pledged asset itself (in the event of appropriation).

A pledge agreement is, in the 1804 tradition, an agreement in rem, meaning that the effective delivery of the pledged asset to the creditor (or to an agreed third party) is a condition for the validity of a pledge (dispossession). The only exception to this dispossession requirement is to be found in the pledge on a business enterprise, governed by the Act of 25 October 1919. The necessity to effectively deliver the pledged asset, in principle, makes it impossible to pledge future tangible assets.

34. Article 4 Act of 10 January 1824.
35. Court of Cassation 19 May 1988, 1988-I Pasicrisie belge 1142, 1988–1989 Rechtskundig Weekblad 572.
36. V. Sagaert, *Volume-eigendom. Een verkenning van de verticale begrenzing van onroerende eigendom*, 46 Tijdschrift voor Privaatrecht 21–102 (2009).

The initiative was taken in Belgium in 2010 to draft a new law on movable security rights. The reform in Belgium is to a large extent based on international models such as the French Law Reform 2006, Article 9 of the American UCC, and the *Draft Common Frame of Reference* in a European context (DCFR, Book IX). The new Belgian Pledge Act of 11 July 2013 will replace the old provisions regarding pledge in the Civil Code (Articles 2071–2091).[37] The new Act will enter into force at a date set by Royal Decree. It is expected that this will be toward the end of 2016, when the new Pledge Register will be, from a technical point of view, operational.

Registration becomes the main form of perfection of the security right, instead of dispossession. The new Pledge Register will be put in place by the Federal Public Service Finance. The registration is broadly speaking in accordance with the principles of the DCFR: available and searchable online, and registration, renewal and deletion may all be done online. The role of the Registrar is strictly passive; only the formal requirements of the filing are examined. Entries in the Register can be made directly by the secured creditor who has to notify the debtor (Article 29). Registration requires the existence of the pledge agreement. As a consequence, advance filing is not possible. One of the reasons for the delay in introduction of the electronic registration is the discussions regarding the open access based on privacy concerns.

However, it will still be possible under the 2013 Act for a security right to be effective against third parties without registration and in other ways, such as by virtue of the taking of possession of the *movable property* by the creditor (Article 39) or the taking of 'control' of *claims* by the creditor (Article 60): the security holder is in 'control' when he is entitled to notify the debtor of the encumbered claim.

The priority ranking of the subsequent pledgees will be determined by reference to the moment they fulfilled the requirement for the enforceability vis-à-vis third parties. The first in time-rule is not without exceptions. A special status ('super-priority') is conferred upon the unpaid seller (Article 58).

[2] Pledge on Receivables

A receivables pledge agreement is, since 1994, in principle valid and perfected vis-à-vis third parties by the mere fact of entering into the agreement. However, the pledge will not be perfected vis-à-vis the debtor of the pledged receivable until the moment such debtor has been notified of the existence[38] of such pledge agreement or such debtor has acknowledged the existence thereof. Prior to the notification or acknowledgement, the debtor of the receivable may be discharged from its obligations under such receivable (to the extent it is acting in good faith) by paying its debt to its initial creditor (pledgor). After the pledge has been notified to the debtor of the receivable or he has acknowledged the pledge, he can only validly pay to the pledgee.

37. Moniteur belge - Belgisch Staatsblad, 2 August 2013 (2nd ed.), www.juridat.be. E. Dirix, *The New Belgian Act on Security Interest in Movable Property*, 23 INTERNATIONAL INSOLVENCY REVIEW 171–180 (2014); E. Dirix & V. Sagaert, *The New Belgian Act on Security Rights in Movable Property*, 3 EUROPEAN PROPERTY LAW JOURNAL 231–255 (2014).
38. It is not necessary to notify the debtor (parts of) the content of the pledge agreement.

Notification or acknowledgement should not mandatorily occur simultaneously with entering into the pledge agreement. However, if the notification or acknowledgement is not performed simultaneously, the risk exists that the pledgor may grant another pledge on the same receivable to another pledgee or can assign the same receivable to an assignee and that the second pledge/assignment is perfected vis-à-vis the debtor of the receivable. This second pledge/assignment would therefore rank prior to the first pledge (to the extent that the second pledgee acts in good faith).

[3] *Title Retention*

Belgian law has for many decades been hostile to the retention of title. A title retention did not affect the validity of the agreement, but Belgian law did not recognise the effectiveness of title retention in relation to third parties. In other words: title retention was considered to be valid, but this clause did not have any proprietary effects. This case law deprived title retention of its usefulness.[39]

The situation dramatically changed when the proprietary effects of title retention have been recognised in the amendment of the Bankruptcy Act of 8 August 1997.

However, the effectiveness of the title retention is subject to the following formalities, which have to be complied with: (i) the clause is in writing; (ii) the parties agreed upon the clause at the latest at the moment of the delivery of the assets; and (iii) the assets are still identifiable in the possession of the (bankrupt) purchaser, have neither become immovable by incorporation nor transformed or commingled with other assets.

The new Pledge Act of 11 July 2013 reinforces the retention of title clause: it provides that the retention of title is effective not only in bankruptcy, but also in other insolvency proceedings. Moreover, retention of title can remain effective after the incorporation of the sold good, subject to the condition that it was registered.

[4] *Fiduciary Transfer for Security Purposes*

Belgian law recognises the validity but not the proprietary effects of a fiduciary transfer of ownership for security purposes, as it was acknowledged in a principled decision of the Court of Cassation.[40] The Court ruled that the ownership of the creditor did not fit within the different types of property right which are recognised and which award protection in case of insolvency. However, this position has been subject to main developments. The EU Financial Collateral Directive 2002/47, implemented in Belgian law by an Act of 15 December 2004, introduced one of the main developments. With regard to financial collateral, the fiduciary transfer of ownership is not only valid, but moreover it is effective against all third parties despite the opening of an insolvency proceeding against the debtor.[41] The fiduciary owner is not subject to any effect of the

39. Court of Cassation 9 February 1933, 1933-I Pasicrisie belge 103.
40. Court of Cassation 17 October 1996, 1996 Arresten van het Hof van Cassatie 930.
41. Article 12 Act of 15 December 2004.

opening of the insolvency proceeding. If the value of the financial collateral exceeds the value of the claim, the remainder must be restituted to the debtor. This is a consequence of the prohibition of unjust enrichment.

It could be argued that this Act of 15 December 2004 has only a limited scope, and that there is already other specific legislation favouring the fiduciary transfer of ownership, especially in the financial sector. However, the scope of the Act is actually very large: the Belgian implementation of the rules in the Financial Collateral Directive is not restricted to financial institutions, but can also ensure a commercial or even civil claim, whatever may be the nature.

More recently, the Court of Cassation ruled that the fiduciary transfer of ownership could not grant more powers to the creditor than the powers pursuant to a pledge agreement.[42] Thus, the fiduciary transfer of ownership could only be upheld as limited property right. This solution has also been adopted, on a more general statutory level, in Article 62 of the new Pledge Act of 11 July 2013 reforming the movable security rights.

[5] Statutory Liens

Statutory liens are rights of priority on movables conferred by the legislature on the basis of the nature of the guaranteed claims. The Belgian legislature makes a distinction between specific liens, granting priority over the proceeds of specific objects, and general liens, covering all the estate of the debtor (or a proportionate part of it). They are not subject to specific publicity measures. For instance, the lessor of an asset can claim priority over the furniture of the asset.[43] If the underlying contract is a sales agreement, the seller will be protected by a statutory lien.[44]

[B] Property Security Rights in Immovables: Mortgages and Immovable Liens

A mortgage ('hypothec') is defined by the legislature as a property right on immovables, allocated to the discharge of an obligation.[45] This definition has been criticised, because it does not comprise the main features of the hypothec, for example: (1) its accessory nature; (2) the absence of dispossession; and (3) the possibility to constitute a hypothec on some movables. In Belgian law, hypothecs are governed by the Mortgage Act of 16 December 1851.

A hypothec can originate in three different ways: it can be either statutory, judicial or conventional. Judicial hypothecs are very exceptional. The absence of dispossession is the most distinctive feature of hypothecs. It has precisely been recognised in order to dribble the requirement of dispossession as it is imposed – until the entry into force of the new Pledge Act of 11 July 2013 – for a pledge. For the sake

42. Court of Cassation 3 December 2010, 2010 Arresten van het Hof van Cassatie nr 712.
43. Article 20, 1, Mortgage Act.
44. Article 20, 5, Mortgage Act.
45. Article 41 Mortgage Act.

of publicity, the dispossession has been replaced by the registration in the Mortgage Register.

Statutory immovable liens are rights of priority on immovables conferred by the legislature on the basis of the nature of the guaranteed claims. An example of a specific lien is the one of the unpaid seller of an immovable, which has to be effective in order to be effective in relation to third parties.[46] General liens on immovables are exceptional, as the legislature was concerned not to impede in the lending capacity of natural persons who generally only can make their immovable goods object of security.

§9.11 ACQUISITION OF PROPERTY RIGHTS

[A] Contractual Transfer of Property Rights

Belgian law has, following French law, a consensual system for the transfer of property rights. Property rights are transferred by the mere consent between the parties.[47] Article 1138 of the Civil Code specifies that an obligation to deliver property is complete by the sole consent of the contracting parties. Neither the handing over of the asset, neither the payment of the price are a requirement for the property transfer.

However, Article 1138 of the Civil Code and its applications only focus on the internal relationship between the transferor and the transferee. Additional requirements are set out in order to perfect the transfer in relation to third parties in good faith. There are, according to Belgian law, different rules for immovables, movables and receivables. In order to 'perfect' the transfer of movables, the physical delivery of the movables to the transferee is required.[48] In order to give third-party effect to a transfer of immovables, registration of the transfer agreement in the Mortgage Register is required. With regard to receivables, the assignment is in principle valid and perfected by mere consent between the assignor and assignee. However, notification (without any formal requirement) is necessary in relation to some, specifically protected third parties, for instance the debtor of the assigned claim, competing assignees and creditors of the assignor.[49]

There are several exceptions to the rule that property rights pass between parties by the mere effect of the agreement. These exceptions can relate to the nature of the assets or the nature of the agreement and the nature of the parties.

---

46. Article 27, 1°, Mortgage Act.
47. We have argued in an extensive analysis that it concerns a fictitious tradition instead of consensualism: V. Sagaert, *Consensus versus Delivery Systems. Consensus About Tradition?*, *in* Rules for the Transfer of Movables. A Candidate for European Harmonization or National Reforms? 9–46 (W. Faber & B. Lurger eds., München: Sellier 2008).
48. Article 1141 Civil Code expresses this third-party protection by providing that 'if the asset which a person has obliged to give to two different persons, is a corporeal movable asset, the one who has first been given possession will prevail and will be considered as owner, even if his title is more recent, at the requirement that his possession is in good faith'. In other words: if A sells a good to B and afterwards A sells and delivers the same good to C, C will be considered as owner at the condition that he is in good faith, i.e., that he did not know and should not have known any previous transfer of the same good.
49. Article 1690 Civil Code; *see supra*.

With regard to *generic goods*, the principle of consensualism cannot be upheld. It is a common principle of property law that property rights can only have as object identified or identifiable goods. This is the so-called principle of specificity. The transfer of generic goods requires a dualistic approach, as the immediate transfer of property rights is excluded.

The same line of reasoning applies to the contractual transfer of *future goods*. A transfer agreement with regard to future goods is in principle valid. The transfer of future goods only operates proprietary effects after the coming into existence of the transferred good.

A major exception to this principle is to be found in Article 931 of the Civil Code: 'all acts containing an *inter vivos* gift shall be executed before *notaries*, in the ordinary form of contracts; and there shall remain the original of them, on pain of annulment'. A prominent exception is that case law has accepted through the decades that a gift of corporeal movables can be effected by mere handing over of the good. It is a *consuetudo contra legem*.

Especially in legal scholarship the opinion gains field that in commercial sale transfer of property and risk take place at the moment of delivery. Case law remains more reserved. The rule is in any case of supplementary law, which implies that parties can agree that transfer of property takes place at another moment.

[B] Acquisitive Prescription

[1] General Rules

Acquisitive prescription entails that a person who has the possession of a property right during a certain period of time, becomes the owner of that right. It consecrates the factual situation into the legal situation. This acquisitive prescription indirectly deprives an owner of his rights, as the acquisition of ownership by one person necessarily deprives the current owner of his entitlement. Normally, acquisitive prescription requires possession of a property right for, at least, thirty years. The general term requires: (1) legal possession for that period; and (2) possession free of defects. These requirements are set out both for the normal prescription as for the abbreviated prescription periods.[50]

The Possession Requirement

Article 2228 of the Civil Code gives a definition of possession: possession is the detention or enjoyment of property or of a right that we hold or exercise by ourselves, or by another who holds and exercises it in our name. Possession requires two essential elements: a material element (*corpus*) and a subjective element (*animus*). A detentor has control over the asset, but does not meet the subjective requirement.

Corpus means that the possessor has the physical control of the asset. This control must however not have been effected in a direct way, indirect control is

50. Article 2230 Civil Code.

sufficient. For instance, if somebody has stolen a car and leaves that car to a garage owner for repair works, the thief remains in possession. The garage holder is the detentor of the car while he effects the repair works. The thief remains possessor. This is called 'indirect possession' or *possessio animo suo, corpore alieno*.

The subjective element means that the possessor also has the intention to exercise this physical control in his own interest, and not in the interest of the owner or a third party (*animus rem sibi habendi*). Belgian law adheres, as French law, to the *Savignan* doctrine according to which the *animus domini* is the main feature of possession. This subjective element, contrary to the material element, cannot be exercised indirectly: it must be assessed on behalf of the possessor himself. However, this subjective element is considered in an objective way: nobody can exercise physical control in his own interest if he has, from the beginning of his physical control, the obligation to make restitution of his asset.

The 'Free of Defects' Requirement

To be able to claim acquisitive prescription, the possessor must have a possession free from defects. A possession that does not meet one or more of the following requirements can never result in acquisitive prescription:

- 'Uninterrupted' means that the possessor undertakes acts of possession in a regular manner, as a normal and diligent owner would have done in the same situation.
- 'Peaceful' has a double meaning. First, it means that the possessor did not use violence to obtain physical control of the property. If the possessor took possession in a violent way, this excludes any subsequent acquisitive prescription. Second, it means that violence used by third parties during the possession, against which the possessor did not react as a normal diligent possessor would have done, also excludes peaceful possession.
- 'Unambiguous' means that there is no doubt concerning the origin of the possession, or concerning its exclusive nature. This problem is, in legal practice, often encountered when a parent or a secretary of a deceased person possesses certain property of the latter after his death and claims that he received it by gift from hand to hand.
- 'Public' means that the possessor does not hide his possession. This requirement must be applied with regard to the nature of the property. The nature of some property does not lend itself to a public possession (for instance, financial instruments, cash money).

However, Article 2265 of the Civil Code provides that, in order to apply the abbreviated term of prescription, additional requirements must be fulfilled: 'A person who acquires an immovable in good faith and under a just title prescribes ownership of it by ten years, where the true owner lives on the territory of the court of appeal within whose limits the immovable is situated; and by twenty years, where he is domiciled outside of the said territory.' In order to invoke an abbreviated term of prescription, two additional requirements have to be satisfied: (1) the possessor is in good faith; and (2) he must have a just title. The latter requirement supposes that the possessor has acquired possession through a title which would have passed ownership if the predecessor had been the legal owner. The only defect in the acquisition is, thus, that the possessor acquired *non a domino*. The abbreviated prescription only applies to immovable goods, as the possessor in good faith of movables acquires ownership immediately (voluntary dispossession) or after three years (involuntary dispossession).[51]

[2] Protection of the Good Faith Possessor of Movables

A specific form of acquisitive prescription can be found in Article 2279 of the Civil Code. According to this provision, the third party who acquired possession of movables in good faith from a non-owner cannot be subject to vindication by the owner. The owner, who had an action in vindication against the transferor, loses this in the case of transfer of the property to a third party in good faith. This is the *possession vaut titre* clause.[52]

However, if the real owner has been involuntarily dispossessed, he does not lose his ownership immediately. The time during which the vindication can be exercised is limited to three years from the moment of the dispossession.[53] Dispossession of movables is involuntary if the movables are lost or stolen. Movables are lost if they have disappeared unintentionally, or if their possession has ended by force majeure (e.g., because of a flood), by accident or even by carelessness.[54]

For lost or stolen banknotes, vindication out of the hands of a possessor in good faith is excluded.[55]

[C] Accession

By means of *accessio*, the owner of property also becomes the owner of everything that this property produces or that incorporates itself into it (*quod accedit*) in a natural or artificial manner. If it is demonstrated that the incorporated property belonged to another person at the moment of the incorporation, *accessio* functions as a way of acquisition of property in favour of the ground owner.[56] The owner of the incorporated property can, however, claim compensation for his loss of property. If the building was built on another's ground in bad faith, the ground owner can opt for a destruction of the building at the expense of the builder.

51. Article 2279 Civil Code.
52. Article 2279, para. 1, Civil Code.
53. Article 2279, para. 2, Civil Code.
54. Court of Cassation 9 February 1982, 1982-I Pasicrisie belge 728.
55. Article 2279, para. 3, Civil Code.
56. Article 533 Civil Code also installs the presumption that the buildings, crops and improvements on or below land belong to the owner of the land. This presumption can be reversed by proving that one has acquired title to this property by prescription or by another title. Court of Cassation 21 April 1866, 1866-I Pasicrisie belge 130.

Accessio implies an incorporation, i.e., a material tie between a main and an accessory movable or immovable.

In the case of *accessio*, the ownership of the accessory property follows that of the main property. The ground is always considered as the main property. Article 577-2, §§9–10, of the Civil Code exceptionally consider the land as one of the accessories to the ownership of an apartment. However, this does not imply that a reversed case of *accessio* is provided by law. Rather, it forms the legal grounds for apartment joint ownership in Belgian law. Moreover, parties can contractually derogate to accession in creating a right of superficies (*see supra*).

§9.12 FEATURES AND ORGANISATION OF THE MORTGAGE REGISTER

As was said, the registration of any transfer, declaration or creation of immovable property rights is necessary in order to make these rights effective in relation to third parties in good faith. Apart from that, not only sales deeds are registered, but also deeds of gift, long lease deeds (more than nine years), easement deeds, building division deeds, seizure measures, etc. The only restriction is that the object of the deed should be an immovable property. There is no similar register in Belgium for movable goods, except for the Pledge Register which will become effective after the entry into force of the new Pledge Act of 11 July 2013 reforming the property security rights on movables (*see supra*).

A sales agreement is, even without publicity in the Mortgage Register, effective vis-à-vis third parties who have knowledge of the existence of this agreement or who ought to have knowledge of the existence of this agreement. Good faith is presumed, bad faith has to be proved by the party who aims to invoke the sales agreement against a third party prior to the publication in the Mortgage Register. If A sells an immovable to B and afterwards A sells the same immovable to C, the latter will prevail if he proceeds as the first one to registration in the Mortgage Register and if he did not know and did not have to know that the immovable had already been sold to B.

There is no unanimity about the question whether the bankruptcy trustee must respect the sales agreement entered into but not registered before the bankruptcy. A creditor seizing an immovable after its sale but before the transcription of the sale, must not take into account the sales agreement either.[57]

The Belgian Mortgage Register is a '*negative*' system: the registration of deeds does not guarantee the validity of the registered rights. The Mortgage Registrar has a sheer passive role: he is not even entitled to verify the validity of the agreement between parties. In other words, the rights that are registered are merely possible rights, and their validity must still be assessed by the person consulting the Register (in most cases: the notary). Belgian mortgage publicity does not protect public faith.[58]

Moreover, the Belgian Mortgage Register is person-based, and not structured as a *Grundbuch*. The Mortgage Register is organised along the identity of the persons

57. Article 1577 Judicial Code.
58. For a critical approach, *see* V. Sagaert, *Het rechtmatig vertrouwen van de schuldeisers in de hypothecaire registers*, *in* Feestbundel Achilles Cuypers 221–236 (Brussels: Larcier 2009).

holding a property right on an immovable property. Hence, searches in the registers can only be effected on the basis of the identity of a person holding rights on the immoveable.

Not all transfers of immovable property are registered in the Mortgage Register.

Only transfers *inter vivos* are registered. The transfer of inherited immovable property is not mentioned in this register. This means that in the given case, the Mortgage Register does not reflect the actual ownership of the premise. With a transfer *mortis causa*, the immovable property passes immediately to the heirs, and not on the basis of a consensual system or on the basis of a notarial deed. Article 777 of the Civil Code states that all acts accepting an inheritance have retroactive force from the moment of the death. The only information regarding the transfer of immovable property *mortis causa* can be found in the competent Registration Office, where the inheritance tax needs to be paid on the basis of a declaration of inheritance. However, the information held in the Registration Office does not offer the same legal guarantees as the Mortgage Register. The information held by this Office has often not been checked by any real estate or family law professional. Needless to say that this forms a major gap in the publicity of immovable property.

Moreover, only consensual acquisition of immovables are the object of publicity. The transfer of immovable property by way of law (acquisitive prescription, accession, etc.) does not figure in the Mortgage Registers. These transfers are automatically (*de iure*) effective vis-à-vis third parties.

§9.13 SELECTED BIBLIOGRAPHY

C. Cauffman & V. Sagaert, *National Report on the Transfer of Movables. Belgium, in National Reports on the Transfer of Movables in Europe* 197–351 (W. Fabert & C. Lurger eds., Munich: Sellier, 2010).

R. Derine, F. Van Neste & H. Vandenberghe, *Zakenrecht*, Boek I–IV (Beginselen van Belgisch Privaatrecht V, R. Dillemans & W. Van Gerven eds., Antwerp: Standaard, 1990–2000).

J. Hansenne, *Les Biens. Précis* (Liège: Collection Scientifique de la Faculté de Droit de Liège 1996).

P. Lecocq, *Manuel de Droit des Biens* (Liège: Larcier 2012–2016).

V. Sagaert, *Goederenrecht* (Beginselen van Belgisch Privaatrecht V, R. Dillemans & W. Van Gerven eds., Mechelen: Kluwer 2014).

CHAPTER 10

Contract Law

Ignace Claeys

§10.01 INTRODUCTION

Belgian contract law is built up around two pivots which most other legal systems share. The first one is that of the life of a contract which serves as the core model to solve contractual issues. Distinct rules govern the subsequent stages of a contract's existence: the negotiation (conception), the formation and validity (birth), the performance (life) and the end (death) of a contract. These contractual stages will be discussed in §10.04. The second pivot is the distinction between contracting parties and third parties, which will be the subject matter of §10.05. Before doing so, in §10.02 we first give an overview of the main sources and principal trends of Belgian contract law and in §10.03 we shortly emphasise the tension between freedom of contract and mandatory law and the relevance of some overriding general principles of law.

This contribution only deals with the general rules of contract law which in principle apply to all types of contracts. Those general rules evidently do not stand on their own. They have to be combined with legislative rules applicable to specific types of contracts which can be found inside and outside the Civil Code, such as sales, services, mandates, leases, security contracts, employment contracts,[1] distribution contracts and commercial cooperation contracts,[2] ... Some of those rules on specific types of contracts deviate from the general rules on contract, others are rather supplementary to those general rules. Some of them are default rules from which parties may freely deviate, others are mandatory rules.

Contract law also does not stand on its own in that it is to be combined with other branches of private law, such as the law on unjustified enrichment and tort law. The issue for example of whether contracting parties can sue each other not only in contract

1. *See infra* Chapter 14, §14.02 [B].
2. *See infra* Chapter 12, §12.05 [A].

but also in tort (the issue of concurrence of contractual liability and tortious or extra-contractual liability) is dealt with in the chapter on tort law.[3]

§10.02 SOURCES AND PRINCIPAL TRENDS

Belgian contract law is spread over multiple sources. The main source of rules is federal or national law. The main body of federal rules is grouped together in the Civil Code. Although most of the relevant rules of the Napoleonic Civil Code are left untouched as they were in 1804, they had to be interpreted and supplemented in an armoury of judgments by civil and commercial courts (the Court of Cassation heading the civil and commercial court hierarchy). But one should look beyond federal law in order to fully grasp Belgian contract law. The regions in Belgium also have jurisdiction to regulate some specific types of contracts, such as leases. More importantly, the EU has been of growing importance to contract law, mainly by way of the legal instrument of directives for business to consumer contracts (B2C). Most comprehensive are the directives on unfair contract terms[4] and on consumer rights[5] which are implemented in the Belgian Code of Economic Law. While the former directive expects from EU Member States to lay down rules to ensure that certain contractual clauses ('unfair terms') are not binding on consumers, the latter directive mainly provides for information duties and rights of withdrawal to the benefit of the consumers for distance and off-premises contracts. Some EU directives are also relevant for business to business contracts (B2B), such as the Late Payments Directive,[6] the e-Commerce Directive[7] and the Services Directive.[8] There are also relevant EU regulations (EU legal instrument other than directives) such as the eIDAS relevant for electronic transactions.[9]

From this general overview of sources of contract law, it is clear that contract law and more generally private law is subject to a growing trend of Europeanisation. Another trend is that of constitutionalisation. There are two types of constitutionalisation of contract law. One type is that the Belgian Constitutional Court may be requested to assess the constitutionality of existing contract law rules. The question often arises whether or not a contract law rule infringes the constitutional principles of equal treatment and non-discrimination. For example, even if a right of a third-party

3. *See infra* Chapter 11, §11.06.
4. Council Directive 93/13/EEC of 5 April 1993 on Unfair Terms in Consumer Contracts.
5. Directive 2011/83/EU of the European Parliament and of the Council of 25 October 2011 on Consumer Rights, amending Council Directive 93/13/EEC and Directive 1999/44/EC of the European Parliament and of the Council and repealing Council Directive 85/577/EEC and Directive 97/7/EC of the European Parliament and of the Council Text with EEA relevance.
6. Directive 2000/35/EC of the European Parliament and of the Council of 29 June 2000 on Combating Late payment in Commercial Transactions, as amended. *See infra* Chapter 12, §12.05 [B].
7. Directive 2000/31/EC of the European Parliament and of the Council of 8 June 2000 on Certain Legal Aspects of Information Society Services, in Particular Electronic Commerce, in the Internal Market.
8. Directive 2006/123/EC of the European Parliament and of the Council of 12 December 2006 on Services in the Internal Market.
9. Regulation (EU) 910/2014 of the European Parliament and of the Council of 23 July 2014 on Electronic Identification and Trust Services for Electronic Transactions in the Internal Market and repealing Directive 1999/93/EC.

beneficiary is subject to a statutory ten-year prescription period as from the day on which the right could be claimed (most often the day of the conclusion of the contract), the third-party beneficiary may nevertheless invoke its right against the promisor even after the expiry of the statutory ten-year prescription period when the third party could not have claimed its right before because it simply did not know and reasonably could not have known of the existence of its contractual right.[10] Whenever the Constitutional Court finds a legislative rule (or the omission of such rule) unconstitutional, it is a delicate question to know whether it is up to the legislature or rather the courts to find a rule that does away with the unconstitutionality.

The other type of constitutionalisation of contract law occurs when a fundamental right permeates the application of an established general rule such as public policy,[11] negligence, the duty to perform a contract in good faith or the prohibition of abuse of a right. The right to leading a life in keeping with human dignity, as embodied in Article 23 of the Belgian Constitution, has for example been successfully used to argue an abuse of a contractual right to an alimony in circumstances where a thirty-year old alimony could no longer be enforced by someone who meanwhile had equivalent sources of income against someone who otherwise would have been left with less income than the minimum wage.[12] The case law of the ECJ in Luxembourg or the European Court for Human Rights (ECtHR) in Strasbourg plays an important role in this constitutionalisation trend.

§10.03 THE TENSION BETWEEN FREEDOM OF CONTRACT AND MANDATORY LAW, INCLUDING SOME GENERAL PRINCIPLES OF LAW

When assessing which rights and obligations contracting parties have, one must always consider both the will of the parties (as interpreted by courts) and the will of the legislature, including the requirements of public policy (as interpreted by courts). Social reality shows the tension that exists between those two wills.

The will of the parties is protected by the principle of freedom of contract. This freedom is generally considered to be part of the freedom to conduct a business. This freedom is not only expressed in the European Charter on Fundamental Rights[13] but also in the Belgian Code of Economic Law: 'Everyone is free to exercise any economic activity to his choice.'[14]

The freedom of contract first of all means that as a rule one is free to conclude a contract or to refuse to do so. It also means that in principle one is free to choose his or

10. Constitutional Court No. 164/2014 of 6 November 2014.
11. Article 6 Civil Code.
12. Court of Cassation 14 October 2010, C.09.0608.F, 2010 Pasicrisie belge 2643, 2010 Arresten van het Hof van Cassatie 2507.
13. Article 16 Charter of Fundamental Rights of the European Union.
14. Article II.3 Code of Economic Law (*see* already Article 7 Décret d'Allarde of 2–17 March 1791).

her contracting party (subject to the prohibition of discrimination[15]). It also means that, subject to the constraints set by the legislature and to public policy requirements, contracting parties are free to determine the content of their contract.

The freedom of contract is however limited. The limits to this freedom is worded as follows in the Belgian Code of Economic Law: 'The freedom of enterprise is exercised taking into account the international treaties in effect in Belgium, the general normative framework of the economic union and the monetary unity as determined by or on the basis of the international treaties and the law, as well as the laws concerning public policy and good morals and the provisions of mandatory law'.[16] A similar wording can be found in the Civil Code: 'Specific contracts may not harm the laws that concern public order and good morals.'[17] An important example of such law restricting the freedom of contract is competition law (as interpreted by national courts and by the Court of Justice).[18]

Apart from specific mandatory regulation for particular contract types or particular industries, freedom of contract is constrained by three overriding general principles of law which have gradually been recognised by the Belgian Court of Cassation. Those principles have in common that in particular circumstances legislative rules or contractual clauses may not be applied between contracting parties. The first general principle of law is known in its Latin expression *fraus omnia corrumpit*. According to that general principle, a person who is acting fraudulently with the intention to harm or to obtain profit will be prevented from invoking an otherwise applicable rule favourable to that party. The second general principle is known as the prohibition of abuse of right (*l'abus de droit - rechtsmisbruik*).[19] Even though a person has a right, he may nevertheless be prevented from exercising that right because of the particular factual circumstances of the case. In the context of contractual rights, this general principle is subsumed under the rule that a contract must be performed in good faith (*see* below).[20] The third general principle of law is that of the prohibition of evasion of law (*la fraude à la loi - wetsontduiking*). According to that general principle, a person is not allowed to intentionally make use of a rule in order to reach a particular outcome that is prohibited by another rule. Especially the two latter principles are very much fact-dependent and rather hard to apply in practice. It is therefore difficult to predict how a court will assess a case under those two principles. Even though the application of those principles is largely a matter of fact, the Court of Cassation sometimes quashes a decision for the wrong application of those principles.[21]

15. See e.g. the Federal Act of 10 May 2007 on Combating Particular Types of Discrimination.
16. Article II.4 Code of Economic Law.
17. Article 6 Civil Code.
18. *See* for example Court of Cassation 18 February 1965, 1965 Pasicrisie belge 621, 1967 REVUE CRITIQUE DE JURISPRUDENCE BELGE 245, on economic boycott as an inacceptable reason for refusing to conclude a contract.
19. *See also infra* Chapter 11, §11.03 [A] [1] [a] [iv].
20. Article 1134, para. 3, Civil Code.
21. For example Court of Cassation 1 February 2016, C.15.0250.F.

§10.04 THE LIFE OF A CONTRACT

[A] Negotiations

Freedom of contract is the leading rule for the behaviour of negotiating parties. Starting up negotiations does not imply a duty to contract. When a person receives an offer to contract, he is not bound to accept the offer. He can refuse or make another offer. However, there are some restrictions on the freedom of contract in the negotiation phase. Below, we give an idea of the four main restrictions.

First, according to the case law of the Court of Cassation, a negotiating party is not allowed to abuse its freedom of contract or, otherwise, he commits a fault for which he may be liable in tort for the damage caused by it.[22] The boundaries between the freedom of contract and the abuse thereof are highly dependent on the assessment of the concrete circumstances of an actual case. In specific circumstances, a blunt refusal to contract may amount to an abuse.[23] The same is true for a situation in which a party abruptly breaks off negotiations without a legitimate motive while he has created the reasonable expectation of the other party that a contract would be concluded. Damages for having abruptly broken off negotiations in a negligent way will most often be restricted to a compensation for costs and expenses, and will generally not include lost profits (the profits which would have been made if the contract had been concluded had negotiations not been broken off).

Second, a negotiating party may be required to disclose some information to the counterparty. It is generally accepted that no general duty to provide information exists and that it again depends on the actual circumstances of the case which information has to be disclosed. One of the main guidelines is that particular information should be provided or searched by the person who can do so for the least cost. The threshold to provide information will also be lower for a professional than for a layman. When the information is not provided to the other party when required, the party having neglected to provide such information or having provided incorrect information commits a pre-contractual fault (*culpa in contrahendo*) and will be liable in tort for the damage thus caused. The pre-contractual liability does not depend on the intention not to give sufficient and correct information. A person will also be liable if he acted merely negligent in the provision of information in the pre-contractual phase.

Third, if a contract is avoided or annulled because of deceit or duress (*see* below), the party having committed deceit or duress will be held liable in tort as well for the damage so caused. If a contract is avoided because of mistake, such mistake may be caused by a negligent behaviour of the other party who will be held liable in tort as well, for example because he provided wrong information or simply did not provide sufficient information to the mistaken party.

Fourth, negotiating parties may have made specific contractual arrangements, such as the promise to keep information exchanged between negotiators confidential

22. Articles 1382–1383 Civil Code.
23. Court of Cassation, 7 October 2011, C.10.0227.F, 2011 Pasicrisie belge 2148, 2011 Arresten van het Hof van Cassatie 2032.

and not to make use of such information (non-disclosure agreement), or the promise of parties to negotiate exclusively with each other and not with another third party (exclusive negotiations agreement). In case of breach of such contract, the liability will be contractual in nature.

[B] Formation of a Contract

As in most other legal systems, a contract is formed as soon as an offer is accepted unconditionally by the addressee of the offer (the offeree) and the offeror can reasonably take knowledge of the acceptance.

A proposal is an offer if the person making a proposal intends to be legally bound by it and the proposal includes all essential and substantial elements. Essential elements are those that are required to characterise a contract as a particular type of contract. For example, a sales contract is characterised by the good to be sold and the sales price. The substantial elements are those that are important subjectively to the party making the proposal, such as the colour of a car to be sold.

It is important to know that, unlike in some other legal systems, an offeror cannot revoke the offer made as soon as the offeree can reasonably take notice of it. The period during which the offeror is thus bound may be fixed in the offer. If such period is not determined in the offer, the offeror is bound for a reasonable term. The reasonability of the term then depends on the particular circumstances of the case, such as the nature of the good (daily or luxury), the price at stake (cheap or expensive), the method of communication (on line or by letter), ...

Whenever a counteroffer is made or an offer is refused by the offeree, the original offer lapses. In the event of a counteroffer, that counteroffer on its turn constitutes an offer. The same is true for a conditional acceptance of an original offer.

As a rule, the formation of a contract does not depend on the fulfilment of formalities or the delivery of a good. As soon as parties reach consent, a contract is formed. If parties come to an oral agreement, a contract exists (be it that parties must still be able to prove its existence and such proof may be formal especially when a contract is invoked against a consumer[24]). Specific types of contracts are however subject to formalities, such as a promise to give gratuitously (*donation* – *schenking*) which is a solemn contract requiring a notarial deed.[25]

[C] Validity of a Contract

The validity of a contract depends on the capacity (*la capacité* – *bekwaamheid*) of the parties and on the quality of their will or consent (*le consentement* – *toestemming*). The contractual obligations also need to satisfy several objective requirements as to their subject matter (*l'objet* – *voorwerp*) and their cause (*la cause* – *oorzaak*).[26]

24. For more details, *see* Article 1341 Civil Code.
25. Article 931 Civil Code. *See supra* Chapter 8, §8.03 [B] [1].
26. Articles 1108 et seq. Civil Code.

As to capacity, in principle every person (whether a natural person or a legal entity) has capacity unless a statutory exception applies.[27] There are instances of general incapacity to exercise one's rights, such as minors.[28] There are also specific instances of incapacity, for instance for spouses to conclude certain sales contracts with each other.[29]

The will of a party is defective when it is tainted by error or mistake, deceit or fraud, or duress. These are the so-called defects of consent. The requirements for mistake, fraud or duress to vitiate the contract are laid down in case law. They all need to be determining for the conclusion of the contract. In other words, if the contract would have been concluded anyway (be it at other conditions) even without the defect, the contract will not be invalid for that reason. A mistake will only vitiate the contract if a reasonable person could have made the same mistake in the same concrete circumstances. This mistake is then said to be excusable. This requirement does not have to be satisfied in the event of deceit. As a rule, deceit must be committed by the contracting party and not by a third party. Duress of a third party to the contrary may invalidate a contract.

In addition, a contractual obligation needs to have a subject matter that needs to be licit or lawful, sufficiently determinable and possible to be performed. The subject matter of an obligation refers to the performance promised by the debtor. The subject matter of the main obligation of an insured for example is the payment of the premium to the insurer.

The most difficult validity requirement is that a contractual obligation also needs to have a cause and that such cause is licit or lawful and not false. The concept of cause is broadly defined as the reasons why a contracting party has engaged into an obligation and without which it would not have done so. Someone pays a price because of the good purchased, for example a tomato. The promised tomato is a cause for the obligation of the purchaser to pay the sales price. But so are the determinant motives why the purchaser buys the tomato (it usually is for eating it but it may as well be for throwing at a bad performer). If one of the determinative motives appears to be false or unlawful, the contract will be subject to avoidance. A cause (or a subject matter) is lawful (or licit) if it does not contradict mandatory law or public policy. According to the case law of the Court of Cassation, a contract may be nullified for unlawful cause even if only one of the parties had an unlawful motive and the contracting party was not aware of it, at least if the general interest is at stake.[30]

In general, courts are considered not to have the power to review the balance of the obligations assumed by parties unless there is an explicit statutory basis for such reviewing power, as is for instance the case for sales of immovable goods when the seller has received a sales price which is less than 5/12 of the value of the good.[31] Under

27. Article 1123 Civil Code.
28. For adults, *see* Articles 488 et seq. Civil Code.
29. Article 1595 Civil Code.
30. Court of Cassation, 12 October 2000, C.99.0136.F, 2000 Pasicrisie belge 1531, 2000 Arresten van het Hof van Cassatie 1564, 2003 REVUE CRITIQUE DE JURISPRUDENCE BELGE 74.
31. Article 1674 Civil Code.

the general theory of abuse of circumstances (*lésion qualifiée - gekwalificeerde benadeling*), a manifest lack of balance of the obligations of the contracting parties may be invoked as a basis of nullity (or, according to some, the modification) of the contract if that imbalance was obtained by an abuse of the weakness or inferiority (such as the illiterateness, the inexperience or the economically or socially weak position) of the disadvantaged contracting party.

If the requirements for the validity of a contract are not satisfied, the contract may be nullified or avoided by a court. Unlike in many other legal systems, a party does not have the power to nullify or avoid a contract unilaterally. A distinction is made between two categories of nullity: relative versus absolute nullity. In the event of relative nullity, only the contracting party that the violated rule is intended to protect has the power to claim the annulment of the contract. For example, only the party under duress may claim the annulment. Third parties are not allowed to claim relative nullity. A contract that is tainted by a ground of relative nullity can be confirmed, in that the party having the right to invoke the annulment has the power to waive the claim for annulment as soon as he no longer finds himself in a position to be protected (e.g., when the situation of duress has come to an end). In the event of absolute nullity, every contracting and third party (to the extent that party can show an interest in obtaining the annulment) has the power to claim the avoidance of the contract. In that event it is not possible for any of the parties to confirm the contract. It is generally accepted that a court has the power to invoke a ground of absolute nullity on his own motion (ex officio), but under the influence of the case law of the ECJ in consumer contracts cases, there is a growing trend to afford the court the same power as regard to grounds of relative nullity.

An important characteristic of the remedy of avoidance of a contract is that parties are not only freed from all obligations arising out of the avoided contract. Avoidance also has a retroactive effect, implying duties to restitute what may already have been performed under the contract. In the event of absolute nullity, however, a court has the power to deny restitution to a party if the denial of restitution is deemed useful to prevent the further conclusion of similar (invalid) contracts or in order to punish one of the parties more severely than the other party (*in pari causa turpitudinis cessat repetitio*).

The remedy of the annulment of a contract will often be combined with that of damages on the basis of tortious liability (Articles 1382–1383 of the Civil Code).[32] If deceit or duress caused damage that is not fully repaired by way of annulment of the contract, they will also bring about tortious liability. In the event of mistake, the mistaken party does not have a duty to pay damages, but may have the right to damages if the other party has caused the mistake due to its negligent behaviour (e.g., the negligent omission to provide relevant information causing the mistake).

Apart from the general rules on validity of contracts, it should be noted that consumer contracts are often subject to additional restrictions of validity of the entire contract or of particular contractual clauses. The EU Unfair Contract Terms Directive is

32. *See infra* Chapter 11, §11.03 [A] [1] and §11.05.

implemented in Belgium in a way that the control of contractual clauses under those rules is limited to consumer contracts to the benefit of the consumer, and therefore does not extend to B2B relations, but it applies to both negotiated B2C contracts as to not individually negotiated contracts and standard terms and conditions.

[D] Content: Interpreting, Supplementing and Correcting

A promise may be stated explicitly or implicitly if it can be inferred with certainty from the circumstances. This implies that the existence or the scope of a contractual promise may be derived from pre-contractual documents (including emails) but also from the way parties have performed the contract in the past.

Contractual documents which lack clarity require interpretation. The Civil Code provides for some rules binding for courts as to how to interpret contracts. The basic rule is that a contract should be interpreted in accordance with the common intention of parties rather than keeping to the literal meaning of the words.[33] Another rule is that a clause should be interpreted in the way that it would have effect rather than that it would not.[34] Only if doubt continues to exist, a clause is to be interpreted against the party who is benefiting of this clause. For example, a clause limiting the liability of a contracting party is to be interpreted - in the event of doubt about the common intention of the parties and in case common reason does not favour one particular interpretation - against the person liable and in favour of the victim.[35] For consumer contracts, unclear clauses are subject to the specific rule that they should be interpreted in the way most beneficial to the consumer.

The content of a contract does not only require interpretation of what contracting parties have stated. Parties do not provide for a rule for every event that may occur during the life of a contract. That is why the legislature provides for a series of default rules which govern the contract if parties have not modified or excluded those rules. The legislature also continues to provide for an array of mandatory rules from which parties cannot validly deviate. Customary rules may also supplement the rules contracting parties have agreed to.

For several decades, case law also accepted the duty to perform contracts in good faith[36] as a legal basis of additional contractual obligations between contracting parties. This is called the supplementary function of the contractual principle of good faith. Those obligations may be of various sorts, such as obligations to provide assistance or information. They require a person to act as a reasonable person in the performance stage of a contract. Good faith sets rules of conduct. For example, if someone has to repair an item and soon after concluding the contract it appears that the cost would equal the purchase price of a new item, the repairer has to first inform the client of the high cost of repair. Good faith is also the basis for the obligation of a party to take the

33. Article 1156 Civil Code.
34. Article 1157 Civil Code.
35. Article 1162 Civil Code.
36. Article 1134, para. 3, Civil Code.

reasonable measures to mitigate damage in the event of a breach by his contracting party.

In some concrete circumstances, the duty to perform a contract in good faith is also the legal basis to deny a contracting party to exercise its contractual rights. This is called the corrective function of the contractual principle of good faith. This function comes into play when a party *manifestly* exceeds the boundaries within which a reasonable party would have exercised its contractual rights in the same circumstances of the case.[37] This is evidently the case if a party merely exercises its rights in order to harm the contracting party, but it is also accepted in situations where such intention is lacking, for example, when a party would exercise a right which would only provide him with a minor benefit while the other party would suffer a disproportionately large disadvantage (proportionality principle). If a contracting party abuses his contractual rights, the exercise of his right may be mitigated or, if not possible, he may be liable for damages. He may even be denied from invoking a particular contractual clause, such as a clause which provides for a fixed amount of damages in the event of a breach.

[E] Breach, Notice and Remedies

The nature of the contractual obligation is the starting point to know whether a debtor failed to perform his contractual obligation. Three categories of contractual obligations are usually distinguished depending on what parties have intended to promise. First, a party may promise an obligation of reasonable or best efforts. In that event, he only promises to make reasonable or best efforts to reach a certain intended outcome, without promising the realisation of that outcome (*obligation de moyen - inspannings-verbintenis* or *middelenverbintenis*). For that category of obligations, a breach requires a fault of the debtor, which has to be proven by the creditor. More intense is the obligation to achieve a particular result. If the debtor does not realise the result promised, there is a breach, and he is liable unless he can prove force majeure (*obligation de résultat - resultaatsverbintenis*). Force majeure is understood to be the situation whereby it is impossible for the debtor to perform a contractual obligation because of a circumstance which is not attributable to him. The most intense obligation is an obligation of guarantee whereby the achievement of a particular result is promised but this time with the understanding that the debtor will not be able to escape liability even if he is able to prove force majeure (*obligation de garantie - garantieverbintenis*). Each contractual obligation has to be analysed separately in order to know whether it is an obligation of best efforts, an obligation to achieve a particular result or an obligation of guarantee. For example, an attorney's obligation to defend a client in court is not an obligation to achieve the result that he will win the case (unless in the rare case that the attorney promised otherwise), while his obligation to appeal a judgment within the statutory time limit is an obligation to achieve the result promised.

37. *See also supra* §10.02 and *infra* Chapter 11, §11.03 [A] [1] [a] [iv].

It is a general principle of Belgian law that the creditor should send a notice (*une mise en demeure - ingebrekestelling*) to the debtor if he wants to claim any of the remedies for breach of contract, at least if performance is still possible and useful for the creditor.

Contrary to some other legal systems, the primary remedy for breach of contract is the actual performance of the obligation that was not or badly performed (*exécution en nature - nakoming in natura*). While a debtor cannot be directly forced to perform (*nemo potest cogi ad factum*), a creditor can ask the court to combine a primary order to perform with a secondary order to pay a substantial amount of money if performance does not occur (*une astreinte - dwangsom*). Such secondary order will usually be a sufficient incentive for the debtor to perform. In cases of urgency, a contracting party may also ask for the provisional performance as an interim remedy (again, combined with such secondary order). In the event of late payments, the court can still give the benefit of an extension of time for the performance by the debtor (*délai de grâce - uitstel van betaling*); this rule cannot be contracted away because it is considered to be an interest of public order.[38]

Damages is another important remedy for breach of contract. Damages in contract are broad in that both losses actually incurred (*damnum emergens*) and the loss of reasonably expected profits (*lucrum cessans*) are subject to compensation. Damages are available for all harm that would not have existed but for the breach. The amount of harm does not have to be foreseeable in order to be compensated in contract. For late payments of debts the amount of which is determined or at least can be determined as from the start (*dette de somme - geldschuld*), a default interest rate is determined yearly by the government.[39] Some debts such as debts between businesses are subject to a higher default interest rate which may vary every half year.[40]

Contracting parties may contractually determine a fixed amount of money or an interest rate as the contractual level of damages (*clause pénale - schadebeding* or *strafbeding*). Such amount should however not be excessive when compared with the damage that parties could foresee at the moment of concluding the contract. Excessive (penalty) clauses are not subject to annulment (except in the context of consumer contracts), but courts do have the power and the duty to mitigate those clauses to a level that may not be lower than the actual damage or the default interest rate.[41]

Parties also have a rather broad possibility to limit their liability for breach of contract. They should however refrain from limiting or excluding their liability for their own intentional faults and from deviating from mandatory liability rules, such as the ten-year liability of general contractors for gross defects.[42] Limitations of liability which render the promise futile are also subject to avoidance. Limitations or exclusions of the liability of a business are subject to stricter restrictions in consumer contracts.

38. Article 1244 Civil Code.
39. The basic rule is set in Article 1153 Civil Code.
40. Federal Act of 2 August 2002 on Combating Late Payments in Commercial Transactions, as amended. *See infra* Chapter 12, §12.05 [B].
41. Article 1231 Civil Code, and for late payments of '*dettes de somme*', *see* Article 1153, last paragraph, Civil Code.
42. Article 1792 Civil Code.

While performance and damages are remedies available for all contracts, termination for breach (*la résolution - ontbinding*) is only available for reciprocal or synallagmatic contracts. Under the default rules of Belgian contract law, a contract can only be terminated for a breach that is sufficiently serious to justify termination. Contrary to many other legal systems, there is no default rule allowing the unilateral termination by the party confronted with a breach. This party is required to claim termination in court, which has the discretionary power to decide whether or not it is expedient to order the termination of the contract.[43] A court may as well extend the term for performing an obligation even though performance is already late.

Termination for breach has a retroactive effect, except for contracts for a long duration which have been performed well during some time. Termination can also be combined with damages on the basis of contractual liability (including compensation for lost profits).

Contracting parties may agree to termination clauses which allow a party to unilaterally terminate the contract in one or more sets of specified breaches (*pacte commissoire - uitdrukkelijk ontbindend beding*). In order to avoid that such clauses are interpreted as to just repeat the termination rule of the Civil Code, the clauses should be drafted in a way that it is clear that a party has the right to unilaterally terminate the contract without prior court intervention (and, if so agreed, without prior notice).

Even without an agreed termination clause, a party may exceptionally consider the contract to be terminated because of the breach of the other party if the situation should be remedied urgently or if there is a complete lack of trust between parties. In that event, they should take all precautionary measures as to avoid the risk that they cannot prove the breach and the surrounding circumstances at a later point of time (in particular in litigation).

Besides performance, damages and termination, it is also possible for the creditor to claim substitution of the debtor by a third party (or the creditor himself). In that event, the additional costs involved must be borne by the breaching debtor.[44] In case of urgency or lack of trust between parties, it may also be possible for the creditor to unilaterally substitute the debtor, but the creditor does so at his own risk and peril.

When confronted with a breach of a reciprocal or synallagmatic contract, the creditor may also have the right to suspend the performance of his own promise arising out of that contract (*exceptio non adimpleti contractus - l'exception d'inexécution - exceptie van niet-nakoming*). A creditor cannot invoke this right to withhold performance if he is obliged to perform before the other party. As any other right, it should be exercised in good faith. A person who has the duty to restitute a good may also have a lien on that good (*un droit de rétention - retentierecht*) if the person to whom the good should be restituted breaches an obligation that has a particular link with that good (even though not necessarily on the basis of the same contractual relationship).

43. Article 1184 Civil Code.
44. Article 1144 Civil Code.

[F] End of Contracts

A contract may come to an end for a multitude of reasons apart from the annulment of the contract due to for example a defect of consent or for termination due to a breach of contract. Evidently, a contract comes to an end if all obligations arising out of it are performed.

A contract may also come to an end without any further declaration of will because its fixed term has lapsed. An exception to that rule is that parties may from the outset have agreed to a clause for the silent extension or renewal of the contract for an additional term unless one of them expresses the will to terminate the contract - usually in a particular formal manner and within a certain timeframe - before the expiry of the original term. A particular rule to the protection of consumers exists for such clauses in services contracts concluded between consumers and businesses. Consumers are free to terminate such contracts at any time giving the notice required in the contract, which cannot be longer than two months, once those contracts are silently renewed or extended.[45] In the event of a contract concluded without a fixed term, it is a rule of public order that each party has the right to terminate the contract at any time, be it that the right should be performed in good faith, and thus with a reasonable term of notice.

Force majeure which is not merely temporary may constitute another reason why a contract comes to an end. However, in the event of a sale of a particular good (*species*), the purchaser is still obliged to pay the purchase price if the good purchased is destroyed due to force majeure after the conclusion of the contract. This is because Belgian law still adheres to the view that a purchaser becomes the owner of the particular good as soon as the contract is concluded (a sales contract is concluded as from consent).[46] The risk of loss of a particular good sold is for the purchaser.[47] It goes without saying that the rules on property and risk transfer are default rules and that in practice contracting parties often deviate from those rules.

Belgian law does not have a general rule that a contract is modified or terminated because of supervening circumstances. Again, this is a default rule from which contracting parties frequently deviate by way of hardship clauses. There are also exceptions for specific types of contracts, such as in the context of public procurement contracts and international sales of goods which are subject to the Vienna Convention on the International Sales of Goods.

Apart from the hypothesis of force majeure, a contract may also come to an end because the subject matter of a contractual obligation disappeared after the conclusion of the contract, for example when a rented house is burnt down. The disappearance of the contract stands apart from a possible liability issue, for example the question whether the lessee is liable for having caused the fire of the house rented.

45. Article VI.91 Code of Economic Law.
46. *See supra* Chapter 9, §9.11 [A].
47. Expressed by the maxim *res perit domino* (the risk is for the owner, viz., the purchaser).

[G] Prescription of Claims

On the basis of the general rule on statute of limitations (prescription), contractual claims are time-barred after the expiry of ten years.[48] That general period of ten years is considered to start as from the moment the contractual obligation can be claimed for.

Prescription periods are subject to suspension or interruption (renewal) for a series of statutory grounds. A writ of summons or the recognition of a debt by the debtor for example has the effect of interrupting the prescription. A simple notice does as a general rule not have an effect on prescription unless for a maximum of one year if the notice letter satisfies a series of formal and substantive requirements and originates from an attorney or a bailiff.[49]

There are hundreds of specific prescription rules.[50] An important example is a claim for the payment of a periodic debt (of one year or less), such as bills for electricity consumption or mobile phone subscriptions. They are time-barred after the lapse of five years.[51] The legislator intended to protect the debtors against the accumulation over time of such periodic debts. Given the multitude of specific rules on prescription, it may not wonder that the Constitutional Court is often asked for a preliminary ruling on the constitutionality of such rules.

§10.05 EFFECTS OF CONTRACTS VIS-À-VIS THIRD PARTIES

The other pivot of contract law is the distinction between contracting parties and third parties. The key rule is called the 'relative effect' of contracts (privity of contract).[52] A contract is only binding for the contracting parties. It does not bind third parties. The rights and obligations arising out of a contract can only be enforced by contracting parties. For example, a contract for the maintenance of a car only binds the parties having concluded the maintenance contract, but not the later purchaser of the car (unless of course all relevant parties have agreed otherwise).

It is therefore important to know who is considered to be a contracting party. Apart from those who conclude a contract directly with each other, whether face to face or on a distance, the heirs of a contracting party may take the position of contracting party. Indeed, a contract does not come to an end because of the death of a contracting party, unless it has been agreed otherwise, the law provides otherwise or the contract is concluded because of the personal characteristics of a contracting party (*intuitu personae*).[53] As in most other legal systems, it is also possible to conclude a contract through an agent who acts in name and on behalf of the principal. The principal then takes the position of contracting party. The Court of Cassation even accepted that a person (an apparent principal) may be bound by a contract which is concluded in his

48. Article 2262*bis*, §1, para. 1, Civil Code.
49. Details in Article 2244, §2, Civil Code.
50. For an overview of prescription rules in Belgium, *see* I. CLAEYS & M. DE RUYSSCHER, PRESCRIPTION EN DROIT BELGE: UBI LEX DISTINGUIT DISTINGUERE DEBEMUS (Mechelen: Kluwer 2011).
51. Article 2277 Civil Code.
52. Article 1165 Civil Code.
53. Article 1122 Civil Code.

name and on his behalf by an apparent agent (someone who acts as his agent although he has no actual agency powers for concluding such contract). Negligence of the apparent principal does not have to be shown as long as the appearance of the powers of the agent, which was credible in the eyes of a reasonable contracting party, is attributable to the apparent principal.

While there are no general exceptions to the rule that a contract cannot bind a third party, there are several exceptions to the rule that a contract cannot benefit a third party. First of all, contracting parties may agree to a third-party beneficiary contract (*une stipulation pour autrui – derdenbeding*).[54] In that event, if all requirements for such contract are satisfied, the third-party beneficiary has a contractual right against the promisor, even though he is not a contracting party. The acceptance of that right by the third party is not required for the existence of that right. However, until such acceptance occurs, the promisee (*le stipulant*) may revoke the third-party beneficiary right.

The legislature also provides for a so-called direct action (*action directe – rechtstreekse vordering*) to the benefit of third parties in some specific circumstances. For example, a subcontractor has a direct action for payment against the client when he is not paid by his own contracting party, the main contractor who has contracted with the client.[55] He can do so by addressing a registered letter to the client (before bankruptcy of the main contractor intervenes). Another important direct action is that of a victim of a damaging event against the liability insurer of the person liable.[56]

As from the end of the nineteenth century courts have also allowed a direct claim for hidden defects in subsequent sales contracts. This implies that an end purchaser may claim damages for hidden defects from the original seller or another seller earlier in the chain of sales contracts even if he has no direct contractual link with such seller. Equally, a purchaser of a house may claim damages directly from the general contractor and the architect having built respectively designed and supervised the construction of that house, although that contractor and architect only had a contract with the seller of the house.[57] According to the Court of Cassation, such claim is deemed to be assigned to the purchaser as an accessory to the house transferred.[58] That is why this theory is called the 'accessory theory'.[59]

Despite the relative effect of contracts, third parties have to accept, and may rely on, the existence of contracts and the effects those contracts have between the contracting parties. This is known as the principle of the 'opposability' of contracts. This principle may play to the detriment or to the benefit of third parties. For example, if a car is sold by A to B, having the transfer of property from A to B as an immediate effect, third parties – such as creditors of A – as a rule have to accept that the property of the car does no longer belong to A but to B. Tax authorities are also third parties to

54. Article 1121 Civil Code.
55. Article 1798 Civil Code.
56. Article 150 Insurance Act of 4 April 2014. *See infra* Chapter 11, §11.01.
57. Court of Cassation 15 September 1989, 1989–1990 Arresten van het Hof van Cassatie 70, 1990 Pasicrisie belge 65.
58. Court of Cassation 5 December 1980, 1980–1981 Arresten van het Hof van Cassatie 382.
59. The theory is based on Article 1615 Civil Code.

the sales contract but nevertheless may invoke the existence of that contract as a basis to conclude that value added tax (VAT) is due. On the basis of the same principle, when a person (A) is bound by a contractual non-compete obligation towards his contracting party (B) and then concludes another contract with a third party (X) in breach of that non-compete obligation, X may be liable in tort towards B for having assisted the breach of the non-compete obligation arising out of the contract between A and B, at least if X knew or had reason to know of the existence of the non-compete obligation of A towards B.

These are also important exceptions to that principle of opposability of contracts. An important one[60] is known by its Latin expression as the *actio pauliana*.[61] If a debtor (B) fraudulently embezzles his assets by concluding a disadvantageous contract transferring a good to a third party (C), his creditor (A) may sue C to obtain a ruling that the contract concluded between B and C cannot be invoked against A. This then allows the creditor A to consider the good transferred by B to C still to be part of the assets of B and not of C. In other words, the contract between B and C will not be opposable to the creditor A.

For some contracts the legislature imposes specific formalities before those parties can be invoked (or 'opposed') against third parties in good faith. This is for example the case for the transfer of property of immovables[62] and the assignments of rights.[63]

§10.06 SELECTED BIBLIOGRAPHY

L. Cornelis, *Algemene theorie van de verbintenis* (Antwerp: Intersentia 2000).

H. De Page, *Traité élémentaire de droit civil belge*, Vol. II & III (Brussels: Bruylant, 1964 & 1967).

J. Herbots, *Contract Law in Belgium* (Brussels: Deventer 1995).

R. Kruithof, H. Bocken, B. De Temmerman & F. Dely, *Verbintenissenrecht (1981–1992) Overzicht van rechtspraak*, 31 Tijdschrift voor Privaatrecht 171–721 (1994).

S. Stijns, *Verbintenissenrecht* (Bruges: die Keure, 2005, 2009 & 2013).

W. Van Gerven & A. Van Oevelen, *Verbintenissenrecht* (Leuven: Acco 2016).

W. Van Gerven, *Algemeen Deel* (Beginselen van Belgisch Privaatrecht I, R. Dillemans & W. Van Gerven eds., Ghent: Story 1987).

W. Van Gerven & S. Lierman, *Algemeen Deel. Veertig jaar later. Privaat- en publiekrecht in een meergelaagd kader van regelgeving, rechtsvorming en regeltoepassing* (Beginselen van Belgisch privaatrecht I, R. Dillemans & W. Van Gerven eds., Mechelen: Kluwer 2010).

P. Van Ommeslaghe, *Droit des obligations* (Brussels: Bruylant 2010).

P. Wéry, *Droit des obligations* (Brussels: Larcier 2011).

60. Another exception is simulation, not dealt with in this contribution (Article 1321 Civil Code).
61. Article 1167 Civil Code.
62. Article 1 Mortgage Act (transcription in the mortgage register). *See supra* Chapter 9, §9.11 [A].
63. Article 1690 et seq. Civil Code (communication to the debtor or acknowledgment by the debtor). *See supra* Chapter 9, §9.11 [A].

CHAPTER 11
Tort Law

Marc Kruithof

§11.01 INTRODUCTION

The core of Belgian civil liability law (*droit de la responsabilité civile - burgerlijk aansprakelijkheidsrecht*) is still based on the five provisions the Napoleonic Civil Code devoted to the subject.[1] The bulk of the substance of this branch of law has been elaborated by the courts, which over the last century have not felt obliged to adhere to the French interpretation of the same statutory texts.[2] Therefore, it would be a mistake to assume that Belgian and French civil liability law have the same content.

Civil liability is a source of obligations. Once liability (*responsabilité - aansprakelijkheid*) is established, one party - the victim (*victime - slachtoffer*) - has a claim for restoration of his harm against the other party - the person held liable (*le responsable - de aansprakelijke*) (*infra* §11.05). According to the traditional analysis, liability requires three constituent elements. First, the claimant has to have suffered damage (*infra* §11.02). Second, there has to have been a fact, linked to the defendant, that is recognised by law as a basis for liability (*infra* §11.03).[3] Third, this fact has to have caused the harm (*infra* §11.04).

The limitations of liability as a system for compensating victims in today's industrialised and consumerised welfare society - where people are vulnerable to more

1. Only two amendments have been made. In 1935, a sixth provision was added to deal with the liability of the mentally ill (Article 1386*bis*), and in 1977, Article 1384, para. 2, was modernised to place the vicarious liability of fathers and mothers for damage caused by their minor children on equal footing.
2. *See supra* Chapter 1, §1.02 [D].
3. In today's French legal literature in Belgium, this fact is called the *fait générateur de responsabilité*.

types of risks causing greater harm but at the same time are less prepared to accept misfortunes and have increased expectations to be shielded from losses – have resulted in the creation of alternative compensation mechanisms in the course of the twentieth century. First, the development of a system of social security, including generalised mutualised and partially publicly financed health insurance,[4] provides compensation for medical costs irrespective of their cause and for lost income in the form of benefits.[5] Second, the popularisation of commercial first party insurance means that victims often can shift the financial burden of harm to their insurer. Third, the legislature has created compensation mechanisms for certain risks – such as industrial accidents, traffic accidents and recently medical accidents (*infra* §11.07). As a result, a large fraction of harm is shifted from the victim to insurance companies, the social security system and different compensation funds.

Many of these institutions are statutorily subrogated in the victim's right to restoration based on civil liability to the extent they have compensated the harm. While civil liability may today in practice be less the primary basis for compensation of victims, it thus remains crucial as the system of allocation of the ultimate financial burden of the compensation of harm.

As nowadays third-party insurance is increasingly used – the legislature has even made such insurance mandatory for certain types of risk – the person held liable can shift the financial burden of this liability to his insurer. Under Belgian law, a victim has a direct claim for compensation based on his own right against the liability insurer of the person liable for his harm.[6] In practice, therefore, civil liability law is more and more a matter relevant for disputes among insurers, appearing both as (subrogated) claimants and as defendants in many of the court cases that have elaborated the principles of this branch of law.[7]

§11.02 HARM OR DAMAGE

[A] General Concept of Recoverable Damage

Civil liability requires harm – called a loss (*perte – verlies*) – that, for it to be recoverable, can legally be qualified as 'damage' (*dommage – schade*). Whether harm is suffered, is a question of fact, to be determined by the courts on the basis of the evidence supplied by the parties. Whether an established harm constitutes damage, however, is an issue to be answered by the court based on the law, under the potential review by the Court of Cassation.

4. Mandatory Health Insurance Act of 14 July 1994.
5. *See infra* Chapter 14, §14.03 [B] [1].
6. Article 150 Insurance Act of 4 April 2014.
7. Even if the defendant in a suit is the person allegedly liable, it often is his insurer that in fact is leading the defence, as Article 143, para. 2, Insurance Act of 4 April 2014 grants the liability insurer the exclusive power to lead the defence in cases where the potential obligation to compensate the claimant falls within the insurance guarantee.

[1] Injury to a Legitimate Interest

Not all harm suffered by a person is protected by civil liability law. However, compared to many other legal systems, Belgian law is very victim friendly in this regard.

It is not necessary for the victim to have had a *right* (*droit - recht*) to something he has lost. Already in 1939 the Court of Cassation ruled that a person who loses the support of the sibling he is living with because this sibling is killed, suffers damage, even though siblings do not have a duty to support each other and he therefore had not lost a right.[8] The existence of damage thus does not require the victim to have a right to something he has lost.[9] Damage consists of an injury to an *interest* (*intérêt - belang*). Injury to an interest is also required for harm to be legally qualified as damage, so the mere infringement of a right without any harm to the rightholder's interests, does not constitute damage.[10]

For harm to be recoverable, the injured interest must be legitimate (*intérêt légitime - rechtmatig belang*).[11] An interest can be illegitimate because it conflicts with the law or public policy, or because it implies an infringement of someone else's right. However, a distinction is made between on the one hand the loss of an advantage that itself is illegitimate, which does not constitute recoverable damage,[12] and on the other hand a loss of an advantage that in itself is legitimate but which was enjoyed by a victim in an illegitimate situation or under illegitimate circumstances.[13]

[2] Resulting Causal Concept of Damage

When the concept of damage is based on the infringement of a right, damage consists of a loss of something the victim had before. When an injury to a mere interest is sufficient, the harm in essence does not consist in something the victim has 'lost', but in the victim not enjoying something which it would have enjoyed but for the accident. In such a counterfactual account, damage consists in the difference between the victim's *actual* interest position after the fact with the *hypothetical* position this victim would have enjoyed if the fact had not happened. On the basis of this line of reasoning,

8. Court of Cassation 16 January 1939, 1939 Pasicrisie belge 15.
9. *See* e.g. Court of Cassation 24 March 1969, 1969 Arresten van het Hof van Cassatie 690, 1969 Pasicrisie belge 655; Court of Cassation 17 June 1975, 1975 Arresten van het Hof van Cassatie 1105, 1975 Pasicrisie belge 999.
10. Court of Cassation 21 June 1990, No. 615, 1990 Pasicrisie belge 1204, 1989–1990 Arresten van het Hof van Cassatie 1358; Court of Cassation 19 March 1991, No. 376, 1990–1991 Arresten van het Hof van Cassatie 755, 1991 Pasicrisie belge 670.
11. Court of Cassation 16 January 1939, 1939 Pasicrisie belge 15. For the development in the Court's attitude towards the legitimacy of the interest non-married cohabitating couples have in their continued mutual support, *see supra* Chapter 7, §7.05 [B] [1].
12. Court of Cassation 27 June 2013 (C.12.0340.F), No. 402, 2013 Pasicrisie belge 1502, 2013 Arresten van het Hof van Cassatie 1644; Court of Cassation 3 October 1997 (C.96.0334.F), No. 387, 1997 Pasicrisie belge 965, 1997 Arresten van het Hof van Cassatie 921.
13. Court of Cassation 2 April 1998 (C.94.0438.N), No. 188, 1998 Arresten van het Hof van Cassatie 407, 1998 Pasicrisie belge 431; Court of Cassation 2 March 2006 (C.05.0061.N), No. 120, 2006 Arresten van het Hof van Cassatie 486, 2006 Pasicrisie belge 483.

the Court of Cassation recently has ruled that wrongful life claims must fail in principle.[14]

What hypothetical position the victim would have been in, is a question of fact.[15] If there is insufficient certainty what the hypothetical position of the victim would have been, the court cannot award full compensation for the ultimate disadvantage the victim claims to suffer. However, the Court of Cassation does allow courts to award compensation for the value of the lost chance the victim had of not suffering the disadvantage.[16] The value of this lost chance will be estimated as a fraction - i.e., an expression of the chance the victim had - of the value of the disadvantage the victim ultimately has suffered.[17] Thus, an underlying causal uncertainty is conceptually reframed as an issue relating to the requirement of damage, to allow the courts to in effect apply proportional liability in certain cases of causal uncertainty.

[3] Types of Damage

Damage can consist of personal injury. Both the loss of functionality and the consequences of disability, such as a loss of income and the value of work performed in the household, are recoverable. Medical costs and cost of care are included. Pain and suffering is considered to be moral damage, and fully recoverable.[18] There are no *a priori* restrictions for harm other persons than the direct victim suffer by repercussion. Thus, the loss of support by a family member who is killed constitutes damage, and so does the emotional distress one suffers when losing a loved one or witnessing a relative's suffering. Harm can also consist in damage to property. Not only loss in value, but also the cost of repair and the loss of use constitute damage.

Because of its broad concept of damage, Belgian civil liability allows claims for economic losses. Not only consequential economic loss - i.e., a financial loss caused by personal injury or property damage - can be recovered, but as opposed to in many other legal systems, there is no *a priori* exclusion of pure economic loss - i.e., lost income or an increased cost that is not the repercussion of a personal injury or property damage.

The broad concept of damage causes problems in how to limit the recoverability of costs connected to a pre-existing legal or contractual obligation triggered as a consequence of the incident. Although it has used different types of reasoning to solve

14. Court of Cassation 14 November 2014 (C.13.0441.N), No. 694, 2014 Arresten van het Hof van Cassatie 2597, 2014 Pasicrisie belge 2541; Court of Cassation 21 April 2016 (C.15.0286.N).
15. Court of Cassation 20 June 1961, 1961 Pasicrisie belge 1148.
16. *See* e.g. Court of Cassation 15 March 2010 (C.09.0433.N), No. 182, 2010 Arresten van het Hof van Cassatie 767, 2010 Pasicrisie belge 839; Court of Cassation 19 January 1984, No. 266, 1984 Pasicrisie belge 548, 1983-1984 Arresten van het Hof van Cassatie 585.
17. Court of Cassation 21 October 2013 (C.13.0124.N), No. 537, 2013 Arresten van het Hof van Cassatie 2159, 2013 Pasicrisie belge 1999; Court of Cassation 17 December 2009 (C.08.0145.N), No. 757, 2009 Arresten van het Hof van Cassatie 3056, 2009 Pasicrisie belge 3045.
18. Court of Cassation 10 October 1972, 1973 Arresten van het Hof van Cassatie 146, 1973 Pasicrisie belge 147; Court of Cassation 3 February 1987, No. 322, 1986-1987 Arresten van het Hof van Cassatie 724, 1987 Pasicrisie belge 644.

the question, the Court of Cassation now rules that expenses that according to the meaning of the contract, regulation or statute are not supposed to remain for the charge of the person who is legally required to make them, constitute recoverable damage.[19] However, careful analysis of the facts reveals that this given rationale is not capable of explaining the actual decisions in all cases, showing that the Court in fact only has allowed the public sector employer to recover the gross salary cost - including social security contributions and paid medical costs - of a civil servant who is disabled because of an accident for which a third party is liable.

The Court even goes further and allows the recovery of the cost of voluntary interventions by third parties, on the condition that they were reasonably intended to help the victim suffering the direct harm without the intention of ultimately bearing the burden.[20]

[B] Personal Damage, Mass Claims and Injury to Collective Interests

Harm is only considered to be damage if the injured interest is personal to the claimant.[21] As a result, shareholders of a corporation cannot claim compensation for the loss in value of their shares as a result of harm suffered by the corporation, for which only the corporation can claim compensation based on civil liability.[22] This also means that a victim whose harm has been restored by a third party free of charge, cannot claim compensation anymore, as its harm has been undone and the related costs are not an injury to the victim's interest but to the interests of this third party.[23] This principle, however, does not preclude a victim's right to compensation for an injury to a personal interest based on civil liability to be transferred to another person, either by succession, subrogation or contract.[24]

Recently, a procedure for mass claims has been created.[25] Such proceedings, however, are limited to personal harm suffered by a group of consumers as a consequence of one common cause, which has to result from a breach of contract or the

19. Court of Cassation 19 February 2001 (C.98.0119.N), No. 96, 2001 Arresten van het Hof van Cassatie 318, 2001 Pasicrisie belge 316; recent: Court of Cassation 4 February 2014 (P.13.0992.N), No. 92, 2014 Arresten van het Hof van Cassatie 352, 2014 Pasicrisie belge 365; Court of Cassation 8 February 2016 (C.15.0170.N).
20. Court of Cassation 6 November 2001 (P.99.1703.N), No. 600, 2001 Arresten van het Hof van Cassatie 1856, 2001 Pasicrisie belge 1790; Court of Cassation 4 March 2002 (C.01.0284.N), No. 154, 2002 Arresten van het Hof van Cassatie 678, 2002 Pasicrisie belge 632.
21. *See* e.g. Court of Cassation 6 January 2010 (P.09.1152.F), No. 5, 2010 Pasicrisie belge 20, 2010 Arresten van het Hof van Cassatie 19.
22. Court of Cassation 23 February 2012 (C.11.0459.N), No. 131, 2012 Arresten van het Hof van Cassatie 459, 2012 Pasicrisie belge 431.
23. Court of Cassation 25 May 2012 (C11.0494.F), No. 340, 2012 Pasicrisie belge 1201, 2012 Arresten van het Hof van Cassatie 1432.
24. Court of Cassation 30 June 1930, 1930 Pasicrisie belge 281; Court of Cassation 26 September 1955, 1956 Pasicrisie belge 38, 1956 Arresten van het Hof van Verbreking 28.
25. Book XVII, Title 2 Code of Economic Law (Articles XVII.35-69). *See also supra* Chapter 5, §5.05 [B] [5].

violation of a rule in a specifically listed statute committed by an undertaking.[26] Thus, no collective claim is possible in case of extra-contractual liability based on negligence.

In case of injury to a public interest, the harm is considered not to be suffered by any individual person. This traditionally has meant that organisations for the protection of the environment cannot claim compensation for environmental damage: the harm they suffer is limited to their moral damage.[27] Recently, the Constitutional Court has ruled that a legal person whose stated purpose is the protection of a collective interest, must be able to recover more than symbolic compensation for the moral damage it suffers because of injury to this collective interest.[28] The Constitutional Court suggested that in estimating the extent of this harm, courts can take into account the legal person's purpose, the extent of its activities and efforts it makes, and the gravity of the injury to the collective interest.

§11.03 BASES FOR LIABILITY

A distinction can be made between fault liability (*infra* §11.03 [A]) and strict liability, usually referred to as objective liability (*infra* §11.03 [B]). Fault liability creates an obligation for the person whose wrongful behaviour caused the harm. Strict liability creates an obligation for a person who is connected to another harm causing fact than his own fault.

[A] Fault Liability

Belgian law knows two types of fault liability. The basic rule imposes liability on he who has been shown to have wrongfully caused the damage (*infra* §11.03 [A] [1]). Separately, vicarious liabilities exist for certain categories of persons who are presumed to have wrongfully caused the damage caused by persons they supervise (*infra* §11.03 [A] [2]).

[1] Liability Based on Proven Fault

Articles 1382–1383[29] of the Civil Code oblige the person who is guilty of a wrongful act that has caused damage to someone else to compensate this harm. The liability is linked to a 'fault' (*faute* – *fout*), which consists of two elements. First, the act itself has to be wrongful in the objective sense (*acte illicite* – *onrechtmatige daad*)[30] (*infra* §11.03

26. Article XVII.36, 1°, Code of Economic Law. The list of statutes can be found in Article XVII.37 Code of Economic Law.
27. Court of Cassation 19 November 1982, No. 172, 1982–1983 Arresten van het Hof van Cassatie 372, 1983 Pasicrisie belge 338; Court of Cassation 19 September 1996 (C.95.0386.F), No. 319, 1996 Pasicrisie belge 830, 1996 Arresten van het Hof van Cassatie 775.
28. Constitutional Court No. 7/2016 of 21 January 2016.
29. In today's interpretation, no difference is recognised between the two provisions in the Civil Code so that most often courts and literature only refer to Article 1382 Civil Code.
30. This objective element is sometimes also referred to as the 'fault' (*faute* – *fout*), which confusion does not render Belgian literature on the subject conceptually very clear.

[A] [1] [a]). Second, the act has to be attributable (*imputabilité - toerekenbaarheid*) to the free will of the actor, so this person is culpable (*culpabilité - schuld*) (*infra* §10.03 [A] [1] [b]).

[a] Objective Element: Civil Wrongs

The traditional rendition of Belgian civil liability law distinguishes two types of wrongs: negligence and the violation of a specific legal rule of conduct.[31]

[i] Negligence

Negligence (*négligence - onzorgvuldigheid*) is not taking the amount of care a 'normally prudent person' would have taken. Care is effort aimed at protecting the interests of others. Such effort can consist of positive action aimed at limiting the risk to others, or of abstaining from undertaking certain conduct which increases this risk to others. Thus, both action and inaction can be negligent. However, there is no requirement to commit all efforts necessary to avoid harm to others: the fact of having caused damage in itself does not constitute negligence.[32] The amount of effort a normally prudent person would have applied, is the amount which is considered 'reasonable'.

This means that in deciding whether behaviour is negligent, all circumstances that influence the extent of the burden of the effort to reduce the risk and the expected resulting limitation of this risk have to be taken into account. Thus, whether an act is negligent can depend on the time and place, the surroundings, the expected behaviour of others involved, the climatologic circumstances, etc. Traditional theoretical consensus holds that these so-called external circumstances should be taken into account, by stating that the standard is the behaviour of a normally prudent person 'placed in the same circumstances'.

One of the most relevant circumstances is the foreseeability (*prévisibilité - voorzienbaarheid*) of the occurrence of harm.[33] Reason only requires one to take into account risks one can be aware of. Therefore, the same behaviour can be negligent in one set of circumstances in which one should have realised certain third parties would be subject to the risk, and not negligent in other in which one would not have expected others to be affected.

Traditional theory states that negligence does not depend on the so-called internal circumstances or the personal characteristics of the person acting.[34] Thus,

31. Court of Cassation 8 December 1994 (C.93.0303.F), No. 541,1994 Arresten van het Hof van Cassatie 1074, 1994 Pasicrisie belge 1063; Court of Cassation 25 March 2010 (C.09.0403.N), No. 219, 2010 Arresten van het Hof van Cassatie 920, 2010 Pasicrisie belge 1007.
32. Court of Cassation 4 May 2012 (C.10.0080.F), No. 276, 2012 Pasicrisie belge 1007, 2012 Arresten van het Hof van Cassatie 1178.
33. Court of Cassation 12 November 1951, 1952 Pasicrisie belge 128, 1952 Arresten van het Hof van Verbreking 118; Court of Cassation 5 May 1971, 1971 Pasicrisie belge 802, 1971 Arresten van het Hof van Cassatie 869.
34. Court of Cassation 24 October 1974, 1975 Arresten van het Hof van Cassatie 259, 1975 Pasicrisie belge 237, stating that the age of the wrongdoer cannot be taken into account.

anybody will be judged by the same standard. However, this principled distinction between external and internal circumstances turns out not always to be strictly applied.

Of course, the professional function and qualification of a person is relevant to judge whether his behaviour was up to standard. To determine whether a surgeon is negligent, her behaviour is compared to the behaviour of a reasonable surgeon in the same circumstances, and not to the behaviour of a normal person. Thus, the state of the art in professions is used as a body of rules to specify the vague content of the general standard of care, applying the principle *spondet peritiam artis, et imperitia culpae adnumeratur*.

Moreover, careful study of case law reveals that courts actually do take certain other personal characteristics into account when determining whether an act is negligent. First, courts tend to lower the standard for people who have physical or mental impairments. Especially when applied to behaviour by the victim contributing to the causation of its harm, the courts tend to be lenient to victims that are especially vulnerable. Second, courts tend to find a person who actually knew of the existence of a risk but chose to ignore it negligent even when a normally prudent person in the same circumstances would not have known this risk and therefore would also not have taken it into account. Actual knowledge by the person whose behaviour is being judged – which is not an 'external circumstance' – is always taken into account. And third, the Court of Cassation has recently refused to reverse a decision of a court that had found a scouts volunteer not negligent because his or her behaviour had not been different from the behaviour to be expected of a normally careful 'young volunteer'.[35] As a result, the exact extent to which personal characteristics are relevant in determining whether behaviour is negligent under Belgian law is at present a point of debate.

[ii] Violation of a Specific Legal Rule of Conduct

As a general principle, Belgian law considers the violation of a statutory or regulatory rule of conduct committed without ground of justification to be per se wrongful,[36] without any negligence required.[37] Thus, even a 'reasonable breach' of a legal behavioural rule is wrong. This means that no foreseeable harm is required. Also, it is not considered to be relevant whether the aim of the violated rule was to avoid the type of harm that actually ensued.[38] Based on this principle, any criminal offence is also a

35. Court of Cassation 5 June 2003 (C.01.0252.F), No. 337, 2003 Pasicrisie belge 1125, 2003 Arresten van het Hof van Cassatie 1337.
36. Court of Cassation 19 December 1980, 1980–1981 Arresten van het Hof van Cassatie 449 No. 241, 1981 Pasicrisie belge 453; Court of Cassation 13 May 1982, 1982 Pasicrisie belge 1056, 1981–1982 Arresten van het Hof van Cassatie 1134 No. 547; more recent: Court of Cassation 16 May 2011 (C.10.0664.N), No. 320, 2011 Arresten van het Hof van Cassatie 1230, 2011 Pasicrisie belge 1339. *See* already Court of Cassation 22 March 1957, 1957 Pasicrisie belge 885, 1957 Arresten van het Hof van Verbreking 610.
37. Court of Cassation 22 September 1988, No. 47, 1988–1989 Arresten van het Hof van Cassatie 94, 1989 Pasicrisie belge 83.
38. As opposed to under Dutch (Article 6:163 of the Dutch Civil Code) and German (§823(2) of the German Civil Code) law.

civil wrong. The victim of a criminal offence can therefore always claim compensation for the damage the offence has caused based on Article 1382 of the Civil Code.

The principle applies to rules imposed by law, irrespective of the formal source of the legal rule. It also applies to an infringement of a right, such as an intellectual property right[39] or someone's privacy,[40] as such infringement necessarily implies the violation of the legal rule granting the subject this right and thereby imposing a duty on all others to respect this.

However, the principle does not apply to behavioural rules which are not imposed by law, i.e., which are not unilaterally imposed by the government on citizens. The violation of a rule of a sports game - a 'foul' - is not necessarily a 'fault' in the sense of Article 1382 of the Civil Code. For a player who has injured another player to be civilly liable, he will have to be shown to have committed a foul which a normal player would not have committed,[41] and one cannot assume that a reasonable person per definition would not commit any fouls.

For the same reason, the violation of a contractual rule of behaviour - a breach of contract - does not *ipso facto* constitute a wrong that leads to extra-contractual liability.[42] The opposite view is considered to be inconsistent with the principle of privity of contract.[43] However, some breaches of contract can be wrongful because they consist of behaviour that apart from a contractual rule also violates a generally applicable standard of care or legal rule.[44] Also, in some types of contracts that are intended to result in benefits for or protection of third parties and where the contract party is aware that his performance directly affects the interests of third parties, the breach of a contractual duty can be considered as negligent and therefore wrongful.[45] The textbook example is the elevator maintenance contract,[46] but also the contract between a corporation and an accountant certifying the accounts can be interpreted this way, resulting in the possibility that third-party victims - users of the elevator in the one case, investors in securities issued by the corporation in the other - can claim damages for the harm they suffer as a consequence of sloppy performance of contractual duties by these service providers.

39. Court of Cassation 3 September 2009 (C.08.0337.N), No. 476, 2009 Arresten van het Hof van Cassatie 1926, 2009 Pasicrisie belge 1782.
40. Belgian case law reveals that the infringement of the right to privacy is considered to be wrongful, even though Belgian law does not know a statutory provision like the one in Article 9 of the French Civil Code. This shows that the violation of a behavioural rule of law constitutes a wrong even if this rule is not imposed by legislation.
41. Court of Cassation 16 June 1969, 1969 Arresten van het Hof van Cassatie 1026, 1969 Pasicrisie belge 950.
42. Belgian law differs from French law, which recognises a breach of contract as a wrong that can serve as the basis for extra-contractual claims by third parties suffering damage caused by this breach. *See* Court of Cassation of France 6 October 2006, 2006 Dalloz 2825.
43. Article 1165 Civil Code. *See supra* Chapter 10, §10.05.
44. Court of Cassation 25 October 2012 (C.12.0079.F), No. 568, 2012 Pasicrisie belge 2039, 2012 Arresten van het Hof van Cassatie 2332; Court of Cassation 11 June 1981, 1980–1981 Arresten van het Hof van Cassatie 1168 No. 583, 1981 Pasicrisie belge 1159.
45. Court of Cassation 22 June 2009, 2009 NIEUW JURIDISCH WEEKBLAD 724.
46. *See* e.g. Brussels Court of Appeal 4 February 1992, 1995 REVUE GÉNÉRALE DES ASSURANCES ET DES RESPONSABILITÉS 12,460.

Recently, however, some doubt has appeared whether the principle that any violation of a specific legal rule of behaviour is per se wrongful still stands. In cases relating to civil liability of a governmental entity, the Court of Cassation has at least issued three rulings which seem hard to reconcile with this general principle.[47] As a result, there is debate possible on the question whether a violation of a specific legal rule at present still can always be unequivocally equated to a wrong.

[iii] Grounds of Justification

A violation of a legal rule of conduct is wrong if there are no grounds of justification (*cause de justification - rechtvaardigingsgrond*). The Court of Cassation has recognised that there are circumstances in which the violation of a statutory or regulatory rule is justified so no liability can attach.[48]

The most obvious ground of justification is force majeure: an event not caused by the defendant that he could not reasonably avoid and that makes it impossible to comply with the legal rule. Another ground is the circumstance that the defendant was legally required to commit the act which violates the rule. Performing a legal duty or obeying an order from the government (*fait du prince*) cannot be wrongful. A third ground of justification is a state of necessity, which means the violation of a rule is required to protect an interest that is valued more than the interest the violated rule protects.[49] Self-defence can be seen as a subcategory of this ground of justification.

A ground of justification can also be found in an unavoidable and invincible mistake.[50] Mere unawareness of the rule is no excuse. Only unescapable ignorance of the law - i.e., *any* reasonable person would not have known - provides an excuse, mere excusable ignorance - i.e., *some* reasonable persons would not have known - does not.[51] The mistake can relate to content of the legal rule or to the factual circumstances determining the applicability of the legal rule.

Some literature and courts invoke grounds of justification to exclude liability in cases involving alleged negligence. This, however, seems to be the consequence of imprecise use of concepts. As in cases based on negligence no behavioural rule was violated, there is no need for justification of the behaviour. In such cases, however, the

---

47. *See infra* §11.03 [D] [1] [a].
48. Court of Cassation 13 May 1982, 1982 Pasicrisie belge 1056, 1981–1982 Arresten van het Hof van Cassatie 1134 No. 547; more recently Court of Cassation 16 May 2011 (C.10.0664.N), No. 320, 2011 Arresten van het Hof van Cassatie 1230, 2011 Pasicrisie belge 1339.
49. Court of Cassation 15 May 1930, 1930 Pasicrisie belge 223; Court of Cassation 20 March 1979, 1979 Pasicrisie belge 842, 1978–1979 Arresten van het Hof van Cassatie 837; Court of Cassation 5 April 1996 (A.94.0002.F), No. 111, 1996 Pasicrisie belge 111, 1996 Arresten van het Hof van Cassatie 247.
50. Court of Cassation 25 October 1999 (S.98.0112.N), No. 559, 1999 Arresten van het Hof van Cassatie 1327, 1999 Pasicrisie belge 1384; Court of Cassation 23 September 2010 (C.09.0220.F), No. 544, 2010 Pasicrisie belge 2367, 2010 Arresten van het Hof van Cassatie 2275.
51. Court of Cassation 20 April 1982, 1981–1982 Arresten van het Hof van Cassatie 1009 No. 486, 1982 Pasicrisie belge 949.

same facts that could lead to justification if a violation of a legal rule were involved, mean that no negligence occurred, as the defendant behaved reasonably in the given circumstances, and so no liability attaches.

[iv] Abuse of Right

The fact that the disputed behaviour was part of the exercise of a right of the alleged wrongdoer, does not shield him from liability. Belgian law recognises that an abuse of right (*abus de droit - rechtsmisbruik*) constitutes a wrong.

An abuse of power is a wrong, leading to liability to restore the resulting damage. Along the same line of reasoning, one can consider using a right with another motive than furthering the protection of the subject's legitimate interests as an abuse of right. The first cases recognised by the courts involved the exercise of a right with the intent to cause damage.[52] The next cases involved a person causing damage by exercising a right without apparent interest in doing so.[53] Then, the doctrine was expanded to cases where the rightholder can choose between two equally advantageous alternatives to exercise his right and he chooses the manner in which he causes more damage.[54]

The Court of Cassation nowadays uses one 'criterion', recognising a general principle of law that exercising a right in a way which *obviously* goes beyond the normal exercise of such right by a reasonable person is an abuse of this right.[55] This rule includes the cases that can be explained on the basis of the principle that rights only allow the rightholder to use them to protect his legitimate interests, but also includes cases where the rightholder does in fact use his right to further his legitimate interests but this causes disproportionate damage, thus introducing an efficiency requirement into the legitimate exercise of rights.[56] The words used by the Court do not seem to be different from the general standard of care applied in negligence, although it is argued that the use of the word 'obviously' (*manifestement - kennelijk*) means that an abuse of right requires some form of 'gross' negligence.

52. Court of Cassation 11 April 1958, 1958 Arresten van het Hof van Verbreking 595, 1958 Pasicrisie belge 867; Court of Cassation 29 November 1962, 1963 Pasicrisie belge 406; 18 February 1965, 1967 REVUE CRITIQUE DE JURISPRUDENCE BELGE 245.
53. Court of Cassation 17 May 2002 (C.01.0101.F), No. 302, 2002 Pasicrisie belge 1169, 2002 Arresten van het Hof van Cassatie 1306; Court of Cassation 17 February 2012 (C.10.0651.F), No. 118, 2012 Pasicrisie belge 369, 2012 Arresten van het Hof van Cassatie 403.
54. Court of Cassation 12 July 1917, 1918 Pasicrisie belge 65, involving the choice exactly how high to hang a neon light at the facade of a department store, blocking the view of the signs of another competitive store down the street.
55. Court of Cassation 10 September 1971, 1972 Arresten van het Hof van Cassatie 31, 1972 Pasicrisie belge 28. More recent: Court of Cassation 6 January 2011 (C.09.0624.F), No. 12, 2011 Pasicrisie belge 44, 2011 Arresten van het Hof van Cassatie 41.
56. Court of Cassation 6 January 2006 (C.04.0358.F), No. 18, 2006 Pasicrisie belge 71, 2006 Arresten van het Hof van Cassatie 71, in which the Court stated that an abuse entails the invocation of a right without 'reasonable and *sufficient* interest'; Court of Cassation 6 January 2011 (C.09.0624.F), No. 12, 2011 Pasicrisie belge 44, 2011 Arresten van het Hof van Cassatie 41, stating that a right is exercised in a way which obviously goes beyond the normal exercise if the caused harm is not in proportion to the benefit the rightholder was pursuing.

[b] *Subjective Element: Culpability*

[i] Concept and General Rule

As opposed to French law, which considers a fault to consist only of an objectively wrongful act,[57] Belgian law requires the wrong to be imputable to the free will of the person who has committed it, for him to be liable. A fault is thus a culpably committed wrongful act.

To be capable of guilt, a person has to possess three characteristics. First, he has to be able to understand what the rule or standard of behaviour is. This means the person has to have moral insight. Second, he has to be able to understand what the circumstances are which might create the risk and what the foreseeable consequences of his behaviour are. This one could call factual insight. Third, he has to have the capacity of actual control over his behaviour, so that he can effectively steer it.

Under Belgian law, everyone is presumed to have these characteristics. This means that lack of culpability is an affirmative defence in civil liability proceedings. If it is not invoked and proven by the defendant, the court cannot exclude liability on this basis.[58] However, this is different if the alleged wrong is a criminal offence: as the defendant in criminal proceedings enjoys the presumption of innocence and the prosecution bears the full burden of proof, the defendant can suffice with showing an element that indicates the possibility for a ground of lack of culpability, for the claimant to have to show his culpability.[59]

Whether a wrong is imputable to a person, is a question of fact, to be determined for each individual case. Capability of guilt, therefore, is not a fixed legal status a person has and keeps, it always is the qualification of the relationship between a specific wrongful act and a specific actor at a specific time in specific circumstances. However, in practice most instances of excuse relate to persons that have systematic and long lasting characteristics that make it impossible to reproach them for their own behaviour: infants and certain mentally ill.

[ii] Infants

Belgian law does not impose a fixed age at which one becomes capable of incurring liability.

The age of legal majority, set at eighteen, is only relevant for the competence of a person to commit legal acts (*acte juridique – rechtshandeling*),[60] such as to enter into

57. French Court of Cassation 9 May 1984 (5 decisions), 1984 Dalloz jurisprudence 525.
58. Court of Cassation 30 October 1980, 1981 Pasicrisie belge 262, 1980–1981 Arresten van het Hof van Cassatie 235 No. 136.
59. Court of Cassation 14 June 1971, 1971 Pasicrisie belge 971, 1971 Arresten van het Hof van Cassatie 1022; Court of Cassation 18 September 1972, 1973 Pasicrisie belge 60, 1973 Arresten van het Hof van Cassatie 65; Court of Cassation 14 December 2001 (C.98.0469.F), No. 705, 2001 Pasicrisie belge 2129, 2001 Arresten van het Hof van Cassatie 2200.
60. A legal act is an act performed with the intent of creating the legal consequences the law attaches to it. For such act to be valid – and thus to have these consequences – the person has to have legal capacity. *See supra* Chapter 10, §10.04 [C].

a valid and thus binding legal transaction.[61] As a wrong is not a legal act but a material fact (*fait juridique - rechtsfeit*),[62] no legal capacity is required. Thus, there is no categorical reason why a juvenile would not be civilly liable for the harm he has wrongfully caused.[63] Certainly the fact that parents are vicariously liable for the damage caused by their minor children,[64] does not preclude these juveniles themselves to be liable.

However, very young children - called *infantes* - will not have the characteristics required to be factually capable of guilt: they will not have sufficient moral insight, factual insight or control over their actions.[65] At which age a child obtains these characteristics, is a question of fact which has to be determined case by case by the court.[66] Reviews of case law, however, have concluded that Belgian courts in general tend to find that children from the age of seven to nine onward can be held liable based on their own fault.

[iii] Mentally Ill

When a wrong is committed by a person with a mental illness, the court will have to decide whether the person is capable of guilt. Again, no fixed legal status exists which implies such incapacity. As it is a question of fact, it has to be determined based on the person's specific capabilities at the time of the disputed act. If a person is considered irresponsible, the wrongs he has committed cannot be imputed to him, and he cannot be liable on the basis of a fault.

As this renders a category of persons who are more likely to behave irrationally and thereby to cause harm in effect immune from fault liability, the legislature has in 1935 decided to insert a specific rule into the Civil Code which makes it possible for mentally ill[67] to be held liable for the damage they wrongfully cause, even though any

61. Article 488 Civil Code. Minors (Article 388 Civil Code) are therefore represented by their parents (Articles 373-374 Civil Code) or a custodian (Articles 389 et seq. Civil Code) in legal transactions.
62. A material fact is either something happening without any interference of a person but it can also be an act of a person that is not performed with the intent of creating the legal consequences the law might attach to it in the given circumstances. Such acts have consequences if they occur, without any 'validity' being required.
63. Court of Cassation 24 January 1985, No. 306, 1984-1985 Arresten van het Hof van Cassatie 682, 1985 Pasicrisie belge 603.
64. *See infra* §11.03 [A] [2] [b].
65. Court of Cassation 30 May 1969, 1969 Pasicrisie belge 879, 1969 Arresten van het Hof van Verbreking 943; Court of Cassation 13 October 1999 (P.99.0861.F), No. 528, 1999 Pasicrisie belge 1308, 1999 Arresten van het Hof van Cassatie 1255.
66. Court of Cassation 3 May 1978, 1978 Arresten van het Hof van Cassatie 1037, 1978 Pasicrisie belge 1012; Court of Cassation 30 October 1980, 1981 Pasicrisie belge 262, 1980-1981 Arresten van het Hof van Cassatie 235 No. 136.
67. The Court of Cassation has refused the application of Article 1386*bis* Civil Code to persons that suffer from a momentary lapse of consciousness as a consequence of a physical condition. Court of Cassation 24 April 1980, 1980 Pasicrisie belge 1055, 1979-1980 Arresten van het Hof van Cassatie 1065 No. 542; Court of Cassation 20 June 1979, 1979-1980 Rechtskundig Weekblad 2901, 1980 Journal des tribunaux 314.

guilt is lacking.[68] Article 1386*bis* of the Civil Code allows the court to leave the burden of the harm completely on the shoulders of the victim or to partially or completely shift it to the wrongdoing mentally ill person based on an equitable judgment, taking into account the (financial) situation of both parties.

Although this has been criticised by scholars, the Court of Cassation has ruled that when the mentally ill person has civil liability insurance, this insurer will be held to full compensation of the harm that was wrongfully caused, as this insurer cannot invoke the grounds for limiting this liability which the mentally ill could.[69]

[2] Vicarious Liability Based on Rebuttable Presumptions

[a] Characteristics of All Vicarious Liabilities

Article 1384 of the Civil Code contains the traditional rules on vicarious liability. As opposed to its French counterpart,[70] the Belgian Court of Cassation has refused to read a general rule of vicarious liability of persons in charge of or supervising another into this provision.[71] In its interpretation, this Article contains an exhaustive list of vicarious liabilities: parents for their minor children (paragraph 2), masters for their servants (paragraph 3), and teachers for their pupils (paragraph 4). These three vicarious liabilities share some characteristics.

First, the person for who the liable person is responsible has to either have committed a wrongful act or to be liable on the basis of a strict liability. This means that the vicarious liability applies even if the juvenile, pupil or servant is not liable because he lacks culpability, such as will be the case with infants,[72] but also with mentally ill persons.[73] It also means that the master is liable for damage caused by the servant even if the servant enjoys immunity.[74]

Second, the vicarious liability does not preclude the personal liability of the juvenile, the pupil or the servant. If the constituent elements are present, both liabilities can co-exist, in which case both parties are held *in solidum*. After compensating the victim, the vicariously liable person can exercise recourse against the person for who he is responsible if the conditions for his personal liability are fulfilled. Also, if the constituent elements of several types of vicarious liability are present - such as if a minor child wrongfully causes harm while under the supervision of a teacher, or if a

68. Article 1 of the Act of 16 April 1935, Moniteur belge - Belgisch Staatsblad 18 April 1935.
69. Court of Cassation 22 September 2000 (C.98.0090.N), No. 489, 2000 Arresten van het Hof van Cassatie 1420, 2000 Pasicrisie belge 1390.
70. French Court of Cassation 29 March 1991, 1991 Dalloz jurisprudence 324, 1992 Gazette du Palais - Jurisprudence 513, 1991 REVUE GÉNÉRALE DES ASSURANCES ET DES RESPONSABILITÉS 11,857.
71. Court of Cassation 19 June 1997 (C.96.0254.F - C.96.0258.F), No. 284, 1997 Pasicrisie belge 700, 1997 Arresten van het Hof van Cassatie 670.
72. Court of Cassation 7 March 1957, 1957 Arresten van het Hof van Verbreking 546, 1957 Pasicrisie belge 806; more recent: Court of Cassation 4 June 2012 (C.10.0734.N), No. 358, 2012 Arresten van het Hof van Cassatie 1527, 2012 Pasicrisie belge 1271.
73. Court of Cassation 18 October 1990, No. 90, 1990–1991 Arresten van het Hof van Cassatie 193, 1991 Pasicrisie belge 171.
74. *See infra* §11.03 [E].

pupil causes harm while under the supervision of a teacher who is the servant of a master - both vicarious liabilities co-exist.[75]

Third, these vicarious liabilities can only be invoked by third parties suffering harm. A parent, teacher or master cannot rely on its own vicarious liability, and neither can a juvenile, pupil or servant invoke this liability against its parent, teacher or master.[76]

Fourth, the claimant does not have to prove any fault of the parent, teacher or master and also does not have to prove that they caused the damage.[77] According to Article 1384, paragraph 5, of the Civil Code, parents and teachers can escape by showing that they did not commit any fault or that their fault did not cause the damage, so for them this vicarious liability remains fault based. Masters, however, are not mentioned in this paragraph 5, so they cannot escape their vicarious liability, which therefore is a strict liability.[78]

[b] Parents for Minor Children

According to Article 1384, paragraph 2, of the Civil Code, parents are liable for the damage caused by their minor children.[79] The basis for this liability is their legally recognised affiliation.[80] Whether this legal parental relationship is based on a (real or presumed) biological affiliation or on adoption, is irrelevant. The liability is not dependent on there being any parental authority.[81] However, if the juvenile is legally emancipated, for instance if he or she is married,[82] the parents no longer are vicariously liable for the harm it causes.[83] Before the amendment of this provision in 1977,[84] the father - and the mother after the death of the father - was only liable if he or she lived together with the minor. This limitation was removed, so now both parents are liable, irrespective with which parent the child lives.[85] The liability of both parents is cumulative, so the victim can claim compensation from both parents, who will be held *in solidum*.

75. Court of Cassation 23 February 1989, No. 356, 1988-1989 Arresten van het Hof van Cassatie 721, 1989 Pasicrisie belge 649; Court of Cassation 21 December 1989, No. 257, 1990 Pasicrisie belge 501, 1989-1990 Arresten van het Hof van Cassatie 560.
76. Court of Cassation 20 June 2008 (C.06.0210.F), No. 385, 2008 Pasicrisie belge 1572, 2008 Arresten van het Hof van Cassatie 1603.
77. Court of Cassation 20 October 1999 (P.99.0652.F), No. 549, 1999 Arresten van het Hof van Cassatie 1305, 1999 Pasicrisie belge 1360.
78. *See infra* §11.03 [B] [2] [a] [i].
79. Articles 388 and 488 Civil Code set the age of legal majority at eighteen.
80. On parental affiliation, *see supra* Chapter 7, §7.02.
81. Court of Cassation 12 November 2002 (P.02.0095.N), No. 598, 2002 Arresten van het Hof van Cassatie 2454, 2002 Pasicrisie belge 2157. On parental authority, *see supra* Chapter 7, §7.03.
82. Article 476 Civil Code.
83. Court of Cassation 11 February 1946, 1946 Pasicrisie belge 62, 1946 Arresten van het Hof van Verbreking 54; Court of Cassation 6 March 1950, 1950 Pasicrisie belge 447, 1950 Arresten van het Hof van Verbreking 449.
84. Act of 6 July 1977, Moniteur belge - Belgisch Staatsblad 2 August 1977.
85. Court of Cassation 12 November 2002 (P.02.0095.N), No. 598, 2002 Arresten van het Hof van Cassatie 2454, 2002 Pasicrisie belge 2157; Court of Cassation 30 May 1984, No. 561, 1983-1984 Arresten van het Hof van Cassatie 1286, 1984 Pasicrisie belge 1200.

This vicarious liability is based on a double presumption. First, if a minor wrongfully causes any damage, his or her parents are presumed to have committed a fault.[86] Second, this fault of the parents is presumed to have caused the damage.[87]

Article 1384, paragraph 5, of the Civil Code allows a parent to escape liability by proving that he could not have prevented the act of the minor. Although over the last decades courts - including the important Brussels Court of Appeal[88] - had begun to adopt a strict interpretation allowing parents only to escape if they prove force majeure, the Court of Cassation has reaffirmed its position that a parent is not vicariously liable if he or she shows not to have committed any fault in supervision and education.[89] The case law shows a varying attitude of judges in accepting such rebutting evidence. Some allow parents to escape as soon as they have shown that they provided a normal education and appropriate supervision. Others seem to consider the wrongful behaviour of the juvenile in itself sufficient evidence of a shortcoming in education (*res ipsa loquitur*), thus in effect excluding all possibilities of rebutting the presumption of fault except by proving force majeure.

[c] Teachers for Pupils

According to Article 1384, paragraph 4, of the Civil Code, teachers and artisans are liable for the damage caused by their pupils or apprentices during the time they are under their supervision. There is no age limit for pupils, so also persons who are teaching adults are subject to this liability.

For this liability to apply, an educational relationship has to exist between the person who has caused the damage and the person held liable. Education in this regard does not only include the transfer of technical and intellectual knowledge in organised courses, but also contains other forms of education of a scientific, artistic, professional, moral and social type.[90] Hence, artisans are considered to be teachers, and apprentices are pupils. No professional status nor structured organisation is required. A person teaching someone to drive a car is subject to this vicarious liability. However, the courts tend to adhere to a strict reading excluding such liability for persons who are merely supervising pupils. Also, the Court of Cassation has held that a school itself is not a teacher, and thus not subject to this vicarious liability for damage caused by its

86. Court of Cassation 20 April 1982, 1981–1982 Arresten van het Hof van Cassatie 1003 No. 484, 1982 Pasicrisie belge 944; Court of Cassation 5 April 1995 (P.94.1363.N), No. 185, 1995 Arresten van het Hof van Cassatie 377, 1995 Pasicrisie belge 390.
87. Court of Cassation 20 October 1999 (P.99.0652.F), No. 549, 1999 Arresten van het Hof van Cassatie 1305, 1999 Pasicrisie belge 1360.
88. *See* e.g. Court of Appeal Brussels 23 October 2007, 2010 Revue générale des assurances et des responsabilités 14,652; Court of Appeal Brussels 24 June 2009, 2009 Revue générale des assurances et des responsabilités 14,554.
89. Court of Cassation 4 March 2015 (P.14.1873.F), No. 159, 2015 Pasicrisie belge 558, 2015 Arresten van het Hof van Cassatie 585; previously: Court of Cassation 23 February 1989, No. 356, 1988–1989 Arresten van het Hof van Cassatie 721, 1989 Pasicrisie belge 649.
90. Court of Cassation 3 December 1986, No. 201, 1986–1987 Arresten van het Hof van Cassatie 442, 1987 Pasicrisie belge 410.

pupils.[91] However, as in many cases the teacher can be legally qualified as a (civil) servant of the school, the school will be vicariously liable as the master or the public entity for damage (presumably) wrongfully caused by its servant.[92]

Teachers can escape this liability by proving that they did not commit any fault, by showing they applied sufficient supervision,[93] or that their (presumed) fault did not cause the actual harm creating event. As many teachers in practice are employees or public servants, enjoying an extensive immunity from civil liability,[94] most teachers can escape this liability by showing that they did not intend to cause harm and did not commit a gross fault or customary - i.e., regularly reoccurring - light fault.[95]

[B] Strict Liability

From the beginning of the twentieth century, the legislature has introduced and the courts have developed several special liability rules that make it possible to hold a person liable for damage that he has not wrongfully caused to occur. Such liability is referred to as objective liability (*responsabilité objective - objectieve aansprakelijkheid*).

[1] Liability for Damage Caused by Lawful Acts

[a] General

In a number of cases, the person held liable has caused the harm, but in doing so he has not committed a wrong. Such liabilities exist for example for damage caused by lawful mining activities,[96] ground water winning,[97] and the exploitation of pipelines.[98]

[b] Nuisance

The most important example of such liability is nuisance (*troubles de viosinage - burenhinder* or *evenwichtsleer*). In such cases, a person is exercising his right without violating any rules or being negligent and the nuisance he has caused to the neighbour is not a type of wrong but a type of damage, consisting in a limitation of the enjoyment

91. Court of Cassation 19 June 1997 (C.96.0254.F - C.96.0258.F), No. 284, 1997 Pasicrisie belge 700, 1997 Arresten van het Hof van Cassatie 670.
92. *See infra* §11.03 [B] [2] [a] [i] and [ii].
93. Court of Cassation 10 October 2003 (C.02.0628.F), No. 490, 2003 Pasicrisie belge 1583, 2003 Arresten van het Hof van Cassatie 1845.
94. *See infra* §11.03 [E] [1] and [2].
95. Court of Cassation 25 January 1993, No. 47, 1993 Pasicrisie belge 91, 1993 Arresten van het Hof van Cassatie 98.
96. Article 33 Flemish Act of 8 May 2009 on the Deep Underground; Article 42 Walloon Mining Act of 7 July 1988.
97. Flemish Act of 24 January 1984; Walloon Act of 24 May 2004 introducing a Book II into the Walloon Environmental Code, called the Water Code.
98. Act of 12 April 1965 on the Transportation of Gasses through Pipelines.

of his right. The Court of Cassation has based this liability on the conflicting property rights of the neighbours, granting each of them in principle an equal opportunity to enjoy their property.[99]

For this liability to attach, the claimant has to have suffered excessive hindrance, which means that the nuisance is significantly more serious than one is normally expected to accept among neighbours in that specific area.

This hindrance has to be caused by the neighbour.[100] More specific, the hindrance has to be attributable to a form of exploitation of the property right on the premise, which can consist in an act or a specific inaction of the person held liable, without this having to constitute a fault.[101] Thus, the liability can only rest on a person who is exercising an attribute of the property right on the neighbouring premise.[102] This can be the owner, but it also can be a tenant. A construction company working in the premises, however, does not exercise an attribute of the property right, and is thus not subject to this liability.[103] If his activities cause damage to a neighbour, he will only be liable if the harm was caused by a fault for which the construction company is responsible. The owner will only be liable based on nuisance if the act of the construction company that caused the hindrance was part of its specific task and thus constituted an exercise of his property right by the owner himself.[104]

Nuisance can only be invoked by a victim that is exercising an attribute of the property right on the premise suffering the hindrance. Thus, the owner of the neighbouring premise is protected, but also for instance a tenant renting those premises.[105]

Nuisance results in an obligation to restore the balance between the enjoyment of the property rights. This means that only the fraction of the hindrance that is considered to be 'excessive' has to be removed.[106] This can result in the court awarding

99. Court of Cassation 6 April 1960 (two decisions), 1960 Pasicrisie belge 920, 1960 Arresten van het Hof van Verbreking 722.
100. Court of Cassation 15 November 2013 (C.11.0656.F), No. 605, 2013 Pasicrisie belge 2222, 2013 Arresten van het Hof van Cassatie 2407.
101. Court of Cassation 3 April 1998 (C.97.0088.F), No. 192, 1998 Pasicrisie belge 440, 1998 Arresten van het Hof van Cassatie 417; Court of Cassation 4 May 2012 (C.10.0080.F), No. 276, 2012 Pasicrisie belge 1007, 2012 Arresten van het Hof van Cassatie 1178.
102. Court of Cassation 10 January 1974, 1974 Pasicrisie belge 488, 1974 Arresten van het Hof van Cassatie 520; Court of Cassation 9 June 1983, No. 561, 1982–1983 Arresten van het Hof van Cassatie 1256, 1983 Pasicrisie belge 1145.
103. Court of Cassation 13 March 1987, No. 416, 1986–1987 Arresten van het Hof van Cassatie 920, 1987 Pasicrisie belge 834.
104. Court of Cassation 25 June 2009 (C.07.0354.F), No. 438, 2009 Pasicrisie belge 1665, 2009 Arresten van het Hof van Cassatie 1821. The neighbour from whose premises the hindrance originate cannot escape this liability because the hindrance was caused by a fault of a third party. Court of Cassation 24 April 2003 (C.01.0371.F), No. 262, 2003 Pasicrisie belge 870, 2003 Arresten van het Hof van Cassatie 1035.
105. Nuisance can be invoked by a tenant of an apartment against the tenant of another apartment in the same building. *See* Court of Cassation 4 June 2012 (C.10.0672.N), No. 357, 2012 Arresten van het Hof van Cassatie 1519, 2012 Pasicrisie belge 1269.
106. Court of Cassation 20 April 2012 (C.10.0103.F), No. 243, 2012 Pasicrisie belge 844, 2012 Arresten van het Hof van Cassatie 1008; Court of Cassation 23 November 2000 (C.99.0104.F), No. 639, 2000 Pasicrisie belge 1789, 2000 Arresten van het Hof van Cassatie 1828.

an injunction forcing one neighbour to limit his use of his property, as long as the court order does not completely preclude the liable neighbour from using his property,[107] as that would only reverse the imbalance between the exercise of the rights involved.[108]

[2] Risk Liability

For a number of specific situations, a strict liability renders a person liable that has not caused the harm. Here, the damage is the realisation of a specific risk, and the person held liable has control over a factor that creates this risk. Only a few examples will be discussed, specifically some forms of vicarious liability and some liabilities for damage caused by things.

[a] Vicarious Liability for Personnel

[i] Masters for Servants

According to Article 1384, paragraph 3, of the Civil Code, 'masters' (*maîtres et commettants - meesters en aanstellers*) are liable for the damage their 'servants' (*domestiques et préposés - dienstboden en aangestelden*) cause in their function. As the master cannot escape this liability by showing that he did not commit any fault,[109] this is a strict liability.

A master-servant relationship is characterised by subordination. This means that the master can supervise and direct the activities of the servant.[110] The subordination does not have to be legally sanctioned: if one person in fact directs the activities of another person, the first will be vicariously liable for the damage caused by the latter.[111] Thus, this vicarious liability is not restricted to employers for damage caused by their employees.[112] On the other hand can the legal possibility of supervision and direction suffice to make one person vicariously liable, even though in fact he has not exercised this authority.[113]

107. *See* e.g. Court of Cassation 8 February 2010 (C.09.0196.F), No. 87, 2010 Pasicrisie belge 388, 2010 Arresten van het Hof van Cassatie 372.
108. Court of Cassation 14 December 1995 (C.93.0354.N), No. 550, 1995 Arresten van het Hof van Cassatie 1125, 1995 Pasicrisie belge 1163.
109. Court of Cassation 27 March 1944, 1944 Pasicrisie belge 275, 1944 Arresten van het Hof van Verbreking 127.
110. Court of Cassation 16 October 1972, 1973 Pasicrisie belge 165, 1973 Arresten van het Hof van Cassatie 165; more recent: Court of Cassation 22 January 2007 (C.04.0343.N), No. 35, 2007 Arresten van het Hof van Cassatie 136, 2007 Pasicrisie belge 122.
111. Court of Cassation 23 January 1964, 1964 Pasicrisie belge 548.
112. Court of Cassation 29 June 2009 (C.07.0611.F), No. 445, 2009 Pasicrisie belge 1698, 2009 Arresten van het Hof van Cassatie 1846. The concept of employer and employee belong to labour law (*see infra* Chapter 14, §14.02 [B] [1]).
113. Court of Cassation 24 December 1951, 1952 Arresten van het Hof van Verbreking 196, 1952 Pasicrisie belge 213; Court of Cassation 16 October 1972, 1973 Pasicrisie belge 165, 1973 Arresten van het Hof van Cassatie 165.

In practice, most employers will be regarded as masters of their employees, but it is possible that an employee is in fact working under the supervision and direction of a client of his employer, in which case this client could be his master.[114] This often happens with temporary agency work. However, only a person acting for his own account can be a master.[115] Thus, an employee who supervises and directs other employees - a foreman, for instance - cannot be held vicariously liable.

The liability covers the damage the servant has caused through his fault, even if it is presumed.[116] It also covers the harm for which the servant according to civil liability law would be strictly liable, for instance as custodian of a defective object[117] or as the user of an animal.[118] Whether or not the servant himself is liable or enjoys immunity,[119] is not relevant.[120]

For this liability to apply, the event has to have occurred in the performance of the servant's function. The courts interpret this broadly, requiring only that the event occurred during the time the servant is working for the master and is related to the performance of this function, even if the connection is indirect or coincidental.[121] This means that the master is not only liable in case of a wrongful performance of the function, but in case of intentional neglect or even an abuse of the servant's position.[122] Thus, employers have been held liable for the damage caused by a criminal offence committed by an employee during his work and at the workplace,[123] and banks have been held liable for the harm suffered by clients who were misled to place savings in a Ponzi scheme organised by an agent of the bank.[124] The fact that the victim knew or should have known that the servant was acting outside of his function does not

114. Court of Cassation 3 January 2002 (C.98.0280.N), No. 2, 2002 Arresten van het Hof van Cassatie 8, 2002 Pasicrisie belge 5; Court of Cassation 21 April 1971, 1971 Arresten van het Hof van Cassatie 778, 1971 Pasicrisie belge 745.
115. Court of Cassation 22 January 2007 (C.04.0343.N), No. 35, 2007 Arresten van het Hof van Cassatie 136, 2007 Pasicrisie belge 122.
116. Thus, the school will be vicariously liable based on Article 1384, para. 3, Civil Code, as the master of the teacher, who is vicariously liable for the damage caused by the pupil based on Article 1384, para. 4, Civil Code. Court of Cassation 28 October 1994 (C.93.0114.N), No. 461, 1994 Arresten van het Hof van Cassatie 895, 1994 Pasicrisie belge 877.
117. *See infra* §11.03 [B] [2] [b] [i].
118. *See infra* §11.03 [B] [2] [b] [iv].
119. *See infra* §11.03 [E].
120. Court of Cassation 18 November 1981, 1982 Revue générale des assurances et des responsabilités 10,459.
121. Court of Cassation 27 March 1944, 1944 Pasicrisie belge 275, 1944 Arresten van het Hof van Verbreking 127; more recent: Court of Cassation 21 March 2013 (C.11.0476.F), No. 202, 2013 Pasicrisie belge 744, 2013 Arresten van het Hof van Cassatie 791.
122. Court of Cassation 19 September 2008 (C.07.0317.N), No. 486, 2008 Arresten van het Hof van Cassatie 1983, 2008 Pasicrisie belge 1978; Court of Cassation 10 February 1958, 1958 Arresten van het Hof van Verbreking 400, 1958 Pasicrisie belge 635.
123. *See* e.g. Court of Cassation 30 September 2015 (P.14.0474.F), 2015 Journal des tribunaux 844, 2016 Revue générale des assurances et des responsabilités 15,287, stating that a master is not only liable for the damage caused by the intentional fault of his employee, but because this was a fraudulent act of the employee also cannot invoke the involuntary fault of the victim (contributory negligence) which allowed the fraud to be possible.
124. *See* e.g. Court of Cassation 26 October 1989, No. 123, 1989-1990 Arresten van het Hof van Cassatie 274, 1990 Pasicrisie belge 241.

preclude the vicarious liability of the master; it can merely result in a reduction of the liability of the master based on contributory negligence by the victim.[125]

The master who has compensated the victim, can have recourse against the servant that is liable for the damage. However, if the servant enjoys immunity,[126] such recourse will fail.

[ii] Public Entities for Civil Servants

The Act of 10 February 2003 on the Liability of and for Members of Personnel of Entities in the Public Sector, which introduced an immunity for civil servants that are not employed on a contractual basis,[127] also provides for a vicarious liability for public sector entities for damage caused by their personnel similar to Article 1384, paragraph 3, of the Civil Code.

[iii] Organisations for Volunteers

When the legislature in 2005 introduced a special liability regime for volunteers,[128] it imposed a strict vicarious liability on organisations for the damage caused by their volunteers in the cases these volunteers themselves enjoy an immunity from liability.[129] Thus – significantly different from the general vicarious liability of Article 1384, paragraph 3, of the Civil Code – this liability is restricted to damage caused by faults which are not an intentional fault, a gross fault, or a with this particular volunteer regularly occurring light fault.[130] Also, this liability is not restricted to subordinated volunteers,[131] but also applies to volunteers in leading functions within the organisation. The organisation is required to have liability insurance covering this liability.[132]

This vicarious liability is only applicable to organisations that are incorporated and to organisations that have at least one employee or that are connected to such an organisation.[133] This limitation was included to avoid the liability and the connected mandatory insurance being applicable to people together entering into some kind of activity without realising they form an unincorporated organisation.[134]

125. Court of Cassation 21 March 2013 (C.11.0476.F), No. 202, 2013 Pasicrisie belge 744, 2013 Arresten van het Hof van Cassatie 791; Court of Cassation 11 March 1994, No. 116, 1994 Arresten van het Hof van Cassatie 247, 1994 Pasicrisie belge 244. On contributory negligence, *see infra* §11.04 [C].
126. For this immunity, *See infra* §11.03 [E].
127. *See infra* §11.03 [E] [2].
128. Federal Act of 3 July 2005 on the Rights of Volunteers.
129. For the extent of this immunity, *See infra* §11.03 [E] [3].
130. Article 5 Act of 3 July 2005 on the Rights of Volunteers.
131. Article 3, 1° & 2°, Act of 3 July 2005 on the Rights of Volunteers.
132. Article 6 Act of 3 July 2005 on the Rights of Volunteers.
133. Article 3, 3° *juncto* Article 5 Act of 3 July 2005 on the Rights of Volunteers.
134. The different treatment of organisations with and without an employee was held to be constitutional. Constitutional Court No. 158/2007 of 19 December 2007.

[b] *Liability for Harm Caused by Things*

The Belgian regime for product liability, holding the producer liable for certain harm caused by defective products he put into circulation, is the implementation of the EU Product Liability Directive,[135] so it will not be discussed in detail. Also the many different types of environmental strict liabilities will not be enumerated.

[i] Defective Objects in General

Since the end of the nineteenth century, the Belgian courts read a strict liability of the custodian for damage caused by a defective thing (*chose vicieuse* – *gebrekkige zaak*) in the first paragraph of Article 1384 of the Civil Code.[136] This liability only applies to material things,[137] but it can also apply to objects composed of several parts, including software. Software itself, however, is not considered to be an object, and neither is information.

The fact that a thing is dangerous, i.e., likely to cause harm, is not sufficient. For this liability to arise, the object has to be defective.[138] The Court of Cassation states that a defect is an abnormal characteristic or state – i.e., the object deviates from the normal model – that causes the object to be capable of causing harm in certain circumstances.[139] The circumstances in which the risk exists have to be a normal, foreseeable use of the object.[140]

The defect does not have to be 'intrinsic' to the object, nor needs the 'structure' of the object to be affected.[141] In fact, the courts often rule an object to be defective if it does not conform to the reasonable expectations one would have and this unexpected condition is what caused the damage.[142] The fact that the specific victim was aware of the condition of the thing, however, does not mean that the object no longer is

135. Council Directive 85/374/EEC of 25 July 1985 on the Approximation of the Laws, Regulations and Administrative Provisions of the Member States concerning Liability for Defective Products, Official Journal L210/29 of 7 August 1985, as amended.
136. This interpretation was approved in Court of Cassation 26 May 1904, 1904 Pasicrisie belge 246; Court of Cassation 25 March 1920, 1920 Pasicrisie belge 110.
137. Court of Cassation 21 April 1972, 1972 Arresten van het Hof van Cassatie 789, 1972 Pasicrisie belge 773.
138. The Court based this on an analogy with other liabilities in the Civil Code: a person is liable when the damage is caused by his 'defective' behaviour (Article 1382), the defective behaviour of a person for whom he is responsible (Article 1384, paras 2–4), or a defect of a his building (Article 1386). Court of Cassation 26 May 1904, 1904 Pasicrisie belge 246.
139. Court of Cassation 23 September 1971, 1972 Arresten van het Hof van Cassatie 88, 1972 Pasicrisie belge 80; recent: Court of Cassation 4 January 2016 (C.15.0191.F), not yet published; Court of Cassation 17 January 2014 (C.12.0510.F), No. 39, 2014 Pasicrisie belge 143, 2014 Arresten van het Hof van Cassatie 161.
140. Court of Cassation 30 January 2003 (C.00.0726.F), No. 70, 2003 Pasicrisie belge 235, 2003 Arresten van het Hof van Cassatie 278.
141. Court of Cassation 13 March 2015 (C.14.0284.N), No. 193, 2015 Arresten van het Hof van Cassatie 737, 2015 Pasicrisie belge 721; Court of Court of Cassation 2 January 2009 (C.08.0074.N), No. 2, 2009 Arresten van het Hof van Cassatie 3, 2009 Pasicrisie belge 2.
142. Court of Cassation 4 January 2016 (C.15.0191.F), not published yet; Court of Cassation 11 March 2010 (C.09.0186.N), No. 171, 2010 Arresten van het Hof van Cassatie 715, 2010 Pasicrisie 777.

defective,[143] resulting in case law that is hard to reconcile with one single explanatory theoretical concept of a defect. The Court of Cassation stresses that the fact that the object creates damage in itself is not a defect.[144] However, the courts tend to be lenient towards the victim if it faces difficulty providing positive evidence of the defect that caused the abnormal behaviour of the object. In general, the courts allow a negative proof, showing that all other reasonably possible causes for the deviant behaviour can be excluded in the particular case.[145]

Liability for damage caused by a defective object attaches to the person who has the thing under his guard. Although this person is referred to as the 'custodian' (*gardien - bewaarder*), this term should not be understood in its legal sense, in which it refers to the party to a contract of custodianship or deposit (*depot - bewaargeving*) who has the obligation to safe keep an object (*depositaire - bewaarnemer*). The custodian, as the term is used in the context of this strict liability, can be the owner but it also can be someone else. Required is that the person had the thing under his detention or used it, and that he had factual control over the object.[146] Thus, a thief will be liable for the harm caused by defective stolen goods.

The custodian is liable, irrespective of whether he has committed any fault and even if he was not aware or could not have been aware of the defect.[147] The cause of the defect is irrelevant. However, if the custodian has compensated the victim, he can have recourse against the person liable for having caused the thing to become defective.[148]

[ii] Collapsing Buildings

Article 1386 of the Civil Code contains a special rule for damage caused by collapsing buildings. The liability only applies to man-made constructions that are durably connected to the ground.[149] The owner is liable for all damage caused by the total or

143. Court of Cassation 17 January 2014 (C.12.0510.F), No. 39, 2014 Pasicrisie belge 143, 2014 Arresten van het Hof van Cassatie 161; Court of Cassation 21 November 2003 (C.02.0619.F), No. 590, 2003 Pasicrisie belge 1878, 2003 Arresten van het Hof van Cassatie 2183.
144. Court of Cassation 24 February 2006 (C.05.0112.F), No. 109, 2006 Pasicrisie belge 442, 2006 Arresten van het Hof van Cassatie 443.
145. Court of Cassation 11 September 2008 (C.07.0200.F), No. 646, 2008 Pasicrisie belge 1916, 2008 Arresten van het Hof van Cassatie 1917; *see* already Court of Cassation 25 March 1943, 1943 Arresten van het Hof van Verbreking 68, 1943 Pasicrisie belge 110.
146. Court of Cassation 13 September 2012 (C.10.0226.F), No. 463, 2012 Pasicrisie belge 1647, 2012 Arresten van het Hof van Cassatie 1923; Court of Cassation 25 March 1999 (C.96.0404.N), No. 183, 1999 Arresten van het Hof van Cassatie 442, 1999 Pasicrisie belge 453.
147. Court of Cassation 3 May 1974, 1974 Arresten van het Hof van Cassatie 989, 1974 Pasicrisie belge 914; Court of Cassation 26 April 2013 (C.12.0286.N), No. 260, 2013 Arresten van het Hof van Cassatie 1010, 2013 Pasicrisie belge 985.
148. Court of Cassation 4 February 2011 (C.10.0236.N), No. 104, 2011 Arresten van het Hof van Cassatie 401, 2011 Pasicrisie belge 429; Court of Cassation 14 February 2013 (C.11.0793.F), No. 109, 2013 Pasicrisie belge 429, 2013 Arresten van het Hof van Cassatie 443.
149. The liability is also applicable to damage caused during construction. Court of Cassation 3 February 1955, 1955 Pasicrisie belge 578, 1955 Arresten van het Hof van Verbreking 436; Court of Cassation 16 June 1995 (C.93.0319.N), No. 305, 1995 Arresten van het Hof van Cassatie 621, 1995 Pasicrisie belge 643.

partial[150] collapse that is the consequence of either a construction defect or of a lack of proper maintenance. The collapse itself is not sufficient, as it can also be caused by force majeure.[151]

This is a strict liability, as it is irrelevant what caused the defect in the construction or who is responsible for the maintenance.[152] The owner remains liable if the defect is caused by an error made by the architect or sloppy work by the construction company,[153] or if a tenant was responsible for the maintenance. The owner who has compensated the victim, however, will be able to have recourse against the person liable for the cause.[154]

[iii] Fire or Explosion in Establishments

A separate statute imposes a liability on the operator of a public establishment for damage caused by fire or explosion.[155] This liability is applicable to a list of establishments, including discotheques, larger restaurants, hotels, larger stores, movie theatres, sports halls and stadiums, amusement parks, hospitals, schools, larger office buildings, train stations and airports, churches and court buildings.[156] The cause of the fire or explosion is not relevant: even if the fire started in a neighbouring building and spread into the public establishment, the operator remains liable. The liability can be invoked by anybody: visitors, but also neighbours and even the members of the staff of the operator, except for the arsonist or the person who wilfully caused the explosion.[157] The operator is legally required to have liability insurance covering this liability.[158] This liability is capped per incident at approximately EUR 24 million for bodily harm and EUR 1.2 million for property damage.[159] After compensating the victim, the insurer can have recourse against the person liable for the fire or explosion.[160]

150. A collapse of an 'important part' of the building is sufficient. Court of Cassation 17 December 1992, No. 802, 1992 Pasicrisie belge 1390, 1991–1992 Arresten van het Hof van Cassatie 1445; Court of Cassation 18 April 1975, 1975 Arresten van het Hof van Cassatie 917, 1975 Pasicrisie belge 828. Whether the part is 'important', is a question of fact.
151. Court of Cassation 8 January 1982, 1981–1982 Arresten van het Hof van Cassatie 586 No. 280, 1982 Pasicrisie belge 573.
152. Court of Cassation 17 December 1992, No. 802, 1992 Pasicrisie belge 1390, 1991–1992 Arresten van het Hof van Cassatie 1445.
153. Court of Cassation 16 June 1995 (C.93.0319.N), No. 305, 1995 Arresten van het Hof van Cassatie 621, 1995 Pasicrisie belge 643.
154. Court of Cassation 23 October 1970, 1971 Arresten van het Hof van Cassatie 176, 1971 Pasicrisie belge 169.
155. Article 8, para. 1, Act of 30 July 1979 on the Prevention of and Liability for Fire and Explosions.
156. Royal Decree of 28 February 1991.
157. Article 8, para. 7, Act of 30 July 1979 on the Prevention of and Liability for Fire and Explosions.
158. Article 8, para. 3, Act of 30 July 1979 on the Prevention of and Liability for Fire and Explosions.
159. Article 1 Royal Decree of 5 August 1991 implementing the Act of 30 July 1979. These amounts are adjusted yearly based on the index of consumer prices. The amounts mentioned are calculated based on the index of September 2016.
160. Article 8, para. 6, Act of 30 July 1979 on the Prevention of and Liability for Fire and Explosions.

[iv] Animals

For damage caused by animals,[161] Article 1385 of the Civil Code places a strict liability on the owner or the person who uses the animal, provided he has in fact the power of control over the animal in the same way an owner has.[162] A person who is a subordinate - and thus a servant in the sense of Article 1384, paragraph 3, of the Civil Code - can be liable based on Article 1385 of the Civil Code if he uses an animal in the course of performing his task and has factual control and mastership over the animal.[163]

The owner or person using the animal cannot escape this liability by showing he has not committed any fault.[164] However, if the harm has been caused by a normal reaction of the animal to a wrongful provocation by the victim[165] or by a third party,[166] the liability does not apply. Courts also tend to refuse to allow a victim that unnecessarily, knowingly and wrongfully exposed itself to the known risk posed by the normal behaviour of an animal compensation on the basis of this liability.[167]

[C] Liability of Legal Persons

Legal persons can only act through their personnel, employees and agents. If the harm is caused by a servant, the legal person will be vicariously liable as the master.[168] If however the damage was caused by a person that is not in a subordinated position, Article 1384, paragraph 3, of the Civil Code is not applicable. Invoking a reasoning that is borrowed from the law of agency, the courts attribute the fault committed by the

161. Article 1385 Civil Code requires no deviant behaviour or 'defect' of the animal. However, the fact that an animal was merely 'involved' in an event causing damage which would not have happened if the animal was not present, apparently does not mean that the event was caused by the animal. Court of Cassation 26 February 1987, No. 383, 1987 Pasicrisie belge 772, 1986-1987 Arresten van het Hof van Cassatie 852.
162. Court of Cassation 18 November 1993 (C.93.01154.F), No. 472, 1993 Pasicrisie belge 970, 1993 Arresten van het Hof van Cassatie 966; Court of Cassation 19 November 2012 (C.09.0379.F), No. 620, 2012 Pasicrisie belge 2253, 2012 Arresten van het Hof van Cassatie 2595.
163. Court of Cassation 5 November 1981, 1982 Pasicrisie belge 316, 1981-1982 Arresten van het Hof van Cassatie 328 No. 159; Court of Cassation 19 November 2012 (C.09.0379.F), No. 620, 2012 Pasicrisie belge 2253, 2012 Arresten van het Hof van Cassatie 2595.
164. Court of Cassation 23 June 1932, 1932 Pasicrisie belge 200.
165. Court of Cassation 20 May 1983, No. 526, 1983 Pasicrisie belge 1061, 1982-1983 Arresten van het Hof van Cassatie 1165.
166. Court of Cassation 19 January 1996 (C.95.0193.F), No. 41, 1996 Pasicrisie belge 85, 1996 Arresten van het Hof van Cassatie 78.
167. *See* e.g. Court of Cassation 12 October 1984, No. 119, 1984-1985 Arresten van het Hof van Cassatie 254, 1985 Pasicrisie belge 220; Court of Cassation 6 January 2012 (C.11.0025.F), No. 15, 2012 Pasicrisie belge 49, 2012 Arresten van het Hof van Cassatie 60. In both cases the behaviour of the animal was not provoked by the victim, but still the Court allowed the fact finding court to exclude all liability, even though the harm was clearly also caused by the normal behaviour of the animal.
168. *See supra* §11.03 [B] [2] [a] [i].

director or the higher officer to the legal person as if it acted itself, so Belgian law allows legal persons to be held liable on the basis of Article 1382 of the Civil Code.[169]

This principle is only applied for damage caused by members of the personnel of the legal person that are called organs (*organe* - *orgaan*). These are the non-subordinated legal representatives of the legal entity, identified by law or by the articles of association. The legal person will only be liable if the organ has acted within its function, i.e., if the action, if performed correctly, would have been within its authority. A legal person is not liable for an action of an organ outside its authority, except if this act from the point of view of *every* prudent and reasonable observer would have been perceived as within its authority.[170]

The liability of the legal person does not preclude any personal liability of the organ.

[D] Liability of Public Authorities

[1] Liability in General

Belgian law has been one of the first to afford citizens the protection of civil liability against actions of the government. Already in 1852 the Court of Cassation ruled that the civil liability provisions of the Civil Code are also applicable to the State and that a governmental agency is only free from such liability if its act is excluded from the province of civil law by a statutory provision or by its political character.[171] In its landmark decision in the *Flandria* case in 1920, the Court decided that the principle of the separation of powers, as it must be understood in Belgian constitutional law, does not preclude the judiciary from judging whether the executive has committed a fault, even when performing its political function.[172]

[a] Damage Caused by the Executive Branch

While the earliest cases involved the liability for damage caused by material acts of the executive,[173] the courts have gradually expanded this liability to harm caused by a regulatory intervention of the executive[174] or by their wrongful neglect to regulate.[175]

169. Court of Cassation 13 December 1923, 1924 Pasicrisie belge 82; Court of Cassation 15 January 1946, 1946 Pasicrisie belge 25, 1946 Arresten van het Hof van Verbreking 23. *See also infra* Chapter 13, §13.04 [B] [5] [d].
170. Court of Cassation 29 May 1947, 1947 Arresten van het Hof van Verbreking 170, 1947 Pasicrisie belge 216; Court of Cassation 19 December 1991, No. 215, 1992 Pasicrisie belge 316, 1991–1992 Arresten van het Hof van Cassatie 364.
171. Court of Cassation 27 May 1852, 1852 Pasicrisie 370.
172. Court of Cassation 5 November 1920, 1920 Pasicrisie belge 193.
173. *See* e.g., the *Flandria*-decision; *see also* Court of Cassation 7 March 1963, 1963 Pasicrisie belge 744.
174. Court of Cassation 26 April 1963, 1963 Pasicrisie belge 905, 1963–1964 RECHTSKUNDIG WEEKBLAD 287, a case about mandatory vaccination.
175. Court of Cassation 23 April 1971, 1971 Arresten van het Hof van Cassatie 786, 1971 Pasicrisie belge 752.

Executive behaviour is wrongful if it violates a specific legal rule of conduct or if it constitutes negligence, using a reasonable executive placed in the same circumstances as the standard.[176] In judging whether governmental behaviour is negligent, the courts respect the constitutional margin of discretion of the executive, which leads commentators to call the review of executive action by the courts to be 'marginal', only sanctioning 'obviously' unreasonable executive behaviour.[177] It was in cases involving the executive that the Court of Cassation formulated the principle that the violation of a legal rule *ipso facto* constitutes a wrong.[178] In recent years, however, the Court has used some reasoning which has created doubt whether there might be a slight diversion from this general principle when the government is concerned. In the first of these decisions, the Court seems to recognise that the executive enjoys some margin of leeway in applying statutes, so that a later finding by a court that the executive did not take the legally required decision does not *ipso facto* mean this decision is wrongful.[179] In the second, most recent decision, the Court has ruled that in deciding whether the violation of a specific statutory rule for which the legislature has not provided a sanction constitutes a wrong, the court has to take the purpose of the violated rule into account.[180] It is not clear whether these decisions are signs of a new development or mere accidental deviations from the rule the traditional doctrine has read into the Court's case law.

While the Court of Cassation seems to be looking for ways to restrict the liability of the government for violations of statutory or constitutional rules by the executive, the legislature has recently done the opposite. As part of the reorganisation of the administrative proceedings before the Council of State, the legislature has now given the Council jurisdiction over claims for compensation.[181] If the Council has found a decision or regulation of the executive to be illegal, the person who has asked the Council to nullify it has the choice between bringing a claim in civil liability before the civil court, invoking the illegality as the fault, and asking for compensation in the proceedings before the Council. Remarkable features of this new basis for compensation are that: (1) no wrong has to be invoked, as the established illegality itself is sufficient; and (2) the Council is not bound to award full compensation but can determine the amount awarded taking into account all circumstances of private and public interest.[182]

176. *See* e.g. Court of Cassation 7 March 1963, 1963 Pasicrisie belge 744.
177. Court of Cassation 4 March 2004 (C.03.0346.N - C.03.0448.N - C.03.0449.N), No. 124, 2004 Arresten van het Hof van Cassatie 392, 2004 Pasicrisie belge 374; Court of Cassation 27 October 2006 (C.03.0584.N), No. 518, 2006 Arresten van het Hof van Cassatie 2132, 2006 Pasicrisie belge 270.
178. Court of Cassation 19 December 1980, 1980–1981 Arresten van het Hof van Cassatie 449 No. 241, 1981 Pasicrisie belge 453; Court of Cassation 13 May 1982, 1982 Pasicrisie belge 1056, 1981–1982 Arresten van het Hof van Cassatie 1134 No. 547. *See supra* §11.03 [A] [1] [a] [ii].
179. Court of Cassation 25 October 2004 (S.03.0072.F), No. 507, 2004 Pasicrisie belge 1667, 2004 Arresten van het Hof van Cassatie 1688.
180. Court of Cassation 10 April 2014 (C.11.0796.N), No. 282, 2014 Arresten van het Hof van Cassatie 962, 2014 Pasicrisie belge 949.
181. Article 6 Federal Act of 6 January 2014 on the Sixth Reform of the State in matters under Article 77 of the Constitution. *See supra* Chapter 4, §4.04.
182. Article 11*bis* Federal Act on the Council of State.

[b] Damage Caused in the Performance of the Judicial Function

Near the end of the twentieth century, the Court of Cassation has recognised that there are no objections to the State being liable for damage caused by faults committed by the judiciary.[183] To avoid such liability claims to render nugatory the procedural system of appeals against court decisions, a limitation was introduced: a liability claim against the State is only admissible if the disputed court decision has been reversed by an appellate court.[184]

The Court has clarified that the fact that a higher court has reversed a decision of a lower court because in its opinion the lower court erred in law does not mean this lower court committed a wrong. The legal rule a court has to interpret and apply to the case can be a specific behavioural legal rule from the perspective of the parties to the dispute, but it is not such a rule for the court.[185]

If no appeal is possible because the alleged wrong was committed by a supreme court, the Constitutional Court has ruled that liability has to be possible if the court has committed a 'sufficiently qualified breach', transplanting a concept from EU state liability law for violations of EU law.[186] This is remarkable, as the Court of Cassation has specifically ruled that limiting wrongs to such qualified breaches violates Article 1382 of the Civil Code.[187]

[c] Damage Caused by the Legislative Branch

More recently the Court of Cassation has allowed courts to find the State liable for damage caused by wrongs committed by Parliament, the legislative branch of government,[188] even if the allegedly wrongful act was part of the legislative function of the government.[189] The Court has decided, however, that a ruling by the Constitutional Court holding a statute unconstitutional and thus establishing the violation of a rule of

183. Court of Cassation 19 December 1991, No. 215, 1992 Pasicrisie belge 316, 1991–1992 Arresten van het Hof van Cassatie 364; Court of Cassation 8 December 1994 (C.93.0303.F), No. 541, 1994 Arresten van het Hof van Cassatie 1074, 1994 Pasicrisie belge 1063.
184. This requirement is fulfilled if no appeal is possible just because the victim lacks procedural interest (Court of Cassation 5 June 2008 (C.06.0366.N), No. 347, 2008 Arresten van het Hof van Cassatie 1442, 2008 Pasicrisie belge 1411), and if the decision has been ruled to be in violation of the ECHR by the European Court of Human Rights (Court of Cassation 25 March 2010 (C.09.0403.N), No. 219, 2010 Pasicrisie belge 1007, 2010 Arresten van het Hof van Cassatie 920).
185. Court of Cassation 26 June 1998 (C.97.0236.F), No. 343, 1998 Arresten van het Hof van Cassatie 762, 1998 Pasicrisie belge 812.
186. Constitutional Court No. 99/2014 of 30 June 2014.
187. Court of Cassation 14 January 2000 (C.98.0477.F), No. 33, 2000 Pasicrisie belge 102, 2000 Arresten van het Hof van Cassatie 104.
188. Court of Cassation 1 June 2006 (C.05.0494.N), No. 306, 2006 Arresten van het Hof van Cassatie 1267, 2006 Pasicrisie belge 1274, involving libel allegedly committed in a Parliamentary report on religious sects.
189. Court of Cassation 28 September 2006 (C.02.0570.F), No. 445, 2006 Pasicrisie belge 1870, 2006 Arresten van het Hof van Cassatie 1848. Before this decision, the ruling precedent was Court of Cassation 27 June 1845, 1845 Pasicrisie belge 392, which held Articles 1382 et seq. Civil Code not applicable to statutes.

law does not imply that the legislature has acted wrongfully. The civil court deciding on liability will have to determine for itself whether the legislature's act constitutes a wrong.[190]

[2] Equal Sharing of Public Burdens

The courts have been willing to apply the rules of nuisance in cases where neighbouring citizens suffer excessive hindrance from activities on public premises. However, instead of judging whether the normal balance between the enjoyment by the respective parties of their property rights on the neighbouring premises has been disturbed - the criterion in nuisance cases between private parties - the courts verify whether the hindrance suffered by this particular neighbour significantly exceeds the amount of hindrance a citizen in general can be expected to accept from activities in the public interest.[191]

This case law is not so much based on the idea underlying the private tort of nuisance, but forms an application of a general principle that all citizens should equally (or better: proportionally, without discrimination) share the burdens of living in society. Recently, the Court of Cassation has ruled that the government is liable to compensate a citizen for the disproportional burden it suffers from an in itself not wrongful act of government, as the burden of such acts in the general interest has to be spread equally over society.[192] This general principle of equal sharing of public burdens has also been recognised as a constitutional principle by the Constitutional Court.[193]

[E] Immunity from Liability

[1] Employees

Employees enjoy social protection under the Employment Contracts Act of 3 July 1978.[194] This Act limits the personal liability of employees to harm caused by their intentional fault,[195] gross fault or for this employee customary - i.e., regularly

190. Court of Cassation 10 September 2010 (F.09.0042.N), No. 508, 2010 Arresten van het Hof van Cassatie 2135, 2010 Pasicrisie belge 2228. This decision seems to be at odds with the reasoning in an earlier decision, holding that a finding by the Council of State of a violation of a statutory or constitutional rule by the executive *ipso facto* established the wrongfulness of the behaviour. *See* Court of Cassation 13 May 1982, 1982 Pasicrisie belge 1056, 1981-1982 Arresten van het Hof van Cassatie 1134 No. 547.
191. Court of Cassation 28 January 1991, No. 281, 1991 Pasicrisie belge 509, 1990-1991 Arresten van het Hof van Cassatie 572; Court of Cassation 4 December 2008 (C.04.0582.F), No. 696, 2008 Pasicrisie belge 2753, 2008 Arresten van het Hof van Cassatie 2831.
192. Court of Cassation 24 June 2010 (C.06.0415.N), No. 453, 2010 Arresten van het Hof van Cassatie 1903, 2010 Pasicrisie belge 2004.
193. Constitutional Court No. 55/2012 of 19 April 2012; Constitutional Court No. 132/2015 of 1 October 2015.
194. *See infra* Chapter 14, §14.02 [B].
195. An intentional fault requires the person to have wanted to cause harm. *See* Court of Cassation 11 March 2014 (P.12.0946.N), No. 193, 2014 Arresten van het Hof van Cassatie 723, 2014 Pasicrisie belge 673.

reoccurring – light fault.[196] This immunity applies to extra-contractual liability for damage caused to third parties and to contractual liability for harm caused to the employer. Thus, the employer who has compensated the victim,[197] cannot have recourse by withholding the same amount on the employee's salary. This also means that a teacher who is an employee can escape his vicarious liability[198] by showing that he did not commit any intentional fault, gross fault or regularly reoccurring light fault.[199] Analogously, an employee will not be liable on the basis of a strict liability when he in the performance of his job is the custodian of a defective object[200] or uses an animal.[201]

[2] Civil Servants

Originally no such immunity existed for civil servants, who do not have an employment contract and therefore do not enjoy the protection of the Employment Contracts Act of 3 July 1978. However, the Court of Arbitration (now the Constitutional Court[202]) has ruled that such different treatment of employees and civil servants and such different treatment of victims of damage caused by employees or civil servants violates the principle of non-discrimination.[203] To remedy this inequality, substantially similar immunities were inserted in the statutes organising the status of several types of public servants. In 2003, a federal statute introduced a general immunity regime identical to the one for employees for subordinated members of personnel of public sector entities.[204]

[3] Volunteers

Since 2005, a comparable immunity regime exists for volunteers working for certain organisations,[205] with the difference that contrary to the regime for employees this

196. Article 18 Employment Contracts Act of 3 July 1978. This immunity has been judged to be consistent with the equality principle: Court of Arbitration No. 20/99 of 17 February 1999.
197. Often, the employer will as a master be vicariously liable for the damage his employees cause to third parties (*see supra* §11.03 [B] [2] [a] [i]), and as a contract party of his customers he will be contractually liable for the harm caused by a bad performance of his contract.
198. Article 1384, para. 3, Civil Code. *See supra* §11.03 [A] [2] [c].
199. Court of Cassation 25 January 1993, No. 47, 1993 Pasicrisie belge 91, 1993 Arresten van het Hof van Cassatie 98.
200. Article 1384, para. 1, Civil Code; *see supra* §11.03 [B] [2] [b] [i].
201. Article 1385 Civil Code; *see supra* §11.03 [B] [2] [b] [iv].
202. *See supra* Chapter 3, §3.12 and Chapter 5, §5.02 [E].
203. Court of Arbitration No. 77/96 of 18 December 1996 (a case about the possibility for the employer to recover damages paid to the victim from the member of personnel), and Court of Arbitration No. 19/2000 of 17 February 1999 (a case about the possibility of the victim to claim damages from the member of personnel).
204. Act of 10 February 2003 on the Liability of and for Members of Personnel of Entities in the Public Sector.
205. Article 5 Federal Act of 3 July 2005 on the Rights of Volunteers.

immunity is also applicable to volunteers performing leading functions within the organisation.[206]

§11.04 CAUSATION

Liability only attaches if the fact for which the defendant is responsible is the cause (*cause - oorzaak*) of the damage.[207]

[A] The Traditional Theory: Equivalence of Conditions

According to generally accepted theory, Belgian law adheres to the doctrine of equivalence of conditions (*théorie d'équivalence des conditions - equivalentieleer*). Under this theory, the court not only is allowed[208] and required[209] to deny causality if it establishes that the invoked fact was not necessary for the harm to occur, it also is allowed[210] and even required[211] to find causality if it has established the invoked fact to have been necessary (*conditio sine qua non*) in the given circumstances for the damage to occur. Causation (*relation causale - oorzakelijk* or *causaal verband*) cannot be denied just because the harm could also have occurred without the invoked fact but in circumstances not present in this particular case.[212] A fact that *in concreto* was necessary for the harm to occur, is a cause even if a later intervening fact was also necessary.[213] Also, a fact that was a necessary condition for the damage to occur the way it did, is a cause even if this damage was not a necessary consequence,[214] this

206. Article 3, 1° & 2°, Federal Act of 3 July 2005 on the Rights of Volunteers.
207. Court of Cassation 14 December 2006 (C.04.0582.F), No. 650, 2006 Pasicrisie belge 2667, 2006 Arresten van het Hof van Cassatie 2605; Court of Cassation 22 April 2004 (C.01.0484.N), 2004–2005 Rechtskundig Weekblad 827.
208. Court of Cassation 7 March 2013 (C.10.0741.F), No. 153, 2013 Pasicrisie belge 565, 2013 Arresten van het Hof van Cassatie 598; Court of Cassation 11 May 1956, 1956 Arresten van het Hof van Verbreking 757, 1956 Pasicrisie belge 962.
209. Court of Cassation 5 June 2008 (C.07.0199.N), No. 350, 2008 Arresten van het Hof van Cassatie 1462, 2008 Pasicrisie belge 1425; Court of Cassation 28 May 1951, 1951 Pasicrisie belge 645, 1951 Arresten van het Hof van Verbreking 554.
210. Court of Cassation 17 December 2009, C.08.0145.N, No. 757, 2009 Arresten van het Hof van Cassatie 3056, 2009 Pasicrisie belge 3045; Court of Cassation 4 December 1950, 1951 Pasicrisie belge 201, 1951 Arresten van het Hof van Verbreking 158.
211. Court of Cassation 6 June 2011 (C.10.0095.F), No. 377, 2011 Pasicrisie belge 1599, 2011 Arresten van het Hof van Cassatie 1478; Court of Cassation 11 June 1956, 1956 Pasicrisie belge 1096.
212. Court of Cassation 24 March 2005 (C.04.0016.F), No. 185, 2005 Pasicrisie belge 703, 2005 Arresten van het Hof van Cassatie 703; Court of Cassation 11 June 1956, 1956 Pasicrisie belge 1094.
213. Court of Cassation 5 March 1953, 1953 Arresten van het Hof van Verbreking 457, 1953 Pasicrisie belge 516; Court of Cassation 28 May 1991, No. 497, 1990–1991 Arresten van het Hof van Cassatie 959, 1991 Pasicrisie belge 843.
214. *See* e.g. Court of Cassation 19 December 1979, 1980 Pasicrisie belge 487, 1979–1980 Arresten van het Hof van Cassatie 488 No. 252; *see* already Court of Cassation 22 December 1947, 1947 Pasicrisie belge 555, 1947 Arresten van het Hof van Verbreking 425.

harm is not the normal consequence,[215] or this harm was not a foreseeable consequence of this fact.[216]

To apply this doctrine, the court has to verify whether the occurrence of the harm can be explained by applying the generally known patterns of events to all the other circumstances in the case apart from the invoked fact. If so, those other circumstances apparently are a sufficient condition for the damage and thus its cause, allowing the court to exclude the element left out in the thought experiment as a cause. Sometimes, applying the generally known patterns to the other facts of the case leaves several outcomes possible, some involving the occurrence of the harm while others not. While in some cases the courts will then decide that there is insufficient certainty to establish causality and therefore refuse to impose liability,[217] in others they find a way around this problem by considering the chance the victim had to avoid the harm as an interest which was lost because of the invoked fact.[218]

[B] The Legal Reality: Not Equivalence of Conditions?

The doctrine of equivalence of conditions necessarily leads to inacceptable decisions. Therefore, Belgian courts do not apply the theory rigorously in cases of remote facts.

For instance, a passenger who knowingly takes a ride with an intoxicated driver or a person that is not allowed to drive or not to have a passenger and is subsequently hurt in an accident, will still be able to recover full compensation from the third party liable for the accident if it was not caused by the state of intoxication of the driver or the reason why he was not allowed to drive or move a passenger.[219] In another category of cases, the harm results from a wrongful failure by a person to avoid a visible irregular circumstance caused by a previous accident or fact.[220] Thus, a careless driver who hits the back of a cue which was caused by an earlier accident, will not be allowed to recover from the person liable for the initial accident which resulted in the jam.[221] Also, if a necessary condition is too remote, the courts tend to neglect it.[222] A typical example

215. *See* e.g. Court of Cassation 23 September 2011 (C.10.0744.F), No. 496, 2011 Pasicrisie belge 2034, 2011 Arresten van het Hof van Cassatie 1909.
216. *See* e.g. Court of Cassation 15 November 2006 (P.06.0308.F), No. 561, 2006 Pasicrisie belge 2336, 2006 Arresten van het Hof van Cassatie 2302.
217. *See* e.g. Court of Cassation 23 September 1974, 1975 Arresten van het Hof van Cassatie 97, 1975 Pasicrisie belge 87; recent: Court of Cassation 29 October 2014 (P.14.0820.F), No. 644, 2014 Pasicrisie belge 2364, 2014 Arresten van het Hof van Cassatie 2374.
218. *See supra* §11.02 [A] [2].
219. Court of Cassation 10 June 2003 (P.02.1358.N), No. 341, 2003 Arresten van het Hof van Cassatie 1355, 2003 Pasicrisie belge 1143; Court of Cassation 16 September 1986, No. 24, 1986–1987 Arresten van het Hof van Cassatie 56, 1987 Pasicrisie belge 53.
220. Court of Cassation 12 October 2001 (C.00.9487.N), 2002 Droit de la circulation – Verkeersrech 414; Court of Cassation 5 November 1996 (P.95.0122.N), No. 413, 1996 Arresten van het Hof van Cassatie 993, 1996 Pasicrisie belge 1066; Court of Cassation 5 November 1996 (P.95.1329.N), No. 414, 1996 Arresten van het Hof van Cassatie 997, 1996 Pasicrisie belge 1070.
221. Court of Cassation 17 June 2003 (P.03.0188.N), not published.
222. *See* e.g. Court of Cassation 23 January 2013 (P.12.0089.F), No. 50, 2013 Pasicrisie belge 164, 2013 Arresten van het Hof van Cassatie 188, a case involving a driver who had committed a hit-and-run after a first accident and was then involved in a second accident.

is the court finding that a car driving too fast was not a cause of the accident when the accident according to the court would also have happened if that car had been driving slower,[223] ignoring that this car would not have reached that position if it had been driving slower.

A large category of cases where the courts systematically take decisions that do not conform to the doctrine of equivalence of conditions, involve wrongful behaviour of the victim that did not cause the accident that resulted in the harm (contributory negligence)[224] but that did cause this damage after it first occurred to increase, the typical example being the passenger not wearing a seat belt or the motorcycle rider not wearing a helmet. A similar set of cases relate to a victim not making reasonable efforts to reduce or limit the damage caused by an event for which a third party is liable.[225] Courts decide in such cases that the victim cannot recover any of this extra harm.

One could therefore conclude that, even though the quasi unanimous Belgian scholarly community keeps repeating the theory that causality is governed by the equivalence of conditions, this might be more a myth than a reality, and that Belgian positive law is not well described by the simple rule of the *conditio sine qua non*.

[C] Plurality of Liable Parties

If the harm can be divided into separate injuries caused by different persons, each of them is liable for the specific injury he has caused. The causality requirement applied in Belgian law, however, also allows for several facts attributable to different persons to be the cause of a single indivisible loss. In that case, the victim is entitled to sue any or all of them for the full amount of his damage, and each is said to be *in solidum* liable for the whole damage.[226]

If one of the liable parties compensated the victim, he can seek 'contribution' from the others.[227] The fraction of the damage each liable party has to bear has to be measured based on the relative role the fact for which it is liable played in causing the harm.[228]

---

223. Court of Cassation 23 February 2000 (P.99.1574.F), No. 140, 2000 Pasicrisie belge 469, 2000 Arresten van het Hof van Cassatie 474; Court of Cassation 3 October 1984, No. 87, 1984–1985 Arresten van het Hof van Cassatie 194, 1985 Pasicrisie belge 167.
224. *See infra* §11.04 [C].
225. A victim does not have to reduce or limit the damage to the extent possible, but if the damage is or remains larger because of his unreasonable behaviour, there is 'shared liability', which means the liability of the third party is reduced. Court of Cassation 14 May 1992, No. 478, 1991–1992 Arresten van het Hof van Cassatie 855, 1992 Pasicrisie belge 798.
226. Court of Cassation 13 February 1970, 1970 Arresten van het Hof van Cassatie 545, 1970 Pasicrisie belge 511; recent: Court of Cassation 16 February 2011 (P.10.1232.F), No. 137, 2011 Pasicrisie belge 529, 2011 Arresten van het Hof van Cassatie 524.
227. Court of Cassation 19 February 1999 (C.94.0246.N), No. 97, 1999 Arresten van het Hof van Cassatie 225, 1999 Pasicrisie belge 232; Court of Cassation 18 January 2007 (C.05.0529.F), No. 27, 2007 Pasicrisie belge 93, 2007 Arresten van het Hof van Cassatie 97.
228. Court of Cassation 4 February 2008 (C.06.0236.F), No. 81, 2008 Pasicrisie belge 329, 2008 Arresten van het Hof van Cassatie 315; Court of Cassation 21 October 2008 (P.08.0561.N), No. 567, 2008 Arresten van het Hof van Cassatie 2322, 2008 Pasicrisie belge 2319; Court of Cassation 2 October 2009 (C.08.0168.F), No. 548, 2009 Pasicrisie belge 2110, 2009 Arresten van

If the victim is also responsible for the harm causing event, such as in case of contributory negligence, 'shared liability' applies,[229] reducing the liability of third parties to the extent the victim has contributed to causing the event.[230] This principle is also applied to next of kin claiming compensation for damage suffered by repercussion.[231]

If a person intentionally inflicts harm to the victim – for instance to obtain an advantage by illegally taking something from the victim – in circumstances in which this could only succeed because of the unintentional fault of the victim, applying the principle *fraus omnia corrumpit* results in the bad faith wrongdoer having to fully compensate the good faith victim that has been taken advantage of.[232] However, if the harm is caused by a combination of intentional and unintentional faults of third parties, they are both *in solidum* liable towards the victim and in dividing the contribution among the third parties, the court can only take the relative causal contribution into account, not the intentional character of one of the faults.[233]

§11.05 OBLIGATION RESULTING FROM LIABILITY: RESTORATION OR COMPENSATION

Liability creates a right to 'reparation' (*réparation du dommage – schadeloosstelling*). The primary obligation is to restore in kind (*in natura*).[234] Only in cases of constructive total loss (*perte totale constructive*), where physical repair is impossible, in cases where actual restoration is conceptually not possible, such as for harm already suffered and moral damage, and in cases where invoking this right to restoration amounts to an abuse of right,[235] as in case of economic total loss (*perte totale économique*) when the

het Hof van Cassatie 2190; Court of Cassation 3 May 2013 (C.12.0378.N), No. 278, 2013 Arresten van het Hof van Cassatie 1099, 2013 Pasicrisie belge 1053.

229. Court of Cassation 9 February 1982, 1981–1982 Arresten van het Hof van Cassatie 741 No. 346, 1982 Pasicrisie belge 716; Court of Cassation 8 September 1999 (P.99.0472.F), No. 443, 1999 Pasicrisie belge 1096, 1999 Arresten van het Hof van Cassatie 1056.

230. Court of Cassation 9 October 2009 (C.07.0080.F), No. 567, 2009 Pasicrisie belge 2195, 2009 Arresten van het Hof van Cassatie 2266; Court of Cassation 9 September 2015 (P.15.0653.F), to be published in reporters.

231. Court of Cassation 19 December 1962, 1963 Pasicrisie belge 491; Court of Cassation 23 January 2012 (C.09.0228.F), No. 62, 2012 Pasicrisie belge 180, 2012 Arresten van het Hof van Cassatie 202. This was approved by Constitutional Court No. 111/2014 of 17 July 2014.

232. Court of Cassation 6 November 2002 (P.01.1108.F), No. 584, 2002 Pasicrisie belge 2103, 2002 Arresten van het Hof van Cassatie 2383. On this basis, the master, who is vicariously liable for damage caused by an intentional fault of his servant, cannot invoke the unintentional fault of the victim to claim 'shared liability': Court of Cassation 30 September 2015 (P.14.0474.F), 2015 Journal des Tribunaux 844, 2016 Revue Générale des Assurances et des Responsabilités 15,287.

233. Court of Cassation 2 October 2009 (C.08.0168.F), No. 548, 2009 Pasicrisie belge 2110, 2009 Arresten van het Hof van Cassatie 2190. The same rule is applied when one of the liable parties is held on the basis of vicarious liability for a person that has committed the *fraus*: Court of Cassation 16 May 2011 (C.10.0214.N), No. 319, 2011 Arresten van het Hof van Cassatie 1227, 2011 Pasicrisie belge 1337.

234. Court of Cassation 26 June 1980, 1980 Pasicrisie belge 1341, 1979–1980 Arresten van het Hof van Cassatie 1365 No. 686.

235. *See supra* §11.03 [A] [1] [a] [iv].

cost of reparation is higher than the value of object,[236] the obligation to restore in kind is replaced by an obligation to compensate the victim by paying damages (*dommages-intérêts - schadevergoeding*).[237] In reality, however, awarding damages is the standard consequence of civil liability, and only rarely can a case imposing restoration in kind be found. Restoration in kind can also be awarded against the government, but the administrative principle of continuity of the public services can preclude the courts from allowing the victim to take the necessary measures itself.[238]

The basic rule is that the awarded damages have to constitute 'integral' reparation of the harm as it occurred. This means that the compensation cannot be smaller than the value of the actual harm, unless the victim has claimed less. In measuring the damage, the circumstances of the case, even characteristics specific to the victim, have to be taken into account.[239]

The damages awarded can also not be larger than the actual harm. Belgian law does not know exemplary or punitive damages. Based on the principle of integral restoration, the Court of Cassation has ruled that a lump sum extra compensation over harm actually suffered by an infringement of an intellectual property right, which consists of the amount of the missed royalties, cannot be based on civil liability.[240] Liability should not result in an enrichment of the victim. This also means that courts also have to look at what the victim may have gained because of the event.[241] Benefits received from third parties that intend to compensate for the damage, such as first party insurance pay-outs or health insurance benefits, have to be subtracted from the victim's loss. The third party that has paid will be subrogated in the rights of the victim, and can thus reclaim from the liable party. If the benefit is not compensation for the damage, such as life insurance pay-outs, it cannot be subtracted.[242] The courts also cannot take into account an increase or decrease of the loss caused by subsequent events that are not related to the fact that originally caused the harm or to the original harm itself.[243]

236. Court of Cassation 23 October 1986, No. 118, 1987 Pasicrisie belge 249, 1986–1987 Arresten van het Hof van Cassatie 266.
237. Court of Cassation 5 May 2011 (C.10.0496.F), No. 299, 2011 Arresten van het Hof van Cassatie 1157, 2011 Pasicrisie belge 1272.
238. Court of Cassation 24 April 1998 (C.97.0252.F - C.97.0253.F), No. 210, 1998 Pasicrisie belge 488, 1998 Arresten van het Hof van Cassatie 462, narrowing the principle invoked in Court of Cassation 26 June 1980, 1980 Pasicrisie belge 1341, 1979–1980 Arresten van het Hof van Cassatie 1365 No. 686.
239. Court of Cassation 13 October 1999 (P.99.0861.F), No. 528, 1999 Pasicrisie belge 1308, 1999 Arresten van het Hof van Cassatie 1255; Court of Cassation 13 April 1995 (C.94.0126.F), No. 201, 1995 Pasicrisie belge 423, 1995 Arresten van het Hof van Cassatie 409.
240. Court of Cassation 13 May 2009 (P.09.0121.F), No. 314, 2009 Pasicrisie belge 1167, 2009 Arresten van het Hof van Cassatie 1254.
241. Court of Cassation 5 March 2015 (C.14.0017.F), No. 162, 2015 Pasicrisie belge 578, 2015 Arresten van het Hof van Cassatie 595; Court of Cassation 1 February 2013 (C.12.0205.N), No. 78, 2013 Arresten van het Hof van Cassatie 317, 2013 Pasicrisie belge 300.
242. Court of Cassation 7 September 2004, (P.04.0315.N), No. 386, 2004 Arresten van het Hof van Cassatie 1320, 2004 Pasicrisie belge 1261; Court of Cassation 15 February 2011 (P.10.1244.N), No. 133, 2011 Arresten van het Hof van Cassatie 506, 2011 Pasicrisie belge 517.
243. Court of Cassation 2 May 2001 (P.00.1703.F), No. 247, 2001 Pasicrisie belge 749, 2001 Arresten van het Hof van Cassatie 778.

If there is no evidence showing the exact value of the harm, the court awards a lump sum, estimating the damages *ex aequo et bono*.[244] This will be so for injuries to interests for which no price exists, such as moral damage[245] and personal injuries. An organisation of judges regularly publishes an 'indicative table', providing non-binding guidelines to estimate damages.[246] The Court of Cassation has ruled that, as the burden of proof rests on the claimant, courts can apply these guidelines if the victim has not provided evidence that its harm differs from the injury normally occurring in similar cases.[247] Compared to other jurisdictions, awards by Belgian courts are low, but they are granted in many instances.

For some specific liabilities, statutory provisions deviate from the general principle of integral restoration, and limit the amount of damages that can be awarded[248] or restrict the obligation to compensate the victim to specific types of damage.[249]

The victim is free to use the damages he receives as he pleases. If he does not want to use the sum awarded to actually repair the property damage, he is free to do so. What the victim uses the money for, in no way influences the amount the court can award.[250]

If the wrongful act on which liability is based consists in an infringement of the victim's right, it can also obtain a court order to force the wrongdoer to undue the infringement or to take the necessary measures to stop the infringement.[251]

244. Court of Cassation 3 March 2008 (C.07.0090.F), No. 149, 2008 Pasicrisie belge 597, 2008 Arresten van het Hof van Cassatie 623; Court of Cassation 2 March 2016 (P.15.0929.F), not yet published in reporters.
245. Moral damages compensate for pain and suffering and are a form of restoration, not private punishment. Court of Cassation 10 October 1972, 1973 Arresten van het Hof van Cassatie 146, 1973 Pasicrisie belge 147; Court of Cassation 13 October 1999 (P.99.0861.F), No. 528, 1999 Pasicrisie belge 1308, 1999 Arresten van het Hof van Cassatie 1255.
246. The most recent version is of 2012, published in the newsletter of the Flemish Bar Association, 8/1 ORDEEXPRESS (10 January 2013), taken from INDICATIEVE TABEL 2012 (J.-L. Desmecht, Th. Papart & W. Peeters eds., Bruges: die Keure 2012). A new version is expected to be published by the end of 2016.
247. Court of Cassation 11 September 2009 (C.08.0031.F), No. 490, 2009 Pasicrisie belge 1847, 2009 Arresten van het Hof van Cassatie 1995.
248. As was mentioned, the liability of a mentally ill person based on Article 1386*bis* Civil Code can be limited or extended, based on the financial situation of this person and the victim. Another example is the Act of 30 July 1979 on the Prevention of and Liability for Fire and Explosions, which limits this strict risk liability to amounts which at present equal approximately EUR 24 million for bodily harm and EUR 1.2 million for property damage. *See supra* footnote 159 and accompanying text.
249. Strict product liability is limited to personal injuries and damage to property that is intended for private use or consumption and that was used by the injured person mainly for his own private use or consumption. Article 11 Product Liability Act of 25 February 1991.
250. Court of Cassation 13 April 1988, No. 489, 1988 Pasicrisie belge 936, 1987–1988 Arresten van het Hof van Cassatie 1016; Court of Cassation 15 February 2010 (C.09.0028.N), No. 101, 2010 Arresten van het Hof van Cassatie 431, 2010 Pasicrisie belge 455.
251. *See* e.g. Court of Cassation 29 June 2000 (C.98.0530.F), No. 420, 2000 Pasicrisie belge 1222, 2000 Arresten van het Hof van Cassatie 1245; Court of Cassation 26 June 1980, 1980 Pasicrisie belge 1341, 1979–1980 Arresten van het Hof van Cassatie 1365 No. 686.

§11.06 TORT AND CONTRACT

Whether extra-contractual liability can exist between parties to a contract (*concours des responsabilités – samenloop van aansprakelijkheid*), is a hotly debated issue in Belgium. This question is very relevant in Belgian law because of its broad concept of damage,[252] resulting in almost any contractual damage also qualifying as recoverable harm in tort. In many cases, the victim has an interest in basing his claim in tort, as that allows him to invoke certain strict liabilities not necessarily available in contract, or this makes it possible to escape a particularly short period of limitation for a contractual claim or – and this is most often the real issue – to avoid the claim being barred by an exoneration clause in the contract.

From the thirties to the early seventies of the last century, the general rule was that extra-contractual liability was not excluded just because the harm was caused at the occasion of a contract between the victim and the wrongdoer.[253] In the nowadays seldom cited *EBES*-decision of 4 June 1971,[254] the Court of Cassation stated that an extra-contractual claim is not possible, however, if the right of which the infringement serves as the basis for the claim only exists because of the contract, and the harm is only a result of the breach of this contract.[255] Then, on 7 December 1973, the Court issued its often cited *stevedore*-decision, which used phraseological units that are open to two distinct interpretations. On the facts, the owner of goods that were damaged during transport was denied an extra-contractual claim against the stevedore, who had been contracted by the carrier to load the ship and who had wrongfully caused the damage.

The specific wording of the ruling was on the one hand interpreted to express a rule that extra-contractual liability between contract parties is only available if both the fact invoked as the basis for liability and the damage for which compensation is claimed are unrelated to the content of the contract.[256] This interpretation is referred to as the 'disappearance theory', as these conditions will only be present in cases where no contractual liability arises, and therefore the concurrence of both types of liabilities is ontologically impossible.

However, according to another feasible reading of the decision, extra-contractual liability between contract parties is available if the fact invoked as the basis for liability is not merely a breach of contract but also a fact recognised as a basis for extra-contractual liability, and if the damage for which compensation is claimed does not merely consist in the loss of the advantage expected from the performance of the

252. *See supra* §11.02 [A].
253. Court of Cassation 13 February 1930, 1930 Pasicrisie belge 115.
254. Court of Cassation 4 June 1971, 1971 Arresten van het Hof van Cassatie 989, 1971 Pasicrisie belge 940.
255. The claim was about damage consisting in not receiving the supply of electricity and harm caused by the interruption of this supply, the archetypical pure economic loss case.
256. This interpretation seemed to be confirmed in Court of Cassation 3 December 1975, 1976 Pasicrisie belge 412, 1976 Arresten van het Hof van Cassatie 417.

contract or in harm caused by the loss of this contractual advantage. This interpretation is referred to as the 'refining theory', as these conditions specify how the older rulings of 1930 and 1971 can be explained by one principle, allowing contractual and extra-contractual liability to concur in certain circumstances.

In 2006, the Court issued a new ruling on the issue.[257] Now, the Court explicitly stated that extra-contractual liability between contract parties can exist if the fact invoked as the basis for liability is *not merely* a breach of contract *but also* a fact recognised as a basis for extra-contractual liability. Hence, this decision could be regarded as choosing sides with the refining theory. However, hope that this decision would have ended the debate turned out to be futile, as the Court added that extra-contractual liability can only be invoked for damage that is 'not the consequence of the bad performance of the contract'. The proponents of the refinement theory argue that this condition merely requires that the damage does not consist of the loss of the advantage expected from the performance of the contract or consequential damage. They read the wording as referring to a type of damage.[258] The proponents of the disappearance theory, however, interpret this wording as referring to a causal requirement: extra-contractual claims are only possible for harm which is not caused by a fact that constitutes a breach of contract, a type of wrong, and thus concurrence remains impossible.

The Court of Cassation has recognised one exception to its rule, but here also debate is possible about its exact meaning. In its original decision on the issue, the Court stated that harm the causation of which constitutes a criminal offence cannot be regarded as mere contractual damage for the sole reason that it was caused by a breach of a contractual duty.[259] This seems to be an application of the concurrence principle recognised by the refinement theory, allowing extra-contractual claims between contract parties for the compensation of harm that is not merely the loss of the advantage expected from the contract. However, the proponents of the disappearance theory read this as a separate exception to their general rule and state that extra-contractual liability can be claimed in any case where the fault invoked as its basis is a criminal offence, irrespective of the type of damage this offence has caused and whether the causation of this type of harm is a constituent element of the offence or not. This also seems to be the interpretation that can be found in a recent decision of the Court.[260]

---

257. Court of Cassation 29 September 2006 (C.03.0502.N), No. 447, 2006 Arresten van het Hof van Cassatie 1863, 2006 Pasicrisie belge 1911.
258. This reading uses the clarification offered in Court of Cassation 25 October 1990, No. 107, 1990–1991 Arresten van het Hof van Cassatie 237, 1991 Pasicrisie belge 210, on the question whether a breach of contract is a wrong resulting in liability towards third parties.
259. Court of Cassation 26 October 1990, No. 110, 1990–1991 Arresten van het Hof van Cassatie 244, 1991 Pasicrisie belge 216. At issue was the offence of unlawful wounding, Article 418 Penal Code.
260. Court of Cassation 10 June 2015 (P.15.0419.F), 2015 Revue de jurisprudence de Liège, Mons et Bruxelles 1740.

§11.07 ALTERNATIVE COMPENSATION REGIMES FOR SPECIFIC ACCIDENTS

[A] General

For some specific types of risks, separate compensation regimes have been developed. For industrial accidents, social law requires employers to contract for first party personal loss insurance for the benefit of their employees.[261] In return for complying with this statutory duty, the employer and his employees receive partial immunity from civil liability for the covered accidents.[262] For medical accidents, recently a Medical Accidents Fund was created, functioning both as a guarantee fund stepping in when for some reason the person who is liable – or his insurer – does not compensate the victim, and as a loss compensation fund for accidents for which nobody is liable, but here only the most serious cases are covered.[263]

[B] Traffic Accidents

Belgian law does not contain a strict liability regime for traffic accidents. In general, liability for traffic accidents is based on general fault liability, with the traffic code to a large extent determining what behaviour is wrongful. This regime is strengthened by a system of mandatory motor vehicle insurance, providing unlimited coverage for traffic accidents and granting the victim a direct right of compensation against the liability insurer.[264]

A Common Guarantee Fund (*Fonds Commun de Garantie Belge, FCGB – Belgisch Gemeenschappelijk Waarborgfonds, BGWF*) covers special cases, such as insolvency of an insurer but also accidents for which the person that caused it is not liable – and hence his insurer is also not bound to compensate the victim – only because of a fortuitous event (force majeure), or accidents wrongfully caused by a driver whose car – and hence its insurance status – could not be identified, the hit-and-run cases.[265] By a much disputed rule,[266] the legislature has also created a system that in an accident for which cannot be established which of the several involved vehicles caused the

261. Industrial Accidents Act of 10 April 1971. *See infra* Chapter 14, §14.03 [B] [1] [a].
262. Article 46, §1, Industrial Accidents Act of 10 April 1971.
263. Federal Act of 31 March 2010 on the Compensation of Damage as a Consequence of Medical Treatment.
264. This direct right of the victim was introduced by the Mandatory Motor Vehicle Insurance Act of 1 July 1956, kept in the Mandatory Motor Vehicle Insurance Act of 21 November 1989, and generalised for all liability insurance by Article 96 Land Insurance Contracts Act of 25 June 1992, now replaced by Article 150 Insurance Act of 4 April 2014 (*see supra* footnote 6 and accompanying text).
265. Article 19*bis*-11, §1, Mandatory Motor Vehicle Insurance Act of 21 November 1989.
266. The rule was introduced after the unequal treatment of a victim in an accident for which no liability can be established because of uncertainty over the facts compared to a victim in an accident for which the known liable party cannot be identified was held unconstitutional. Constitutional Court No. 96/2000 of 20 September 2000.

accident, the victim can obtain compensation from all insurers of the vehicles involved whose driver's liability cannot be excluded with certainty.[267]

Near the end of the twentieth century, the general liability system was complemented by a special compensation regime for damage resulting from bodily harm caused by a traffic accident involving a motor vehicle.[268] The regime grants compensation to any victim that is not a driver of a motor vehicle involved in the accident,[269] so not only to people that are participating in traffic – like pedestrians, bicycle-riders and passengers of motor vehicles – but also to people that without participating in traffic get hurt by a traffic accident. The victim has a direct claim against the liability insurer of any motor vehicle that is involved in the accident. If the vehicle is connected to rails, the compensation is owed by the owner of the vehicle.

This compensation regime is not based on fault. The insurer is obliged to pay, even though the insured person did not commit any wrong and is not liable. More even, the vehicle involved in the accident does not have to have caused the accident: it is sufficient that it played a role in the totality of the accident.[270] The victim has a right to compensation even if it has wrongfully caused the accident itself. The only exception is the case of a victim over fourteen years old intentionally causing the injury, i.e., cases of suicide or self-mutilation.[271]

After compensating the victim, the insurer can have recourse against the insurers of all other cars involved, and the total burden will be shared equally between them.[272] If the conditions for liability are present, however, the insurer, who by compensating the victim is subrogated in its rights, can have full recourse against the person who is liable for the accident or against this person's liability insurer.[273]

---

267. Article 19*bis*-11, §2, Mandatory Motor Vehicle Insurance Act of 21 November 1989.
268. Article 29*bis* Mandatory Motor Vehicle Insurance Act of 21 November 1989, inserted by the Act of 30 March 1994 and immediately amended by the Act of 13 April 1995.
269. Article 29*bis*, §1 *juncto* §2, Mandatory Motor Vehicle Insurance Act of 21 November 1989.
270. Court of Cassation 3 October 2008 (C.07.0130.N), No. 524, 2008 Arresten van het Hof van Cassatie 2138, 2008 Pasicrisie belge 2131; Court of Cassation 15 November 2012 (C.11.0523.F), No. 615, 2012 Pasicrisie belge 2229, 2012 Arresten van het Hof van Cassatie 2568. If there was contact with the vehicle, this vehicle is involved. Court of Cassation 28 April 2011 (C.10.0492.F), No. 286, 2011 Pasicrisie belge 1195, 2011 Arresten van het Hof van Cassatie 1107. However, a vehicle with which there was no contact, can also be involved.
271. In such a case, also the persons suffering harm by repercussion, cannot claim compensation under this regime. Court of Cassation 26 June 2008 (C.07.0494.N), No. 407, 2008 Arresten van het Hof van Cassatie 1709, 2008 Pasicrisie belge 1698.
272. This recourse will be based on Article 1251, 3°, Civil Code. Court of Cassation 4 October 2007, 2008 Bulletin des assurances – Tijdschrift voor Verzekeringen 150; Court of Cassation 28 September 2012 (C.11.0404.N), No. 501, 2012 Arresten van het Hof van Cassatie 2081, 2012 Pasicrisie belge 1787.
273. Article 29*bis*, §4, Mandatory Motor Vehicle Insurance Act of 21 November 1989. Court of Cassation 6 October 2005 (C.03.0377.N), No. 489, 2005 Arresten van het Hof van Cassatie 1853, 2005 Pasicrisie belge 1852; Court of Cassation 23 January 2012 (C.09.0228.F), No. 62, 2012 Pasicrisie belge 180, 2012 Arresten van het Hof van Cassatie 202.

§11.08 SELECTED BIBLIOGRAPHY

H. Bocken, I. Boone & M. Kruithof, *Inleiding tot het schadevergoedingsrecht. Buitencontractueel aansprakelijkheidsrecht en andere schadevergoedingsstelsels* (Bruges: die Keure 2014).

L. Cornelis, *Beginselen van het buitencontractueel aansprakelijkheidsrecht*, Vol. I, *De onrechtmatige daad* (Antwerp: Maarten Kluwer 1989).

L. Cornelis, *Principes de droit belge de la responsabilité extra-contractuelle, L'acte illicite* (Brussels: Bruylant 1991).

R.O. Dalcq, *Traité de la responsabilité civile, in Les Novelles, Droit Civil*, vol. V-1 & V-2 (Brussels 1962 & 1967).

D. de Callataÿ & N. Estienne, *La responsabilité civile. Chronique de jurisprudence 1996–2007*, Volume 2: *Le dommage* (Les Dossiers du Journal des tribunaux No. 75, Brussels: Larcier 2009).

B. Dubuisson, V. Callewaert, B. De Conink & G. Gathem, *La responsabilité civile. Chronique de jurisprudence 1996–2007*, Volume 1: *Le fait générateur et le lien causal* (Les Dossiers du Journal des tribunaux No. 74, Brussels: Larcier 2009).

M. Kruithof, *Belgium, in International Encyclopaedia for Tort Law* (I. Boone ed., Alphen aan den Rijn: Wolters Kluwer, loose-leaf, forthcoming).

H. Vandenberghe, *Aansprakelijkheid uit onrechtmatige daad (2000–2008). Deel 2: Foutvereiste*, 47 Tijdschrift voor Privaatrecht 1749–2145 (2010).

H. Vandenberghe, *Aansprakelijkheid uit onrechtmatige daad (2000–2008). Deel 3: Kwalitatieve aansprakelijkheid & Deel 4: Samenloop en co-existentie*, 48 Tijdschrift voor Privaatrecht 349–656 (2011).

P. Van Ommeslaghe, *Droit des obligations*, vol. II (Brussels: Bruylant 2010).

M. Vanquickenborne, *Aansprakelijkheid uit onrechtmatige daad (2000–2007). Deel 1: Oorzakelijk verband*, 47 Tijdschrift voor Privaatrecht 283–359 (2010).

T. Vansweevelt & B. Weyts, *Handboek buitencontractueel aansprakelijkheidsrecht* (Antwerp: Intersentia 2009).

Responsabilités: traité théorique et pratique (Diegem: Kluwer, loose-leaf).

CHAPTER 12

Commercial Law and Business Transactions

Eddy Wymeersch & Diederik Bruloot

§12.01 LEGAL FRAMEWORK FOR BUSINESS ACTIVITIES: AN OVERVIEW

This chapter introduces the reader into the main sources and concepts of the rules affecting Belgian business life. Although considerable progress has been made in this respect over the last few years, there is no single set of rules organising business activities in Belgium. Besides by the rules of civil law, applicable to all persons alike, and commercial law, only applicable to those entities qualified as 'commercial', business is increasingly governed by rules of what is, in a continental context, called 'economic law'. Furthermore, there are other fields of law that do play an important role for business activities. These are, however, left out of this overview, either because they are the subject of a separate chapter in this book,[1] or because they are highly specialised and only affect a limited number of businesses (like financial law, insurance law or competition law).

[A] Commercial Law

From a historical perspective, most of the rules affecting Belgian business life could be found in the Commercial Code, introduced in Belgium under the French regime in 1807. This Code imposes a dual legal regime, distinguishing between civil and commercial rules, the latter only being applicable to those entities that qualify as 'commercial'. These commercial entities or merchants (*commerçants – handelaars*)

1. *See infra* Chapter 13 on company law and Chapter 14 on tax law.

can be both individuals (natural persons) or companies (legal persons). The difference between commercial and civil entities is currently still in place, but it lost much of its practical importance (*infra*).

According to Article 1 of the Commercial Code, 'merchants' are those that engage in business that is defined as commercial. This 'business'-concept relates to different forms of economic activity, not including however activities relating to land (mines, real estate), nor to the agricultural sector, the non-profit sector and the so-called liberal professions. The last group predominantly consists of physicians, dentists, attorneys, notaries, auditors and architects. According to the recent legal definition of the concept, it concerns natural or legal persons who exercise, in an intellectual independent way and under their own responsibility, a professional activity that mainly consists of intellectual services that require special qualifications and continuous training, and for which they are supervised by a disciplinary committee established by statute.[2] Note that this division between commercial and non-commercial activities has become rather ambiguous and can only be understood against its historical background, which goes back several centuries. In any case it should be clear that currently, according to Belgian law, not all economic activity is subject to traditional commercial law.

Technically, a firm is a merchant if it engages in one of the commercial activities listed in Articles 2 and 3 of the Commercial Code. This list contains references to traditional trading (like the distribution or the production and distribution of goods and services, including transportation, banking, insurance and maritime activities), or to specific transactions (such as the establishment of a firm or the drawing of cheques or bills of exchange). All transactions, undertaken by merchants, are deemed subject to commercial law, and all claims and liabilities arising out of these transactions will be subject to the specific rules of commercial law, referred to below. As the description of the ambit of commercial law does not correspond to a systematic analysis of a theoretical concept, it is advisable to refer to the list of Article 2 of the Commercial Code to identify which transactions will be deemed commercial.

Today, 'commercial law' can be defined as the rules applicable to commercial firms, or more precise to those entities that do qualify as 'merchants' according to the Commercial Code. Originally, all rules of commercial law were codified in the Commercial Code. The original Code has, however, been substantially modified over time, and an increasing number of rules have been transferred to separate statutes, leaving the original Code behind as an almost empty shell. As a result, most rules of commercial law can be found outside the Commercial Code. The most important examples in this respect are:

- the Bankruptcy Act of 8 August 1997;
- the Continuity of Undertakings Act of 31 January 2009;[3] and
- the Cheques Act of 1 March 1961.

2. *See* Article I.8, 35°, Code of Economic Law.
3. This is the act on business reorganisations.

All rules on company law – in Belgium traditionally regarded as partially commercial law and partially civil law – were also removed from the Commercial Code and can nowadays be found in a standalone Companies Code.[4] A similar exercise has been undertaken for the rules regarding insurance law, which historically were seen as an important part of commercial law as well.[5]

[B] Economic Law

Over the last decades, an increasing number of statutes has been adopted that regulates certain aspects of business life, but for which the choice was made not to use the Commercial Code's concept of 'merchant' to define their scope of application. Instead, these statutes make use of the broader concept of an 'undertaking' (*entreprise – onderneming*), which is largely derived from European Law. According to its legal definition, an undertaking is every natural or legal person that pursues an economic goal in a sustainable way.[6] According to the interpretation by the EU Court of Justice, this concept must be very broadly understood, encompassing all entities that offer goods or services on the market, regardless their legal status or the way in how they are financed.[7] Besides commercial firms or 'merchants', as defined by the Commercial Code, this also includes farming enterprises, non-profit entities with economic activities and liberal professions.

The shift towards the 'undertaking'-concept first occurred predominantly for those matters traditionally seen as aspects of economic law *sensu stricto*, which can be defined as the rules by which the government unilaterally intervenes in the operation of the market. The most important examples in that respect are competition law and the legislation on market practices and consumer protection. Consequently, for quite a long time it remained possible to make a clear distinction between commercial law, based on the concept of merchants, and economic law, based on the concept of an 'undertaking'. Since a couple years, however, this distinction has become completely blurred, as the concept of an 'undertaking' was increasingly used by the legislature to redefine the scope of rules traditionally belonging to commercial law. Examples in this respect are the law on business registers and the legislation regarding the jurisdiction of the commercial courts.[8] This evolution gave rise to the development in the legal literature of the concept of 'economic law *sensu lato*'. This category of rules goes beyond the rules by which the government intervenes in the markets (economic law *sensu stricto*) and encompasses all rules that affect business life in some way and which are using the 'undertaking' concept to define their scope of application.

In 2013 the legislature finally decided to make an end to the proliferation of separate statutes regulating business life and started an operation to codify almost all

4. *See infra* Chapter 13.
5. *See* Insurance Act of 4 April 2014.
6. *See* Article I.1, 1°, Code of Economic Law.
7. *See* in particular *BKK Mobil Oil*, ECJ C-59/12, ECLI:EU:C:2013:634.
8. *See* for both items *infra* §12.03 [A] and [B].

existing legislation in the area of economic law *sensu lato* into one single new Code of Economic Law.[9] Apart from the rules of economic law *sensu stricto*, the Code contains plenty of other rules that do regulate certain aspects of business life. All rules are centred around the 'undertaking' concept, thus further diminishing the importance of the Commercial Code's notion of 'merchants'. The Code of Economic Law consists of eighteen different subdivisions called 'books', dealing with an exceptionally wide range of topics: from the business register and accounting over competition law and consumer protection to intellectual property law and consumer credit law. Important to note, however, is that, for reasons that sometimes remain unclear, several statutes regulating certain – quite crucial – aspects of business life were left out of the Code of Economic Law so far.[10] It concerns:

- the Bankruptcy Act;
- the Continuity of Undertakings Act;
- the (remainder of the) 1807 Commercial Code;
- the Companies Code; and
- important parts of banking and financial law.

[C] Civil Law

The rules of civil law are applicable to all persons, irrespective the type of activities they engage in, thus including both commercial and non-commercial entities. Therefore, these rules can be referred to as constituting the common core of the legal system. In the absence of specific rules in a commercial statute or in the Code of Economic Law, one should refer to the Civil Code as the primary source of applicable law. Rules of commercial or economic law, however, do prevail if they contain specific rules. The impact of the rules specifically applicable to merchants or undertakings is considerable in practice, important examples being for instance the rules on bankruptcy or the rules of evidence.

§12.02 RULES EXCLUSIVELY APPLICABLE TO 'MERCHANTS'

A first set of rules is exclusively applicable to those entities that qualify as commercial according to the Commercial Code. As mentioned before, the number of rules of this kind has dramatically decreased over time. Although the concept of commerciality is still relevant for the rules of insolvency law as well, we will deal with these in a separate subsection for reasons of clarity.

9. *See* Act of 28 February 2013 introducing the Code of Economic Law.
10. It is however expected that, at some point in time, these separate acts will be incorporated into the Code of Economic Law.

[A] Commercial Evidence

With respect to claims arising out of contracts subject to commercial law, more flexible rules of evidence are applicable.[11] For dealings of non-commercial parties, the rules on evidence have been strictly regulated in the Civil Code. These rules mainly rely on written evidence, and apply strictly. They tend to protect the debtor, the purpose being that the inexperienced layperson should be shielded against the too-flexible rules of evidence applicable to commercial firms. In commercial matters, debtors are considered more sophisticated and better able to fend for themselves. Therefore, all types of evidence are declared admissible (including testimony, witnesses, and oaths). Evidence of a debt arising out of contract between commercial firms can in the first place be produced by an invoice: provided the debtor has not protested the invoice within a short, reasonable period of time, the invoice will constitute conclusive evidence. Evidence of commercial claims can also be derived from the accounting records: if these have been kept properly, a creditor may even be allowed to prove his claim on the basis of his own accounting records. But in all cases, the court will decide whether it considers the evidence produced as credible.

The rules of evidence in commercial matters apply in cases between two or more merchants, and may be applied moreover by non-commercial entities delivering evidence against a commercial entity. Evidence introduced against a non-commercial entity must in all cases comply with the civil law regime, resulting in a potentially asymmetric treatment of both parties in a dispute, thus clearly illustrating the protective role of the rules on evidence.

[B] Joint Liability

Although Article 1202 of the Civil Code states that joint liability is not to be presumed, there is generally accepted old case law declaring commercial debtors that have the same obligation towards the creditor, not only jointly held to that obligation but also jointly liable in case of breach. This principle of customary law goes back to medieval merchants, and aims to reinforce creditors' confidence in commercial affairs. Note that it is assumed this rule can only be applied to individuals or legal persons that do qualify as merchant according to the Commercial Code, thus making all other entities that do engage in economic activities as well, subject to several liability.

[C] Duty to Open a Bank Account

Commercial firms are obliged, before starting their business, to apply to a bank and open a 'giro account'.[12] Mention of the account number is to be made on all

11. *See* Article 25 Commercial Code.
12. Royal Decree No. 56 of 10 November 1967 regarding the promotion of the use of transferable money.

correspondence, invoices and other documents. Third parties can assume to be entitled to pay into this account.

The same regulation obliges merchants to accept cheques, giro payment and other payment forms by money transfer for payments above EUR 250. However, the creditor can suspend delivery of the goods or services, until the amount has effectively been credited to his account.

§12.03 OTHER TRADITIONAL TOPICS OF COMMERCIAL LAW

Under this subtitle we collected two types of rules. A first category concerns rules that are traditionally perceived as belonging to commercial law, but for which the legislature (recently) decided to broaden their scope of application by using the 'undertaking' concept instead of the qualification as commercial according to the Commercial Code.[13] A second category of rules consists of a limited number of matters that are deemed to be commercial, irrespective of whether the parties involved are merchants or not. The latter applies particularly to liabilities arising out of bills of exchange, promissory notes and cheques.

[A] Disclosures

Before starting any business activity, one must register at the central enterprise database (*Banque-Carrefour des Entreprises – Kruispuntbank van Ondernemingen*).[14] Although originally typical commercial, the scope of this rule has been broadened to all undertakings and even beyond.

Upon registration the undertaking, whether an individual or a company, obtains its unique 'undertaking number', which it must expressly state on all its outgoing documents. Besides identifying all undertakings, the duty to register serves to collect information about their proposed activity. In connection to the latter, it is a key element in the enforcement of the rules on establishment for certain business activities, as no registration can be obtained except by producing evidence that the applicant has the required authorisation to engage in the business proposed. Such authorisation requirement applies to a quite elaborate list of activities, including central heating contractors, second-hand car dealers, bakeries, banks, insurance brokers, etc.

[B] Commercial Courts

Belgium has maintained the French system of having separate courts with respect to disputes between or against merchants. These commercial courts (*tribunaux de*

13. *See* in this respect already *supra* §12.01 [B].
14. *See* in this respect Book III, Title 2 of the Code of Economic Law. This was previously the commercial registry.

commerce – rechtbanken van koophandel) are staffed by professional judges who are assisted by lay judges, being business people recruited from the local business community. This formula has proven quite successful, as law suits brought before the commercial courts are generally decided in a more swift way than in civil courts. In all other respects these courts function according to the general rules of civil procedure, while appeals against their decisions go to the courts of appeal, which hear all appeals in civil and commercial matters, and which are composed of professional judges only.

Until recently, the jurisdiction of the commercial courts was defined making use of the concept of 'merchant' as used in the Commercial Code. In 2014, however, the legislature decided to broaden the scope of the commercial courts' jurisdiction. Since then, the commercial courts are in charge of deciding disputes between 'undertakings', under the condition that the dispute is related to an action performed within the context of their economic activities.[15] Furthermore, lawsuits by private persons against undertakings can also be voluntarily brought before a commercial tribunal. The concept of 'undertaking' that applies here is equal to the one as defined in de Code of Economic Law.[16]

Finally, for some matters the commercial courts have jurisdiction, irrespective of the capacity of the parties. To mention in this respect in particular are all disputes regarding bankruptcy procedures and reorganisations, as well as all disputes about companies that are controlled by the Companies Code.

[C] Bills of Exchange, Promissory Notes and Cheques

Bills of exchange, promissory notes and cheques once were crucial documents for day-to-day business life. Nowadays, however, their use has become rare and in fact is limited to certain sectors of (international) commerce. Cheques are still used for significant transactions under the form of bank certified cheques (for instance for paying the price of a real estate purchase or a car).[17] The rules on bills of exchange and promissory notes are part of the Commercial Code. This part of the Code was substantially modified in 1953 by implementing the Uniform Law on Bills of Exchange and Promissory Notes.[18] A similar approach was followed for implementing the Geneva Convention on Cheques,[19] which, however, was not made part of the Commercial Code as such. As a consequence, Belgian law is largely identical to the rules of these uniform laws. However, with respect to both bills of exchange and cheques, the Belgian legislature introduced a few additional provisions, mainly continuing previously followed business practices. The present overview will be limited to the rules and practices that differ from these uniform laws.

15. *See* Article 573, 1°, Judicial Code.
16. Cf. *supra* §12.01 [B].
17. As cash transactions are no longer or only to a very limited extent allowed in that respect by the anti-money laundering legislation.
18. Adopted in Geneva on 7 June 1930 and introduced in Belgium by the Act of 10 August 1953.
19. Adopted on 19 March 1931, implemented in Belgium by the Act of 1 March 1961.

[1] *Bills of Exchange*

Belgian practice uses a uniform model form for the bill of exchange (*lettre de change – wisselbrief*), which has been rendered mandatory by way of a technical norm. According to this form, reference has to be made to the invoices to which the bill relates. However, a footnote mentions that this reference only serves the purposes of discounting the bills and does not affect the independence of the bill in relation to the commercial transaction to which it relates.

The main differences in the Belgian statute in comparison with the uniform law relate to the continuing role attributed to the 'provision' or the claim of the drawer against the drawee. The holder of a bill is entitled to a direct right of action against the drawee, for the sums due to the drawer; however this claim is based on the underlying contract and not on the bill itself and, therefore, the drawee will not be held to more than he was due to the drawer. In order to safeguard his position, the holder can forbid the drawee to dispose of the provision. To mention further is that the holder, taking recourse against the drawer, also is a privileged creditor in the drawer's liquidation, including his bankruptcy.

[2] *Cheques*

The Belgian Cheques Act largely conforms to the uniform law. However, it also contains some *addenda*, and banking practices have drifted away at some points from the scheme on which the uniform law is based.

Cheques cannot be drawn on parties other than credit institutions. The Act imposes no specific formula for drawing a cheque; however, most banks require their clients to use the forms which they have issued. Drawee banks should hold funds during the entire period of presentation of the cheque, being eight days. The drawing of cheques without the drawer holding funds available is a serious criminal offence.

'Visum' and 'certification' are techniques aimed at securing payment of the cheque. The bank may declare that funds are available at the moment of applying its 'visa', without implying that these funds will still be available upon presentation of the cheque. Under 'certification', the bank blocks the funds in a separate subaccount. The drawee bank can validly pay any cheque presented, except if the payment is fraudulent or grossly negligent. The bank should verify the signature of the drawer, and cannot exonerate itself of this obligation, which belongs to the essence of the client-bank relationship.[20] In case of forgery, the bank will not be liable if the forgery could not be easily detected; however, if the bank has been warned about theft or loss of the cheque or cheque forms, its payment would not be valid. If neither the drawer, nor the bank have been negligent, the final risk flowing from the unauthorised use of the cheque forms is imposed on the holder of the account to which the forms were issued.

The cheque is valid for a six-month period. Presentation should take place within eight days, for cheques drawn and presented for payment in Belgium; for cheques

20. Court of Cassation 27 September 1990, 1992 Revue de la banque – Bank- en Financiewezen 37.

drawn outside Belgium, this period is extended to 20 days, or 120 days for cheques issued outside Europe. Within this period, the drawer is barred from revoking the cheque. Afterwards, his revocation will be effective. This bar does not prevent the drawer, nor the holder to oppose against the payment of any cheque. Cheques become stale after a six-month period. Off course the holder might retain his claim on the basis of the underlying contract, in light of which the cheque was drawn.

§12.04 INSOLVENCY LAW

[A] Overview

Probably the most important remaining difference between the legal regime applicable to commercial and non-commercial persons relates to the possibility of the former to be subject to bankruptcy. Persons that are not commercial according to the Commercial Code, cannot be declared bankrupt and thus are in principal subject to compulsory liquidation following seizures on a first come, first served basis. For firms encountering financial difficulties without being insolvent already, a set of reorganisational measures has been introduced. Since the last overall amendment of the legislation on reorganisations in 2009, its scope of application has been broadened. Besides commercial entities as meant in the Commercial Code, a limited number of other types of undertakings are subject to these rules as well (*see infra*).

The bankruptcy procedure is governed by the Bankruptcy Act of 8 August 1997. In addition to compulsory liquidation, as provided for in the Bankruptcy Act, the Companies Code further contains provisions on voluntary liquidation. Voluntary liquidation, however, would not protect an insolvent company from being declared bankrupt. The regime on reorganisation procedures and other measures targeted to save firms that are nearing insolvency, can be found in the Continuity of Undertakings Act of 31 January 2009. This Act completely amended the earlier legislation to make it more debtor friendly. Note that, according to the European Insolvency Regulation, Belgian insolvency law is applicable to all firms that have their centre of main interests (COMI) in Belgium.[21]

Before sketching the main characteristics of the bankruptcy and reorganisation procedures, we will briefly pinpoint some protective measure that can be taken with regard to companies acting (wrongfully) in the vicinity of insolvency.

[B] Urgent Protective Measures

According to the Bankruptcy Act, commercial court are entitled to suspend all or some of the debtor's rights with respect to all his assets, provided that this measure appears 'absolutely necessary', and provided there are concurring indications that the debtor is

21. EU Regulation (EC) No. 1346/2000 of 29 May 2000 on Insolvency Proceedings, Official Journal L160 of 30 June 2000.

'virtually bankrupt'.[22] The court designates a provisional administrator, who will act on behalf and *in lieu* of the debtor. This measure is essentially designed to avoid virtual bankrupt debtors to hide or remove the firm's assets.

Further protective measures can be found in the Continuity of Undertakings Act. Very similar to the provisional administrator, who can be appointed when the firm is virtually bankrupt, a 'judicial trustee' can be appointed by the court to fully or partly replace the firm's management when it is demonstrated that serious shortcomings of the firms' management endanger its ability to further pay its debts and that the measure can be effective in avoiding this situation.

[C] Bankruptcy

Merchants that are chronically unable to honour their debts can be declared bankrupt by the commercial court of their place of business, or for legal persons, of their seat. Bankruptcy (*faillite – faillissement*) results in compulsory liquidation for the benefit of the creditors, under judicial scrutiny. It is a measure of public order aimed at eliminating deficient firms that could no longer be saved by imposing a halt on their liabilities.

The measure should normally be triggered by a voluntary filing by the owner of the firm, or, if it is a corporation, by its board of directors. This filing is required under threat of criminal sanctions. Creditors may also claim bankruptcy, and ultimately the public prosecutor is entitled to submit a request in bankruptcy to the court. However, the court may always find that the firm can still be saved and postpone its decision to start a reorganisation procedure, or simply dismiss the filing, claim or request.

Bankruptcy is essentially a judicial procedure. The liquidation is managed by a liquidator called '*curator*', appointed by and reporting to the court. A judge – most often a lay judge[23] – is appointed to supervise the procedure. Under the present Act, once bankruptcy has been pronounced by the court, there is a clear preference for a speedy liquidation, creditors having little or no say in the way the procedure is handled; employees are treated as creditors, with statutory liens protecting their financial claims.

The bankruptcy declaration leads to a so-called *concursus creditorum*, whereby all unsecured creditors are entitled to a share of the proceeds of the remaining assets on a *pari passu* basis. Therefore, all claims against the debtor must be halted, execution being suspended, and interest calculation stopped. The curator will draw up the inventory of the assets, call on the creditors to file their claims within a one month period, settle remaining claims or submit these for decision to the court, and proceed to the sale of the assets. The proceeds are then divided among the creditors, in principle on a proportional basis. Many creditors – such as the employees, claims for unpaid social security contributions, the State for the collection of taxes, and others – enjoy

22. *See* Article 8 Bankruptcy Act.
23. *See* on this concept *supra* §12.03 [B].

preferences over the ordinary creditors in the form of statutory liens.[24] As a result, the unsecured creditors often receive only a small fraction of their claim. In practice, remaining assets in many cases are even too low to justify the costs connected to the liquidation procedure itself, and the curator will immediately stop the liquidation. This is all the more true as the curator's fees are paid out of the estate.

Some creditors are not entirely subject to this collective liquidation procedure: creditors with statutory liens on specific assets (such as unpaid sellers), or with collateral - particularly pledges and mortgages - will be able to recover their claim on the assets subject to their security right. These secured creditors can take execution in their own hands, but they do have to wait a certain period after the bankruptcy declaration before they can unilaterally start the procedure to sell the assets at stake. Some creditors are entitled to recover - or vindicate - property from the bankrupt estate title of which had not passed to the bankrupt person. This is the case with all assets sold to the bankrupt firm with retention of title to the seller: provided certain formalities have been complied with,[25] these items can be recovered if the curator refuses to pay the purchase price. The same applies to items rented to or deposited with the bankrupt.

At the end of the bankruptcy procedure the court will decide whether the bankrupt natural person can be 'excused', that is morally exculpated: in this case, the bankrupt person will be freed from all debts, and could restart a business. When the bankrupt debtor is not excused, creditors can seize all later-acquired property. The bankrupt person being excused is the rule, not the exception. Corporations, however, cannot be excused. The closing of the bankruptcy procedure leads to their dissolution and immediate closing of their liquidation.

[D] Reorganisations

[1] Access to the Procedure

All firms whose continuity have been jeopardised are eligible to enter a reorganisational procedure as governed by the Continuity of Undertakings Act.[26] Limited liability companies whose net-assets have fallen below half of the amount of their stated capital are presumed to be in that situation. The Continuity of Undertakings Act is, off course, applicable to commercial firms as mentioned in the Commercial Code. Furthermore the Act has been made applicable to farmers and to all companies, irrespective whether they qualify as merchant or not. Still excluded, however, are companies of practitioners of liberal professions.[27] Also excluded are companies in certain specific sectors, like the banking, insurance and investment services industry, to which specific resolution rules apply.

24. *See supra* Chapter 9, §9.10 [A] [5].
25. *See* Article 101 Bankruptcy Act.
26. The Act as well as the procedure in itself are mostly referred to by their acronym LCE in French (*Loi relative à la continuité des entreprises*) or WCO in Dutch (*Wet continuïteit ondernemingen*).
27. *See* on this concept *supra* §12.01 [A].

The reorganisation procedure can only be initiated by the undertaking itself, not by third parties. The owner of the firm or the board of directors if it is a corporation are the only persons entitled to file a request for reorganisation. Other bodies, such as the works council,[28] creditors or the public prosecutor, cannot file a request.

[2] First Stage: Preliminary Term of Protection

The acceptance by the court of the firm's request leads to a stay of all creditors' execution measures against the debtor for an initial period not exceeding six months, during which the debtor drafts a restructuring plan. If necessary, the initial period of protection can be prolonged. The total duration of the protection period, however, may never exceed twelve months.[29] In practice, it appears to be common that a first stay of two to four months is being granted, after which the duration of the protection period is being prolonged several times with additional periods of some extra months, taking into account the debtor's actual financial situation. Important to mention is that the stay of all creditors' execution measures only applies to creditors whose claims matured before the opening of the procedure. Creditors whose claims originated after the start of the start of the procedure (the so-called new creditors) can still pursue the execution of their claims.

Since the introduction of this new legislation on reorganisations in 2009, Belgian law fully adheres to the debtor-in-possession principle. The debtor remains principally competent to carry out whatever transaction he wants to. He may incur new liabilities, sell assets or pay debts which actually fall under the protection regime. The only supervision the debtor must accept is the supervision by the court, through a so-called delegated judge – usually a lay judge – who is responsible for following up the firm's situation, without however being able to interfere in the debtor's decisions. In some rather exceptional circumstances, a judicial trustee (*mandataire de justice – gerechts-mandataris*) can be appointed. The competences of this trustee, usually being a qualified attorney, must be defined by the court. They range from merely providing assistance to the debtor to actually replacing the debtor's management.[30]

[3] Second Stage: Execution of the Reorganisation Plan

Once a debtor is admitted to the first stage of the procedure, he can choose between three different regimes according to which he can achieve his reorganisation.

A first option is trying to use the initial stay to reach an amicable settlement with at least two or more of his creditors. Once formally approved by the court, such an agreement cannot be called into question in a later stage, which is particularly helpful when the reorganisation would fail and the firm ultimately goes bankrupt.

28. On this council, *see infra* Chapter 14, §14.02 [E] [1] [b].
29. Except in extraordinary circumstances; Article 38, §2, Continuity of Undertakings Act.
30. *See* Article 27 *v.* Article 28 Continuity of Undertakings Act.

The second – and most common – option for firms to manage their reorganisation is trying to establish an overall reorganisation plan on which the creditors must vote. The plan is considered accepted by the creditors if a majority of the creditors present during a special session before the commercial tribunal that represent at least half of the unsettled debts of the firm, vote in favour of the proposed plan. Once accepted by this double majority, the plan must receive a final approval by the court. The plan may provide for a debt rescheduling, a partial reduction of debts, or a conversion of debts into capital. However, except in case they individually agree, the plan may not impinge upon specific property security rights of secured creditors, such as statutory liens on specific assets, mortgages or financial collateral. The period during which the plan must be implemented may not exceed five years. If the firm fails to stick to its commitments made in the reorganisation plan, creditors fully regain their rights to launch execution measures or to take action to have their debtor declared bankrupt.

A third option available to institute a firm's reorganisation is based on a transfer of the firm as a whole or at least of an important part of its activities 'under judicial authority'. Unlike the other reorganisation schemes, the competences of the firm's management are fairly limited under this scheme, as they may not organise the transfer of the firm's assets themselves. In this variant, the appointment of a judicial trustee[31] is mandatory. The trustee must try to collect several bids for the activities to be transferred in order to guarantee a minimal level of competition. Within this procedure, special attention is addressed to the rights of the firm's employees.[32] The final approval of the transfer must be given by the court. Once the transfer has been approved and effectuated, the creditors must be paid out of the amount received in return for the firm's assets.

§12.05 RULES RELATING TO COMMERCIAL AND FINANCIAL TRANSACTIONS

Besides the special rules on evidence,[33] commercial transactions (i.e., B2B contracts) are basically governed by the rules of general contract law.[34] In a B2B-setting contractual freedom prevails: firms are supposed to be able to adequately protect themselves. Some types of contracts that are frequently used in a commercial setting, however, are subject to an extra set of rules, predominantly aimed at protecting the rights of the party with the weakest bargaining power. The extent to which these rules interfere with the parties' contractual freedom, remains nevertheless limited. This starkly contrasts with the regulation of B2C contracts, which are subject to a very extensive set of rules that fundamentally deviate from general contract law.[35]

The following paragraphs start with a brief overview of the rules that were adopted relating to certain frequently used commercial contracts and then turn to the

31. *See supra* §12.04 [D] [2].
32. *See* Article 61 Continuity of Undertakings Act.
33. *See supra* §12.02 [A].
34. *See supra* Chapter 10.
35. *See* Book VI on 'market practices and consumer protection' of the Code of Economic Law.

Belgian implementation of the EU directive on combating late payments in commercial transactions. Finally, an overview will be given of the rules applicable to credit contracts that are most frequently used by businesses.

[A] Commercial Contracts

Book X of the Code of Economic Law contains specific rules regarding three different commercial contracts that can be used by firms in order to organise the distribution channels for the goods or services they supply. The rules are all aimed at protecting commercial intermediaries, which often have a far less favourable bargaining position compared to the principal. We will discuss the rules for commercial agency: (1), for exclusive distributorship contracts; (2) and for franchise contracts; (3). For a last category of commercial intermediaries, brokers and commission agents; (4), the legislature did not provide a separate set of rules, thus making those contracts basically subject to the rules of general contract law only. Note, however, that commercial intermediaries in several sectors are subject to an extra layer of sector-specific regulation, which predominantly deals with professional requirements, permits and supervision. This holds particularly true for intermediaries in the financial sector, the transport business and the real estate sector. These sector-specific regulations will not be dealt with here.

[1] Commercial Agency

A first type of contract for intermediaries that is specifically regulated in the Code of Economic law is the contract between enterprises and self-employed commercial agents (*agent commercial – handelsagent*). These Belgian rules transpose an EU Directive.[36] The rules are predominantly aimed at ameliorating the position of commercial agents with respect to their remuneration and in case of termination of the contract. Note that, besides these specific rules for commercial self-employed agents, agents are basically subject to the general rules of the agency contract in the Civil Code (*mandat – lastgeving*), as far as these rules are compatible with the specific rules of the Code of Economic Law.

The Code defines 'commercial agents' as self-employed persons who have continuing authority to negotiate and possibly conclude contracts on behalf of and in the name of a principal.[37] A first crucial element in order to qualify a contract between a principal and an intermediary as a commercial agency contract is that the intermediary must be self-employed, which means that there may not be any authority – in the legal sense – of the principal over the intermediary, as in that case the relationship would be qualified as an employment contract for a sales representative.[38] A second

36. EEC Directive 86/653 of 18 December 1986 on the Coordination of the Laws of the Member States relating to Self-Employed Commercial Agents, Official Journal L382/17 of 31 December 1986.
37. *See* Article I.11, 1°, Code of Economic Law.
38. *See infra* Chapter 14, §14.02 [B] [2].

element which distinguishes commercial agency from brokerage, concerns the presence of a continuing - and thus not merely occasional - relationship between the principal and the intermediary. This does, however, not require an exclusive relationship between the agent and the principal: a commercial agent can work for several principals. A third element, which is actually thought to be inherent to the commercial character of the contract, is that the intermediary's activities are remunerated. A fourth characteristic element concerns the contents of the intermediary's task, which can either be limited to negotiating contracts for the principal or can be expanded to the actual conclusion of the negotiated contracts. The nature of the negotiated contracts is irrelevant: sale or purchase of goods or services, rental contracts, contracts with regard to movable or immovable property, etc. A fifth and final characteristic of commercial agency concerns the legal relationships between the principal, the intermediary and the third party. The commercial agent acts on behalf of and in the name of its principal, so that no contractual relationship exists between the agent and the third party. The latter can only act against the principal and *vice versa*, for instance in case of default. An exception to this rule of great practical importance concerns the use of so-called *del credere* clauses. When including such a clause in the agency contract, the agent actually guarantees the payment by the third party to his principal.[39]

The Code contains detailed rules regarding agents' remuneration, particularly when it takes the form of commissions.[40] The rules on commissions are of an imperative nature, making it impossible to deviate from them by contract. A distinction is made between the conditions under which an agent becomes entitled to the commission,[41] and the moment the commission is actually due.[42]

A second element of the contractual relationship between a self-employed commercial agent and his principal, which is regulated in detail, is the termination of the agency contract. Agency contracts can basically be terminated in three different ways. A first option is termination according to the rules of general contract law,[43] which means particularly the termination in case of death or insolvency of the agent, in case of mutual consent, or in case of force majeure. A second - and in practice the most important - way of terminating the relationship between a commercial agent and his principal is the termination by unilateral notice by one of both parties.[44] A third way how the contract can come to an end is by immediate termination in case of serious breach of contractual obligations or in case of exceptional circumstances that make

39. *See* Article X.23 Code of Economic Law, which contains several conditions these clauses must meet in order to be lawful.
40. That is every part of an agent's remuneration which varies with the number or value of business transactions.
41. Articles X.8 and X.9 Code of Economic Law, transposing resp. Articles 7 and 8 of EEC Directive 86/653 of 18 December 1986 on the Coordination of the Laws of the Member States relating to Self-Employed Commercial Agents, Official Journal L382/17 of 31 December 1986.
42. Article X.11 Code of Economic Law, transposing Article 10 of EEC Council 86/653 of 18 December 1986 on the Coordination of the Laws of the Member States relating to Self-Employed Commercial Agents, Official Journal L382/17 of 31 December 1986.
43. *See supra* Chapter 10, §10.04 [F].
44. The period of notice is one month for the first year of the contract, two months for the second year commenced, three months for the third year, and so one, without however being ever longer than six months.

future cooperation between the parties impossible.[45] Upon the termination of a commercial agency contract, distinction must be made between different types of compensation that can be due.

[2] Exclusive Distributorship

Agreements of exclusive distributorship (*concessions de vente exclusive - concessies van alleenverkoop*) are contracts in which one party - a producer or importer - grants the other party exclusive rights to distribute, in his own name and at his own risk, certain of the producer or importer's products, within an agreed territory. Such contracts are subject to specific rules, predominantly dealing with the untimely termination of the contract by the producer or importer.[46] The purpose of the rules is to protect the distributor, who often has made large investments in setting up his sales organisation and who, after the unanticipated termination of the contract, might see his efforts continually benefiting the producer or importer, who in effect takes over the distributorship for his own account.

A first rule imposes a reasonable period of notice or a fair indemnity in case of termination of the contract. In addition, an indemnity will be due by the producer or importer covering the loss of goodwill for the distributor, which in any case benefits the producer or distributor. This indemnity must be calculated according to the rules of the Code, and provide for the goodwill accrued to the distributor and the expenses laid out by the distributor. Expenses laid out for laying-off of employees should also be refunded.

These rules basically only apply to distributorship contracts for indefinite periods of time. In order to avoid that the rules could be easily circumvented, contracts that have been concluded for a definite period of time are, in the case of absence of specific contractual clauses in that respect, automatically turned into a contract for an indefinite period if the parties did not give notice three months before the expiration of the fixed term. Furthermore, contracts for definite periods will in any case be turned into contracts for indefinite periods at the moment of their third renewal.

[3] Franchise Contracts

A third type of commercial contract which is subject to specific rules in the Code of Economic Law is the so-called franchise contract.[47] However, the Belgian legislature chose not to use this name and preferred instead to use the broader denomination 'commercial cooperation agreement' (*accord de partenariat commercial - commerciële samenwerkingsovereenkomst*). They are defined as contracts between two or more parties in which one party (the franchisor) grants the right to the other party (the franchisee) to use a commercial formula in the context of the sale of goods or services

45. *See* Article X.17 Code of Economic Law.
46. *See* Articles X.35–40 Code of Economic Law.
47. *See* Articles X.26–34 Code of Economic Law.

by the franchisee. The Code further specifies that the use of a commercial formula can follow from one or more of the following facts: the use of a common sign or name, the transfer of knowhow, or the provision of commercial or technical assistance. Another element that is typical for franchise contracts, without however being essential in order to be qualified as such, is the fact that the franchisee must pay royalties in return for the use of the franchisor's commercial formula.

The legislature intervened in the contractual relationship between potential parties to a commercial cooperation agreement in order to protect the interests of franchisees. The approach taken with regard to these contracts, however, is completely different compared to the rules applicable to commercial agency contracts or agreements of exclusive distributorship (*supra*). The Code does not contain rules relating to the duration or the termination of the franchise contract. Instead, the focus is on the pre-contractual stage, with a view to avoid that franchisees would rashly enter into commercial cooperation agreements not being aware of the far reaching (financial) implications these can have for franchisees.

[4] Brokers and Commission Agents

A fourth category of commercial intermediaries consists of brokers and commission agents. Contrary to the other intermediaries, contracts between brokers and commission agents and their principals are not subject to a separate set of statutory rules. Issues not dealt with by contract, thus have to be solved based on the rules of general contract law.

The broker (*courtier – makelaar*) is the party, often from a specialised firm, acting on his own behalf, in charge of searching a suitable contract for his principal, preparing the contract terms and finally bringing the parties to the negotiation table. The resulting contract is entered into between the principal and the other contract party directly. In those sectors where brokerage is most common – like the insurance, banking or real estate sector – brokers are subject to additional sector-specific rules.

A different type of commercial intermediary is the so-called commission broker or commission agent (*commissionaire – commissionair*). These are agents acting on behalf of a principal but, contrary to a regular agent, acting in their own name. By doing so, they are commercial traders in their own right. They may be in charge of selling or buying the goods of their principal, presenting themselves to clients as selling or buying for their own account. Stock exchange brokers, for instance, are usually acting as commission agents for the orders they execute on the markets. Their transactions are binding for themselves, and only indirectly on their principals. Their right against the principal is secured by a lien on the assets or sums held for the latter, both in respect of their fee and the sums due by the principal.[48] In case of bankruptcy of the commission broker, the principal is entitled to vindicate his goods, if still present in the broker's premises.

48. *See* Article 14 Act of 5 May 1872 on the Revision of the Rules on Pledges and Commissions, as inserted into the Commercial Code.

[B] Rules on Combating Late Payment in Commercial Transactions

Since 2002 Belgian law contains specific rules trying to cope with the issue of late payments in commercial transactions.[49] These rules transpose an EU Directive on the subject.[50] Central to these rules, which are perceived to be quite effective, are a uniform default payment period and a high uniform default interest rate in case of late payment.

The rules apply in the first place to the relationship between undertakings, and only as far as commercial transactions are concerned, thus excluding payments in other contexts, like damages due based on liability. Commercial transactions are in this context understood as transactions which lead to the delivery of goods or the provision of services in return for remuneration. The concept of an undertaking is broadly defined in this respect and slightly deviates from the general definition of the concept in the Code of Economic Law.[51] In this context, any organisation, other than a public authority, acting in the course of its independent economic or professional activity, qualifies as an undertaking, even where that activity is carried out by a single person. Besides the traditional B2B-relationship, the rules on combating late payments are further targeted towards contracts between an undertaking and a public authority as well, be it only for those cases where the latter is the undertaking's debtor as a result of a commercial transaction.

The default payment period as foreseen in the rules on combating late payments amounts to thirty calendar days, basically starting from the date of receipt by the debtor of the invoice.[52] Nevertheless, it remains possible for the parties to deviate from this default rule and to agree on a longer or shorter period. The rule is slightly more severe when a public authority is the undertaking's debtor. In those cases the payment period can in no case be longer than sixty calendar days.

If there is no payment within the default payment period or another period agreed on, the creditor is entitled to interest for late payment. The specific rules on combating late payments deviate in this respect in two ways from the general rules of civil law.[53] First, the creditor is entitled to interest without having to send a reminder. The expiration of the payment period is sufficient in itself. Second, a particularly high default interest rate is applicable. This special interest rate is calculated by adding eight percentage points to a reference interest rate, the latter being the interest rate applied by the European Central Bank to its most recent main refinancing operations. The rate must be rounded off to the nearest half percentage point. In a mere B2B-context parties still have the possibility to agree on a higher or lower interest rate. This is not the case

49. *See* Act of 2 August 2002 on Combating Late Payment in Commercial Transactions.
50. Originally Directive 2000/35/EC, which has been replaced in 2011 by Directive 2011/7/EU of the European Parliament and of the Council of 16 February 2011 on Combating Late Payment in Commercial Transactions, Official Journal L48 of 23 February 2011, hereinafter the 'Late Payments Directive'.
51. Cf. *supra* §12.01 [B].
52. Note that some nuances can apply, *see* Article 4 Act of 5 May 1872 on combating late payment in commercial transactions, implementing Article 3, para. 3, Late Payments Directive.
53. *See supra* Chapter 10, §10.04 [E].

when a contract between an undertaking and a public authority is at stake. In those cases, the special interest rate is mandatory.

A last feature of the rules on combating late payments is that, in all cases in which the creditor is entitled to interest for late payment, he is automatically also entitled to obtain from the debtor a fixed sum of EUR 40 as compensation for his recovery costs. Additionally, the creditor remains entitled to obtain full compensation for all recovery costs exceeding the amount of EUR 40 which are incurred due to the debtor's late payment.

[C] Credit Contracts

[1] General Overview

Like all other contracts dealt with earlier, credit contracts entered into by undertakings are in the first place subject to the general rules of civil law. For a very long time, loans to undertakings were thus predominantly subject to the freedom of contract, as the Civil Code contains only a few strict provisions in this respect. There was - and still is - for instance full freedom to fix the interest rate, provided the lender does not abuse his position and calculate an interest rate that is exorbitant in relation to the prevailing market rate and the risk taken on the debtor (prohibition of usury).[54] Also it is allowed to calculate interest on a capitalisation basis, as a composite rate, a technique clearly prohibited with non-commercial parties.[55] Since 2014, however, a new small and medium-sized enterprise (SME) Financing Act brought some important limits to the freedom of contract that existed before.[56]

Besides traditional *instalment loans*, credit to smaller firms in Belgium usually takes the form of *overdraft facilities*. These allow the beneficiary to draw funds up to the limit agreed. The contract is analysed as a credit contract, allowing the client to call the funds. Usually the credit is revolving. This aspect, however, is not considered to be a natural part of the credit, and therefore should be expressly stipulated. Furthermore, larger firms frequently use so-called *straight loans*, which can be analysed as short term credits, renewable until notice.

Both straight loans and overdraft facilities, together with instalment loans, do fall within the scope of the aforementioned SME Financing Act if the beneficiary qualifies as an SME (cf. *infra*). This holds not true for some other popular forms of credit, such as *leasing*. Leasing contracts are, as a result, not regulated as such, irrespective of whether the lessee qualifies as an SME. They are nevertheless subject to some requirements which follow from the conditions leasing companies should comply with in order to get their administrative registration.[57] Leasing contracts frequently contain

54. *See* Article 1907*ter* Civil Code. This situation is completely different with regard to consumer credit contracts, for which the law imposes a maximum interest rate.
55. *See* Article 1154 Civil Code (prohibition of anatocism).
56. *See* Act of 21 December 2013 with regard to diverse regulations on SME financing, hereinafter referred to as the 'SME Financing Act'.
57. *See* Royal Decree No. 55 of 10 November 1967.

the clause that a lessor who fails to pay the agreed terms, owes, by way of liquidated damages, the entire amount of the remaining periodic payment. However, case law has invalidated so drastic a clause, and reduced it to the actual value of the future terms.

Another type of credit contract which is excluded from the scope of application of the SME Financing Act and which thus remains basically subject to contractual freedom is *factoring*. Factoring is practised in Belgium only by a few specialised companies. The transfer of the invoices is being effectuated according to the general rules on the transfer of claims,[58] which means that the transfer is to intervene *solo consensu*, without any formalities as between transferor and transferee. The debtor must be informed, but this information can be given in any form.[59]

Yet another type of credits that can be mentioned in this respect are *documentary credits*, and all like credit transactions that make use of letters of credit. Usually they are issued with an express reference to the Uniform Customs and Practice for Documentary Credits (UCP) issued by the International Chamber of Commerce and even when they are not, some case law declares the UCP applicable in the absence of an express contractual reference. Frequently used in Belgian commercial practice are, furthermore, *bank guarantees* or first-demand guarantees. Again there is no specific legislation on this point, but the validity of these guarantees is generally accepted. Their independence in relation to the underlying contract is recognised: the guarantee can be called at first demand, without the beneficiary having to prove non-execution of the underlying contract. In cases of blatant abuse, the courts have been willing to grant a stop to the payment under guarantee.[60]

Finally, certain credit techniques should be mentioned that are based on the use of bills of exchange or promissory notes.[61] There is no legislation relating to discounting bills, so general contract law applies. In its basic form, this transaction implies a drawer of a bill of exchange transferring the bill to his bank, in exchange for the nominal value, minus the interest, calculated as a discount, entitling the bank to claim against the drawee who has accepted the bill, or to take recourse against the drawer or his guarantor. Recourse in case of non-payment is based on the bill or on the underlying credit contract. Another frequently used scheme in this respect is the one in which the bill, when accepted by the drawee, is handed over to the drawer, supplier of merchandise to the drawee. The drawer then discounts the bill at the drawee's bank against full nominal value, the interests and expenses being charged to the drawee, the beneficiary of the credit opened by the bank. Upon the drawee's failure to honour the bill, the bank can take recourse against the drawer.

[2] Act on SME Financing

As mentioned before, the principle of freedom of contract with regard to loans to businesses has been largely curtailed in 2014 at the time the SME Financing Act entered

58. *See* Article 1690 Civil Code.
59. *See supra* Chapter 9, §9.11 [A].
60. The same is true moreover in the context of letters of credit.
61. *See supra* §12.03 [C] [1].

into force.[62] Framed as legislation aimed at stimulating SME's access to finance in the post-financial crisis era, it constituted an elaborate legal framework for loans to businesses predominantly aimed at protecting the interests of the latter. Remarkably, notwithstanding the quite different relationships at stake, most of the adopted rules are very similar to rules that already existed before in the context of consumer credit.

The Act applies to credit agreements concluded between a borrowing undertaking that qualifies as an SME on the one hand and a professional 'provider of credit' on the other. The latter concept is the only one of which the precise meaning is not really discussed: only professional lenders, in particular banks, are envisaged. What concerns the meaning of 'credit agreements', the potential list of credit contracts that could qualify as such has been importantly narrowed down in the Act's Explanatory Memorandum. The legislature actually only wanted the new legislation to be applicable to 'financial credits', by which is essentially meant instalment loans and overdraft facilities. The Explanatory Memorandum explicitly excludes factoring and leasing contracts, as well as documentary credits, just like arrangements on deferred payments of invoices or intra-group loans.[63]

The most debated aspect of the Act's scope of application is the concept of 'undertaking qualifying as an SME'. Although the reference to SMEs looks like another important limitation of the Act's scope, this is not the fact at all, as SMEs are so broadly defined that almost 99% of all Belgian businesses belong to this category. 'Undertakings' in the Act refers in the first place to undertakings as defined in the Code of Economic Law.[64] Furthermore, the Act explicitly refers to persons exercising liberal professions as well.[65] Both do however only fall within the scope of the Act if they can be considered as 'small' businesses according to the criteria of Article 15 of the Companies Code. As the latter criteria are specifically developed to distinguish between small and large *companies* - not undertakings - their application in this context is not always unambiguous. In a company law context, for companies operating as corporate groups, the criteria must be applied on a group level. By lack of an express reference to this principle in the SME Financing Act, it is assumed that the criteria in this context must be applied on a non-consolidated, company only basis, even if the borrowing undertaking is part of a larger group of undertakings.

The SME Financing Act consist of three main parts. A first and most elaborate part contains a framework of duties which are imposed on lenders in the pre-contractual stage. They can be summarised as a duty of care, a duty to inform and, finally, a suitability obligation. The duty to inform consists of several detailed obligations which lenders must fulfil before concluding the contract, like handing over a standardised information document and a draft copy of the credit agreement. Also in case of refusal of a credit demand, the client must be informed about the reasons on which the lender's decision is based. The suitability obligation implies that lenders are required to choose, among the types of credit agreements they usually offer, the type of credit that

62. Cf. *supra* footnote 56.
63. *See* Explanatory Memorandum, 24 October 2013, Doc 53K3088/001.
64. Cf. *supra* §12.01 [B].
65. Cf. *supra* §12.01 [A].

is most suitable for the undertaking at stake, taking into account the undertaking's financial situation and the purpose of the agreement.

A second part of the Act contains a list of prohibited contract terms with a view to enhance contractual fairness in credit agreements concluded between professional lenders and undertakings.[66] Terms that would constitute a violation of the prohibition are null, without making the contract itself entirely null. The list of prohibited clauses is quite short compared to a similar list which exists in the context of consumer contracts. The Act is targeted towards three specific clauses that are thought to constitute a disequilibrium between the parties' rights, particularly with regard to the lender's right to unilaterally terminate the contract.

The third and most discussed part of the SME Financing Act deals with the early repayment of loans falling under the Act's scope. In fact, it has been the high number of disputes regarding this topic, that has been the real trigger for the legislature to adopt this Act. The early repayment of loans is only very partially regulated in the Civil Code. Only for those loans qualifying as instalment loans, the Civil Code contains a limitation on the indemnification clauses that can be applied in case of an early repayment. Parties cannot stipulate an indemnity fixed at a rate higher than the agreed interest rate, over a period of six months, based on the amount repaid.[67] In all other cases, particularly in the case of overdraft facilities, no such limitation applied in the past. Thus, in those cases very high amounts of damages could be due by undertakings if they wanted to repay their credit early, for instance in the case of a refinancing operation, which were very often at stake over the last decade given the trend of decreasing interest rates.

The aforementioned situation, which was perceived by entrepreneurs as highly frustrating, has fundamentally changed since the adoption of the SME Financing Act. The starting point of the new rules is an unconditional right of undertakings to repay at any time partially or in full the amount of principal outstanding under every credit agreement falling under the Act's scope.[68] When a borrower decides to make use of this right, the lender may ask for an indemnity. The amount of this early repayment fee and all related fees (so-called break costs), however, may not exceed the amount of six months of interest over the repaid sum, calculated at the interest rate of the contract. This limitation to six months of interest leads to amounts substantially differing from the penalties formerly claimed and which were calculated according to the so-called funding loss-method. Besides credit agreements falling outside the scope of the Act, only one real exception to the limitation of the indemnity to six months of interest exists: for other contracts than instalment loans, particularly overdraft facilities, exceeding an amount of EUR 1 million, the parties to the contract remain free to determine the amount of the early repayment penalty.[69] For instalment loans the

66. *See* Article 13 SME Financing Act.
67. *See* Article 1907*bis* Civil Code.
68. *See* Article 9 SME Financing Act.
69. Be it within the boundaries as set in a code of conduct which was adopted at the joint initiative of representatives of the financial sector and the SMEs; *see* Article 10 SME Financing Act.

maximum threshold of six months of interest applies irrespective the amount of the contract.

Note that the new rules on early repayment can only be applied for credit contracts concluded after 10 January 2014. Contracts concluded before that date are only subject to the Civil Code, which means that only in case of instalment loans a limitation applies to the indemnity for early repayment.

§12.06 SELECTED BIBLIOGRAPHY

K. Byttebier & T. Wera, *Handboek handels- en ondernemingsrecht* (Bruges: die Keure 2016).

P. De Vroede & H. De Wulf, *Overzicht van rechtspraak. Algemeen handelsrecht en handelspraktijken 1998–2002*, 42 Tijdschrift voor Privaatrecht 111–299 (2005).

E. Dirix, R. Steennot & H. Vanhees, *Handels- en economisch recht in hoofdlijnen* (Antwerp: Intersentia 2014).

L. Fredericq & S. Fredericq, *Handboek van Belgisch handelsrecht* (Brussels, Bruylant 1976).

G. Schrans & R. Steennot, *Algemeen deel van het financieel recht* (Antwerp: Intersentia 2003).

J. Van Ryn & J. Heenen, *Principes de droit commercial* (2nd ed., Brussels: Bruylant 1988).

I. Verougstraete, *Manuel de la continuité des entreprises et de la faillite* (Antwerp: Kluwer 2010).

Commercial Practices (J. Stuyck & G. Straetmans eds., 2nd edition, Brussels: Larcier 2015).

Handels- en economisch recht. Commentaar met overzicht van rechtspraak en rechtsleer (R. Steennot, J. Stuyck, H. Vanhees & E. Wymeersch eds., Antwerp: Kluwer, s.d., loose-leaf).

Handels- en economisch recht, Deel 1, *Ondernemingsrecht* (B. Tilleman & E. Terryn, eds., Beginselen van Belgisch privaatrecht XIII, R. Dillemans & W. Van Gerven eds., Antwerp: Kluwer 2011).

Het Wetboek van economisch recht: van nu en straks? (B. Keirsbilck & E. Terryn eds., Antwerp: Intersentia 2014).

Traité pratique de droit commercial (2nd ed., C. Jassogne ed., Waterloo: Kluwer 2009).

[illegible] and before six months or at least 20 [illegible] the amount [illegible].

[illegible] the [illegible] order [illegible] applied [illegible] [illegible] the [illegible] date [illegible] applied to the Court (§§ [illegible]) which [illegible] [illegible] applies [illegible].

SELECTED BIBLIOGRAPHY

- [illegible] W., *[illegible]* (Antwerp, [illegible], 2016).
- De Wulf, H. & De Wulf, [illegible], *Algemene [illegible]* [illegible] 2012, [illegible] Privaatrecht [illegible] [illegible] [illegible] [illegible] Antwerp, [illegible].
- [illegible] (Antwerp/[illegible], 2011).
- [illegible] (Brussels, [illegible] 1998).
- [illegible] (Brussels, [illegible]).
- [illegible], 2nd edition, Brussels, [illegible].
- [illegible] [illegible] [illegible] [illegible] Kluwer, [illegible].
- [illegible] [illegible] Van Gerven [illegible] Antwerp, Intersentia, 2011).
- [illegible] (B. Kepbiler [illegible] Antwerp, Intersentia, 2014).
- [illegible] (Waterloo, Kluwer, 2009).

CHAPTER 13

Company Law

Hans De Wulf

§13.01 INTRODUCTION

[A] Basic Concepts: The Companies Code

In Belgium the three main legal forms of private organisations are companies, associations and foundations. This Chapter only discusses companies. A company is defined in Article 1 of the Belgian Companies Code as a contract on the basis of which two or more persons agree to contribute assets in order to pursue one or more precisely defined activities and with the intention to provide direct or indirect material benefits to the shareholders or partners. This definition, which essentially goes back to the definition of 'company' in the Napoleonic Civil Code of 1804, stresses that companies are for-profit organisations: they pursue profits and – this is the essential feature – the intention is to distribute those profits among shareholders/partners. The Belgian concept of company (*société – vennootschap*) covers both partnerships and corporations as these words are used in American and British legal parlance.[1]

Associations are also considered to be contracts aiming at cooperation among the members, requiring at least three founders for the most commonly used form of association: the *ASBL-VZW* (*association sans but lucrative – vereniging zonder winstoogmerk*). But associations are essentially non-profit-organisations: if they make a profit, this may in any case not be distributed directly (through dividends) or indirectly (such as through service contracts between members and the association) among members. Another fundamental difference between companies and associations under Belgian law is that the latter

1. *See infra* §13.01 [B].

may not be used to pursue activities that are deemed commercial pursuant to the list of commercial activities in Article 2 of the Commercial Code.[2]

Foundations are legal persons to which assets are assigned by the founder(s). They have no members. The assets are administered under the responsibility of a board (at least three members are required) in accordance with the wishes of the founder as set forth in the document of incorporation, which must be a notarial deed. Foundations may engage in commercial activities, but just like associations, foundations can only be used as non-profits: any profits a foundation makes, must be ploughed back into the purpose of the foundation. Foundations may not distribute profits to founders, board members or third parties except, in the latter case, when this is essential to attaining the goal set for the foundation by the founder.[3] Foundations come in two varieties: private and public foundations. Public foundations can only be used for a closed list of activities enumerated in Article 27 of the Associations and Foundations Act of 1921. This includes the support of philanthropic, scientific, religious, pedagogical and cultural activities. They only attain legal personality upon approval of their articles by royal decree. They are largely exempt from income taxation. Private foundations can be used for any non-profit purpose that is not illegal. They did not exist as a legal form in Belgium until 2001.

By Act of 7 May 1999, which became effective on 6 February 2001, Belgian company law was codified in the so-called Companies Code (*Code des sociétés – Wetboek van vennootschappen*).[4] This Companies Code contains all statutory rules about Belgian company law in the strict sense, by which I mean outside the realm of capital markets law and securities regulation. It is accompanied by a Royal Decree of 30 January 2001 on the Implementation of the Companies Code,[5] which mainly deals with details concerning disclosures to be made upon registration of the company or changes to its articles of association, accounting rules and the format of annual statutory and consolidated accounts, auditor independence and detailed rules on squeeze-outs, as well as some less important matters. The Companies Code is subdivided into 'books'. The first four books deal with general principles and partnerships; next, each major company type gets its own book; after that books on mergers and some special company types follow.

2. For the general definition of association, *see* Article 1, para. 3, Act of 27 June 1921 on Associations, International Associations and Foundations, hereinafter referred to as the 'Associations and Foundations Act of 1921'. For comments on Article 2 Commercial Code, *see supra* Chapter 12, §12.01 [A].
3. *See* Article 27 of the Associations and Foundations Act of 1921 for the general definition of foundation and the requirement of a notarial deed.
4. In this book, we will use the English expression Companies Code even though we realise that Companies Act is a more common expression, because Belgian legal terminology does distinguish between a code and an act, the idea being that a code is a comprehensive and coordinated collection of all legislation relevant for a certain area of the law. To the best of our knowledge, there is no English translation available of the Belgian Companies Code (certainly not an official version, but even major law firms do not seem to have a full translation).
5. In Belgian law, royal decrees can contain legislation, even though they are enacted by the executive and do not need to be approved by Parliament. They are often taken on the basis of an enabling clause in a statute and in such cases implement and complement the rules in the act of Parliament.

Associations and foundations, on which this Chapter will say nothing more from now on, are governed by the Associations and Foundations Act of 27 June 1921, as fundamentally reformed by an Act of 2 May 2002.

[B] Some General Features of Belgian Company Law

[1] One Company Definition, Fourteen Company Types

Article 1 of the Companies Code contains a general definition of company. An entity or contract is not a company if it does not conform to this definition and any entity that has all the features of the definition is a company.

In the UK the word 'company' is reserved for incorporated firms – i.e., legal persons, distinct from the shareholders – with limited liability – i.e., shareholders are not liable for the company's obligations/debt – and there is, apart from some oddities, only one company type, which comes in two varieties, the private company limited by shares and the public company limited by shares. Unincorporated firms or corporate entities with unlimited liability of members for the entity's debt are called partnerships, and partnerships are not considered to be companies. In the US the situation is very similar: a distinction is made between corporations (legal person, limited liability, transferable shares held by shareholders), of which there is only one type although de facto but not legally one can distinguish between closed and public corporations, and partnerships (unlimited liability, partners not shareholders). Over the past few decades hybrids have developed in both countries, such as the limited liability partnership (LLP) and the limited liability company (LLC).

The situation in Belgium is different, and similar to that in most European countries outside Scandinavia and the UK. There is one generally applicable definition of company, but this word (*société – vennootschap*) covers both what Americans would call partnerships and corporations (and includes company types that are very similar to LLPs or LLCs). In addition, Article 2 of the Companies Code lists fourteen different company forms, each subject to its own rules. There is therefore no uniform company type along the British or American model. It cannot even be said that the two commercially most important company forms, the *SA–NV* and the *SPRL–BVBA* correspond to the plc (public company) or the ltd (private company) in the UK. In the UK plc and ltd are two varieties of an essentially uniform legal form. Even though *SA–NV* and *SPRL–BVBA* are both governed by one Companies Code, they are in separate books within that Code and the difference is very much like the difference between a German *Aktiengesellschaft* (*AG*) and *GmbH*, or a French *SA* and *SARL* respectively.

[2] Companies Are Still Considered to Be Contracts

From this it follows that each company needs at least two shareholders, both at the moment of its foundation and during its entire existence. Cooperative companies even need three shareholders.[6] The only exception is the possibility to set up a one person *SPRL–BVBA*,[7] a legal form Belgium was forced to introduce by the Twelfth EU Company Law Directive and which is mostly used by professionals for tax reasons and in order to limit their professional liability. Even for this company type, the Companies Code provides that the sole shareholder must be a natural person.[8] In requiring two shareholders for almost all companies, Belgian law comes across as very old-fashioned in a comparative perspective. While some legal scholars have criticised the view that companies are contracts, there is no denying that Article 1 of the Companies Code explicitly states that they are, and that there is near universal agreement that gaps in the law left by statute can be filled with the help of principles from contract law.

[3] Companies Are for Profit

Belgian law is also quite old-fashioned in a comparative perspective in that as a rule, only for-profit entities are considered to be companies. Once it has been established that an entity is a company, the company's organs (i.e., decision-making bodies) may not lawfully take any decisions that cannot potentially contribute to generating profits – for instance donations are outlawed – a principle that is sometimes and with some measure of success used before courts to invalidate intra-group guarantees provided by a subsidiary for the benefit of its parent or vice versa, without any apparent countervailing benefit for the guarantor.[9]

The for-profit principle is formulated in Article 1 of the Companies Code but is further elaborated in Article 32 of the Companies Code (the ban on so-called leonine clauses, i.e., arrangements awarding the lion's share of profits to one shareholder). This article contains two rules. The first one is that no shareholder may be excluded from sharing in the company's profit and that any arrangement that undermines this principle (and the corresponding rule that no shareholder may be awarded all or virtually all profits) is null and void. This nullity cannot be waived by shareholder or anybody's consent. The second rule in Article 32 of the Companies Code is unique to Belgium and France. It says that no shareholder may be excluded from sharing in the company's losses. The idea is that contributions of assets to companies have to be risk-bearing. This second rule was repeatedly used, from the mid-1980s onwards, to try and invalidate share (put) option agreements that gave one party the right against another shareholder to force that other shareholder to buy the first party's shares at a price which guaranteed that the first party would not lose money on its initial contribution to the company. In a whole string of judgments[10] the Court of Cassation has, in a reaction, curtailed the reach of Article 32, paragraph 2, of the Companies

6. *See* Article 351 Companies Code.
7. *See* Article 211 Companies Code.
8. *See* Article 212 Companies Code.
9. For example Court of Cassation 7 April 2005, 2006 TIJDSCHRIFT VOOR RECHTSPERSOON EN VENNOOTSCHAP 597; Court of Cassation 30 September 2005, 2006 REVUE DE DROIT COMMERCIAL BELGE – TIJDSCHRIFT VOOR BELGISCH HANDELSRECHT 1028.
10. Still relevant today is Court of Cassation 5 November 1998, 1999 REVUE PRATIQUE DES SOCIÉTÉS – TIJDSCHRIFT VOOR RECHTSPERSOON EN VENNOOTSCHAP 79 ('*Torrespapel*').

Code. According to the Court contracts between shareholders that guarantee one party that it will not make a loss on its contribution are not illegal as far as they are compatible with the company's interest.[11] Most scholars and practitioners seem in favour of abolishing at least the second rule of Article 32 of the Companies Code.

[4] *The Public SA–NV Corporate Form Is Often Used for Small,* De Facto *Closed Firms Instead of the Private SPRL–BVBA Form, but This Is Changing*

When the first Belgian legislation concerning the public corporation in the form of the *SA–NV* was introduced in 1873, the *SA–NV* was intended for the large, capital-intensive industrial firms that were coming about as a result of the industrial revolution. After the First World War, it was mainly shopkeepers and the like who lobbied for the introduction of a private company type modelled on the German *GmbH* (1899), and this was introduced as the *SPRL–BVBA* in 1935. Even so, until recently, the *SA–NV*, intended as a public company, that would attract a large number of investors, was very often used by small and medium-sized business, in spite of its higher minimum capital requirements and more extensive set of mandatory rules. The main reason for this is obvious: tax advantages. The *SA–NV* was he only company type that could issue bearer shares, and such shares not only helped guarantee anonymity for shareholders in general, they can also be donated (such as by parents to their children who will take over the firm) without going through a notary who would then have registered the donation with the tax authorities and levied the taxes due by the parties to the donation. The popularity of the *SA–NV* for this tax reason led to a situation where there were many more Belgian *SA*'s (*NV*'s) than German *AG*'s, even though the two corporate forms are equivalent on paper and the German economy is of course several times the size of the Belgian one. However, since bearer shares were gradually phased out from 2005 onwards (and were totally abolished by 1 January 2014), statistics show that the private *SPRL–BVBA* is becoming more popular compared to the *SA–NV* and is outpacing it when one looks at new company formations.

[5] *The Influence of the European Directives: Goldplating and Creditor Protection*

Belgium has of course implemented all EU company law directives, leading to substantial harmonisation in some areas of the law for limited liability companies with other EU countries. Belgium therefore shares at least two features with other EU countries that strike anyone who compares EU corporate law with US corporate law: as a result mainly of the Second Company Law Directive, the tendency of company legislation in European countries – whose firms traditionally relied more on bank finance than on capital markets – to contain rules aimed at the protection of company

11. The current state of affairs is represented by Court of Cassation 29 May 2008, 2008 Tijdschrift voor Rechtspersoon en Vennootschap 655.

creditors has been reinforced. A second feature, which was influenced by mainly the Second and First Company Law Directives, is that certain decisions, and especially decisions to amend the articles of incorporation and anything having to do with legal capital, have mandatorily been declared the exclusive prerogative of the general meeting of shareholders (whereas in other legal systems, and in particular in the US State of Delaware, the board may intervene in these areas). Belgium, far more so than for instance the UK and the Netherlands, has engaged in extensive 'goldplating' of EU directives, at least until recently. The most prominent example is the extension of the rules contained in the Second Company Law Directive to private companies of the *SPRL–BVBA* type and even, to a large extent to cooperative companies, even though the Directive itself only envisaged public companies of the *SA–NV* type.

[6] The Close Link Between Accounting and Tax Rules

While accounts mainly have a function as a source of information for entrepreneurs themselves, investors and creditors – with the latter traditionally getting priority over investors in the way European accounting rules are constructed – they are also used to determine the taxable base for companies. However, in many if not most countries, separate accounts need to be drawn up for tax purposes. In Belgium there is still a close link, among non-listed firms, between the financial accounts and the tax accounts, in fact normally no separate accounts need to or may be drawn up for tax purposes. This sometimes leads to accounts that are arguably less informative for investors or really anyone, because the content is distorted by tax considerations.

[7] Concentrated Ownership

Even in listed firms, ownership in most firms is highly concentrated in one or more often closely knit groups of dominant shareholders, sometimes family members. In combination with sometimes opaque multi-layered pyramidal holding structures, this led to suspicions about relatively widespread 'tunnelling', i.e., the extraction of private (not shared between all shareholders) benefits of control for the dominant shareholder group. Over the past twenty years or so, many corporate group structures have, however, been simplified, perhaps because the firms involved were trading at a discount. But concentrated ownership as such has remained.

[8] The Importance of Shareholder Agreements

Shareholder agreements between a number of shareholders are very common in Belgian companies. They are used to create voting blocks, but there are also coalitions the members of which grant each other pre-emption rights. The two often go hand in hand. This can lead to situations where the shareholder agreement deviates from the provisions in the articles which leads to difficult questions – which we cannot go into here – to what extent this is and should be permitted. Although I am not aware of statistics, it seems shareholder agreements are also quite common in listed companies.

[9] Little Enthusiasm for Substance Over Form

Belgian courts are reluctant to deviate from black letter law and while they have sometimes developed doctrines that have given them powers that are not explicitly provided for in statute – the most important example being that of the power to appoint a 'provisional administrator' replacing part or all of the directors in companies where decision-making is completely blocked or serious fraud is apparently being committed[12] – they have not been very active in developing doctrines that allow them to look at the substance of corporate transactions or structures when black letter law limits itself to the outer form. Veil piercing, while prevalent in the 1960s and 1970s, does not happen anymore after it was rejected by the Court of Cassation,[13] and outside the tax context there are no rules on 'hidden distributions', that is rules that would treat as dividend distributions transactions between a company and some of its shareholders or directors that are used to channel value/money from the company to the other party in another way than through a dividend payment. Another example is that Belgian courts do not subordinate shareholder loans.

§13.02 TYPES OF COMPANIES

[A] Incorporated or Not

Article 2 of the Companies Code contains a list of all company types that can be set up in accordance with Belgian law. §1 indicates that there are three unincorporated company forms, whereas all other company types (listed in §2) are legal persons. Article 2, §1, of the Companies Code lists the following unincorporated partnership forms:

- simple partnership (*société de droit commun – maatschap*);
- temporary partnership (*société momentanée – tijdelijke handelsvennootschap*); and
- silent partnership (*société interne – stille handelsvennootschap*).

These company types are mere contractual arrangements between partners.[14] We discuss them here instead of in the section on partnerships. Partners have agreed to contribute assets to the company's purpose, with the overarching aim of generating a

12. The best treatment of this topic is still E. Pottier & M. De Roeck, *L'administration provisoire: bilan et perspectives*, 1997 Revue de droit commercial belge – Tijdschrift voor Belgisch Handelsrecht 322 et seq.
13. *See* especially Court of Cassation 1 June 1979, 1978–1979 Arresten van het Hof van Cassatie 1153; 1979 Pasicrisie belge 1129, and Court of Cassation 12 February 1981, 1981 Pasicrisie belge 653.
14. Specific rules for these company types are listed in the very short Book III of the Companies Code (Articles 46–55), but in fact most rules in Book II of the Companies Code (general principles applicable to all companies unless later books deviate from them for a specific company type) were originally (in 1804) written with mainly these companies in mind. In addition, general rules of contract law and the law of agency are also applicable.

profit and distributing that profit among themselves. Contractual freedom governs this form of cooperation, including what kind of contributions a partner offers, the valuation of these contributions, the rights of partners such as voting power and profit rights, transfer of 'shares' (i.e., the legal position as partner).

These partnerships are not legal persons. Therefore, they are not legal subject, in the sense that they are transparent not only for tax purposes but also at the level of civil ('common') law: when 'the company' enters into an obligation, for example enters into a contract, legally this means that all partners enter into the obligation because someone (another partner, a director who usually will be a partner but may also be an outsider) had received legal authority to enter into the contract on behalf of the partners. This authority can be derived from statute - Article 36 of the Companies Code states that all partners are presumed to have granted each other power of attorney to represent the other partners in the management of the company's affairs - from the articles of incorporation, or from a common law agency contract. Since obligations and rights are not attached to a legal person but to the partners, they are personally liable with their personal assets for the obligations that had been validly entered into on their behalf. For simple partnerships this liability will only be joint and severally when the purpose of the partnership is commercial in the sense of Article 2 of the Commercial Code.[15] The partners of the other two types of unincorporated partnerships are always jointly and severally liable for company debt.[16]

Assets that 'the company' has acquired (through contributions or otherwise) are common property of all partners. One result is that no partner can transfer any asset of the company without the consent of all other partners, unless the articles say otherwise, or the asset is unimportant to the company and transferring it is part of the daily management of the company, or the partner is at the same time a director of the company, in which latter case (s)he can dispose of the assets within the bounds set by the articles and the company's purpose.

Since this type of partnership is not a legal person, they cannot as such sue or be sued, but must be represented according to the rules of agency.

Partnerships that are not legal persons can in theory be the result of a merely oral agreement. In practice, a written memorandum or charter (*acte de constitution - oprichtingsakte*) is almost always drawn up, but it need not take the form of a notarial deed, as is required for limited liability companies. If a written charter containing the articles of association is drafted, it will never be registered with a court registry, as this would mean the company becomes a legal person whether it intended this or not, and would thereby be transformed from an unincorporated partnership into an incorporated partnership, i.e., a company that is a legal person but with unlimited personal liability for company debts. Parties often have recourse to a notary of their own accord, because they hope this will result in a well-drafted document.

The differences between the simple partnership and the other two unincorporated partnership are not completely negligible but still very limited.

15. *See* Article 52 Companies Code.
16. *See* Articles 53–54 Companies Code.

A temporary partnership is exactly the same as a simple partnership, except that the Companies Code defines it as having been entered into with a view to a specific 'work'.[17] It is dissolved automatically when this 'work' has been achieved, unless the articles provide otherwise, as they usually do. Also, partners are always jointly and severally liable, even if the purpose of the company is not commercial.[18] In practice, temporary partnerships are very often used, mainly in the construction sector, when construction firms that are themselves limited liability corporations set up a temporary partnership in order to jointly bid for a big project that they will jointly perform (such as the construction of big infrastructure works). The professions, especially large accounting firms, also sometimes use temporary partnerships as tax transparent, very flexible structures to structure a cooperation in a joint venture like way. In spite of the fact that they are not legal persons, temporary partnerships need to keep accounts that are separate from the accounts of their partners.

A silent partnership is a so-called merely internal company. To the outside world they do not look like a partnership, since they consist of someone, the unlimited partner, engaging in a (usually commercial) venture and one or more silent or limited partners limiting themselves and thereby their liability to contributing a certain amount of money or other assets to the venture of the unlimited partner, in exchange for a share in the profits that the venture generates (hence the distinction, not always easy to make in practice, between a limited partner and a creditor extending for instance a loan: the latter is of course entitled to a legally fixed claim, whereas a silent partner only shares in profits). The unlimited partner is exposed to unlimited liability for his venture – i.e., he is responsible with his personal private assets for the debts flowing from the venture –, since he runs the business and the business is not incorporated. Naturally, the silent partner's liability for the debts and obligations associated with the venture is limited to the amount of assets that he agreed to contribute to the venture.[19] His personal assets cannot be seized by the creditors of the unlimited partner. This does not change when these creditors or the outside world know that the limited partner has a share in the unlimited partner's business. If, however, the unlimited partner does not stick to his role as a mere financier but engages in legal acts with third parties (for instance suppliers or customers of the unlimited partner) on behalf of the venture/unlimited partner, he will engage his personal liability and will in fact have turned himself into a unlimited partner.

Article 2, §2, of the Companies Code contains the following list of incorporated companies:

- the general partnership (*société en nom collectif* or *SNC* – *vennootschap onder firma* or *VOF*);
- the limited partnership (*société en commandite simple* or *SCS* – *gewone commanditaire vennootschap* or *Comm.V*);

17. *See* Article 47 Companies Code.
18. *See* Article 53 Companies Code.
19. *See* Article 54 Companies Code.

- the limited partnership with shares (*société en commandite par actions* or *SCA - commanditaire vennootschap op aandelen* or *Comm.VA*);
- the public limited liability company (*société anonyme* or *SA - naamloze vennootschap* or *NV*, henceforth *SA-NV*);
- the closely held (or 'private') limited liability company (*société privée à responsabilité limitée* or *SPRL - besloten vennootschap met beperkte aansprakelijkheid* or *BVBA*, henceforth *SPRL-BVBA*);
- the cooperative company with limited liability (*société coopérative à responsabilité limitée* or *SCRL - coöperatieve vennootschap met beperkte aansprakelijkheid* or *CVBA*);
- the cooperative company with unlimited liability (*société coopérative à responsabilité illimitée* or *SCRI - coöperatieve vennootschap met onbeperkte aansprakelijkheid* or *CVOA*), and
- the Economic Interest Grouping (*groupement d'intérêt économique* or *GIE - economisch samenwerkingsverband* or *ESV*).

By far the most widely used and therefore most important company types are the *SA-NV* and the *SPRL-BVBA*. The main differences (in addition to a great many other which are also important in practice, of course) between a *SA-NV* and *SPRL-BVBA* are twofold:

- The shares in an *SA-NV* are freely transferable and transfer restrictions are only permitted to a limited extent,[20] whereas the Code itself limits the sale or transfer of shares in a *SPRL-BVBA*, and these statutory limitations cannot be watered down in the articles.[21] As a sort of extension of these rules, *SPRL-BVBA* companies can never be listed on an exchange and more broadly, public offerings of their shares are outlawed.[22]
- The *SA-NV* must have a collegiate board consisting of at least three directors who can always be dismissed at will by a simple majority at general meeting,[23] whereas for a *SPRL-BVBA* it is sufficient to have one managing director and if there are several, they can act independently and need not form a collegiate board; in addition they can be protected against easy dismissal by shareholders.[24]

Companies become legal persons upon registration of the corporate charter with the registry of the commercial court that is territorially competent for the district in which they have their registered office.[25]

20. *See* Article 510 Companies Code.
21. *See* Article 249 Companies Code.
22. *See* Article 210 Companies Code.
23. *See* Article 518 Companies Code.
24. *See* Articles 255 & 257 Companies Code.
25. *See* Article 2, §4, Companies Code.

For limited liability companies, the corporate charter needs to be a notarial deed; for other companies this is not required.[26] The rule is sanctioned by nullity.[27]

Within fifteen days after registration, an excerpt[28] of the articles of incorporation is published in the Annexes to the Moniteur belge - Belgisch Staatsblad.[29] As a result, the company can rely against third parties on those sections of the articles and other data[30] that have been disclosed.[31] Article 77 of the Companies Code states that when the appointment of a company organ (such as the directors) has been published in the Annexes to the Moniteur belge - Belgisch Staatsblad, irregularities in such appointments (for instance the nullity) cannot be relied upon against third parties until corrective disclosures have been made.

[B] Civil or Commercial

Belgian law is old-fashioned in that it still distinguishes between commercial and non-commercial activities. Even though this distinction has already lost much of its importance in favour of the difference between consumers and persons acting in a professional capacity,[32] it is still on the books.

Article 2 of the Belgian Commercial Code contains a list of activities that are deemed commercial. Basically al activities that common sense tells one are commercial (producing goods or services to sell them, transport, insurance, banking, distribution, ...) are also commercial from a legal point of view, except traditional agricultural activities and the professions.[33]

A company is deemed to be commercial, i.e., a merchant (*commerçant - handelaar*), as soon as its objects clause contains a commercial activity.[34] Whether the company actually engages in such an activity or whether these commercial activities are less important than other, civil activities mentioned in the objects clause, is irrelevant.

There is no relationship under Belgian law between the form a company takes (such as a *SA–NV* or cooperative company) and whether it is commercial or not: all company forms can choose between civil (non-commercial) and commercial activities (this was different before 1996) and no company is commercial simply because it takes a certain form (no principle of *Formkaufmann*).

---

26. *See* Article 66 Companies Code.
27. *See* e.g., Article 227 Companies Code for the *SPRL–BVBA*.
28. For the minimum content, *see* Article 69 Companies Code.
29. *See* Article 73 Companies Code.
30. Article 74 Companies Code details certain events or decisions that have to be disclosed, in addition to the excerpt from the initial corporate charter. The most important item are the decisions concerning the appointment and dismissal of the persons who have the power to represent the company, such as the board. The Companies Code contains many scattered provisions concerning additional mandatory disclosures.
31. *See* Article 76 Companies Code.
32. *See supra* Chapter 12, §12.01 [B].
33. Doctor, lawyer, accountant, auditor, architect, ... *See supra* Chapter 12, §12.01 [A].
34. *See* Article 3, §2, Companies Code.

The main relevance of the commercial-civil distinction is that most non-commercial companies cannot be declared bankrupt,[35] and the strict rules on proof and evidence from the Civil Code do not apply to commercial transactions when evidence is brought against a merchant.[36]

[C] Listed and Public or Private

As in all other countries, only a small percentage of Belgian companies finance themselves through the capital markets, but these are often large and economically important entities. The public issue of shares or bonds as such will (usually) be subject to the prior approval of a prospectus by the Belgian Financial Markets Supervisory Authority (FSMA). When a company is listed, it becomes subject to a whole range of additional rules of securities regulation/capital markets regulation, such as rules on insider dealing, market manipulation. The same goes for its directors, and the general meeting is organised in a different way as well. The Belgian corporate governance code[37] will become applicable to the company, on a comply or explain basis.

We cannot discuss securities regulation in this Chapter. In any case, the Companies Code only defines the concepts of 'listed'[38] and 'public'[39] company for purely corporate law purposes: the Companies Code contains some additional rules specifically for such companies, but mainly rules that deviate from the rules for unlisted or non-public companies. By contrast, the rules on prospectuses, market abuse, public take-over bids, transparency of ownership of public companies and other rules of securities regulation are contained not in the Companies Code but in separate acts, each with its own ambit and sometimes using the same concepts of public and listed company as the Companies Code, but more often than not amending these concepts for the purpose of the specific act.

Private companies limited by shares (*SPRL–BVBA*) may not issue securities (neither shares nor other securities) to the public.[40] Therefore, they cannot be listed. While this ban is understandable for the shares of a *SPRL–BVBA*, there seems no sound policy reason why this company type may not issue debt securities publicly.

In practice the vast majority of listed companies take the form of a *SA–NV* but, except for the *SPRL–BVBA*, in theory all companies that are legal persons could be listed, provided their articles are adapted to make their shares freely transferable.

Simplifying the rules somewhat, the two basic concepts are that of 'listed company' as defined in Article 4 of the Companies Code and 'public *SA–NV*' as defined in Article 438 of the Companies Code. The two categories overlap to a large extent, but not completely.[41]

---

35. *See supra* Chapter 12, §12.04.
36. *See supra* Chapter 12, §12.02 [A].
37. This Code can be found (in English) at www.corporategovernancecommittee.be/en.
38. *See* Article 4 Companies Code.
39. *See* Article 438 Companies Code.
40. *See* Article 210 Companies Code.
41. For an up-to date and comprehensive overview of the different concepts of public and listed company under Belgian law and which rules are applicable to which type of public company, *see*

Article 4 of the Companies Code defines a listed company as a company whose shares have been admitted to trading on a regulated market.[42] As indicated, any company other than a *SPRL–BVBA* can in theory be listed, but in practice almost all are of the *SA–NV* type, with also a few *SCA–Comm.VA*. Listing is only possible after the approval of a listing prospectus and acceptance of the listing rules of the relevant market.

'Public companies' as defined by Article 438 of the Companies Code can, by contrast and somewhat confusingly, only be of the *SA–NV* type. A public *SA–NV* is a company that is either listed or that has publicly issued shares or other securities. So some companies are unlisted, but have nevertheless issued shares to the public, usually bonds. Such companies become subject to certain company law rules that deviate from regular company law or add rules to it. They have to adapt their articles to these different rules, and the articles and every piece emanating from the company must mention that it is a public company.[43] Once a company has issued securities to the public, it becomes a public company forever until the company proves that its securities are no longer spread among the investing public. Engaging in a squeeze-out - which is only possible for shares, not for debt securities - is sometimes the only possibility to attain this goal.

To complicate matters further, there is a trend in recent legislation to make certain additional or deviating rules applicable only to companies the shares of which have been listed. For instance, certain rules on the organisation of shareholder meetings apply to all listed companies,[44] others (those rules that were adopted as a result of the implementation of the EU Shareholder Rights Directive) apply only to companies whose shares have been listed[45] (and therefore not to companies that only had debt securities listed, but not shares). The latter also goes for, for example, certain rules concerning executive pay[46] and intra-group conflicts of interests (related party transactions[47]).

In order to define the concept of 'public' for purposes of Article 438 of the Companies Code, the Code essentially refers to the rules on prospectuses.[48] To vastly oversimplify matters: this essentially means the company has offered its securities to more than 150 investors, discounting certain professionally qualified investors and

---

H. De Wulf & X. Dieux, *Publieke versus besloten vennootschappen: de noodzaak aan rationalisatie en vereenvoudiging van de regulering*, in De Modernisering van het vennootschapsrecht 91–202 (BCV ed.), Brussels: Larcier 2014), also published in French in the same volume.

42. A market is a Belgian regulated market once it has been recognised as such by a royal decree. A list of various markets can be found on the website of the FSMA, *see* www.fsma.be/en/Site/Repository/lijsten/gm.aspx.
43. *See* Article 438 Companies Code.
44. For example Article 533*bis* Companies Code, concerning the content of the proxy materials for (all) listed companies; but the way the meeting has to be called/the proxy materials distributed is only different for companies the shares of which are listed, *see* Article 533, §2, Companies Code.
45. For example Articles 533 and 536 Companies Code.
46. *See* Articles 520*bis* & 520*ter* Companies Code.
47. *See* Article 524 Companies Code.
48. *See* Article 202 of the Royal Decree of 30 January 2001 implementing the Companies Code, with a reference to Article 3 of the Prospectus Act of 16 June 2006.

offerings where the minimum required investment is very large. Offers limited to current or former employees or directors of the company do not cause the company to gain the status of a 'public company' in the sense of Article 438 of the Companies Code, even if the offer was public for the purposes of prospectus legislation. As indicated, we leave out many crucial details.

[D] For Profit or Not

Since a 1995 change in the law, all company types with legal personality, except the 'agricultural company',[49] can choose to organise themselves not as companies pursuing a profit but as a 'company with social objective' (*société à finalité social* or *SFS – vennootschap met sociaal oogmerk* or *VSO*) if they comply with all of the requirements set forth in the Code.[50] The legislature thought it necessary to create this organisational form for entities from the social economy that engage in commercial economic activities and pursue profits, but where making a profit is not the main aim. Allegedly such organisations had less access to bank loans when they organised themselves as associations instead of as companies.

These companies do not have to pursue profit for their members, may only distribute a small part of any profits they make (the percentage, currently at less than 2%, is set by a government agency), must allow their employees who so wish to become shareholders after one year of employment, may not allow anyone to exercise more than 10% of the vote at a general meeting and come close to non-profit associations (*association sans but lucratif* or ASBL – *vereniging zonder winstoogmerk* or *VZW*). Minimum capital requirements for these companies are lower than for for-profit companies. Almost all *SFS–VSO* take the form of a cooperative company. When this type of company was introduced in 1996, tax benefits were promised, but the necessary tax legislation was never adopted. The *SFS–VSO* is not very successful: there are fewer than 1,000 such companies, in spite of the fact that the legislature introduced rules that enable non-profit associations (*ASBL–VZW*) to transform themselves, without break in legal personality and in a tax-neutral way, into *SFS–VSO*. The company with a social objective is mainly used by companies that mainly employ mentally handicapped people, whereas hospitals and other parts of the 'social economy', for which this form of company was actually intended, have largely stuck to the pure non-profit association as their preferred organisational form.

§13.03 PARTNERSHIPS

As already indicated, the traditional partnership-corporation distinction that is a feature of common law jurisdictions like the US and England has no equivalent in continental European or Belgian law. We use the word 'partnership' in this section to indicate companies in which at least some shareholders are personally liable for the

---

49. Defined in Article 789 Companies Code.
50. *See* Article 661 Companies Code for these requirements.

company's debt, either because the company is not a legal person or, in case it does enjoy legal personality, statutory provisions determine that these shareholders are liable for the company's debt.

Incorporation does have practical impact, especially in civil procedure, but the difference between incorporated and unincorporated partnerships is not very important. A far more important *summa divisio* in Belgian company law is that between partnerships and corporations in the sense of limited liability companies.

We have already discussed the main distinguishing features of unincorporated partnerships and the implications of them not being legal persons in §13.02 [A]. Here we focus on the general features of partnerships, and on incorporated partnerships.

The general features of partnerships mainly follow from the fact that they are considered to be contracts *intuitu personae*, that is regular contracts, aimed at personal cooperation, in which the identity of each partner is deemed to be an essential feature of the contract for every other partner.

From this most other salient features simply follow:

(1) Like for every contract, at least two parties are required, not only at the moment the partnership is entered into, but for the whole duration of the partnership. If the number of surviving partners drops below two, the company is automatically dissolved.

(2) No notarial incorporation document is required for the setting up of the partnership. Indeed, for unincorporated partnerships, no written 'incorporation' document is required, even though in practice it is almost always drawn up. For incorporated partnerships, a written incorporation document (which will then have to be registered with the commercial registry in order for the company to come into existence) is required, but this does not need to be notarial.[51] But in practice parties often have recourse to a notary, even for a *société simple – maatschap*. Also, when real estate or real rights are contributed to the partnership, a notarial deed will be required to register ownership in the name of the company.[52]

(3) Membership rights –'parts' – cannot be transferred, except with unanimous consent of all partners, unless the articles provide otherwise.[53] This also applies to transfers to heirs upon death, but heirs who are not accepted as partners have a claim to the value of the shares of the *de cuius*.

(4) If a partner 'drops out'– because of death, incapacity or personal insolvency – the partnership is automatically dissolved,[54] except if, as is common, the articles provide otherwise. Two types of such clauses are common:[55]

51. *See* Article 66 Companies Code.
52. *See supra* Chapter 9, §9.11 [A].
53. *See* Article 38 Companies Code.
54. *See* Article 39, 3°, Companies Code.
55. These clauses are also recognised in Article 42 Companies Code.

- The first clause determines that the company is not dissolved nor wound up, but will be continued with the heirs, if any, of the deceased partner. The validity of clauses that thus automatically accept certain but not all heirs is contested.
- The second type of clause determines that the company is not wound up, but continues with the remaining partners, to whom the share of the deceased partner is awarded pro rata.

(5) The articles of association can only be changed with unanimity among partners, unless the articles provide otherwise.

(6) Profit rights of partners are proportionate to the value of the contribution made by the partner;[56] each partner has one vote at the partners' (general) meeting. These are default rules and as long as each partner shares in profits and losses, every kind of deviation is permitted (such as non-voting partners or, more commonly, partners with veto rights or multiple votes; profit rights that are not proportionate to value of contribution).

(7) Partners have the default right to act as directors, i.e., to take decisions on behalf of the company/their co-partners and to represent the company/their partners against third parties.[57] This is called the 'managing partners' approach. No separate 'class' of directors need to be appointed. If, however, as is common, one or more persons are appointed as directors, they have the exclusive power to represent the company.[58] The director will usually be a(n important) partner, but there is no legal requirement for this to be so. In case of multiple directors, they have a mandate to act independently, unless the articles provide otherwise (e.g., provide that the company is not bound by acts of directors unless two of them have signed, or unless directors have acted as a collegiate body).

(8) The ordinary rules of agency law apply to the representation towards third parties of the partnership.[59]

(9) In view of the unlimited liability for the partnership's debt, there is of course no need for minimum capital requirements or rules limiting profit distributions, nor for rules on mandatory valuation by independent experts of contributions. Such rules are therefore lacking from Belgian partnership law.

(10) The Companies Code contains virtually no mandatory rules on partnerships, except the rules that at least two partners are required at all times, that each partner must share in profits and losses and that partners are jointly liable for the company's debts towards third parties (creditors), except in civil simple partnerships (unlimited liability, but debt obligation is split in equal parts among partners). Apart from this, freedom of contract prevails, meaning that parties can deal with issues as they see fit in the articles.

---

56. *See* Article 30 Companies Code.
57. *See* Article 36 Companies Code.
58. *See* Article 33 Companies Code.
59. The so-called *Prokura* doctrine (*see infra* §13.04 [B] [5] [b]), which applies to corporations, is not applicable to partnerships.

In case of unincorporated partnerships, assets are co-owned by all partners; if the partnership is a legal person, the assets are of course owned by that legal person.

Liabilities that are said to be partnership liabilities – because they emanate from contracts (validly) entered into on behalf of the partnership or some other source of liabilities that can be attributed to the partnership – are at the same time liabilities of the company and of the partners. The partners are not a sort of second-line debtors: they are debtors of partnership liabilities at the same level as the partnership. Therefore, the companies' creditors can choose whose assets they seize (if necessary) in order to receive payment of their claims: the partnership's or the partners'. Partners are jointly liable towards company creditors, except in the civil *société simple – maatschap*.

Personal creditors of partners can seize the share of the partner, but cannot seize the assets of the partnership, not even when the partnership is not a legal person. The fact that these assets were contributed to the partnerships and have therefore become the collective property of the partners, so that a creditor of an individual co-owner cannot seize or attach the assets which are partly owned by people who are not his debtors, can be relied upon against third parties including creditors (absent fraud). Neither can they sell the share, since this would require consent of the partners in the partnership, just like for every sale or transfer or assignment of such a share.

As indicated, *company creditors* can of course seize the assets of the company. They can also seize the assets of the partners or one of the partners (e.g., the most visibly solvent one). Title (for instance a judgment) against the company is title against the partners, even if the title document does not mention the partners. As indicated, there is no ranking between the partnership on the one hand and the partners on the other (or among partners, for that matter) as debtors towards the partnerships' creditors: creditors are by no means obliged to first exhaust their possibilities against the company before they can seize assets of the partners. In order to avoid the situation where partnership creditors would seize assets of partners when it is uncertain that there actually is a partnership debt towards a certain creditor, Article 203 of the Companies Code provides that in an incorporated partnerships, a judgment against partners ordering them to pay partnership debt is not possible if the partnership itself has not 'first' – but this may happen in the same judgment – been condemned to pay this debt. So if a creditor sues only partners before a court, without at the same time (or previously) suing the company, the court should reject the claim. But once the court has ruled that the company owes a creditor a certain debt, the judgment can be executed against the partners without first having recourse to the company's assets.

In case of transfer of shares, the transferor remains liable for partnership debt that existed at the time of the transfer until five years after the transfer.[60] The Code does not answer the question whether the transferee is also liable for debts from the period preceding him becoming a partner, but the Court of Cassation recently decided that such a 'new' partner is also liable for 'old' debt.[61]

60. *See* Article 209 *juncto* Article 198 Companies Code.
61. *See* already Court of Cassation 24 May 2012, 2013 Rechtspraak Antwerpen Brussel Gent 52, and more clearly Cassation 7 November 2013, 2014 Revue de droit commercial belge – Tijdschrift voor Belgisch Handelsrecht 846.

Incorporated partnerships are not very often used nowadays. Especially the *SNC–VOF*, however, is sometimes used to structure joint ventures (the partners then are corporations, with limited liability for these partners' shareholders). The *SNC–VOF* is also used by really small firms, like firms in which two brothers or a father and son cooperate as decorators or electricians, or for small car repair shops (not for large dealerships). Also, firms that are not capital-intensive and where liability risk is deemed low, like certain types of advisory boutiques, are structured as incorporated partnerships, enjoying the low costs (no legal capital) and great flexibility these forms offer.

§13.04 CORPORATIONS

[A] Introduction: Cooperative Companies and Limited Partnerships by Shares

The word 'corporation' is here understood to mean a company that is a legal person and whose shareholders enjoy limited liability. In addition to 'European' company types such as the SE (*societas europaea* - European Company) and the European cooperative company, which this Chapter does not discuss at all, Belgian law knows four types of corporations. The 'public company' limited by shares (*société anonyme* or *SA – naamloze vennootschap* or *NV*) and the private company limited by shares (*société privée à responsabilité limitée* or SPRL - *besloten vennootschap met beperkte aansprakelijkheid* or *BVBA*) are by far the most widely used. The main differences are that shares of a public company are freely transferable whereas share transfers are always restricted in a private company; in addition, one director is sufficient for a private company, and the articles or contract can make it very difficult for the shareholders to dismiss this director, whereas a *SA–NV* needs a board consisting of at least three directors, who can always, notwithstanding any other rule in the articles or private agreement, be dismissed at will by a vote of the general meeting with a simple majority among votes cast. In the past another important difference was that only the *SA–NV* could issue bearer shares, whereas the *SPRL–BVBA* had and has to use registered shares. Since the general ban on bearer shares this is of no importance anymore, also because very few unlisted *SA–NV* issue dematerialised shares (not allowed in *SPRL–BVBA*). As indicated in the introduction, the nineteenth century legislature had intended the *SA–NV* for large industrial firms, but in practice *SA–NV* and *SPRL–BVBA* have always been used interchangeably by SMEs.

The two other corporate forms in Belgium are cooperative companies and the *SCA–Comm.VA*. We will say a few words about those now and focus the rest of our text on the *SA–NV* and *SPRL–BVBA*.

A cooperative company[62] is subject to many of the same rules as a *SPRL–BVBA*. The main differences is that a cooperative needs at least three shareholders at all

62. Defined in Article 350 Companies Code, the first article of Book VII of the Companies Code, which deals with cooperatives.

times[63] and, more importantly, has a variable legal capital.[64] That is, shareholders have a statutory right of appraisal,[65] meaning that they can demand that the company buy back their shares, at a price determined in the articles or, if the articles provide nothing, at 'the value as it appears from the balance sheet of the accounting year during which the shareholder exited the company'.[66] As a result of such an appraisal, the shares will be annulled and legal capital will automatically decrease with an amount corresponding to the face value of these shares. It is therefore said that cooperative companies have a 'variable capital': legal capital fluctuates on the occasion of shareholders exiting or entering the company without recourse to the rules and procedures on capital decreases and capital increases. However, every limited liability cooperative company[67] also needs a fixed legal capital. The amount of the latter is at least EUR 18,550.[68] Appraisal is only possible if the company has the financial means to buy out the shareholder demanding his exit without touching this amount of fixed capital.[69] Also, shareholders must demand their exit/appraisal in the first six months of the accounting year.[70] It is generally accepted that the articles of association may limit the appraisal right, or even completely exclude it. Cooperative companies are the only company type in Belgium where a statutory appraisal right exists.[71]

In addition to this 'variability of legal capital', as Belgian scholars call it, the other defining feature of cooperative companies compared to private or public corporations is the extreme flexibility of governance arrangements and share transfers: whereas a cooperative company is subject to virtually the same rules as a *SPRL–BVBA* concerning the fixed part of their legal capital,[72] virtually any arrangement is allowed concerning the powers of directors and the general meeting, the rights attached to shares and their transfer. For instance, multiple voting rights or veto powers for certain shareholders at general meetings are banned in the SPRL–BVBA or SA–NV, but are allowed in the cooperative. Concerning shares transfers, the default rules are restrictive: shares may only be transferred to a person belonging to a category of persons as described in the articles of association and provided the specific transferee has been approved as a new shareholder by the general meeting or, if the articles so provide, the directors. But these

63. *See* Article 351 Companies Code.
64. *See* Article 392 Companies Code.
65. *See* Article 367 Companies Code.
66. *See* Article 374 Companies Code.
67. There is also a cooperative company with unlimited liability for shareholders – *see* Article 352 Companies Code, indicating that the articles have to indicate which type of cooperative was chosen by the company's founders – which we do not discuss here and which has hardly been used in the past few decades.
68. *See* Article 390 Companies Code.
69. *See* Article 427 Companies Code.
70. *See* Article 367 Companies Code. If they ask for appraisal in the second half of the year, this will be treated as an exit for the subsequent year.
71. Outside the context of cross-border mergers.
72. Including the rules on what kind of contributions are permitted and how they have to be valued and the rules on capital decreases and increases.

are default rules, and any other type of arrangement in the articles or shareholder agreements is permitted.

Originally, when cooperative companies were first officially regulated in Belgium by an act of 1873, the idea was that the cooperative form would mainly be used by organisations for cost-saving purposes rather than to maximise profits. The default rule was that every partner had one vote, irrespective of the value of its contribution. Profits would be distributed not proportionate to the number of shares held by a cooperative partner, but based on the contribution to turnover generated by this partner. A small number of cooperatives that still operate along these lines and in accordance with a detailed set of rules set forth in royal decrees, can apply for recognition by the National Council for Cooperatives as 'genuine' cooperatives. This brings important tax benefits. It is sometimes said that tradition and politics play a more important role in the recognition process than any genuine 'cooperative spirit'. Some important firms (in banking and insurance, in agriculture, ...) have been organised as cooperatives and corporate advisors are at long last rediscovering the flexibility that the cooperative form offers.

The least often used corporate form is the so-called limited partnership with shares (*société en commandite par actions* or *SCA – commanditaire vennootschap op aandelen* or *Comm.VA*),[73] which is in fact subject to all the rules applicable to the *SA–NV*,[74] apart from the fact that it is required to have only (but at least) one director who must be a shareholder, and whose liability as a shareholder for the company's debt is unlimited. For this last reason, one often uses limited liability companies as directors, namely a single member *SPRL–BVBA*. The director has a very strong position, as he cannot be dismissed by a vote of the other shareholders and can in practice only be removed by a court order invoking 'just grounds'. Irrespective of how many shares he holds, he can veto decisions of the general meeting that bear on the relations of the company with third parties. It is generally accepted that the decision on his own forced dismissal as director is such a decision. The *SCA–Comm.VA* is not very commonly used, but has nevertheless enjoyed a small renaissance since 1989 (when it was almost abolished), when practitioners realised, after the first hostile takeover attempt in Belgium, that it could be used to combine the advantages of a *SA–NV*, including free transferability of the shares and the possibility to list them on a stock exchange, with the possibility of putting one person (for instance the *pater familias*) or more commonly family in a virtually unassailable position.[75] It is also frequently used as the legal vehicle for listed real estate investment funds (REIT-like structures).

73. *See* Book IX of the Companies Code, Articles 654–660.
74. *See* Article 657 Companies Code.
75. The multinational Solvay group is a well-known example of a large company where large shareholders have cemented control with the help of Comm.VA companies. Recently (2016), when the huge supermarket chains Delhaize (Belgium) and Ahold (The Netherlands) merged, thereby mainly combining their dominant US operations, the Belgian parts of Delhaize were transformed into a Comm.VA with Ahold Netherlands as its parent.

[B] *SA–NV* and *SPRL–BVBA*: Public and Private Corporations as the Most Widely Used Economic Entities

[1] Formation in General

The public company is founded by at least two members, physical or legal persons, together contributing at least EUR 61,500 to its capital, fully paid up. For shares issued against a contribution of money, at least 25% of legal capital needs to be paid up upon issuance.[76]

The private company can be founded by one single physical person ('one man company'),[77] but several founders are of course permitted. It requires a minimum starting capital of EUR 18,550, only EUR 6,200 of which must be paid up at the moment of formation. Apart from that least 20% of the face value of each share issued against a contribution of money has to be fully paid up upon formation of the company.[78]

In order to combat the use of English private ltds. by Belgian entrepreneurs and as part of the general trend towards lowering minimum capital for private companies, the Belgian legislature introduced the '*société privée à responsabilité limitée starter – vennootschap met beperkte aansprakelijkheid starter*', or '*SPRL-S – S-BVBA*' for short, a 'light' version of the *SPRL–BVBA*.[79] All *SPRL–BVBA* rules apply to it, except that it can be set up with a minimum capital of EUR 1. However, if the legal capital of such a starter company is still below EUR 18,550 three years after its incorporation, the shareholders are personally liable for company debt for an amount equivalent to the difference between EUR 18,550 and the actual legal capital. Starter companies must retain at least 25% of their profits and cannot decrease their legal capital as long as the latter has not reached EUR 18,550. Only firms with fewer than six employees are eligible for *SPRL-S – S-BVBA* status. The reform has not been a success: few *SPRL-S – S-BVBA* have been set up. One reason is that thinly capitalised SPRL–BVBA are taxed at a higher rate than similar small SPRL–BVBA with a thick(er) equity cushion.

If after a public company has been validly formed, the number of shareholders drops below two, this does not lead to the dissolution or nullity of the company: the sole remaining shareholder has twelve months to either find a second shareholder or to transform the public company into a private one; failing this, the sole shareholder becomes jointly liable with the company for all company debts which came into existence after the number of shareholders had fallen below two.[80]

Both company types (public and private) have to be founded by notarial deed,[81] mentioning the company's name – to be freely chosen, but different from any other company's name, irrespective of whether the companies are competitors – its registered office, its purpose and its capital. If any of these data is not mentioned in the deed,

76. *See* Articles 439 and 448 Companies Code.
77. *See* Article 211 Companies Code.
78. *See* Articles 214 and 223 Companies Code.
79. Introduced by an Act of 13 January 2010, Moniteur belge – Belgisch Staatsblad 26 January 2010. *See* mainly Articles 211*bis*, 212*bis* and 214, §2, Companies Code.
80. *See* Article 213 Companies Code for the *SARL–BVBA*.
81. *See* Article 66 Companies Code.

the company may be declared null and void. Articles 453 (public company), 226 (private company) and 69 (both types) of the Companies Code contain lists of other things which must be mentioned in the articles of incorporation. If these data are omitted, however, this does not lead to the nullity of the company, but only to possible liability of the founders for damage caused.

The notary will only draft the notarial deed if (s)he is first presented with at least the following two documents:

- A written declaration by a bank, attesting that the starting capital of the company, to an amount of at least the legal minimum amount, has been put into an account in the name of the company. Only the company can dispose of the money in the account, once it has acquired legal personality.[82]
- A 'financial plan', i.e., a document, which the notary will keep in his archives, in which the founders of the company justify the amount of starting capital of the company, in light of the planned activities and related financing needs for the first two years of existence of the company.[83] The financial plan requirement was introduced in order to force company founders to give careful thought to the financing needs of the corporation, but it has proven largely ineffective. Usually this 'financial plan' or draft budget takes the form of two simplified balance sheets and profits and loss accounts. If a company goes bankrupt within three years after it has been set up, the court can declare the founders of the company jointly liable for all company debts if the bankruptcy *curator* can prove that the initial 'capital' (here understood in the sense of financial means, so including debt finance and of course equity in the broadest sense) was manifestly insufficient for the planned activities for the first two years. In these proceedings, the financial plan often plays an important role, either to help prove that the founders paid insufficient attention to the financial needs of their company or that on the contrary, they should not be held personally liable for company debts because it appears from the plan that they had thoroughly considered the financial needs of the future company.

After the notary has made sure a small registration tax has been paid and within fifteen days of the date of the notarial deed, a copy and an excerpt of the deed must be deposited with the registry of the commercial court in whose judicial district the company has chosen its registered office.

It is upon this registration with the commercial court's registry that the company becomes a legal person and comes into existence. Before this, its organs (board of directors, general meeting, ...) cannot exercise their legal powers.

The excerpt is kept at the registry of the commercial court, together with all changes to it and certain other documents related to the company, such as the acts by

82. For all this, *see* Article 449 Companies Code.
83. *See* Article 440 Companies Code for the *SA–NV*.

which directors were appointed or dismissed.[84] There is a separate file for each company, which can be consulted at no cost by anyone interested (photocopies have to be paid for, at an expensive rate). Since 1 July 2003, the Annexes to the Moniteur belge - Belgisch Staatsblad can be consulted online.[85]

Within fifteen days of the deposition of the excerpt, the minimum contents of which is listed in Article 69 of the Companies Code, it has to be published in the Annexes to the Moniteur belge - Belgisch Staatsblad. This publication has as a consequence that in principle, the contents of the articles can be relied upon against third parties.[86]

One more word on corporate documents. The 'founding act' (as the Dutch expression is '*oprichtingsakte*') of the company will be called (corporate) charter (of incorporation) in this Chapter. In Belgian practice, this document usually consists of three parts. The first part concerns the actual foundation of the company: it lists the name, address and company form of the company, followed by the names of the initial shareholders, the contributions they made and the number of shares awarded to each of them, and contains a declaration that the shareholders wanted to set up and incorporate the company. The second part of the charter are the articles of association. They contain the main rules governing the functioning of the company. The articles can later be amended, always by a decision of the general meeting, usually requiring unanimity (partnerships) or a 75% majority of votes cast (corporations). Every time the articles are amended, a coordinated version of the new articles must be filed with the court registry, and the actual changes must be published in the Annexes to the Moniteur belge - Belgisch Staatsblad. The third and final part of the charter are 'temporary' provisions: the appointment of the first directors, possibly (in large firms) of an auditor, the approval by the founders of pre-incorporation acts by the company's promoters, the length of the first accounting year and related matters. For companies that are legal persons, the charter will be submitted to the court registry, and the company comes into existence at the moment of registration (and does not exist before that). The only part of the charter that can later be amended are the articles, the first and third part of the charter always remain as they were at the moment of incorporation/founding.

In Belgian law, the distinction between the articles of association - which can only be amended by the general meeting - and by-laws - which can be amended by the board - does not exist. By-laws or any similar document simply do not exist under Belgian law. Any rules the company adopts on its functioning that are not in the articles of association ('articles' for short) at the most have the status of a mere contract and can therefore never be binding on shareholders (let alone outside parties like creditors) who were not parties to that contract or document.

84. *See* Articles 74 & 75 Companies Code for acts to be published in addition to the original excerpt of the notarial deed.
85. *See* www.ejustice.just.fgov.be/tsv/tsvf.htm (French) or www.ejustice.just.fgov.be/tsv/tsvn.htm (Dutch), but only the issues from 1 September 2002 onwards are available.
86. *See* Article 76 Companies Code.

[2] *Formation: Capital and Contributions*

In order to become a shareholder, a contribution is required. Contributions may be in cash or in kind. Any contribution that does not consist of cash pure and simple ('pure cash' includes wire transfers into a bank account) is a contribution in kind. Thus, in case of a debt-equity swap, a contribution in kind takes place: legally this amounts to the contribution of the claim the creditor has to have his loan or credit facility paid back, and claims are not cash.

Contributions in kind must be valued by an independent auditor or accountant, in order to avoid overvaluation of the contribution in exchange for which shares are issued.[87] The incorporators are not bound by the valuation report of the auditor, but this report is filed with the registry of the commercial court, where it can be consulted by anyone interested. The incorporators are liable for any damages caused to third parties by a manifest overvaluation of contributions in kind, and this overvaluation can be proven with the help of the auditor's report. In order to combat easy circumvention of the rule, a corporation may within two years after its incorporation only acquire (for instance by way of a sale of goods) assets from a founder, director or shareholder with the prior approval of the general meeting and provided these assets are first valued by an independent auditor. The rule only applies if the payment by the company represents at least 10% of its stated capital, and is not applicable to transactions in the ordinary course of business.[88]

Limited liability corporations may not accept an undertaking by any person to perform work or services for the company as a contribution in exchange for shares which represent the capital of the company.[89] The rule follows from the Second EU Directive and is inspired by the (unconvincing) idea that such a contribution cannot be seized by creditors and is hard to value. In a *SA–NV*, however, the company may issue so-called profit-sharing certificates (*parts bénéficiaires – winstbewijzen*), which are shares that do not represent the company's legal capital.[90] The rights attached to these profit-sharing certificates are freely determined by the articles,[91] but they must share in the company profits in some way and may carry no more than one voting right (per profit certificate).[92] In a *SA–NV*, therefore, the contribution of an undertaking to perform future services can be compensated through such certificates. In other corporations than the *SA–NV*, only shares that represent legal capital are allowed.

[3] *Formation: Nullity of the Company and Liability of Founders*

A corporation, once formed, can only be declared void on the four grounds listed in Article 454 of the Companies Code:

87. For example Article 444 Companies Code for the *SA–NV*.
88. *See* Article 445 Companies Code.
89. *See* Article 443 Companies Code.
90. *See* Article 483 Companies Code for this definition.
91. *See* Article 483 Companies Code.
92. *See* Article 542 Companies Code.

- when the corporate charter (founding act) did not take the required form, for example when no notarial deed was used to set up a limited liability corporation;
- when the charter contains no data at all concerning the corporation's name, object, the contributions or the amount of its legal capital;
- when the objects clause in the articles of association contains activities that are illegal; and
- when there were fewer than two validly bound founders at the moment of incorporation[93] (as mentioned, a *SPRL–BVBA* can always be set up by one person).

For other company types than corporations, the common law grounds of nullity apply. But for any company with legal personality, nullity (always the result of a court decision) never has retroactive effect. The effect of the nullity is that the company is wound up and has to be liquidated by a court-appointed liquidator.

The above rules for corporations imply that the nullity of a contribution of a founding shareholder does not normally entail the nullity of the whole company (unless the number of founders drops below two as a consequence). The defects in the contribution of one of the founders will usually be covered by the statutory rules on the liability of the founders/incorporators. One of these rules states that when a contribution is invalid, the other founders are jointly and severally liable for the obligations of this contributor.[94]

Belgium has a set of rules on so-called founders' liability which is probably unique in Europe if not the entire world. They are mainly contained in Articles 456 (*SA–NV*) and 229 (*SPRL–BVBA*) of the Companies Code. The overarching purpose of these rules is to make sure that if something goes wrong with capital formation, there is a group of people on whom the corporation and its creditors can fall back to make sure the company is provided with the equity it is entitled to. The rules are mandatory and cannot be changed through the articles. Liability attaches to all 'founders', that is every person who either appeared in person before the notary executing the corporate charter upon the company's formation, or who was represented on that occasion. In the *SA–NV* (and only in that type of corporation) it is, however, possible to exclude founders' liability for certain people who acquired shares upon the formation of the company. Such original shareholders are called 'mere subscribers' and must be explicitly mentioned as such in the corporate charter. At least one third of a company's initial legal capital must be contributed by people who do bear full founders' liability, so that it is impossible to set up a *SA–NV* with nobody being subject to such liability. It is incompatible with the status of 'mere subscriber' to receive so-called founder's benefits, an undefined statutory notion but which in any case comprises a position as director or an award of profit-sharing certificates. Also, persons who have made contributions in kind are not eligible.

93. If the number of shareholders drops below two after incorporation, this does not lead to nullity, but to unlimited liability for the company's debt if the situation persist for more than twelve months.
94. *See* Article 456 Companies Code.

The main rules on founders' liability can be summarised as follows:

(1) Founders are jointly and severally liable for, and are legally presumed to have subscribed to:
   - shares that have not been validly subscribed (for instance someone subscribed as a result of being misled in a fraud, a minor subscribed to the shares without the necessary approval of its parents, or a subsidiary subscribed to the shares of its parent, something which is outlawed under Belgian law); and
   - shares making up the difference if the amount of legal capital represented by the validly subscribed shares is lower than the amount of minimum capital required by law.
(2) Founders are jointly and severally liable to fully pay up:
   - the statutory minimum capital, if for some reason this has not been fully paid up upon formation;
   - 20% (*SPRL–BVBA*) or 25% (*SA–NV*) of the face value of each share if this has not been immediately paid up upon issuance of the share; and
   - the shares to which they are legally presumed to have subscribed as a result of the rules on founders' liability mentioned under the first bullet.
(3) Founders are jointly and severally liable to restore the damage arising from:
   - the nullity of the company;
   - the failure to mention all mandatory data in the charter of incorporation; and
   - manifest overvaluation of contributions in kind.
(4) Founders are jointly and severally liable towards the bankruptcy *curator* for all corporate debt that cannot be paid with the proceeds of the company's assets if the *curator* can show in court that the insolvency of the company is at least partly due to the starting capital having been manifestly too low to finance the intended activities of the firm for two years after it had been set up. This liability can only come into play if the company is declared bankrupt within three years after it has been set up. Although the Companies Code refers to insufficient 'starting capital', in practice courts look at the amount of equity and debt, i.e., the complete financing picture, to determine liability.

In practice, the grounds for liability mentioned under the first and the last bullet are the most important ones. The others are rarely applied. Liability for manifest undercapitalisation is, alas, not very rare among small firms that are declared bankrupt.

When new shares are issued during a capital increase, a liability regime very similar to founders' liability attaches to the directors who proposed the capital increase.[95]

95. *See* Article 610 Companies Code for the *SA–NV*.

[4] Shares and Other Securities

A corporation may issue different kinds of shares.

A first distinction is between bearer shares, registered shares and dematerialised shares.[96] Belgium was a forerunner in outlawing bearer shares. They were gradually phased out starting in 2006 and the last ones were transformed by force of law into registered shares on 1 January 2014.

The existence of the registered shares appears from the charter of incorporation or from the share registry which every company which issues registered shares must keep. Shareholders get a certificate proving their registration in the share registry, but these certificates are not the shares, and their transfer does not imply transfer of the shares.

Dematerialised shares are book-entry shares that are created electronically and held in a securities account. Only public companies (*SA–NV*) may issue such shares. They are used by virtually all listed companies, but very rarely by unlisted *SA–NV* because of the costs banks charge for operating the securities account system.

Apart from the *SA–NV* – who can issue profit sharing certificates, which are shares that do not represent the stated legal capital of the company[97] – all shares in corporations represent a part of the capital. Which part of the capital a share represents, is expressed by its fractional or nominal value, collectively called the 'par value' of the share. This 'value' bears no relation to the economic or book value of the share, but is the expression of the relation between a share and the total amount of legal capital issued by a company, and plays a crucial role in determining the voting and profit-sharing rights attached to a share. Nowadays, most shares have a fractional value, i.e., their capital value is not expressed nominally by a specific amount such as EUR 100, but is expressed by a fraction, for example 1/10,000th, which means the share represents such a fraction of the company capital, and its fractional value is calculated by dividing the capital by the number of shares.

In principle the voting and profit-sharing rights attached to a share are proportionate to the part of the capital it represents. In the *SPRL–BVBA* this rule is absolute, since all shares must have the same value.[98] In the *SA–NV* the rule is mandatory as far as voting rights are concerned,[99] but profits may be distributed among shares/shareholders according to other rules set forth in the articles of incorporation, the only limit being that no shareholder may be totally excluded[100] from sharing in profits (or losses). In the cooperative company the proportionality-rule is merely a default rule for both voting rights and profit distribution.

Corporations may issue non-voting capital shares, which are also called preference or preferential shares, because the Companies Code obliges *SA–NV* and

96. *See* Articles 462–475*ter* Companies Code (*SA–NV*) for the rules tied to these different forms of shares.
97. *See supra* §13.04 [B] [2].
98. *See* Articles 238–239 Companies Code.
99. *See* Article 541 Companies Code.
100. *See* Article 32 Companies Code.

SPRL–BVBA to compensate the lack of voting rights attached to these shares by a preferential treatment of these shares for the distribution of profits and liquidation surpluses compared to voting shares. No more than one third of company capital may be represented by non-voting shares.[101] They are not commonly used in Belgium, because the Companies Code contains the mandatory rule that non-voting shares must be allowed to vote on certain important decisions and because generally the same goals can be achieved in a far more flexible way by using profit-sharing certificates.

Shares may not be issued for a price below their par value. But Article 582 of the Companies Code Allows a SA–NV that has issued shares with a fractional value to issue new shares at a price below the par value of the existing shares and still attach the same voting and profit (and other) rights to those new shares as to the old ones. The company will do this when the economic (book and market) value of the existing shares is lower than their par value. Because too large such a discount would dilute existing shareholders (who are shareholders prior to the capital increase) to an unnecessary extent, and too small a discount would be detrimental to new subscribers, Article 582 of the Companies Code mandates the board to draw up a detailed report justifying the issue price; an independent auditor or accountant needs to check the reliability of the financial data used in the report, and only the general meeting may decide on such an issue of new shares, never the board using authorised capital.

Conversely, it is of course permitted to demand a share premium when new shares are issued, i.e., the company may issue shares for a subscription price that is higher than the par value of the shares. The board will try to do this when the book and market value of the (existing and also of the) new shares is clearly higher than the par value of the existing shares.

Shares in a *SA–NV* or *SCA–Comm.VA* are freely transferable. Shareholder agreement or the articles may temporarily exclude the transfer of shares, provided this restriction can be justified by the interest of the company.[102] Pre-emption rights (right of first offer or right of first refusal) and the need to obtain approval of a company organ or third party are also permitted, provided that they do not have as an effect that the share cannot be transferred for longer than six months.[103] Essentially this means that even if approval is not forthcoming, the shares can be transferred after six months. This is why an approval clause is almost always accompanied by a pre-emption right.

In the *SPRL–BVBA* shares can only be transferred (sold, donated, inherited, ...) with the prior approval of half the shareholders who represent at least 75% of the capital, not counting the shares to be transferred.[104] Between existing shareholders and certain classes of family members, shares can be freely transferred. These rules can be made stricter in the articles, but may not be relaxed. Shareholders who do not obtain the necessary approval to transfer their shares may go to court.[105] If the court finds that

101. For all these rules, *see* Article 480 Companies Code.
102. *See* Article 510 Companies Code.
103. *See* Article 510 Companies Code.
104. *See* Article 249 Companies Code.
105. *See* Article 251 Companies Code for principle and procedure.

the refusal of approval was 'unreasonable', the potential seller/transferee may demand that his shares are bought within two months by the shareholders who objected to the transfer. If this buy-out does not happen within two months, the transferee can apply for the dissolution of the company. In case heirs are refused as shareholders, they will immediately have the right to be bought out by the shareholders who objected against their admission as shareholders.[106]

In the cooperative company, shares may only be transferred to those persons belonging to a category of persons indicated in the articles (and transfers are free among existing shareholders).[107] The transferee additionally needs approval of the general meeting (or board of directors if the articles so provide) in order to be able to exercise his rights as a shareholder. The articles are free to deviate from these rules.[108]

In all company types, the donation (gift) of shares is in principle only valid if it is enacted in a notarial deed. But the same effect as gift can be reached, for dematerialised shares, by transferring the shares between securities accounts and then drawing up a document which cannot be construed as being the gift document itself, but which nevertheless clearly expresses the *animus donandi*, i.e., the intent to transfer ownership over the shares. Although the issue is not completely uncontested, the largely dominant opinion is that such indirect gifts are not possible for registered shares (so simply registering a so-called gift in the share register is not deemed a valid gift by the vast majority of lawyers).

In public companies (in the sense of listed companies or companies the securities of which have been offered to the investing public) squeeze-outs are permitted: a shareholder who has obtained 95% of all shares, can force the remaining shareholders to sell their shares to him. By going through the squeeze-out procedure, the shares will be transferred to the bidder by operation of law. The vast majority of squeeze-outs take place in the wake of a successful public take-over bid, but an 'independent' squeeze-out is possible.[109]

In 1996, important and very successful, often invoked conflict resolution rules were introduced.[110] Shareholders have a statutory right to force each other out of the company, or to demand their own buy-out by another shareholder. Each holder of shares in a public or private corporation (*SA–NV* or *SPRL–BVBA*) who, alone or together with other shareholders, owns 30% of the issued shares to which voting rights are attached, can ask the court to order another shareholder to sell his shares to him, the plaintiff, provided the plaintiff proves that he has 'serious grounds' to demand this. These 'serious grounds' need not necessarily pertain to the defendant as such; often, a situation of deadlock is sufficient. But the difficulties that are invoked as 'serious grounds' must materialise at the level of shareholder relationships: difficulties at the level of the board alone are never sufficient, nor are mere marital troubles between

106. *See* Article 252 Companies Code.
107. *See* Article 362 Companies Code.
108. For all these rules, *see* Article 366 Companies Code.
109. For the basic rules on squeeze-outs, *see* Article 513 Companies Code.
110. *See* Articles 635–644 Companies Code for the *SA–NV*, Articles 334–342 Companies Code for the *SPRL–BVBA*.

shareholders if they do not spill over to the company and affect its functioning at the level of shareholders' meetings. The compulsory transfer will take place on the conditions fixed by the court, and the purchase price will be determined by the court with the help of an expert.

Conversely, each shareholder – irrespective of the percentage of shares it holds – can ask the court to force one or more other shareholders to buy his shares at a price fixed by the court on the advice of an expert, provided the plaintiff proves the existence of 'serious grounds' that pertain to the defendant(s). Usually, the plaintiffs are shareholders who feel they are the victim of minority oppression. Courts will not grant the demand if they feel the problem is not systematic, but can be solved in a less radical way, such as having one decision of a general meeting declared null and void.

These rules are mandatory for all Belgian public and private corporations. They are not applicable to companies that are listed or have otherwise issued shares in a public offering.

[5] Governance: General Meeting and Directors

[a] General Meetings

All corporations have a general meeting as a company organ. It has only those powers explicitly conferred on it by the Companies Code. All other powers are vested in the board of directors (or the auditor). The main powers of the general meeting are:

- appointing and dismissing the board of directors, deciding on whether to sue directors for negligent behaviour, and setting directors' remuneration (i.e., what they receive in their capacity as directors; the pay executive directors receive as managers is, subject to the rules on conflicts of interest, set by the board, of which these executives themselves are members);
- approving the annual accounts as drafted and proposed under the responsibility of the directors, including the decision to declare a dividend or not; and
- changing the articles of incorporation; this includes, among other issues, capital increases and decreases, name or seat changes, dissolution, change of the objects clause, changes to the rights attached to a certain class of shares, transformations, mergers and related transactions.

In companies whose shares have been listed on a regulated stock market, the approval of the general meeting is needed for certain executive pay packages ('say on pay'-rules, for instance contracts between an executive and the company awarding a right to severance pay exceeding twelve months' worth of pay).[111]

All shareholders may attend general meetings, either in person or by proxy, and may vote. Bondholders may also attend but may not vote. The directors (all of them)

---

111. *See* Articles 520*bis* and 520*ter* Companies Code are the most important rules concerning say on pay.

must be present, the external auditor must attend if one of his reports will be discussed.[112]

At least once a year, a general meeting must be held ('ordinary general meeting' or 'annual general meeting') at a day, hour and place set forth in the articles of incorporation.[113] The main purpose of this annual general meeting is to offer the possibility to shareholders to call directors to account. Therefore, the Companies Code mandates a discussion and a vote on the annual accounts during this meeting. The annual accounts contain the board's proposals concerning distribution or retention of profits (if any). Provided the annual accounts have first been approved (this requires a simple majority of 50% plus one vote of votes cast), the general meeting will be asked to vote on a discharge of liability for the directors for any breaches of duty they might have committed during the period to which the annual accounts pertain (i.e., the previous accounting year). In case this discharge is approved, the company itself can no longer hold the directors liable for breaches of duty committed during the relevant accounting year.[114] The waiver does not affect the right of others than the company to sue the directors and does not prevent derivative actions by minority shareholders (indeed, the statutory rules only allow derivate actions if directors have obtained discharge of liability; the suit can only be initiated by shareholders who did not vote in favour of the discharge). If the company becomes insolvent because of gross negligence of directors, these can still sued by the bankruptcy *curator*.

Any general meeting of shareholders other than the annual general meeting is called an 'extraordinary general meeting'. These are usually called when there is no time to wait until the next annual general meeting for a vote, usually an amendment to the articles such as in case of capital increases or mergers.[115]

A general meeting can be convened by the board, the auditor and by shareholders representing at least 20% of the capital.[116] Unless all shareholders are present and unanimously agree to discuss other subjects, the meeting can only discuss subjects mentioned in the agenda which must be distributed together with the notice whereby the meeting is called. Shareholders can ask questions, to which the board must answer,[117] about any point on the agenda, and may submit shareholder proposals on these agenda points or propose to add certain points to the agenda, but the directors are only obliged to add shareholder proposals emanating from 5% of shareholders in listed companies and 20% in unlisted companies. In listed companies shareholder proposals are therefore rare.

Decisions are taken by simple majority (of the votes of present or represented shareholders), and for regular general meetings there is no minimum attendance requirement for a valid meeting. If the general meeting wants to change the articles of

112. *See* Articles. 536–538 Companies Code (*SA-NV*) for the rules on who may attend a general meeting.
113. *See* Article 552 Companies Code.
114. *See* Article 554 Companies Code for the basic rules on discharge.
115. *See* Article 558 Companies Code.
116. *See* Articles 532–535 Companies Code on the calling of general meetings.
117. *See* Article 540 Companies Code.

incorporation, however, it can only validly deliberate if at least 50% of capital is represented. If this threshold is not reached, a second meeting with the same agenda may be called, for which no minimum attendance is required. In any case, changes to the articles are only adopted if they approved by 75% of the votes present.[118] These rules cannot be relaxed by the articles. Changes to the objects clause, or transformation of the corporation in another type of corporation (for instance from *SPRL–BVBA* to *SA–NV*) require an 80% majority of votes cast.[119]

If all shareholders agree to do so, a general meeting may be held in writing, i.e., without any sort of physical meeting between shareholders.[120] This is an interesting possibility for the Belgian subsidiaries of foreign companies. However, written resolutions can only be adopted by unanimity, and a regular meeting is required for all decisions which according to the Companies Code have to be enacted in a notarial deed. This means that all changes to the articles, such as capital increases and decreases or dissolutions, have to be decided by a regular general meeting.

Article 551 Companies Code recognises the validity of shareholder voting agreements as long as they are limited in time and compatible with the interest of the company,[121] the latter being defined by the Court of Cassation as the collective interests of shareholders to make a profit.

Article 64 of the Companies Code contains a closed list of grounds for nullity of general meeting decisions. Shareholders (and theoretically others who show a legitimate interest) can demand the nullity before a court but must do so within six months after the general meeting decision became reliable against them (either because they were at the general meeting, or the decision was disclosed or they became aware of it). Essentially decisions can be nullified, first, if the rules on the calling of the meeting or its organisation and proceedings were not respected and the plaintiff shows that the irregularity potentially had an effect on the outcome of the vote. There is no need to show this latter aspect, of course, if the plaintiff can show intent. Also, if certain board reports listed in the Companies Code were not submitted to shareholders, this obviates the need to show any potential influence on the vote. This influence is always assumed.

Decisions of the general meeting can also be declared null and void if the general meeting took a decision about matters it could not lawfully decide upon (because they were the competence of the board, usually), when the content of the decision is incompatible with any mandatory legal rule, or in cases of 'abuse of power'. The latter category covers situations where the majority vote at the meeting was inspired by untoward motives - such as to harm minority shareholders - or more generally, according to the Court of Cassation, when majority shareholders have exercised their voting rights in a 'manifestly unreasonable manner'.

118. *See* Article 558 Companies Code.
119. *See* Article 559 Companies Code.
120. *See* Article 536 Companies Code.
121. In addition, certain types of agreement as detailed in Article 551 Companies Code whereby a shareholder commits himself to voting in accordance with the instructions of the company, its board or its parent, are null and void.

[b] *Directors: Appointment, Dismissal and Powers*

Management of the *SA–NV* is vested in a board of at least three directors, elected by the general meeting and revocable at will and without notice.[122] The board is a collegiate body,[123] meaning it can only validly take decisions if at least half of its members are present at a meeting and if the decisions is approved by a simple majority of those present. Individual directors have no powers to take decisions, nor to represent the company to the outside world in e.g., contracts or court proceedings (but *see* below about daily managers and managing directors).

In other companies than the *SA–NV*, such as the *SPRL–BVBA*, one or more directors must be appointed, who separately have the power to manage and represent the company, unless the articles provide otherwise.

Directors in a *SA–NV* are appointed for a maximum term of six years.[124]

In other companies and corporations than the *SA–NV*, there is no term limit for directors, and they may be appointed for life or the duration of the company. The latter rule is the default rule for directors mentioned by name in the articles of association. These (as a default rule) can only be dismissed against their will either by a unanimous vote at the general meeting (which will be impossible if, as is almost always the case, the director himself also is a shareholder) or with a 75% majority at the general meeting provided 'justified grounds' can be invoked. The latter will almost always be contested before a court. For directors not mentioned by name in the articles, the default rule is that they can be dismissed at will by the general meeting, by a simple majority vote. However, any other arrangement is allowed.[125]

Legal entities may be directors, but they must appoint a natural person as their permanent representative who is liable as if he were a director in his own name.[126]

The board or the directors in other corporations than the *SA–NV* have the widest powers to manage the company: they have all powers which the Companies Code does not expressly reserve for the general meeting or the auditors. This even extends to the sale of all or virtually all assets. Restrictions of this power in the articles of incorporation are permitted - and are a signal from the shareholders to the directors about the desirable limits to their autonomy - but cannot be relied upon against third parties acting in good faith.[127]

In the *SA–NV*, in addition to the mandatory board, further optional management bodies may be set up, who all have the status, like the board, of company organs, with as a consequence that the *Prokura* doctrine (*see infra*) applies to them:

122. *See* Article 518 Companies Code.
123. *See* Article 61 Companies Code.
124. *See* Article 518, §3, Companies Code.
125. *See* Articles 255-257 Companies Code for the rules on appointment, dismissal and basic competences of directors in the *SPRL–BVBA*. For other companies, both partnerships and cooperatives, the Companies Code contains very similar rules.
126. *See* Article 61, §2, Companies Code.
127. *See* e.g., Article 522, §1, Companies Code.

- 'daily management',[128] i.e., one or more persons, directors or not, who have been entrusted with daily management in the literal, restricted sense of the word; the Court of Cassation has construed the concept of 'daily management' in an unrealistically narrow way; most daily managers are not aware of this and take decisions that far exceed the bounds of what the Court deems legitimate; only rarely does this lead to legal problems;
- an executive committee (*comité de direction – directiecomité*),[129] composed of at least two persons, directors or not, which can be entrusted with all powers of the board except 'general policy' and those powers, such as approving the draft annual accounts before they are submitted to the general meeting, which have been expressly reserved for the board by the Companies Code;
- one or more 'managing directors'.[130] These persons are in fact either the CEO of the company, or have the same powers of representation as the CEO. According to the statutory system, the articles can confer the same powers of representation as are vested in the full board in a single managing director – who must be a board member – but at the same time this managing director may not take decisions that exceed the bounds of daily management, as narrowly defined by the Court of Cassation. In reality the CEO often takes decisions that far exceed the legal daily management concept and such decisions are then later ratified by the full board. At the same time, few Belgian companies vest the full power of representation in one single person like the CEO. Almost always, the articles provide that a second director, or a top manager such as the CFO, must co-sign with the managing director. This requirement of a co-signatory can be relied upon against third parties, even under the *Prokura*-system (*infra*).

Corporations are represented, through 'legal acts' like contracts or decisions concerning civil procedures, by their board or directors. As indicated, in a *SA–NV* individual directors have no powers of representation unless they have been made managing directors[131] or daily managers. The organs of daily management or the executive committee have powers of representation concerning the matters on which they may take decisions.

In other companies than the *SA–NV*, individual directors have the power to represent the company unless the articles provide otherwise.

Needless to say, in virtually all companies the board/directors delegate part of their powers of representation to people lower down the hierarchy, such as ordinary employees. This is not permitted on a permanent basis for decisions that exceed the concept of daily management.

The so-called *Prokura* doctrine, originating in the First EU Company Law Directive and intended to protect the interest of persons who contract with a corporation, applies to the powers of representation of the corporate organs of public and

128. *See* Article 525 Companies Code.
129. *See* Article 524*bis* Companies Code.
130. *See* Article 522, §2, Companies Code.
131. *See* Article 522, §2, Companies Code.

private companies (*SA–NV* and *SPRL–BVBA*). This doctrine, embedded in various provisions of the Belgian Companies Code such as Articles 522, §2, 525, and 526 (*SA–NV*), boils down to the following rule: if a company organ acts within the bounds of its statutorily established maximum powers of representation, the company will be bound by the act of representation. Third parties may disregard the articles, they may assume the default statutory rules apply. If the articles of association limit the powers of representation of a company organ, such a limitation has a merely internal effect; it cannot be relied upon against third parties such as co-contractors, unless the company proves that the third party is acting in bad faith, meaning that it actually knew of the limitation. However, the disclosure/publication of the relevant sections of the articles in the Annexes to the Moniteur belge – Belgisch Staatsblad is by no means sufficient to prove such knowledge. Thus, limitations of the powers of the board by demanding shareholder approval, in the articles, for certain decisions, limitations of the power of the managing director to certain amounts of money or certain subject matters, cannot be relied upon against third parties, even though it is of course a breach of duty for the company organ to disrespect the limitation. The same goes for the objects clause: a decision that is incompatible with the objects clause is nevertheless binding on the company. However, the clause in the articles that certain directors may not act individually but need the co-signature of one or more co-directors or managers, can be relied upon against third parties if it has been published in the Annexes to the Moniteur belge – Belgisch Staatsblad.[132]

For non-organs or other companies than the *SA–NV* and *SPRL–BVBA*, the regular general rules of agency apply to the representation of companies. This implies that as a rule, clauses in the articles concerning the power of representation of directors can be relied upon against third parties, so that the company will not be legally bound by a contract entered into by a director who did not, according to the articles, have the power to bind the company over such matters, even if according to the default statutory rule the director would have had the power to bind the company.

[c] Directors' Conflicts of Interest

The Belgian Companies Code contains statutory rules on conflicts of interest of directors of the *SA–NV* and *SPRL–BVBA*.[133] There are no statutory rules on conflicts of interest in cooperative companies.

The rules only apply when it appears on the occasion of a decision that the board or the individual director is about to take on behalf of the company, that a director has a personal interest of a financial nature in such a decision, and that (according to the wording of the statutory provision) this interest conflicts with the interests of the company. 'Purely functional' conflicts are not caught by the rule; these are situations where a director acts on both sides of a transaction, and is therefore serving two

132. *See* Article 522, §2, Companies Code.
133. *See* Article 259 Companies Code for the *SPRL–BVBA*, Article 523 Companies Code for the *SA–NV*.

masters (companies) who themselves have conflicting interests, but where the director does not stand to lose or gain anything financially himself.

Conflicted directors must inform their colleagues and the auditor, if there is one, about the conflict. Remarkably, in non-listed companies they are allowed to take part in the decisions that give rise to the conflict; in listed companies they have to abstain from taking part in deliberations about the matter. In the *SPRL–BVBA*, the same procedure applies as in the *SA–NV* if the corporation has organised a collegiate board (which in practice is rare). When, as is the normal case, the directors of the *SPRL–BVBA* have individual decision-making powers, the conflicted director must inform the shareholders of his conflict and they will appoint a special company representative to take the decision. If, however, there is only one shareholder who is also the director, he may still act even when conflicted, but must register the decision in a special register.

If the procedural rules on conflicts are not respected, directors may be held liable by the company or third parties for the damage they cause.[134] In addition, the company may demand the nullity of the decision. But going through the motions of the procedure is not sufficient: if on the occasion of a conflict of interest at least one director has obtained unjustified benefits to the detriment of the company, all directors are jointly liable to compensate the company, even when all the formal procedural rules concerning conflicts of interest have been respected.[135]

[d] Civil Liability of Officers and Directors

Directors are contractually liable towards the company.[136] They are liable if they behave (take decisions or omit to take decisions when they should) in a manner different from what may be expected of the ordinarily careful professional in the same circumstances. If the board or an individual director has discretionary powers to decide in one sense or the other (typical example: investment and divestment decisions), in other words, if there is no 'bright line' legal rule which applies according to statute or generally accepted practice (such as for instance insuring company buildings against fire, even though there is no statutory obligation to do so), then directors can only be deemed to have violated their duty of care if no reasonable director in the same circumstances would have contemplated such a decision. In a literal translation of the Dutch legal terminology, the standard is 'the utterly unreasonable decision'. This standard was introduced in order to avoid judges being wise after the facts (hindsight bias), such as deducing from the fact that an investment has resulted in big losses that the decision to invest was wrong in the first place. It does not, however, offer directors the same level of protection as the business judgment rule under US law.

Directors are liable both towards the company and *vis-à-vis* third parties for violations of the Companies Code or the articles of incorporation.[137] The accounting

134. *See* Article 528 Companies Code for the *SA–NV*.
135. *See* Article 529 Companies Code for the *SA–NV*.
136. *See* Article 527 Companies Code for the *SA–NV*.
137. *See* Article 528 Companies Code.

rules contained in the Royal Decree complementing the Companies Code are deemed to be part of the Code.

Whereas the liability for ordinary violation of the duty of care is in principle a personal one, all directors are jointly and severally liable for violations of the Companies Code or the articles. But if a director can prove that he did not take part in a decision or opposed it (the burden of proof is on him), he can escape liability (only) if he has brought the breach of duty of his colleague(s) to the attention of the first general meeting after he became aware of it.

The annual general meeting of shareholders has in principle to decide on the discharge of the directors.[138] If discharge is granted, this means the director can no longer be held liable by the company for any of the breaches of duty he committed during the previous accounting year. No valid discharge can be given unless first the annual accounts have been approved, and these accounts contain no mistake or omissions which are liable to mislead shareholders about the financial implications of directors' decisions.

If no discharge is given, the general meeting can decide, by ordinary majority, to institute a claim against the directors. The practical aspects of instituting the claim can of course be left to the care of a special agent appointed by the general meeting. It bears repeating that only the general meeting, not the board, has the power to decide to hold a director liable towards the company.

If directors are discharged, shareholders who did not vote in favour of the discharge and who represent at least 1% of total voting rights the company has issued, or shares representing at least EUR 1,250,000 of capital, can launch a so-called minority claim, that is, a derivative action. If the claim is successful, the damages that may be awarded go to the company, not to the minority shareholders, who are deemed to have acted on behalf of the company. Derivative actions are very rare in Belgium.[139]

Directors have contractual duties towards the company and therefore normally only the company, through its general meeting, can hold them liable. Directors are not liable towards others than the company itself, such as creditors or individual shareholders, for ordinary violations of their (contractual) duty of care.

But in some cases directors commit breaches of duty that do not merely amount to a violation of their duty to carefully 'manage' the corporation (i.e., exercise their functions as directors).

A first basis of liability here is Article 528 of the Companies Code concerning violations of the Companies Code or the articles of association. This provision has already been discussed above (liability towards the company).

Directors can moreover be liable towards third parties on the basis of a tort. The main example is the *culpa in contrahendo* of a director: the director negotiating a contract with a third party on behalf of the company commits some sort of fraud (e.g., knowingly presenting misleading versions of the annual accounts to a potential buyer

138. *See* Article 554 Companies Code.
139. For the technical rules, *see* Articles 562–567 Companies Code for the *SA–NV*.

of shares), or the director contracting in the name of the company knowing that the company will not be able to honour its obligations arising out of this contract/knowing that it is likely that the company will become insolvent in the foreseeable future behaves negligently.

Directors are personally liable for torts they commit, even if they commit the tort while exercising their powers as directors. In addition, when a director does commit a tort while acting on behalf of the company and within his powers as a director, the company itself will also be presumed to have committed this tort. However, in case of a company with a collegiate board, the latter is only true if the board, as the company's organ, has committed the tort, not if an individual director who is not a company organ has committed the tort. The liability of the company as a result of tortious behaviour by a director is traditionally explained by invoking the so-called organ theory as developed by the Court of Cassation.[140]

If something goes wrong with the subscription or paying up of new shares created through a capital increase, directors will be liable in the same way as incorporators are for problems with capital formation upon incorporation of the company. The specific rules are set forth in Article 610 of the Companies Code.

If a company goes into bankruptcy and, as is usually the case, its liabilities exceed its assets, the court has discretion to rule, on application of the bankruptcy *curator*, that all or some of the directors are jointly and severally liable for all the unpaid debts of the company.[141] There is one important condition, however: the bankruptcy *curator* must prove that the directors he wants to hold liable have committed a 'manifestly grave mistake that contributed to the bankruptcy' of the company. Not making sure that the company pays its taxes or social security contributions while it is able to, or organising tax fraud, are typical examples of 'manifestly grave mistakes'. There is no need to prove a formal causal link between the mistake and bankruptcy, and in practice courts, once convinced of the manifestly grave nature of a mistake, are not reluctant to assume that this mistake has contributed to bankruptcy. Not only directors can be held liable under Article 530 of the Companies Code, but also shadow or 'de facto' directors, i.e., persons who were never formally appointed as directors but who in reality exercise directorial powers.

It should be noted that discharge granted by the general meeting can never be invoked against third parties. A bankruptcy *curator* will in the great majority of cases be regarded as a third party.

[6] Profits and Losses

If a company makes a profit, it has three options, which can be combined. It can either distribute them among shareholders, retain ('reserve') them, or transfer them to the next accounting year. The general meeting decides with ordinary majority, but it is

140. For example., building on earlier cases, Court of Cassation 30 January 1961, 1961 Pasicrisie belge 570; Court of Cassation 27 May 1963, 1963 Pasicrisie belge 1033. *See also supra* Chapter 11, §11.03 [C].
141. *See* Article 530 Companies Code.

possible to limit the discretionary power of the general meeting in the articles, for example by providing that at least 20% of profits have to be reserved or on the contrary, have to be distributed. Additionally, each corporation is statutorily required to each year reserve 5% of its profits until it has accumulated a so-called statutory reserve amounting to 10% of its capital.

The general meeting decides on profit distributions, but is bound by the proposals made by the board/directors. It can only reject or approve the proposals, not amend them.

Under certain circumstances, the board of directors (not the general meeting) of an *SA–NV* (not allowed in other company types) may distribute interim dividends, which are dividends taken from the profits of the running accounting year instead of, as is normally the case, the pervious accounting year. The basic condition is that the existence of these profits has been proven by an interim financial report, and that the annual accounts of the previous year have already been approved by the general meeting.[142]

Annual profits must first be set off against previous losses, and only the surplus may be distributed. Article 617 of the Companies Code formulates this rule in a more technical way: no profit may be distributed by way of dividend or otherwise, if, at the date of closure of the previous accounting year, the net assets as they appear in the accounts are worth less or would, as a consequence of the profit distribution, become less than the amount of the paid-up capital plus all reserves that may not be distributed according to statutory rules or the articles. Net assets are total assets minus provisions and debt. This is a statutory balance sheet test. The Belgian Companies Code does not contain a liquidity test, but there seems general agreement among lawyers that it would be a breach of a director's duty of care to approve or perform a distribution if the director should clearly have known that such a distribution would create liquidity problems for the company, i.e., threaten its capacity to pay its debt as it becomes due.

If a company incurs losses, these must of course be mentioned in the accounts and must be transferred to the next accounting year. If a company incurs losses during two consecutive years, the board must devote a section of its report to the annual general meeting to the question whether it is still justified to consider the company a going concern. If, as a consequence of losses, the net assets of the company have become worth less than 50% of the capital amount, then the board should make sure a general meeting convenes within two months after the board knows or should have known about this situation. Dissolution of the company must be put on the agenda, but the board may at the same time propose other measures, such as capital increases, renegotiations of debt etc.[143] If the net assets have become worth less than the amount of the legal minimum capital, then every interested party may ask the court to dissolve the company.[144]

142. *See* Article 618 Companies Code.
143. *See* Article 633 Companies Code.
144. *See* Article 634 Companies Code.

[7] Capital Movements; Capital Protection

Here we can, for brevity's sake, refer the reader to the Second EU Company Law Directive. Belgium has basically copied its provisions, which the Directive intended for the public company (*SA–NV*), but has extended them to the private company (*SPRL–BVBA*).

Very briefly, this means that the general meeting is the competent body to decide on capital increases or decreases, in accordance with the rules on changes to the articles of association (75% majority, notarial deed, disclosure in Annexes to Moniteur belge – Belgisch Staatsblad).[145] In the *SA–NV* authorised capital clauses are standard (not permitted in other companies), delegating the power to increase capital (not to decrease it) to the board for a maximum of five years at a time and within the bounds (amounts; price per share, ...) set by the general meeting.[146] Pre-emption rights apply and cannot be excluded in the articles but can be excluded by a general meeting decision limited to a specific capital increase with a 75% majority and provided the board shows in a written report that this is warranted in the interest of the company.[147]

Real capital decreases, in which shares are annulled and money or other assets are paid to shareholders,[148] rarely happen. If they do – usually because a shareholder needs money or wants to exit the company – creditors can demand additional sureties for outstanding debt that had not become due yet.[149] Far more common are 'formal capital reductions', in which losses are wiped off the balance sheet by compensating them with legal capital.[150] This is usually done immediately before a capital increase in which an investor injects new equity into the company, in order to mitigate the immediate dilution of this financial saviour.

Belgium has copied the rules on share buy-backs[151] and financial assistance[152] from the Second Directive. Financial assistance is allowed, but under the strict conditions set forth in the Directive, meaning that in practice companies almost never apply the procedure set forth in Article 629 of the Companies Code to engage in lawful financial assistance, but either do not provide financial assistance or use one of the many techniques considered to be more or less lawful evasions of the rules.

Concerning share buy-backs Belgium has limited the amount of shares that can be bought back in one transaction to 20% of legal capital. The transaction needs to be approved by the general meeting with an 80% majority. Violation of the statutory rules on buy-backs leads to nullity of the shares, a sanction considered to be odd by many commentators since it is also deemed to prevent the possibility to have the buy-back itself declared null and void.

---

145. *See* Article 302 Companies Code (*SPRL–BVBA*) and Article 581 Companies Code (*SA–NV*) for capital increases.
146. *See* Article 603 et seq. Companies Code.
147. The rules on pre-emption rights are found in Articles 592–599 Companies Code for the *SA–NV* and Articles 309–310 Companies Code for the *SPRL–BVBA*.
148. *See* Articles 612 (*SA–NV*) and 316 (*SPRL–BVBA*) Companies Code.
149. *See* Article 613 Companies Code.
150. *See* Article 614 Companies Code.
151. *See* Article 520 Companies Code.
152. *See* Article 629 Companies Code.

§13.05 SOME PRIVATE INTERNATIONAL LAW REMARKS: BRANCHES OF FOREIGN COMPANIES

A company is considered to be Belgian and therefore subject to the Belgian Companies Code if it has its 'real seat', that is head office, in Belgium, which means that the company is actually managed from Belgium.[153] In the same way, a company is considered to be foreign if it is managed from abroad. Thus, under Belgian law the place of incorporation, the registered office, only creates a presumption as to the nationality of a company – that is: which companies law, Belgian or foreign, governs the internal affairs of the company – which may be rebutted by third parties. Belgium can of course only apply its own corporate law to corporations incorporated in other EU jurisdictions but having their head office ('real seat') in Belgium insofar this is compatible with the rules on freedom of establishment as elaborated by the ECJ in cases ranging from *Centros* to *Vale* and *Kornhaas*. This issue cannot be discussed here.

Belgium's highest courts have always had a very liberal approach towards corporate migrations. It was recognised from the 1960s onwards that foreign corporations could move their registered office to Belgium and thereby become Belgian without interruption in their legal personality, as long as their country of origin recognised this possibility and as far as they adapted their articles to some essential rules of Belgian company law.[154] Conversely, it was recognised that Belgian companies could emigrate without break in legal personality by moving their head office abroad.[155]

All companies with a branch in Belgium will be subject, in accordance with the Eleventh EU Company Law Directive, to local rules concerning disclosure requirements, such as the mandatory publication of the act of incorporation, the articles, the appointment of directors, and the annual accounts,[156] all in the official language of the region where the establishment is located (Dutch in Flanders, French in Wallonia, either of these official languages in Brussels). Some of these disclosures concern the foreign company (for instance its annual accounts), others the branch itself (such as its address and activities). All letters, invoices and other documents emanating from the local branch of a foreign corporation must mention the data listed in Article 86 of the Companies Code (mainly name, legal form and address of the head office and the latter's undertaking number[157]).

Not every form of presence on the Belgian territory constitutes a branch. A branch is a permanent establishment, which has no separate legal personality, through which contacts are made with third parties and – this is the crucial aspect – in which at least one agent is present who can bind the company he represents, even though the powers of attorney of this agent can be limited.[158]

153. *See* Article 110 Belgian Code of Private International Law. *See also infra* Chapter 16, §16.05 [G].
154. Court of Cassation 12 November 1965, 1965–1966 RECHSTKUNDIG WEEKBLAD 911.
155. Council of State No. 28,267 of 29 June 1987, 1989 TIJDSCHRIFT VOOR RECHTSPERSOON EN VENNOOTSCHAP 110.
156. For a full list of data to be disclosed, *see* Articles 81–82 Companies Code.
157. *See supra* Chapter 12, §12.03 [A].
158. *See* Court of Cassation 18 December 1941,1941 Pasicrisie belge 467.

The persons in charge of managing the Belgian branch of a foreign company are liable according to the same rules as if they were directors of a Belgian company.[159]

Companies setting up a subsidiary or branch in Belgium must respect the Act on the Use of Languages in Administrative Matters, as coordinated by Royal Decree of 18 July 1966. This basically means that all 'official documents' as defined in this Act, must be drawn up in the language of the region of establishment. Examples of 'official documents' include the articles of association, the minutes of the general meeting of shareholders, but also employment contracts. Companies are of course free to draw up an extra copy in another language, but these translations have no legal value. In Flanders, the official language is Dutch, in Wallonia it is French, while in the Brussels-Capital Region both languages may be used. Violations of the 1966 Act are sanctioned by the nullity of the contract or other document that was not drawn up in the correct language. The rules are mandatory, and no agreement (e.g., between the company and an employee) can deviate from them.

§13.06 DISSOLUTION AND WINDING UP

Under Belgian law, companies can be dissolved (*dissolution – ontbinding*) in three ways, and subsequently be wound up (*liquidation – vereffening*).

Dissolution can theoretically happen by operation of law, i.e., automatically upon certain events. In practice the cases mentioned in Article 39 of the Companies Code almost never occur, except the death of a partner in a partnership, but as a rule the articles of association of the partnership will exclude this as grounds for dissolution.

Dissolution by a court also rarely happens, except for the hundreds of companies that are each year dissolved upon request of the public prosecutor because they have not filed annual accounts with the National Bank for three consecutive years.[160] The other possibility is for a court to dissolve a company upon the request of a shareholder on 'grave grounds', meaning in practice a deadlock situation or other situation that makes it permanently impossible for the company to attain its stated purpose (as defined in the objects clause).[161] Judges have always been reluctant to dissolve companies because of fundamental shareholder conflicts, because this also impacts employees and creditors, and they have become even more reluctant since the introduction of the statutory conflict resolution mechanism which allows forced exits of shareholders while maintaining the company.[162]

By far the most common form of dissolution is voluntary dissolution, decided by the general meeting in accordance with the rules for changes to the articles of incorporation, meaning the meeting has to be held in the presence of a notary and the decision requires a 75% majority. In addition, several reports as detailed in Article 181 of the Companies Code need to be submitted to the meeting.

159. *See* Article 59 Companies Code.
160. *See* Article 182 Companies Code.
161. *See* e.g., Articles 45 (general principle), 343 (*SPRL–BVBA*) and 645 (*SA–NV*) Companies Code.
162. *See* Article 635 Companies Code for the *SA–NV*.

As an immediate consequence of the decision to dissolve the company, the board loses all its powers, and is replaced by a liquidator, who will to the extent necessary sell the assets of the company in order to pay the creditors. The general meeting can only take decisions relevant for the liquidation. The company must mention on all documents that it is in liquidation.

Once the liquidator thinks his task is finished, he must call a second general meeting in order to officially close the liquidation (simple majority).[163] This can only happen, however, after the liquidation accounts have been approved by a court. With the closing of the liquidation, the company disappears as a legal person, although creditors that have been overlooked still have five years to sue the company by assigning its former liquidator[164] – or to sue the liquidator within five years of the date on which he committed a breach of duty that resulted in the non-payment of the creditors.[165] Shareholders (in limited liability companies) are never liable for unpaid debts after closing of the liquidation (no successor liability), not even if they received assets from the liquidation (except in cases of fraud).

§13.07 SELECTED BIBLIOGRAPHY

H. Braeckmans & R. Houben, *Handboek vennootschapsrecht* (Antwerp: Intersentia 2012).

M. Coipel, *Disposition communes (à toutes les formes de sociétés commerciales)* (Brussels: Larcier 1980).

L. Frédéricq, *Traité de droit commercial belge*, Vol. IV, V & VI (Ghent: Rombaut-Fecheyr 1950).

K. Geens & M. Wyckaert, *De vennootschap*, Vol. A, *Algemeen deel* (Beginselen van Belgisch rivaatrecht IV, R. Dillemans & W. Van Gerven eds., Mechelen: Kluwer 2011).

J. Malherbe, Y. De Cordt, Ph. Lambrecht & Ph. Malherbe, *Droit des sociétés. Précis. Droit européen. Droit belge* (4th ed., Brussels: Bruylant 2011).

J. Ronse, Algemeen deel van het vennootschapsrecht (3d ed., Leuven: Acco 1975).

T. Tilquin & V. Simonart, *Traité des sociétés* (3 Vol., Brussels: Bruylant, 1996 – 1997 – 2005).

D. Van Gerven, *Handboek vennootschappen. Algemeen deel* (Brussels: Larcier 2016).

J. Van Ryn, *Principes de droit commercial*, Vol. I & II (Brussels: Bruylant 1954).

Code des sociétés annoté (Kluwer, loose-leaf and electronically available).

Vennootschappen en verenigingen. Artikelsgewijze commentaar met overzicht van rechtspraak en rechtsleer (H. Braeckmans, K. Geens en E. Wymeersch eds., Kluwer, loose-leaf and electronically available).

Wet & duiding vennootschappen (D. Bruloot, K. Byttebier, J. Cerfontaine, H. De Wulf & K. Maresceau eds., 2nd ed., Brussels: Larcier, 2016).

163. *See* Article 194 Companies Code.
164. *See* Article 198, §1, 3d indent, Companies Code.
165. *See* Article 198, §1, 4th indent, Companies Code.

CHAPTER 14
Labour and Social Security Law

Willy van Eeckhoutte

§14.01 INTRODUCTION

Social law, as the branch of law is known in Belgium, in fact encompasses two separate law disciplines that have a common origin and cover quite some common ground: labour or employment law and social security law. Both are covered in this chapter, with the main emphasis on employment.

Compliance with social law is enforced by way of the social enforcement law, which contains supervisory measures and sanctions.

§14.02 EMPLOYMENT AND LABOUR LAW

Employment law can be roughly divided into six sections.

[A] Employment Policy

[1] Stimulation of Employment

In the last twenty years, a huge number of measures to stimulate employment has been set up. These measures vary from granting premiums or tax benefits and reducing social security contributions, through to making the rules more flexible and the promotion of education and training. The latter includes professional training, practical training of young people and an apprentice system.

[2] Recruitment and Selection

In Belgium, recruitment and selection are regulated not by rules imposed by the government but by the collective bargaining agreement No. 38 concluded within the National Labour Council. Notably, only a few of the provisions of this collective bargaining agreement were subsequently declared generally binding by the government and can therefore be generally enforced. The majority of its rules are formulated as recommendations. Violation of these rules cannot lead to any effective sanction. The prohibition on discrimination is one of the binding rules, but is also regulated by separate statutes.

[3] Finding of Work and Job Placement

In Belgium, public job placement falls within the jurisdiction of the regions: Flanders, Wallonia and Brussels.[1] They organise the employment services.

Everyone can register himself as looking for work at the regional public employment offices. These offices search the labour market to find job opportunities. They also inform and coach people seeking work and assist employers in the pre-selection of the candidates.

Private employment offices are also permitted and do exist.

[4] Temporary Employment Agency Work and Hiring Out

Employment agency work is legally only allowed for permitted temporary work and for recruitment purposes. Permitted temporary work consists in the replacement of a permanent employee whose employment contract has been suspended (e.g., due to illness or pregnancy) or summarily terminated, or in responding to a temporary increase in work or exceptional work that falls outside of normal company operations. Temporary employment agency work may also be called upon to fill a vacant position if the intention is to hire the temporary employment agency worker afterwards in the same job.

In all cases, making use of agency employment work is subject to a strict procedure and is limited in time.

A specific employment contract is drawn up between the temporary agency worker and the employment agency that places the worker at the disposal of the agency's client, called the 'user', on the basis of a separate agreement between the latter and the agency. The law guarantees the temporary agency worker the same working conditions as those of the permanent workers of the user.

Outside temporary employment agency work, hiring out employees to third parties is forbidden in principle. If this prohibition is violated, the employment contract between the employer and the hired out worker is terminated by law, while the worker

1. *See supra* Chapter 3, §3.09 [D].

and the third-party user are held to an imputed employment contract with unlimited duration from the start of the work.

[5] Outplacement

Employees made redundant and entitled to a notice period of at least thirty weeks or who are at least 45 years of age, are entitled to outplacement counselling at the expense of the employer.

[6] Foreign Workers

As in any EU Member Country, subjects of other Member Countries or countries of the European Economic Area (EEA) enjoy free movement of employees. This right implies a ban of all discrimination on the basis of nationality in what concerns entry to the job market.

To all other foreigners the Foreign Workers Act applies, which in essence provides that no employer can employ a foreign worker without first obtaining an employment authorisation, and no foreign worker can work without first obtaining a work permit (work card).

For the employment of workers who are not already residing legally in Belgium, employment authorisations and work permits are only delivered upon the presentation of a medical certificate and a signed employment contract drawn up according to a certain model. But there are of course exceptions to this rule, for example, for people who come to assume a management function in a subsidiary of a company from their own country, for highly educated personnel, etc.

[B] Employment Contracts

[1] Understanding, Form and Proof

In the private sector, work is performed either on the basis of an employment contact or on the basis of self-employment. In the first case, employment law is applicable, in the second it is not. Civil servants have a legal status[2] to which employment law is only partially applicable, for example the rules on health and safety at work.

According to the Employment Contracts Act of 1978 an employment (or labour) contract is an agreement in which one party, the employee, commits himself to the other party, the employer, to carry out work in return for pay, as a subordinate or under the authority of the employer. The Employment Relations Act of 2006 sums up the criteria according to which subordinate workers can be discerned from self-employed workers. These can be summarised as the presence of a right to give orders and to

2. *See supra* Chapter 4, §4.03 [B].

supervise. Notwithstanding this essentially legal approach, it remains a matter of fact whether in a given situation there is authority or not. The Act provides a system of social rulings by the authorities, in order to avoid requalification of the relationship afterwards.

In principle, it is not necessary for an employment contract to be in writing for it to be valid. However, there are certain types of employment contracts that must be in writing, such as fixed-term contracts. Also some clauses have to be drawn up in writing.

[2] Types of Employment Contracts

Employment contracts can be categorised according to the type of work performed, the duration, and the extent of the employment.

The Employment Contracts Act of 1978 differentiates between employment contracts for *blue-collar* workers, *white-collar* workers, *sales representatives* and *domestic servants*. In addition, specific statutes exist for employment contracts for seamen, professional sportsmen and temporary agency employment workers. Until 2014 the distinction in legal protection between white- and blue-collar workers was most significant. The Unique Status Act of 2013 harmonised the until then existing substantially different terms of notice. Nonetheless some of the legal distinctions according to whether the employee performs mainly intellectual work or manual work, subsist. The Employment Contracts Act of 1978 also contains specific provisions for students and home workers.

An employment contract can be concluded for an *indefinite* period or with a time stipulation. As employment contracts for an unspecified duration offer the employee the best safeguards in terms of job security, the Act requires that an employee who starts work under a *fixed-term* employment contract be given prior notice in writing of the temporary nature of the employment. By concluding several consecutive employment contracts for a definite period of time, the employer could attempt to bypass the rules concerning the terms of notice. For this reason, the Act restricts the number of successive separate employment contracts for a definite period that can be concluded, the duration of each of them and the total duration of the successive contacts. In all other cases, when the parties have concluded various successive employment contracts for definite periods, they are legally presumed to have concluded a contract for an indefinite duration, except when the employer can present concluding evidence that the multiple agreements were justified due to the type of work or to other legitimate reasons. A specific type of open-ended *replacement* contract permits to stipulate the contract ends at the moment the replaced employee resumes his job.

Lastly, an employment contract can be concluded for *full-time* or *part-time* work. The latter must be laid down in writing for each individual employee, at the latest when the employee starts work under the agreement. The document must mention the agreed part-time working hours and the working schedule.

[3] Terms of the Employment Contract

In principle, the parties of the employment contract are free to select their own terms. But employment law is laid down to protect the employee, who is considered to be the economically weaker party. It is clear that this protection would be worthless if the parties were allowed to deviate from it to the disadvantage of the employee. Therefore, that kind of deviations are explicitly declared null and void by the Employment Contracts Act of 1978. Of course, deviations from the legal requirements that are to the advantage of the employee, do not infringe on the intended protection, and are therefore allowed.

A number of possible terms that can be included in an employment contract are specifically regulated by law.

The already mentioned Unique Status Act of 2013 has abolished the possibility to include a *probation clause* or a *trial period stipulation* in the employment contract: the reduction of the notice periods by this Act was deemed to make such clauses superfluous. Reintroduction of the legality of such clauses is being considered, however.

A *competition stipulation* is a clause in which the employee agrees not to practise any similar activities after leaving the employer, either by setting up his own business or by taking employment with a competing employer, by which he can possibly cause harm to the company he is leaving, by using the industrial or commercial knowledge that belongs to said company that he gained from it, for his own purposes or for the benefit of a competing company. A competition stipulation seriously limits a former employee's professional possibilities. Therefore, the Act only allows a competition stipulation under well-defined, strict conditions: the employee's wage has to reach a certain level, the stipulation must apply to similar activities, it must be limited in time (maximum twelve months) and in territorial scope, and grant the employee who is not a sales representative a lump-sum compensation equal to the wages due for half the duration of the competition restrictions. In addition, a competition stipulation does not apply when the employee is dismissed by the employer, unless it is a dismissal for just cause. Deviation from some of these requirements is possible in companies with an own research department and an international scope of activities.

[4] Liability

The Employment Contracts Law of 1978 restricts the employee's liability. When an employee causes harm to his employer or to a third party during the execution of his employment contract, he is only liable for gross fault, deceit and recurring minor faults.[3] In most instances, third parties suffering damage because of a fault by an employee can claim compensation from the employer, who is held to strict vicarious liability as the master for his servants.[4]

---

3. *See supra* Chapter 11, §11.03 [E] [1].
4. *See supra* Chapter 11, §11.03 [B] [2] [a] [i].

[5] Suspension of the Employment Contract

An employment contract is suspended when the parties temporarily stop executing the employment contract without the contract coming to an end. For example, the employment contract is suspended in cases of force majeure and because of annual holidays, maternity leave, and bad weather (only for manual workers). Some causes of suspension require particular attention.

Every employee can be absent from work, with full pay, for one of more days due to certain family events, such as a wedding or funeral, or to fulfil civil responsibilities, such as jury service.

The employment contract is also suspended when the employee is unable to work as a result of illness or an accident. In that case he must inform his employer immediately of his incapacity for work. The employee only needs to present a medical certificate when required to do so by an applicable collective bargaining agreement, by the work rules, or when requested by the employer. During the first month of work incapacity the employee retains his full pay; in the case of manual workers, this is partly carried by the health insurance. Given that the employer bears the burden of the absence from work of the incapacitated employee and that he has to continue to pay his wages for some time, the employer has the right to have the claimed incapacity of his employee verified by way of a medical examination carried out by a physician appointed and paid by the employer.

A system of paid educational leave has been set up to allow employees to further their training or to retrain themselves. This gives employees the right to be absent for a number of working hours with full pay in order to follow courses that provide them with general or professional training.

Very common causes of suspension of the employment contracts are the different forms of professional career breaks, of which the so-called time credit system is the most important. The aim of these breaks is to enable employees to take a temporary full or part-time break – i.e., a reduction of the number of working hours – from their professional career for personal reasons. In some cases, under certain conditions and for a limited period, the career breaker receives a 'break allowance' paid by the social security agency competent for unemployment benefits.

As all EU Members States, Belgium has implemented parental leave in compliance with EU-Directive 96/34. The right to parental leave upon the birth of a child exists until the child has reached the age of eight. During the parental leave, the employment contract is fully suspended, although it also can be suspended in part for a longer period by reducing the number of working hours.

Finally the employment contract can be suspended for several days or weeks because of lack of work due to economic circumstances. In this case, the employee receives unemployment benefits from social security although his contract of employment subsists and he remains on the payroll of his employer.

[6] Termination

The ways in which an employment contract can be terminated are very diverse. First, an employment contract can be terminated as any other contract, viz. by expiry of the term of a fixed-term contract or the completion of the work agreed upon, by mutual agreement, force majeure, and annulment. In addition, the Employment Contracts Act of 1978 provides a number of specific ways to terminate an employment contract.

There are also a large number of termination injunctions and restrictions in the Belgian employment law. Finally, good faith (bona fides) forbids the employer to abuse his right to dismissal.

[a] Employment Law-Based Ways of Termination

[i] Dismissal and Resignation: Power and Right

Under Belgian employment contracts law, each party has the power to impose unilaterally the termination of the employment contract on the other party, who cannot prevent this by demanding to maintain the employment relation and cannot claim its restoration. This is called the power to terminate a contract of employment, which is acknowledged to both the employer - by dismissal - and the employee - by resignation.

However, this does not mean that each party always has the right to make an end to the employment contract. For this, a lawful dismissal or resignation is required, i.e., a unilateral act of termination that complies with all relevant requirements laid down by law. To be lawful, the dismissal or resignation must take the form of a notice of termination (for employment contracts for an indefinite period and within the first half with a maximum of six months of a fixed-term contract of employment) or a summary dismissal or resignation for just cause (for 'urgent causes') (for all types of employment contracts).

[ii] Notice of Termination

Notice of termination is the normal, the ordinary way to lawfully terminate an employment contract for an indefinite period of time and fixed-term contracts during the first half of their term. Notice must always be in writing. The type of document required differs according to whether the notice is on the part of the employer or the employee. If the employee gives notice, notification is given:

- either by giving the employer a document made up in duplicate, the duplicate of which is signed by the employer to serve as proof of receipt of the notification;

- or by sending a letter by registered mail that takes effect on the third working day following the date of posting;
- or by serving a writ.

If notice is given by the employer, the notification can only take place in the last two ways.

The letter of notice must contain mention of the start and the length of the notice period. The notice period is the period during which the employment contract subsists after notice of termination is given. It always commences on the Monday following the week during which notice of termination was given.

A motive for the dismissal must not be given. However, collective bargaining agreement No. 109 concluded in the National Labour Council compels employers of the private sector to communicate to the employee who so requests by registered letter within two months after the end of the employment contract, the actual dismissal reasons under penalty of compensation equal to two weeks' wages.

The length of the notice period is fully determined by the seniority of the employee, being the length of uninterrupted service with the same employer. It varies furthermore according to who is the initiator of the termination of the contract of employment, the employer or the employee.

Although the system has been reformed by the already mentioned Unique Status Act of 2013 and this Act has harmonised the terms of notice for blue- and white-collar workers, the calculation remains complicated because of the fact that the unification only works to its full extent for employees who have not been employed by the same employer before 1 January 2014. For them the length of the notice period is calculated in weeks according to the months and years of service with the same employer. In case of dismissal, it starts with two weeks for employees with less than three months seniority and ends with eighty-seven weeks after forty-five years seniority. The resigning employee has to respect a term of notice varying between one week (less than three months seniority) and thirteen weeks (length of service of eight years or more).

In case of dismissal of or resignation by an employee who has built up seniority with the same employer before 1 January 2014, the calculation described above has to be applied on the service period from that date. The resulting term of notice has to be added to a second one, resulting from the application of the modified former rules on the seniority up to 31 December 2013. According to these former rules there was a different way of calculation for blue- and white-collar workers. For the former, one has to calculate the length of the notice period in days, for the latter, in months.

In case an employer gives notice to an employee of sixty years or older, the maximum length of the term of notice is twenty-six weeks. In case the employment contract is terminated by the employer and the employee finds other employment, he can give counter-notice with a reduced term.

Both parties keep the right to give notice to terminate an employment contract in a period of suspension of the contract of employment, for instance in case of disability of the employee, except in cases where termination restrictions or prohibitions apply.

But upon notice by the employer, in most cases, the notice period is extended with the duration of the suspension.

[iii] Dismissal and Resignation for Just Cause

The Employment Contracts Act of 1978 gives each party the right to terminate the employment agreement summarily, with immediate effect and without severance pay in the event of a so-called urgent reason. This kind of termination is always possible, irrespective of the type of employment contract concluded, and also during periods of suspension of the employment contract or during the notice period already running because of an earlier termination. As dismissal or resignation for just cause has wide-reaching consequences for the affected party, this is seen as an exceptional type of termination that can only be invoked when all conditions are fully satisfied.

The law describes just cause or 'urgent reasons' as serious shortcomings that render all professional cooperation between employer and employee instantly and permanently impossible. Whether a shortcoming classifies as a just cause, must first be judged by the person who wishes to dismiss or resign. In the event of dispute, a court will make the final judgment. The party who invokes an 'urgent reason' must provide evidence of such.

Dismissal or resignation for serious shortcomings is not subject to any requirements of form. It just has to happen within three working days following the day on which the initiator has gained sufficient knowledge of the facts.

Only reasons of which notification is given within three days after the dismissal or resignation can be used to justify the termination for just cause. Dismissal or resignation and notification can occur simultaneously but then within three working days following the acquaintance with the facts. At any rate, the notification of the 'urgent reasons' must take place, under penalty of nullification:

- either by way of letter sent by registered mail;
- by serving a writ;
- or by the other party returning one of the two duplicates of a document to the originator signed for receipt.

The aim of the notification is to give the other party the possibility to prepare his defence against the claims made against him and to enable the court to verify that the reasons put forward are the same as those brought against him. The courts therefore require that the reasons be described in great detail and with extreme accuracy and precision.

[iv] Unlawful Termination

If unilateral termination of the employment contract does not take the form of a lawful termination – i.e., a regular notice of termination or a regular dismissal or resignation for 'urgent reasons' – then the unilateral act does have the instant and permanent effect of terminating the contract, but as this is unlawful, it allows the other party to claim compensation. Cases of unlawful termination are:

- an explicitly given dismissal or resignation that is not a regular dismissal or resignation for 'urgent reasons';
- notice to terminate without compliance with all requirements of form;
- notice to terminate with notification of too short a notice period (the unlawful dismissal/resignation takes place at the end of the too short period);
- unfounded or unlawful (termination too late, too late or incorrect notification of the reason, too vague description of the reason) dismissal or resignation for 'urgent reasons';
- implicit dismissal or resignation, constituting an act that is considered to be equal to termination of the contract of employment (a shortcoming in a contractual obligation coupled with the will to terminate, or an important one-sided change to an essential part of the employment contract).

The party who unlawfully terminates an employment contract with unlimited duration is obligated to pay compensation to the other party that is called severance pay. The severance pay is an amount equal to the current wage and benefits due according to what is agreed upon, corresponding to the length of the notice period or, when this has already been partly completed, with the remaining part thereof.

In case a fixed-term employment contract is unlawfully terminated, then compensation is owed equal to the current wage and benefits for rest of the period of the contract, with a maximum of twice the notice period that should have been notified if the contract had been concluded for an indefinite period.

[b] *Dismissal Prohibitions and Restrictions*

Belgian employment law contains a whole series of dismissal prohibitions and restrictions for the employer, set up by statute or by collective bargaining agreement. However, violation of the dismissal prohibition or restriction does not influence the effect of the dismissal: the employee who was dismissed although this was not permitted by law or forbidden by collective bargaining agreement, remains dismissed and has no right to retain his employment relationship, nor can he demand to be reinstated. Violation of a legal dismissal prohibition or restriction only results in compensation owed to the employee affected. In case the prohibited dismissal is also unlawful as such, because it does not take the form of a regular notice to terminate or a regular dismissal for 'urgent reasons', this could consist of an additional compensation, i.e., compensation that is over and above the normal termination compensation that is owed due to the unlawfulness of the dismissal.

There are two types of dismissal prohibitions and restrictions: either the employee cannot be dismissed for certain reasons, or he can only be dismissed for certain reasons. Furthermore there is a protection against manifestly unreasonable dismissal.

[i] Prohibition of Dismissal for Specific Reasons

The main dismissal prohibitions that belong to the first category, are the following:

- a female employee may not be dismissed in case of pregnancy, except for reasons that are not related to her physical condition as a result of her pregnancy or childbirth;
- employees who have filed a complaint or brought a legal action for discrimination, sexual harassment or bullying at work, may not be dismissed except for reasons that are not related to the complaint or the legal action;
- in the case of a 'career break', the employer may not dismiss the employee for reasons that are related to, or ensue from, the career break;
- the employee receiving paid education leave may not be dismissed for reasons that are related to his application;
- trade union representatives may not be dismissed for reasons that concern the execution of their mandate;
- a company medical officer may not be dismissed for reasons which are recognised as harming his technical or moral independence;
- the employee who does night work may not be dismissed during the trial period that he is accorded to switch from night to daytime work, except for reasons that do not relate to his request to end his night-time employment;
- the employer may not undertake any actions towards terminating the working relationship with an employee who has applied for parental leave except for an urgent reason or a sufficient reason, being one found to be such by the court which does not concern or ensue from the suspension of the employment contract or the reduction of the working hours resulting from the exertion of the right to parental leave.

The compensation is a fixed amount which normally equals six months' wages.

[ii] Protection Against Dismissal of Personnel Delegates

The second type of dismissal prohibition protects members of, and non-elected candidates for, the works council and the occupational health and safety committee ('committee for prevention and safety at work'). They can only be dismissed for 'urgent reasons' that have to be accepted beforehand by the labour court or for economic or technical reasons that have to be recognised beforehand by the proper joint committee. The personnel representative who is dismissed with violation of this protection has two options: he can decide to apply for his reinstatement within the company, or not to do so. When the personnel representative or the union that has presented his candidacy does not apply for reinstatement, the employer has to pay him compensation equal to his current wage for:

- two years, if he has less than ten years of service;
- three years, if he has between ten and twenty years of service;
- four years, if he has twenty or more years of service in the company.

When the employee, or the union that has presented his candidacy, applies for his reinstatement and this is refused by the employer, the latter has to pay him the same compensation increased by the pay for a period equal to the remaining part of the mandate of the sitting personnel representatives, which lasts in its entirety four years.

[iii] Protection Against Manifestly Unreasonable Dismissal

Lastly, the employer may not abuse his right to dismissal. A right is abused when it is exerted in a way that clearly goes beyond the normal exertion of it by a careful and concerned person.[5] According to the rules of civil law, it is the employee who has to prove the abuse of right and who has to show the damage it caused him.

The collective bargaining agreement No. 109 concluded in the National Labour Council specifies and improves this protection offered by civil law by introducing the formal notion of 'manifestly unreasonable dismissal'. A manifestly unreasonable dismissal is defined as a dismissal for reasons that are unrelated to the suitability or behaviour of the employee or that are not due to the necessary operation of the company, and on the basis of which a normal and reasonable employer never would decide to dismiss. In case of dispute, the employer, who has not communicated the real reasons for the dismissal to the employee who has asked for it, has to provide convincing evidence of the existence of reasons which legitimate the dismissal. If he does not, he owes the employee compensation equal to three to seventeen weeks' pay.

[C] Protection in the Execution of Work

[1] Working Time Regulations

According to the Belgian Labour Act of 1971, the term 'working time' is understood to be the time during which the members of personnel are at the disposal of the employer. Working hours are therefore seen as different to the time actually worked, the presence on the work floor and the right to wage. In accordance to the EU Working Time Directive and its interpretation by the EU Court of Justice, the Belgian courts distinguish between waiting periods to be spent in the workplace and waiting time beyond. Only the first is considered as working time.

The working time rules use two methods of setting maximum working hours. If the employee is employed under a *fixed-time arrangement*, the working hours cannot be more than eight hours a day (nine hours in a five-day week) or thirty-eight hours a week. These legal maximum limits can be shortened by collective bargaining agreements. In case of a *flexible time arrangement*, a collective bargaining agreement or the work rules can permit to exceed the fixed working time limits by setting working hours on an annual basis and by respecting an average of weekly working hours.

Overtime is only allowed in well-defined cases, clearly described by law. In addition, employees are entitled to compensation in the form of compensatory leave

5. *See supra* Chapter 11, §11.03 [A] [1] [a] [iv].

and extra wages (a supplement of 50% or 100% is due, depending on whether the overtime occurs on Sundays or public holidays or not).

The working hours rules are not applicable to all employees. They do not apply, for example, to employees who hold a management position or fill a post of responsibility, or to domestic servants and sales representatives.

[2] Night Work

The Belgian Labour Act of 1971 describes night work as work that is carried out between 8 p.m. and 6 a.m. In principle, it is forbidden to work at night. There are several exceptions to this prohibition.

An employment arrangement for night work can only be entered into via a well-defined procedure.

[3] Sunday Rest

It is forbidden to employ workers on Sundays. As is the case with night work, there is a whole series of exceptions to this prohibition.

Employees who work on Sundays are entitled to compensatory leave during the six days following the Sunday in question.

[4] Public Holidays

The employee cannot be employed on the ten legal public holidays or substitute days, except in those cases where Sunday work is permitted.

When an employee is employed on a legal public holiday or substitute day, he is entitled to compensatory leave.

The employee is entitled to pay for each legal public holiday or substitute day during which he was not employed and for each day compensatory leave.

[5] Annual Holidays

The number of the statutory annual holidays of employees is determined by the number of effective days they have worked and of days of inactivity assimilated to those days, such as days of disability or maternity leave, in the previous year. The maximum number of legal annual holidays for twelve months' employment or assimilated days in the previous year is twenty or four weeks.

The statutory annual holiday pay consist of two parts: a so-called single holiday pay and a double holiday pay, each time equal to the normal wages for the already mentioned maximum of four weeks.

Annual holiday allowance is paid to blue-collar workers by the National Office for Annual Holidays or by a private holiday fund. It is financed by an employer's contribution on the employee's wages, paid to the National Social Security Office.

The holiday pay for white-collar workers is financed and paid directly by the employer.

[6] Well-Being at Work

Health and safety are but two aspects of what the Belgian Workers' Health and Safety Act ('Well-Being at Work Act') of 1996 provides to protect workers in the execution of their work. Apart from the many detailed requirements that must be met with respect to safety and health, much attention is paid to the protection of the worker against psychosocial risks, including violence and psychological and sexual harassment at work.

A couple of bodies assist the employer in the elaboration and application of the policy the law imposes on him in the area of well-being at work.

First of all every employer is obligated to set up an *internal* occupational health and safety *service*, ('service for prevention and protection at work'), which consists of one or more prevention advisors who are employees in the company. In the event this internal service is not able to carry out all its assignments, the employer must supplement it by calling in a recognised *external* service for prevention and protection at work. This is mostly the case for the medical examinations within the framework of labour relations, which are executed by prevention advisors who are physicians, called prevention advisors competent for occupational medicine.

In companies that usually employ an average of at least fifty employees, a health and safety *committee* ('committee for prevention and protection at work'), composed of both employer's and employee's delegates, the latter elected for a mandate of four years, is set up in addition.

[7] Equal Opportunities

The general Anti-Discrimination Act of 2007 prohibits in principle any direct and indirect discrimination in labour relations on the basis of age, sexual orientation, civil status, birth, wealth, religion or belief, political opinion, trade union affiliation, language, current or future state of health, disability, physical or genetic traits, or social origin. Making a distinction on the basis of age is considered not to be a forbidden discrimination when it is objectively and reasonably justified by a legitimate objective, for example encouragement of the employment of younger or elderly people.

The law provides a range of instruments victims of discrimination can use. All agreements that violate the non-discrimination principle are null and void. Victims also can bring an action in court to enforce equal treatment or to claim compensation. These actions and claims can also be made by trade unions.

Finally EU law forbids a subject of a Member Country, on the territory of another Member Country, to be treated differently to the national employees with respect to all employment and working conditions.

[8] Protection of Young People and Women

Finally there is a whole series of particular protection measures in favour of young people and women, two categories of employees who, since days of old, have received special attention in employment law.

In principle, it is forbidden for minors who are still subject to compulsory full-time education, to be put to work or allowed to perform any activities outside the framework of their education or training.

The protection of motherhood consists in the granting of fifteen weeks maternity leave, protection against dismissal on this ground, and the prohibition of certain activities. During the period of maternity leave, the employee receives a maternity benefit within the health insurance scheme. The employer may not dismiss an employee from the moment she informs him of her pregnancy to one month to the end of the maternity leave, except for reasons not relating to her physical condition resulting from the pregnancy or childbirth. If he still does so, he owes her compensation equal to six months' pay.

[D] Wages

[1] The Concept of Wage and Right to Pay

Wage, in the general meaning of the word, is the reward for work that is carried out by an employee in the execution of an employment contract. The difference between benefits that are the reward for work and therefore forms part of the wage and benefits that are not is of practical importance in the question of right to pay. Indeed, since wage is paid in consideration of work, an employee is, in principle, not entitled to wages when he is not working. Therefore, the employee whose employment contract is suspended has, in principle, no right to pay during this period. In many suspension cases though, the law does grant wages in spite of the absence of work, for example during the first month of disability of the employee. These are referred to as 'guaranteed' wages, which means that the right to pay is guaranteed although no work is carried out.

[2] Pay Determination

In Belgium, it is a tradition that the wage level and the minimum wages are not set by the government but by the employers and employees or their organisations. In the last decades, these agreements were thwarted repeatedly by legal measures whereby the government intervened in the process of free wage determination. The governmental intervention consists of a compulsory restraint in pay rises.

The level of the wage and the form in which that wage is made up and the way it is paid, are the main subject of a consensus between the parties and are therefore defined principally in the employment contract. However, pay can also be determined for a company on a collective basis by way of a collective bargaining agreement.

In terms of rate of pay, there are in Belgium binding minimum standards laid down in collective bargaining agreements, drawn up at industry or interprofessional level, which prevail over the will of the parties and from which, therefore, individual and collective bargaining agreements concluded on a lower level cannot deviate. At the interprofessional level, there is a collective bargaining agreement of the National Labour Council No. 43, which grants an average minimum monthly income to every employee of the private sector. In addition, in most industries levels of minimum pay are determined by collective bargaining agreements made in the joint committees. The structure of these bodies (still often separate committees do exist for white- collar and blue-collar workers in the same business sector) explains that wage determination is usually performed differently for manual and intellectual workers. For manual workers, there is often hourly pay, for intellectual workers more often monthly pay. The rates of the minimum wages, which vary according to the class of function and/or the number of years of service with the same employer, are laid down in scales.

Belgium is one of the few countries that still have an automatic linkage of the wages to the consumer price index. This means that an adjustment of the amount of the wages occurs according to a pre-defined formula, without appraisal of the desirability or possibility of the adjustment, as happens in other countries. The index link is not made on a statutory basis but by collective bargaining agreements made at industry level.

[3] Wage Protection

The Wage Protection Act of 1965 has the objective of guaranteeing the employee a maximum availability of the wage he is entitled to. Therefore, the employer is prohibited to limit in any way the freedom of the employee to dispose of his wage as he sees fit. To this end, the Act includes requirements concerning the payment of wages in kind, the frequency of payment, the measurement of work, the amounts that can be deducted from pay, seizure and transfer of pay, etc.

Given its objective, it is logical that this Wage Protection Act adopts a broader definition of wage than the general definition, being the reward for the work carried out in execution of the employment contract. Indeed, the employee must also enjoy maximum availability of the benefits to which he has a right upon suspension or termination of an employment contract, as well as the payment of costs; if not, his livelihood, and that of his family, could be threatened.

[E] Collective Labour Law

[1] Social Dialogue

[a] Social Partners

Among the most important worldwide acknowledged social basic rights, are the right to free trade unions and the right to collective bargaining.

In Belgium, the Freedom of Association Act of 1921 safeguards the freedom of unions. This Act states that no one can be forced to join or to leave a union. Violation of this Act is a criminal offence.

The Belgian trade unions are, as most employers' organisations, unincorporated associations, missing legal personality. Therefore, they for instance cannot be sued in court to be forced to pay damages for a strike. Nevertheless, the law grants them a whole range of powers that enable them to participate in social, economic and even judicial matters, as they are represented in the labour courts.

This so-called limited functional legal personality is only granted to certain unions that are recognised as being representative by law. Only the three large 'traditional' unions - the Confederation of Christian Trade Unions, the General Federation of Belgian Labour, and the General Confederation of Liberal Trade Unions of Belgium - are recognised as such.

[b] Levels of Social Dialogue

Typical of the Belgian social dialogue are the different levels at which this takes place.

First of all, there is the interprofessional level, which contains all industries of the private sector. On this level the dialogue mainly takes place in the National Labour Council, which is made up jointly of the recognised representative employers' and workers' organisations. They give advice to the executive and the legislature and negotiate about and conclude collective bargaining agreements that have effect across the private sector of the whole country.

The sectoral level is that of the industries. The social dialogue at industry level takes place in joint committees. In these too, collective bargaining agreements are concluded by employers' and workers' organisations.

At company level, no less than three separate consultation bodies can exist. First, there is the *trade union delegation*, composed solely of employees of the company. The setting up and operation of this delegation is regulated by collective bargaining agreements on the industry level that are concluded in implementation of the inter-professional collective bargaining agreement No. 5 of the National Labour Council. In order to set up a trade union delegation, one or more representative workers' organisations have to make a request to the head of the company. The trade union delegation is to be considered as the representation of the trade union affiliated personnel to the employer. The power of the trade union delegation can, contrary to that of the works council, be described as demanding, contesting and vindicating: the trade union delegation negotiates collective bargaining agreements with the employer at company level, monitors the observance of employment law, and plays an important role in conflict situations.

In business units with at least 100 employees, the employer must take the initiative to set up a *works council*. This council is a two-part body: it is composed of an employer's and an employees' representation, without there having to be the same number of representatives on each side; only the number of employees' representatives should not be higher than that of the employer's representatives. The former are elected every four years by way of social elections held in the enterprises. The works council has advisory powers in social affairs, it has the right to receive information concerning economic and financial affairs and to debate about it, and it has limited decision powers in drawing up of the work rules, and management responsibilities concerning the so-called social works of the enterprise. The council is convened by the head of the company. It meets at least once a month. The members of the works council who represent the employees must be given the necessary time and facilities to fulfil their task satisfactorily.

Lastly, every employer with a business unit of at least fifty employees is obligated to set up on that level a committee for prevention and protection at work. This committee is, as is the works council, a two-part body composed of representatives of the employer on the one hand, and of the employees on the other. It complements the service for prevention and protection at work by providing advice in that area.

[2] Collective Bargaining Agreements

In many cases, social dialogue leads to the conclusion of collective bargaining agreements. A collective bargaining agreement is an agreement reached between one or more workers' organisations on the one hand, and one or more employers' organisations or one or more employers (at the company level) on the other hand, and whereby the individual and collective relations between employers and employees in companies or industries or for the whole private sector of the country are set out, and the rights and responsibilities of the contracting parties are specified.

The *parties* in a collective bargaining agreement on the side of the employees are always one or more representative workers' organisations or trade unions. On the side of the employers, one or more representative employers' organisations can be involved but also only one employer. In the latter case, the collective bargaining agreement is concluded at company level.

A collective bargaining agreement can indeed be concluded at various levels. Above the company level, there is the sectoral or industry level. Lastly, a collective bargaining agreement can be concluded for the whole private sector of the country, within the National Labour Council.

The content of a collective bargaining agreement consists in the regulation of two matters: the relations between employers and employees on the one hand (called normative provisions), and the rights and responsibilities of the contracting parties on the other hand (called obligatory provisions). The normative provisions define binding standards for employees and employers. Individual normative provisions contain regulations that are taken up in the individual employment contract, such as working hours and wages. The obligatory provisions only bind the contracting parties who, on the side of the employees, are always workers' organisations. A number of obligatory provisions are considered to be inherent in every collective bargaining agreement and therefore are part thereof, even if they were not expressly agreed. These are the so-called information, influence and peace obligations, which mean that the representative organisations that concluded the collective bargaining agreement, will inform their rank and file of the existence and the contents of the agreements they have concluded, encourage their members to comply with them, and refrain from collective action against the said collective agreements.

The originality of the collective bargaining agreement phenomenon shows itself mainly in their *binding force*. Binding force should be understood as the parties being held to responsibilities that are laid down in the collective bargaining agreement, but also being entitled to claim the rights that it grants. In principle, the normative provisions of a collective bargaining agreement bind the employers who are members of the employers' organisations that concluded the agreement. On the side of the employees, the normative dispositions of a collective bargaining agreement are primarily binding for all employees of a committed employer. Individual employees can therefore refer to the provisions of a collective bargaining agreement when their employer is bound by that agreement, regardless of whether they are member of an workers' organisations or not. The latter effect is the result of the legal representativeness of the workers' organisations, which are considered to represent all employees. Even if an employer is not affiliated with an employers' organisation, he and his employees are bound by the provisions of the collective bargaining agreements the employers' organisations concluded, unless they agree to deviate from it in writing in the individual employment contract. Finally most collective bargaining agreements concluded in the National Labour Council or in joint committees are made generally binding. This happens by royal decree at the request of the body or of an organisation represented therein. A collective bargaining agreement, which is declared generally binding, is mandatory for all employers and employees who fall within the domain of either the National Labour Council, i.e., the entire private sector, or the joint committee and within the scope as defined in the agreement. Such an agreement, therefore, has almost the same binding force as law, although it originates from and remains in essence a contract.

Finally, it must be mentioned that violations of a collective bargaining agreement that has been declared generally binding constitute a criminal offence.

[3] Industrial Conflicts

In Belgium, Article 6.4 of the European Social Charter is the legal basis of the right of every individual employee to strike. Dismissal of an employee due to participation in a strike is therefore unlawful.

Strikes are often accompanied by other means of action, such as the occupation of company premises, a blockade of the company premises, a blockage of traffic routes and junctions, etc. In some cases, the actions are quite serious and include destruction, arson, violent acts, kidnapping, etc. These kind of actions are not legitimised by the right to strike. Some are even actual criminal offences. An exception should be made for strike picketing, being the exertion of pressure on work-willing employees to encourage them to stop work. Although some courts condemn picketing as illegal and forbid it when petitioned by an employer, there is also a well-established legal practice that accepts this phenomenon as part of the right to strike.

Since some strikes can cause serious harm to the economy and even to society as a whole, the Essential Services Act from 1948 ('Act on Services of Public Interest in Peacetime') empowers the government to proceed, under certain conditions, to requisitions in order to guarantee essential services.

But traditionally in Belgium, a lot of attention is paid to conciliation and mediation for solving industrial conflicts. These take place mainly via the trade union delegation, the joint committees and the 'social mediators' of the Federal Public Service Employment, Labour and Social Dialogue. As industrial conflicts almost never are disputes about rights but rather cases of conflicting interests, they cannot be settled on the basis of the available legal rules. Therefore, the courts are also powerless in that they cannot decide on such disputes in favour of one of the parties, by for example prohibiting a strike. This does not mean, though, that the judiciary has no say at all in these kind of conflicts. Of course, the labour courts can and do decide in individual disputes whose origins can be found in a collective dispute. In addition, the civil courts have the power to order in case of emergency measures that temporarily intervene in strike accompanying circumstances, such as an order to remove a blockade.

[4] Work Rules

The work rules specific to each company are also a source of law in employment relations. They codify the practices and applications of the employment legislation that are related to the company. The more employment legislation has been extended, the less important the work rules of companies have become. The work schedules and disciplinary sanctions are the main provisions of work rules.

Drawing up and modifying the work rules of a company must take place according to a well-defined procedure that varies depending on whether there is or is not a works council in the company. In the first instance, the works council draws up the work rules; in the second, the employees must be consulted via the publication of a draft.

The employees must at all times be able to acquaint themselves with what is contained in the work rules. Furthermore, every employee must receive a copy of these rules.

[F] Company Restructuring

[1] Closure of Enterprise

Belgian legislation concerning *closure of enterprises* comprises three large parts that involve a central public organisation, the Compensation Fund for Employees Made Redundant as a Result of the Closure of Enterprises, in short the Closure Fund. For the financing of this fund, all employers are irrevocably held to pay a contribution via the National Social Security.

The first of its assignments concerns the granting of a specific compensation for closure to certain employees affected by closure when the employer fails to pay it.

A second guarantees every employee who is affected by a company closure payment of any other amounts owed to him by the employer.

Finally, a transitional compensation is granted to employees of companies that are declared bankrupt and whereby the assets and employees are taken over within six months.

[2] Collective Dismissal

Collective dismissal is dismissal due to economic or technical reasons that affects a minimum number of employees during a period of sixty calendar days. The minimum is, in principle, 10% of the number of employees of the previous calendar year.

The employer who is intending to move to collective dismissal is obliged to inform and consult the works council, or in the absence thereof, the trade union representation. Upon non-adherence to these requirements, the employer will have to continue to pay wages until he has provided the necessary information and completed the necessary consultation.

Further to the information and consultation of his personnel, the employer has to notify his intention to proceed to a collective dismissal to the authorities. He is not allowed to dismiss the employees earlier than the end of a period of thirty days, which can be extended to sixty days, starting from the day of the notification of intention.

The employees subject to collective dismissal who benefit from unemployment benefit, receive in addition compensation for collective dismissal at the expense of the employer.

[3] Transfer of Enterprise

The collective bargaining agreement No. 32*bis* concluded in the National Labour Council has a twofold objective:

- on the one hand, it safeguards the employees' rights in all cases of change of employer due to transfer of an enterprise or part of an enterprise;
- a less stringent protection is guaranteed to the employees in case of the take-over purchase of assets after bankruptcy of the employer.

The first is in keeping with EU Directives 77/187 and 2001/23. The principle that applies is that the rights and responsibilities of the transferor resulting from the existing employment contracts at the time of transfer are carried over by the transfer to the receiver. This means that the transferee must take over from the transferor all employees who are employed at the time of the transfer, with preservation of all of their rights. Furthermore, it is stated that the change of employer itself provides no grounds for dismissal either for the transferor or the transferee. Employees who change employer can only be dismissed for just cause ('urgent reasons') or for economic, technical or organisational reasons that bring about changes to the employment.

In the case of transfer of employees upon a take-over of assets following bankruptcy, the regime is somewhat different. It only applies when the take-over takes place within six months from the date of bankruptcy. First – and contrary to what is the case for transfers of enterprise outside the context of bankruptcy – the transferee can choose which of the employees, in service at the time of the transfer, he will take over. Second, only the rights guaranteed by collective bargaining agreements that bound the previous employer are transferred to the new employer, be it that changes therein can be made under mutual agreement. Also, the seniority built up by the employee with his previous employer is transferred to the new employer, with any period of interruption due to bankruptcy being taken into account.

§14.03 SOCIAL SECURITY LAW

[A] In General

Belgian social security is of the Bismarckian, i.e., professional kind, and not of the Beveridgeian, i.e., universal kind. This means that the right to social security support stems, in principle, from work and is not based on citizenship. This approach has an effect on the method of financing. The latter involves a certain reciprocity: the protection offered by social security is considered in a certain way as the return on the contribution to the collectivity made by work. This is also shown in the fact that the benefits granted are mostly in proportion to the lost income from the professional activity, although the application of a wage or income limit in the calculation of the social security benefits leads to flat-rate replacement incomes for bigger earners. Finally the scope of application of some social security schemes is extended to certain categories of non-professionally active people, and some benefits, such as the compensation for health care expenses and family allowances, have even an almost universal nature.

The professional structure of the Belgian social security is actually made up of three social security systems: one for employees, one for the self-employed, and one for civil servants. With regard to certain social security provisions, the civil servants' system strongly resembles that of the employees or is even incorporated in it. The system for the self-employed provides lower social protection, resulting from a more limited source of financing by the independent workers themselves.

In addition, there is a system of social assistance that provides support according to the level of need in certain situations.

[B] Social Security Provisions

[1] Schemes and Benefits

[a] Industrial Accidents and Professional Diseases

The industrial accidents and professional diseases provisions are two schemes of Belgian social security that exist only for employees and public servants, not for the self-employed. The latter have to claim from the health insurance in the event of an accident or an illness that originates from a professional context.

The two schemes of insurance of professional risks only compensate the damage resulting from injuries to the physical or mental condition of the employee or civil servant, in other words, the damage caused by death or by personal injuries, disability or medical care. In the event of death, the damage suffered by some survivors as a result of the loss of the victim's way is compensated; in the event of work incapacity, compensation is provided for the loss of income or of the employment potential of the victim. In all cases, all medical expenses are fully compensated.

The compensation for incapacity to work and death is computed on the basis of the wages of the victim of the last year, which are seen as representing the value of his economic potential on the general labour market. In the event of permanent disability, the claiming employee receives lifelong a percentage of this wages that corresponds to the degree of permanent work incapacity. In the event of death, the surviving partner receives an annuity equal to 30% of the said wages, whilst other relatives, such as children, receive a lower amount for a limited time.

[b] Family Allowances

The family allowances scheme, which comprises maternity (or adoption) allowance and child benefits, is in transition in Belgium. It used to be a branch of the federal social security system, but since the Sixth Reform of the State in 2013, it falls within the jurisdiction of the regions.

At the occasion of this transfer of powers, the former separate systems for employees, civil servants and self-employed workers have been unified in one, be it transitory, system.

At the time of finalising this text, none of the three regions already completed its own family allowances scheme.

[c] Pensions

The pension systems for employees, civil servants and self-employed persons grant an old age or retirement pension as well as a survivor's (widow's/widower's) pension. The latter is granted to the surviving husband or wife without a substantial proper income, in the event of the death of his or her spouse, after at least one year of marriage.

In the two systems of the private sector (for employees and self-employed persons), both kinds of pensions are calculated on the basis of the number of years worked, increased by the periods of inactivity assimilated to periods worked (e.g., periods of disability or unemployment), and on the wages or income (up to a certain limit) earned during these years or flat-rate fictive wages for the assimilated periods. Retired persons with a dependent spouse, receive a so-called family pension, being 75% of the (limited) average wages or income of their entire professional career. The retirement pension of the others and the survivor's pensions are calculated at 60%.

Although pensions for the self-employed are calculated in a similar way, the result obtained has to be multiplied by a percentage that reflects the difference between the pension contributions of the self-employed and those of the employee pension system, which results in a substantial reduction of the pension amount.

Finally, pensions for civil servants are calculated on the basis of the pay during the last ten years of service. For them, there is no difference between the retirement pension of a married and that of a single person: all retirement pensions are calculated at the same rate as the 'family' pensions of the private sector, even if the retired civil servant is single.

[d] Compensation for Health Care Expenses and Work Incapacity

The Belgian mutual health insurance system encompasses a partial compensation of the medical care expenses (for quasi all residents in Belgium) and the payment of a replacement income in the event of incapacity to work or disability (due to non-professional causes for employees, whatever the cause for self-employed persons).

The first scheme of the mutual health insurance covers a large part of most *medical expenses* a citizen can make. A personal share of approximately 25% is to be supported by the beneficiary, in order to reduce medical consumption.

A *work incapacity benefit* is granted to every employee whose earning capacity has been decreased by at least two thirds. It is calculated as a percentage of his wage and varies according to the family circumstances of the employee and the period of work incapacity (the first year, called primary work incapacity period, and later periods, called invalidity periods), and starts at 60% of a limited salary. The self-employed only receive a work incapacity benefit after one month. Their benefit varies as that of the employees, but the amounts are fixed and low.

Pregnant employees and self-employed workers receive a *maternity benefit* during the period of maternity leave, which is fifteen weeks long for the former, eight weeks for the latter.

For work incapacity and motherhood, civil servants are subject to status regulations that guarantee the preservation of their salary to be paid by their public employer.

[e] Unemployment Benefits

Unemployment benefits only exist for employees. To have a right to unemployment benefits, the employee must present evidence of a number of days worked, or days of inactivity assimilated to days worked, during a waiting period that varies in length according to age, and number of days worked or days of inactivity that are considered equal to days worked (e.g., illness).

Unemployment benefits are only granted to the employee who is involuntarily unemployed and is not entitled to any wage. He must register himself as seeking work, be capable of work, actively seek work, be available to the job market, accept any suitable job offered, reside in Belgium and subject himself to control.

As the work incapacity benefit of the mutual health insurance, the amount of unemployment benefit varies according to the family situation of the unemployed person and the duration of unemployment. It is a percentage of the last wage lost, limited to a certain amount. The percentage starts at 60%, but is degressive.

In principle, unemployment benefits are granted for an unlimited period. Only those who can fall back on the income of another member of the family can, under certain conditions, lose their right to benefit due to the length of their unemployment.

The self-employed can receive a time-limited flat-rate benefit in the event of bankruptcy or economic difficulties.

[2] Structural Aspects

[a] Field of Application

The social security system for *employees* is applicable, in principle, to those bound by an employment contract. However, others who find themselves in a legally or economically inferior position have been brought, in part or in full, into the social security system for employees. This is the case, for example, for some self-employed taxi and truck drivers.

As a rule, *self-employed* have their own social security system. It applies to all physical persons who perform a business activity outside any relationship of subordination. This social security system also applies to so-called helpers who assist or replace self-employed workers without being themselves under the authority of the latter.

Lastly, *civil servants* enjoy in part the same social security protection as employees. For the remainder, they are protected by their own social security or employment status, to an effect which is at least equal to that of employees.

[b] Financing

Social security for *employees* is mainly financed by contributions from employees and employers, calculated as a percentage of the wages earned and paid, which are withheld from the wages or paid over and above the wages, respectively. Many supplementary benefits, such as luncheon vouchers, are exempted from social security contribution to a certain amount and under certain conditions. The administration of the contributions is the exclusive responsibility of the employer, who transfers both his own contributions and the withheld contributions of his employees periodically to a central collection body, the National Social Security Office. Private employers' organisations, called social secretariats, can assist and represent the employers. There are various types of reductions in employers' contributions that aim to stimulate employment.

The *self-employed* pay their social security contributions to so-called social insurance funds for independent workers, which are private organisations that they can freely select. The contributions are a percentage of their professional income. The contribution rates vary according to the level of income and are not owed on professional income that exceeds a certain amount.

Lastly, the social security provisions for civil servants are only partly financed by contributions, especially compensation for medical care expenses. For the main part, the provisions are directly funded by the public employer.

[c] Administrative Organisation

The administrative organisation of the Belgian social security contains various levels.

At the top, social security for employees is managed by the Federal Public Service Employment, Labour and Social Dialogue (for the unemployment insurance) and the Federal Public Service Social Security (for the other schemes).

Both the social security system for employees and that for the self-employed have a central public institution that manages all the financing. This is the National Social Security Office on the one hand, and the National Institute for Social Insurances of the Self-employed on the other hand.

Each social security scheme is managed, under the trusteeship of the above-mentioned central public organisation, by a specific national office, institute or fund that in turn is a public institution: the National Employment Office, National Health Insurance Institute ('National Institute for Sickness and Invalidity Insurance'), National Pension Office and the Federal Agency for Professional Risks.

The scheme-specific public offices for employees are managed by joint representation, this means by an (mostly) equal number of representatives of the employers' and workers' organisations, under chairmanship of independent person. The social security for the self-employed is managed by the organisations of the self-employed workers.

The private organisations that are historically at the basis of some social security schemes - health insurance funds, unemployment benefit funds and the family allowances funds ('child benefit funds') - have been retained as part of the administrative organisation of the Belgian social security system: they actually pay the social security benefits to the beneficiaries.

As far as industrial accidents for employees of the private sector are concerned, every employer must take out insurance from a private insurance company. The premium paid by the employer varies according to the risks created by his business and the kind of prevention policy enforced by the employer, so that prevention is encouraged.

The Social Security Crossroads Bank co-ordinates the communications between the various social security bodies. It is not a central database of social security data, but a public institution that has a reference register of social security information. Every actor within the social security system can, via the Crossroads Bank, obtain electronically the information he requires, without having to ask the beneficiary for it. Of course, severe privacy protection measures are in force within the system.

For the beneficiaries, the formalities are greatly simplified by the use of his electronic identity card containing a microchip that gives social security bodies access to the relevant information they need. The legally entrenched 'Charter of the Socially Insured' ensures a transparent and efficient communication between the beneficiaries and the panoply of social security actors.

[C] Social Assistance

Despite the extensiveness and the steady improvement of Belgian social security, a number of people continue to slip through the safety net. The concern to eliminate the resulting poverty has led to a number of schemes that aim to provide a minimum income for those people who due to circumstances are unable to work or obtain social security benefits, or who can only claim insufficient benefits. So there is a 'minimum income guarantee for the elderly', a system of allowances to disabled persons, and a residuary subsistence allowance called 'living wage'.

Social assistance provisions are not based on the payment of contributions but on the solidarity of the community: they are usually financed with money from the public purse. They are therefore reserved for Belgians, EEA-subjects and foreigners of equivalent status, and support is only granted in the event of real need, i.e., they provide means-tested benefits.

The amounts of these benefits are flat-rate and relatively low.

§14.04 SOCIAL ENFORCEMENT LAW

The Belgian Social Criminal Code contains the measures by which the authorities monitor and enforce the compliance with the social law.

The monitoring of the compliance with employment and social security law is carried out by a body of specialised inspectors. These so-called social inspectors can issue warnings and set time limits for regularisation. *Pro Justitia* reports from their hand can lead to prosecution, which can result in administrative fines imposed by the Federal Public Service Employment, Labour and Social Dialogue or criminal penalties imposed by the criminal courts.

§14.05 SELECTED BIBLIOGRAPHY

J. Clesse & F. Kéfer, *Manuel de droit du travail* (Brussels: Larcier 2014).

J.F. Funck, *Droit de la sécurité sociale* (Brussels: Larcier 2006).

P. Humblet & M. Rigaux, *Belgian Employment Law* (Antwerp: Intersentia 2010).

P. Humblet & M. Rigaux, *Belgian Industrial Relations Law* (Antwerp: Intersentia: 2005).

G. Vanden Avyle, *Guide social permanent. Commentaire droit du travail et Commentaire droit de la sécurité sociale* (Waterloo: Kluwer, loose-leaf).

W. van Eeckhoutte, *Mémento social* (Waterloo: Kluwer, biannually a new edition).

W. van Eeckhoutte, *Handboek Belgisch arbeidsrecht* (Mechelen: Kluwer 2014).

W. van Eeckhoutte, *Compendium social – Droit du travail* (Waterloo: Kluwer, annually a new edition).

W. van Eeckhoutte, *Sociaal compendium socialezekerheidsrecht* (Mechelen: Kluwer, annually a new edition).

J. Van Langendonck, Y. Stevens & A. Van Regenmortel, *Handboek socialezekerheidsrecht* (Antwerp: Intersentia 2015).

CHAPTER 15

The Belgian Tax System

Miguel De Jonckheere[*]

§15.01 INTRODUCTION

[A] The Belgian State Structure and the Tax System

[1] The Constitutional Reforms

For a good understanding of the Belgian tax system, some preliminary remarks have to be made concerning the Belgian form of government. Several constitutional reforms since 1970 have transformed the unitary State into a federal form of government. Between the State and the local authorities (provinces and municipalities), two new government levels have been created: the communities and the regions.[1] Because of these constitutional reforms, the powers that were formerly allocated to the unitary State have been split up between the federal State, the communities and the regions. Each of these government levels has its own legislative assembly and executive. The matters that have been withdrawn from the federal State's powers are rather important because of both their budgetary extent and their impact on the daily life of the citizens. Education, one of the main components of the country's public expenditure, has become a competence of the communities. The regions are competent for matters such as public works and infrastructure, urbanisation, environmental policy and regional economy.

* The author based this text on the original chapter on the Belgian tax system by A.J.J. Spruyt in the first edition of this book, published in 2001.

1. *See supra* Chapter 3, §3.09 [D].

[2] *Constitutional Tax Powers*

As part of this constitutional reform, the constitutional right to levy taxes originally granted to the (federal) State and the local authorities was extended to the communities and the regions. Each of these government levels has a constitutional right to levy any tax it chooses to install. However, to avoid clashing tax systems, Article 170 of the Constitution has given the federal legislature the option of restricting the taxation powers of the communities and the regions in case of proven necessity. As a result, the federal legislature has forbidden the communities and regions to levy any tax on areas already taxed at the federal state level.[2] Since statutes at the (now federal) state level had already introduced most types of modern taxes, the effective extent of the constitutional tax-levying authority of the communities and the regions is strongly reduced. Moreover, the tax-levying competence of the Flemish and French communities remain purely theoretical, since no system was installed to determine which inhabitants of the bilingual Brussels-Capital Region are part of the Dutch Community and which belong to the French Community. Only the regions have therefore effectively been able to use their constitutional taxation powers by introducing their own system of – mostly environmental – taxes. Even here, their tax-levying options have limitations, since the constitutional reforms emphasise the principle of economic and monetary union implying a total ban on internal excise duties or measures with the same extent between the subdivisions of the Belgian State.

As opposed to the regions, the constitutional tax competence of local authorities is not limited by a general statute but only by several specific statutory provisions. The most important is to be found in the Income Tax Code and forbids provinces and municipalities to levy additional taxes on top of the federal income taxes or similar taxes on the base of these income taxes. Although the legislation concerning provincial and municipal institutions became a regional competence in 2002, the boundaries of the local tax-levying competences remain a matter for the federal legislature.

[3] *Allocated Tax Powers and Transferred Tax Proceeds*

Next to the constitutional tax powers, regions and local authorities also have specific tax competences allocated by statute. Local authorities may levy an additional tax on the real property withholding tax and municipalities can also levy an additional tax on the personal income tax. These additional taxes provide over 80% of the municipal tax income. Next to that income from taxation, local authorities are financed through funding by the regional governments. Municipalities obtain about 52.5% of their total income from taxes.

2. Act of 23 January 1989 concerning the Taxation Powers meant in Article 110, §§1 and 2 (Article 170, §§1 and 2 in the coordination of 1994) of the Constitution, Moniteur belge – Belgisch Staatsblad, 24 January 1989.

Regions have been granted the proceeds and regulating powers in a dozen previously existing state taxes, which were transformed into regional taxes by the Special Finance Act of 16 January 1989.[3] Amongst those regionalised taxes are the real property withholding tax, the inheritance tax, most registration duties, taxes on gaming and betting, the radio and television tax and the motor vehicle taxes. The regulating powers statutorily transferred to the regions originally depended on the specific tax, which led to a very complex situation. This was resolved by the fifth state reform of 2002. Since then, regions have the jurisdiction to determine the taxable base, the tax rate and the exemptions of all regionalised taxes. They however still cannot modify the taxable matter[4] and are only competent for the procedural provisions of the regionalised taxes they collect themselves. Because the concepts of taxable matter, taxable base, tax rate and exemptions were not clearly defined, the repartition of competences caused numerous issues of real or alleged transgressions of powers. The Belgian Constitutional Court mostly decided in favour of the regions, thus aiding in the gradual growth of regional tax competences.

Until recent, the regions also received an important part of the proceeds of the personal income tax due by their inhabitants, and they could levy surcharges or grant a discount on that tax. The sixth state reform of 2012, which resulted in the Special Act of 6 January 2014,[5] transformed this transfer of proceeds in an independent right for regions to levy an additional tax on the reduced federal personal income tax, with the possibility to levy surcharges or to grant reductions or tax credits.

The Special Act now also states that regions must use their allocated tax powers while respecting the principles of federal loyalty, economic and monetary union, free movement of persons, services, goods and capital, double tax avoidance and the exclusion of disloyal tax competition. Again (some of) these concepts were not clearly defined, leaving space for future issues of possible transgressions of power.

Communities have no allocated tax powers but receive an important part of the proceeds of certain federal taxes. This is the case for the VAT and for the federal personal income tax. Although a large portion of the proceeds of these federal taxes is transferred to the communities, they have no right to legislate in these matters. The distribution of the proceeds is not based on the origin of the transferred tax innings, but on the financial need and the number of students in each community.

3. Special Act of 16 January 1989 organising the Financing of the Communities and Regions, as modified by the Special Act of 16 July 1993, the Special Act of 13 July 2001 and the Special Act of 6 January 2014. The term 'special act' refers to the qualified majority that is required for the approval or any modification of this type of statute (*see* Article 4 Belgian Constitution).
4. Only the 'special' federal legislature can change this taxable matter.
5. Special Act of 6 January 2014 modifying the Special Act of 16 January 1989 Organising the Financing of the Communities and Regions, Moniteur belge – Belgisch Staatsblad, 31 January 2014.

[4] *Some Figures*[6]

OECD Revenue Statistics	
Taxes on Personal Income, Profits & Gains	47,454
Taxes on Corporate Income & Gains	11,679
Social Security Contributions	54,787
Payroll Taxes	0
Taxes on Property	12,873
Indirect Taxes	42,495
of which VAT	26,862
Other	1,357
TOTAL	**170,645**

Federal Tax Revenues		*Regional Tax Income*			
Direct Taxes	55,787.6		Flanders	Wallonia	Brussels
Personal Property Withholding Tax	5,307.5	Regionalised Taxes			
Pre-emptive Payments	9,971.6	Real Estate Withholding Tax	103.81	31.07	20.21
Personal Income Tax Assessment Notes	-4,736.3	Tax on Gaming and Betting	30.44	19.46	23.62
Corporate Tax Assessment Notes	1,712.5	Tax on Gaming Machines	26.01	20.63	10.21
Payroll Levies	42,785.5	Registration Duties	4,942.59	2,001.15	1,246.64
Indirect Taxes	47,976.1	Motor Vehicle Tax	993.20	462.10	135.72
Import and Excise Duties	9,999.2	Motor Vehicle Registration Tax	200.20	132.00	43.17
VAT	27,472.8	Euovignet	79.95	56.00	4.38
Other	1,781.7	Inheritance Tax	1,399.41	642.71	433.62
TOTAL	**103,763.7**	Radio & Television Tax	0.00	105.00	0.00

6. Numbers for 2014 in millions of EUR. For sources, *see* www.oecd.org/tax/revenue-statistics-Belgium; http://financien.belgium.be/nl/Statistieken_en_analysen/statistieken/belgische_federaal_geïnde_fiscale_ontvangsten; www.begroting.be/NL/figures/Pages/databank.aspx; www.belfius.be/publicsocial/NL/Expertise/Studies/LokaleFinancien/.

	Regional Tax Income		
	Proper Regional Taxes		
Non-Allocated	161.19	44.55	115.95
Allocated	125.73	55.80	

Regions	*Allocated Personal Income Tax*
Flanders	6,255.26
Brussels	3,743.81
Wallonia	1,249.28

Communities	
Allocated Personal Income Tax and VAT	22,737.36
Dutch Speaking Community	13,603.98
French Speaking Community	9,024.95
German Speaking Community	6.27
Community Organs in Brussels	102.16

Municipalities	*Flanders*	*Wallonia*	*Brussels*
Total Tax Revenue	3,650.00	2,192.00	1,026.00
Total Tax Revenue per Inhabitant	664.00	655.00	917.00
of which			
Surcharges on Real Estate Withholding Tax	290.00	242.00	509.00
Surcharge on Personal Income Tax	271.00	238.00	189.00
Other Additional Taxes	15.00	12.00	10.00
Local Taxes	87.00	130.00	209.00
% Own Levies as Part of Total Income	54.60	48.00	53.00

[B] General Principles of Tax Law Laid Down in the Constitution

[1] The Fiscal Principle of Legality

Article 170 of the Constitution contains the fiscal legality principle. According to this principle, there is no taxation without representation. This means that only the federal and regional *parliaments* and the provincial and local *councils* have the competence to raise taxes and to determine the key components of the regulations. Federal tax statutes, regional tax statutes and local tax regulations must therefore determine the tax subject, the taxable object, the taxable base, tax rates, exemptions and the fundamentals of the tax procedure.

As a rule, those competences cannot be delegated to the executive branches. However, history has shown that there have been times when the federal Parliament itself accorded special powers to the executive, allowing it to create new taxes and to modify or abolish existing taxes by means of royal decrees. These special powers are mostly given within specific limits and conditions and for a short period. The Belgian Constitutional Court has allowed this delegation of competence in case of proven necessity (the normal parliamentary procedure being to slow), and on the condition that the royal decrees are afterward ratified by the Parliament within a predetermined limited period of time, thus assuring the supremacy of the legislature over the executive.

One of the main consequences of the tax principle of legality lies with the interpretation of tax laws. Since tax debts generate from the law, tax laws must be interpreted in a strict manner. They may not be applied by way of analogy to situations the legislature did not clearly intend to tax.

[2] The Annuality Principle

The principle of annuality includes the obligation for the executives to annually request the permission from the legislatures to levy taxes based on the existing tax legislation. Article 171 of the Constitution states that the rules that determine the taxes of the State, the communities and the regions only remain valid for one year, so that the legislature annually must vote the renewal of the tax legislation. Thus, the power of the purse remains with the legislature. Tax debts cannot originate unless the Parliament has renewed the application of the existing tax laws.

Therefore, the annual budget act expressly provides that the taxes existing on the last day of the previous budget year may be levied during the new budget year. With this provision, the legislature not only grants the permission to collect taxes during the next budget year (Article 174 of the Constitution), but also proclaims that the existing tax rules remain in force during that next year (Article 171 of the Constitution).

There is no constitutional annuality principle for local taxes, but a budgetary annuality principle within the legislation concerning provinces and municipalities causes a somewhat comparable result.

[3] The Equality Principle

According to Article 172 of the Constitution, no privileges with regard to taxes can be established. Moreover, no exemption or reduction of taxes may be granted except by statute. This means that the executive cannot grant any exemption or reduction of taxes and that every tax exemption or reduction must have an explicit legal base. The principle of tax equality means that all persons who find themselves in the same position must be taxed equally. Law may create categories of taxpayers if the criterion for distinction relies on an objective and reasonable justification. It is generally accepted that Article 172 of the Constitution is an application of the general non-discrimination and equal treatment principles (Articles 10 and 11 of the Constitution) in tax matters. In the last decades, the equality requirement has considerably gained attention since the Constitutional Court has jurisdiction to review federal and regional (tax) acts on their compatibility with the constitutional principle of non-discrimination and equal treatment, and can nullify a discriminatory tax measure.

§15.02 FEDERAL TAXES

[A] Income Taxes

[1] Introduction

The Belgian income tax contains four different tax systems depending on the subject of the tax. The first is the (Federal) personal income tax, which is a progressive tax levied from resident individuals and based on their worldwide income from all sources. Both regions and municipalities may levy a surcharge on this tax. The second one is the corporate income tax to which domestic companies are subject on their worldwide income. The corporate income tax is normally levied at a fixed rate of 33%. Next there is the income tax for non-resident individuals and companies, who are only taxable on their Belgian-source income. Tax rates are the same for resident and non-resident taxpayers.

Finally there is the legal entities income tax, levied on specific types of income received by legal entities that are not engaged in a business or in profit-making activities, such as public authorities, non-profit organisations and several entities explicitly mentioned by name. Often the legal entities income tax equals the withholding tax that was previously levied.

[2] (Federal) Personal Income Tax

[a] Tax Liability

The personal income tax applies to all resident individuals irrespective of their nationality. An individual is considered a resident if he has established his domicile or the seat of his wealth in Belgium. The Income Tax Code contains two legal presumptions of residence. First, people registered in the 'National Register of Individuals' are deemed residents of Belgium until proof of the contrary is provided. Furthermore, married couples and legal cohabitants are deemed to have their tax domicile where the household is established.

The personal income tax is based upon the worldwide income of the individuals, though their foreign-source income often is exempt due to double taxation treaties, but with a progressive reserve. This means that the foreign income is exempt from taxation in Belgium, but it is taken into account to determine the marginal tax rate applicable to the taxable income. In some cases, the municipal surcharge will be due notwithstanding the double taxation treaty exemption.

The assessment normally is based on the taxable income of a calendar year (e.g., income year 2015) and the tax is due the following year (e.g., tax year 2016), based on the legislation that applies for this tax year. The taxable income of a resident individual may consist of income from real estate, income from personal property, professional income and miscellaneous income.

[b] Real Property Income

This type of income is generated by real property that is not professionally used by the owner.[7] It is not always taken into account for its actual amount. To a large extent it is calculated on a lump sum basis, the so-called cadastral income representing the estimated net rental value of immovable property on a one-year basis. It derives its lump sum character from the fact that it is determined according to market standards at a fixed date and remains unchanged for a long period. Presently, the cadastral income is still determined according to market standards of 1 January 1975. As of 1991 the cadastral income is subject to an annual 'indexation'. This adjustment based on the retail prices index is intended to avoid a further widening of the gap between the cadastral income and the actual rental value of immovable property. For the tax year 2016, the index-coefficient is 1.70.

The taxable income upon which the owner is taxed for a second residence and for properties rented for private habitation purposes, amounts to the indexed cadastral income plus an increase of 40%.

If the tenant is a company, an individual who uses the rented property for business purposes or a non-profit organisation, the taxable income of the owner is based upon the actual net rent received. In this case, the indexed cadastral income increased by 40% constitutes the minimum taxable amount. The actual net rent is equal to the real amount of income minus a lump sum deduction for expenses of 10% for land and 40% in case of constructed property. This 40% deduction may however not exceed 2/3 of the 'revalorized' cadastral income. The revalorising-coefficient is based on the evolution of rental value of commercial property and is 4.23 for the tax year 2016. This upper limit is meant to neutralise excessive deductions which might result from exorbitant rents.

Real property income is exempt from personal income tax if the owner or non-profit inhabitant has designated the real property for a.o. educational or religious purposes, as a hospital or for another charitable purpose. The real property income of the 'personal residence', meaning the dwelling inhabited by the owner or that the owner cannot inhabit due to some specific circumstances, is also exempt. Reductions are granted in case of involuntary unproductivity.

Interest paid on debts incurred for the sole purpose of acquiring or maintaining real property is deductible from the individual's (total) real property income. Next to this regular interest deduction there is an additional regional tax deduction for single personal residences and an additional federal tax deduction for not personally occupied residences.

7. Income from professionally used real property is considered to be professional income.

[c] Personal Property Income

Income from personal property includes such income from private investment as interest, dividends, royalties and rentals. Interest derived from certain regulated saving deposits is exempt from tax for the first EUR 1,880 per year (tax year 2016). Interest paid on loans contracted in order to acquire or preserve an individual's personal property income is not deductible.

Individual taxpayers may refrain from declaring personal property income in their income tax returns if such income has been subject to the Belgian personal property withholding tax. In most cases, this withholding tax constitutes the final tax on an individual's personal property income. Its basic rates amount to 27% and in some cases 15%. For income paid or attributed as of 1 January 2017, the standard withholding tax rate for dividends, interest and royalties is increased to 30%.

Since 2008, income derived from publications and copyright – which previously qualified as professional or miscellaneous income – is taxed as a personal property income if it does not surpass EUR 57,207 (tax year 2016). After a generous lump sum deduction for expenses, the tax equals to the withholding tax rate of 15%.

Capital gains are normally not taxable in the personal income tax regime, provided they are the result of a 'normal management' of the individual's private equity estate. Capital gain taxes are however levied on sales of substantial holdings in a Belgian company to non-European companies.

[d] Professional Income

The concept of professional income includes any income directly or indirectly resulting from a professional occupation. A professional occupation implies a repeated activity with a normal and continuous nature. It is not required that the activity is profit seeking.

Professional income consists of:

- profits from industrial, commercial and agricultural business enterprises carried out by individuals;
- gains resulting from a liberal profession;
- profits and gains from a former independent/business or professional activity;
- wages and salaries of employees, company directors, active partners or other individuals with a similar leading position in a company; and
- pensions and similar payments compensating a permanent loss of profits, gains and wages.

Professional income is widely defined and includes all fringe benefits provided by the employer, such as the private use of a company car, stock options, housing allowances,... For example, the annual taxable benefit for the private use of a company car is presumed equal to 6/7 of the catalogue value of the car multiplied by a percentage in function of the age of the car (from 100% to 70%) and a percentage linked to the car's CO_2 emission rate (from 4% to 18%). On the other hand, some social or cultural allowances are exempt from taxation (e.g., birth allowance, ICT-allowance, allowances for commuting by bike or by public transport ...).

Next to the profits of the actual activity, professional income also includes capital gains on the sale of assets used for the exercise of a business enterprise or a liberal profession, both when acquired during the activity or on its discontinuation. However, these capital gains often enjoy a favourable tax treatment such as an exemption (e.g., gains on farming land) or an advantageous fixed rate of 16.5% or 33% (instead of the progressive tax rate). The exemption may be permanent or temporary (delayed taxation). In the latter case, the exemption is only granted on condition of a qualifying reinvestment.

Every type of professional income is only taken into account for its net amount, i.e., after subtraction of compulsory social security contributions and after deduction of professional expenses and losses. Professional expenses are computed on an itemised basis or as a lump sum. For employees, the lump sum deduction is calculated on a sliding scale, going from 29.35% for the first EUR 5,760 to 3% for professional income above EUR 19,390 and with a total maximum of EUR 4,090 (tax year 2016). For remunerated directors, the lump sum deduction is a flat 3% and cannot exceed EUR 2,380.

Professional expenses computed on an itemised basis must be substantiated, and several specific expenses are not (e.g., clothing) or only partially (e.g., use of motorcars, restaurant expenses) deductible. Losses incurred in one type of professional activity (e.g., a liberal profession) may be set off against the positive results of the other activities of the taxpayer. Losses realised in a tax year may be carried forward indefinitely. There are no carry back provisions.

Finally, enterprises and liberal professions can benefit from specific tax incentives in the form of a deduction from the tax base in case of engagement of highly qualified staff members, low qualified personnel and trainees. An investment deduction is also granted for general and specific types of investment, going from 3.5% to 20.5% of the investment (tax year 2016).

[e] Miscellaneous Income

Presently this source of taxable income consists of a dozen different income types such as revenues from occasional operations, speculations or services rendered to third parties. Alimony payments are also taxed as miscellaneous income if they are paid in accordance with specific provisions of the Civil Code. Taxation of alimony is limited to 80% of the amount received. The debtor is entitled to a 80% tax deduction.

Miscellaneous income also consists of several types of capital gains on specific privately held assets. Capital gains realised upon the transfer for valuable consideration of unbuilt real property are subject to tax if such property was acquired for consideration within a period of less than eight years. Gains realised more than eight years after the acquisition are not taxable. Capital gains on built property are taxed when such property was acquired for consideration less than five years before the realisation of the capital gain. Taxpayers who acquire a piece of land on which they start the construction of a building within five years will also be taxed with respect to capital gains realised on the transfer for consideration of this built property if the latter occurs less than five years after the first occupation of the building.

Gains on transfers of privately held shares in Belgian companies may also constitute miscellaneous income if the transferor owned directly or indirectly at any time during the five years preceding the transfer a substantial (i.e., more than 25%) holding of the shares of such company. However, only transfers to corporations or entities not located in the EEA are taxable.

Miscellaneous income is also taken into account for its net amount, i.e., after deduction of itemised expenses. With respect to particular types of miscellaneous income such as capital gains on unbuilt real estate, the taxpayer may choose for a lump sum cost deduction.

[f] Tax Incentives

Before the sixth state reform that led to the Special Act of 6 January 2014, the Belgian Income Tax Code contained a long list of specific expenses deductible from the total income taxable in the personal income tax. Following the sixth state reform, which gave regions the right to levy an additional tax on the reduced federal personal income tax, all these deductions were transformed into tax reductions, which are mostly situated on the regional level. The alimony paid to near relatives or a separated spouse is the only remaining tax base deduction. The expenses for which tax reductions are granted, concern for example life insurance premiums, pension-savings contributions, payment of services performed by local employment agencies, energy savings investments, child custody expenses, charitable contributions, etc.

[g] Personal Exemption

For every taxpayer, the Belgian tax legislation provides a tax-free basic amount which, for the tax year 2016, equals to EUR 7,380 if the income does not exceed EUR 26,360 and is EUR 7,090 if the income exceeds EUR 26,360. An additional personal tax-free amount is granted for dependent children, and is equal to EUR 1,510 for one child, climbing to EUR 14,060 for four children and an additional EUR 5,370 per extra child. For other dependent persons, the additional tax-free amount is EUR 1,510.

These tax-free amounts are subtracted from the income that is subject to the lowest marginal tax rates. If the tax is levied from married couples and legal cohabitants, the additional tax-free amount for dependent persons is granted to the spouse with the highest taxable income.

[h] *Tax Calculation and Tax Rates*

[i] Married Couples and Legal Cohabitants

Although married couples and legal cohabitants receive a joined tax note on both their names, since 2005 the income of each spouse or legal cohabitant is taxed completely separately. However, special rules exist for one-income families or if one of the partners only has a limited income.

For one-income families, 30% of the gross taxable earnings is imputed to the non-working spouse and taxed in that spouse's own name. The imputation of income for one-income families is limited to a maximum of EUR 10,230 (tax year 2016). If one of the spouses is self-employed or is engaged in a liberal profession and is effectively assisted by the other spouse, an income equal to a maximum of 30% of the net earnings may in some cases be attributed to the assisting spouse.

These rules also apply if both spouses receive earned income, but the earnings of one spouse exceed 70% of their total earnings whilst the earnings of the other spouse does not reach EUR 10,230. Income may then be attributed to the lesser earning spouse, until 30% of total earnings is reached without exceeding the maximum of EUR 10,230 (tax year 2016).

[ii] Tax Rates

The individual income tax was basically meant as a progressive tax on the individual's aggregated income, regardless of its source and/or nature. The personal income tax therefore normally is calculated by applying a progressive tax rate on the net taxable income base described above, and divided in a sliding scale. Tax brackets normally are indexed every year. For tax year 2016, the tax brackets and rates are as follows:

Income Brackets (in EUR)	*Tax Rate*
0–8,710	25%
8,710–12,400	30%
12,400–20,660	40%
20,660–37,870	45%
over 37,870	50%

However, over the years, an increasing amount of income types have been excluded from the progressive taxation and have been subjected to (twelve) fixed tax rates going from 5% to 33%, but only if this benefits the taxpayer. There are also two specific tax rates equal to the average rate of the previous and of the current tax year.

[iii] Tax Calculation

The sixth state reform that allowed regions to levy an additional tax on the reduced federal personal income tax had an important influence on the way the personal income tax is calculated. The Special Finance Act of 16 January 1989, as last modified by the Special Act of 6 January 2014, gives a detailed description of that calculation.

The first step consists of determining the 'state tax'. This is done by assessing the globally taxable base (subject to the progressive rates) and the separately taxable bases (subject to fixed rates) and by applying those tax rates. The tax calculated on the globally taxable base is then reduced with the tax calculated on the personal tax-free amount(s) and the reductions grated for pensions and for foreign income. The remaining global tax and the separate taxes are then added, after which the tax levied on certain types of income that may not be taxed by the regions (dividends, royalties, some capital gains ...) is subtracted. The remaining amount is called 'state tax'.

The next steps consists of determining the 'reduced state tax' and – following – the 'federal personal income tax', the 'regional personal income tax' and the additional municipal personal income tax.

The 'reduced state tax' is determined by deducting an amount equal to 25.99% of the state tax from that state tax. This is the so-called autonomy-factor (valid for the tax years 2015–2017). The 'federal personal income tax' is formed by the reduced state tax and the tax on dividends, royalties, some capital gains ..., and with subtraction of the federal tax reductions that were not yet deducted (charitable contributions, pension-savings contributions...).

The 'regional personal income tax' starts with a surcharge calculated on the reduced state tax. The Special Act temporarily set the surcharge at a flat 35.11%, but it is for the regions to determine this rate or rates, since the surcharge can also be differentiated following self-determined tax brackets. Differentiated surcharge rates are however subject to some specific limitations. On this surcharge, regions can thereafter grant fixed tax deductions, proportional or fixed tax reductions, proportional tax increases and proportional or fixed tax credits. The reductions, increases and credits must be related to the regions non-taxation competences. Regions are among other things exclusively competent for tax reductions concerning the acquirement of a 'personal residence', the protection of residences against burglary and fire, energy savings investments for residences, payment of services performed by local employment agencies or paid with service-checks, etc. The 'regional personal income tax' consists of the regional surcharge on the reduced state tax minus the fixed tax deductions, proportional or fixed tax reductions and plus proportional tax increases. The federal and regional authorities must decide if a possible surplus of tax reduction will be lost or can be compensated with the personal income tax due to the other government level.

The so-called total tax is reached by adding the federal personal income tax and the regional personal income tax. It is on this total tax that the additional municipal tax is finally calculated (usually varying from 0% to 9%).

[i] Procedural Provisions

The assessment and levying of the personal income tax, with inclusion of the regional and local surcharges, is a purely federal competence and is done by the federal tax administration. Starting point is the tax return that is sent during the tax year by the tax authorities and in which subjects of the personal income tax must annually report their worldwide income. Spouses and legal cohabitants must normally file a joined tax return.

After a brief or more thorough tax audit, the tax authorities send an assessment note within eighteen months starting from the first of January of the tax year. Tax dues must be paid within two months following the sending of the assessment note. Interest for late payment mount up to 7% per year. In reality, the personal income tax is to a large extent levied through a payroll withholding tax, whilst the assessment notes mostly consist of tax refunds.

The period during which the tax authorities can perform a tax audit and adjust the taxable basis normally is three years starting from the first day of the tax year. This period is however extended to seven years in case of fraud. A tax audit normally starts with a request for information from the tax inspector. The taxpayer must provide the data requested within a month. Any documentary evidence considered relevant to the audit can be requested and reviewed by the authorities. Third parties – under certain conditions also including banks – can also be requested to provide information. Once the tax inspector has completed his audit, any adjustment he deems necessary is proposed in a notification of amendment outlining the reasons for the proposed adjustment. The taxpayer has thirty days to react to this notification, on penalty of an ex officio assessment of the tax due. The tax inspector then sends the assessment note, taking into account the remarks of the taxpayer.

Following the assessment note, the taxpayer has six months to contest the note in an administrative appeal that must be introduced before the regional director of taxes. The regional director has six, sometimes nine months to make a decision. If the appeal was rejected or if no timely decision was taken, the assessment note may be appealed and litigated under the ordinary judicial procedure before the courts of the judiciary.

[3] Corporate Income Tax

[a] Tax Liability

Domestic companies are subject to the corporate income tax on their worldwide income. All companies, associations, establishments or institutions that meet each of the following three conditions are defined as domestic companies for income tax purposes:

- they have legal personality;
- they are engaged in a business or in profit-making activities;
- they have their statutory seat, their principal establishment or their seat of management or administration in Belgium.

The scope of this definition is very broad and does not only cover company types that can be found in the Belgian Companies Code, such as the *SA–NV* and the *SPRL–BVBA*, but can also make non-profit organisations liable to the corporate income tax if they are regularly engaged in a business or in profit-making activities. However, many types of non-profit associations and public entities are explicitly exempt from the corporate income tax and subjected to the legal entities income tax, which mostly generates a lower tax pressure. On the other hand, certain entities such as agricultural companies and European economic interest groupings, which have legal personality for company law purposes, are treated as fiscally transparent for income tax purposes. This means the net result from the activities of such an entity is taxable as income of its members.

The corporate income tax is based on the taxable income of a financial year. If the financial year corresponds with the calendar year, the tax year is the following calendar year. If the financial year does not correspond with the calendar year or the closing date is not 31 December, the tax year coincides with the calendar year during which the financial year ends.

In corporate income tax, there are quite some differences in the tax regime that applies to SMEs and the system applicable to large companies. SMEs are companies with an average annual workforce of less than fifty, an annual turnover smaller than EUR 9 million and a balance sheet total inferior to EUR 4.5 million. Different tax rules can for example be found on the matter of amortisation, the investment reserve, the investment deduction, the notional interest deduction, the tax on capital gains, the fairness tax, etc.

[b] Taxable Income

Domestic companies are subject to corporate income tax on their worldwide income. Every asset a company owns is considered to serve its business purpose. All of its income is therefore treated as business income. All of a company's operations and assets contribute to its results.

According to Article 183 of the Income Tax Code, the taxable income of a corporation is the same as the profits from industrial, commercial and agricultural business enterprises of individuals. The taxable profits of a company could therefore be determined according to the rules that apply to profits. The corporate income tax, however, uses a more practical method of determining the companies' taxable income.

Starting point is that companies are taxed on the total amount of profit that is revealed in the company's financial statements held according to the Belgian Generally Accepted Accounting Principles (GAAP) and that is translated in the increase of the company's equity during the tax income year and in the total amount of dividends paid to the shareholders. The increase of equity is however corrected since some types of reserves enjoy a (temporary) tax exemption, whilst other components – that do not qualify as reserves in accounting – are considered taxable reserves for tax purposes. Moreover, a number of expenses made and booked in the financial statements are not deductible for tax purposes, so they will have to be added to the accounting result in the form of 'disallowed expenses'.

After adding the 'taxable increase of reserves', the 'paid dividends' and the 'disallowed expenses', this 'tax result' is subsequently reduced by a number of tax base deductions meant as economic incentives, to avoid double taxation or to deduct losses from the past. These deductions are made in a strict order of proceeding, since some deductions can be carried forward to following years, whilst other will be lost in case of a lack of taxable income to deduct them from.

[c] *From Accounting Result to Tax Result*

[i] Corrections to the Increase of Equity

As mentioned, the starting point for determining the taxable income is the increase of equity during the income year, which is determined by adding the increase of taxable reserves, of retained earnings and of taxable provisions, which are all elements that can be found in the financial accounting. This total must be increased with the 'invisible reserves', such as fiscally unaccepted or excessive depreciations, overestimations of liabilities and underestimations of assets. Other components must however be subtracted because of their unconditional tax exemption, which is realised by increasing the initial state of the reserves. Components exempt from taxation in this way are for example (some) capital gains on shares, investments (tax shelter) in audio-visual works, qualifying regional grants and subsidies and a part of the capital gains on cars.

[ii] Tax-Free Reserves

Another number of reserves that can be found in the financial statements are the tax-free reserves, containing profit components that enjoy a temporary tax exemption as long as they remain untouched. Here we find qualifying write-downs on trade receivables (bad debt reserves), tax-free provisions for risks and expenses, a temporary exemption for investments (tax shelter) in audio-visual works, an investment-reserve tax exemption for SMEs and a number of capital gains such as monetary capital gains, expressed but unrealised capital gains, capital gains on qualifying vehicles, barges and ships.

There is also a temporary exemption for capital gains on tangible fixed assets and (depreciable) intangible assets that have been held by the company for over five years, if the total proceeds of the transfer is reinvested in tangible or intangible assets subject to depreciation in the EEA within three or sometimes five years' time. This capital gain is then subject to a deferred and spread taxation based on the depreciation percentages of the assets in which was reinvested.

A last tax-free reserve, contains the 20% cost deductions above 100%, which is granted for some specific expenses, such as electric cars, collective commuting and bike-commuting.

[iii] Disallowed Expenses

Disallowed expenses are expenses that were made and therefore booked in the financial statements but that are not deductible for tax purposes because they do not fulfil the criteria to be accepted as a professional expense, or because the tax legislature refuses their deductibility. Disallowed expenses are for example the corporate income tax paid and all what goes with it (tax increases, interest, advanced payments, withholding tax...), regional taxes based on the constitutional regional tax competence, fines and penalties, some disallowed pension contributions, a part of the car expenses and of the fuel costs, a part of restaurant and representation expenses, gifts and charitable contributions, paid interest that are excessive, that were paid to specific beneficiaries or that fall under the 'thin cap' regulations, social benefits, meal-, sports-, culture- and Eco-vouchers and non-declared payments to tax heavens.

Two categories mentioned in the disallowed expense rubric of the tax return form, do not really fit. The first contains the reversal of previously granted tax deductions, if some conditions are no longer met (e.g., deductible amount for the engagement of high-qualified staff members). The second contains the abnormal or gratuitous benefits the company gave to third parties and that must be added to its own profit unless certain conditions are met.

[d] From Tax Result to Taxable Profit

[i] Determining (and Splitting) the Tax Result

As mentioned above, the taxable profit is determined after a series of operations, using a strict order of proceeding. The first operation consists of assessing the tax result of the activity during the income year, by determining, correcting and adding the increase in reserves, the paid dividends and the disallowed expenses.

[ii] Splitting the Tax Result

In the second operation, the company's profits are broken down according to their source: Belgian profits, foreign profits exempt by tax treaty, and foreign profits not exempt by a tax treaty.

There is, however, also a partition between the tax results on which the operations mentioned hereafter can apply, and components of the tax result on which no deductions are allowed. The legislature indeed decided that no deductions may be made on the part of the tax result originating from abnormal or gratuitous benefits received from a group member, on received bribe-commissions, on some specific disallowed expenses and on some profits subject to the fairness tax or a separate tax rate. Those profit components are therefore subtracted from the tax result on which the tax base deductions are subsequently made, to be re-added to the remaining result after the final operation.

[iii] Deduction of Foreign Profit and Tax-Free Components

The third operation consists of the deduction of foreign profits that are exempt according to a double tax treaty. This operation is also the place for a number of other tax deductions such as qualifying charitable contributions and the deductible amounts granted in case of engagement of highly qualified staff members, low qualified personnel and trainees. Worth mentioning is that these deductions are not transferable and are therefore lost in case of insufficient taxable income to deduct them from.

[iv] Dividend Income Deduction

In the fourth operation dividends received by a Belgian company or its permanent establishments – which are first included in its taxable base – are removed from the (remaining) taxable base as 'definitively taxed income' for up to 95% of their amount. Conditions for this dividend income deduction are that the distributing company is subject to a corporate income tax, that the shareholding in the latter company amounts to at least 10% or an acquisition value of at least EUR 2.5 million in the capital of the distributing company and that the beneficiary of the dividend must have the full legal ownership of the underlying shares for at least one year.

Until June 2009, dividend income deductions that could not be subtracted by lack of taxable income to deduct them from, could not be carried forward and were lost. After having been condemned by the EU Court of Justice, the legislation was changed and unused parts of the dividend income deduction can now be carried forward unlimited in time, if of course the dividends were received from a subsidiary located in a Member State of the EEA.

[v] The Notional Interest Deduction

The 'notional interest deduction' was introduced in the tax year 2007, and is a deduction based on the capital of the company. It was introduced to 'compensate the disparity' caused by the fact that paid interest constitutes a deductible expense, whilst dividends form a part of the taxable profit.

The deduction is calculated on the adjusted capital, formed by the company's share capital and its retained earnings, but minus among other things the tax net value of financial fixed assets qualifying as participations and other shares, of participations and shares that qualify for the dividend income deduction, and various other abuse-avoiding corrections. The percentage of the notional interest deduction is determined annually and may not exceed 3% (3.5% for SMEs). The notional interest deduction rate for tax year 2016 is 1.63% and 2.13% for SMEs.

Until tax year 2012, the notional interest deduction that could not be subtracted due to a lack of taxable income, could be transferred to the following years for a maximum of seven years. Whilst this still remains in effect for the 'stock' of excess notional interest deduction build up in the past (with some limitations), since tax year 2013 new excess notional interest deduction can no longer be carried forward and is therefore lost. The subtraction of the 'old notional interest deduction-stock' was transferred to a new, ninth operation. Starting from tax year 2016, the notional interest deduction is limited for insurance companies.

[vi] Deduction of Carry-Over Losses

The losses the company had during one or more previous taxable years, are deductible from the income of the taxable period. There is no possibility for a carry back of the losses. The taxpayer cannot postpone the tax recovery of his losses. Since tax year 1991, the previous losses are recoverable without any time limit.

However, limitations were introduced to counter the abuse of loss deductions. Previous business losses will for instance no longer be deductible in case of acquisition or change of control of a company that does not comply with a legitimate economic or financial need. The notion of 'control' includes the power to exercise a decisive influence on the appointment of the majority of the directors or managers of a company, or the orientation of its policies.

[vii] Investment Deduction

The investment deduction that may be applied consists of a percentage of the value of qualifying investments. For a long time, the normal investment deduction has been reduced to nil. Only recently did the Belgian government introduce a new 'normal' investment deduction percentage of 8% for qualifying investments by SMEs. 'Specific' investment deductions for investments in patents, environmentally friendly research and development investments and energy-saving investments, however, were never restricted and now apply to all companies. Companies benefit from a one-off investment deduction of 13.5% (tax year 2016) of the acquisition value of qualifying investments. For investments in qualifying environmentally friendly research and development assets, they can also opt for a spread investment deduction of 20.5% of the depreciation on that asset.

Investment deduction that could not be subtracted by lack of remaining taxable profit can be carried forward without any limitation in time or in amount. Just like with the carry-over losses, the carried forward investment deduction can be lost in case of acquisition or change of control of a company that does not comply with a legitimate economic or financial need.

[e] Tax Rates

The basic rate of the corporate income tax is 33%, increased by a 3% crisis surtax, thus totalling 33.99%.

Reduced basic rates are available to companies with a taxable income not exceeding EUR 322,500 (not subject to indexation). Including the crises surtax, they amount to 24.98% on the first EUR 25,000 of taxable profit, 31.93% on taxable profit between EUR 25,000 and EUR 90,000 and 35.54% on the taxable profit between EUR 90,000 and EUR 322,500. Corporate income tax rates are not increased with a local surcharge.

Next to the abovementioned basic rates, there are 'specific basic rates' for the profit of some specific companies (21%), for some specific profits such as agricultural subsidies (5%) and some capital gains on shares (0.4% and 25%).

Next to these basic tax rates, some special tax rates apply in certain conditions. A special 'secret commissions' tax rate of 103% (or 51.5% if the beneficiary is a legal entity) applies on paid commissions, fees, bonuses, benefits, remunerations etc. for which no documents were made identifying the beneficiary of these expenses. The secret commission tax is also due for hidden profits discovered during a tax audit and for payments done in view of public or private, domestic or international corruption.

Other special tax systems are the so-called fairness tax and the carat tax. The fairness tax was introduced in tax year 2014 and is a tax of 5.15% levied on a part of the dividends paid by large companies that enjoy important tax base deductions due to the subtraction of notional interest deduction and carried forward tax losses. The carat tax is a flat tax rate of 0.55% on the turnover of companies active in the diamond sector and should take effect as of tax year 2017.

[f] Advance Payments

The corporate income tax must be paid in the form of advance tax payments in view to avoid a surcharge. The advance payments can be made in quarterly instalments. Depending on the quarter the payments were done, they give rise to a tax credit of 1.5%, 1.25%, 1% and 0.75%. If the total tax credits exceeds the surcharge, no surcharge is due. There is no surcharge for SMEs during the first three years of their activity.

[4] Other Income Taxes

[a] The Legal Entities Income Tax

Public legal entities such as the State, the communities and regions, the provinces and municipalities are subject to this particular type of income tax. This is also the case for legal persons excluded from the scope of the corporate income tax as well as for legal persons with principal seat in Belgium that are not engaged in a business nor in profit-making activities of any kind.

There is no general concept of income under the legal entities income tax. Its taxpayers are only taxable on specific types of income as defined for individual income tax purposes, such as income from real estate or personal property. However, the results of their activities do not qualify as taxable income.

The tax pressure generated by the legal entities income tax is mostly considerably smaller than is the case for the other income taxes. Taxation is either limited to the level of the real property or the personal property income withholding tax or equal to the fixed rates applicable under the individual income tax to the same type of income.

[b] Non-resident Income Tax

Subject to this tax are the non-resident individuals, foreign entities engaged in profit-making activities and foreign non-profit entities.

Taxable income is limited to Belgian-source income. Income from real property is considered Belgian income if the property is situated in Belgium. Personal property income is as a rule taxable if the debtor of such income is a taxpayer in one of the Belgian income taxes. However, specific exemptions may apply. With respect to salaries of employees and company directors, Belgian non-resident income tax is generally due when they are at the expense of a taxpayer subject to one of the Belgian income taxes. Salaries to the account of a foreign enterprise with respect to the Belgian activities of an employee or company director are also subject to this tax if the beneficiary resided in the country for more than 183 days during the taxable period. Income from business activities is taxable if it is realised through a Belgian establishment of a non-resident taxpayer. However, some profits are subject to the non-resident income tax even if they are not realised through a Belgian establishment. This applies among other things to business profits resulting from the disposal or renting of Belgian real property and to profits derived by foreign insurance companies collecting insurance contracts in Belgium other than reinsurance contracts. Gains from a liberal profession are subject to tax if they are generated by such activity exercised in the country.

The non-resident tax liability is computed according to the rules applicable to the personal income tax, the corporate income tax and the legal entities income tax. However, a global assessment of non-resident income tax is only established with respect to specific types of income. This is for instance the case for non-resident individuals whose Belgian real property income is aggregated with their Belgian occupational and miscellaneous income in order to be taxed at the same progressive rates as those applied under the individual income tax. With respect to other income of non-resident individuals, no assessment is established since the tax due is deemed to correspond to the Belgian withholding tax already paid at source. For foreign legal entities with profit-making activities and realising Belgian business income through a Belgian establishment a global assessment is made and the non-resident income tax is calculated at the same rates as the corporate income tax.

[B] Value Added Tax

The VAT is a sales tax levied on turnover and not profit. It is also a fractional sales tax, meaning it is levied on each stage of production, distribution and services. VAT is by far the most important indirect tax. Belgium first introduced the VAT in 1969, thus implementing the European directives on the subject. VAT indeed is essentially a European creation, which was transposed into Belgian law. The European legal basis is now to be found in Directive 2006/112/EC of 28 November 2006 on the Common System of Value Added Tax (VAT Directive).

VAT is a tax on the supply of goods and services mentioned in the VAT Code and done in the course of an independent exercise of any economic activity, regardless of the place where the economic activity is pursued and regardless if the activity is profit seeking. Such supplier of goods and/or services qualifies as taxable person.

A taxable person is usually required to charge VAT to its customers. On the other hand, he may claim credit for the VAT he has paid to his own suppliers. Only the positive balance of VAT on outgoing invoices over the VAT on incoming invoices is payable to the tax administration. Some services supplied by persons carrying on an independent economic activity qualify for an exemption. This for example is the case for medical services and certain banking and financial services. Although these suppliers still qualify as taxable persons, they are not required to charge VAT to their customers nor can they claim credit for VAT paid to their suppliers for goods and services used within their exempt services.

There are several types of taxable transactions. The first is the supply of physical goods, both movable and immovable, when provided for consideration, and some assimilated transactions such as the withdrawal for non-economic purposes. Second, there is the supply of services, being every economic activity that is not considered a supply of goods by the VAT Code. A third type of VAT-taxable activity is the import of goods into the country from outside the EU, even if the importer is not carrying on an independent economic activity. A next type of activity subject to VAT is the so-called intra-Community acquisition of goods by a taxable person or by a non-taxable legal person such as public authorities without any economic activity. An intra-Community acquisition is an acquisition whereby the goods are moving from one EU Member State to another EU Member State. The taxable activity in principle is done by the taxable person acquiring the goods, meaning the tax will be due in the Member State of arrival, whilst the goods will under certain conditions be VAT exempt in the Member State of departure. Intra-Community acquisition implies that both the supplier and the acquirer have the status of VAT-taxable person - with or without the right to credit for VAT incurred - or by non-taxable legal persons such as public authorities without any economic activity. Finally, there is the intra-Community acquisition of services.

For each type of taxable transaction, there are specific rules for determining the place where the transaction takes place and VAT is due. For VAT purposes, the transaction does not necessarily take place where it can be located materially. Only if the place of the taxable transaction is located in Belgium, the act may be subject to Belgian VAT.

The present Belgian standard VAT rate is 21%. This rate applies to all taxable transactions that are not subject to a reduced VAT rate. Lower rates are 12% (e.g., for margarine, some restaurant and catering services, social housing, phytopharmaceutical products), 6% (e.g., for food, medical products, renovation of immovable property, public transport services, distribution of drinking water), and 0% (e.g., newspapers and magazines, gold for investment).

[C] Customs and Excise Duties

Custom duties are taxes levied on some goods at their border crossing on the occasion of their import and export. Custom duties are largely a European tax, which is however levied by the Belgian administration.

Excise duties burden the domestic consumption of some goods and are levied on the occasion of their production or import. A distinction is made between the Community and the national excise duties. The first are levied on alcohol, tobacco products and mineral oils and have already been the subject of a European harmonisation, meaning the same procedures (excise applications, suspension regimes) apply in all EU Member States. The EU also determines the minimum and maximum excise duty-rates between Member States. The Belgian national excise duties relate to coffee and soft drinks.

§15.03 REGIONAL TAXES

[A] Regional Taxes in the Special Finance Act

[1] General

As mentioned before, regions have two types of taxes, namely the 'proper' taxes based on their constitutional tax powers, and the 'derived' tax competences granted by the Special Finance Act of 16 January 1989 that transformed a dozen previously existing State taxes into regional taxes. The most important derived tax competences concern the inheritance tax, the registration duties, the real property withholding tax and, since tax year 2015, the regional personal income tax.

[2] Inheritance Tax

An inheritance tax is due following the net transfer of property caused by the death (or an equivalent event) of a resident person, that must be paid by heirs or legatees and that is calculated on the net amount inherited by each recipient of the estate of the deceased. For non-resident persons having Belgian immovable property, a transfer duty upon death is due. Neither the place of death, nor the nationality or residence of the heirs affects the applicable inheritance tax.

Certain asset transfers are subject to inheritance tax although there is no transfer by virtue of the death. This is for instance the case for movable property gifts within three year preceding the death of the donor, if there is a presumption that a transaction includes a gratuitous benefit, in case of benefits granted by third parties (life insurances), etc. These gifts and life insurance benefits must therefore must be reported in the tax return.

The inheritance tax is normally levied at a progressive rate on each heir's share in the total net amount of the deceased's worldwide estate. The rates vary according to the degree of kinship between the heir and the deceased and increase progressively with the inherited amount. Tax exemptions or special rates exist for the inheritance of the family business (0% in the Flemish and Walloon region, 3% in the Brussels region) and for the inheritance of the main residence by the surviving spouse.

The inheritance tax is calculated upon the worldwide assets of the deceased resident, the value of which (at the date of death) must be assessed by the heirs. Liabilities and debts that can be considered as a part of the estate may be subtracted from the assets in the declaration note. Debts that occurred after death are in principle not deductible, save for funeral expenses and the cost of the executor.

As mentioned above, the inheritance tax and the transfer duty upon death were transformed into regional taxes. Presently the full proceeds of the inheritance tax go to the region according to the domicile of the deceased at the time of death, or to the region where he was located the longest in the five years preceding his death. Each of the three regions has legislative powers with respect to the taxable base, the rates and the exemptions of the tax. Since the Flemish Region also collects its own inheritance tax since 2015, it is also competent for the procedural provisions. Next to the differences this competence caused for the applicable tax rates in the different regions, the Flemish Region decided to apply its (new) tax rates separately to the net value of the inherited immovable and the movable estate, whilst preferably subtracting the liabilities form the value of the movable estate. In this system, the structure of the deceased's estate (personal and/or real property and/or debts) may considerably influence the tax pressure and the applicable inheritance tax law.

In 2016, the tax rates are as follows:

	Flanders			Wallonia				Brussels-Capital Region			
	Children, Spouse, Partner	*Brothers & Sisters*	*Third Parties*	*Children, Spouse, Partner*	*Brothers & Sisters*	*Uncles, Aunts, Nieces & Nephews*	*Third Parties*	*Children, Spouse, Partner*	*Brothers & Sisters*	*Uncles, Aunts, Nieces & Nephews*	*Third Parties*
0.01–12,500	3%	30%	45%	3%	20%	25%	30%	3%	20%	35%	40%
12,500.01–25,000	3%	30%	45%	4%	25%	30%	35%	3%	25%	35%	40%
25,000.01–50,000	3%	30%	45%	5%	35%	40%	60%	3%	30%	35%	40%
50,000.01–75,000	9%	30%	45%	7%	35%	40%	60%	8%	40%	50%	55%
75,000.01–100,000	9%	55%	55%	7%	35%	55%	80%	8%	40%	50%	55%
100,000.01–125,000	9%	55%	55%	10%	35%	55%	80%	9%	55%	60%	65%
125,000.01–150,000	9%	65%	65%	10%	50%	55%	80%	9%	55%	60%	65%
150,000.01–175,000	9%	65%	65%	14%	50%	55%	80%	9%	55%	60%	65%
175,000.01–200,000	9%	65%	65%	14%	65%	70%	80%	18%	60%	70%	80%
200,000.01–250,000	9%	65%	65%	18%	65%	70%	80%	18%	60%	70%	80%
250,000.01–500,000	27%	65%	65%	24%	65%	70%	80%	24%	65%	70%	80%
Over 500,000	27%	65%	65%	30%	65%	70%	80%	30%	65%	70%	80%

[3] *Registration Duties and Gift Taxes*

Most registration duties and gift taxes have become regionalised taxes, meaning that the regions determine the tax rates, the calculation base and the exemptions. The Flemish Region is also competent for the procedural provisions, since it collects its own registration duty-revenues. Regions are competent based on the location of the purchased or transferred real estate or, in case of gift taxes, the domicile of the donor or the region he was located the longest in the past five years.

Registration duties are taxes on certain deeds due on the occasion of the registration of those deeds.[8] Mandatory registration exists for deeds made by public officials (notaries, bailiffs, etc.), for written documents containing certain types of transactions (e.g., written tenancy agreements concerning Belgian property), or because of the type of legal transaction that is made (purchase or transfer of real estate, public sales of tangible movable property). Depending on the content of the act, the registration duty may be a flat tax (usually EUR 50), a proportional tax rate (e.g., 1% on the creation of a mortgage) or a progressive rate.

Registration duties are mostly levied on the purchases and transfers of real estate, including buildings. The tax rate amounts to 10% (Flemish Region) or 12.5% (Walloon Region and Brussels-Capital Region) of its conventional value (transfer price plus charges imposed upon the buyer). However, the market value of the real property serves as the minimum base for the registration tax. New buildings are subject to VAT and are therefore exempt from registration duties.

Gifts made by notarial deed are also subject to registration duty (gift tax). This is always the case when *real property* is transferred. Gift tax here usually is levied at a progressive rate varying according to the amount of the gift and the relation between the donor and the donee. Rates range from 3% to 80%. Special rates exist in Flanders for the gift of building land and in the Brussels-Capital Region for the gift of the main residence between spouses or legal cohabitants.

A gift of *tangible* personal property does not require a notarial deed. However, if parties do ask a notary to intervene, a gift tax is due. It is levied at progressive rates varying according to the amount of the gift and the degree of relationship between the donor and the donee. Gift tax rates vary based on the region where the gift is registered. In the Flemish Region and the Brussels-Capital Region registered gifts of movables are taxed at a reduced flat registration rate of 3% for gifts between spouses, children, grandchildren, parents, grandparents, and cohabiters, and 7% for gifts between other individuals. Gifts of the family enterprise often enjoy a tax exemption.

[4] *Real Property Withholding Tax*

Originally, the real property withholding tax was meant as an advance payment of the income tax due on the lump sum based income of real property, which was afterwards

8. In the Flemish Region, the registration duty is levied following a tax assessment note made up after the actual registration.

deducted from the global annual income tax due. However, the real property withholding tax gradually evolved into an independent tax on (the income of) immovable property, with no ties with the actual income taxes, except for the use of the indexed cadastral income as its tax base. This evolution was completed when the real property withholding tax became a regional tax, the regions being able to modify its calculation base, its rate and the exemptions.

The real property withholding tax is an annual tax, which for now in all three regions still is based on the indexed cadastral income as determined by the federal tax administration. As described above, this is the estimated net rental value of immovable property on a one-year basis, as assessed on 1 January 1975 and as indexed since 1992. A cadastral income exists for unbuilt land, for (different types of) immovable constructions, but also for machinery and equipment that in certain cases is considered to be immovable property. The real property income tax is still levied by the federal tax administration, except for the Flemish Region where it is levied by the Flemish Tax Service.

The real property income tax is due by the owner, usufructuary, leaseholder ... of the immovable property on 1 January of the tax year. The tax rate depends on the region and is 1.25% in the Walloon Region and in the Brussels-Capital Region and 3.97% in the Flemish Region, with a reduced rate for social housing in all regions. Cadastral income related to machinery and equipment is often subject to a reduced rate or even an exemption. However, these basic regional tax rates are only a very small part (about 15%) of the actual annual real property withholding tax, since provinces and municipalities can and do levy surcharges that by far exceed the basic tax.

Depending on the region, tax exemptions exist for real property used for education and religious or other charitable purposes, for forest and nature parks, monuments, for foreign public property and for qualifying national public property. Exemptions or reductions are sometimes granted in case of involuntary unproductivity. Reductions are sometimes granted for modest homes, low-energy buildings, for (war) disabled persons and for families with plural dependent children.

[5] Regional Personal Income Tax

As mentioned above, since tax year 2015 the regions are competent to levy a surcharge on the reduced federal personal income tax. The Special Act temporarily set the surcharge at a flat 35.11%, but it is to the regions to determine this rate or rates, since the surcharge can also be differentiated following self-determined tax brackets. Differentiated surcharge rates are however subject to some specific limitations, such as the condition that they may not limit the progressive rate system, except for a limited percentage and with limited consequences.

On this surcharge, regions can subsequently grant fixed tax deductions, proportional or fixed tax reductions, proportional tax increases and proportional or fixed tax credits. The fixed tax deductions must apply to all tax subjects, whilst the reductions, increases and credits must be related to the regions non-fiscal competences.

The Special Finance Act of 16 January 1989 states that the regions are exclusively competent for tax reductions concerning the acquirement of a 'personal residence', the protection of residences against burglary and fire, energy savings investments for residences, payment of services performed by local employment agencies or paid with service-checks, etc.

Proposals of regional acts using these fiscal competences must be presented to the Federal Government in view of their technical feasibility, the regional personal income tax still being levied by the federal tax administration, and to the Belgian Court of Auditors (*Cour des comptes - Rekenhof*) to assess the respect of the progressivity-rules.

[B] Proper Regional Taxes

Next to tax competences granted by the Special Finance Act of 16 January 1989, the regions can also introduce their own new taxes based on their constitutional tax-levying powers.

The Flemish Region has been quite active with the introduction of various taxes. Taxes that can be mentioned are among others:

- the tax on waste treatment (now included in a Flemish Act of 23 December 2011);
- the tax on waste water treatment (included in the Federal Act of 26 March 1971);
- the fee on environmental permits (now included in a Flemish Act of 25 April 2014);
- water intake permits (Flemish Act of 21 December 1990);
- the levy on gravel (Flemish Act of 14 July 1993);
- the tax on subsurface water intake (Flemish Act of 24 January 24);
- the tax on neglected and/or vacant manufacturing and business accommodations (Flemish Act of 19 April 1995, now included in the Flemish Tax Code);
- the tax on neglected buildings and neglected, unappropriated or unhealthy housing (Flemish Act of 22 December 1996, now included in the Flemish Tax Code);
- the ground destination modification tax (Flemish Act of 18 May 1999, now included in the Flemish Code on Territorial Planning); and
- electricity and gas levies (Flemish Acts of 17 July 2000 and 6 July 2001).

The Brussels-Capital Region has been less active in imposing new regional taxes, but took over most previously existing provincial taxes. Mention may among others be made of the following taxes:

- the tax on building-users and on owners of non-residential buildings (Brussels Act of 23 July 1992);

- the former provincial taxes on banks and ATMs, car dumps, advertising boards and signs, gas pumps, horse betting agencies, dangerous activity-permits (Brussels Act of 22 December 1994);
- the tax on taxi services and hiring limousines (Brussels Act of 27 April 1995); and
- the environmental levy (Brussels Act of 5 June 1997).

The Walloon Region finally did not launch many new taxes, but 'took over' a series of previously existing municipal and provincial taxes as part of so-called tax pacts with these government levels. Taxes worth mentioning are:

- the tax on waste prevention and valorisation (Walloon Act of 22 March 2007);
- the tax on water pollution (Walloon Act of 27 May 2004);
- the tax on drinking water (Walloon Act of 27 May 2004);
- the tax on ATMs (Walloon Act of 19 November 1998);
- the tax on neglected manufacturing and business accommodations (Walloon Act of 27 May 2004); and
- the ground destination modification tax (Walloon Act of 24 April 2014).

Contrary to derived taxes, regions must determine their own procedural tax rules for their proper taxes. They can arrange these procedural rules either globally for all proper taxes, as happened for the Walloon Region in the Walloon Act of 6 May 1999, or individually for each tax, which until recent was the choice of the Flemish Region. With the introduction of the Flemish Tax Code by the Flemish Act of 13 December 2013, the legal provisions and formal tax law-rules of most proper and derived regional taxes were grouped in this Code.

Procedural tax rules regulate the (annual) tax returns, ex officio tax levies, rules on the burden and means of proof, the investigation powers, the administrative and criminal sanctions, the tax assessment and re-evaluation period, the administrative appeal and the recovery procedure including mortgages and limitations. In principle however, rules concerning legal appeal and legal proceedings remain a federal competence.

§15.04 LOCAL TAXES

Contrary to most countries, local authorities in Belgium do not have assigned taxation competences, but have constitutional jurisdiction to levy every tax they choose to install, except for limitations introduced by the federal legislature. This explains why there exist over a hundred different types of local taxes, whilst local taxes with the same name moreover very often contain small or big differences.

Nevertheless, the two most important local taxes – in terms of tax revenues – are not constitution based but are legislation based. These are the municipal additional tax on the personal income tax and the municipal and provincial additional tax on the real property withholding tax. Together, both surcharges provide over 80% of the income the local authorities derived from taxation.

Legal limitations of the tax competence of local authorities concern the taxable bases of the federal income taxes (Article 464 of the Income Tax Code), taxes on cars and vehicles, gaming and betting and on automatic entertainment devices. There are also some very specific limitations, such as the ban on taxes on the transport of deceased persons or on the use of the public domain by telephone operators, and limitations that exempt certain institutes or legal persons from all or specific local taxes. Next to the legal limitations, there are some local taxes regulated by – nowadays regional – legislation, thus indirectly limiting the local tax competence. This applies for local taxes on taxies, on unbuilt land and on neglected or vacant premises.

Local authorities must of course also obey constitutional and basic legal principles, such as the principle of legality, the principle of equal treatment and the prohibition of discrimination, the territorial competence limitation, the prohibition of retroactive legislation and the European and international rules that often indirectly limit tax competences. The latter was for instance the case for local taxes on satellite dishes.

Contrary to the tax competence itself, local authorities are not considered able to decide independently upon their own procedural tax rules, nor is it any longer a competence of the federal legislature. Since 2002, the regions are competent to determine if and when local authorities can demand a tax return, can make an ex officio tax assessment, to determine what are the rules on the burden and means of proof, if and which investigation powers local tax administrations have, what sanctions can be imposed in which cases, if there is an administrative appeal, etc. The Walloon Region has done so in its Code of Local Decentralization and Democracy of 2004, the Flemish Region in the Flemish Act of 30 May 2008 and the Brussels-Capital Region in the Brussels Act of 3 April 2013. Here too, rules concerning legal appeal and judicial proceedings remain a federal competence.

To give a small overview of existing local taxes, those taxes can be divided in a number of categories.

A first category consists of taxes due for – or (politically) justified by – services rendered by local authorities. Here we for example find levies on the issuing of building permits, permits concerning dangerous establishments, the issuing of administrative documents, the urbanisation tax, the tax on buildings connected to public water supply or connected to the sewer system, levies on the culling of wastewater tanks, on the collection of domestic waste and on the retrieval of industrial waste, on garbage bags, on illegal dumping, on burials, assert in columbarium, grave concessions and excavations, on the transport of persons who cause nuisance, on the retrieval of derelict cars and goods and on the preservation of seized vehicles, on false alarms, on parking spaces, parking spaces for taxies and cabs, etc.

A second category contains taxes on economic activities. Existing local taxes are levied on employed staff, bar-personnel, the electric power of industrial engines, on quarries, liquor stores, tobacco stores, peddling, bookmakers, private clubs, on illuminated signs and billboards, on banks and financial institutions, hotels, night shops and phone shops, on public entertainment and shows, on scrap yards, camping grounds, advertising booklets and sheets, on market places, carnivals, fairground stalls, terraces, petrol pumps, automatic dispensers, masts and pylons, offices, etc.

A third group of local taxes can be linked to the ownership or the use of real property and contains taxes on the laying of pavements and sewers, on unbuilt grounds or undeveloped industrial land, on the absence of parking spaces, on second residences, vacant houses and buildings, uninhabitable or abandoned dwellings, etc.

The fourth group consists of taxes on luxury items, like swimming pools, luxury horses, dogs, pigeon houses, hunting and firearms licenses...

Next, there are a number of more general taxes due by every inhabitant or economically active person in the municipality, with however various denominations such as general municipal tax, general business tax, overall family tax, environmental tax ...

Finally, there are the additional taxes, such as the additional personal income tax, the additional tax on the real property withholding tax, the additional motor vehicles tax and surcharges on regional or provincial taxes.

§15.05 SELECTED BIBLIOGRAPHY

M. Bourgeois & S. Garroy, *Impôts sur les revenus*, 59 Chroniques notariales 353–581 (2014).

C. Chevalier, *Vademecum vennootschapsbelasting 2014* (Ghent: Larcier 2014).

P.F. Coppens, *L'entreprise face au droit fiscal belge* (Brussels: Larcier, 2009).

J. Couturier, B. Peeters & N. Plets, *Belgisch belastingrecht* (Antwerp: Maklu 2015).

A. Culot, *Manuel des droits d'enregistrement* (Brussels: Larcier 2013).

D. Darte, N. Honhon & L. Van Acker, *L'impôt des personnes physiques* (Limal: Anthemis 2013).

M. De Jonckheere, M. Delanore & M. Maus, *Basisbegrippen fiscaal recht* (Bruges: die Keure 2016).

M. De Jonckheere, M. Delanore, M. Maus & E. Van Dooren, *De fiscale procedure* (Bruges: die Keure 2014).

I. Lejeune & E. Cortvriend, *Memento T.V.A. 2016* (Mechelen: Kluwer 2016).

A. Mayeur (mise à jour par M. Petit), *Droits de succession 2014–15* (Mechelen: Wolters Kluwer 2014).

V. Sepulchre, *Mémento de la fiscalité locale et régionale 2015* (Mechelen: Kluwer 2015).

X. Tiberghien, *Manuel de droit fiscal 2015–16* (Mechelen: Wolters Kluwer 2015).

CHAPTER 16

Private International Law

Johan Erauw

§16.01 INTRODUCTION

This survey of Belgian private international law is intended as an overview of the general theory and then of the branches of international jurisdiction, of choice of law and of recognition of foreign decisions and authentic documents. The law on Belgian nationality is explained very briefly. To the new Belgian law of international commercial arbitration I give no more than a reference.

Treaties play a major role in the field, making it necessary for me to point to the main aspects of those treaties. Evolutions under treaties were, generally speaking, influential in our law. Some treaties have introduced uniform rules giving them universal application, such as for the sale of goods, the applicable law for maintenance payments and for traffic accidents.

The expansion of EU law in the entire field of private international law has been most remarkable in the past fifteen years. Our analysis of the private international law of Belgium must thus point to those broader European sets of rules, as they are part of the law in Belgium. Their description must however be strictly limited to the mention of the sources and the main characteristics for some of those effective European regulations. This chapter of this Introduction to Belgian Law should for that purpose be combined with reading up on European legal sources, because in the field of trans-frontier relationships there is simply too much substantive law. I do give the references to each such regulation or directive holding European rules of jurisdiction and recognition, as necessary information for the reader – and as a caution. Only when one understands how the European rules apply, it will next become understandable how, in the margin of their application, there are other national rules that apply to relations *ad extra Europa*. It will hereafter be explained how the gaps are filled for the questions not covered by them.

Belgium is representative for the continental thinking about the problems of trans-frontier relations under private law. The Belgian legal practice for conflicts jurisdiction grew to be internationalist in spirit throughout the nineteenth and twentieth Centuries. It established itself as 'open' to foreign rules and as flexible in terms of diverse legal cultures. The notion that it is legitimate to apply different laws for the benefit of different foreign citizens has long been taken in stride. But Belgium grapples, since decades now, with the problems of immigration and of floods of foreign documents in a mobile and wired or networked world. Our open, friendly attitude to the neighbours' laws brought grave consequences at the logistic level. The call for more application of local law became louder. Also inherently, as to legal precepts, limits in adaptability were seen to lie where 'human rights' come in. The equal rights of women, for example, in marriage and beyond, justify deviation from some of the aspects of Islamic law; in that area the 'public policy' of the country guards the basic rights, also in international cases. Techniques to deviate from the conflicts rule do however exist.

Furthermore, one can find cases in which the content of foreign law, to be researched ex officio, was not readily found, whence Belgian law was applied as substitute. Often also a mandatory principle under domestic law was relied upon; where especially in the family law area with justices of the peace and courts of first instance were and possibly still are overpowered by the foreign cases. Administrative authorities like the immigration department of the Department of the Interior, the town and city 'civil registrars' (*état civil – burgerlijke stand*), social support services and pension administration; all cope with the same practical challenges.

In international business law the evolution over the past decades has brought a great increase in the number of transactions with foreign partners. In legal practice strong emphasis is placed on jurisdictional issues; lawyers' efforts necessarily go towards practicing a round of 'shopping' for the best forum or to defend against such strategies of the opponent. To cope with procedural issues is as much a task as with substantive problems under the law.

In the context of increasing importance of private international law, a group of scholars took the initiative in the middle of the 1990s to clarify and where necessary to adapt the rules of jurisdiction, of conflicts of law, respectively of recognition and enforcement, in a comprehensive Code of Private International Law.

§16.02 THE BELGIAN CODE OF PRIVATE INTERNATIONAL LAW (2004)

The Belgian Code was introduced as the Act of 16 July 2004 holding the Code of Private International Law.[1] It became applicable on 1 October 2004. This national Code contains the field of the law described in this Chapter. It must be understood as prescribing solutions that are in hierarchy surpassed by the relevant European rules. The Code counts 140 articles. The interpretation of the text is helped by a lengthy

1. The official source in Dutch and French is: Moniteur belge – Belgisch Staatsblad, 27 July 2004, last amended by Act of 18 December 2014, Moniteur belge – Belgisch Staatsblad, 23 December 2014.

Explanatory Report that goes with the Code.[2] In due time doctrine caught up, bringing analysis, illustrations and further questions.[3] When it comes to divorce, successions and contractual obligations, there are presently EU regulations, and for traffic accidents Belgium ratified a treaty; all those have universal application and make national conflicts rules redundant in those named fields.

The Code of Private International Law was promulgated in both Dutch and French versions. An unofficial English version of the Code was published;[4] it is also available in German,[5] Polish[6] and Chinese.[7]

One aspect of Belgium's openness for foreign law is that courts are obliged to research the foreign law ex officio[8] although only after allowing party deliberations[9] and accepting that judges are excused from this obligation in the case of urgent, ancillary measures.[10]

Belgium for a very long time accepted '*renvoi*' in personal status, in family law, in succession and in company law. In a new approach, the Code only adheres to this theory of *renvoi* in three specific areas viz. general status, succession (where an EU regulation took over, containing also a *renvoi*) and company law.

The Code also offers escape techniques. The *ordre public*-exception[11] is inspired by the typical clause found in Hague Conventions, but adds elements to be taken into account. This provision seeks to offer a working method that requires first that one must evaluate the incompatibility of foreign law depending on the effects concerned in the particular case ('*effet atténué*').[12] In a second step one must look at how strong the

2. Moniteur belge - Belgisch Staatsblad, 27 July 2004. The Department of Justice offered a further circular letter with guidelines for the application of the newly codified rules in matters of family law and the law of persons on 23 September 2004 (Moniteur belge - Belgisch Staatsblad, 28 September 2004), last amended on 29 May 2007 (Moniteur belge - Belgisch Staatsblad, 11 May 2007).
3. *See infra* and *see* the Selective Bibliography, for sources in English.
4. *See* P. Torremans & C. Clijmans (translators), *Belgium: Law of 16 July 2004 Holding the Code of Private International Law (status April 2010)*, VI YEARBOOK OF PRIVATE INTERNATIONAL LAW 2004 319–375.
5. In Royal Decree of 12 October 2009, Moniteur belge - Belgisch Staatsblad, 10 November 2005. *See also* S. Francq, *Das belgische IPR-Gesetzbuch*, 2006 RABELSZEITSCHRIFT 235–278.
6. In 2005 KWARTALNIK PRAWA PRYWATNEGO (K.P.P.) part 3 (translated by S. Van Den Bogaerd).
7. Shan Hailing & Liang Min, [Chinese] 'The Code of Private International Law of Belgium', 2006 YEARBOOK OF CHINESE PRIVATE INTERNATIONAL LAW AND COMPARATIVE LAW 559–606 (Beijing: Law Press).
8. Court of Cassation 9 October 1980, 1981-I Pasicrisie belge 159, and Court of Cassation 3 December 1990, 1991-I Pasicrisie belge 329.
9. Court of Cassation 15 September 1982, 1982–1983 Arresten van het Hof van Cassatie 72; 1983-I Pasicrisie belge 254.
10. Court of Cassation 12 December 1985, 1986-I Pasicrisie belge 478. The rule is now laid down in Article 15 Code of Private International Law.
11. Article 21 of the Code says: 'In determining this incompatibility, special consideration is given to the degree in which the situation is connected with the Belgian legal order and to the significance of the consequences produced by the application of the foreign law.'
12. For example, regarding a polygamous marriage: asking to celebrate such a marriage in Belgium or for the respect of the duty of cohabitation, would be a too 'grave' effect, while asking for maintenance, or declaring a parent-child relationship would be acceptable.

situation is connected to the Belgian legal order. The Code also holds a general rule which allows judges to divert from the hard and fast conflicts rule.[13]

The Belgian Code of Private International Law offers no rule on the technical issues surrounding characterisation issues. It has long been accepted that the forum law determines the categories or building blocks of our construction of private international law. Defining a legal question or an action in terms of the system of private international law requires classification in terms of Belgian law; the forum determines how it applies the conflicts rules. That of course may result in difficulties because the concepts and their content differ in foreign law. We will need to allow substitution of legal phenomena with the functional equivalents in other legal systems and we must be open to adaptation and be flexible. The Code inevitably contains flexible, open concepts, like 'habitual residence', a connecting factor open to interpretation in the individual case. This progressively replaces 'nationality' as connecting factor in family law, as an illustration of the proximity principle.[14]

§16.03 JURISDICTION AND PROCEDURAL MATTERS

[A] International Treaties and Bilateral Conventions

Only few treaties contain rules on jurisdiction. References below often go to an important international convention concluded at Lugano with the members of the European Free Trade Association (EFTA), formulated in close parallel with the EU Brussels *Ibis* Regulation. Belgium has other treaties containing jurisdictional grounds, like the multilateral treaties in the field of transportation or air-travel or international law of the sea.

Belgium is still bound in a few older bilateral treaties, concluded with France, The Netherlands, Germany and Italy – which are applicable in the now narrow margin left by the European regulations mentioned above, in regard to disputes over filiation that are not subject to a European regulation.

[B] European Union Regulations

[1] The Brussels Ibis *Regulation Covering Civil and Commercial Disputes in General and Its Parallel Treaties*

Belgium was a founding party to the first European jurisdiction convention, viz. the Brussels Convention of 27 September 1968 concluded between six countries – plus its rules on interpretation on appeal before the ECJ. This Convention gained in importance

13. Article 19 Code of Private International Law, similar to the Swiss Private International Law.
14. To define 'habitual residence', the Code lists a series of factors for the court to appreciate in the individual case (Article 4). For legal persons, it imposes a hierarchy between these elements, indicating that the place of administration be the main factor, in the line of the 'real seat' rule.

as more and more Member States acceded to the EU, whilst with each phased accession amended versions were introduced. This multinational convention was replaced by a EU community instrument, namely the Regulation on Jurisdiction and on Recognition and Enforcement of Foreign Court decisions in Civil and Commercial Matters, which was revised in its version No. 1215/2012 of 12 December 2012, applicable since 10 January 2015 (the 'recast' version of 'Brussels I*bis* Regulation').[15] Hereinafter I refer to the articles of the regulation in its version of late 2012. This version binds twenty-eight Member States.[16]

In the relations between EU Member States and Switzerland, Iceland, or Norway (EFTA countries and as such members of the EEA), the Treaty of Lugano (2007) was concluded which lays down the same rules of jurisdiction (as well as recognition) so that a wide European space is created in which parties find the grounds for jurisdiction of national courts comprehensively spelled out.[17] The Regulation and conventions are all important for practice and for their wider influence on thinking about jurisdictional and procedural issues.

The temporal application of those rules in conventions, resp. regulations, was a regularly returning issue, because of the consecutive enlargements through accession and the metamorphoses into a regulation; then rewritten as version I*bis*... now recently switching to the 'recast Brussels I*bis*', with some changes in content and all new numbers of articles. The new version applies to proceedings instituted after 9 January 2015.[18]

The material field of application of the Brussels I*bis* Regulation and identically the treaties with Denmark and other states under the Lugano variant is broad. They notably cover most or all liquidated claims (contract and tort) in civil and commercial conflicts, including consumer and insurance disputes, plus labour conflicts of a private nature as well as claims among shareholders and partners in corporations or other legal entities. All European regulations cover, besides jurisdiction, also their second main

15. Originally the European *Convention* Regarding Jurisdiction and the Enforcement of Decisions in Civil and Commercial matters including the Protocol and the Common Declaration, was signed at Brussels on 27 September 1968; after amendments it was replaced by Regulation No. 44/2001 of 20 December 2000 – the source for the latest version is: Official Journal L351-1 of 20 December 2012, amended Official Journal L54-1 of 20 November 2014.
16. Ireland and the UK have opted out, but both accepted its application. When the UK exits the EU, it will have to be agreed whether and how it could accept to remain bound and be subject to decisions of the ECJ, without being a member/partner therein. Denmark had first opted out of the automatic application of the EU regulations on jurisdiction to its territory or courts. It then concluded an agreement with all the Member States, first laid down in an EU Council Decision, which contained the same rules; thereafter in a second embodiment by Council Decision 2006/325 of 27 April 2006, Official Journal L120 of 5 May 2006 – now superseded.
17. Convention on Jurisdiction and Recognition and Enforcement of Judicial Decisions, signed at Lugano on 16 September 1988, last amended on 30 October 2007, in force since 1 January 2010. Careful: the rules of the Convention accord with the 2000-version and have not been adapted to the latest 2012-version of the Brussels I*bis* Regulation, applicable since January 2015.
18. Article 66 Brussels I*bis* Regulation. That transitory rule is for determining jurisdiction thereafter commencing, but just as well for the recognition and enforcement of decisions taken much later in such instituted proceedings (as well for authentic instruments drawn up after that date). This leaves the version of Regulation No. 44/2001 (applicable since end of 2000) covering quite a good number of court decision taken or to be taken on or after 10 January 2015.

subsection: the automatic recognition and easy enforcement of court decisions from other Member States.[19]

As main rule, the national courts of the country of domicile of the defendant have jurisdiction to decide (Article 4 contains the general ground of '*forum rei*' or: court at the residence of he who is called - independent of the party's nationality). Articles 62 and 63 define the manner of determining whether the domicile is located in the country of the judge addressed.

But the country or court to which parties have referred their disputes by contractual agreement, takes precedence (the agreed court - under the conditions of Article 25). Such an agreed forum is exclusive. The notion of consensual jurisdiction is stretched to cases where a defendant is hailed to a Member State court and does not protest the jurisdiction in its first defence.[20] Party agreed jurisdiction is however not allowed when a number of specific topics are litigated for which the framers imposed mandatory and exclusive *fora* as mentioned in Article 24, notably actions in rem over real estate located inside a European Member State or actions over rental agreements for such plots or premises and, lastly, in regard to corporations with their seat in Europe, we have the intra-societal claims about the valid constitution, the functioning and the resolution or liquidation of the legal person, as well as disputes regarding the decisions by its principal organs; all exclusively subject to handling and deciding at the *forum* where the entity is established.[21]

In claims against someone with 'domicile' in the Regulation's territory, alternatives to the defendant's *forum* are allowed. Claimant thus gets options; jurisdiction is broad and virtually concurrent. But in this survey I must, in order to remain within bounds, not expand more on these European rules.

Judges need only control ex officio the respect for the jurisdictional criteria in the case of mandatory *fora* imposed by Article 24 and in case the defendant did not enter an appearance. In other instances the defendant must introduce a defence against lack of international jurisdiction or would otherwise be deemed to accept the jurisdiction by submission.[22]

Non-residents of this 'European area' of judicial cooperation are not given the safe haven within the area created for those residing in one of the twenty-eight Member States bound.[23] If a person residing *outside* the Union's territory is sued in Belgium, the international jurisdiction is determined by Belgian national rules provided in the Code of Private International Law - and this, indeed, is done without discrimination of claimants;[24] the older, national exorbitant grounds for jurisdiction (such as the forum of claimant's domicile) are no longer exercised, because the national common law has

19. *See infra* §16.06 [B].
20. Article 26 Brussels I*bis* Regulation.
21. Article 24.2 Brussels I*bis* Regulation.
22. Article 26 Brussels I*bis* Regulation.
23. The discriminatory treatment of persons residing in third states was mitigated by the earliest EC jurisdiction cooperation of the Brussels Treaty, 27 September 1968 (Article 59), respected all through Article 72 Brussels I*bis* Regulation.
24. Article 6 Code of Private International Law.

taken up principles very similar to those we know from the conventions of European regulation.

[2] Other EU Regulations

- The Brussels IIa Regulation No. 2201/2003 of 27 November 2003,[25] often referred to as 'Brussels IIa', regards matters of jurisdiction for marriage annulment, divorce and all aspects of parental authority (custody, rights of access, guardianship, placing with foster parents, protection of a child or its property and abduction).
- The EU Regulation No. 4/2009 of 18 December 2008[26] regarding claims over maintenance obligations, puts jurisdiction optionally with the court of the place where either the defendant or the creditor is habitually resident, or with the court competent for the proceedings over the status or the matter relating to parental responsibility to which the maintenance is related.[27]
- The EU Regulation No. 650/2012 of 4 July 2012 regards successions and last wills or 'disposition of property upon death'.[28] This replaces the Belgian grounds for international jurisdiction of the Code of Private International Law. The EU legislature made an effort to obtain a parallel between competent forum and applicable law – in order that the countries with jurisdiction to decide, shall apply their own law as the singular national law of the succession.
- The EU Regulation No. 655/2014 of 15 May 2014 determines jurisdiction for obtaining a Union preservation order to prevent transfers or withdrawals for certain amounts from bank accounts.[29]

25. Regulation No. 2201/2003 of 27 November 2003 Regarding Jurisdiction and Recognition and Enforcement of Decisions regarding Marital Affairs and Parental Authority (which replaced EU Regulation No. 1347/2000), Official Journal L338 of 23 December 2003, amended by Regulation No. 2116/2004, Official Journal L367 of 14 December 2004.
26. Regulation No. 4/2009 of 18 December 2008 Regarding Jurisdiction, Applicable Law, Recognition and Enforcement of Decision and Cooperation in the Field of Maintenance Obligations, Official Journal L7-1 of 10 January 2009, rectified and last amended by Regulation No. 2015/228 of 17 February 2015, Official Journal L49-1 of 20 February 2015. It applies to all EU Member States except Denmark, Ireland and the UK, which are thus, in terms of the regulation, not 'member states'.
27. Exceptionally also in the country of which both parties are nationals or before national courts with which the case has sufficient connection.
28. Regulation No. 650/2012 of 4 July 2012, on Jurisdiction, Applicable Law, Recognition and Enforcement of Decisions and Acceptance and Enforcement of Authentic Instruments in Matters of Succession and on the Creation of a European Certificate of Succession, Official Journal L201 of 27 July 2012, entered into force on 17 August 2015.
29. Regulation No. 655/2014 of 15 May 2014 establishing a European Account Preservation Order to facilitate cross-border debt recovery in civil and commercial matters, Official Journal L189 of 27 June 2014, applicable from 18 January 2017.

- The EU Regulation No. 1346/2000 of 29 May 2000[30] on insolvency proceedings has had a huge impact on insolvency administration inside the Union. It took effect on 31 May 2002 and was repealed by the new 'recast' version: EU Regulation No. 2015/848 of 20 May 2015 on insolvency proceedings, to become applicable in 2017.[31]

[C] National Law on Jurisdiction of Belgian Courts

[1] General Rules on International Jurisdiction

The Code of Private International Law introduced a complete system of grounds for international jurisdiction for claims introduced in Belgium after 1 October 2004. These national grounds have lost some importance since they apply only when a dispute does not fall under one of the EU regulations. That means they apply *inter alia* when the defendant is not domiciled in the EU territory and by definition for disputes not covered under any of the above-mentioned EU regulations.

The Code also honours as the main rule *forum rei* – accepting jurisdiction when either the defendant's domicile or his habitual residence lies in Belgium.[32] The national sovereign determination of jurisdiction, under the Code, is of course only unilateral; the text only has authority for Belgian courts and it can only have effect here.[33] For co-defendants, eventually residing outside Europe, the Belgian domicile/resp. residence of one of them suffices.

We allow party autonomy of consensual forum clauses (jurisdiction agreements) when they appoint Belgian courts[34] as well as when they de facto exclude Belgian courts (derogation) by preferring to give competence to one or more foreign courts.[35] In this context, *vis-à-vis* a party not resident in the EU territory, a court may deny jurisdiction notwithstanding the parties have mutually agreed on jurisdiction of Belgian courts, if any relevant connection with Belgium is lacking (this is the forum non conveniens principle).

30. EU Regulation No. 1346/2000 of 29 May 2000 on Insolvency Proceedings, Official Journal L160-1 of 30 June 2000, last amended by EU Regulation No. 663/2014 of 5 June 2014, Official Journal L179-4 of 19 June 2014 – *see* the consolidated version at http://eur-lex.europa.eu. Denmark has opted out.
31. EU Regulation No. 848/2015 of 20 May 2015 on Insolvency Proceedings, Official Journal L141-19 of 5 June 2015 – most Articles of this Regulation enter into force on 26 June 2017; *see* a summary at http://eur-lex.europa.eu.
32. Article 5 Code of Private International Law. But, in effect, if the substance of the claim is covered by an EU Regulation, then defendant's domicile in Belgium (a European Member State) would normally cause the Regulation to be applicable... so this general national rule only works for *marginal* matters such as claims over paternity (filiation).
33. *See* Article 2 Code of Private International Law.
34. Article 6 Code of Private International Law for the rare agreements materially not covered by EU regulations.
35. Article 7 Code of Private International Law. The Code provides that the court addressed must declare itself without jurisdiction unless it has not been able to assess that the foreign court's decision over the matter will be recognisable in Belgium, and must postpone its own decision to reject jurisdiction until such assessment is possible.

Counterclaims are allowed before the competent court. Further there are complementary grounds for cases where a third party is called as warrantor or a third party asks to intervene.[36]

For hypotheses in which the defendant(s) is (are) domiciled *outside* European countries, the Code offers other, 'alternative' grounds. There is then for example also a contractual forum in Belgium (including when a contract was concluded in Belgium). See also other alternative opportunities to sue a foreign party in Belgium, below, for some of the specific topics. The Code also provides that urgent or interlocutory relief may be sought in Belgium through protective attachment or garnishment of goods situated in Belgium (*forum arresti*).[37]

The Code introduced the novelty that Belgian judges can take up jurisdiction based on the notion of the necessity to intervene, to avoid denial of justice, where suing before foreign courts holds no promise for justice to be done for the claimant - such as when the natural foreign forum would accept jurisdiction, but where we see perhaps civil war or wide-spread corruption (*forum necessitatis*).

[2] Specific Jurisdictional Grounds

Status and Certain Matrimonial Causes

Belgian courts accept broad jurisdiction for questions of status or relating to our civil registrars; also for declarations on the validity of marriage or for disputes between partners in marriage or cohabiting. EU Regulation No. 2201/2003 on divorce has diminished the field.

Claims Regarding Parentage

Alternatively, jurisdiction for establishing or disputing parentage is taken up in Belgium when the descendant (child) or the ascendant has domicile/resp. residence here; or when both claimant and defendant possess Belgian nationality).[38]

International Estates

Because we have the EU Succession Regulation No. 650/2012 with truly broad criteria of jurisdiction,[39] the rules in the Belgian Code of Private International Law are basically superseded except in successions of persons who died before 17 August 2015.

Contractual Obligations and Torts Beyond the Ambit of the Brussels I*bis* Regulation

For contractual obligations, the national rules would still apply to trust agreements or certain family relationships in dispute. Below, I will refer to those fields in which

36. Article 8 Code of Private International Law.
37. Article 10 Code of Private International Law.
38. Article 61 Code of Private International Law.
39. *See supra* §16.03 [B].

mandatory rules have a bearing on the jurisdiction issue. For the very specific torts of defamation and damage through nuclear radiation, national rules would apply.

Property Claims

Alternative jurisdiction against a person not residing inside EU territory is provided before the courts at the place of location of property (or hypothetical location for immaterial goods or bank-accounts) at the time suit is introduced, for claims regarding rights in rem in such property[40] and for claims about the protection of intellectual property rights on Belgian territory.[41]

Insolvency Beyond the Scope of the EU Regulation

Because EU Regulation 1346/2000 only covers insolvency for entities with their establishment (COMI) in a Member State and – in that hypothesis – not comprising the claims relating to secondary establishments *ad extra*, Belgian law fills those gaps. It grants jurisdiction to the Belgian forum of the centre of main activity in relation to foreign branches; it adds jurisdiction for Belgian secondary branches when the main forum would be *ad extra Europa* and then works out solutions of mutual respect and cooperation plus recognition and enforcement in parallel to the European principles.[42]

[D] *Lis Alibi Pendens* and Related Proceedings

Under the EU Brussels I*bis* Regulation regarding general claims, as well as under the Brussels IIa Regulation on annulment of marriage, divorce and parental authority, Regulation 4/2009 on maintenance obligations, and Regulation 1346/2000 on insolvency, the effect of introducing a claim first in one Member State has strict mandatory consequences for all the other Member States. A new claim elsewhere cannot be accepted if there is a foreign case pending on the same cause.

There is – on the other hand – no obligation to respect foreign proceedings introduced in countries with which there are no reciprocal treaty obligations. The Belgian Code of Private International Law in essence copies and expands the notions of EU law on *lis pendens*, to become the general law.[43] It means that parties may simultaneously pursue their judicial claims in Belgium and in another country (unless treaty-bound) hoping to win first and to appeal thereafter for recognition of such a beneficial judgment. But the Belgian judge may find it is wiser to stay the cause of action in anticipation of what the general rules of recognition could bring.

40. Article 85 Code of Private International Law.
41. Article 86 Code of Private International Law.
42. Articles 116–121 Code of Private International Law.
43. Article 14 Code of Private International Law.

[E] Service of Process Abroad

Belgium is a member of the Hague Service Convention of 15 November 1965, binding sixty-nine countries. This Treaty organises the service of process through national central authorities (for some cases, through consular authorities) that communicate by using standard multilingual forms.

The improved EU Regulation No. 1393/2007 of 13 November 2007[44] regarding service of judicial and non-judicial documents in civil and commercial matters, covers exchanges of such documents between Member States. Transmitting and receiving agencies were installed.[45]

When it exceptionally applies, Belgian general law provides rather liberal rules of service.[46]

[F] Obtaining of Evidence Abroad and Rules Regarding Proof

European Regulation No. 1206/2001 of 28 May 2001 governs cooperation between courts of Member States for obtaining proof.[47] It intends to improve, simplify and accelerate cooperation between courts in the taking of evidence. The communication is directly between courts, either asking for the other's help or for permission to go in and obtain evidence. Requests for information may go to the Central Authority.[48]

Presently, the only aid we offer or receive for obtaining evidence in relation with countries outside the EU is the questionable cooperation under the decrepit Hague Convention of 1 March 1954 on Civil Procedure with its burdensome diplomatic procedure for rogatory commissions.

The *lex fori* as law governing the procedure controls the use of different modes of proof; it may for example allow the oath or witness declarations in certain matters.

[G] European Payment Order and Small Claims Procedures

EU Regulation No. 1896/2006 of 12 December 2006[49] created a European order for payment procedure allowing creditors to recover their uncontested civil and

44. Regulation No. 1393/2007, Official Journal L331-21 of 10 December 2008, repealing Regulation No. 1348/2000 - in force since 13 November 2008. Denmark has opted out, but under an agreement its rules apply similarly in relation to Denmark.
45. Transmitting agents are also court clerks and public prosecutors; for receiving the Central Body is the National Chamber of the Federation of Bailiffs, at www.huissiersdejustice.be.
46. Articles 40 and 46 Judicial Code.
47. Regulation No. 1206/2001 of 28 May 2001, Official Journal L174 of 27 June 2001, in force since 1 January 2004.
48. In Belgium: the Federal Department of Justice. The standard request form and supporting documents must be brought in the language (French or Dutch or German, as the case may be) of the judicial district of the Court of First Instance to which the request is sent.
49. Regulation No. 1896/2006 of 12 December 2006 creating a European Order for Payment Procedure, Official Journal L399 of 30 December 2006; all information on courts with jurisdiction, languages and communication was last consolidated on 11 July 2014. Denmark has opted out.

commercial claims, based on a uniform procedure that operates on the basis of standard forms. The procedure does not require presence before the court. The claimant only has to submit his application, after which the procedure will lead its own life.

EU Regulation 861/2007 of 11 July 2007[50] established a European small claims procedure, which seeks to improve and simplify procedures in civil and commercial matters where the value of a claim does not exceed EUR 2,000 (from mid-2017: EUR 5,000). It is a written procedure operating on the basis of standard forms. The Regulation prescribes time limits to speed up litigation.

§16.04 INTERNATIONAL COMMERCIAL ARBITRATION

Belgium is a jurisdiction open to the application of foreign law. It is a multilingual environment affording good secretarial services, communication and transportation. Brussels is an important political and legal centre because of the concentration of the administrations of the EU Commission and Council and the location of the EU Parliament, and NATO has its headquarters there too. It has an internationally oriented bar.

Belgium is a member state to the international treaties about arbitration and thus also offers assurances for respect of arbitration agreements, for respect of the basic tenets of arbitration, and for ease of trans-boundary enforcement of the resulting awards. We are bound in the impressive group of 156 member states of the Convention of New York of 10 June 1958 regarding the recognition and enforcement of foreign arbitral awards of arbitral tribunals. This gives an indication of how wide the network is for the advanced cooperation.[51] Also significant is the European Convention of Geneva of 21 April 1961, which binds Belgium as one of thirty-two member states.[52] Its rules apply to arbitration proceedings over contracts between parties who have residence in the territories of a member state. These rules exist besides the rules of the New York Convention.

Those convention rules determine how we may call on the exception against a state court's competence (*exceptio arbitrandi*). They indicate which law is applicable to the validity of the agreement and to the legal question whether the subject matter of the dispute may in principle be subjected to arbitration by private tribunals ('arbitrability'). They supply detail about the capacity of public law entities to enter into

50. Official Journal L199 of 31 July 2007. Denmark has opted out. The European e-Justice Portal provides all information as well as a tool for filling in the forms. *See infra* §16.06 [B], *i.a.* for the amendment of 16 December 2015.
51. *See* https://treaties.un.org/ for text and status of ratifications and accessions. Belgium is also party to the Geneva Convention of 26 September 1927, largely replaced by this New York Convention, but possibly still binding for some of the territories depending for their foreign relations on the United Kingdom.
52. *See* https://treaties.un.org/ for text and status. Belgium ratified on 19 July 1975 (Moniteur belge – Belgisch Staatsblad, 17 February 1976).

arbitration and about how courts afford support in composing tribunals. They also determine the conflicts of law rules to be used for deciding the merits of the case and they impose the general rule of motivation of the awards. The Geneva 1961 Convention goes further to reduce the grounds for denial of enforcement abroad, in a member state (even though the New York Convention of 1958 may be applicable) in case of annulment of an arbitration award in the country where it was decided.

For the settlement of disputes over investments, between states and subjects of other states, Belgium is party to the Washington Convention of 18 March 1965 (instating the International Center for the Settlement of Investment Disputes, ICSID).

The Federal Act of 24 June 2013 has rewritten Belgian arbitration law, with drafting delegated to an expert commission within CEPANI - the Belgian Centre for Arbitration and Mediation.[53] Belgium may now be counted among the countries that adhere to the UNCITRAL Model Law on Arbitration,[54] even though the Belgian Act does contain some particularities.

The space is lacking here to discuss the law and the practice of commercial arbitration, notwithstanding the importance of the issues for the field of private international relations.

§16.05 CHOICE OF LAW OR APPLICABLE LAW

[A] National Law of a Person and Belgian Nationality Law

Nationality is used as a distinguishing factor in deciding the capacity of persons and still some elements of family law.[55]

For the use of nationality as a connecting factor, conflicts of nationality are resolved in accordance with the principles formulated in the Hague Convention of 12 April 1930, taken up in Article 3, §2 of the Belgian Code of Private International Law, viz.: When Belgian nationality is one of the accumulated nationalities of a person, then only the Belgian nationality is regarded. When a person holds two foreign nationalities, then the most effective nationality is sought out for use in private international law, considering all elements but with domicile in a country being a strong indication of the prevalence of that nationality. For those who have been given the status of United Nations fugitive and who have thus essentially lost subjection to a former motherland, as for those who are stateless following the UN Convention, Belgium's treaty

53. Law introducing a new version of Chapter VI (Article 1676–1722) Judicial Code, Moniteur belge - Belgisch Staatsblad, 28 June 2013, entered into force on 1 September 2013, for all proceedings commenced after that date. *See* the English version (translation by Federal Department of Justice, M. Price & H. Verbist) of the Act, in the brochure of CEPANI, Arbitration Rules (containing also the new arbitration rules of CEPANI) in its Schedule IV, Brussels, CEPANI - Stuiversstraat/Rue des Sols 8, 1000 Brussels, 2013, p. 64–84.
54. *See* www.uncitral.org.
55. *See infra* §16.05 [B] [1].

obligations bring us to apply the law of the domicile as a substitute personal law,[56] the reference in the Code of Private International Law to nationality is thus replaced by the subject's habitual residence.[57] If a person's nationality cannot be determined, his habitual residence takes its place.[58]

Under the Code on Belgian Nationality,[59] Belgian nationality is allotted on the basis of a mixture of elements pertaining to descent, place of birth, volition connected to the length of residence on Belgian territory and – since the amendment of 2012 – based on proven integration. Men and women are treated equally, irrespective of their status as having been born in or out of wedlock. Thus husband and wife, resp. father and mother are treated equal. After the Act of 1 March 2000 liberalised and sped up irresponsibly the way our nationality was given (sometimes referred to as the 'quick-Belgian law'), winds of change set in, with stricter conditions introduced in 2006 and 2007, and more recently through the Act of 4 December 2012 'amending the Code on Belgian Nationality to make it neutral as to migration',[60] by which essentially integration must come before acquiring nationality and the latter is not given in the hope of speeding up the first. Place is lacking to explain the rules of Belgian nationality.

[B] Persons and Family

[1] Personal Status and Capacity of Persons in General

A person's status and capacity are determined by the law of that person's nationality.[61] In this case, if the conflicts rule of the national law were to refer back to Belgian law, such *renvoi* is accepted. That covers the reduced capacity for minors, and their personal emancipation through adulthood.

The national law of a person determines the declaration of absence in case of his disappearance,[62] while his assets are managed according to the law of his habitual residence at the time he disappeared, or if that lacks interim protection measures, then following Belgian law.

The gender of a person is a question of his national law. So is the legal adaptation of gender after a sex-change, where Belgian law would set aside a law that forbade adaptation.[63]

---

56. *See* respectively the Conventions of Geneva (28 July 1951 – Article 12) and of New York (28 September 1954 – Article 12).
57. Article 3, §3, Code of Private International Law.
58. Article 3, §4, Code of Private International Law.
59. By the Act of 28 June 1984 the Code of Nationality Law was introduced, Moniteur belge – Belgisch Staatsblad, 12 July 1984, effective 1 January 1985 and amended by Acts of 1991, 1993, 1995, 1998, 2000, 2006, 2007 – then end of 2012.
60. Moniteur belge – Belgisch Staatsblad, 14 December 2012, in force on 1 January 2013. Some call this the 'better-Belgian law'.
61. Article 34 Code of Private International Law. Capacity to make a will or to commit a tort, falls under the law applicable to the relationship (Article 34, §2).
62. Article 41 Code of Private International Law.
63. Article 35*ter* Code of Private International Law.

[2] The Name of Persons

Belgium adheres to a principle of permanence of the name. The original formation of the family name and the given name of a person – for the administration at time of birth or in case a request to determine the name is introduced in court – is governed by the national law of that person. If a person's nationality changes, the law of the new nationality determines the effects this can have on his name.[64] Changing a name, voluntarily or through operation of law, comes under the national law at the time of the purported change. The name forms a distinctive category always decided independently, which leaves the names of married spouses to be decided individually per each partner's person law, eventually leading to different names for the two of them. The law is strict on changes to a person's name acquired in a foreign country; denial of recognition would follow if the substantive rules of name-law as in Belgian law were not respected in that change abroad. But under pressure of EU law as interpreted by the ECJ, the name of a person as formed, changed or registered under the law of a Member State of the EU must be recognised, so as not to obstruct the free movement of persons.[65]

[3] Guardianship of Children: Parental Authority – Protection of Persons

When it comes to guardianship and to the authorities that are competent to organise the appointment of a guardian and to control his or her performance, the governing law is that of the habitual residence of the minor at the time such guardianship must be organised. The exercise of guardianship as well as of parental authority is governed by the law of the ward's, resp. the child's place of habitual residence at the time a measure is taken.[66] An eventual system of a specific protective incapacity regime for adults and regarding their assets, falls under the same law of habitual residence of the individual – with further subsidiary rules. The Hague Convention of 19 October 1996 was ratified by Belgium and prevails.[67] It similarly applies when a Belgian court has jurisdiction over a person less than 18 years old, on the basis of the Brussels IIa Regulation regarding matrimonial causes and parental *responsibility*.

Many bilateral consular conventions impose the obligation on Belgian authorities to inform the national authorities if one of their citizens died in Belgium (and the inverse, if a Belgian died in that country), or when a minor with its nationality is left orphaned. If those national authorities do not organise guardianship, then Belgian

64. Article 37 Code of Private International Law.
65. Article 39 Code of Private International Law.
66. Article 35, §1, Code of Private International Law.
67. For persons less than 18 years old the rules of the international Convention of The Hague of 19 October 1996 regarding parental responsibility (comprising parents, guardians and other legal representatives of children) and protection of children prevail over national rules for jurisdiction, applicable law and enforcement (Article 35, §3). This Convention binds Belgium and forty other countries; it subjects the member states' nationals of less than 18 years old to measures under the law of the place of habitual residence (including if there were a non-member state's law (Article 20 of the Convention of 1996).

authorities must take initiative, following the minor's national law. Urgent protective measures to physically safeguard a child can be taken in Belgium according to our law, when the child is present here.

Effective controls over the exercise of parental authority and the abduction of children by a parent, confront us with problems of recognition and enforcement of foreign judicial decisions.

[4] Marriage and Partnerships

If a breach of promise to marry or of 'engagement' is considered, the law of the country in which both parties have habitual residence at the time of the breach applies; lacking such, the law of common nationality applies, and lacking that connection as well, then Belgian law applies.[68]

For the valid conclusion of marriage, each party shall fulfil the conditions applicable to himself or herself in his, respectively her personal law, but national law not allowing same-sex marriage would be disregarded.[69] The conditions of formal validity are those at the place where the ceremony is held.[70] The question whether the marriage before religious authorities constitutes legal marriage is such a question relating to form. Since Article 7 of the new Belgian Consular Code,[71] in force since 15 June 2014, with the list of consular competencies, Belgians can no longer conclude marriage before their diplomatic or consular representatives in a foreign country; they can marry in Belgium, even if they are domiciled abroad. A Belgian citizen may not marry through the office of a foreign diplomatic representative in Belgium.

The national law that imposes a condition for valid conclusion of marriage is also the law that decides over the type of sanction when that condition is violated. However, a scam marriage in which the intent to marry was absent in the mind of at least one party – for instance when consent was feigned in order to obtain access to or residence in the country, or to acquire nationality – is, in the Belgian view, null and void based on fraud.[72]

---

68. Article 45 Code of Private International Law.
69. Article 46 Code of Private International Law.
70. Article 47 Code of Private International Law.
71. Act holding the Consular Code of 21 December 2013, Moniteur belge – Belgisch Staatsblad 21 January 2014, entered into force on 15 June 2014, last amended by Act of 10 August 2015, Moniteur belge – Belgisch Staatsblad 24 August 2015 – effective on 5 January 2016. The competencies of Belgian consular agents for the field of civil law lie in functioning as registrar to receive declarations or to file (foreign) public documents relating to the status of Belgian citizens, and to perform certain notarial functions (officiating deeds in regard to immovable goods in Belgium, closing marital agreements or accepting last wills) – Article 7–25 Consular Code. Those are activities accepted under the Treaty on Consular Relations concluded in Vienna on 24 April 1963 (Article 5).
72. There was much to do about the number of persons evading Belgian law through scam relationships of marriage (or partnership), that they would conclude in Belgium: a substantive rule was introduced in the Civil Code; later a cause of nullity was added for marriage under duress by threat or violence (*see* Article 146*bis* Civil Code (1999) about seeking immigration advantage; Article 146*ter* (2007) about duress). Recognition of *foreign* marriages and partnerships on the basis of a foreign official document, has put us before the more difficult policing

The law applicable to the effects of marriage is that of the habitual residence both spouses have in the same country, or if not, their common national law, and if that is absent too, Belgian law.[73] First, independent of the law applicable, the personal freedom and equal capacity of women is a matter of international public policy. Belgian domestic law states that some effects of marriage are mandatory for every marriage, whichever the property regime of the couple.

A growing number of couples live in marriage-like unions, such as partners living in a trial-marriage or in a de facto-marriage. These are a type of contractual relationship that create legal problems when they end. Verifying whether a bond is equivalent to marriage is left to the court: if yes, the choice of law rule on marriage is to be applied. It belongs to the forum to decide whether a 'partnership' under the law of a Scandinavian country, Dutch law, Swiss law or German law is equivalent to marriage.[74] The Code of Private International Law adds a definition of what is a lesser or another form of union, namely a 'relation of cohabitation', saying it 'refers to a situation of co-habitation that requires registration with a public authority and that does not create a bond equal to marriage'.[75] Belgium allows its unilateral termination. Such registered cohabitation exists in comparative law in several functionally equivalent forms. The legal consequences are to be found in the national law of the place of first registration.[76] For the variant of a not-registered cohabitation, the loosest form, the effects on the couple's patrimony could be conceived in parallel to unincorporated partnership. The issues should however preferably be resolved as in a family-like relationship, governed by the same conflict rules as for marriage and its effects.

[5] Property Regime of Spouses and Partners in Cohabitation

The property regime of married persons, husband and wife or same-sex spouses, as well as among partners in a registered relation of cohabitation, is settled in the Code of Private International Law. Europe has not intervened. The conflicts rule described above for the effects of marriage covers a number of legal issues concerning rights of spouses that are simple effects of marriage.[77] That is the case, notwithstanding several effects are of a pecuniary nature, and touch a couple's assets and the capacity to manage them.

For the marital property regime, the reference is to a chosen national law, with restricted autonomy (only the law of where the couple will establish their first habitual

issues, to defend against the same fraudulent creation of scam relations abroad with the intention of evading Belgian immigration laws or nationality law and social security law (*see infra*).

73. Article 48 Code of Private International Law.
74. Instructions published by the Department of Justice declare that most of those partnerships are equivalent to marriage, except the Dutch one because Netherlands' law explicitly leaves to the parties the choice to conclude either a marriage or a partnership - Circular letter of 29 May 2007, Moniteur belge - Belgisch Staatsblad 31 May 2007.
75. Article 58 Code of Private International Law.
76. Article 60 Code of Private International Law.
77. Article 48 Code of Private International Law.

residence; or a national law or a residential law of a party).[78] A choice must be in writing[79] and must relate to all the goods of the spouses, having only effects for the future.[80] If spouses did not choose, then we apply the law of the place where both spouses established their first habitual residence after the celebration of the marriage; absent such, the law of the common nationality at the time of marriage if applied, and absent that, in other cases, the law of the state where the marriage was celebrated will apply.[81] The scope of application comprises the composition, management and liquidation and division of property, liabilities, change of regime and also the formal validity of the marital agreements.[82] The position of third parties comes under the same law. The law of the place where a relationship of cohabitation was first registered is applicable to the effects of the relationship for the assets of parties.[83] Under Belgian substantive law, cohabiting partners have a complete property regime, as in marriage.

Because many marriages need to be regarded that exist from before the entry into force of the Code of Private International Law on 1 October 2004, the temporal application of the conflicts law is at issue, under its general rule, which gives the new rules immediate effect on individual actions taken and individual transactions made relating to property and liabilities after their entry into force.[84] But over and above that, the law chosen as applicable by the parties prevails independent of the time of choosing;[85] a chosen regime shall cover all assets. The transitory rules thus result in an eventual split in the regime of marital property under a regime of a previous period and then a new regime after the given transition date, with a virtual dissolution, liquidation and a re-distribution on the date of transition to start anew.

[6] Divorce and Separation[86]

The EU Regulation No. 1259/2010 of 20 December 2010 implementing enhanced cooperation among sixteen participating EU Member States in the area of the law applicable to divorce and legal separation, entered into force on 22 June 2012.[87] It is referred to as the 'Rome-III Regulation'. Notwithstanding the rule was not generally accepted in the EU, the makers had the ambition to make it universal – so it demands application whether or not it is the law of a *participating* Member State or, for that

---

78. Articles 49–50 Code of Private International Law.
79. Article 52 Code of Private International Law.
80. Article 50 Code of Private International Law.
81. Article 51 Code of Private International Law.
82. Article 53 Code of Private International Law.
83. Article 54 Code of Private International Law with regard to protection of third parties (*supra*) applies by analogy. In the event that the relationship of cohabitation does not exist in the designated law, the law of the state on the territory of which the relationship is registered applies.
84. Article 127, §1, Code of Private International Law.
85. Articles 127, §2, and 50, §1, Code of Private International Law.
86. For jurisdictional criteria, on the basis of EU Brussels IIa Regulation – *see supra*.
87. Published in Moniteur belge – Belgisch Staatsblad 29 December 2010, 343-10. It applies to legal proceedings instituted after 21 June 2012 and to agreements regarding choice of law concluded thereafter; but Article 18, §1, would validate an earlier choice if it complied.

purpose, a non-member state.[88] It covers issues relating to divorce or separation and conversion of separation into divorce; it does not include issues summed up in Article 1, §2, such as capacity, validity of marriage or its annulment, name, property consequences or parental authority.[89]

The rule looks first at a national divorce law or separation law resulting from a choice made by agreement between spouses - written, dated and signed by both spouses and concluded before the introduction of the claim.[90] The free choice of applicable law is limited to that of the common residence or former common residence or to the law of either party's nationality law or to *forum* law.[91] Those precautions must protect a weaker, impressionable spouse. The freely appointed law also decides for itself whether the expressed choice of law is indeed valid.[92] If no choice was made, then the default rule is, that the law of the place of common habitual residence, or lacking such, the law of the former common place of residence,[93] or, lacking also such law, then the law of common nationality or if not: finally the court's own law.[94] Exceptions are found in Articles 10 and 13 of the Rome-III Regulation.

Belgian private international law under the Code of 2004 would only apply in procedures commenced before 21 June 2012.[95]

[7] Legitimacy, Legitimation and Adoption

The maternal parentage is deemed to exist by operation of law, based on the birth certificate. A mother's national law will decide. The mother's husband who would dispute his paternity, may rely on his national law. Indeed, the law of the parent is applicable to legitimacy and legitimation in her/his regard. But when looking at the issue whether a child shall be asked to consent, the law of the place of habitual residence of the child governs.[96] The applicable law decides who may claim parentage or affiliation, what the statute of limitations is, which conditions apply, and who carries the burden of proof.

The rules regarding adoption of minors underwent significant change when Belgium ratified the Convention of the Hague Conference on Private International Law, concluded on 29 May 1993.[97] That Convention stated that it was largely preferred that children would be raised in the member state country of origin. The convention for

88. Article 1, §1, and Article 4 Rome-III Regulation.
89. It follows, that the consequences of a divorce in relation to matters outside this Regulation's field must be brought under the applicable national laws to which the respective specific rules point.
90. Article 7 Rome-III Regulation spells out which national formal requirements apply.
91. Article 5 Rome-III Regulation.
92. Article 6 Rome-III Regulation.
93. If the habitual residence there goes back less than one year and one spouse still has residence in that country.
94. Article 8 Rome-III Regulation.
95. *See* Article 55 Code of Private International Law.
96. Article 62 Code of Private International Law. Article 62, §2, states how an eventual double paternity under two applicable national laws, is to be resolved.
97. Convention on Protection of Children and Co-operation in Respect of Intercountry Adoption. *See* for all data of the Hague Conference on Private International Law at www.hcch.net.

administrative cooperation introduced preliminary controls exchange of files between authorities set up in the country of origin and country of destination. Only with all conditions fulfilled and after the particular child is matched to the parents, can a child be displaced from its motherland across a national border, preferably after an adoption procedure in the child's country.

Only if adoption would follow in Belgium would the national conflict rule require application. Adoptions that have come about in respect of this Convention would profit from a remarkably liberal recognition in other member states, based solely on authentic documentation by the competent national authority of the country where adoption took place.

After the introduction of this stringent approach between Belgium and treaty-bound member states of the Hague Convention, the numbers of adoptions of foreign children has steadily diminished, to only seventy adoptions with foreign element for the entire year 2015. Belgian general rules on conflict of laws are laid down in federal law, namely a special statute of private international law, in which the rules distinguish between adoptions under the Hague Convention and outside the scope of the convention.[98] It is a complicated set of articles. Besides those basic principles in the Belgian Civil Code and the role the federal Department of Justice fulfils as 'Central Authority' under the Convention, we find the institutions at the levels of the four cultural communities (the Flemish Community, the French Community, the German Community, and the Brussels Community) with most influence and effective power in the field. The different levels of legislatures in Belgium, all having promulgated numerous provisions by statute, each with its own treaty-making powers, make the subject of adoption most complex. There are formidable hurdles for prospective adoptive parents.

[8] Maintenance Payments[99]

The rules regarding maintenance obligations between parents and children or for those who must support a creditor of under 21 years of age and in relations between spouses have been upset since mid-2011, when the EU Regulation No. 4/2009 became effective. The Hague Convention of 24 October 1956 that had been in force was replaced by a new Hague Protocol, applied provisionally. The conflicts rules of the Belgian Code of Private International Law of 2004 were replaced as well – except where they relate to

98. *See* Act of 24 April 2003, Moniteur belge – Belgisch Staatsblad, 16 May 2003, amended by Act of 27 December 2004, Moniteur belge – Belgisch Staatsblad, 31 December 2004, in force on 1 September 2005, introducing Articles 343–368(8) and 369–370 into the Civil Code; *see also* Act of 13 March 2003, Moniteur belge – Belgisch Staatsblad, May 2003, amending the Judicial Code; and *see* Royal Decree of 24 August 2005, Moniteur belge – Belgisch Staatsblad, 29 August 2005 providing measures for execution of the Act. I do not try to cite all the decrees on the level of Cultural Communities. For a Dutch-language analysis, *see* J. ERAUW & H. STORME, INTERNATIONAAL PRIVAATRECHT 565–603 (Beginselen van Belgisch Privaatrecht XVII, R. Dillemans & W. Van Gerven eds., Mechelen: Kluwer 2009).

99. For matters of jurisdiction *see* Articles 3–14 EU Regulation 4/2009 on Maintenance and Article 5(2) Lugano, plus the agreement with Denmark.

recognition and enforcement of decisions from states not bound by the Regulation – per definition, from the world beyond Europe.

EU Regulation No. 4/2009 of 18 December 2008[100] makes clear it takes up the full regulating competence, representing henceforth the Member States in foreign relations for the field of maintenance payments. It covers claims based on parentage or on marriage and other affinity relations, plus maintenance payments after divorce or separation[101] and covers claims accessory to a dispute over establishing such status relationships.[102] As regards the rules appointing the applicable law, the Regulation refers to the Protocol which the EU signed at the Hague Conference of Private International Law on 23 November 2007 as a 'Regional Economic Integration Organisation'.[103] The Protocol as such only became effective on 1 August 2013. It gives conflicts rules that apply universally,[104] i.e., independent of whether the applicable law is that of a member state; thus making all conflicts rules in Belgian domestic conflicts law obsolete. It applies also to maintenance claims over periods preceding the formal application in time.

[C] Successions and Wills

[1] Successions[105]

The EU has entered this field of personal and family asset management out of concern that many successions have a multi-state character, justifying intervention to improve the fluidity of assets all around, which private international law does, indeed, now coherently for a group of partner countries. The EU Regulation No. 650/2012 of 4 July 2012 on Succession, applies to a person deceased on or after 17 August 2015.

As for rules of conflict of laws, the Regulation applies universally, independent of the deceased last residing outside the European territory, or goods being located outside Europe; thus, independent of it resulting in a reference to the law of a third state.[106] Except if the deceased had made a choice of law for his entire succession, the law applicable to the succession, as a whole, is the law of the state in which he had his habitual residence at the time of death. This rule is rebuttable, exceptionally, if at death

100. Regulation 'on jurisdiction, applicable law, recognition and enforcement of decisions and cooperation in matters relating to maintenance obligations', Official Journal L7/1 of 2009, entered into force on 18 June 2011. It does not bind Denmark and UK – similarly not bound by the Hague Protocol 2007 – to be mentioned.
101. Article 74 of EU Regulation No. 4/2009.
102. Article 73 of EU Regulation No. 4/2009.
103. In its Articles 15 and 76 Maintenance Regulation. *See* Article 24 Protocol. 2007 for this EU representation of Member States. It signed on for all Member States except Denmark and the UK We therefore only look at this Protocol of 23 November 2007 on the law applicable to maintenance obligations. The Regulation lets existing treaties remain in force, but the Hague Protocol replaced the Hague Convention of 24 October 1956 to which Belgium was a party, for obligations towards children (Article 18 Protocol of 2007).
104. Article 2 of the 2007 Protocol.
105. The rules for jurisdiction are given *supra* §16.03 [B].
106. Article 20 of EU Regulation No. 650/2012. Denmark, Ireland and the UK are not part of the territorial field.

the deceased was manifestly more closely connected with another state, for instance if he had recently moved.[107] Only one law applies.[108] Express choice, in the form of a last will, can be made for the law of the deceased's nationality (present or at time of death), also as a whole.[109] Add to this, however, a limited *renvoi*. The Regulation provides an exemplary list of issues that come under the scope of application of the law of the succession.[110] An important new facet of the Regulation No. 650/2012 is the introduction of the European Certificate of Succession ('ECS'), produced on a standard European form, which helps considerably in providing all the required information.[111]

The rules on recognition and enforcement of Regulation No. 650/2012 relate only to decisions from Member States for persons deceased after 17 August 2017.[112] For earlier deaths and for a court decision originating from either Denmark, Ireland or the UK (not part of the EU cooperation) or from any other part of the world outside Europe, the Belgian general rules still apply. The same is true for foreign deeds with regard to successions.

[2] Dispositions of Property upon Death

A last will can take the place of the rules that name the beneficiaries in the law of intestate succession. Several types of 'dispositions of property upon death' are possible. EU Regulation No. 650/2012 defines such disposition as 'a will, a joint will or an agreement as to succession'.[113] That would cover stipulations in view of death, which couples could make in a marital agreement.

Articles 24–27 of Regulation No. 650/2012 state the applicable law. A disposition of property upon death[114] shall be governed, as regards its admissibility and *substantive* validity (including interpretation of its terms), by the law which, under this Regulation, would have been applicable to the succession if the person had died on the day he made it. A person may also choose the law that shall govern the admissibility, substantive validity and effect of his 'last will' among the laws he could chose to cover his succession. As regards the *formal* validity of a last will, the Regulation leaves the existing treaty unchanged,[115] whilst in fact the solutions are the same: the Hague

107. Article 21 of EU Regulation No. 650/2012.
108. Article 23, para. 1, of EU Regulation No. 650/2012.
109. Article 22 of EU Regulation No. 650/2012. The choice can have consequences for the jurisdiction: a court at the residence of the deceased may then decline jurisdiction in favour of proceedings in the country of which the law is applicable. Article 6 of EU Regulation No. 650/2012.
110. Article 23, para. 2, of EU Regulation No. 650/2012.
111. Article 62 et. seq. of EU Regulation No. 650/2012. For its elaborate contents, *see* Article 68 of EU Regulation No. 650/2012.
112. Even for Member States, the cooperation, the recognition and enforcement of decisions relating to the succession of a person who *died before 17 August 2015*, came under the general Belgian rules.
113. Article 3, §1, (d), of EU Regulation No. 650/2012.
114. As regards application in time: disposition upon death made before August 2015 are valid if they comply with the new rules *or* with the old rules via the then applicable rules of conflict of laws (Article 83).
115. Article 75, §2, of EU Regulation No. 650/2012.

Convention of 5 October 1961 is thus still effective for Belgium, independent of reciprocity – in all cases, for the issue of formal validity of wills.[116] A last will is formally valid if it is made in compliance with the formalities prescribed in either one of several national laws (law of the place where it was made, or law of the country of the nationality or domicile or residence of the testator, either at the time it was executed – in writing – or altered, or at the time of death, et al.).[117]

Whichever is the law applicable to a will or agreement, the national law that governs the succession keeps determining the measure of freedom to bequeath or devise by will; imposing minimum obligatory proportions for some persons and then establishing the modes of reconstituting those shares through return of gifts or devises and eventually through reduction of inheritance share.[118]

In Belgium, dispositions of property upon death must only be registered if they are in notarial form.

[D] Property

The law applicable to property and other rights in rem in respect of an asset, movable or immovable, is the law of the country on the territory of which the asset is located when those rights are invoked.[119] That location is amenable to change for movable goods, as when they cross a boarder. The law clarifies that the acquisition and loss of these rights is governed by the law of the state on the territory of which the assets are located when the final action or fact that is invoked in the law as basis of the acquisition or the loss occurs. In a country like Belgium, where the transfer of property is constituted by sole consensus, the time of agreement is when one must locate the good; for other national law systems it is the time of delivery. The scope of issues resolved under that law is broad.[120] Security rights in rem fall under the same law of the *situs*. Attachment for security, seizure of goods, as well as government confiscation of assets are all limited within the territorial realm of the judiciary and other authorities.

Intellectual property rights are also judged on a territorial basis, because the prevailing notion is that protection is afforded at the place where it is sought and where it is obtained through formal application for industrial property rights – subject to registration. For copyright that would be the place where communication is performed and where the question of protection is raised. Applying local law splits up the protection per country, whereby commentators agree that a question of principle, viz. the question of who is original owner or has original title to an invention, should be decided by just one law. That must be preferably the law of origin of a creation or an invention. This is the national law that governs the relationship under which the

116. All data plus reference to commentary at: www.hcch.net.
117. Belgium is party to the international convention that introduced as one specific form of will, the so-called international will (Washington Convention, 26 October 1973, Moniteur belge – Belgisch Staatsblad, 11 October 1983).
118. Article 23, para. 2, of EU Regulation No. 650/2012.
119. Article 87, §1, Code of Private International Law.
120. Article 93 Code of Private International Law.

creative work was performed, such as the labour law applicable to the employment relationship or the law of the contract for work.

Several goods can form a whole, with a special purpose, like a portfolio or a business. This patrimony is deemed to be located on the territory with which it has the closest connections.[121]

Rights in rem in respect of a receivable and the effects of the transfer of the receivable are governed by the law of the territory on which the party that created the rights or that transferred rights has its habitual residence.[122] The Code of Private International Law also gives detail for the law applicable to rights in rem regarding negotiable instruments.[123]

For cultural goods and stolen goods an alternative choice is offered to the country from which a good was removed illegally, or to the party who suffered loss through theft, for the rules of replevin, reclaiming or protection of property: they may assert their rights under either the law of the place of the original location or under that of the place where the asset is present when the claim is brought.[124]

[E] Contractual Obligations[125]

[1] EU Conflicts Law for Contracts under the Rome-I Regulation

Belgium introduced the conflict rules of the Rome Convention of 19 June 1980 on the law applicable to contractual obligations by Act of 14 July 1987.[126] These rules first became effective 1 January 1988 as Belgian law, for contracts concluded after that date. Later, on 1 April 1991, it became applicable as the 'Convention'. Still later, from 17 December 2009 onwards, these conflict rules govern as EU Regulation, referred to as 'Rome-I'.[127] The conflicts principles of this Regulation thus apply to most contracts over time. Its substantial field is all contracts except when Article 1 of the Rome-I Regulation has excluded its application, like for family relationships, succession or incorporated ventures.

This Convention signed in Rome (1980) and its successor Regulation (2008) have been praised, for good reasons. It gives a two-legged rule: first, parties may choose freely the applicable law, and second, if they did not agree on a choice, then the law of the country with something like the closest connection to the contract prevails. This connection is made predictable by the introduction of, on the one hand, eight more specific conflicts rules for named specific contracts (sale of goods, services, transfer of rights in immovable goods, rental agreements, franchising, distribution agreement,

121. Article 87, §2, Code of Private International Law.
122. Article 87, §3, Code of Private International Law.
123. Article 91 Code of Private International Law.
124. Articles 90 and 92 Code of Private International Law.
125. For the European jurisdictional criteria, *see supra* §16.03 [B].
126. Moniteur belge - Belgisch Staatsblad, 9 October 1987.
127. EU Regulation No. 593/2008 of 17 June 2008 regarding the law applicable to contractual obligations, Official Journal L177-6 of 4 July 2008, corrected in Official Journal L309-87 of 24 November 2009.

auction sale and finally sales of financial instruments in a multilateral banking system),[128] on the other hand, by a presumption for the place of habitual residence of the party who performs characteristically.[129] The eight specific rules and the latter presumption are rebuttable, if the court finds that a closer connection exists. When there is not one party with, economically speaking, the characteristic performance, such as for joint ventures or barter agreements, we shift to the national contract law with the 'closest connection'.[130]

The Regulation clarifies all questions pertaining to exercising free choice and the limits to the freedom, whilst filling in the objective or default rule with sufficiently clear and flexible general rules.

Rome-I furthermore offers detail as to formal validity with an alternative reference, validating the contract as to form, if requirements were honoured under any of the local laws at places from where the parties (not in one another's presence) or their agents acted to express consent.[131] The list of issues covered in the field of application is helpful, comprising interpretation, performance, effects of breach, termination and effects of avoidance; to which is added that the law of the place of performance may be consulted for issues surrounding performance.[132]

Extension of these conflicts rules to other agreements or issues not explicitly covered by the Rome-I Regulation (jurisdiction or arbitration clauses) occurred under Article 98, §1, of the Belgian Code of Private International Law.

[2] Public Policy Exception and Mandatory Rules

If a foreign contract law were to allow the creation or performance of substantive obligations that infringe on elements of public policy or would eventually hold egregious rules, the court sets aside those aspects with the general exception of public policy.[133]

The role of mandatory provisions that intervene in the conflicts mechanism is different; it has been much debated. Article 9 of the Rome-I Regulation defines what are those overriding mandatory rules.[134] It states how they apply based on the country's policy in the particular circumstances of a relationship. Naturally the mandatory rules of the normally applicable law of the contract apply; besides that, especially those of the court's forum (*lex fori*). Also, overriding mandatory rules from the country of the

128. Article 4.1 Rome-I Regulation.
129. Article 4.2 Rome-I Regulation. For corporate entities the place of business is defined in Article 19 as the effective place of business establishment, like a branch office, involved in the transaction.
130. Article 4.4 Rome-I Regulation.
131. Article 11 Rome-I Regulation.
132. Article 12 Rome-I Regulation. Contracts concluded before 1 January 1988 (like old labour contracts) fall under the old common law.
133. Article 20 Rome-I Regulation.
134. Article 9(1) says: '... are provisions the respect for which is regarded as crucial by a country for safeguarding its public interests, such as its political, social or economic organisation, [...]applicable to any situation falling within their scope, irrespective of the law otherwise applicable...'.

place of performance as third foreign country, can eventually be applied – even though in practice that is a rare thing – if they would render the performance unlawful and if the judge considers it appropriate to apply them, taking into account nature, purpose and consequences of their application.

The specific conflicts rule for consumer contracts protects the consumer in all cases according to the law of the place of his habitual residence and similarly for employment contracts the imperative rules that protect the employee in the law of the habitual place of work shall be safeguarded notwithstanding a choice of law.[135]

[3] Specific Contracts

The *sale of movable goods,* the single most important business contract, comes under the Rome-I Regulation, where free choice applies, if exercised, otherwise the law of the place of the seller's residence is applicable.[136] However, conflicts will only emerge in the margin of the field of the Vienna Convention for the International Sale of Goods of 11 April 1980 (CISG), and if CISG does not decide on the particular issue in dispute.[137]

Consumer contracts may be governed by a law chosen by the parties, but such choice is limited in effect, because it may not diminish the protective rules of the normally applicable law, namely the one indicated by the default rule. The latter refers to the place of residence of the weaker party if he was approached for the contract in that residence.[138] The rules on *insurance contracts* make difficult distinctions, whereby large risks (excluding life insurance) allow more freedom of choice, but the other risks leave little place for a choice of only specifically connected national regimes. Absent a choice of law, the law of the place of the location of the risk is applicable. *Employment agreements* (with equally diminished freedom of choice) are covered by the law of the place of habitual work.[139] The *assignment of intangible movable goods* that are receivables in a broad sense, is covered by the Rome-I Regulation.[140] As to *agreements*

135. For very long-running labour contracts, not within the scope of the European rules, we also struggled with imperative laws. Belgian courts applied Belgian rules to labour contracts when the particular national rule for large redundancy payments as sanction for severance of contract, was classified as a rule that 'policed' contracts (the old Article 3, para. 1, Civil Code – labelled them '*lois de police*').
136. Article 4, §1 Rome-I Regulation. On 1 September 1999, the Belgian Government denounced the Hague Convention of 15 June 1955.
137. *See* www.uncitral.org. CISG was ratified by Belgium on 1 November 1997 with no reservations. The convention succeeded for Belgium the uniform rules on international sales under the two United Nations conventions (ULIS and ULFIS) of 1 June 1964. For a good commentary, *see* UN CONVENTION ON CONTRACTS FOR THE INTERNATIONAL SALE OF GOODS (CISG) – COMMENTARY (S. Kröll, L. Mistelis & P. Perales Viscasillas eds., Munich: C.H. Beck 2011). Belgium is also a member of the Convention of Vienna of 14 June 1974 amended on 11 April 1980) on the Statute of Limitations for Sale of Movable Goods. *See* the texts of both conventions at www.uncitral.org.
138. Article 6 Rome-I Regulation. Several European Directives have resulted in the promulgation of a plethora of national rules to protect consumers: the Doorstep Selling Directive 85/577; Package Travel Directive 90/314; Unfair Contract Terms Directive 93/13; Timeshare Directive 2008/122/EC; Distance Selling Directive 97/7; Price Indication Directive 98/6; Injunctions Directive 98/27 and the Consumer Sales Directive 99/44 (*see* www.eu-consumer-law.org).
139. Article 8 Rome-I Regulation.
140. Article 14 Rome-I Regulation.

for air-travel, a 'denied-boarding compensation system' exists for delays in air-travel, cancellations and overbookings, plus for claims regarding damage to, loss or delay of luggage.[141] It applies to flights within the EU and from outside EU with an EU airline.[142]

Belgian domestic law is of influence in imposing substantive mandatory conditions to certain or all international contracts: commercial distributorships (called 'sale *concessions*') and commercial agency as well as author or copyright agreements and mortgage loans. The European Rome-I Regulation has primacy, but those strict national rules have relevance in connection with Article 9 of the Rome-I Regulation. International agreements of *exclusive distribution of goods* in Belgium through independent holders of a sales concession come under such a mandatory rule.[143] For *negotiable instruments*, Belgium is a party to the Convention of Geneva of 7 June 1930 on the law applicable to bills of exchange and promissory notes and the Convention of Geneva of 19 March 1931 on the law applicable to cheques.

For *trust agreements* and the management of a trust, the Code of Private International Law provides a separate section.[144] The conflicts rule, inspired by the convention of The Hague of 1 July 1985 on trusts, would apply the law chosen by the settlor of the trust, with an exception.

[F] Torts

The EU 'Rome-II' Regulation largely covers this field.[145] This Regulation covers *inter alia* the pre-contractual relationship (for which the breach is qualified throughout Europe mostly as a tort), as well as unjust enrichment and *negotiorum gestio*.[146] Those rules apply to torts, including a tort threatening to occur, universally for all countries involved – independent of the indicated law being that of a EU Member State or not.[147]

141. EU Regulation No. 261/2004 of 11 February 2004, Official Journal L46-1 of 17 February 2004, establishing common rules on compensation and assistance to passengers in the event of denied boarding; it also affords equal rights in ticket-pricing. *See also* EU Regulation No. 2027/97 modified by Regulation No. 889/2002 of 13 May 2002, Official Journal L140 of 30 May 2002 concerning liability for passengers and their baggage.
142. The initiative to revise air-passenger rights is pending; *see* the Proposal for a Regulation amending Regulation (EC) No. 261/2004 establishing common rules on compensation and assistance to passengers in the event of denied boarding and of cancellation or long delay of flights and Regulation (EC) No. 2027/97 on air carrier liability in respect of the carriage of passengers and their baggage by air, COM/2013/0130 final – 2013/0072 (COD), at http://eur-lex.europa.eu.
143. Act of 27 July 1961, Moniteur belge – Belgisch Staatsblad, 5 October 1961 and the 1971 amendment published 21 April 1971. For an English version of this Act, *see* YEARBOOK OF COMMERCIAL ARBITRATION 1979, 254. From 31 May 2014, the text was recast in Book X Code of Economic Law (Art. 39) in which a disposition regarding commercial agents (Art. 25) raises similar questions regarding its mandatory nature.
144. Chapter 12, Articles 122–125 Code of Private International Law. To approach the trust phenomenon under a foreign law, the Code gives a definition narrowing down its reference more specifically to types of actual 'Anglo-Saxon' trust that have three named characteristics.
145. EU Regulation No. 864/2007 on the law applicable to non-contractual obligations, Official Journal L199-40 of 31 July 2007.
146. Articles 10–12 Rome II Regulation.
147. Article 3 Rome II Regulation.

This leaves only a small class of torts to the national conflicts rules (below). Because this is general EU law of conflicts, I - again - refrain from going into detail.

For traffic accidents, the Rome-II Regulation does not prejudice existing treaty obligations.[148] Belgium had ratified the Hague Convention on the Law Applicable to Traffic Accidents.[149] The Convention makes the law of the place of the registration of the vehicle applicable (nationality of the car's number plate) in several instances and less often the law of the place. In the meantime the EU Rome-II Regulation would offer a more flexible and attractive rule, but the Convention prevails, lacking denunciation by Belgium.

Little space remains in this field for Belgian national rules of the Code of Private International Law: A few types of torts are excluded from the field of application of the Rome-II Regulation: non-contractual obligations arising out of family or matrimonial relations, out of a trust relationships or in relations within companies and other bodies corporate or their winding-up, personal liability of officers or auditors to a company. The Belgian Code would apply the more specific conflicts rule for that sector, under which liabilities would be covered. At the same time, the Rome-II Regulation gives no rule for non-contractual obligations arising out of nuclear damage, nor for violations of privacy and rights relating to personality, including defamation. In these exceptional matters the Code would bring the law of the place where the claimed damages occurred,[150] and, specifically for defamation: the law chosen as the preferred statute by the claimant, as either the law of the place of wrongful action or of the place of the damaging impact, except if this latter place was not foreseeable.[151]

[G] Corporations

The Belgian present rule of private international law for legal persons points to the law of the state on the territory of which the entity had its 'main establishment' since the time of the incorporation.[152] That is close to what used to be the 'real seat' of the entity under the earlier Article 197 of the Commercial Code. For companies constituted in Belgium, the seat of main establishment is the same as the registered office, but not necessarily so for companies constituted elsewhere or whose seat is deemed to be 'foreign'. This '*real*' or effective seat is primarily tied down to the place from where the management operates. Indeed, the Code of Private International Law lines up, in a clear hierarchy, three elements to fill in the notion of main establishment: 'For the purposes of the present Act the main establishment of a body with separate legal entity is determined by taking into account primarily the place of administration, as well as

148. Article 28 Rome II Regulation.
149. Convention of 4 May 1971 applicable in Belgium since 3 June 1975 (Moniteur belge - Belgisch Staatsblad, 7 May 1975). *See* al materials at the Hague Convention website: www.hcch.org.
150. Articles 99 et seq. Code of Private International Law.
151. Article 99, §2, Code of Private International Law.
152. Article 110 Code of Private International Law. *See also supra* Chapter 13, §13.05.

the centre of its business and activities, and in subsidiary order the registered office'.[153] This approach may be changed in the future.

The conflicts rule is given for either corporations or other legal entities, such as charitable institutions or non-governmental bodies or organisations with a legal status, either of private or of public law. The choice of law rule thus refers equally to a foreign place of administration. Foreign corporations and charitable institutions are fully respected in Belgium as legal persons if they are validly constituted and existing under the law of their seat.[154] Foreign corporations enjoy the right to sue and may be sued before Belgian courts. Their representation follows their 'national' law, as the Code now states: the law at the place of their (central) administration (*lex societas*). A specific rule of *renvoi* is added, in order to avoid inconsistency in regard to the question of valid incorporation or legal existence.[155]

The law of the corporation has a wide scope of application.[156] The transfer of the seat as main establishment from one state to another can only take place without interruption of its legal personality, if done with due regard for the conditions under which the law of the two states permit this. The new law applies as of the time of transfer.[157] Mergers require the law of the corporations involved to be respected.[158] Cross-border mergers are thus conceivable (but burdensome). Claims resulting from a public issue of titles are governed, at the choice of the security holder, by the law applicable to the legal entity or by the law of the state on the territory of which the public issue took place.[159]

[H] Insolvency

The subject has been totally transformed in the last fifteen years. The European Regulation No. 1346/2000 was introduced on 30 May 2002, with a major impact in the field. It has in the meantime been 'recast', taking consideration of the various remaining problems. The new Regulation No. 2015/848 on insolvency will for most of it become applicable on 1 June 2017.[160]

The Belgian Code of Private International Law expanded the European Regulation, wishing to complement the administration of insolvencies in the identical manner when assets were located outside European Member States. That same intention remained present where for example a liquidator from a non-EU member state where the COMI was located, would want to act in Belgium or where secondary proceedings

153. Article 4, §3, Code of Private International Law.
154. The Court of Cassation upheld, for example, the legal personality and accepted the corporate shield of an Algerian company whose possessions were claimed by a creditor of another, similar company, because they were separate entities under their national law.
155. Article 110, para. 2, Code of Private International Law.
156. *See* Article 111 Code of Private International Law.
157. Now Article 112 Code of Private International Law. First decided in Court of Cassation 12 November 1965, 1966-I Pasicrisie belge 336.
158. Article 113 Code of Private International Law.
159. Article 114 Code of Private International Law.
160. *See* the summary of these regulations in §16.03 [B].

might be started in Belgium or in a non-member state. The law encourages cooperation and exchange in good comity – if such is returned from outside.[161]

Because insolvency and similar proceedings are essentially considered a matter of court-administered winding-up, the court's rules apply. Once jurisdiction is accepted in a court we basically have found the means of administering the sought insolvency proceedings. The law applicable to insolvency is the law of the *forum*,[162] with a broad scope of application summed up. The EU Regulation as well as the national Belgian statutory provision that follows it,[163] then introduce a series of exceptions, to assure that for instance existing priority rights in rem for certain assets are respected, or for rights to immovable goods, for set-off such as in financial markets, or that rights of workers in an employment relationship stay privileged – each under different applicable laws. The national law of the competent court even applies where each separate secondary proceeding was introduced.[164]

The rules on recognition and enforcement, a key element in trans-frontier cooperation (to acknowledge the powers of the liquidator/administrator) and enforcement (to close on the basis of a foreign court decision), are discussed in the relevant section, below.

§16.06 RECOGNITION AND ENFORCEMENT OF FOREIGN DOCUMENTS AND JUDICIAL DECISIONS

[A] Treaty Obligations

The Lugano Convention of 30 October 2007 binds Belgium to Norway and Switzerland with regard to the issues of recognition and eventual forced execution of judicial decisions, in terms copied from the 2000 version of the Brussels I Regulation (below). Other treaties exist, such as those in regard to transportation by air, rail and sea, or on ocean pollution.

For *parental responsibility and child abduction*, we have the European Convention of 20 May 1980 (Luxembourg) on recognition of decisions regarding custody over children and restoration of custody, which is in force since 1986.[165] However, it now only operates with contracting parties that are not Member Countries of the EU.[166] The 'world treaty' on the same topic was signed at The Hague Conference, *viz.* the Convention of 25 October 1980 on the *civil aspects of international child abduction*.[167]

161. *See also supra* §16.03 [C] [2].
162. Article 4 of EU Regulation No. 1346/2000 or Article 7 of Recast EU Regulation No. 2015/848.
163. Article 119 Code of Private International Law.
164. Article 28 of EU Regulation No. 1346/2000 or Article 35 of Recast EU Regulation No. 2015/848.
165. European Convention on Recognition and Enforcement of Decisions concerning Custody of Children and on Restoration of Custody of Children, signed in Luxembourg on 20 May 1980 under the auspices of the Council of Europe, in: Council of Europe Treaty Series (Coetser) 1980.
166. Belgium declared that a judgment given in a court of a Member State of the EU, in respect of a matter relating to the Convention, shall be recognised and enforced in Belgium by application of the relevant internal rules of Community law; others follow the procedure of common law.
167. *See* www.hcch.net for all information. In force for Belgium since 1 May 1999. The Belgian Central Authority is the Federal Department of Justice.

The Convention of The Hague of 19 October 1996 *on protection measures for children* also works for Belgium.[168]

Another treaty obligation that holds facilitated rules of recognition and enforcement with a view to *collecting maintenance payments* is the very elaborate Hague Convention of 23 November 2007 on the international recovery of child support and other forms of family maintenance, applicable since 1 August 2014.[169]

[B] European Law of Recognition and Enforcement

The Brussels I*bis* Regulation was mentioned above as the most important source for jurisdictional criteria inside the EU Member States.[170] Another just as important aspect is that it allows trans-boundary effect of money-judgments with such ease, that we have in the EU come close to a mutual 'full faith and credit'. Since 10 January 2015 the recast I*bis*-version is in force for court decisions taken and public acts or documents made up after that date.[171] First, recognition of Member States' judgments goes automatically, without prior seal or judicial approval. This implies that other judges than the normally competent 'exequatur court' may need to respect the res judicata from abroad and may apply set-off for amounts allotted under such foreign authority. Second, even court-ordered execution may be obtained for EU-judgments without first requesting an 'exequatur', meaning, that in the Member State addressed it is enforceable without any declaration of approval or enforceability being required through any procedure, on condition that the decision is enforceable in the Member State of origin.[172] If a debtor of a decision wishes to oppose, it is he who must introduce a *request to deny* enforcement,[173] under procedural rules of the addressed Member State.[174] If the law of this country does not know the measures imposed in the decision, it must seek functionally equivalent measures.[175] The grounds for rejection are limited; no retrial of the merits is allowed,[176] and the jurisdiction of the court of origin is not to be controlled (except for the mandatory criteria of Article 26 of the Brussels I*bis* Regulation).

Other more specific European regulations have introduced the same principles and rules to facilitate the flow of court decisions and public documents across the borders of Member States. *See* above, §16.03 [B], for the special regulations and their

168. Convention on Jurisdiction, Applicable Law, Recognition, Enforcement and Co-operation in Respect of Parental Responsibility and Measures for the Protection of Children; *see* www.hcch .net for all information. Belgium's ratification became effective 1 September 2014; it declared that the Central Authority was exclusively the Federal Department of Justice for requests made under of Article 34, para. 1. A matter relating to the Convention shall be recognised and enforced in Belgium by application of the relevant internal rules of Community law.
169. *See* for all information www.hcch.net.
170. *See supra* §16.03 [B].
171. No longer applicable to maintenance matters in the family relations – *see* the Maintenance Regulation – *infra*.
172. Article 39 Brussels I*bis* Regulation.
173. Article 46 Brussels I*bis* Regulation.
174. Article 47.2 Brussels I*bis* Regulation.
175. Article 54.1 Brussels I*bis* Regulation.
176. Article 52 Brussels I*bis* Regulation.

fields of application: the subject matters are *decisions on annulment of marriage, divorce or separation and parental responsibility* ('Brussels IIa' Regulation No. 2201/2003),[177] decisions on *maintenance obligations* (Regulation No. 4/2009), *successions* (Regulation No. 650/2012) and *insolvency* (Regulation No. 1346/2000 to be repealed by the recast version, starting June 2017). Those contain recognition rules resulting in full faith and credit of EU decisions throughout the territory (except Denmark) and enforcement without prior procedure (but not under the regulation on succession).

We have seen the creation of a special payment order that can cross the borders of European Member States with ease. Regulation No. 805/2004 of 21 April 2004 *creating a European Enforcement Order for Uncontested Claims*,[178] introduced a truly European 'executory title' for certain money claims of a civil or commercial nature. When a claim was uncontested[179] and was laid down in a judicial decision, a court settlement or authentic instruments, it can, by using standard forms of the Regulation, be enforced as a foreign judgment within the EU without the need of any intermediate proceedings, such as exequatur. We also have the EU Regulation No. 861/2007 of 11 July 2007 *establishing a European Small Claims Procedure*.[180] It introduced a written procedure that deals with claims under EUR 2,000 specifically for cross-border disputes. The purpose is to provide for the enforcement of decisions in any of the Member States, on the standardised forms, without formal exequatur. That procedure was amended by EU Regulation No. 2015/2421 of 16 December 2015,[181] effective 14 July 2017, so that claims not exceeding EUR 5,000 would be included, with enhanced efficiency measures such as communication by electronic means and reduction of court costs. Lastly, the EU Regulation No. 655/2014 of 15 May 2014[182] allows a creditor, wishing to seize or preserve a debtor's bank assets, to obtain a preservation order that is valid throughout the EU; to apply from 18 January 2017.

177. As to a judicial penalty payment intended to ensure compliance with the rights of access granted to the father of a child, the ECJ decided on 9 September 2015, case C 4/14, *Christophe Bohez v. Ingrid Wiertz* (2015 ECR 563), that enforcement in a Member State must be sought through the EU Regulation 'Brussels IIa' on the rights of access, applicable to the matter that lay at the base of the lawsuit and not through the regulation regarding money judgments; clarifying also that a court penalty was only enforceable if it had been fully determined.
178. Official Journal L143 of 30 April 2004, followed by Regulation No. 1869/2005 of 16 November 2005, (Official Journal L300 of 17 November 2005) amending the Annexes to the Regulation No. 805/2004; was itself amended, effective 14 July 2017, by Regulation No. 2015/2421 of 16 December 2015, Official Journal L341 of 24 December 2015 introducing a change to Article 17.
179. 'Uncontested' is defined as a claim to which the debtor has expressly agreed (by admission or by a settlement approved by a court); or to which he did not object when the claim came before a court; or regarding which, his conduct in court amounted to a tacit admission of the claim or of the facts alleged by the creditor; or in case where the debtor agreed to the claim in a signed and authenticated document (Article 3 Regulation).
180. Official Journal L199 of 31 July 2007.
181. EU Regulation (EU) 2015/2421 of 16 December 2015 amending Regulation (EC) No. 861/2007 establishing a European Small Claims Procedure and [...], Official Journal L341-1 of 24 December 2015.
182. Regulation No. 655/2014 of 15 May 2014, Official Journal L189 of 27 June 2014, establishing a European Account Preservation Order to facilitate cross-country debt recovery in civil and commercial matters.

[C] National Law of Recognition and Enforcement

Belgian domestic law on foreign judicial decisions and foreign authentic documents is laid down in the Articles 22–29 of the Code of Private International Law.

Automatic or de jure full recognition without prior court approval is offered to court decisions in all matters, personal as well as for payment-decisions, coming from anywhere in the world.[183] But the recognition of a foreign decision comes only after it has been checked whether the conditions of Article 25 were fulfilled. There we find a list of nine items to check, being nine possible grounds for refusal:[184]

- infringement of public policy;
- breach of a party's rights of defence;
- fraud in a matter not at parties' disposition;
- the decision being still open for appeal or review;
- whether the decision goes against a prior decision in Belgium;
- if the suit was introduced after identical proceedings that are still pending commenced in Belgium between the same parties;
- if the Code gives Belgian judges exclusive jurisdiction (think company issues or disputes over immovable);
- if foreign jurisdiction was accepted on the sole basis of temporary presence of the defendant or of location of his assets unrelated to the case at hand; and finally
- whether other grounds for denial of recognition were present in more specific cases.

For a foreign authentic public instrument the same is true; it shall be recognised by any authority in Belgium without the need for any procedure if the validity is established in accordance with the law applicable by virtue of the present statute, adding that a finding of fraud or conflict with public policy must result in rejection.[185] We allow the evidentiary value a public document as provided in the country of its origin to seamlessly flow through and have effect in Belgium. No other practice is feasible, knowing how big the flow of documents is. If the public instrument could lead to enforcement at its original home, then enforcement can be obtained in Belgium by following the foreseen procedure of exequatur.[186]

The recognition without court approval typically allows other judges then the competent court addressed with a request for exequatur, who intervene on status matters or in regard to maintenance obligations or marital issues, to resolve a recognition issue as preliminary and interlocutory issue. Their controls and their

183. Article 22, §1, para. 2, and §3, 2°, Code of Private International Law.
184. The Code refers to its own more specific rules on: decisions that would change the name of a Belgian citizen, divorce by '*talaq*' or unilateral declaration by the male partner, foreign adoptions, decisions over registration or validity of foreign intellectual property rights, the matter of validity or winding up for corporate entities, lastly decisions in insolvency proceedings.
185. Article 27, §1, Code of Private International Law.
186. Article 27, §2, Code of Private International Law.

prejudicial choice about recognition, in case it is a material motive for the judicial decision that they take, based on their judgment on that issue, possesses force *of* res judicata for the exequatur, definitive for the recognition in Belgium.[187] The recognition 'outside court' allows administrative departments such as pension administrations or tax authorities to also control the requirements for recognition of foreign court decisions that change or confirm the status of a person. They need to do so for their own needs, as a preliminary issue before they decide on allocation of a benefit or imposition of a tax. It allows notaries (for instance when they distribute assets of an estate) or civil registrars (e.g., when asked to register parentage or to conclude a marriage) to judge for themselves over the recognition of for example a foreign parentage decision or foreign adoption or foreign divorce. They must do the controls for the particular administrative purpose, under the rules of law, being the criteria of Article 25 of the Code of Private International Law, mentioned above. But this control by officers of administration or by notaries is always precarious, always rebuttable, pending a possible intervention of the exequatur court - which might be called by a party (typically, if a functionary denies recognition; or if a partner in the status relationship disputes recognition) to judge the matter with finality. Only a court can bring such finality. The recognition of foreign court decisions or administrative instruments by town registrars before they make on entry in any of the official registries for status or residence permission based thereupon, gets a special mention.[188] The question of the nature of such 'precarious' registration has caused much debate and doubts. With different functionaries making different evaluations of a decision or public document, this remains an issue of contention; one must advise to go to the exequatur court in case of uncertainty.

When there is doubt or a dispute arises over full recognition, a legal claim for recognition or for denial of recognition is offered to those who have a personal interest in a foreign decision or public document.[189] If enforcement would be needed in Belgium, then *surely* the procedure of exequatur must be followed, because prior court approval and attachment of the seal of enforceability is indeed necessary under the common law.[190] The procedure is started up by unilateral request signed by a lawyer and proceeds as in summary proceedings; local competence lies with the court of first instance of the place of defendant's domicile or residence or the place of enforcement.[191]

As to the external formal requirements of foreign documents or authentic instruments, *legalisation* is a condition for granting them their evidentiary power. Belgium is a member state of the Convention of The Hague of 5 October 1961 abolishing the requirement of legalisation of foreign public documents, binding sixty-eight countries. The convention reduces the formalities of legalisation, to a

187. For the binding power of the specific *dictum* in such interlocutory decisions, *see* Court of Cassation 15 March 1991, 1990–1991 Arresten van het Hof van Cassatie 739; 1991-I Pasicrisie belge 656.
188. Article 31 Code of Private International Law.
189. Article 22, §2, Code of Private International Law.
190. Article 22, §1, resp. Article 27, §2, Code of Private International Law.
191. Article 23 Code of Private International Law. Article 24 describes the documents to be supplied.

competent authority placing an 'apostille'-stamp on the document.[192] For some specific documents and for some countries there are treaties that have altogether suspended the obligation to legalise. The Code of Private International Law fills in the blanks:[193] it confirms that an obligation to legalise does exist, and it provides for the common law method of legalisation via the competent Belgian diplomatic personnel in or for the state of origin of a document. The Code adds that a foreign public document provides proof in Belgium as under the law where it was made up, if it fulfils the requirements under the foreign law and the formal requirements of the Code - just mentioned.[194]

§16.07 SELECTED BIBLIOGRAPHY

E. Apers, *Recognition and Enforcement of Foreign Judicial Decisions: Belgium's Codification Explored*, 2014/4 Nederlands Internationaal Privaatrecht (NIPR) 573–580.

A. Dickinson & E. Lein, *The Brussels Regulation Recast* (Oxford University Press 2015).

J. Erauw, *Brief Description of the Draft Belgian Code of Private International Law*, IV Yearbook of Private International Law 2002 145–161 (P. Šarčević & P. Volken eds., Dordrecht 2003).

J. Erauw, *Arbitrability of Distribution Agreements in Belgian Law, in Liber Memorialis Petar Šarčević – Universalism, Tradition and the Individual* 411–438 (J. Erauw, V. Tomljenovic & P. Volken eds., München: Sellier European Law Publishers 2006).

J. Erauw & M. Fallon, *Flexibility and Conflict Justice in the Belgian Code of Private International Law, in The Belgian Reports at the 2010 Conference of Washington of the International Academy of Comparative Law* 227–276 (E. Dirix & Y.-H. Leleu eds., Brussels: E. Bruylant 2011).

P. Hollander, *The New Belgian Arbitration Law*, 2013/4 Les cahiers de l'arbitrage - The Paris Journal of International Arbitration 1013–1023.

G. Keutgen, G.-A. Dal & M. Dal, *Belgium, in International Handbook on Commercial Arbitration*, Suppl. 82 (Kluwer Law International 2014).

The New Belgian Arbitration Law (B. Den Tandt ed., Bruges: die Keure 2015).

M. Pertegás Sender, *The Belgian Code on Private International Law: A Tour d'horizon*, 2006 Praxis des Internationalen Privat- und Verfahrensrechts 53–61.

D. Philippe, *Modernisation of the Belgian Law on Arbitration*, 2014/109 Le droit des affaires - Het ondernemingsrecht (Brussels) 5–20.

M. Piers & D. De Meulemeester, *The New Belgian Arbitration Law*, 2013/3 ASA-Bulletin (Swiss Arbitration Association, Geneva) 597–602.

192. *See* the Conference of The Hague for Private International Law, at www.hcch.net, for all information on authorities and for guidance.
193. Article 30 Code of Private International Law circumscribes or 'defines' legalisation as relating to the confirming the correctness of signature; the quality in which the person signed and the authenticity of a seal that was used.
194. Article 28 Code of Private International Law.

M. Piers & D. De Meulemeester, *The Adoption of the UNCITRAL Model Law Encourages Arbitration in Belgium*, 2013/2 b-Arbitra - Belgian Review of Arbitration 367–404.

H. van Houtte, *Updating Private International Law? The Belgian Experiment, in Liber Memorialis Petar Šarčević – Universalism, Tradition and the Individual* 65–73 (J. Erauw, V. Tomljenovic & P. Volken eds., München: Sellier European Law Publishers 2006).

H. Verbist, *New Belgian Arbitration Law of 24 June 2013 and New CEPANI Arbitration Rules of 1 January 2013*, 30 Journal of International Arbitration (The Hague) 597–618 (2013).

Index

G

M

N

O

P

R

S

U

V

W

www.ingramcontent.com/pod-product-compliance
Lightning Source LLC
LaVergne TN
LVHW020646300926
849161LV00004B/843